TOOL ENGINEERING AND DESIGN

By the same Author :

1. Machine Design
2. Machine Drawing
3. Geometrical Drawing
4. Machine Tool Engineering
5. Metal Forming Processes
6. Material Science
7. Power Plant Engineering

Dedicated to
My Late Respected
Father

TOOL ENGINEERING AND DESIGN

G.R. NAGPAL

B.Sc., B.Sc. Engineering (Mechanical)
M.Tech. (Mech. Engineering)
Retd. Asstt. Prof. in Mech. Engg. Department
Y.M.C.A. Institute of Engineering
Faridabad (Haryana)

KHANNA PUBLISHERS

Operational Office
B-35/9, G.T. Karnal Road Industrial Area,
(Near Telephone Exchange), Delhi-110033
Phones : 011-27224179, 011-45033819 • *Mob*. 09811541460
email : contactus@khannapublishers.in

Published by :
Romesh Chander Khanna & Vineet Khanna
for **KHANNA PUBLISHERS**
2-B, Nath Market, Nai Sarak
Delhi- 110 006 (India)

Website : www.khannapublishers.in

Hologram & Description

To all readers of our books, from yourself if being defrauded by pirates to prevent, please make sure that there is an Hologram on the cover of our books with the below specifications. If you find any book without Hologram and Description, please mail us at **contactus@khannapublishers.in**

Thanking you

ISBN No. 978-81-7409-203-8

First Edition : 2000
Sixth Edition :
Ninth Reprint : 2020

***Price :* ₹ 299.00**

PREFACE

The aim of this book is to present knowledge and skills needed for the effective design of tools. The tool designer should thoroughly understand the concept and theories involved in before he attempts the actual design of tools and fixtures. The kind of tools, the decision he makes and results he achieves depend upon this understanding.

The subject matter has been presented in a simple and understandable way. The text includes many theory questions, numerical problems, discussion of important considerations in tool design and the manner in which they affect production economy and feasibility.

The author is thankful to the Publishers for the most pains taking and cooperative attitude for bringing this book in a very short period.

G.R. NAGPAL

CONTENTS

6. Press Tool Design

0

Introduction

0.1. Tooling

It refers to the hardware necessary to produce a particular component. Tooling consists of a vast array of cutting devices, jigs, fixtures, dies, gauges etc. used in normal production. The common classification of types of tooling is as follows :

(*i*) Cutting tools such as
  (*a*) Single point cutting tools
  (*b*) Multi-point cutting tools.

(*ii*) Press tools

(*iii*) Dies for die-casting

(*iv*) Forging dies

(*v*) Jigs and fixtures

(*vi*) Gauges.

0.2. Cutting Tools

The purpose of the cutting tool is to remove metal under controlled conditions. Therefore, the tool must be harder than the material which is to cut. This efficiency with which a tool will remove metal from the material is a function of the following :

(*i*) Relative hardness between the work and tool materials

(*ii*) Sharpness of the tool

(*iii*) Tool Geometry

(*iv*) Forces applied

Cutting tools are designed with sharp edges to minimise rubbing contact between the tool and the work piece. Variations in the shape of cutting tool influences the following :

(*i*) Tool life

(*ii*) Surface finish of the workpiece

(*iii*) Amount of force required to shear the metal from the parent metal.

The cutting tools can be broadly classified into two major graphs

(*i*) Single point cutting tools

(*ii*) Multi point cutting tools.

The basic requirements of a cutting tool are as follows :

(*i*) Cutting tool should be harder than the material to be cut.

(*ii*) Tool and workpiece must be held rigidly so that tool can penetrate the workpiece when forces are applied.

0.3. Tool Design

Tool design is the process of designing and developing the tools, methods, and techniques necessary to improve manufacturing efficiency and productivity.

Design of cutting tools depends on the function to be performed by the cutting tool. Metal cutting involves interaction of four namely:

(*i*) Workpiece (*ii*) Cutting tool

(*iii*) Work Holder

(*iv*) Cutting tool holding and guiding devices.

The physical composition and shape of workpiece will greatly influcence the selection of machining methods and tool material and tool geometry. The work piece holder will depend on the geometry of workpiece.

The cutting tool should be easy and safe to operate. It should be made as economically as possible and it should have simple geometry. Tool design depends on the following factors :

(*i*) Overall size and shape of the part

(*ii*) Type and condition of workpiece material

(*iii*) Type of machining operation and sequence of operations

(*iv*) Degree of a accuracy required

(*v*) Numbers of components to be made

(*vi*) Locating and clamping surfaces

(*vii*) Type and size of machine tool

(*a*) Single Spindle machine tool

(*a*) Multi spindle machine tool

(*viii*) Should the tool be capable of performing more than one operation.

0.4. Duties of Tool Design Engineer

The tool design engineer should know the manufacturing procedures to make a component. He should understand how tools perform their functions. Tool designer must have a knowledge of standard. Tools can be designed economically by using standard parts like screws, bushings, handles, clamps etc. While designing a tool the tool engineer should take into considerations the following:

(*i*) Manufacturing methods to be used.

(*ii*) Work piece material

(*iii*) Cutting tool materials

(*iv*) Life of tool

(*v*) Cutting fluids to be used

(*vi*) Degree of accuracy required

(*vii*) Locating and clamping surfaces on part.

After designing a tool, the engineer should supply the following:

(*i*) Detail drawing of each part of tool

(*ii*) List of parts needed to make a tool

(*iii*) Assembly drawing.

For success of any component the product designer, tool designer and process planning engineer should work in close coordination. The extent of planning in a tool design greatly affects the success/failure. All of information and specifications pertaining to the proposed product should be evaluated to arrive at the most efficient and cost efficient and cost effective tool design.

0.5. Human Factor Involved

Some of the human factors to be considered while designing a tool are as follows :

(*i*) Tool should erate smoothly

(*ii*) Controls and clamps should be convenient for the operator to use

(*iii*) Use of foot can be made to lessen hand and arm fatique (*iv*) All controls clamps should be located within easy reach of the operator

(*v*) Levers and handles, should be large enough to reduce hand fatique

(*vi*) Tool should be completely safe to operate

(*vii*) Tool body should be rigid enough to resist all cutting forces.

0.6. Jig and Tool Department

Fig 0.1 shows a typical lay out indicating the division of responsibilities of a Jig and tool department.

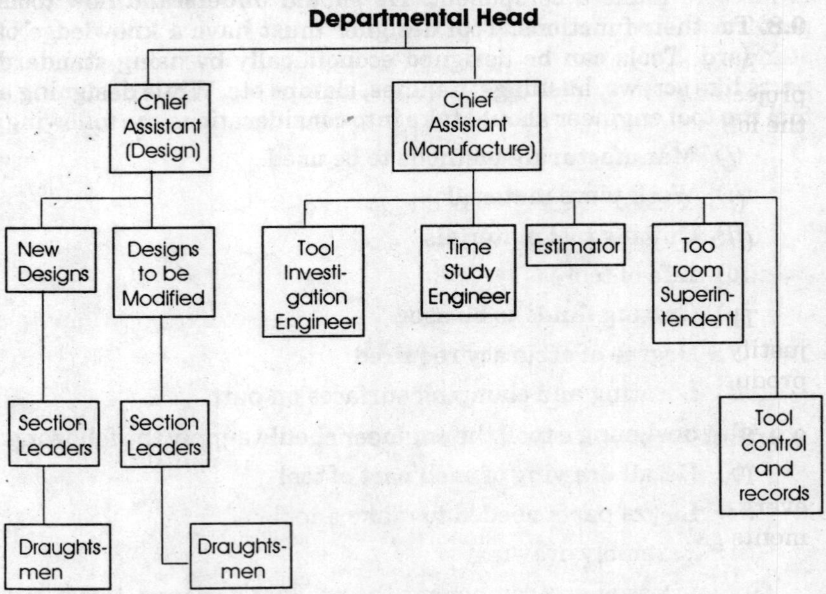

Fig. 0.1.

The main purpose of design section is to prepare new designs. However alterations in design to be made in the existing equipment is equally important. The responsibility of the tool investigation engineer is to examine draw backs and troubles in manufacture and to propose remedies.

0.7. Tool Design Objectives

The main objective of tool design is to lower manufacturing cost while maintaining quality and increased production.

Various objectives of tool design are as follows :

(*i*) To provide simple, easy to operate tools for maximum efficiency

(*ii*) To design tools which consistently produce parts of high quality

(*iii*) To design tool to make it fool proof and to prevent improper use

(*iv*) To select materials which will give adequate tool life

(*v*) To provide in the design of the tools for maximum safety of the operator.

0.8. Tool Cost Estimation

A tooling estimate includes the estimated cost of the tool and projected savings over alternate methods. The cost of tool involves the following costs.

(*i*) Cost of tool material

(*ii*) Cost of labour needed to fabricate the tool

(*iii*) Cost of designing the tool

The estimate also includes any special conditions which may justify the cost of tooling such as close tolerances or high volume production.

0.9. Safety as Related to Tool Design

The tool should be safe to operate. Safety should be planned into every tool design details. A tool should satisfy the following requirements as far as safety is concerned

(*i*) It should be easier to load and unload the tool

(*ii*) All sharp edges on tool should be chamfered

(*iii*) All controls and clamps should be located within easy reach of the operator

(*iv*) Chip guards should be provided to protect the operator

(*v*) Tool clamping devices should not loosen during tool operation

(*vi*) Tool body should be rigid enough to resist all cutting forces

0.10. Lead Time

It is the time spent between the design and fabrication of a part or assembly.

PROBLEMS

1. Write short notes on the following :

(*i*) Tooling (*ii*) Cutting tools

2. What is tool design state the factors which affect design of tools.

3. Discuss the duties of tool designer.

4. List the human factors which should be considered while designing a tool.

5. List the safety factors to be considered during design of a tool.

6. Describe tool design objectives.

7. Write short notes on the following :

(*a*) Tool cost estimation

(*b*) Safety as related to tool design

(*c*) Lead time.

8. Discuss the duties of jig and tool department.

1

Process of Metal Cutting

1.0. Metal Cutting

Metal cutting process consists in removing a layer of metal from blank to obtain a machine part of the required shape and dimensions and with the specified quality of surface finish.

A metal cutting tool is the part of a metal cutting machine tool that, in the cutting process, acts directly on the blank from which the finished part is to be made. The metal cutting process accompanied by deformation in compression, tension and shear by a great deal of friction and heat generation is governed by definite laws. In order to cut the material from blank the cutting tool should be harder than material to be cut, the tool should penetrate the blank and the tool should be strong enough to withstand the forces developed in cutting.

Metals are given different usable forms by various processes. These processes are of two types.

(*a*) Chip removal processes.

(*b*) Non-chip removal processes (Chipless processes).

1.1. Chip Removal Processes

In chip removal processes the desired shape and dimensions are obtained by separating a layer from the parent workpiece in the form of chips. The various chip forming processes are as follows :

(*i*) Turning
(*ii*) Shaping
(*iii*) Boring
(*iv*) Drilling
(*v*) Milling
(*vi*) Honing
(*vii*) Grinding.

During the process of metal cutting there is a relative motion between the workpiece and cutting tool. Such a relative motion is produced by a combination of rotary and translatory movements either of the workpiece or of cutting tool or of both. This relative motion depends upon the type of metal cutting operation. Table 1.0 indicates the nature of relative motion for various continuous cutting operations.

Table 1.0

Operation	*Motion of Workpiece*	*Motion of Cutting Tool*
Shaping	Fixed	Translatory
Turning	Rotary	Translatory
Drilling	Fixed	Rotary as well as translatory
Milling	Translatory	Rotary

1.2. Chipless Processes

In chipless processes the metal is given the desired shape without removing any material from the parent workpiece. Some of the chipless processes are as follows :

(*i*) Rolling
(*ii*) Forging
(*iii*) Spinning
(*iv*) Stamping.

1.3. Metal Cutting Principle

Metal cutting is one of the most important processes carried out in an industry. The purpose of any metal cutting operation commonly called machining is to produce a desired shape, size and finish of a component by removing the excess metal in the form of chips from a rough block of material. Consequently the primary objective in metal cutting is the production of chips, although these chips are only a means to an end and are discarded. They may constitute more than 50% of the initial workpiece material. The machining process should be carried at high speeds and feeds and least cutting effort and at lowest cost. The cutting operation whether being carried out on lathe, milling machine or any other machine tool is based on theory which is same for all processes. A number of inter-related factors affect metal cutting, the more important factors being as follows :

(*i*) The properties of work material.

(*ii*) The properties and geometry of the cutting tool.

(*iii*) The interaction between the tool and the work during metal cutting.

The exact mechanism of metal cutting briefly stated is that a cutting tool exerts a compressive force on the workpiece. Under this compressive force the material of the workpiece is stressed beyond its yield point causing the material to deform plastically and shear off. The plastic flow takes place in a localised region called shear plane (Fig. 1.1) which extends from the cutting obliquely up to the uncut surface ahead of tool (Fig. 1.2). The sheared material begins to flow along the cutting tool face in the form of small pieces called chips. The compressive force applied to form the chips is called cutting force. The flowing chips cause wear of cutting tool. Heat is produced during shearing action. The heat generated raises the temperature of the work, cutting tool and chips. The temperature rise in the cutting tool tends to soften it and causes loss of keenness in the cutting edge leading to its failure. The cutting force, heat and abrasive wear are thus the basic features of the material cutting process.

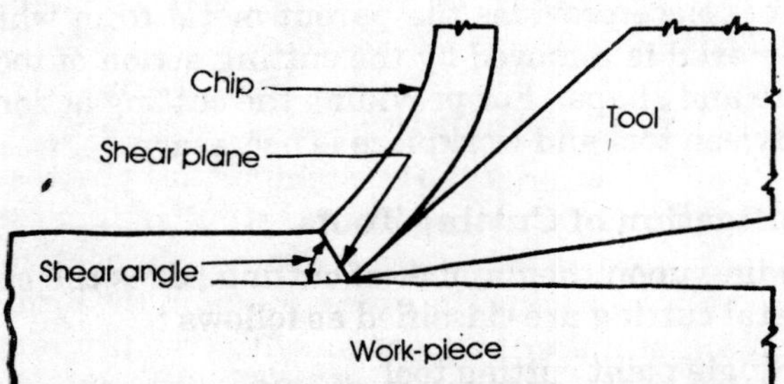

Fig. 1.1.

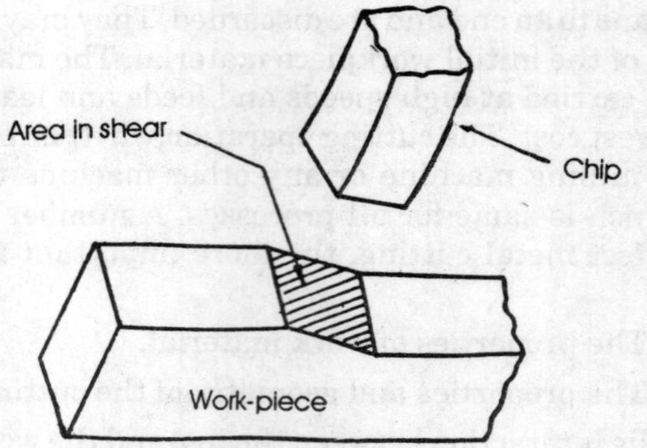

Fig. 1.2.

During cutting process the following properties of the work-piece material are quite important:

(*i*) Hardness

(*ii*) Toughness

(*iii*) Inherent hard spots and surface inclusions

(*iv*) Abrasive qualities

(*v*) Tendency to weld.

On the other hand the tool material should be hard, strong, tough and wear resistant.

1.3.1. Basic Elements of machining. The basic elements of all machining operations are as follows :

(*i*) Workpiece.

(*ii*) Cutting tool.

(*iii*) Chip.

The workpiece provides the parent metal from which the unwanted material is removed by the cutting action of tool to obtain desired size and shape. For providing the cutting action a relative motion between tool and workpiece is necessary.

1.4. Classification of Cutting Tools

Depending upon the number of cutting edges the cutting tools used in metal cutting are classified as follows :

(*i*) Single point cutting tool

(*ii*) Multipoint cutting tool.

(*i*) **Single point cutting tool.** This type of tool has an effective cutting edge and removes excess material from the workpiece along the cutting edge. Single point cutting tool is of the following types:

(*a*) Ground type

(*b*) Forged type

(*c*) Tipped type

(*d*) Bit type.

In ground type the cutting edge is formed by grinding the end of a piece of tool steel stock. Whereas in forged type the cutting edge is formed by rough forging before hardening and grinding. In tipped type cutting tool the cutting edge is in the form of a small tip made of high grade material which is welded to a shank made up of lower grade material. In bit type, a high grade material of a square, rectangular or some other shape is held mechanically in a tool holder. Single point tools are commonly used in lathes, shapers, planers, boring machines and slotters.

Single point cutting tool may be left handed or right handed type. A tool is said to be right/left hand type, if the cutting edge is on the right or left side when viewing tool from the point end. Lathe tools, shaper tools, planner tools and boring tools are single point tools.

(*ii*) **Multipoints cutting tools.** They have more than one effective cutting edge to remove the excess material from the workpiece. Milling cutters, drills, reamers broaches and grinding wheels are multipoint cutting tools.

1.5. Tool Geometry

The desirability of getting the maximum use from a tool before it needs regrinding is one of the objectives of tool technology. Tool life is defined as the length of time, a tool will operate before its failure occurs. There are many factors that contribute to cutting tool efficiency. Among the most important of these are the following :

(*i*) The shape of the cutting edge that removes the excess material.

(*ii*) The correct selection of the type of cutting tool for the material to be machined.

(*iii*) The correct choice of cutting speed and feed.

(*iv*) The proper setting of cutting tool relative to work.

(*v*) The correct choice and proper application of coolants.

Unless the cutting tools is ground to the correct shape with correct angles and unless it is ground with a keen, smooth cutting edge, time will be wasted, accuracy will be impossible and a poor finish will result.

The optimum tool geometry depends upon the following factors:

(*i*) Workpiece material

(*ii*) Machining variables

(*a*) Cutting speed

(*b*) Feed

(*c*) Depth of cut.

(*iii*) Material of the tool point

(*iv*) Type of cutting.

Tool geometry refers to the tool angles, shape of the tool face and the form of the cutting edges.

Fig. 1.3 shows a typical single point tool. The most important features are the cutting edges and adjacent surfaces. Fig. 1.6 shows various angles of single point tool.

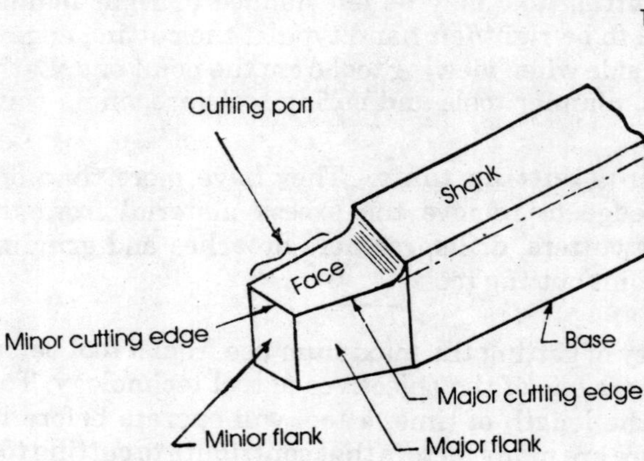

Fig. 1.3.

Fig. 1.4 shows the principal plane and cutting plane with reference to a single point cutting tool with respect to velocity taken along. Z axis whereas Fig. 1.5 shows principal and cutting planes in relation to working surface.

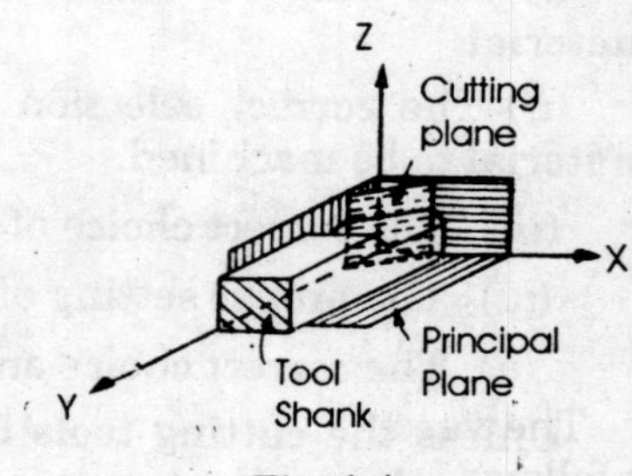

Fig. 1.4

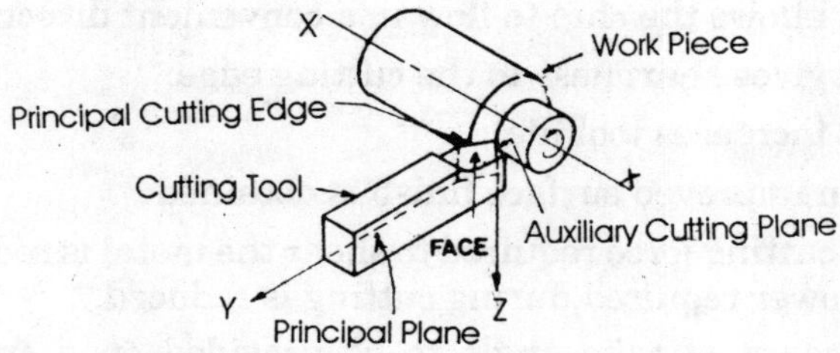

Fig. 1.5

1.5.1. Terms and definitions.

(*i*) **Face**. The face is the surface over which the chip flows.

(*ii*) **Cutting edge.** The cutting edge carries out the cutting.

(*iii*) **Nose.** The nose is the corner, arc or chamfer at the junction of the major and minor cutting edges.

(*iv*) **Flank.** Flank of the tool is the surface below the cutting edge.

(*v*) **Tool angles.** The various angles influence tool performance to a considerable extent and therefore their value should be selected with great care and consideration.

Fig. 1.6 shows the geometry of single point tool.

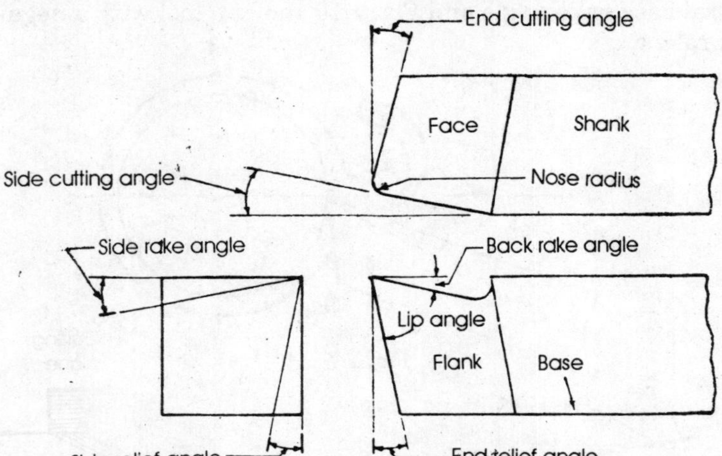

Fig. 1.6.

The various functions of the rake or slope of the tool face are as follows :

(*i*) It allows the chip to flow in a convenient direction.

(*ii*) It gives sharpness to the cutting edge.

(*iii*) It increases tool life.

(*iv*) An improved surface finish is obtained.

(*v*) The cutting force required to shear the metal is reduced, and therefore power required during cutting is reduced.

The amount of rake angle to be provided on a cutting tool depends upon the following factors :

(*i*) Material of the workpiece

(*ii*) Material of cutting tool

(*iii*) Rigidity of the machine tool

(*iv*) Depth of cut.

(*vi*) **Back rake angle.** It measures the downward slope of the top surface of the tool from the nose to the rear along the longitudinal axis. Its purpose is to guide the direction of the chip flow. It also serves to protect the point of the cutting tool. (Fig. 1.7). The size of the angle depends upon the material to be machined, the softer the material the greater should be positive rake angle. Aluminium requires more back rake angle than cast iron or steel. Back rake angle may be positive, neutral or negative. Fig. 1.8 shows a tool with a positive back rake angle. Fig. 1.9 shows a tool with a neutral back rake angle and Fig. 1.10 shows a tool with a negative back rake angle.

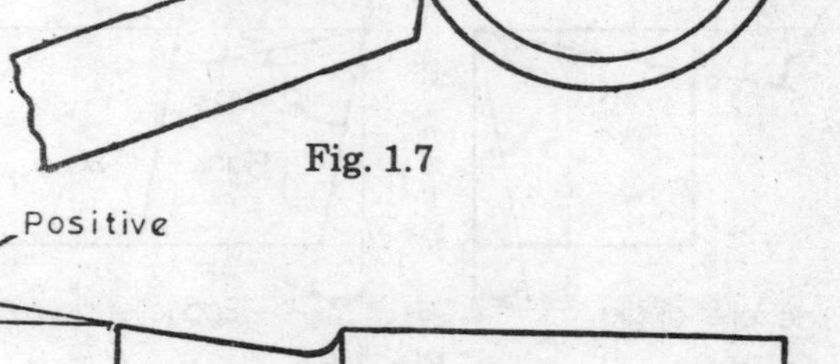

Fig. 1.7

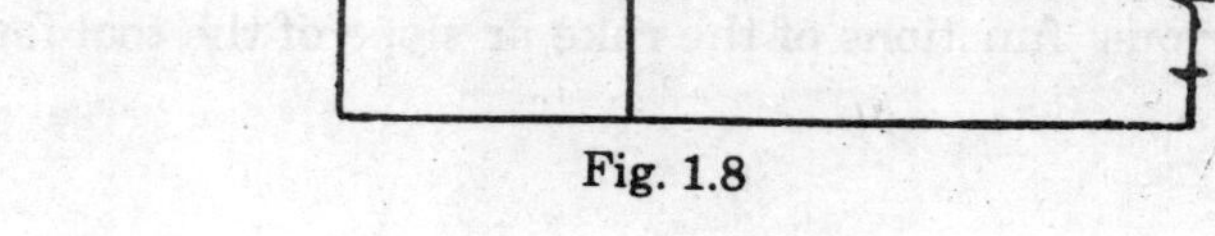

Fig. 1.8

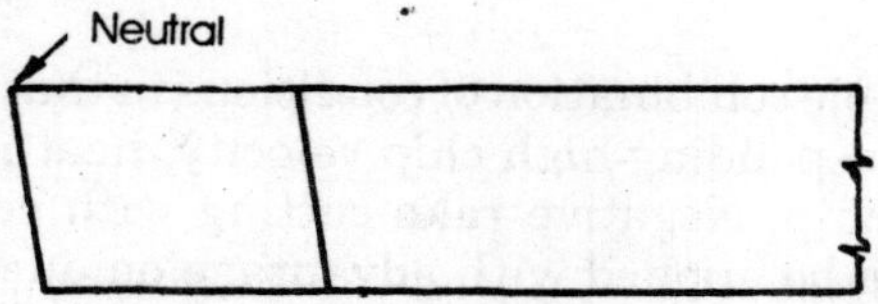

Fig. 1.9

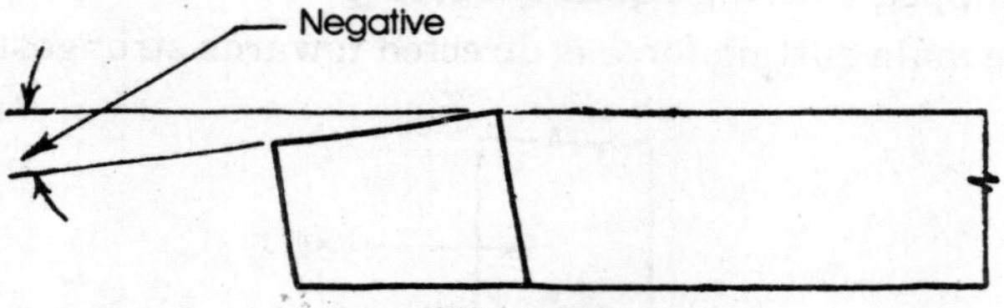

Fig. 1.10

Higher value of rake angle weakens the cutting edge. A negative rake angle increases tool forces to some extent but this minor disadvantage is off set by the added support to the cutting edge. This is particularly important in making intermittent cuts and in absorbing the impact during the initial engagement of the tool and work.

Cemented carbide cutting tools are normally given negative rake because cemented carbide possess very high compressive strength and comparatively very low tensile and shear strength.

The advantages of negative rake cutting when using sintered carbide or ceramics tool under suitable conditions are as follows :

(*i*) Higher cutting speeds may be used.

(*ii*) There is a less tendency for a built up edge to form on the tool.

(*iii*) The heat conductivity of the working part of the tool is improved.

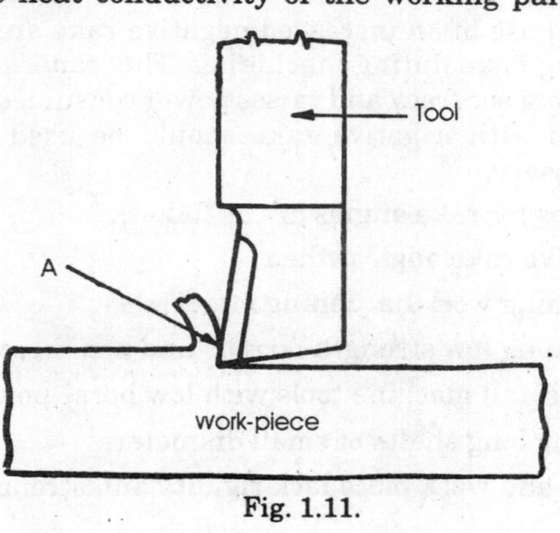

Fig. 1.11.

(*iv*) Favourable combination of conditions in that at high cutting speeds and corresponding high chip velocity, heat is carried away rapidly by the chip. Negative rake cutting with sintered carbide cutting tools can be applied with advantage on ductile steels. The machine tools using such tools must possess considerable rigidity and be equipped with high quality bearing.

(*v*) The main cutting force is directed towards strongest part of the tool.

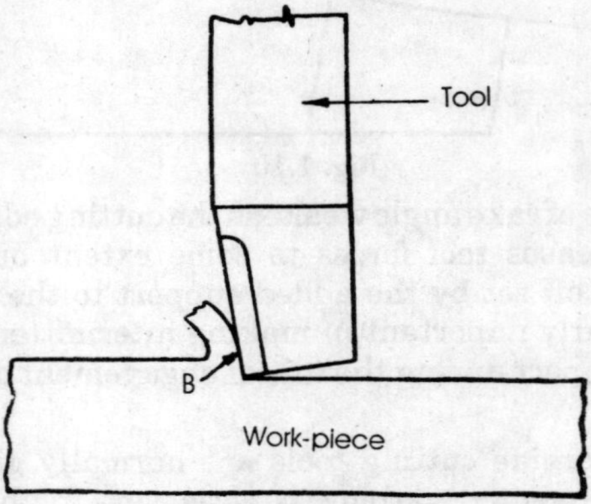

Fig. 1.12.

A cutting tool with positive rake (Fig. 1.11) results in a force component in the direction of arrow *A* which tends to shear the edge of tool. When the cutting tool is provided with a negative rake (Fig. 1.12), the main force component is directed at the strongest rake section of the tool, as shown by arrow *B*. Cutting tools with negative rake angle are stronger and are used to cut high strength alloys.

However the use of an increased negative rake angle leads to increased cutting force during machining. This causes vibrations, reduces machining accuracy and raises power consumed in cutting. Therefore tools with negative rake should be used only when absolutely necessary.

General rules for rake angles are as follows :

1. Use positive rake angles when

(*i*) Machining work hardening materials

(*ii*) Machining low strength ferrous and non-ferrous metals

(*iii*) Using small machine tools with low horse power

(*iv*) Turning long shafts of small diameters

(*v*) Set up and work piece lack rigidity and strength

(*vi*) It is necessary to machine below recommended cutting speeds.

2. Use negative rake angles when

(*i*) Machining high strength alloys

(*ii*) Interrupted cuts and heavy feed rates are to be used

(*iii*) Machine tools are more rigid.

(*vii*) **Side rake angle.** It measures the slope of the top surface of the tool to the side in a direction perpendicular to the longitudinal axis. It also guides the direction of the chip away from the job. The amount that a chip is bent depends upon this angle. With increase in side rake angle, the amount of chip has to bend decreases and hence the power required to part and bend the chip decreases. Larger side rake angle produces smooth surface finish. Fig. 1.13 shows side rake angle.

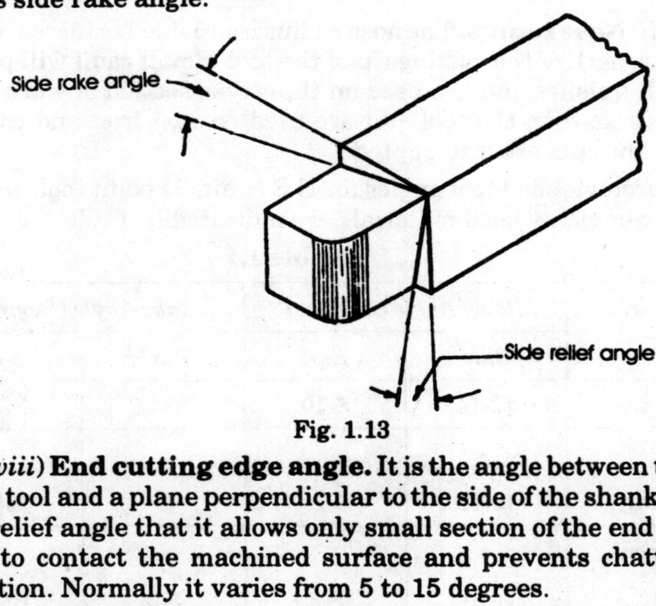

Fig. 1.13

(*viii*) **End cutting edge angle.** It is the angle between the face of the tool and a plane perpendicular to the side of the shank. It acts as a relief angle that it allows only small section of the end cutting edge to contact the machined surface and prevents chatter and vibration. Normally it varies from 5 to 15 degrees.

(*ix*) **Side cutting edge angle.** It is the angle between the side cutting edge and the longitudinal axis of the tool. It avoids formation of built up, edge, controls the direction of chip flow and distributes the cutting force and heat produced over larger cutting edge.

(*x*) **Side relief angle.** It is the angle made by the flank of the tool and a plane perpendicular to the base just under the side cutting edge. This angle permits the tool to be fed side-way into the job so that it can cut without rubbing. If the side relief angle is very large the cutting edge of the tool will break because of insufficient support whereas if the side relief angle is very small the tool can not be fed into the job, it will rub against the job and will get overheated and become blunt and the finish obtained on the job will be rough.

(*xi*) **End relief angle.** It is the angle between a plane perpendicular to the base and the end flank. This angle prevents the cutting tool from rubbing against the job. If the angle is very large the cutting edge of tool will be unsupported and will break off. Whereas if this angle is very small the tool will rub on the job, cutting will not be proper and poor finish will be obtained on the job. Its value varies from 6 to 10°.

(*xii*) **Nose radius.** The nose radius is provided to increase finish and strength of the cutting tip of the tool. Small radii will produce smooth finishes and are used on thin cross-section of work. Large radii strengthen the tool and are used on cast iron and castings, where the cuts are interrupted.

Recommended tool angles for H.S.S. single point tools for some of the commonly used materials are indicated in Table 1.1.

Table 1.1

Material	*Relief Angle (Degrees)*		*Rake Angle (Degrees)*	
	Side	*End*	*Back*	*Side*
Aluminium	12-14	8-10	30-35	14-16
Brass, (Free cut)	10-12	8-10	0	1-3
Cast Iron, (Gray)	8-10	6-8	3-5	10-12
Copper (Commercial)	12-14	12-14	14-16	18-20
Steel	7-9	6-8	5-7	8-10

Recommended tool angles for carbide single point tool are indicated in Table 1.2.

Table 1.2

Material	*Relief Angle*		*Rake Angle*	
	(degrees)		*(degrees)*	
	Side	*End*	*Back*	*Side*
Aluminium	6-10	6-10	0-10	10-20
Copper	6-8	6-8	0-4	15-20
Brass	6-8	6-8	0-(-5)	8-(-5)
Cast Iron	5-8	6-8	0-(-7)	6-(-7)
Steel	5-10	5-10	0-(-7)	6-(-7)

1.5.2. Methods of holding tool. There are different ways of holding single point cutting tools. Tool directly fitted into tool holder is shown in Fig. 1.14 whereas Fig. 1.15 shows a tool fitted in a tool post.

The tool hold by a clamp is shown in Fig. 1.16 and tool insert brazed to a tool shank is shown in Fig. 1.17.

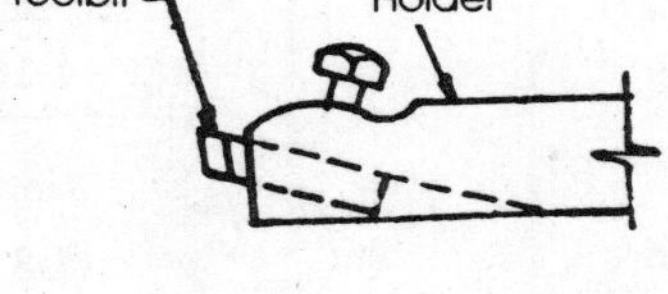

Fig. 1.14

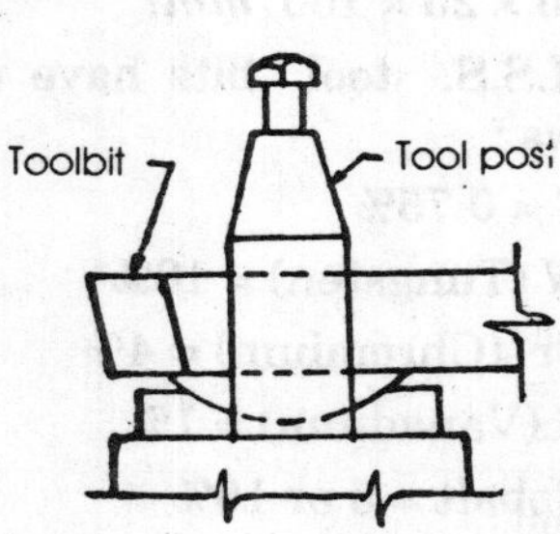

Fig. 1.15

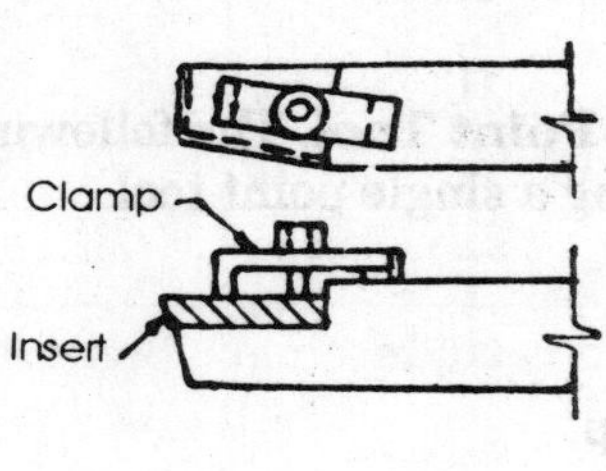

Fig. 1.16

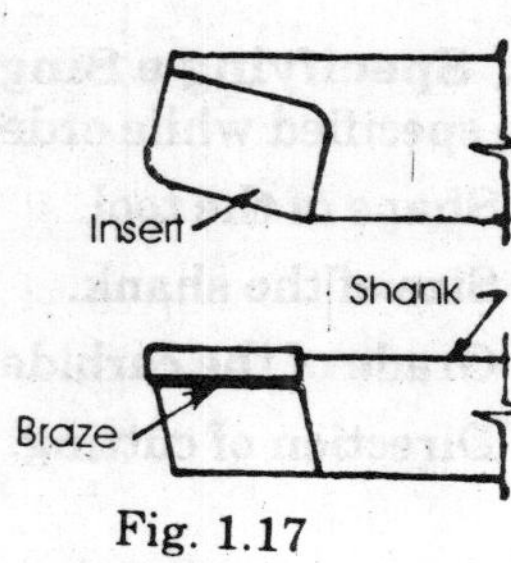

Fig. 1.17

1.5.3. Carbide inserts clamping methods. Fig. 1.17.1 shows types of seats for cemented carbide inserts.

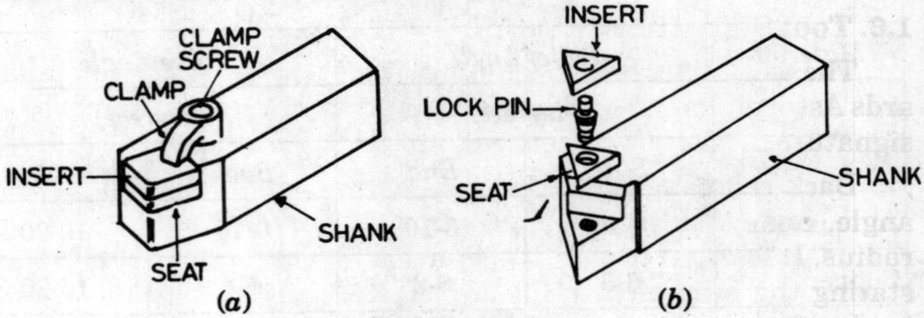

Fig. 1.17.1.

1.5.4. High Speed Steel (H.S.S.) Tools Bits. The hardened and ground H.S.S. bits are available in the following general sizes.

6 × 6 × 100 *mm*.

8 × 8 × 100 *mm*.

10 × 10 × 100 *mm*.

12 × 12 × 150 *mm*.

16 × 16 × 150 *mm*.

20 × 20 × 150 *mm*.

25 × 25 × 150 *mm*.

H.S.S. tool bits have an average chemical composition as follows :

C = 0.75%

W (Tungsten) = 18%

Cr. (Chromium) = 4%

V (Vanadium) = 1%

Cobalt = 5 or 10%

(5% cobalt H.S.S. is used for free machining steel whereas 10% cobalt H.S.S. is used for high tensile steel).

1.5.5. Specifying a Single Point Tool. The following details should be specified while ordering a single point tool.

(*i*) Shape of the tool.

(*ii*) Size of the shank.

(*iii*) Grade of the carbide tip.

(*iv*) Direction of cutting.

(*a*) Right Hand (R.H.)

(*b*) Left Hand (L.H.)

1.6. Tool Signature

The tool angles have been standardised by the American Standards Association (ASA). The seven important elements comprise the signature of the cutting tool and are stated in the following order.

Back rake angle, side rake angle, end relief angle, side relief angle, end cutting edge angle, side cutting edge angle and nose radius. It is usual to omit the symbols for degrees and mm, simply stating the numerical value of each element. For example a tool having tool signature as 10, 10, 6, 6, 8, 8, 2 will have the following angles :

Back rake angle = 10°

Side rake angle = 10°

End relief angle = 6°

Side relief angle = 6°

End cutting edge angle = 8°

Side cutting edge angle = 8°

Nose radius = 2mm

1.6.1. Requirements of a cutting tool. A cutting tool intended for high production machining should possess the following requirements :

(*i*) It should be amply strong and rigid.

(*ii*) It should be keenly sharpened with a high class finish.

(*iii*) It should have optimum geometry.

(*iv*) It should be producible in manufacture and convenient in use.

1.7. Two Systems of Defining the cutting Angles of a Single Point Tool

The cutting angles of a single point tools are commonly defined in two systems called *L-M-N* planes and *X-Y-Z* planes. The *L-M-N* plane system is chosen in reference to three mutually perpendicular planes. The plane *L* called as cutting plane being a vertical plane is tangent to the cutting edge of the tool. The plane *M* called as orthogonal plane being a vertical plane is perpendicular to *L* plane. The plane *N* called as base plane is a horizontal plane being perpendicular to L and M planes. The various angles according to this shown in Fig. 1.18 are as follows :

α = Side relief angle.
β = Wedge angle.
γ = Orthogonal rake angle.
δ = Cutting angle.
$= \alpha + \beta$
ϕ_1 = Auxiliary cutting edge angle.
θ = Nose angle.
ϕ = Plan approach angle. (Principal cutting edge angle)
λ_1 = Inclination angle.
α_1 = End relief angle.
β_1 = Side wedge angle.
γ_1 = Side rake angle.

This system is also known as International Orthogonal System (I.O.S.) of designating tool angles.

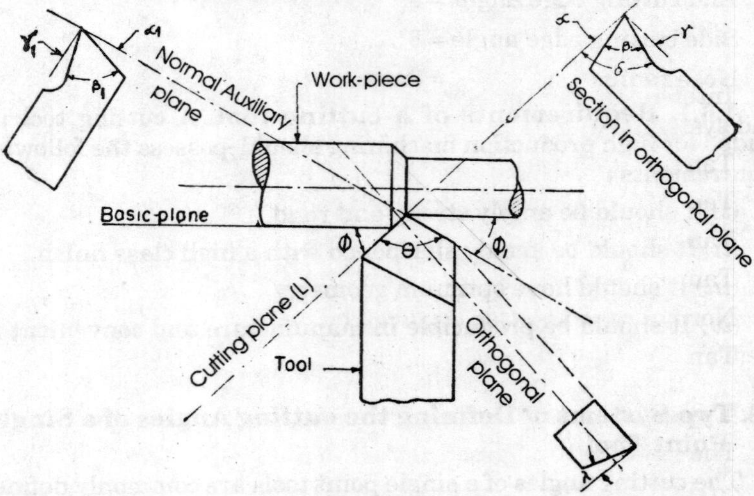

Fig. 1.18. Tool angles in L–M–N plane.

The various angles in X–Y–Z systems are shown in Fig. 1.19. The system is the most popular system. This system is also called American system of tool nomenclature.

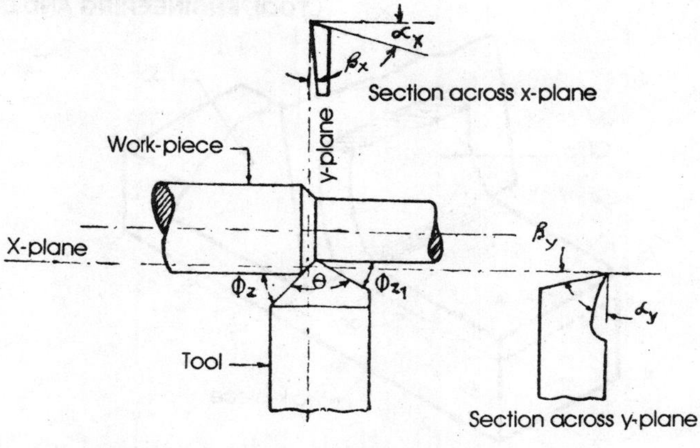

Fig. 1.19. Tool angles in X–Y–Z planes.

α_y = Back rake angle.

β_y = End relief angle.

α_x = Side rake angle.

β_x = Side relief angle.

θ = Nose angle.

ϕ_z = Side cutting edge angle.

ϕ_{z1} = End cutting edge angle.

Inter-relationship between different angles of system L–M–N and system X–Y–Z is as follows :

$$\text{Tan } \lambda = \tan \alpha_y \sin \phi - \tan \alpha_x \cos \phi$$

$$\text{Tan } \alpha_x = \sin \phi \tan \gamma - \cos \phi \tan \lambda$$

$$\text{Tan } \alpha_y = \cos \phi \tan \gamma + \sin \phi \tan \lambda$$

$$\text{Tan } \gamma = \tan \alpha_y \cos \phi + \tan \alpha_x \sin \phi$$

Normal rake angle (γ_n) is given by

$$\text{Tan } \gamma_n = \tan \gamma . \cos \lambda$$

1.8. Types of Metal Cutting Process

The metal cutting processes are of two types :

(*i*) 2Orthogonal cutting process (two dimensional cutting).

(*ii*) Oblique cutting process (three dimensional cutting).

Orthogonal cutting. Orthogonal (two dimensional) cutting occurs when the major cutting edge of the tool is presented to the work piece perpendicular to the direction of feed motion. Orthogonal cutting involves only two forces and this makes the analysis of cutting motion much easier. (Fig. 1.20).

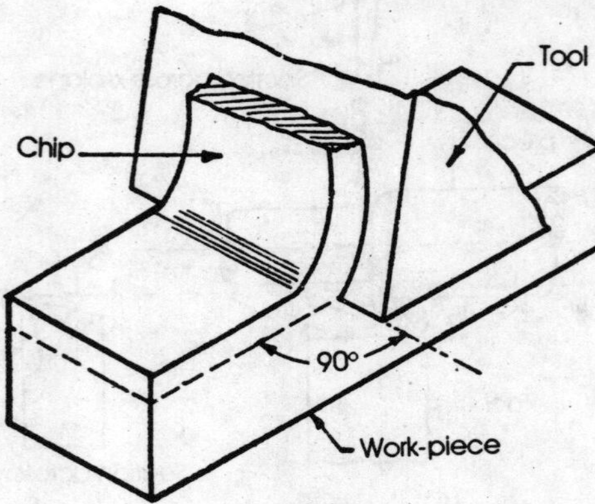

(*a*)

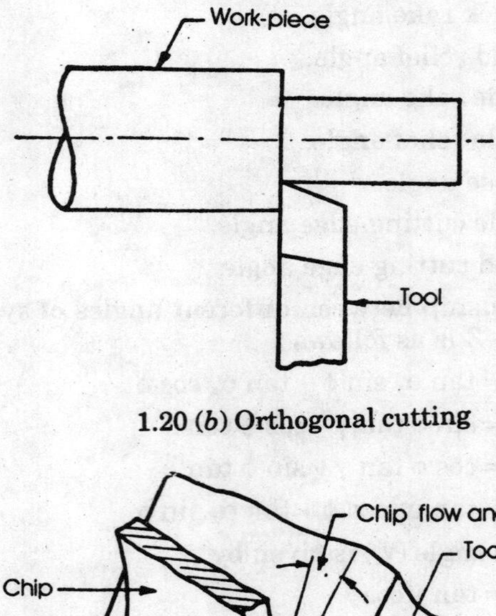

1.20 (*b*) Orthogonal cutting

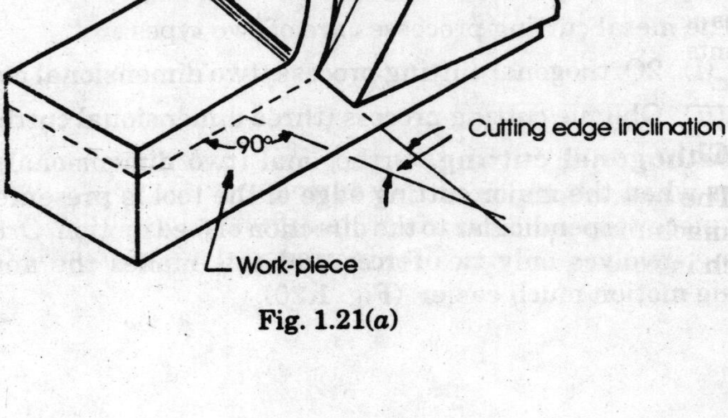

Fig. 1.21(*a*)

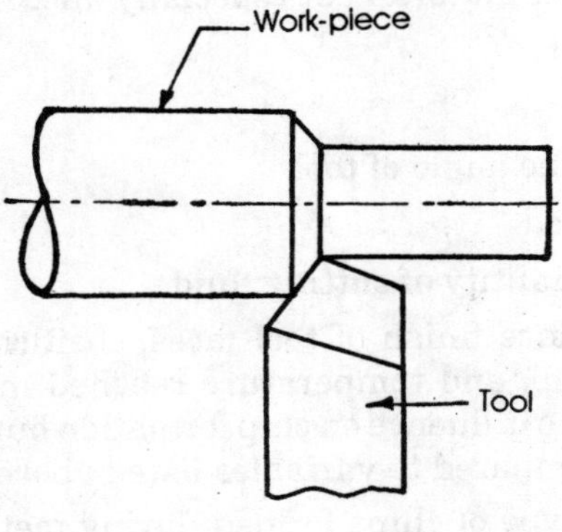

(*b*)

1.21. Oblique cutting.

Oblique cutting. This form of cutting occurs when the major edge of cutting tool is presented to the work piece at an angle which is not perpendicular to the direction of feed motion. (Fig. 1.21).

1.8.1. Comparison of orthogonal and oblique cutting. These two methods are compared as follows :

Orthogonal cutting	*Oblique cutting*
(*i*) The cutting edge of the tool remains normal to the direction of tool feed.	The cutting edge of the tool is inclined at an acute angle to the direction of tool feed
(*ii*) The direction of chip flow velocity is normal to the cutting edge of the tool.	The direction of chip flow velocity is at an angle with the normal to the cutting edge of the tool.
(*iii*) The cutting edge clears the width of the work-piece on either ends.	The cutting edge may or may not clear the width of the workpiece.
(*iv*) Only two components of cutting forces act on the tool. These two components are prependicular to each other.	Three mutually perpendicular components of cutting forces act at the cutting edge of the tool.

1.9. Chip Formation

The type of chip produced during metal cutting depends upon the machining conditions and material being cut. The variables which influence the type of chip produced are as follows :

(i) Properties of material cut especially ductility
(ii) depth of cut
(iii) feed rate
(iv) effective rake angle of tool
(v) cutting speed
(vi) type and quantity of cutting fluid.

Factors like surface finish of tool faces, coefficient of friction between tool and chip, and temperature reached in the region of cutting also have some influence on chip formation but are generally less significant as compared to variables listed above.

Three different type of chips formed during metal cutting are as follows :

(i) Continuous chips
(ii) Discontinuous chips
(iii) Continuous chip with a built up edge.

Continuous chip. A continuous chip is obtained when cutting ductile materials such as low carbon steel, aluminium and copper. This chip is severly deformed and either comes off in the form of a long string, or curls into a tight roll. (Fig. 1.22).

Some very soft and ductile materials with a low strength tend to tear away form the parent metal of the workpiece rather than shear clearly. This results in a rough surface that has to be cleaned up by a very keen cutting edge. In addition to ductile workpiece material the other conditions which favour their formation are fine feed, sharp cutting edge, higher cutting speeds and larger rake angles.

Discontinuous chip. Brittle materials such as grey cast iron lack the ductility necessary for appreciable plastic chip formation. Consequently the compressed material ahead of tool fails in a brittle manner along the shear zone producing small fragments. Such chips are called discontinuous chips. (Fig. 1.23). Lower cutting speeds and insufficient rake angles cause the formation of such chips.

Continuous chips with a built up edge. When during cutting, the temperature and pressure is quite high it causes the chip material to weld itself to the tool face near the nose (Fig. 1.24). This is called "Built up edge". This accumulated build up of chip material will then break away, part adhearing to the underside of the chip and part to the workpiece. This process gives rise to a poor finish on the machined surface and accelerated wear on the tool face. High friction at tool face, coarse feed, low take angle and ineffective use of cutting fluid produce such chips.

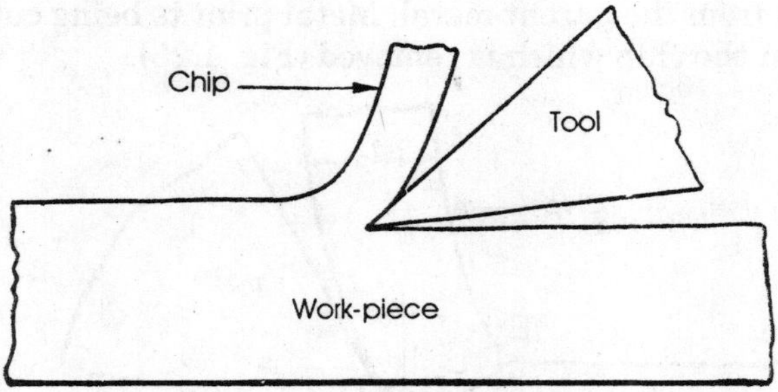

Fig. 1.22. Continuous chip.

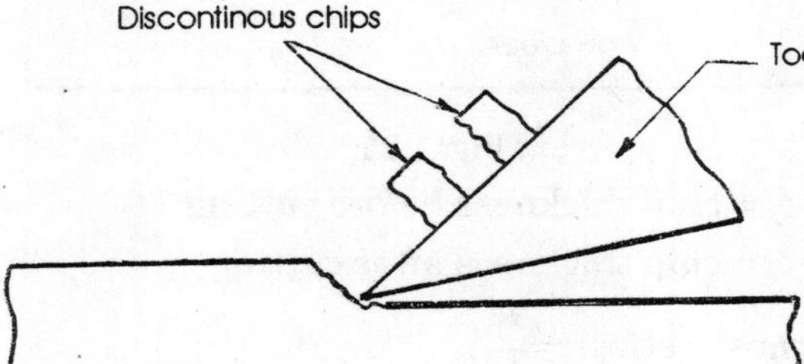

Fig. 1.23. Discontinuous chip.

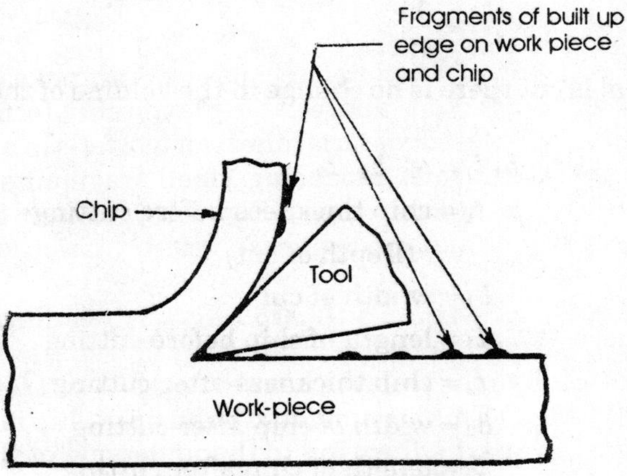

Fig. 1.24.

1.10. Chip Thickness Ratio

The outward flow of the metal causes the chip to be thicker after separation from the parent metal. Metal prior to being cut is much longer than the chip which is removed (Fig. 1.25).

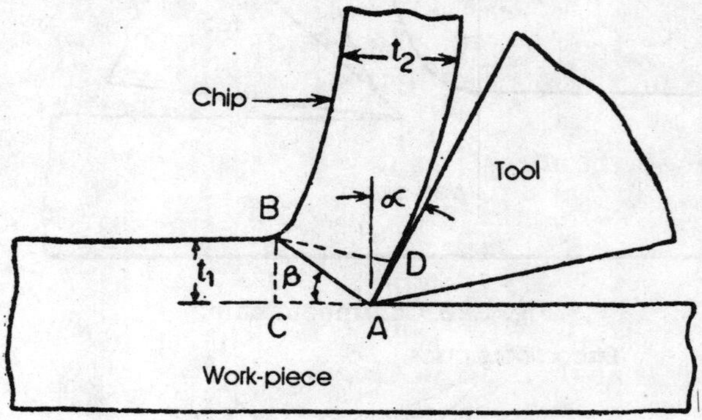

Fig. 1.25.

Let t_1 = chip thickness before cutting

t_2 = chip thickness after cutting

chip thickness ratio, $r = \frac{t_1}{t_2}$

The chip thickness ratio or cutting ratio is always less than unity. If the ratio r is large, the cutting action is good. A ratio of 1 : 2 yields good results.

$$k = \text{chip reduction coefficient} = \frac{1}{r}$$

When metal is cut there is no change in the volume of the metal cut.

$$t_1 \cdot b_1 \, l_1 = t_2 \cdot b_2 \cdot l_2$$

where
t_1 = chip thickness before cutting (Depth of cut)
b_1 = width of cut
l_1 = length of chip before cutting
t_2 = chip thickness after cutting
b_2 = width of chip after cutting
l_2 = length of chip after cutting

It is observed that $b_1 = b_2$

$$\therefore \quad t_1 \cdot l_1 = t_2 \cdot l_2$$

$$\frac{t_1}{t_2} = \frac{l_2}{l_1} = r.$$

Although chip thickness ratio can be obtained by measuring chip thickness (t_2) and depth of cut (t_1) this is not the most precise procedure. Chip thickness ratio can be easily obtained by measuring l_1 and l_2.

From the right angle triangle ABC (Fig. 1.25) we have

$$\frac{BC}{AB} = \sin \beta$$

$$AB = \frac{BC}{\sin \beta} = \frac{t_1}{\sin \beta} \qquad ...(i)$$

From right angle triangle ABD

$$\frac{BD}{RB} = \sin(90 - \beta + \alpha) = \cos(\beta - \alpha)$$

or

$$\frac{t_2}{AB} = \cos(\beta - \alpha)$$

$$\frac{t_2}{\cos(\beta - \alpha)} = AB \qquad ...(ii)$$

From (*i*) and (*ii*) we get

$$\frac{t_1}{\sin\beta} = \frac{t_2}{\cos(\beta - \alpha)}$$

$$\frac{t_1}{t_2} = r = \frac{\sin \beta}{\cos(\beta - \alpha)}$$

$$= \frac{\sin \beta}{\cos \beta \cos \alpha + \sin \beta \sin \alpha}$$

$$r = \frac{\sin \beta}{\cos \beta \cos \alpha + \sin \beta \sin \alpha}$$

$$\frac{r \cos \beta \cos \alpha}{\sin \beta} + \frac{r \sin \beta \sin \alpha}{\sin \beta} = 1$$

$$\frac{r \cdot \cos \alpha}{\tan \beta} + r \sin \alpha = 1$$

$$\frac{r \cos \alpha}{\tan \beta} = 1 - r \sin \alpha$$

$$\tan \beta = \frac{r \cos \alpha}{1 - r \sin \alpha}$$

Shear angle can be measured by measuring chip thickness, depth of cut and rake angle of tool. This can be most conveniently solved with the help of nomograph shown in Fig. 1.26 for determining shear angles.

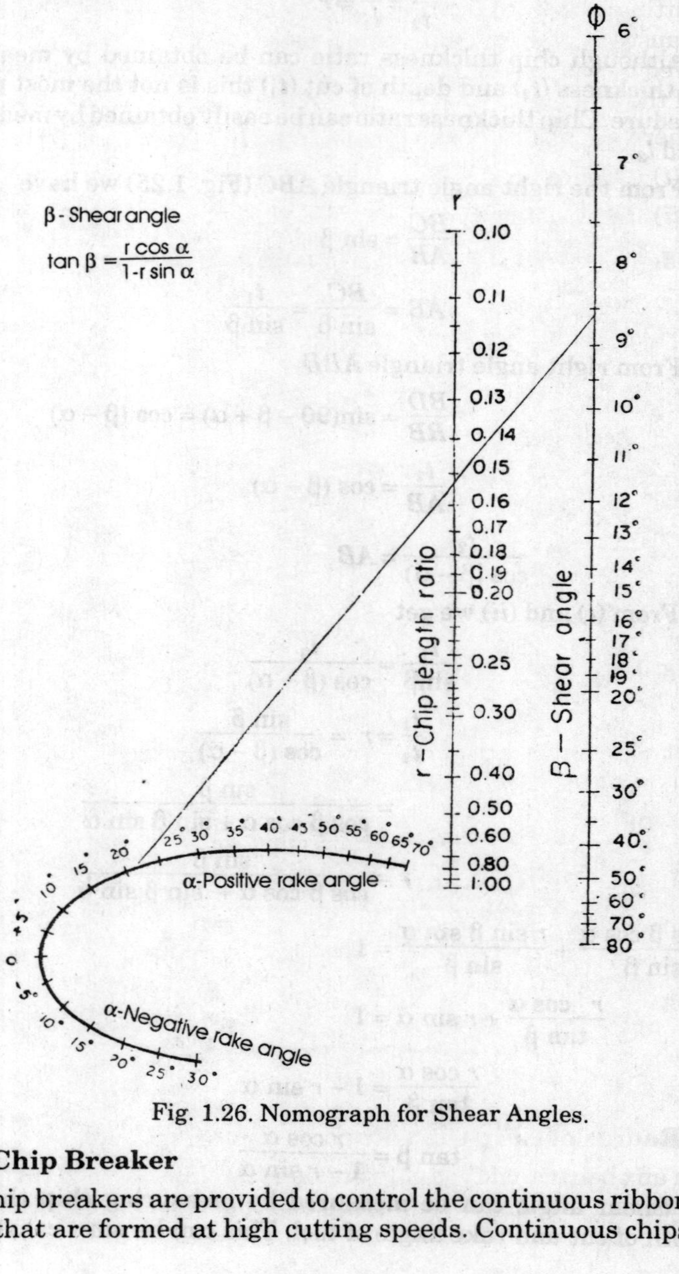

Fig. 1.26. Nomograph for Shear Angles.

1.11. Chip Breaker

Chip breakers are provided to control the continuous ribbonlike chips that are formed at high cutting speeds. Continuous chips are dangerous to the operator of the machine. These chips are hard, sharp and hot. They become entangled around the revolving job and the cutting tool. The chip breaker deflects the chip at a sharp angle and causes it to break into small pieces. So that they are easily removed by the coolant or air or simply allowed to fall into the chip pan of the machine.

There are basically two types of chip breakers :

(*i*) Groove type

(*ii*) Obstruction type.

Fig. 1.27 shows the groove type chip breaker.

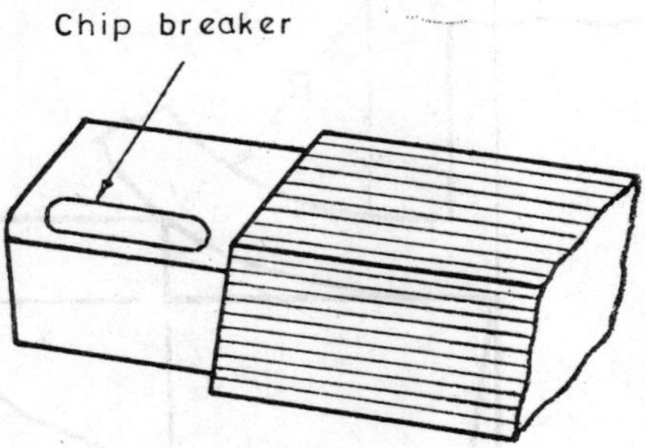

Fig. 1.27.

Fig. 1.28 shows an obstruction type chip breaker.

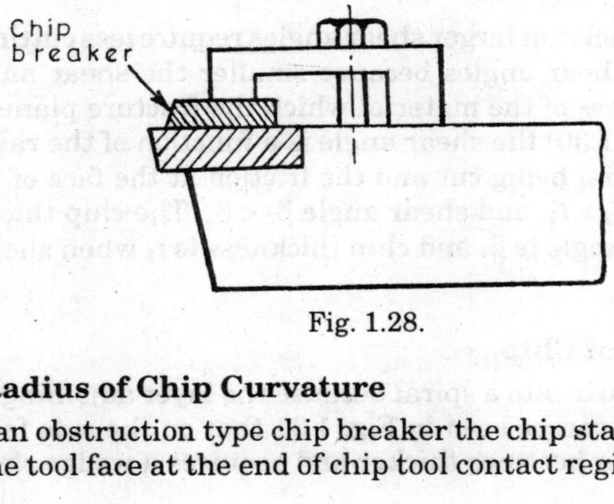

Fig. 1.28.

1.12. Radius of Chip Curvature

In an obstruction type chip breaker the chip starts to curl away from the tool face at the end of chip tool contact region and that the chip then maintains a constant radius of curvature until it clears the chip breaker. (Fig. 1.29). The radius of the chip curvature can be found by the following formula.

$$R = \frac{(S-H)^2}{2h} + \frac{h}{2}$$

where R = Radius of chip curvature

S = Chip breaker distance

H = Length of chip tool contact

h = Chip breaker height.

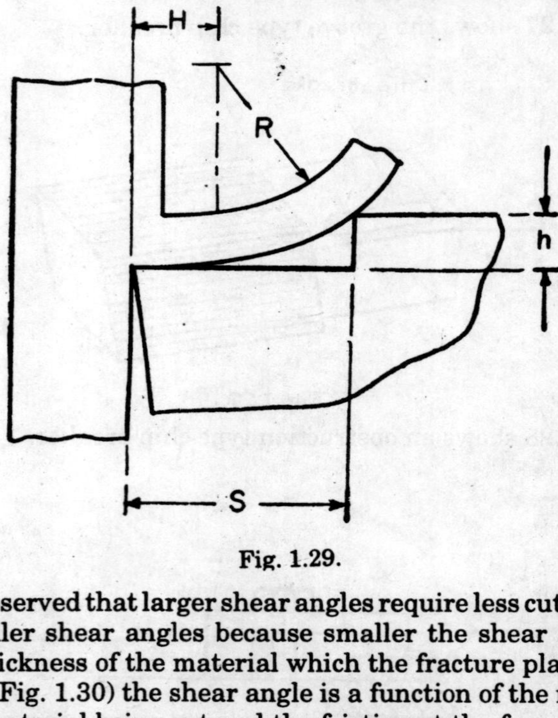

Fig. 1.29.

It is observed that larger shear angles require less cutting forces than smaller shear angles because smaller the shear angles the greater thickness of the material which the fracture plane need to traverse. (Fig. 1.30) the shear angle is a function of the rake of the tool, the material being cut and the friction at the face of the tool. As shown $t_3 > t_2 > t_1$ and shear angle $\beta_2 < \beta_1$. The chip thickness is t_2 when shear angle is β_1 and chip thickness is t_3 when shear angle is β_2.

1.13. Curling of Chip.

The chip curls into a spiral because the layer adjoining the tool is deformed. It can be seen in Fig. 1.31 that on the side facing the force P the layer becomes thicker and acquires a wedge shape as a result of which the curvature (curling) is produced. Another reason for curling the chip is that in meeting the tool face a change in its direction of flow away from tool face takes place curling is also produced by the non-uniform cooling of the chip throughout its thickness. Depending upon the machining conditions the chip may curl into a flat (logarithmic) spiral or into a helix.

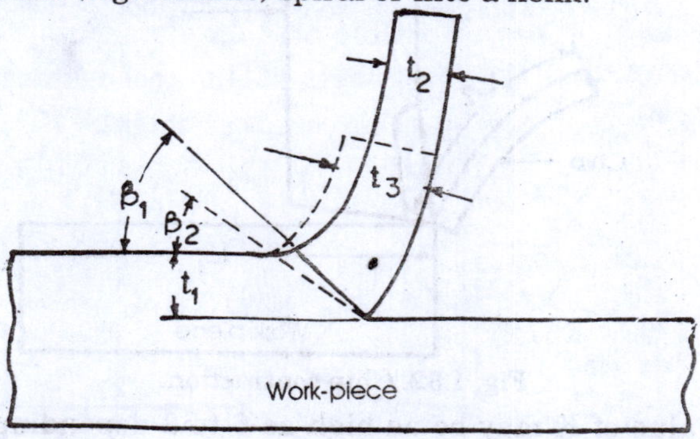

Fig. 1.30.

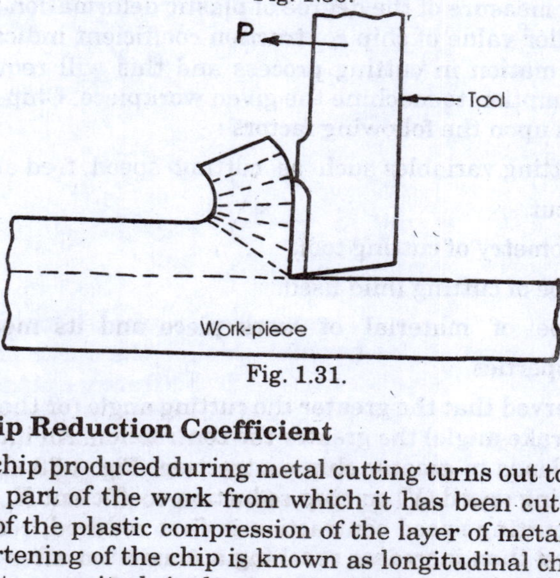

Fig. 1.31.

1.14. Chip Reduction Coefficient

The chip produced during metal cutting turns out to be shorter than the part of the work from which it has been cut (Fig. 1.32) because of the plastic compression of the layer of metal being cut. This shortening of the chip is known as longitudinal chip contraction and its magnitude is characterised by the coefficient of contraction.

Let, $K =$ Chip reduction coefficient

$L_1 =$ Length of the section of the work from which chip was removed in mm

L_2 = Length of chip cut from the section in mm

$$K = \frac{L_1}{L_2}$$

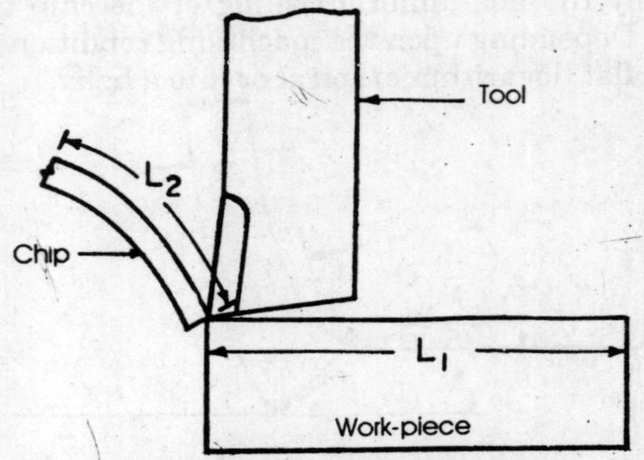

Fig. 1.32. Chip contraction.

The value of K may be as high as 6 to 8 depending upon the machining conditions. The coefficient of chip contraction is a certain quantitative measure of the degree of plastic deformation in metal cutting smaller value of chip contraction coefficient indicates less plastic deformation in cutting process and this will require less power consumption to machine the given workpiece. Chip contraction depends upon the following factors :

(*i*) Cutting variables such as cutting speed, feed and depth of cut.

(*ii*) Geometry of cutting tool.

(*iii*) Type of cutting fluid used.

(*iv*) Type of material of work piece and its mechanical properties.

It is observed that the greater the cutting angle (or the smaller the positive rake angle) the greater the contraction. An increase in nose radius leads to greater chip contraction. Fig. 1.33 shows the effect of cutting speed (V) on chip reduction coefficient K. With an increase in cutting speed contraction is first reduced, reaching a minimum and then increases reaching a maximum after which it drops again. Fig. 1.34 shows variation of chip reduction coefficient with feed upon an increase in feed coefficient of chip reduction is usually reduced.

The effect of surface active cutting fluids is clearly manifested on the reduction of chip contraction (Fig. 1.35).

1.15. Cutting Speed, Feed and Depth of Cut

Cutting speed. It is the travel of a point on the cutting edge relative to the surface of the cut in unit time in the process of accomplishing the primary cutting motion. For example in lathe work when a workpiece of diameter D rotates at a speed N revolutions per minute the cutting speed (V) is given by the relation

$$V = \frac{\pi \cdot D \cdot N}{1000} \text{ m per min.}$$

where D = Diameter of workpiece in mm.

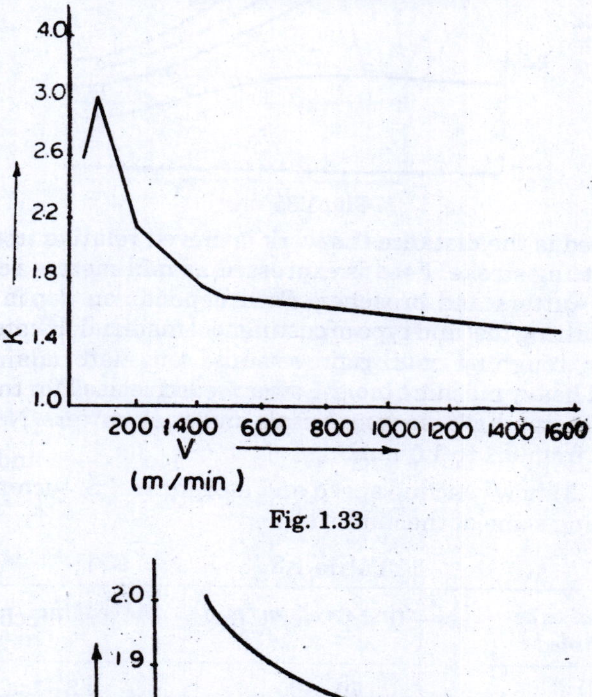

Fig. 1.33

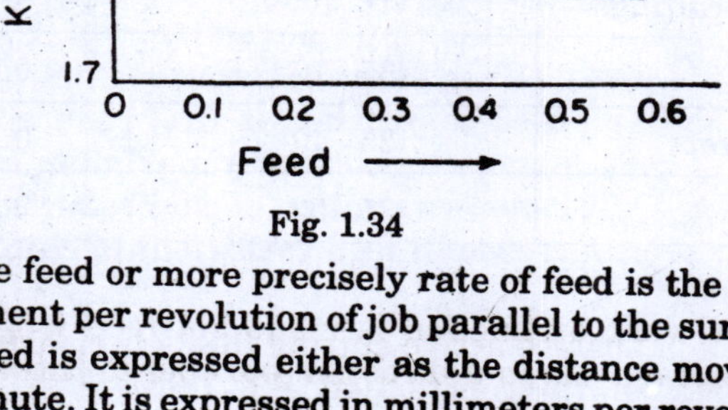

Fig. 1.34

Feed. The feed or more precisely rate of feed is the amount of tool advancement per revolution of job parallel to the surface being machined. Feed is expressed either as the distance moved by the tool in one minute. It is expressed in millimeters per revolution. On

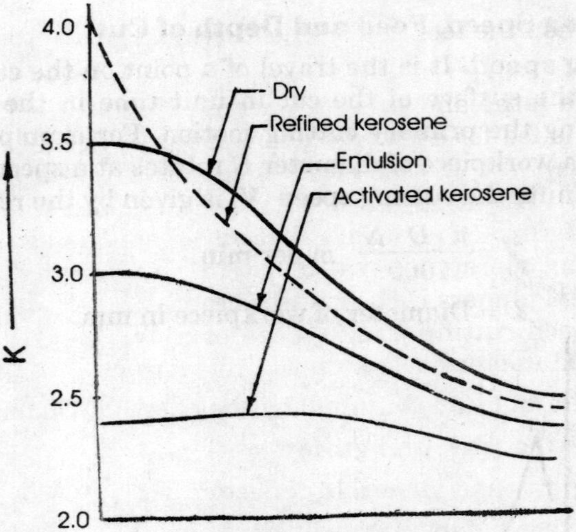

Fig. 1.35

a shaper feed is the distance the work is moved relative to the tool for each cutting stroke. Feed is expressed as millimeters per tooth for milling cutters and broaches. Feed depends on depth of cut, rigidity of cutting tool and type of cutting tool material. Higher feeds are used in roughing cuts, rigid set-ups, soft materials, rugged cutters and heavy machine tools. Lower feeds are used for finishing cuts, frail set-ups, hard work materials and weak cutters. Normally feed varies from 0.1 to 1.5 mm.

Table 1.3 shows cutting speed and feed for H.S.S. turning tools for machining some of the materials.

Table 1.3

Material to be machined	*Cutting speed (m / min)*	*Feed (mm / rev.)*
Aluminium	70 - 100	0.2 - 1.00
Brass (Free cutting)	70 - 100	0.2 - 1.5
Copper	35 - 70	0.2 - 1.00
Grey Cast Iron	25 - 40	0.15 - 1.7
Mild Steel	35 - 50	0.2 - 1.00

In lathe work distinction is made between longitudinal feed when the tool travels in a direction parallel to the work axis and cross feed when the tool travels in a direction perpendicular to the work axis.

Feed of a lathe and similar machine tools is the distance the cutting tool is fed for each revolution of work. The feed of drilling machine is the rate at which drill is advanced into the work piece per revolution of drill. The feeds for reaming operation is usually higher than that used for drilling because reamers have more teeth and a reaming operation is used for sizing and finishing. The feed of shapers and planers is the distance the cutting tool advances at the end of each cutting stroke. Feed of a milling machine is expressed in millimeter per minute of table movement.

The maximum feed is limited by the following factors :

(*i*) Cutting edge strength

(*ii*) Rigidity and allowable deflection

(*iii*) Surface finish required

(*iv*) Tool chip space.

Use of proper cutting fluid permits higher feeds and increased cutting speeds as well as attainment of better surface finish.

Depth of cut. It is the thickness of the layer of metal removed in one cut or pass measured in a direction perpendicular to the machined surface. The depth of cut is always perpendicular to the direction of the feed motion.

In external longitudinal turning it is half the difference between the work diameter (D_1) and the diameter of the machined surface (D_2) obtained after one pass.

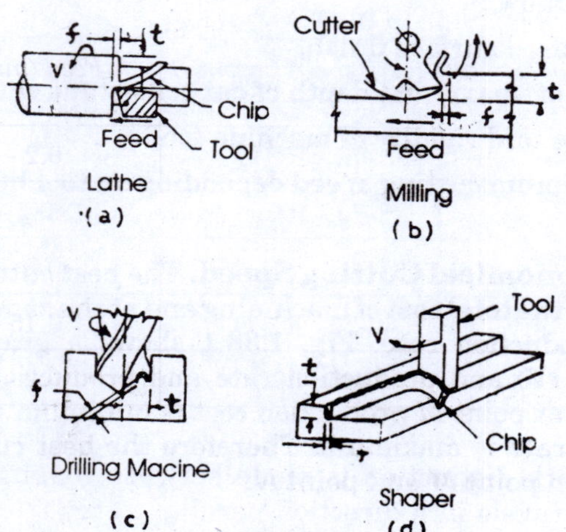

Fig. 1.36.

$$t = \text{Depth of cut} = \frac{D_1 - D_2}{2} \text{ mm}$$

Fig. 1.36 shows cutting speed (v), depth of cut (t) and feed (f) for lathe, milling machine, drill machine and shaper.

In general speed and feed depend upon the following factors :

(*i*) Type of material of workpiece.

(*ii*) Type of material of cutting tool.

(*iii*) Quality of finish desired.

(*iv*) Type of coolant used.

(*v*) Rigidity of the machine tool.

Table 1.4 shows typical lathe turning speeds for ceramic tools.

Table 1.4

Material to be cut	*Roughing (m / min)*	*Finishing (m / min)*
Upto 0.2 Carbon Steel	130 - 260	320 - 420
0.2 to 0.3 Carbon Steel	100 - 200	260 - 320
0.3 to 0.4 Carbon Steel	80 - 160	230 - 300
0.4 to 0.6 Carbon Steel	65 - 100	130 - 200
Cast Iron (BHN 217)	160 - 320	320 - 500

To achieve higher machining efficiency it is desired to use high feed that will allow :

(*a*) Required surface finish.

(*b*) Use of maximum depth of cut consistant with available power and rigidity of machine tool.

(*c*) Maximum cutting speed depending on tool life.

1.15.1.Economical Cutting Speed. The best cutting speed is which reduces the total cost of machining and at the same time gives maximum production rate. Fig. 1.36.1 shows a graph between cutting speed (V) and production rate and production cost. It is observed that at point M production cost is minimum and at point N production rate is maximum. Therefore the best cutting speed will be between point M and point N.

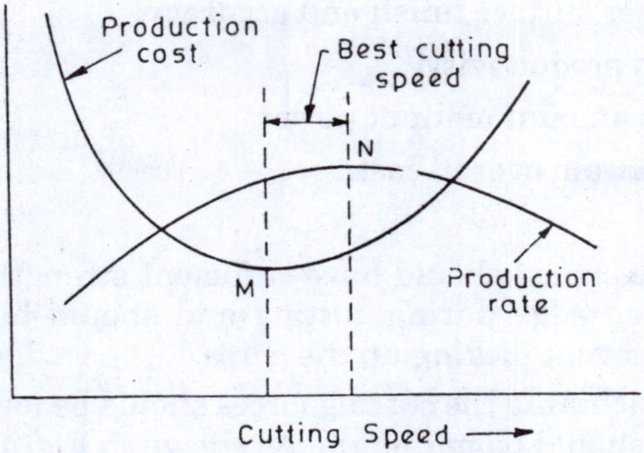

Fig. 1.36.1.

Tool design depends on the following factors :

(1) Type of machining operation such as

(*i*) Turning

(*ii*) Milling

(*iii*) Drilling

(*iv*) Shaping

(*v*) Slotting etc.

(2) Type of material of tool such as

(*i*) H.S.S.

(*ii*) Cemented Carbide.

(3) Type of work piece material

(4) Machining variables such as

(*i*) Cutting speed

(*ii*) Feed

(*iii*) Depth of cut

(5) Cutting force

(6) Accuracy to be obtained on work piece.

(7) Heat treatment and surface finish of tool.

1.16. Objectives of a Good Tool Design

A cutting tool should be made up of proper material and should be accurately designed in order to achieve the following objectives.

(*i*) Easy chip flow.

(*ii*) Proper surface finish and accuracy.

(*iii*) High productivity.

(*iv*) Less amount of input power.

(*v*) Minimum overall cost.

The tool designed should have sufficient strength to maintain a sharp cutting edge during cutting and should have sufficient hardness to prevent picking up the chips.

During machining the cutting forces should be low and the cost of production should be minimum. As shown in Fig. 1.36.2 .

In zone A cutting forces are very high due to the low cutting speed. Therefore cutting edges of brittle material like carbide may break. In zone C the cutting edge temperature will be very high due to the high cutting speed which will lead to rapid plastic deformation of the cutting edge. Zone B is, therefore, ideal for working with carbides where cutting forces are more or less independent of change in cutting speed. Cutting speeds vary with the machineability factor of the material being machined. Normally we employ higher cutting speeds for softer, and lower cutting speeds for harder materials. Therefore, it is advisable to use lower speeds within Zone B combined with higher feeds to achieve low cutting tool costs.

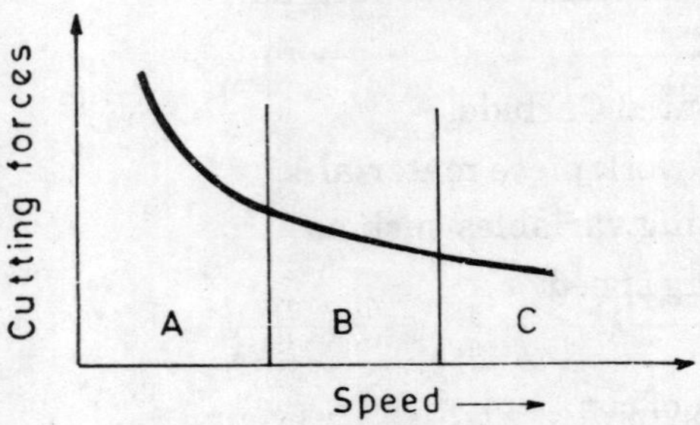

Fig. 1.36.2.

Though the tool life can be increased by using lower cutting speeds, the objective generally is to have that cutting speed which will give us the lowest cost of production. The cutting speed so selected is called economical cutting speed as shown in Fig. 1.36.3.

1.16.1. Re-sharpening Allowance. Allowance for re-sharpening of single point tools is indicated in Table 1.4.A.

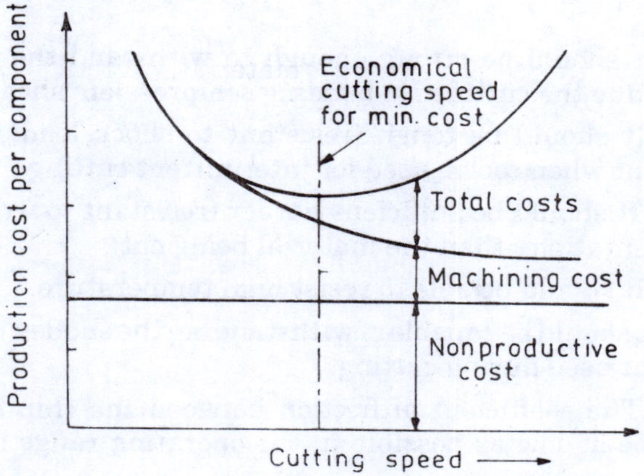

Fig. 1.36.3.

Table 1.4.A.

Tool Types	Tool material	Surface to be ground	Resharpening allowance, millimeters						
			Tool cross section, mm × mm						
			10 × 16	12 × 20	16 × 25	20 × 30	25 × 40	30 × 45	40 × 60
For single tool lathes	Cemented carbid	Face and flank	0.2	0.2	0.3	0.3	0.4	0.4	0.5
	High speed steel	Face and flank	0.3	0.4	0.5	0.5	0.6	0.6	0.6
For multi tool lathes	Cemented carbide	Flank	0.6	0.6	0.7	0.7	0.8	0.9	--
	High-speed steel	Flank	--	0.7	0.8	0.8	0.9	--	--
For circular foming tools	High-speed steel	Face	1.1	1.1	1.1	1.1	1.1	1.1	1.1

Tools used on multiple lathes are ground only on flanks whereas forming tools are ground on their faces.

1.17. Cutting Tools Materials

The purpose of cutting tool material is to remove metal under controlled conditions. Therefore the tool must be harder than the material which it is to cut. The cutting tools are made up of different materials. The cutting tool material should possess the following requirements :

(*i*) It should be strong enough to withstand the forces being applied due the cutting *i.e.* bending compression, shear etc.

(*ii*) It should be tough (resistant to shock loads). It is quite important when tool is used for intermittent cutting.

(*iii*) It should be sufficient harder (resistant to wear, abrasion and indentation) than the material being cut.

(*iv*) It should be able to resist high temperature.

(*v*) It should be capable of withstanding the sudden cooling effect of coolant used during cutting.

(*vi*) The coefficient of friction between the chip and the tool should be as low as possible in the operating range of speed and feed.

(*vii*) It should be easily formed to the required cutting shape.

Material chosen for a particular application will depend on the material being machined, the quantity of components to be produced, the cost of cutting tool materials, the type of machining operation (intermittent or continuous roughing or finishing, high or low speed etc.), the tool design details (cutting and clearance angles method of holding rigidity etc.) and the general conditions of machine tool.

Several materials exhibiting above properties in varying degrees have been developed for use in cutting tools.

The following metals suitably heat treated wherever required (tungsten carbide and ceramics are not heat treatable) are used in the manufacture of cutting tools :

(*a*) Carbon tool steel.

(*b*) High speed steel.

(*c*) Cemented carbides.

(*d*) Ceramics.

(*e*) Diamonds.

1.17.1. Carbon tool steels. Carbon steels are limited in use to tools of small section operating at lower speeds. A typical plain carbon steel used for cutting tool has the following composition.

$$\begin{aligned} C &= 0.8 \text{ to } 1.3\% \\ SI &= 0.1 \text{ to } 0.4\% \\ Mn &= 0.1 \text{ to } 0.4\% \end{aligned}$$

Such steels when hardened and tempered have good hardness, strength and toughness and can be given a keen cutting edge. Tools made up of plain carbon steels can be used for machining soft materials such as free cutting steels and brass. This material starts loosing its hardness at about 250°C and is therefore not used when the operational temperature is more.

Table 1.5(*a*) indicates percentage composition of typical medium alloy tool steels.

Table 1.5(a)

C	*Mn*	*Si*	*Cr*	*W*	*Mo*
1.2	0.6	0.3	0.5	-	-
1.2	0.7	0.3	0.5	-	0.5
1.2	0.3	0.3	0.7	1.5	0.3
1.3	0.3	0.3	0.7	4.0	-

Medium alloy tool steels are similar to carbon tool steel. However in medium alloy tool steels elements like chromium, molybdenum and tungsten are added. Chromium and molybdenum are added to increase hardenability of steel whereas tungsten is added to improve wear resistance.

1.17.2. Alloys and their effect on tool steels. Plain carbon steels when used as cutting tools lack certain necessary characteristics such as

(*i*) Red hardness
(*ii*) Impact strength
(*iii*) Abrasive resistance.

Addition of alloying elements such as

(*i*) Chromium
(*ii*) Vanadium
(*iii*) Tungsten
(*iv*) Cobalt
(*v*) Titanium
(*vi*) Molybdenum
(*vii*) Nickel
(*viii*) Manganese
(*ix*) Silicon

Helps in achieving the following properties :

(*i*) Improving toughness

(*ii*) Improving tensile and impact strength

(*iii*) Improving wear resistance

(*iv*) Improving hardenability

(*v*) Increasing high temperature resistance (red hardness)

(*vi*) Improving corrosion resistance.

Table 1.4.2. indicates case hardening temperature (T) and hardness (HRC) obtainable for some of Die Steels.

Table 1.4.2.

Type	T (°C)	HRC
En - 8	830 - 840	38 - 48
En - 9	830 - 860	45 - 55
En - 24	850 - 870	55 - 60
En - 30	900 - 920	50 - 60
En - 31	850 - 860	58 - 60
En - 36	900 - 920	50 - 60
En - 56	860 - 870	55 - 58
Spring steel	840 - 850	60 - 64
OHNS	860-880	60-62

1.17.3. High speed steels. High speed steel tools give improved cutting performance and higher metal removal rates. High speed steel is widely used for drills, many types of general purpose milling cutters and single-point tools.

Although several types of high speed steels are in use but 18-4-1 high speed steel containing tungsten 18%, chromium 4% and vanadium 1% is quite commonly used. This type of material gives excellent performance over a great range of materials and cutting speeds and it retains its hardness upto around 600°C. The coolant should be used freely to increase tool life. The chief characteristics of high speed steels are superior hardness and wear resistance.

Sometimes, the surface of high speed steel tools are treated by the following methods to reduce friction and to increase wear resistance.

(*i*) Super finishing (to reduce friction).

(*ii*) Chromium of electrolytic plating (to reduce friction).

(*iii*) Oxidation (to reduce friction).

(*iv*) Nitriding (to increase wear resistance).

Table 1.5 indicates some of the carbon tool steels.

1.17.4. Cemented carbides. They consist of tungsten, tantalum and titanium carbides together with a binder usually cobalt all mixed together as fine powders. These powders are compacted (compressed) into the required shape and subjected to a high temperature treatment known as sintering. During this process the cobalt binder is fused to the carbides, producing a hard, dense substance.

Tools made up of cemented carbides are extremely hard having Rockwell hardness varying from 90-93 HRC. They can be used at cutting speeds 200 to 500% greater than those used for high speed steel. They have virtually replaced high speed steels in high speed and high production machining. Cemented carbides are very hard and the usual practice is to confine the size to a relatively small shape known as an "insert" which is clamped to a tough steel shank or holder. This has the advantage that the tool bit is well supported to resist the cutting forces. The insert may have three to eight edges and is so designed that each of its cutting edges can be used in turn. It may then be discarded and replaced with a new tool bit giving low maintenance and breakdown time.

The general characteristics of carbide tools are as follows.

(*i*) They have high thermal conductivity, low specific heat and low thermal expansion.

(*ii*) They have high hardness over a wide range of temperature (upto 900°C).

(*iii*) Their compressive strength is more than tensile sthrength.

(*iv*) They are very stiff. Their Young's modulus is about three times than steel.

Tungsten carbide cutting tools containing only tungsten carbide and cobalt with no other elements added are referred to as the straight grades. The only variables in this case are the grain size of the tungsten carbide particles and the percentage of cobalt. Any change of these variables affects the hardness and transverse rupture strength (toughness) of the carbide insert. In turn, any reduction of hardness would reduce the abrasion resistance of the tool, and a reduction in toughness would result in a more brittle tool. In other words, the tougher the grade, the lower its wear resistance and vice versa.

Table 1.5. Carbon Tool Steels

IS : 1570/1961	*Nominal Chemical Composition*						
Designation	*C%*	*Mn%*	*Si%*	*S%*	*P%*	*Cr%*	*V%*
T 70	0.70	0.25	0.20	0.03	0.03	—	—
T 80	0.80	0.25	0.20	0.03	0.03	—	—
T 90	0.90	0.25	0.20	0.03	0.03	—	—
T 103	1.00	0.25	0.20	0.03	0.03	—	—
T 118	1.15	0.25	0.20	0.03	0.03	—	—
T 133	1.30	0.25	0.20	0.03	0.03	—	—

Table 1.6 shows some of popular grades of high speed steels used for making tools.

Table 1.6. High Speed Steel

IS:1570/1961	*Nominal Chemical Composition*									
Designation	*C%*	*Mn%*	*Si%*	*S%*	*P%*	*Cr%*	*Ni%*	*Mo%*	*W%*	*V%*	*CO%*
T70W18Cr4VI	0.70	0.40	0.35	0.25	0.025	4.15	—	—	18.25	1.20	—
T75W18Co6 Cr4VIMo75	0.75	0.40	0.35	0.25	0.025	4.20	—	0.75	18.25	1.25	5.50
T83Mo6W6Cr4V2	0.83	0.40	0.35	0.25	0.025	4.10	—	5.50	6.00	1.90	—

The effect of the variables in the straight carbide grades is as follows :

An increase in grain size

(a) lowers the hardness

(b) increases the transverse rupture strength (toughness).

An increase in cobalt content

(a) lowers the hardness

(b) increases the transverse rupture strength.

Maximum wear resistance is obtained from using a small grain size and a low cobalt content. When chipping of the tool occurs, the toughness is increased by increasing the grain size and cobalt content at the expense of wear resistance.

1.17.5. Ceramics. Aluminium oxide and boron nitride powders mixed together and sintered at 1700°C form the ingredients of ceramic tools. These materials are very hard with good compressive strength. Ceramics are usually in the form of disposable tips. They can be operated at from two to three times the cutting speeds of tungsten carbide and cutting speeds on cast iron in the order of 1000 m/min are not uncommon. They resist cratering, usually require no coolant. However in order to take full advantage of their capabilities special and more rigid machine tools are required.

Ceramic and cemented carbide cutting tools should be sharpened to a high degree of surface finish to minimise friction between tool and chip. This will improve the efficiency of the cutting process and less power will be absorbed and there will be a less tendency for a built up edge to form on the cutting face of the tool.

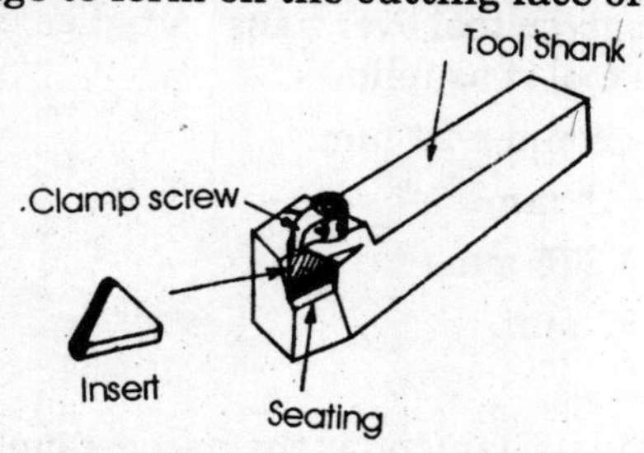

Fig. 1.37.

Cemented carbide or ceramic tips can be brazed to medium carbon steel shank and resharpened by grinding when necessary. For many applications it is more economical to clamp the tip to the shank (Fig. 1.37). The technique enables a tip to be thrown away (called throw away tips) at the end of its useful life and new tip to be clamped to the existing shank.

The various conditions for the effective use of carbide or ceramic tool are as follows :

(*i*) Rigidity of tool and workpiece.

(*ii*) Highly finished surface on cutting tool.

(*iii*) High cutting speeds.

(*iv*) Use of machine tool having high quality bearings.

(*v*) Use of effective chip bearings.

(*vi*) Elimination of any unbalanced forces.

(*vii*) Chip guards are essential when using these tools.

Appropriate reliefs and clearances are ground on carbide inserts as shown in Fig. 1.37(*a*).

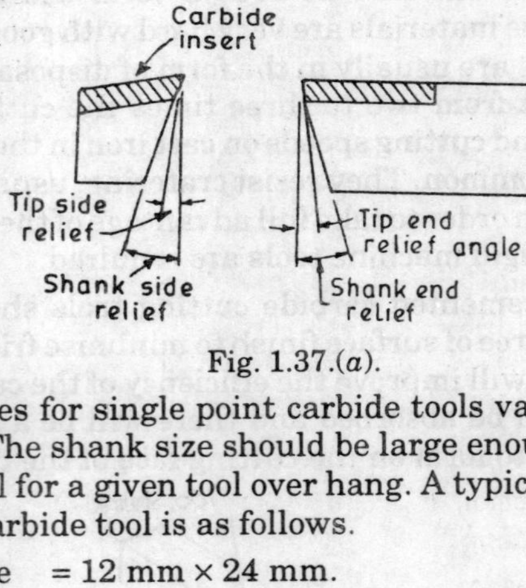

Fig. 1.37.(*a*).

Shank sizes for single point carbide tools vary from 12 mm to over 50 mm. The shank size should be large enough to support the load of the tool for a given tool over hang. A typical shank size for a single point carbide tool is as follows.

Shank size = 12 mm × 24 mm.

when depth of cut = 3 mm.

Feed = 0.375 mm.

Over hang = 36 mm.

1.17.6. Diamonds. Diamond is the hardest material known. It has a low coefficient of friction, high compressive strength and is extremely wear resistant. It is used mainly for cutting very hard materials, such as glass, plastics, ceramics etc. Diamond tools produce a very good surface finish at high speeds with good dimensional accuracy. Diamond tools are small and are best suited for light cuts and finishing operations. Other application for diamond is that it is used for truing the grinding wheels. The general properties of diamond may be summarised as follows :

1. It is the hardest known substance.
2. It has lowest thermal expansion of any pure substance.
3. It has high heat conductivity.
4. It has poor electrical conductivity.
5. It has very low coefficient of friction against metals.

Since very high hardness is always accompanied by brittleness a diamond tool must be cautiously used to avoid rupturing the point. This usually limits the use of diamond tools to light continuous cut in relatively soft metals and low values of rake angle are usually used to provide a stronger cutting edge.

The main disadvantages of diamonds are their brittleness and high cost.

1.17.7. Multi-coated cemented carbide inserts. Cemented carbide inserts coated with layers of optimum thickness of Titanium Carbide, Titanium Carbonitride, and Titanium nitride have more life. Layer coating is carried out by chemical vapour deposition process.

Various advantages of multiple coatings are as follows :

1. A hard, binderless layer of TIN, acts as a diffusion barrier and eliminates the possibility of chip welding and chemical diffusion on insert Rake face, thereby **increasing crater resistance.**
2. Reduced Flank wear.
3. Lower frictional resistance and reduction in cutting forces upto 10-15%. This also allows higher cutting speed.
4. Higher Thermal conductivity.
5. Superior surface finish on machined parts.

1.18. Variation of Hardness with Temperature

Fig. 1.38 shows the variation of hardness with temperature for the tools made up of different materials.

1. A plain carbon tool steel tool.
2. An 18-4-1 high speed steel tool.
3. A cast alloy tool.
4. A cast iron grade cemented tungsten carbide tool.

1.19. Economic Comparison of Tool Materials

The principal tool materials are high speed steel, cemented carbide and ceramics in increasing order of hardness and reducing order of toughness. High speed steel is quite commonly used as it can be used to manufacture complicated shaped cutting tools such as drills, taps, reamers, dies and milling cutters. Cemented carbide because of its high cost and need to form it in its final shape has limited applications and is generally used for rough or finish turning and face milling operations. Ceramic tool material is brittle, cannot withstand high force and is generally used in finish turning operations.

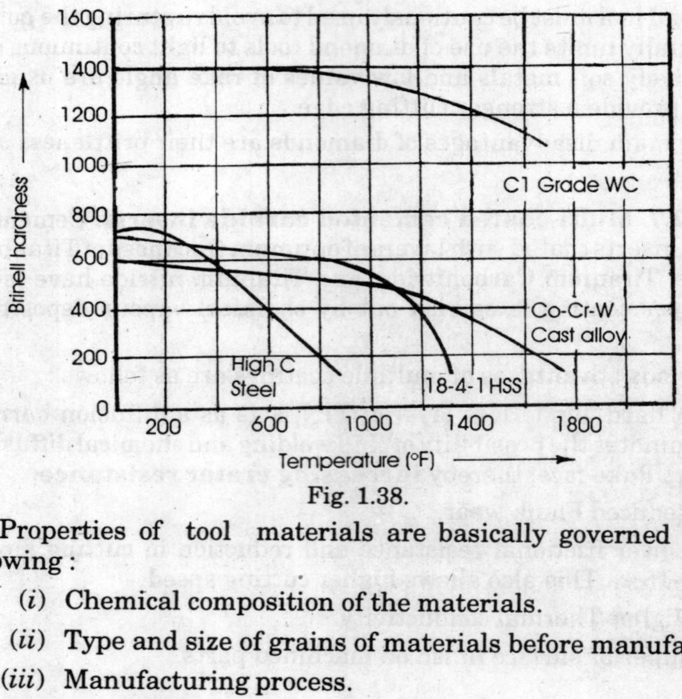

Fig. 1.38.

Properties of tool materials are basically governed by the following :

(*i*) Chemical composition of the materials.

(*ii*) Type and size of grains of materials before manufacture.

(*iii*) Manufacturing process.

(*iv*) Finishing treatments.

1.20. Multi-edge Cutting Tools

Multi-edge cutting tools present more than one cutting edge to the work. They have a higher metal removal rate than single edged cutting tools and also the life of the multi-edge cutting tool is raised by increasing the number of cutting edges. The different multi-edge cutting tools are divided into two groups as shown in Table 1.7.

A grinding wheel is also a form of multi-edge cutting tool.

Table 1.7

Group	*Machines*	*Cutting Tools*
A	Drills	Twist drills
	Capstan	Reamers
	Lathe	Multi flute core drills
	Turret	Counter bores spot
	Lathe	Facing cutters.
B	Milling	Saws and slotting
	Machines	Cutters
		Side and face cutters
		Slab mills
		End mills
		Face mills
		Form-relieved cutters.

The tools in group *A* have their cutting edges in continuous engagement with the work and are fed axially at a uniform feed per revolution. The underformed chip thickness is therefore constant and directly proportional to the feed/rev. The geometry and mechanics of cutting are then identical with those discussed for single point tools. The various tools in group *B* have their cutting edges intermittently engaged with the work and are fed in a plane parallel or perpendicular to the cutter axis of rotation.

1.21. The Twist Drill

It is used to produce a hole in the workpiece. Its sole purpose is to remove the maximum volume of metal in a minimum period of time. The finish obtained by a drill is not so fine. If a hole of accurate size and good finish is required the drilled hole should be finish machined by means of a reamer or by single point boring tool. Twist drills are usually made of high speed steel. High carbon steel can also be used to manufacture drills. Drills with cemented carbide cutting tips (tips are brazed) are used at very high speeds for drilling operations on non-ferrous metals but are not recommended for ferrous metal particularly steels because the tips are not supported as effectively as in case of single point cutting tools or milling cutters. A twist drill consists of a cylindrical body carrying two helical grooves into it to from the flutes. The flutes run the full length of body of twist drill and perform the following functions.

(*i*) They provide the rake angle.

(*ii*) They form the cutting edges.

(*iii*) They provide a passage of the coolant.

(*iv*) They facilitate swarf removal.

1.22. Elements of a Twist Drill

A twist drill is shown in Fig. 1.39. The various elements of a twist drill are as follows :

(*i*) **Body.** It is the part of the drill that is fluted and relieved.

(*ii*) **Shank.** It is the part held in the holding device.

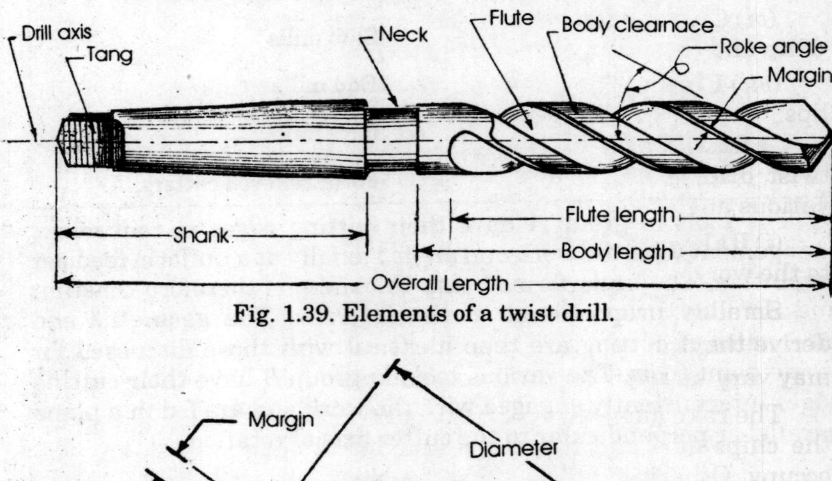

Fig. 1.39. Elements of a twist drill.

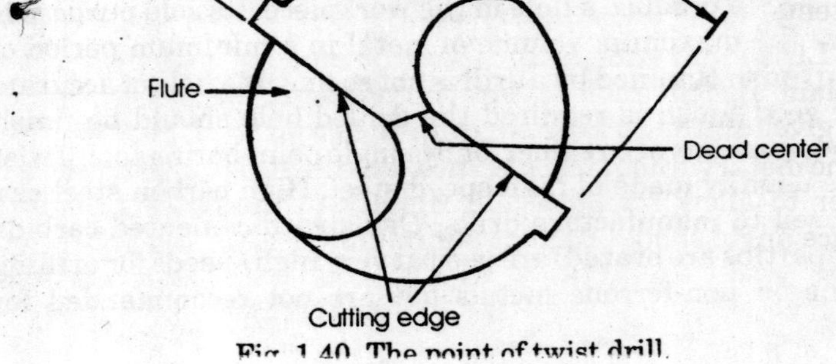

Fig. 1.40. The point of twist drill.

The most common types of shanks are the taper shank and the parallel shanks. Small drills up to about 12.7 mm diameter are provided with parallel shanks and the larger size drill have tapered shanks. Tapered shank drill carry a tang at the end of the shank to ensure a positive grip. The straight shank drills are held in a drill machine by a chuck. The jaws of the chuck are tightened around the drill by means of a key or wrench. The point of a drill is the entire cone shaped surface at the cutting end of the drill. (Fig. 1.40).

(iii) **Dead centre.** The dead centre or chisel edge of the drill is the sharp edge at the extreme tip end of the drill. It should always be in the exact centre of the axis of the drill.

(iv) **Lip.** Lip or cutting edge is formed by the intersection of the flank and face. Both the lips of the drill should be of equal length and should be at the same angle of inclination with the drill axis. This will enable to produce a perfectly round smooth and accurate hole. Unequal lips will result in an oversize hole.

(v) **Flank.** Flank is the surface on a drill point which extends behind the lip to the following flute.

(vi) **Chisel edge corner.** The corner formed by the intersection of lip and the chisel edge is called chisel edge corner.

(vii) **Flutes.** The grooves in the body of the drill which provide lips.

1.22.1. Twist drill angles. Lake any other cutting tool the twist drill is provided with correct tool angles (Fig. 1.41). The various angles are as follows :

(i) **Rake angle or helix angle.** It is the angle of flute in relation to the work.

Smaller the rake angle greater will be the torque required to derive the drill at a given speed. Its usual value is 30° although it may vary up to 45° for different materials.

The rake angle also partially governs the tightness with which the chips curl and hence the amount of space which the chips occupy. Other conditions being the same, a very large rake angle makes a tightly rolled chip, while a rather small rake angle makes a chip tend to curl into a more loosely rolled helix.

(ii) **Lips clearance angle.** It is the angle formed by the flank and a plane at right angle to the drill axis. Lip clearance is the relief that is given to the cutting edges in the order to allow the drill to enter the metal without interference. This angle is 12° in most cases. In order to allow strength and rigidity to the cutting edge the clearance angle should be kept minimum.

(*iii*) **Cutting angle or point angle.** It is the angle included between the two lips projected upon a plane parallel to the drill axis and parallel to the two cutting lips. It is observed that the best point angle is 118°.

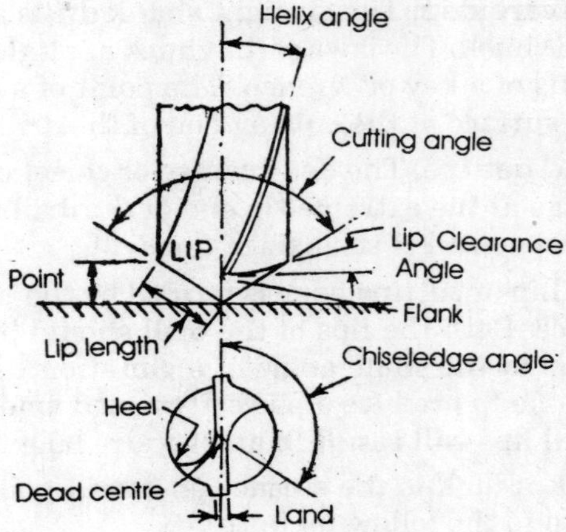

Fig. 1.41.

(*iv*) **Chisel edge angle.** It is the angle included between the chisel edge and the lip as seen from the end of the drill.

The various angles for a drill are shown in table 1.8.

Table 1.8

Material	*Point angle (Degrees)*	*Lip clearance angle (Degrees)*	*Chisel edge angle (Degrees)*	*Helix angle (Degrees)*
Aluminium	**90-140**	**8-12**	**120-135**	**24-48**
Brass	**111**	**8-15**	**120-135**	**0-27**
Copper	**100-118**	**8-15**	**120-135**	**28-40**
Cost iron hard	**118**	**8-12**	**120-135**	**24-40**
Steel	**118**	**8-12**	**120-135**	**24-32**
Stainless Steel	**125-135**	**10-12**	**120-135**	**24-32**

Fig. 1.41(*a*) shows a carbide tip. embedded in the shank. The tool flank must be designed in such a way as to minimise sharpening

costs. The flanks of almost all carbide tips are bevelled to an angle of 20°. Fig. 1.41(*b*) shows shape of flank surfaced of carbide tipped tool without tip over hang whereas Fig. 1.41(*c*) shows shape of flank surface of carbide tipped tool with tip overhang.

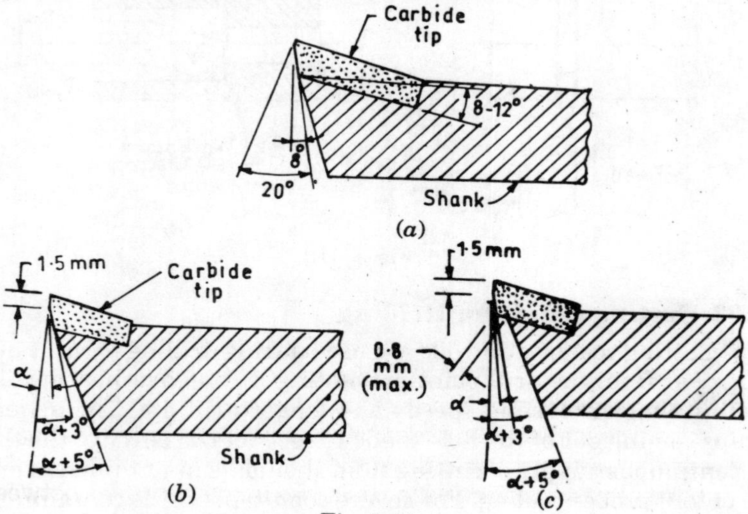

Fig. 1.41

Tipped tools are preferable when expensive cemented carbides or high speed steels are used : then, the point is made of a metal-cutting material, while the shank is of structural carbon steel.

Cemented-carbide tips are brazed or clamped mechanically, while tips of highspeed steel are clamped.

An as-brazed tip may protrude from the shank for as much as 1.5 millimetres, but in tool sharpening this over-hang should be reduced to within 0.8 millimetre. This will enable carbide tips to be sharpened by diamond wheels, keeping the latter out of touch with the shank.

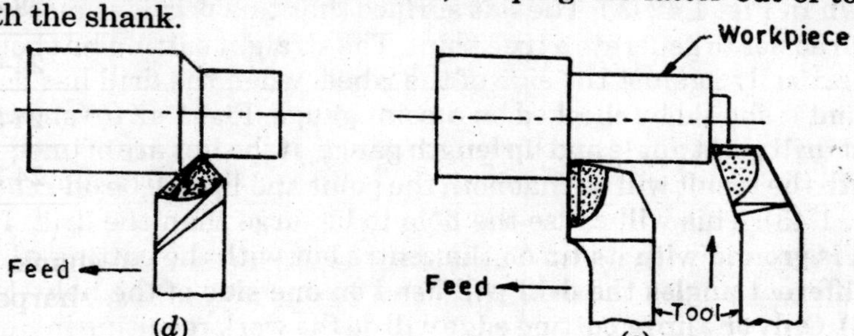

Fig. 1.41(*d*) shows a turning tool whereas a facing tool is shown in Fig. 1.41(*e*). A parting tool used to cut off the material is shown in Fig. 1.41(*f*). A boring tool is shown in Fig. 1.41(*g*).

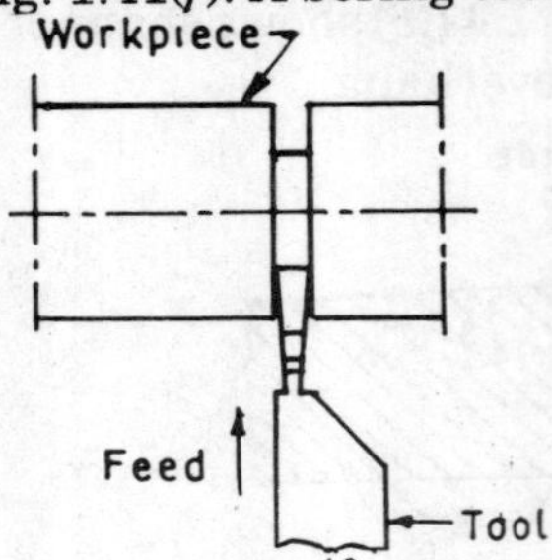

(*f*)

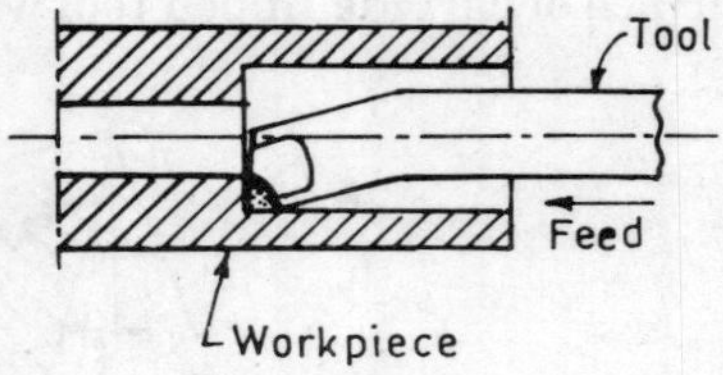

(*g*)

Fig. 1.41.

1.23. Cutting Fluids for Drilling

Cutting coolants and oils are used during drilling to carry away the heat from the drill point preventing it from overheating. This permits higher cutting speeds and longer drill life. The action of chips coming out of the hole tends to restrict the entry of the fluid. A continuous supply of cutting fluid should be maintained in order to obtain proper cooling. For severe conditions drills containing oil holes have a considerable advantage. In such case not only the fluid is supplied near the cutting edges but the flow of fluid aids in chip removal from the hole.

Practically all metals require the use of coolant when being drilled except cast iron which may be machined dry.

1.24. Twist Drill Grinding

It is very important that drills are properly ground. The drill point must be in the centre of rotation of the drill. The lips should be of equal length and at correct angle with the axis. The twist drill is ground on the side of grinding wheel of the grinding machine as shown in Fig. 1.42 (*a*). The flat surface that this provides makes it much easier to generate a true point. The straight cutting lip should lie vertically against the side of the wheel when the drill has been ground it should be checked on a point gauge. Fig. 1.42 (*b*) shows a twist drill point angle and lip length gauge. If the lips are of unequal length the result will be that both the point and lip will be off-centre (Fig. 1.43). This will cause the hole to be large than the drill. If a drill is ground with its tip on the centre but with the cutting edges at different angles the drill will bend on one side of the hole (Fig. 1.44). Only one lip or cutting edge will do the work resulting in rapid wear on that edge and the hole will be larger than drill.

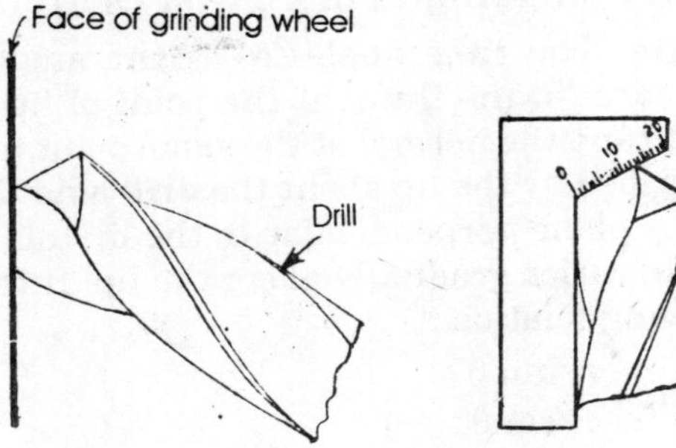

Fig. 1.42.

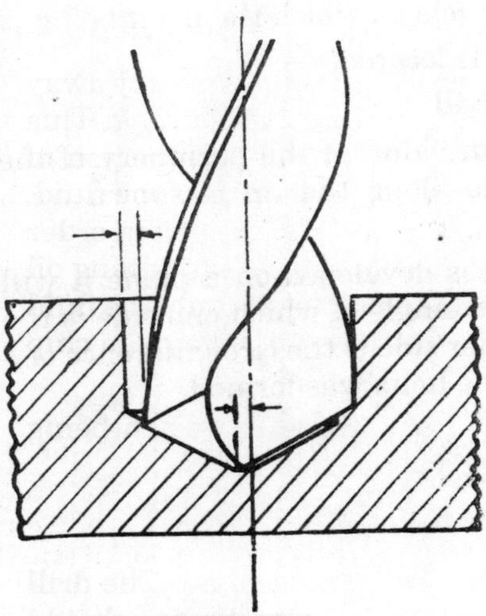

Fig. 1.43.

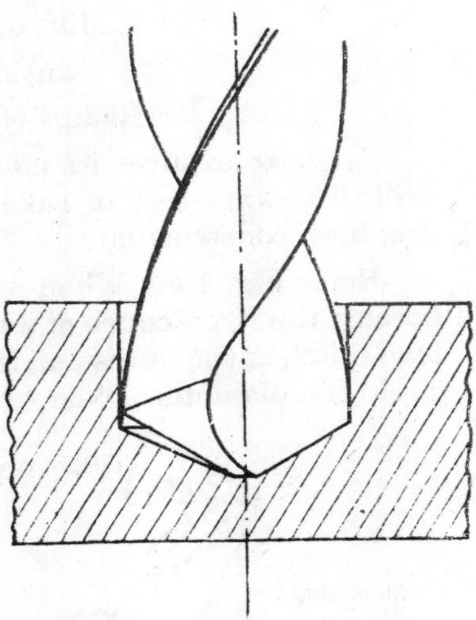

Fig. 1.44

1.24.1. Twist drill failure. A twist drill will suffer an early failure or produce holes that are dimensionally inaccurate, out of round and poor finish for the following general reasons :

(*i*) Incorrect speed and feeds

(*ii*) Incorrect grinding of the point

(*iii*) Mishandling

(*iv*) Lips of unequal length.

1.25. Rake and Relief Angles of a Twist Drill

Rake Angle. The rake angle (α) is the angle between the tangent to the face (in the flute) at the point of lip (cutting edge) being referred to and the normal at the same point to the surface of revolution described by the lip about the drill axis. The rake angle is measured in a plane perpendicular to the lip (plane MM in Fig. 1.45). This angle varies gradually along the lip. It can be found by using the following relation :

$$\tan \alpha_x = \frac{r_s \tan \beta}{R \sin \theta}$$

where β = Helix angle of flutes

R = Radius of drill.

θ = One half of the point angle.

rx = Radius of the circle on which the point being considered is located.

R = Radius of the drill

Angle α acquires its maximum value at the periphery of the drill. The variation of rake angle along the lip is shown by a graphical construction.

Refer Fig. 1.46. When a helix is developed on a plane it will become the hypotenuse of a right triangle of which one side is the lead (pitch of the flutes and the other side is the circumference of a circle of a diameter (D) on which the helix was formed.

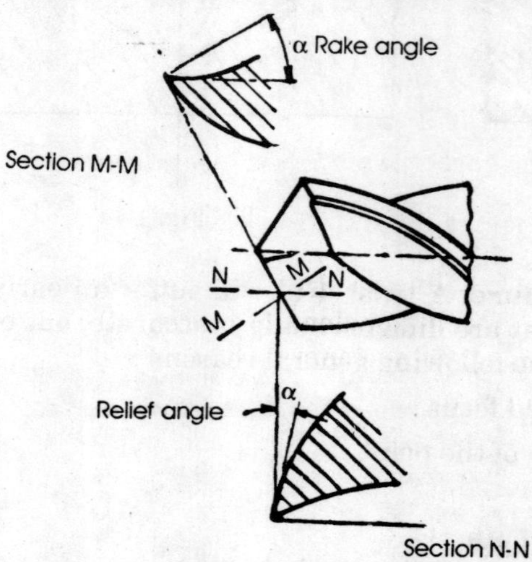

Fig. 1.45.

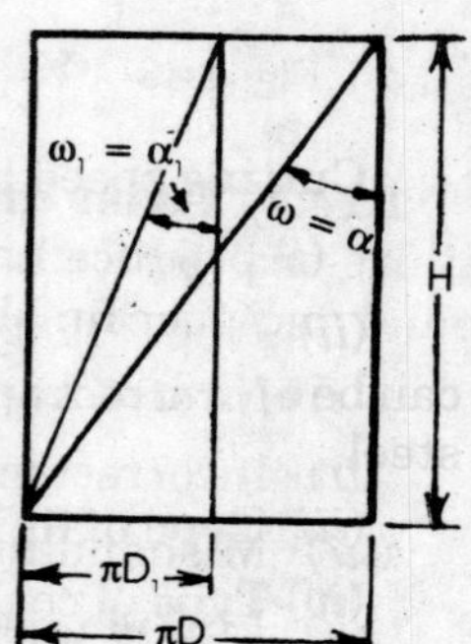

Fig. 1.46.

Relief Angle γ. It is the angle between a tangent to the flank or lip relief surface at the point being considered on the lip and a tangent at the same point to the circle the point describes as it rotates about the drill axis. This angle is measured in plane *NN* (Fig. 1.45) which is tangent to the cylindrical surface on which the above mentioned point on the lip lies.

1.26. Drill Specifications

According to Indian Standard System, twist drills are specified by the diameter, the I.S. number, the material and the series to which they belong. The drills are made in three types :

(*i*) Type *N*--for normal low carbon steel.

(*ii*) Type *H*--for hard materials.

(*iii*) Type *S*--for soft and tough materials.

For example a parallel shank twist drill 12 mm diameter and made up of high speed steel and conforming to IS : 5101 with a point angle of 118° and of N-type is designated as 12.00--IS : 5101 HS-N-118.

Unless otherwise mentioned in the designation it should be assumed that drill type is N and point angle is 118°.

1.26.1. Drill Size. In metric system the drills are made in diameters from 0.2 mm to 100 mm.

1.27. Cutting Speed, Feed and Depth of Cut

(*i*) **Cutting speed.** It is the peripheral speed of a point on the surface of the drill in contact with the work piece. It is usually expressed in metres per minute.

Let D = Diameter of drill in mm.

N = R.P.M. of drill spindle.

V = Cutting speed in metre per minute.

$$V = \frac{\pi D N}{1000} \text{ metre per minute.}$$

Cutting speed mainly depends upon the following factors :

(*i*) Type of material to be drilled.

(*ii*) Type of material of drill. Twist drill made of high speed steel can be operated at about twice the speed of drill made of high carbon steel.

(*iii*) Type of finish required.

(*iv*) Type of coolant used.

(*v*) Capacity of machine and tool life.

Table 1.9 shows cutting speed for high speed steel drill.

Table 1.9

Material being drilled	*Cutting speed (m / min)*
Aluminium	70--100
Brass	35--50
Phosphor Bronze	20--35
Grey Cast Iron	25--40
Copper	35--45
Mild Steel	30--40
Alloy Steel (High tensile)	5--8

(ii) **Feed.** It is the distance the drill moves into the work at each revolution of the spindle. It is expressed as millimeter per revolution.

It may also be expressed as feed per minute.

Let N = R.P.M. of drill spindle.

f = feed in mm /rev.

f_1 = feed in mm per minute.

$= N.f.$

Table 1.10 shows feed for high speed steel drill of various diameters.

Table 1.10

Drill diameter (mm)	*Feed (mm / rev.)*
1.0--2.5	0.04--0.06
2.6--4.5	0.05--0.10
4.6--6.0	0.075--0.15
6.1--12.00	0.75--0.25
12.1--15.0	0.20--0.30
15.1--18.0	0.23--0.33
18.1--21.0	0.26--0.36
21.1--25	0.28--0.39

A twist drill gives satisfactory performance if it is run at correct cutting speed and feed. The following factors help in running the drill at correct cutting speed and feed.

(*i*) The work is rigidly clamped.

(*ii*) The machine is in good condition.

(*iii*) A coolant is used if required.

(*iv*) The drill is correctly selected and ground for the material being cut. The selection of drill depends upon the following.

(*a*) Size of drill hole

(*b*) Material of workpiece

(*c*) Point angle of drill.

The rates of feed and cutting speed for twist drill are lower than most other machining operations because of the following reasons.

(*i*) The twist drill is weak compared with other cutting tools.

(*ii*) It is relatively difficult for the drill to eject chips.

(*iii*) It is difficult to keep the cutting edges cool when they are enclosed in the hole.

(*iii*) **Depth of cut.** It is equal to one half of the drill diameter.

D = Diameter of drill in mm.

t = Depth of cut in mm.

$$= \frac{D}{2} \text{ mm.}$$

1.28. Machining Time

Machining time in drilling is calculated as follows (Fig. 1.47)

Let T = Machining time in minutes

l = Thickness of workpiece in mm.

h = Approach of drill = 0.3 D in mm.

D = Diameter of drill in mm.

L = Length of axial travel of drill = $l + h$.

f = Feed/rev. in mm.

$$T = \frac{L}{N \times f}.$$

1.29. Forces Acting on a Drill

The various forces acting on a drill are shown in Fig.1.48. All the elements of a drill are subject to certain forces in drilling. Resolving the resultant forces of resistance to cutting at each point

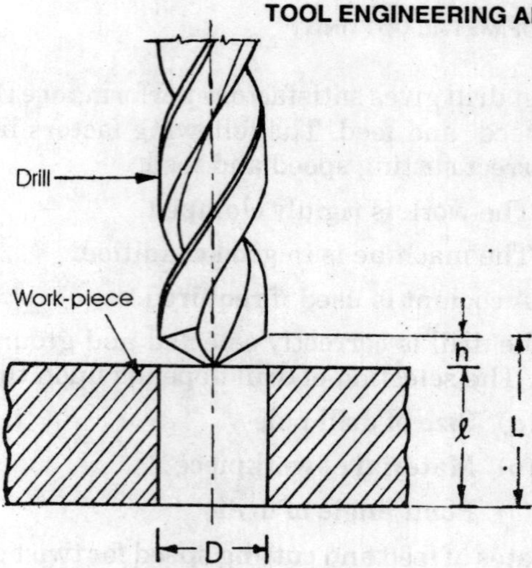

Fig. 1.47

of the lip we obtain three forces F_Z F_V, and F_H acting in directions mutually perpendicular to each other. The horizontal forces F_H acting on both lips are considered to counter balance each other. The vertical force F_V also called as thrust force comprises of the forces F_{V1}, F_{V2}, F_C and F_m. (The forces F_C and F_M are not shown). The force F_{V1}, acts on the web. This force is quite large and is about 60% of the total thrust force. This force F_{V2} act on each of the two lips and forms the real cutting force which depends upon the work material, cutting variables and cutting point geometry and is about 37% of total thrust force. The F_c and E_m are of smaller magnitude. The force F_c is due to the rubbing of the chips, flow from the hole against the sides of the hole and flutes on the drill. This force is about 1% of the total thrust force. The force F_M is due to the rubbing action of margin of the drill against the sides of the hole and is about 2% of thrust force.

In order that the drill is to penetrate into the work piece the thrust force F applied to it by the machine must over come the sum of resistances acting along the drill axis.

$$F > \Sigma\,(F_{V_1} + 2Fv_2 + F_C + F_m)$$

The force F_Z sets up the moment of resistance (M_r)

$$M_r = F_Z \,.\, S$$

The total moment of the forces of resistance (M) to cutting is made up of the following moments.

(*i*) Moment of forces F_Z *i.e.* M_r.

(*ii*) Moment of forces due to scraping and friction on the chisel edge (M_c).

(*iii*) Moment of the friction forces on the margins (M_m).

(*iv*) Moment of the forces of friction of the chip on the drill and on the machined surface.(M_d)

$$M = M_r + M_c + M_m + M_d$$

The total moment of resistance should be overcome by the available torque of the drilling machine.

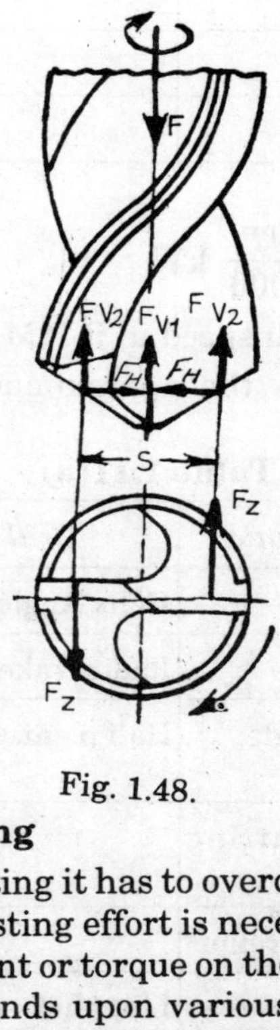

Fig. 1.48.

1.30. Power of Drilling

When a drill is cutting it has to overcome the resistance offered by the metal and a twisting effort is necessary to turn it. The effort is called turning moment or torque on the drill. The torque required to operate a drill depends upon various factors. The relationship between torque, diameter of drill and feed is as follows :

$$T_1 = C.f^{0.75}\ D^{1.8} \text{ newton metres}$$

where T_1 = Torque in newton metre.

f = Drill feed in mm/rev.

D = Diameter of drill in mm.

C = Constant depending upon the material being drilled. The values C are given In table 1.11 for different materials.

Table 1.11

Materials to be drilled	*Value of C*
Aluminium	0.11
Soft brass	0.084
Cast Iron	0.07
Mild steel	0.56
Corbon tool steel	0.4

$$\text{Power} \quad (P) = \frac{2\pi N T_1}{60{,}000} \text{ kW}$$

where N = Drill speed in R.P.M.

Table 1.11 (a) shows the approximate equivalents of tool geometry.

Table 1.11(a)

Lathe and planer	*Milling cutter*	*Drill*	*Broach*
Back rake	Axial rake	Helix Angle	Hook angle
Side rake	Radial rake	Radial rake	Side rake
Side cutting edge angle	Corner Angle	Half point Angle	
End cutting edge angle	End cutting angle		
Side relief	Peripheral relief		Clearance
End relief	End relief	Lip relief	Clearance

1.31. Milling Cutters

Milling is an operation in which metal cutting is carried out by means of multi-teeth rotating tool called cutter. The cutters are manufactured in a variety of shapes and size each made for a specific purpose. In milling cutters each tooth after taking a cut comes into operation again after some interval of time. This allows the tooth to cool down before the next cutting operation is done by it. This minimises the effect of heat developed in cutting on cutting edges. A coolant is helpful when milling steel for producing a good surface finish. The coolant may be oil or an emulsion of oil and water. The form of each tooth of cutter is same as that of a single point tool.

Many types of milling cutters are used on a milling machine. Most of them are considered standard and are available in many sizes. High speed steel is the material commonly favoured for cutters. They are also available with carbide tips at cutting edges. Cutters should be kept sharp. Cutters which are sharpened frequently usually last longer than those which are allowed to become dull.

A milling cutter is a multiple tooth tool and therefore higher requirements are made to its construction, sharpening and operation. The cutter should be reliably and rigidly clamped on the spindle. Milling cutters may be solid, inter locking, carbide tipped solid cutters and inserted blade cutters with high speed steel or carbide tipped blades.

The various advantages of carbide tipped cutters either solid or inserted blade type are as follows :

(*i*) They have high production capacity.

(*ii*) They produce surface finish of high quality.

(*iii*) They can machine hardened steels.

(*iv*) Their use leads to reduction in machining costs.

1.30.1. Milling operations. With cylindrical cutters the two methods of milling operations commonly used are as follows :

(*i*) **Up or conventional milling.** In this process the cutter rotates against the direction in which the work is feeding (Fig. 1.49).

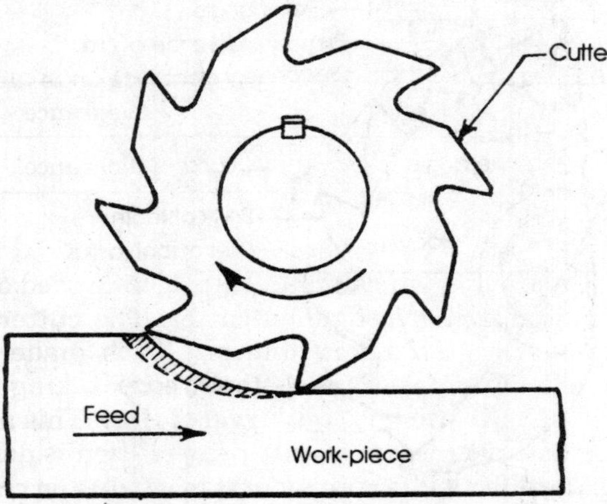

Fig. 1.49. Up milling.

(*ii*) **Down milling or Climb milling.** In this process the cutter rotates in the same direction as that in which the work is feeding (Fig. 1.50). The machine in which high velocity milling is to done should not only be capable of operating at high speeds and feeds but should also possess ample rigidity. The cutter should be reliable and rigidly clamped on the spindle.

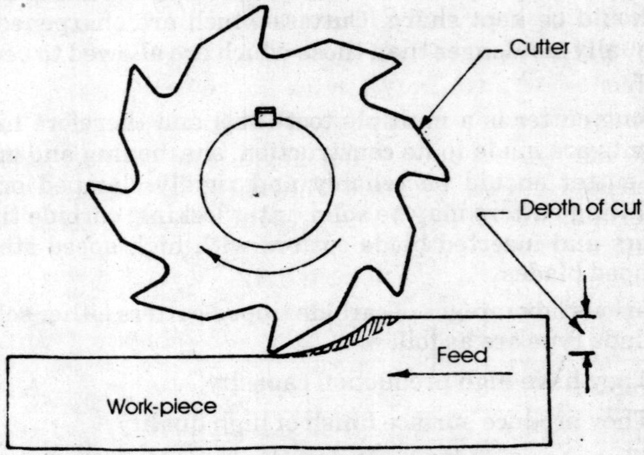

Fig. 1.50. Down milling.

1.32. Elements of a Plain Milling Cutter

A milling cutter may have either straight teeth *i.e.* parallel to the axis of ratation or in helical shape. A milling cutter can be considered as a built up unit of a number of single point cutting tools

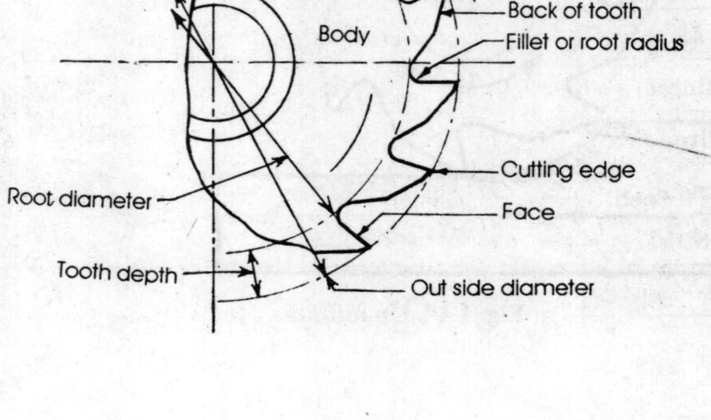

such that each tooth of the cutter is a single point cutting tool. Fig. 1.51 shows a plain milling cutter. The various parts of the cutter teeth are face, cutting edge, fillet, and body.

The various elements of the cutter are as follows :

(i) **Lip angle.** It is the angle included between the land and the face of the tooth or it is the angle between the tangent to the back at the cutting edge and the face of the tooth.

(ii) **Relief angle.** The angle in a plane perpendicular to the axis which is the angle between the land of a tooth and the tangent to the outside diameter of cutter at the cutting edge of that tooth.

The main function of relief angle is to prevent interference between land and work surface. The relief angle varies with the type of material being milled. Table 1.12 indicates the relief angles for different materials.

Table 1.12

Material	*Relief angle (Degrees)*
Cast Iron	4-7
Mild Steel	3-6
Brass	10-12
Aluminium alloys	10-12

(iii) **Rake angle (Radial).** It is the angle measured in the diameteral plane between the face of the tooth and radial line passing through the tooth cutting edge. It facilitates free cutting by tool allowing the chip to flow smoothly. This ensures less power consumption and better surface finish, less wear and hence more life of tool. It may be positive, negative or zero.

Table 1.13 indicates the rake angles in degrees for different materials to be milled.

Table 1.13

Material	*Cemented carbide cutter*	*H.S.S. Cutter*
Aluminium alloys	10-12	20-35
Cast Iron Hard	0-3	8-10
Soft cast iron	3-6	10-15
Mild Steel	0-(-5)	10-15
Brass	3	10

(*iv*) **Primary clearance angle.** It is the angle between a line passing through the surface of the land and a tangent to the periphery at the cutting edge. This angle is provided to prevent the back of tooth from rubbing against the work. It is 4 to 7° for C.I. and 10 to 12 degrees for aluminium and brass.

(*v*) **Secondary clearance angle.** This angle is generally ground back of the land to keep the width of land within proper limits. It is usually 3 degrees greater than primary clearance angle.

(*vi*) **Land.** It is the narrow surface back of the cutting edge resulting from providing a clearance angle.

(*vii*) **Face.** Tooth face is the surface upon which the chip is formed when the cutter is cutting. It is may be flat or curved.

(*viii*) **Back of tooth.** It is created by the fillet and secondary clearance angle.

A milling cutter is a multiple tooth tool and therefore higher requirements are made to its construction, sharpening and operation. The cutter should be railably and rigidity fixed on the spindle. The machine in which high velocity milling is to be done should not only be capable of operating at high speeds and feeds but possess ample rigidity.

Figure 1.51(*a*) shows a high-speed steel milling cutter.

Relief and rake angles are applied to milling cutters in the same manner in which they were applied to tool bits. The milling cutter is actually a multiple tool bit arrangement.

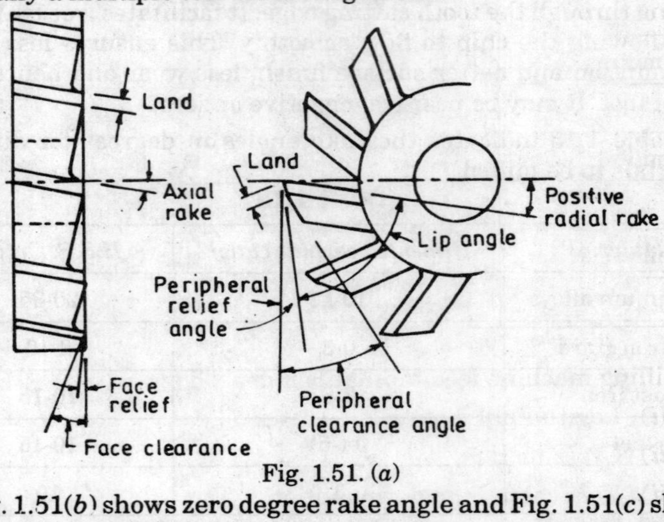

Fig. 1.51. (*a*)

Fig. 1.51(*b*) shows zero degree rake angle and Fig. 1.51(*c*) shows negative rake angle on tooth.

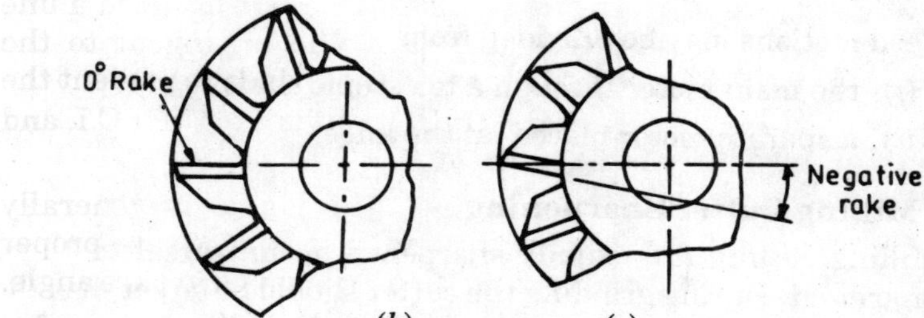

Fig. 1.51.

1.32.1. Milling Cutter Teeth

Following formula may be used to find number of teeth on a milling cutter $Z = \frac{D}{12} + 8$ provided D is more than 50 mm.

where D = cutter diameter in mm.

1.32.2. Feed for milling cutter

Feed per tooth for milling steel with H.S.S. cutters and cemented carbide cutters is indicated in table 1.14*a*. The feed can be increased 1.5 to 2 times the feed values for milling steel.

Table 1.14(*a*)

		Feed in mm.tooth for a depth of cut		
Types of cutter		up to 3 mm	3 to 5 mm	5 to 8 mm
Plain milling cutter	H.S.S.	0.08-0.05	0.08-0.05	0.05-0.03
	Carbide	0.15-0.12	0.12-0.10	0.10-0.05
Face milling cutter	H.S.S.	0.12-0.10	0.10-0.05	0.06-0.03
	Carbide	0.25-0.20	0.20-0.15	0.10-0.12
End milling cutter	H.S.S.	0.05-0.10	0.02-0.050	0.08-0.04
	Carbide	0.06-0.04	0.05-0.03	0.04-0.03

Milling machine feed mechanism is used for

(*i*) Logitudinal motion.

(*ii*) Cross motion.

(*iii*) Vertical up and down motion.

(*iv*) Rapid traverses for all the above motions.

Feed motions may be provided from

(*i*) the main motor through a telescopic shaft.

(*ii*) a sparate motor placed at the knee.

1.33. Milling Cutter Sharpening

Milling cutters are usually sharpened on universal tool and cutter grinder. During grinding the cutter should be so set that the tooth can be advanced to the grinding wheel. Grinding is done with the face of a cup wheel. The cutter tooth should be positioned in respect to the wheel so that required relief angle (γ) is obtained. The tooth face bears on a stationary tooth rest. Fig. 1.52 shows sharpening a face milling cutter by grinding the tooth flanks. The amount of offset (*S*) is determined by using the following relation.

$$S = \frac{D}{2} \sin \gamma$$

where *D* is the cutter diameter in mm.

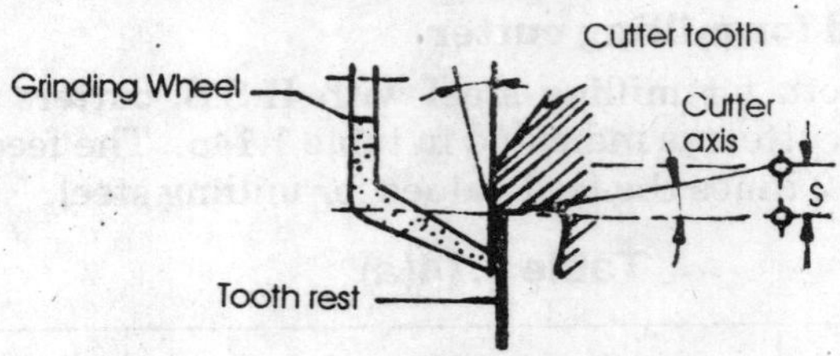

Fig. 1.52.

1.34. Materials for Milling Cutters

The common materials used for manufacturing milling cutters are as follows :

(*i*) High carbon steel

(*ii*) High speed steel

(*iii*) Cemented carbides

(*iv*) Stellite

(*v*) Ceramics.

High carbon steel is not commonly used except for a few cutters used for small scale production. High speed steel containing 18% tungsten is quite commonly used. Cemented carbides are very commonly used when milling cutters are to be run at higher speeds. Stellite is very useful material for milling cutters, when particularly machining hard metals, forgings and castings. Tips made of ceramics are also used in milling cutters. Such cutters, because of their brittleness, are used for finishing operations and smaller cuts. They are commonly used to machine cast iron and bronze.

Cemented carbide tipped cutters have the following advantages

(*i*) Their production capacity is high.

(*ii*) They can produce surface finish of high quality.

(*iii*) Hardened steels can be machined by them.

(*iv*) Their use leads to reduction in machining cost.

1.35. Number of Teeth in a Cutter

Milling cutters may be coarse tooth *i.e.* cutters with a large pitch and a small number of teeth or fine tooth *i.e.* cutters with a small pitch and a large number of teeth. The teeth are stronger in cutters with a coarse pitch. Coarse tooth straight flute cutters do not operate smoothly. Fine tooth cutters remove chips of relatively less thickness and are commonly used for finishing operation whereas coarse tooth remove thicker chip, resulting in removal of more metal in each cut and are used for roughing milling operation various empirical formulas are used to determine number of teeth in a cutter. A typical formula for calculating the number of teeth suitable for a cutter is as follows :

$$Z = A\sqrt{D}$$

where Z = Number of teeth

D = Diameter of cutter in mm

A = Constant

It depends upon the construction of cutter and machining conditions. Values of A are given in Table 1.14

Table 1.14

Type of cutter	*θ(Helix angle)*	*A*
Solid cutters		
(*a*) Fine tooth	15 to 20°	2
(*b*) Coarse tooth	Upto 30°	1
Inserted blade cutters		
(*a*) Find tooth	20°	0.9
(*b*) Coarse tooth	45°	0.8

1.36. Cutting Speed and Feed for Milling Cutter

Cutting Speed. It is the distance travelled per minute by the cutting edges of the cutter. It is expressed in metre per minute.

The cutting speed for milling cutter is found in the same way as for turning and drilling.

Let, D = Diameter of cutter in mm

N = R.P.M. of cutter

V = Cutting speed

$$= \frac{\pi DN}{1000} \text{ metre/minute}$$

The cutting speed should be as high as possible constant with economical cutter life before it needs regrinding.

Feed. It is the rate at which the workpiece advances past the rotating cutter. Three types of feed are distinguished.

(*a*) Feed per tooth (f_1)

(*b*) Feed per cutter revolution (f_2).

(*c*) Table feed per minute (f_3).

These feeds are related by following equations.

Let T = Number of teeth on cutter

N = R.P.M. of cutter

f_1 = feed per tooth in mm

$f_2 = f_1 \times T$

$f_3 = f_2 \times N = f_1 \cdot T \cdot N$ mm/min.

Table 1.15 shows feed per tooth possible with various types of milling cutters.

Table 1.15. Feed for H.S.S. Cutters

Cutter	*Feed per tooth (mm)*
Form cutter	0.05 to 0.2
Slotting cutter	0.5 to 0.15
End mill	0.1 to 0.25
Face mill	0.1 to 0.5
Spiral mill	0.05 to 0.2

The average value of cutting speed in metre per minute for H.S.S. cutter and cemented carbide cutter are shown in Table 1.16.

Table 1.16

Material to be machined	*Tool material*	
	H.S.S.	*Cemented carbide*
Aluminium	180-240	400-450
Brass soft	45-55	140
Copper	45-55	140
Gray cast iron	18-24	60
Cast iron hard	10-12	45
Mild steel	18-25	60
Hard steel	10-12	30

For a multipoint cutting tool such as milling cutter the maximum feed per tooth is limited by the following factors :

(*i*) Cutting edge strength.

(*ii*) Rigidity and allowable deflection.

(*iii*) Surface finish required.

(*iv*) Tool chip space.

With increase in feed, the cutting force gets increased and this causes greater deflection between tool and work piece. Accuracy can not be maintained if deflection is large. Proper cutting fluid can permit higher feeds and increased speeds as well as attainment of better surface finish. Cutting fluid should be directed to the exact point where cutting is taking place.

For setting up the operating conditions for any multipoint cutting tool there are three important variable that can be adjusted. They are as follows :

(*i*) Cutting speed.

(*ii*) Feed per cutting edge.

(*iii*) Cutting fluid.

1.37. Power Required at the Cutter

The horse power ($H.P_c$) required at the cutter depends on the volume of metal to be removed by the cutter per minute and varies for different materials.

$$H.P_c = \frac{Kfdb}{1,00,00}$$

where f = Feed in mm/min.

d = Depth of cut in mm.

b = Width of cut in mm.

K = Constant varying according to thematerial being cut.

The values of K are shown in Table 1.17.

Table 1.17

Material to be cut	*Constant (K)*
Light alloy (Positive rake)	1.3
Copper (Positive rake)	2.6
Brass (Positive rake)	3.0
Cast iron (Positive rake)	3.0
Bronze (Positive rake)	5.0
Steel (Negative rake),	
Low carbon	5.0
High carbon	8.5

$$H.P_m = \text{Horse power at motor} = \frac{HP_c}{\eta}$$

The efficiency (η) of various milling machines is shown in Table 1.18.

Table 1.18

H.P. of the machine	*Efficiency (%)*
3	40
5	48
10	52
15	52
20	60
25	65
30	70
40	75

1.38. Machining Time

The machining time for plain milling and face milling is calculated at follows.

(*i*) **Plain Milling.** Fig. 1.53 shows milling operation being carried out by using plain milling cutter.

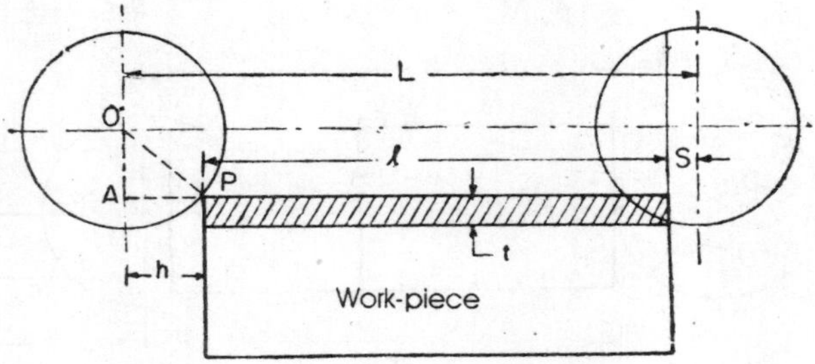

Fig. 1.53.

Let h = approach in mm.

l = Length of workpiece in mm.

s = Overrun of cutter in mm.

L = Total cutter travel in mm. $= h + l + s$

D = Diameter of cutter

t = Depth of cut

f = Feed/rev. in mm.

N = R.P.M.

Then T = Machining time $= \dfrac{L}{N \times f}$

The approach h can be calculated as follows.

In triangle AOP

$$OP^2 = OA + AP^2$$

$$\left(\frac{D}{2}\right)^2 = \left(\frac{D}{2} - t\right)^2 + h^2$$

$$h = \sqrt{t(D - t)}$$

(*ii*) **Face milling.** Fig. 1.54 shows milling operation being carried out by face milling cutter.

l = Length of workpiece in mm.

h = Approach in mm.

$$s = \text{Overrun of cutter.}$$

$$L = l + h + s$$

$$f = \text{Feed in mm /rev.}$$

$$N = \text{R.P.M.}$$

$$T = \frac{L}{f \cdot N}$$

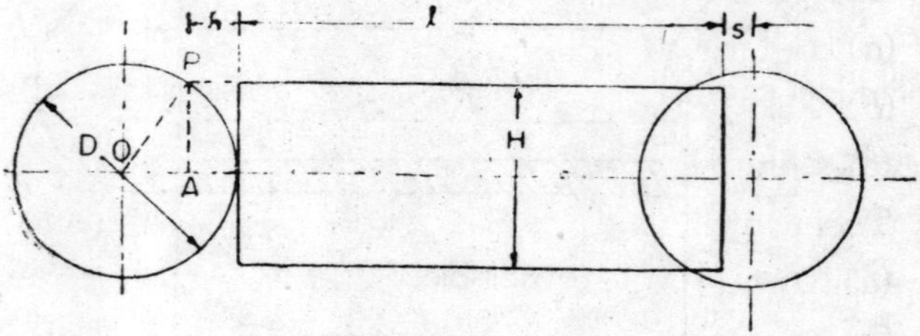

Fig. 1.54.

The approach h is can be calculated as follows.

$$H = \text{Width of workpiece}$$

$$D = \text{Diameter of cutter}$$

$$OP^2 = OA^2 + Ap^2$$

$$\left(\frac{D}{2}\right)^2 = \left(\frac{D}{2} - h\right)^2 + \left(\frac{H}{2}\right)^2$$

$$h = \tfrac{1}{2}\left[D - \sqrt{D^2 - H^2}\right]$$

1.38 Turning/Milling data sheet. This data sheet indicates the following details of machine tool such as lathe, milling machine and cutting tool, workpiece etc.

1. Machine tool details
   - (*i*) Type
   - (*ii*) Make
   - (*iii*) Power
   - (*iv*) Rigidity (*a*) Good (*b*) Fair (*c*) Poor
   - (*v*) Stiffness
   - (*vi*) Coolant.
2. Workpiece details
   - (*i*) Material
   - (*ii*) Strength
   - (*iii*) Hardness

(*iv*) Dimensions

(*v*) Tolerance

(*vi*) Surface conditions.

3. Tool details

(*i*) Material (*a*) Insert being used.

(*ii*) Tool geometry/approach angle

(*iii*) Tool holder condition

(*a*) Good

(*b*) Fair

(*c*) New

(*iv*) Tool overhang

(*a*) Normal

(*b*) Excessive.

4. Operation details

(*i*) Nature

(*a*) Turning

(*b*) Copy turning

(*c*) Face milling

(*d*) End milling etc.

(*ii*) Stage

(*a*) Roughing

(*b*) Semi-finishing

(*c*) Finishing.

5. Machining data

(*i*) Spindle speed

(*ii*) Cutting speed

(*iii*) Feed (*a*) Handfeed (*b*) Autofeed

(*iv*) Depth of cut

(*v*) Metal removal rate

(*vi*) Surface finish

(*vii*) Machining time

(*viii*) Number of parts made for insert

(*ix*) Wear pattern.

6. Chips

(*i*) Type

(*a*) Short

(*b*) Long

(*c*) Broken

(*d*) Curved

(*e*) Ribbon type

(*ii*) Colour

(*a*) Grey

(*b*) Blue

(*c*) Burnt.

1.38.1. Broaching Tool. A broaching tool or a broach has a series of multiple teeth. The main elements of a broaching tool are shown in Fig. 1.55. The first teeth are designed to do the heaviest cutting and are called roughing teeth. Next teeth are semi-finishing teeth which are followed by finishing teeth. The finishing teeth carry out finishing operation Fig. 1.56 shows teeth details. The rake angle (face angle) of the tooth depends on the material to be cut and its hardness, toughness and ductility.

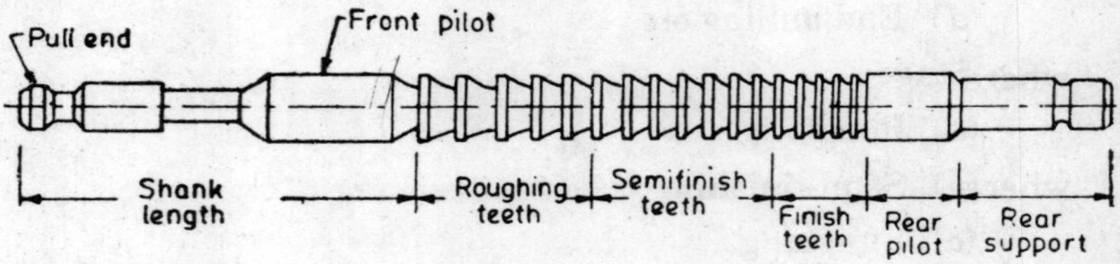

Fig. 1.55.

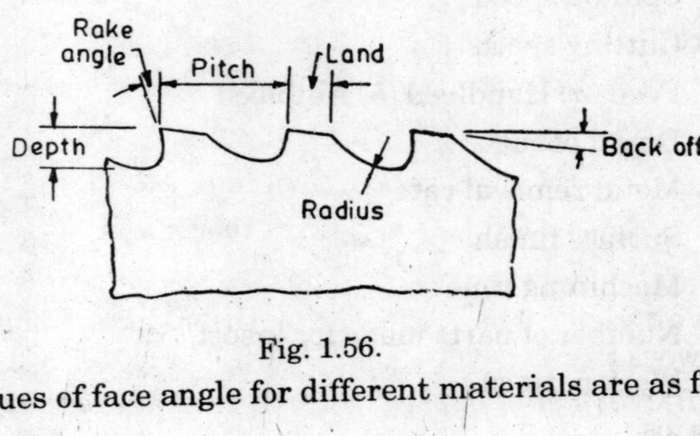

Fig. 1.56.

The values of face angle for different materials are as follows :

Material	*Face angle (Degrees)*
Aluminium	10
Brass	-5 -5
Cast iron	6 -8
Steel (hard)	8 -12
Steel (soft)	16 -20

The land of tooth determines its strength. The pitch determines the length of cut and chip thickness which a broach can handle.

During broaching operation the broach is either pulled or pushed by the broaching machine past the surface of the workpiece. In doing so each tooth of broach takes a small cut through the metal surface. Most broaches are made from 18-4-1 high speed steel, ground after hardening. Carbide broaches are used extensively in broaching cast iron.

1.38.2. Design elements. (*i*) *Length of broach.* The length of broach is calculated as follows :

$$L = L_1 + L_2 + L_3 + L_4 + L_5$$

where L_1 = Length of cutting portion

$= p_1 \cdot Z_1$

where p_1 = pitch of cutting teeth

Z_1 = Number of cutting teeth

L_2 = Length of finishing teeth

$= p_2 \cdot Z_2$

where p_2 = pitch of finishing teeth

Z_2 = Number of finishing teeth

L_3 = Length of pull end

L_4 = Length of neck

L_5 = Length of rear pilots

Values of L_3, L_4, L_5 depend on the standards, broaching fixture and work piece.

(*ii*) *Number of teeth.* The teeth provided on a broach are calculated as follows :

$$Z = \text{Total number of teeth}$$
$$= \frac{A}{d} + Z_1 + Z_2$$

where A = Amount of material to be removed

d = Depth of cut

Z_1 = Number of finishing teeth = 3 or 4

Z_2 = Number of safety teeth

(*iii*) *Pitch of teeth.* It is determined as follows

p = pitch

$= (1.25 \text{ to } 1.50)\sqrt{L}$ for plain broach

$= (1.45 \text{ to } 1.90)\sqrt{L}$ for progressive broach

where L = Length of broached surface in mm.

(*iv*) *Cutting force* (P_C). The cutting force in broaching is found as follows

$$P_C = F\Sigma M$$

where P_C = Cutting force

F = Cutting force per mm of cutting edge length (kgf /mm)

ΣM = Total length of cutting edges of all the teeth in operation simultaneously (mm)

$$\Sigma M = \frac{\pi D Z_s}{Z_g} \text{ for cylindrical holes.}$$

where D = Maximum diameter of teeth in mm

Z_g = Number of teeth in a group.

Z_s = Number of teeth in operation simultaneously

$$\Sigma M = \frac{BN}{Z_g} \text{ for spline holes and key ways.}$$

where

B = Width of broached surface on work piece in mm.

N = Number of splines on key ways

The maximum broaching force is found as follows

$$P_{max} = k_1 \cdot k_2 \cdot d \cdot b \cdot \frac{l}{p}$$

where k_1 = Coefficient that takes into account friction

$= 1.1$ to 1.3

k_2 = Specific cutting resistance (kg/cm^2)

d = Depth of cut per tooth in cm.

b = Width of cut in cm.

l = Length of tool entry in cm.

p = Pitch of cutting edges in cm.

(*v*) *Power required for broaching.* The power required during broaching is determined as follows

$$P = \text{Power}$$

$$= \frac{P_C V}{7200} \text{ k. Watt.}$$

where P_C = Cutting force in N

V = Cutting speed in m/min.

(*vi*) *Cutting speed.* The cutting speed is the speed of broach movement. It depends on material and type of surface being broached.

$$V = \frac{EK}{T^x S^y} \text{ m /min.}$$

where

E = Co–efficient characterising the processing conditions

K = Co–efficient that takes into account broach material

T = Tool life in minutes

S = Cut per tooth in mm.

Values of x, y depend on broach material and other processing conditions.

For broaching round holes in steel

$$E = 12, \; x = 0.6, \; y = 0.6$$

$$K = 1 \text{ to } 1.5 \text{ and } T = 80 \text{ to } 100 \text{ minutes.}$$

Value of cutting Speed in broaching usually varies from 1.5 m to 20 m per minute.

(*vii*) *Rise per tooth.* Rise per tooth depends on the following factors.

(*a*) Shape of hole

(*b*) Type of material of work piece

(*c*) Force available at the machine

(*d*) Size of hole.

h = Rise per tooth.

= 0.025 mm to 0.16 mm.

(*viii*) *Depth of tooth (H)*

$$H = 1.13\ \sqrt{fL\,k}$$

where

f = Difference in height between two successive cutting teeth
= 0.02 to 0.12 mm.

L = Length of work piece

K = Constant

= 3 to 5 for surface broaches

= 6 to 10 for internal broaches.

(*ix*) *Neck diameter.* It is 0.3 to 1.0 mm less than shank diameter.

(*x*) *Width of land.* It varies between 2.5 to 4.5 mm.

(*xi*) *Groove radius.* It varies between 2.5 to 5 mm.

(*xii*) *Broaching allowance.* It is calculated as follows

A = Broaching allowance

$= 0.005D + (0.1 \text{ to } 0.2)\sqrt{L}$

where D = Basic diameter of hole in mm.

L = Length of hole to be broached in mm.

In terms of pitch the following commonly used values may be adopted.

Tooth height = (0.35 to 0.40) p.

Land width = (0.3 to 0.4) p.

Groove radius = (0.2 to 0.25) p.

Flute angle = 30° to 36°

Groove angle = 45° to 50°.

1.39. Improving Cutting Efficiency

The cutting efficiency during machining can be improved by using following methods.

(*i*) Reduction of tool-face friction.

(*ii*) By reducing chip length by means of chip breakers.

(*iii*) By improving surface finish of tool face by honing or chrome plating.

(*iv*) By increasing cutting speeds.

(*v*) Increased depth of cut increases cutting efficiency by a small amount.

1.40. Power Distribution

Out of total power supplied to the machine tool the power available at the cutter depends upon the type of machine tool. A typical power distribution for a milling machine and a lathe is as follows.

Milling Machine

Electrical power input	= 100%
Losses in motor	= 16%
Losses in spindle transmission	= 18%
Power to feed	= 21%
Power available at cutter	= 45%

Lathe

Electrical power input	= 100%
Losses in motor	= 11%
Losses in machine	= 18.5%
Power to feed	= 0.5
Power available at tool	= 70%

1.41. To Determine Power Rating of Electric Motor

The required power of main drive is determined on the basis of useful power calculated for the most effective cutting conditions. In designing general purpose machine tools the useful power is calculated for the maximum cutting speeds and feeds.

N_m = Required power rating of electric motor

$= N + N_f$

where N = Useful power

N_f = Power lost in overcoming friction

η = Efficiency of main drive.

$$= \frac{N}{N_m}$$

The efficiency (η) may range from 0.7 to 0.85 for machine tools with a rotary primary motion having a single motor drive.

1.42. Cutting Tool Design

The design of a cutting tool means determination of all the dimensions and shapes of all the elements of a cutting tool by carrying out calculations and graphical construction. The cutting of metals with a single point cutting tool is fully applicable to any kind of cutting tool since all tools remove a certain layer of stock and impart the required shape, size, and surface finish to the machined part. The cutting teeth of all cutting tools whatever may be their shapes and purpose resemble to the point of single point tool.

The common procedure carried out during the design of cutting tool consists of following calculations :

(*i*) To determine forces acting on cutting surface of the tool.

(*ii*) To find out optimum tool geometry.

(*iii*) To select suitable material for making cutting elements of the tools.

(*iv*) To find suitable shapes of cutting and mounting elements of tool and to determine the tolerance on the dimensions of cutting and mounting elements of tool depending on machining accuracy required on work piece.

(*v*) To determine strength and rigidity of mounting and cutting elements of tool.

(*vi*) To prepare a working drawing of tool.

1.43. Friction between Chip and Tool

Friction between the chip and tool plays a significant role in cutting process. It should be as low as possible friction can be reduced in the following ways :

(*i*) Improved tool finish and sharpness of the cutting edge.

(*ii*) Use of low friction tool material.

(*iii*) Improved tool geometry.

(*iv*) Use of cutting fluids.

(*v*) High sliding speeds.

1.44. Design of a Single point Lathe Tool

The design on the cutting tool depends upon the cutting forces acting on the cutting surfaces of the tool and rigidity of the machine on which cutting tool is used. The shank of a single point tool may be rectangular, square or rounding cross-section. The rectangular cross-section is commonly used because the reduction in strength of shank (at section YY of a single point cutting tool as shown in (Fig. 1.56 (*a*) is less than for a square shank when a seat is cut for a tip.

Let
$$F_H = \text{Cutting force}$$
$$B = \text{Width of shank}$$
$$H = \text{Height of shank.}$$

For rectangular cross-section the relations between B and H are as follows :

$$\frac{H}{B} = 1.25 \text{ for roughing operations}$$

$$\frac{H}{B} = 1.6 \text{ for semifinishing and finishing operations.}$$

The minimum permissible size of the shank cross-section on strength basis is calculated by equating the actual bending moment to the maximum moment permitted by cross-section of the shank.

$$M_1 = \text{Bending moment due to cutting force } F_H$$
$$= F_H \times l$$

where
$$l = \text{Cutting tool overhang.}$$
$$(l = 1 \text{ to } 1.5\ H)$$
$$M_2 = \text{Maximum moment permitted by the cross-section of the shank}$$
$$= f \times Z$$

where f = Permissible bending stress for the shank material

Z = Section modulus of the tool shank

$$\therefore \quad M_1 = M_2$$
$$F_H \times l = f \times Z$$

For rectangular cross-section of tool shank

$$Z = \frac{BH^2}{6}$$

$$\therefore \quad F_H \times l = f \times \frac{BH^2}{6}$$

$$BH^2 = \frac{6\,F_H \cdot l}{f}$$

$$H = \sqrt{\frac{6F_H \cdot l}{f.B}}$$

For square cross-section shank

$$B = H.$$

$$F_H \times l = f \cdot \frac{BH^2}{6}$$

$$= f \cdot \frac{B \cdot B^2}{6}$$

$$B^3 = \frac{6F_H\, l}{f}$$

$$B = \sqrt[3]{\frac{6F_H \cdot l}{f}}$$

For round cross-section shank

$$Z = \frac{\pi}{32} D^3$$

where D = Diameter of shank.

$$l \times F_H = fZ.$$

$$= f \cdot \frac{\pi}{32} D^3$$

$$D^3 = \frac{32 \cdot F_H \cdot l}{\pi \times f}$$

$$D = \sqrt[3]{\frac{32F_H \cdot l}{\pi f}}$$

Square shank tools are commonly used for boring machines, screw machines and turret lathes. Round shank tools are generally used for boring and thread cutting operations.

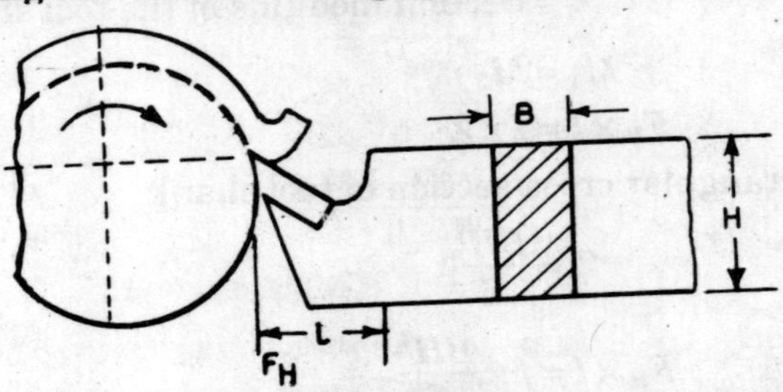

Fig. 1.56 (a)

Example 1.0. *In orthogonal cutting of a mild steel bar on a lathe the feed (f_1) used is 0.3 mm per revolution and the depth of cut (t) is 2 mm. Determine the cross-section of a rectangular tool shank if the* *allowable stress in the shank material is 7 kg/m² and the cutting force (F_H) can be calculated by the relation $F_H = 200 \times f_1^{0.75} \times t$.*

Solution. Let $H =$ Height of a shank

$B =$ Width of shank

$$\frac{H}{B} = 1.16 \text{ (assume)}$$

we know $H = \dfrac{\sqrt{6F_H \cdot l}}{f \cdot B}$

where $F_H =$ cutting

$$= 200 \times f_1^{0.75} \times t$$

$$= 200 \times 0.3^{0.75} \times 2$$

$$= 170 \text{ kg.}$$

$l =$ Cutting tool overhang.

$= 1.25\,H$ (assume)

$f = 7 \text{ kg/mm}^2$

$$H = \sqrt{\frac{6 \times 170 \times 1.25H}{7 \times \dfrac{H}{1.6}}}$$

$$H = 17 \text{ mm.}$$

$$B = \frac{H}{1.6} = \frac{17}{1.6} = 10.6 \text{ mm.}$$ **Ans.**

Example 1.1. *Determine the spindle speed for a high steel drill 12 mm diameter cutting medium carbon steel at 28 m / min.*

Solution. $V = 28$ m/min

$D =$ Diameter of drill = 12 mm.

$N =$ R.P.M. of spindle

$$V = \frac{\pi DN}{1000}$$

$$28 = \frac{\pi \cdot 12 \cdot N}{1000}$$

$N = 743$ R.P.M. **Ans.**

Example 1.2. *Determine the machining time to drill a hole of 20 mm diameter in a workpiece 25 mm thick by a drill at a cutting speed of 30 metre / min with a feed of 0.2 mm / rev.*

Solution. $L =$ Length of axial travel of drill in mm.

$= $ Thickness of workpiece $+ 0.3\,D$

where $D =$ Hole diameter

$L = 25 + 0.3 \times 20 = 25 + 6 = 31$ mm

$V =$ Cutting speed = 30 metre per min.

$$V = \frac{\pi DN}{1000}$$

$$30 = \frac{\pi \times 20 \times N}{1000}$$

$N = 477$ R.P.M.

$T =$ Machining time

$f =$ feed/rev = 0.2 mm /rev.

$$T = \frac{L}{N \times f} = \frac{31}{477 \times 0.2} \text{ minute}$$

$$= \frac{31 \times 60}{477 \times 0.2} = 19.5 \text{ seconds.}$$ **Ans.**

Example 1.3. *A 30 mm H.S.S. drill is used to drill a hole in a cast iron block 100 mm thick. Determine the time required to drill the hole if feed is 0.3 mm/rev. Assume an over travel of drill as 4 mm. The cutting speed is 20 metre/min.*

Solution. $D =$ diameter of drill = 30 mm

$$V = \text{cutting speed} = \frac{\pi DN}{1000}$$

$$20 = \frac{\pi \cdot 30 \cdot N}{1000}$$

$N = 202$ R.P.M.

$h =$ approach

$= 0.3\,D$ (assume) $0.30 \times 30 = 9$ mm

$s =$ over travel = 4 mm

$L =$ Total length

$= h + S +$ Thickness of work piece

$= 9 + 4 + 100 = 113$ mm.

$$T = \text{Machining Time} = \frac{L}{fN} = \frac{113}{0.3 \times 202}$$

where $f =$ feed

$T = 1.85$ minutes.

Example 1.4. *Calculate the power required to drill 20 mm diameter hole in mild steel at a feed of 0.25 mm/rev and at a drill* *speed 300 R.P.M. Determine also the volume of metal removed per unit of energy.*

Solution. $D =$ hole diameter $= 20$ mm

$f =$ feed $= 0.25$ mm/rev.

$N = 300$ R.P.M.

$T_1 = \text{Torque} = C \cdot f^{0.75} D^{1.8}$

where, $C =$ Constant $= 0.36$ for mild steel

$$T_1 = 0.36 \times 0.25^{0.75} \times 20^{1.8} = 27.96 \text{ newton–m.}$$

$P =$ Power

$$= \frac{2\pi N T_1}{60{,}000} = \frac{2\pi \times 300 \times 27.96}{60{,}000} = 0.879 \text{ kW.}$$

Volume of metal removed per minute

$= \text{Area of hole} \times \text{Feed} \times \text{Speed}$

$$= \frac{\pi}{4} \times 20^2 \times 2.25 \times 300$$

$= \mathbf{23550\ mm^3}$.

$$\text{Energy consumption} = \frac{23550}{879} \quad \textbf{Ans.}$$

$= 21$ mm^3/watt minute.

Example 1.5. *(a) A carbide face milling cutter of 200 mm diameter is used take one cut across the face of a block of aluminium which is 200 mm wide. The length of block is 450 mm. If a feed of 0.75 mm / rev is used how long will it take to machine one cut on the block. The total travel is 12 mm. The cutting speed is 320 meter / minute.*

(b) Calculate the time taken if the diameter of cutter is 300 mm.

Solution.

(*a*) $D =$ Diameter of cutter $= 200$ mm.

$H =$ Width of block $= 200$ mm

$l =$ Length of block $= 450$ mm

$f =$ Feed $= 0.75$ mm/rev.

$s =$ Overrun of cutter $= 12$ mm.

As the diameter of cutter is equal to width of block, (Fig. 1.57).

$\therefore$ $h =$ Approach

$$= \frac{D}{2} = \frac{200}{2} = 100 \text{ mm.}$$

$N =$ R.P.M. of cutter

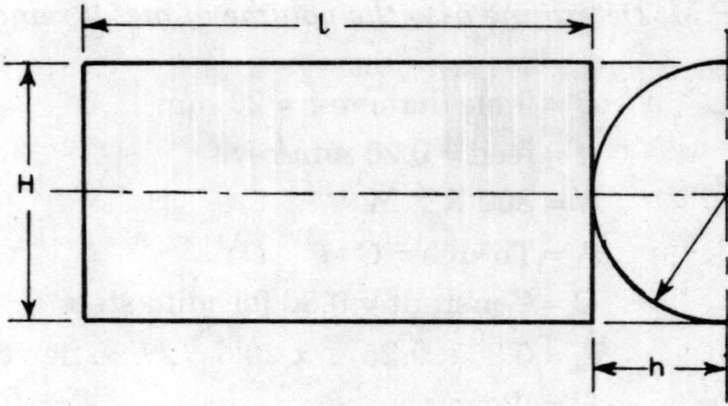

Fig. 1.57.

$$V = \text{ cutting speed} = \frac{\pi DN}{1000}$$

$$320 = \pi \times \frac{200}{1000} \times N$$

$$N = 510 \text{ R.P.M.}$$

Total length, $L = l + h + s = 450 + 100 + 12$

$= 562$ mm.

$$T = \text{machining time} = \frac{562}{0.75 \times 510}$$

$= 1.45$ minute **Ans.**

(*b*) D = Diameter of cutter = 300 mm.

In this case the diameter of cutter is more than the width of block

$\therefore$ $h = \text{Approach} = ½[D - \sqrt{D^2 - H^2}]$

$= ½[300 - \sqrt{300^2 - 200^2}] = 38$ mm.

$\therefore$ $L = \text{Total length} = l + h + S$

$= 450 + 38 + 12 = 500$ mm.

$$V = \frac{\pi DN}{1000}$$

$$320 = \frac{\pi \times 300 \times N}{1000}$$

$$N = 340$$

T = Machining time

$$T = \frac{L}{f.N.} = \frac{500}{0.75 \times 340}$$

$= 1.97$ minutes **Ans.**

Example 1.6. *A carbide milling cutter 250 mm in diameter is used to cut a block of mild steel with a plain cutter .The block is 500 mm long. If the feed is 0.50 mm / rev and depth of cut is 1.2 mm determine the time required to take one cut. The over travel is 16 mm. The cutting speed is 80 metre per minute.*

Solution. D = Diameter of cutter = 250 mm.

f = feed = 3.5 mm/rev.

l = Length of block = 500 mm.

t = Depth of cut = 1.2 mm

s = Over travel = 16 mm

V = cutting speed = 80 metre/minute

N = R.P.M.

$$V = \frac{\pi DN}{1000}$$

$$80 = \frac{\pi \cdot 250 \cdot N}{1000}$$

N = 102 R.P.M.

$$h = \text{Approach} = \sqrt{t(D - t)}$$

$$= \sqrt{1.2(250 - 1.2)} = 17.3 \text{ mm.}$$

$$L = \text{Total length} = l + h + s$$

$$= 500 + 17.3 + 16 = 533.3 \text{ mm.}$$

T = Machining time

$$= \frac{L}{f \cdot N} = \frac{533.3}{0.5 \times 102}$$

$$= 10.45 \text{ minute}$$ **Ans..**

Example 1.7. *Determine the horse power required to face mill a block of grey cast iron 125 mm wide, using a tungsten carbide cutter 150 mm in diameter and having eight tooth. The depth of cut is 3 mm and a chip thickness of 0.25 mm is to be used. The cutting speed is 60 m / min and the specific horse power required for cast iron is 0.30 H.P./cm³/min.*

Solution. V = cutting speed = 60 m/min.

Now $$V = \frac{\pi DN}{1000}$$

$$60 = \frac{\pi \times 150 \times N}{1000}$$

where D = cutter diameter

N = R.P.M. of cutter

$\therefore \quad N = 128$

Now $\quad f_1$ = feed per tooth (chip thickness)

$= 0.25$ mm.

f_2 = feed per cutter revolution

$= f_1 \times$ Number of teeth

$= f_1 \times 8 = 0.25 \times 8$

f_3 = feed per minute $= f_2 \times N$

$= 0.25 \times 8 \times 128$ mm/minute

$= 256$ mm/minute $= 25.6$ cm/minute.

The metal removal rate (w)

w = Width of workpiece × Depth of cut × feed per minute

$= 125 \times 0.3 \times 25.6$ cm^3 /minute

$= 96$ cm^3 /minute

Horse power required

$= 96 \times 0.03 = 2.88$. **Ans.**

Example 1.8. *The feed of an 8-tooth face mill cutter is 0.325 mm per tooth at 200 R.P.M. The material cut is 300 BHN Steel.*

If the depth of the cut is 3 mm and width is 100 mm calculate the following :

(*a*) *B.P. at the cutter.*

(*b*) *H.P. at the motor.*

Solution . $$H.P._c = \frac{K \cdot f \cdot d \cdot b}{10,0000}$$

where K = Constant = 8.5 (From table 1.11)

f = Feed $= 0.325 \times 8 \times 200$

$= 520$ mm/minute.

d = Depth of cut in mm

$= 3$ mm

b = Width of cut = 100 mm.

$$HP_c = \frac{85 \times 520 \times 3 \times 100}{10^5} = 12.48 \qquad \textbf{Ans.}$$

Let the efficiency of the machine be 50%

HP_m = Horse power at the motor

$$= \frac{HP_c}{0.5} = \frac{12.48}{0.5} = 25. \qquad \textbf{Ans.}$$

Example 1.9. *Determine the power required by a milling cutter to take a cut 100 mm wide 3 mm deep at 75 mm/min feed for an alloy steel. If the cutter diameter is 100 mm and cutting speed is 15 meter/min, find the mean torque at the arbor.*

Solution. The horse power required at the cutter is given by

$$HP_c = \frac{K \cdot f \cdot d \cdot b}{10{,}0000}$$

Now $K = 8.5$ (From table 1.11.)

$f = 75$ mm/min.

$b = 100$ mm.

$d = 3$ mm.

$$HP_c = \frac{8.5 \times 75 \times 100 \times 3}{100{,}000} = 1.9.$$

Mean force at the periphery of the cutter,

$$F = \frac{HP_c}{V} \times 4500$$

where V = cutting speed = 15 metre / min.

$$F = \frac{1.9 \times 4500}{15} = 570 \text{ kg}.$$

Mean torque at the arbor.

$$T = F \times \text{ Radius of cutter}$$

$$T = 570 \times \frac{50}{1000} = 28.5 \text{ kg–m}. \quad \textbf{Ans.}$$

Example 1.10. *During turning a mild steel component with a 0-10-7-7-8,-9-1.5 mm shaped orthogonal shaped tool a depth of cut of 1.8 mm is used. If feed is 0.18 mm/rev. and a chip thickness of 0.36 mm is obtained determine the following :*

(*a*) *Chip thickness ratio.*

(*b*) *Shear angle.*

Solution. r = chip thickness ratio $= \frac{t_1}{t_2}$

where t_1 = chip thickness before cutting

= 0.18 mm.

t_2 = chip thickness after cutting

= 0.36 mm.

$$r = \frac{0.18}{0.36} = 0.5$$

(*b*) β = Shear angle

α = Back rake angle = 0° (given)

$$\tan \beta = \frac{r \cos \alpha}{1 - r \sin \alpha}$$

$$= \frac{0.5 \times \cos \theta}{1 - 0.5 \sin \theta} = \frac{0.5}{1} = 0.5$$

$$\beta = 26^\circ - 34$$

Example 1.11. *Determine the power required for milling a mild steel workpiece with a cutter of 80 mm diameter having 9 teeth and rotating at 120 R.P.M. The workpiece has a width of 60 mm. Depth of cut is 4 mm and tooth feed is 0.03 mm.*

Solution. P = Power in kW /cm² /min.

It is given by the following formula

$$P = \frac{C}{\left[f\sqrt{\frac{d}{D}}\right]^n}$$

where f = feed per tooth

C = Material constant

d = Depth of cut in mm.

The values of C and n depends upon material to be cut. The values are as follows :

Mild Steel : C = 0.02 *to* 0.03.

n = 0.28

Bronze : C = 0.006–0.007

n = 0.4

Now C = 0.02 (say)

$$f = \text{Feed per tooth} = \frac{F}{T}$$

where F = Feed rate, mm /min.

T = Number of teeth on cutter

f = 0.03 mm.

d = Depth of cut = 4 mm.

D = Diameter of cutter = 80 mm.

n = 0.28

$$P = \frac{0.02}{\left[0.03\sqrt{\frac{4}{80}}\right]^{0.28}} = 0.245$$

P_1 = Power in kW

$= P \times b \cdot d \cdot f \cdot T \cdot N$

where b = width of workpiece = 6 cm.

N = R.P.M. = 120

$P^1 = 0.245 \times 6 \times 0.4 \times 0.003 \times 9 \times 120$

= 1.9 kW.

Example 1.12. *Determine the power required to cut a brass bar on a lathe when the cutting speed is 18 metres per minute, feed is 0.06 mm per revolution and depth of cut is 0.058 cm. Assume that the power lost in friction is 30%.*

Solution. H.P. = Total horse power required

$P_1 + P_2$

where P_1 = Power required for cutting action

P_2 = Power lost in friction

= 30% of P_1

∴ H.P. = 1.3 P_1

$$= \frac{1.3 \times K \cdot d \cdot f \cdot V}{4500}$$

where K = constant = 12000 for brass

d = depth of cut in cm.

= 0.058 cm. = 0.58 mm

f = 0.06 mm per revolution

V = cutting speed = 18 metres per minute.

The value of K depends on material being machined. The values of K are as follows.

Metal to be cut	K
Aluminium	6700
Brass	12000
Cast iron	8600
Steel	11000

$$\text{H.P.} = \frac{1.3 \times 12000 \times 0.58 \times 0.06 \times 18}{4500}$$

= 2.17 **Ans.**

Example 1.13. *Estimate the power of electric motor for a drilling machine to drill a hole 15 mm diameter in cast iron (soft) work piece at 450 R.P.M. and 0.2 mm feed. The specific power is 0.03 kW and efficiency of motor is 80%.*

Solution. D = Hole diameter

= 15 mm

N = 450 R.P.M.

F = feed = 0.2 mm/rev.

S = specific power

= Power required to remove material of one cubic centimeter per minute.

= 0.03 kW

η = Efficiency of motor = 0.8

V = volume of metal to be cut during drilling

$$= \frac{\pi}{4} D^2 \times f \times N$$

$$= \frac{\pi}{4}\left(\frac{15}{10}\right)^2 \times \frac{0.2}{10} \times 450$$

= 15.9 cu cm/min

P_1 = Power required at the drill

$= V \times S = 15.9 \times 0.03$

= 0.477 kW

P = Power of electric motor

$$= \frac{0.477}{\eta} = \frac{0.477}{0.8}$$

= 0.6 kW **Ans.**

Example 1.14. *A broach is used to cut a key way 8 mm wide, 5 mm deep in a boss 64 mm long. Determine*

(*a*) *cutting length of broach*

(*b*) *Number of teeth on broach.*

Solution. L = Length to be broached in mm = 64 mm

p = pitch

$= 1.5\sqrt{64} = 12$ mm.

d = Depth of cut = 5 mm

h = rise per tooth

= 0.0875 mm (Assume)

Z_1 = Number of teeth

$$= \frac{d}{h} = \frac{5}{0.0875} = 57$$

Z_2 = Number of finishing teeth

= 13 (say)

Z = Total number of teeth

$= Z_1 + Z_2 = 57 + 13 = 70.$

$p_1 = p$ Pitch for finishing teeth

$$= \frac{p}{2} = \frac{12}{2} = 6 \text{ mm.}$$

(The pitch for finishing teeth is usually half of that adopted for cutting teeth)

L = Total effective length (cutting length) of broach = $L_1 + L_2$

where L_1 = length of roughing teeth

L_2 = length of finishing teeth

$$L = 57 \times p + 13 \times p_1$$

$$= 57 \times 12 + 13 \times 6$$

$$= 762 \text{ mm.}$$

Example 1.15. *Calculate the cutting times for each of the following maching operations :*

(*a*) *Work piece-grey cast iron, cutting speed 20 m / min, depth of cut is 2.5 mm, dimensions of surface to be machined 50 mm long × 70 mm wide over run of cutter = 10 mm*

cutter (i) Helical mill 76 mm diameter and 45 degree helix

(ii) Face mill 100 mm diameter.)

Solution. (*a*) *For helical milling*

D = cutter diameter

= 76 mm

α = Helix angle

= 45°

d = Depth of cut

= 2.5 mm

Z = Number of teeth in cutter

$$= \frac{4\pi D}{D + 4d} \times \cos\alpha = \frac{4\pi \times 76}{76 + 4 + 2.5} \times \cos 45$$

$$= 8$$

f = feed/tooth

= 0.25 mm (From table 1.15)

h = Approach

$= \sqrt{d(D-d)}$

$= \sqrt{2.5(76-2.5)}$

= 13.6 mm

N = R.P.M. of spindle

V = cutting speed = 20

$$20 = \frac{\pi DN}{1000}$$

$$= \frac{\pi \times 76 \times N}{1000}$$

N = 84 *R.P.M.*

S = over run of cutter = 10 mm

F = Table feed

$= N \times Z \times f$

$= 84 \times 8 \times 0.25$

= 168 mm/min

L = length of cut

= length of workpiece + h + s

= 50 + 13.6 + 10 = 73.6 mm.

$$T = \text{Time for one cut} = \frac{L}{F}$$

$$= \frac{73.6}{168}$$

= 0.44 min.

(*b*) *For face milling*

b = width of component (cut) = 70 mm.

$$Z = \frac{2\pi D}{b}$$

$$= \frac{2\pi \times 100}{70}$$

= 9

d = Depth of cut

= 0.3 mm (From table 1.15)

D = cutter diameter = 100 mm.

$$h = \text{Approach}$$

$$= \frac{D}{2} - \sqrt{\frac{D^2}{4} - \frac{b^2}{4}}$$

$$= \frac{100}{2} - \sqrt{\frac{100^2}{4} - \frac{70^2}{4}}$$

$$= 14.3 \text{ mm}$$

$$V = 20 = \frac{\pi DN}{1000}$$

$$20 = \frac{\pi \times 100 \times N}{1000}$$

$$N = 64 \text{ R.P.M.}$$

$$F = \text{Table feed}$$

$$= N \times Z \times f$$

$$= 64 \times 9 \times 0.3$$

$$= 172.8 \text{ mm/min}$$

$$L = \text{Length of component} + h + s$$

$$= 50 + 14.3 + 10$$

$$= 74.3 \text{ mm}$$

$$T = \text{Time for one cut}$$

$$= \frac{L}{F}$$

$$= \frac{74.3}{172.8}$$

$$= 0.43 \text{ minutes.}$$

Example 1.16. *The bore of an alloy steel component is to be finish broached to* $21.75^{+0.01}$ *mm diameter, the bore prior to broaching being* $21.24^{+0.05}$ *mm diatermeter-Determine*

(*a*) *Pitch of teeth*

(*b*) *Length of cutting portion*

(*c*) *Force to pull broach through work if length of hole is 36 mm and rise per tooth is 0.025.*

Number of finishing teeth is 3 and force to remove 1 mm² of metal is 4800 N.

Sketch the broach.

Solution. L_1 = hole length

$$= 36 \text{ mm}$$

p = pitch

$= 1.5\sqrt{36} = 9$ mm.

Z = Number of finishing teeth = 5

L = Length of cutting portion of broach

$$= P\left(\frac{T}{h} + Z\right)$$

where T = metal to be removed by roughing teeth

$$= \frac{21.76 - 21.24}{2}$$

$= 0.26$ mm.

h = Rise per tooth = 0.025 mm.

$$L = p\left(\frac{T}{h} + Z\right)$$

$$= 9\left(\frac{0.26}{0.025} + 5\right)$$

$= 144$ mm.

The first cutting tooth will be 21.24 mm diameter, second will be 21.26 mm diameter. The rest of cutting teeth will rise in steps of 0.05 mm on diameter and finishing teeth will be 21.76 mm diameter.

F = Force to pull broach = $\pi D Z_1 h K$

where D = Finish diameter

$= 21.76$ mm.

Z_1 = Maximum number of teeth cutting at a time

$= 3$

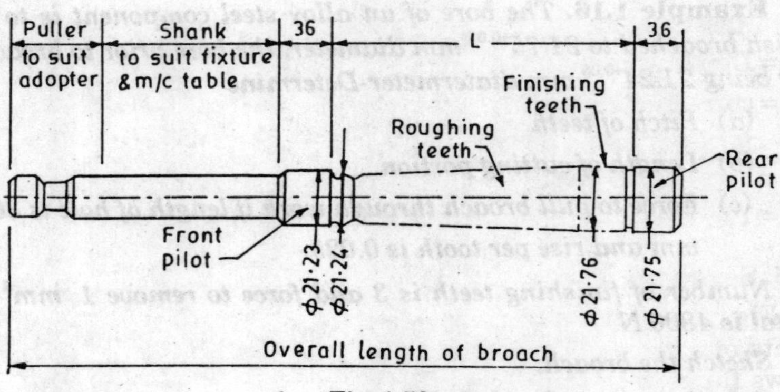

Fig. 1.58.

K = Force required to remove 1 mm^2 of metal at given rise / tooth

$= 4800\,N$

h = Rise per tooth = 0.025 mm.

$F = \pi \times 21.76 \times 3 \times 0.025 \times 4800$

$= 25581\text{ N} = 25.581\text{ kN}$

Fig. 1.58 shows sketch of broach.

Example 1.17. *A mild steel rod is machined on a lathe. Find power of motor using following data.*

Cutting speed = 90 m/min

Feed = 0.5 mm/rev.

Depth of cut = 2.54 mm

Correction factor = 0.5

Solution. The formula for calculating power of motor is as follows:

P = Power (kW)

$$= \frac{v \cdot f \cdot d \cdot F}{6000 \times \eta}$$

where v = cutting speed = 90 mpm

f = Feed = 0.5 mm / rev.

F = specific resistance

$= 270 - 300\text{ kg/mm}^2$ (assume) for steel

d = Depth of cut = 2.54 mm

η = correction factor

$$p = \frac{90 \times 0.5 \times 2.54 \times 280}{6000 \times 0.5}$$

$= 10.7$ kW.

1.45. Screwing Tap

Fig. 1.59 shows various elements of a screwing tap. Fig. 1.60 shows flutes with right hand (RH) helix and flutes with spiral point. Fig. 1.61 shows various types of rake for the tap teeth.

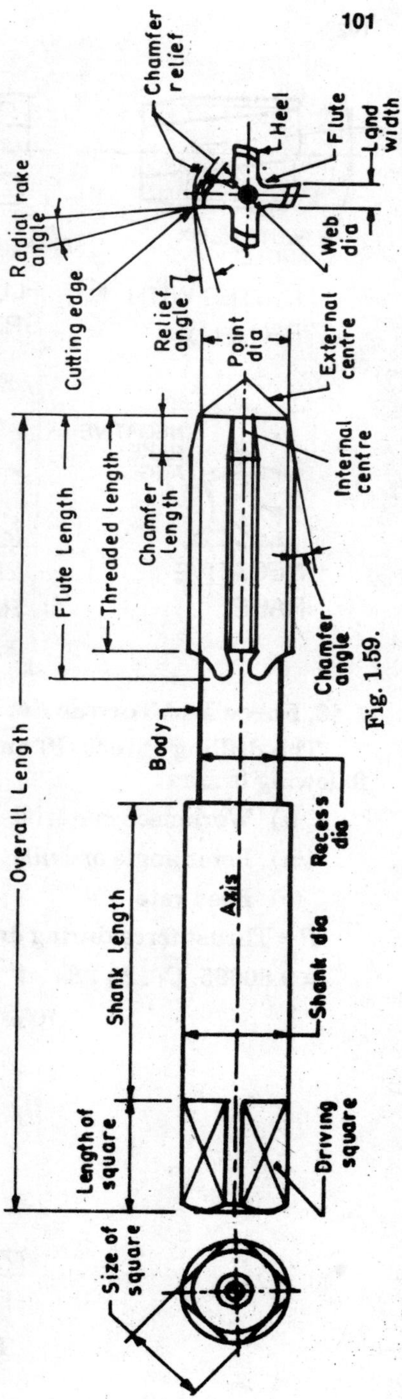

Fig. 1.59.

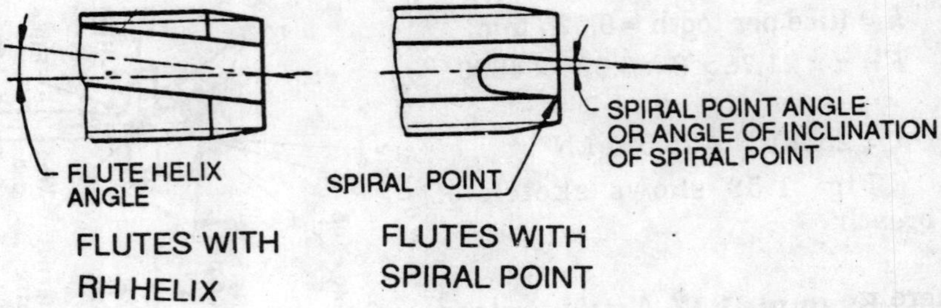

Fig. 1.60.

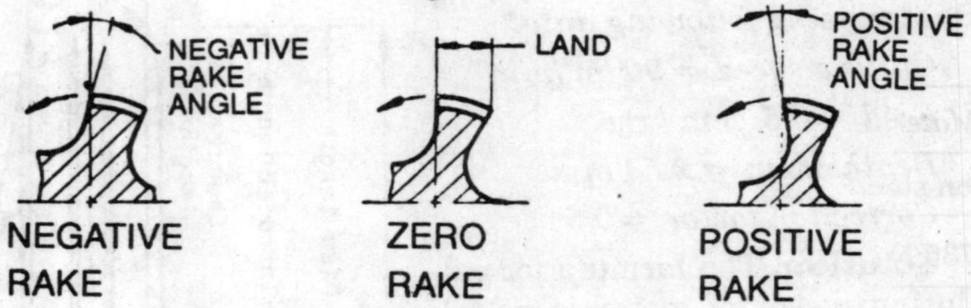

Fig. 1.61.

1.46. Force and Torque during Drilling

The drilling thrust (P) and drilling torque (T) depend on the following factors :

(*i*) Workpiece material (*ii*) Hardness

(*iii*) Point angle of drill (*iv*) Drill diameter

(*v*) Feed rate

P = Thrust force during drilling as shown in Fig. 1.62.

$= 9.80665 . C_1 . K_1 . K_2 . d^x . s^y$ Newton.

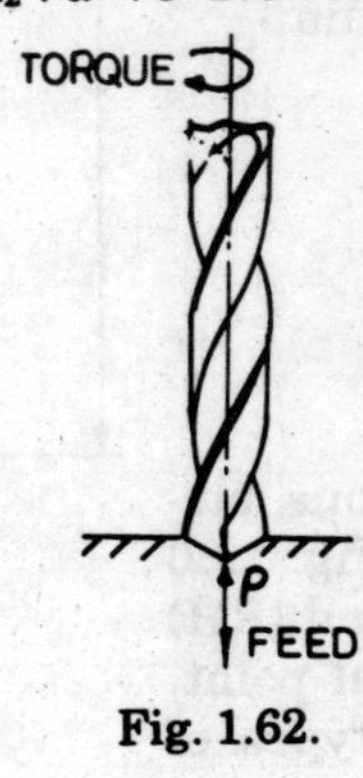

Fig. 1.62.

where C_1 = Material constant.
K_1 = Brinell hardness coefficient.
K_2 = Drill point angle coefficient.
d = Drill dia meter in mm.
S = Feed rate in mm /Rev.
T = Drilling torque.
$= 9.80665.\ C_2\ .\ K_1\ .\ K_2\ .\ d^m\ s^n$ (N–mm)

where x, y, m and n are constants.

The values of c_1, c_2, x, y, m and n are shown in Table 1.19.

Table 1.19

Materials	C_1	C_2	x	y	m	n
Carbon steel						
$\sigma_u = 735$ N /mm^2	85	34	1	1.9	0.7	0.8
C.I. *HB* = 190	52	20	1	1.9	0.8	0.8
Bronze	31	12	1	1.9	0.8	0.8
Alloy steel :						
$\sigma_u = 112$ N /mm^2	270	75	1.15	2.1	0.77	0.76
$\sigma_u = 686$ N /mm^2	163	55	1.0	2.0	0.62	0.76

The values of K_1 is indicated in Table 1.20

Table 1.20

HB	130	150	170	190	210	220	250	270
K_1	0.80	0.87	0.94	1.00	1.96	1.13	1.18	1.25

The values of K_2 are indicated in Table 1.21.

Table 1.21

½ point angle	*P*			*T*		
degree	45	60	75	45	60	75
Steel	0.97	1.0	1.04	1.23	1.0	0.82
Cast iron (K_2)	0.73	1.0	1.27	1.25	1.0	0.88

1.47. Brazing of Carbide Tools

For carbide tools a suitable shank material is carbon steel with a tensile strength of about 70 kg/mm^2. So that the least possible stresses shall occur, the ratio between the thickness of the carbide tip and the height of the shank material beneath the tip should be about 1 : 3 as shown in Fig. 1.63.

Grind the brazing areas of the tip on a silicon carbide or diamond wheel. Another reliable method is hard blasting with steel shot. De-grease the tip, and when necessary the tip-seating of the shank as well, with, for instance, trichlorethylene, acetone or carbon tetrachloride.

Arrange the seating of the tip so that the brazing stresses are as small as possible. 'Open' seatings of the tip generally give the best result. Onlt the underside of the tip and one side face (max. on-third of the tip's thickness) should come into contact with the tool shank. Then carbide tip is brazed on the seat.

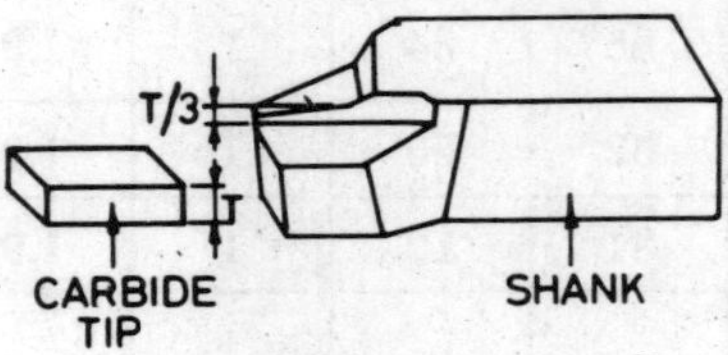

Fig. 1.63.

Re-grinding is facilitated and the carbide tip's thickness is better preserved if the tip is set at an inclination greater than that which the top-rake angle requires. Tip-seating angle for most turning tools is greater by 2° than the top rake angle.

The brazed joint has two functions. It has to hold the carbide tip in position despite heavy shearing forces and high temperatures. It must also be capable of minimizing the stresses which occur during the heating and cooling of the tool material.

1.48. Cutting Tool Wear

For a given metal cutting operation the metal removal rate and the tool life are controlled by cutting parameters. By a judicious selection of cutting data one could get the maximum rate of metal removal and optimum tool life.

Under usual cutting conditions when the form stability of the cutting edge has been achieved, wear due to interaction between the chip and the tool and between the workpiece and the tool are the main processes by which the cutting tool wears out. These types of wear are called crater wear and flank wear respectively.

1.48.1. Tool wear mechanism. Tool wear is a complex phenomenon in which the following actions take place simultaneously :

(*i*) Molecular diffusion between workpiece material and tool material. Carbon and cobalt move from tool surface to flow zone of the workpiece. Iron moves from work material to tool surface. Structural changes in the surface region of a carbide tool lead to its deterioration. By providing thin diffusion barriers the wear can be reduced.

(*ii*) Chemical affinity between the nascent layer of the workpiece material and the cutting tool material.

(*iii*) Mechanical abrasion between the micro constituents and matrix of the workpiece material and the layer of the cutting tool.

(*iv*) Pressure welding of workpiece material to cutting tool surface followed by micro transfer of small particles from the cutting tool matrix adhering to workpiece material.

All the above actions in tool wear phenomena result in two predominant types of tool wear-crater wear and flank wear.

1.48.2. Tool Wear Types. (*i*) *Flank Wear*. This occurs on the relief side and nose radius of the cutting edge. It is due to the action of abrasion and resultant heat generated between the tool and the workpiece. This increases the cutting forces, ruins the surface finish and dimensional accuracy.

(*ii*) *Crater Wear*. When turning long chipping materials like steel, the hot chips under pressure have a tendency to weld to the top face as the chip moves over it. These welded granules in turn get loosened along with some carbide particles and are carried away by passing chips. This triple action of welding, uprooting and carrying away leads to cratering. The development of a crater results in premature cutting edge failure. Higher cutting speed wear out tools faster than higher cutting feeds.

1.49. Carbide Tool Failures and Remedies

Premature tool failure problems should be checked to increase tool life. Some of the commonly observed porblems and their solutions are as follows :

Problem	Reommended Solution
1. Wear	(*i*) Decrease speed
	(*ii*) Increase feed
	(*iii*) Decrease lead angle
	(*iv*) Check that tool is not above centre height.
	(*v*) Tool should be of proper grade and hardness.
	(*vi*) Increases one or both relief and clearance angle.
2. Poor surface finsih	(*i*) Increase nose radius
	(*ii*) Increase lead angle
	(*iii*) Tool should be properly clamped
	(*iv*) Increase speed
	(*v*) Decrease feed
3. Chatter	(*i*) Decrease nose radius
	(*ii*) Decrease rake angle
	(*iii*) Increase relief and clearanance angle
	(*iv*) Decrease overhang.
	(*v*) Check the condition of spindles and slides of the machine.
	(*vi*) Decrease cutting speed
	(*vii*) Increase feed
	(*viii*) Check that workpiece is properly held and clamped.
4. Crater	(*i*) Use coolant of good lubricating qualities
	(*ii*) Use harder grade tool
	(*iii*) Increase speed
	(*iv*) Decrease feed
	(*v*) Positive rake angle may be used.
5. Built up edge	(*i*) Increase speed

	(*ii*) Use positive rake
	(*iii*) Use coolant with good lubricating properties
6. Chipping Cracking and Breakage	(*i*) Increase nose radius
	(*ii*) Increase lead angle if possible
	(*iii*) Use negative rake.
	(*iv*) Increase speed
	(*v*) Decrease feed
	(*vi*) Check the tool for looseness
	(*vii*) Check rigidity of workpiece
	(*viii*) Decrease tool overhang

Terms Relating to Reamers

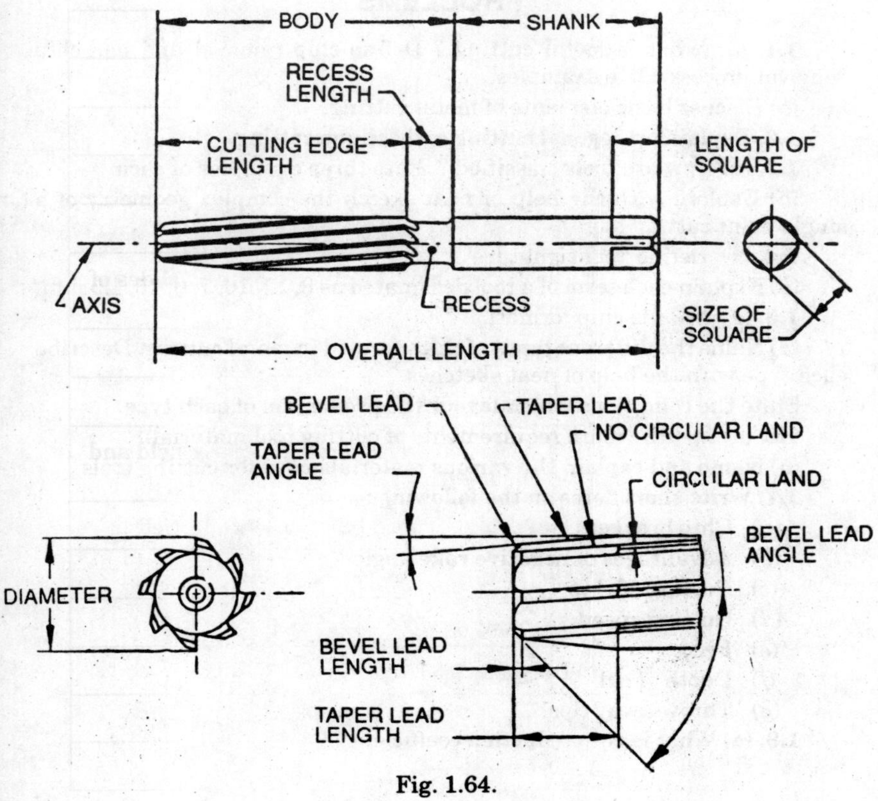

Fig. 1.64.

Only one solution or number of solutions listed above may be used to run the tool smoothly to increase life of tool, to obtain proper surface finish, production rate etc.

1.50. Cast Alloy Tools

They contain no iron and are cast into their final shape . They consists of cobalt, chromium, tungston, and carbon, the carbide phase being about 25 to 30 per cent by volume of the matrix. These tools can be used at slightly higher speeds than high speed steels and have less tendency to form a built up edge during machining. They are commonly used in machining of cast iron, malleable iron and hard bronzes.

1.51. Reamer

It is used to produce an accurate hole. Reaming is carried out after drilling.

Fig. 1.64 shows various elements of a reamer.

PROBLEMS

1.1. (*a*) What is metal cutting ? Define chip removal and non-chip removal process. Give examples.

(*b*) Discuss basic elements of metal cutting.

1.2. Explain orthogonal cutting and oblique cutting.

1.3. (*a*) How are tools classified ? State three examples of each.

(*b*) Explain with the help of neat sketch the complex geometry of a single point cutting tool.

1.4. (*a*) Define 'tool signature'.

(*b*) Explain each term of a tool designated as 8, 12, 10, 7, 0, 15, 1.5 mm.

1.5. (*a*) What is chip formation ?

(*b*) Name the different types of chips formed in metal cutting. Describe each type with the help of neat sketches.

State the conditions which favour the production of each type.

1.6. (*a*) List the main requirements of cutting tool material.

(*b*) Name and explain the various materials used for cutting tools.

1.7. Write short notes on the following :

(*a*) Chip breakers
(*b*) Advantages of negative rake angle
(*c*) Curling of chip
(*d*) Cutting speed
(*e*) Feed
(*f*) Depth of cut
(*g*) Throw-away tips.

1.8. (*a*) What is chip reduction coefficient ?

(*b*) What are the effects of cutting variable on the chip reduction coefficient.

1.9. (*a*) What is a multipoint cutting tool ?

(*b*) Sketch a twist drill and describe its various elements.

1.10. (*a*) Make a neat sketch of a twist drill, showing various angles.

(*a*) Define the following angles of a twist drill.

(*i*) Rake angle

(*ii*) Lip clearance angle

(*iii*) Point angle

(*iv*) Chisel edged angle.

1.11. Write short notes on the following :

(*a*) Cutting fluids for drilling

(*b*) Twist drill grinding

(*c*) Twist drill failure

(*d*) Drill specifications.

1.12. Analyse the forces acting on a drill.

1.13. What are the parameters which affect the drilling torque.

1.14. What factors decide the cutting speed of a drill.

1.15. (*a*)What is a milling cutter

(*b*) Sketch and explain

(*i*) Up milling

(*ii*) Down milling.

1.16. Sketch a plain milling cutter and explain the various elements of the cutter.

1.17. Write short notes on the following :

(*a*) Milling cutter sharpening

(*b*) Number of teeth on a cutter

(*c*) Cutting speed

(*d*) Coarse tooth and fine tooth milling cutters.

1.18. Explain how to calculate machining time in

(*a*) Plain milling

(*b*) Face milling.

1.19. A stab milling operating is carried out with a 60 inch diameter inserted carbide tooth cutter having 10 teeth at a cutting speed of 400 feet/min and a feed of 40 inches per minute. If the depth of cut is 0.02 inch and width of cut is 4.5 inch and the following relation is assumed :

$$F = -32000\, b \cdot d^{0.8} f^{0.7}$$

where F = Tangential fcrce on cutter

d = Depth of cut in inch

b = Width of cut in inch

f = Feed in inches per tooth

Determine the following :

(*a*) Tangential force exerted by the cutter.

(*b*) Torque transmitted by the cutter.

(*c*) Total H.P. required at the drive end of milling machine at a mechanical efficiency of 7%.

(*d*) Specific H.P. required at the arbor.

1.20. Determine the depth of cut taken on a lathe while turning brass at a feed of 0.625 mm per revolution and cutting speed of 24 metre/min if 3 horse power is available and 20% of power is lost in friction.

1.21. Estimate the time required for a single cut in each of the following machining operations.

(*a*) To turn 25 mm dia 100 mm long with cutting speed 30 m/min and a feed of 0.25 mm/rev.

(*b*) To turn 3 mm deep recess in a 50 mm dia and shaft using a 6 mm wide form tool with a cutting speed of 12 m/min and a feed of 0.05 mm.

1.22. (*a*) State the characteristics of carbide tools.

(*b*) Describe the power distribution in a milling machine and a lathe.

1.23. Write short notes on the following :

(*a*) Requirements of cutting tool.

(*b*) Power required at milling cutter.

1.24. Write short notes on the following :

(*a*) Improving metal cutting efficiency.

(*b*) Power distribution in the following machines.

(*i*) Lathe

(*ii*) Milling machine

1.25. Discuss the design of a cutting tool.

1.26. Explain the following terms with reference to a plain milling cutter :

(*i*) Radial rake angle

(*ii*) Lip angle

(*iii*) Relief angle

(*iv*) First clearance angle

(*v*) Second clearance angle.

1.27. Sketch a broaching tool and describe its construction.

1.28. Write short notes on the following :

(*a*) Friction between chip and tool.

(*b*) Power rating of electric motor.

(*c*) Improvement of cutting efficiency during machining.

(*d*) Design of a single point cutting tool.

(*e*) Common sizes of H.S.S. tool bits.

(*f*) Specification of a single point tool.

1.29. Determine the total production time for a batch of 400 components to be milled two at a time in a fixture on a horizontal milling machine given that

Length of workpiece	= 180 mm
Approach	= 25 mm
Over run	= 10 mm

Feed/tooth = 0.25 mm
Number of teeth on cutter = 10
R.P.M. of cutter = 80
Time allowed for loading, unloading and cleaning is 1 1/2 min/cycle and other allowances amount to 1/2 min/cycle.

1.30. Determine the production quantity at which the manufacturing costs of the following two alternative manufacturing methods break-even :

Numerically controlled miller and Conventional miller

(*i*) Computer cost Rs. 80, -
(*ii*) Programming cost Rs. 60, -
(*iii*) Machining time $\frac{1}{2}$h and $1\frac{1}{2}$h
(*iv*) Setter operator rate Rs. 12/h and Rs. 10/h
(*v*) Set up time $\frac{1}{2}$h and 1 h
(*vi* Over heads Rs. 9/h and Rs. 7/h
(*vii*) Depreciation Rs. 15/h and Rs. 8/h

1.31 Write short notes on the following :

(*i*) Tool wear
(*ii*) Carbide tool failure and remedies
(*iii*) Cast alloy tools
(*iv*) Sketch a reamer and name its parts
(*v*) Brazing of carbide tools
(*vi*) Screwing tap.

2

Mechanics of Metal Cutting

In any metal cutting process, considerable forces are involved and in order to design machine tool holders and work holders that will withstand these forces, it is important to establish the magnitude of these forces and the directions in which they act. According to Ernst and Merchant the chip is assumed to behave as a rigid, body held in equilibrium by the action of the forces transmitted across the chip tool interface and across the shear plane. A number of attempts have been made to study the mechanics of the cutting process starting with Mallock in 1881. The theory suggested by Ernst and Merchant and later developed by Merchant considers orthogonal cutting with a flow type having no built up edge. The mode of plastic deformation is considered to be one of simple shear across a plan extending from the tool cutting edge to the junction of the chip with the original work surface. Lee and Shaffer in 1949 obtained a solution to the problem of the mechanics of metal cutting by using the slip-line field theory which was developed for studying the stress distribution in a body undergoing plastic deformation in two dimensions.

2.1. Cutting Forces in Orthogonal Cutting

The forces acting on a single point cutting tool are of fundamental importance in the design and of cutting and machine tools. For a conventional turning process the force system is shown in Fig. 2.1. The resultant cutting force *P* represented by *OA* acting on the tool is considered to be as vector sum of three component cutting forces mutually at right angles.

(i) Feed force F_x acts in a horizontal plane but in the direction opposite to the feed.

(ii) Thrust force F_y acting in the direction perpendicular to the generated surface.

(iii) Cutting forces F_z in the direction of the main cutting motion.

The relationships between forces F_x, F_y and F_z depend upon the cutting variables, geometry of the tool point, the work material, tool wear etc.

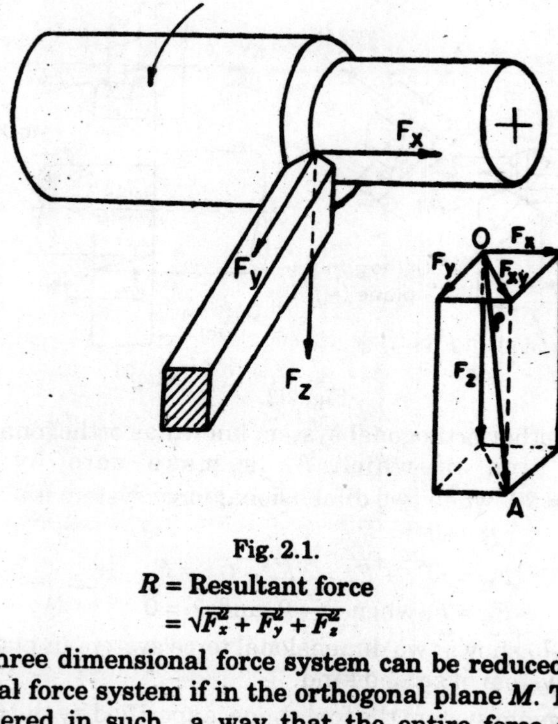

Fig. 2.1.

$$R = \text{Resultant force}$$
$$= \sqrt{F_x^2 + F_y^2 + F_z^2}$$

This three dimensional force system can be reduced to a two dimensional force system if in the orthogonal plane M. The forces are considered in such a way that the entire force system is contained in the considered state, when

$$R = \sqrt{F_z^2 + F_{xy}^2}$$
$$F_{xy} = \sqrt{F_x^2 + F_y^2}$$

For this $\lambda = 0$ and F_{XY} is contained in orthogonal plane M. This system is then known as orthogonal system of first kind for which the conditions are as follows :

(i) $\lambda = 0$

(ii) $0<\phi<90$

(iii) Chip flow deviations are small.

The various forces for the orthogonal system of first kind are shown in Fig. 2.2 (*a*).

where ϕ = Principal cutting edge angle

λ = Inclination angle.

In orthogonal system of first kind

$$F_x = F_{xy} \sin \phi$$
$$F_y = F_{xy} \cos \phi$$

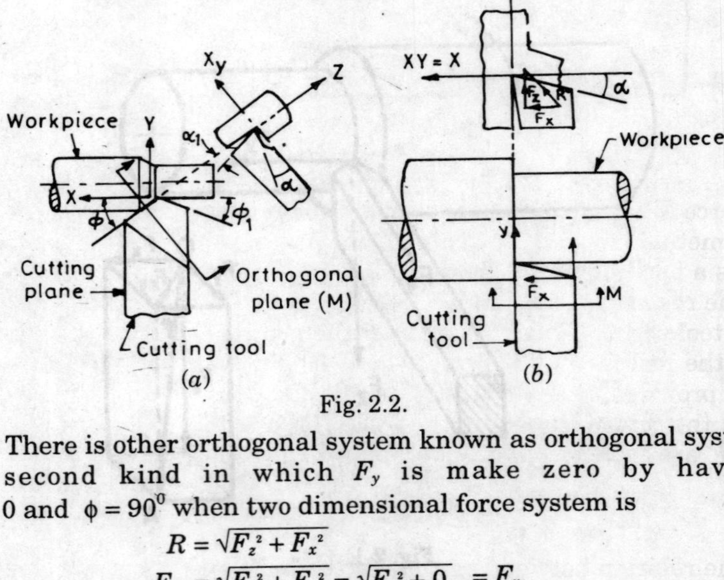

Fig. 2.2.

There is other orthogonal system known as orthogonal system of second kind in which F_y is make zero by having $\lambda = 0$ and $\phi = 90^0$ when two dimensional force system is

$$R = \sqrt{F_z^2 + F_x^2}$$
$$F_{xy} = \sqrt{F_x^2 + F_y^2} = \sqrt{F_x^2 + 0} = F_x.$$
$$F_{xy} = F_y \text{ when } \phi = 0 \text{ and } \lambda = 0$$

Fig. 2.2 *(b)* shows two dimensional force system in plane *M* for orthogonal system of second kind.

In orthogonal system the tool shape is specified by the following terms stated in order.

(i) Inclination angle.

(ii) Orthogonal rake angle (α).

(iii) Orthogonal clearance angle (α_1).

(iv) Auxiliary orthogonal clearance angle.

(v) Auxiliary cutting edge angle (ϕ_1).

(*vi*) Principal cutting edge angle (ϕ).

(*vii*) Nose radius in millimeters.

The chip may be considered as a separate body held in equilibrium by the various forces shown in Fig. 2.2.

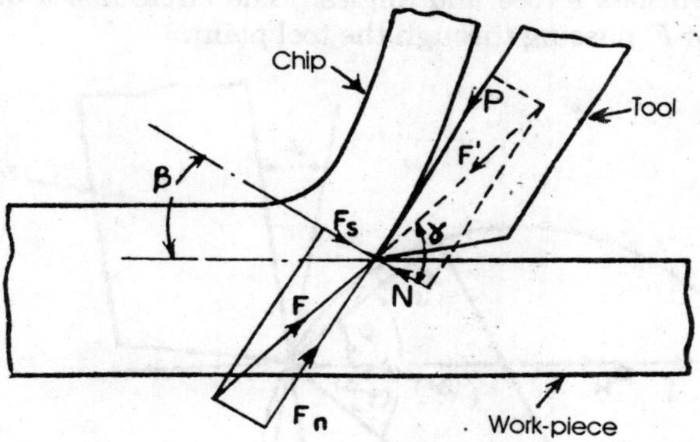

Fig. 2.2.

Force F_s acts along the shear plane and is the resistance to shear of the metal in forming the chip. Force F_n is normal to shear plane. This is a backing up force on the chip provided by the work piece. F is the resultant of F_s and F_h. Force P is the frictional resistance of the tool acting downward against the motion of chip as it moves along the tool face. The normal force N is normal to the tool face and is provided by the tool. The resultant of these two forces is F' and is the force exerted by the tool on the workpiece. The force F andF' are equal in magnitude, opposite in direction and collinear.

$$\vec{F} = \vec{F_x} + \vec{F_n}$$

$$F' = \vec{P} + \vec{N}$$

The relation between various forces have been worked out by Merchant with a large number of assumptions as follows :

(*i*) The chip behaves as a free body in stable equilibrium under the action of two equal, opposite and collinear resultant forces.

(*ii*) Continuous chip without built up edge is produced.

(*iii*) The cutting velocity remains constant.

(*iv*) The cutting tool has a sharp cutting edge and it does not make any flank contact with the workpiece.

2.1.1. Merchant circle of forces. Merchant suggested a compact and easiest way of representing the various forces inside a circle having the vector F as diameter. Fig. 2.3 shows Merchant circle diagram which is convenient to determine the relation between the various forces and angles. The circle has a diameter equal to F or F' passing through the tool point.

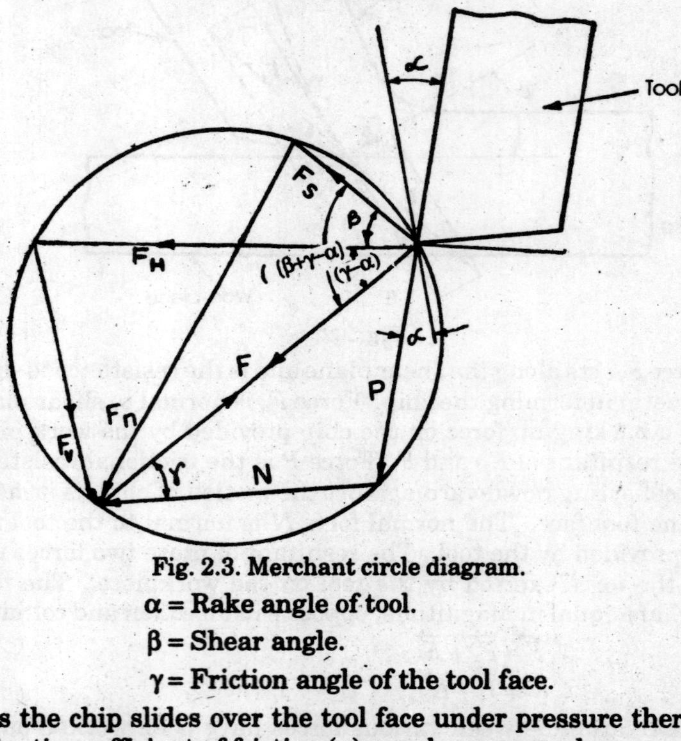

Fig. 2.3. Merchant circle diagram.

α = Rake angle of tool.

β = Shear angle.

γ = Friction angle of the tool face.

As the chip slides over the tool face under pressure therefore the kinetic coefficient of friction (μ) may be expressed as

$$\mu = \frac{P}{N} = \tan \gamma$$

F_H = Cutting Force

F_v = Feed Force

The cutting force F_H and feed force. F_V can be measured with a cutting tool dynamometer and then the other forces can be determined in terms of F_H and F_V. Shear angle β can be obtained from the equation.

$$\text{Tan } \beta = \frac{r \cos \alpha}{1 - r \sin \alpha}$$

Chip thickness ratio,

$$r = \frac{t_1}{t_2}$$

where t_1 = Chip thickness before cutting

t_2 = Chip thickness after cutting

P = Friction resistance

$$= F_H \sin \alpha + F_V \cos \alpha$$

N = Normal force

$$= F_H \cos \alpha - F_V \sin \alpha.$$

$$F = \sqrt{F_H^2 + F_V^2}$$

F_H = Cutting force

$$= F \cos (\gamma - \alpha)$$

Also $F_S = F \cos \theta$

$$\therefore \quad F = \frac{F_S}{\cos \theta}$$

where $r = \beta + \gamma - \alpha$

$$\therefore \quad F_H = \frac{F_S \cdot \cos (\gamma - \alpha)}{\cos \theta}$$

$$= \frac{F_S \cos (\gamma - \alpha)}{\cos (\beta + \gamma - \alpha)}$$

μ = Coefficient of friction

$$= \tan \lambda = \frac{P}{N}$$

$$= \frac{F_H \sin \alpha + F_V \cos \alpha}{F_H \cos \alpha - F_V \sin \alpha}$$

$$= \frac{F_H \cdot \tan \alpha + F_V}{F_H - F_V \tan \alpha}$$

The relationships for F_s and F_n are as follows :

$$F_S = F_H \cos \beta - F_V \sin \beta$$

$$F_n = F_V \cos \beta + F_H \sin \beta.$$

Cutting force depends on the following :

(*i*) Material to be cut

(*a*) Hardness of material

(*b*) Strength of material

(*ii*) Depth of cut

(*iii*) Feed

(*iv*) Tool geometry.

2.2. Stress and Strain in the Chip

During machining the chips are produced due to the plastic deformation of the metal and are subjected to stress and strain.

Let F_S = Shearing force

f_S = Shear stress in the shear plane.

A_1 = Cross sectional area of chip before cutting.

A_2 = Area of shear plane.

Now $$f_S = \frac{F_S}{A_2}$$

$$A_2 = \frac{A_1}{\sin \beta}$$

$$\therefore \quad f_S = \frac{F_S}{A_1} \sin \beta$$

$$= \frac{(F_H \cos \beta - F_V \sin \beta) \sin \beta}{A_1}$$

$$= \frac{F_H \cos \beta \sin \beta - F_V \sin^2 \beta}{A_1}$$

where $A_1 = b_1 \cdot t_1$

and b_1 and t_1 indicate width and thickness of chip respectively (Fig. 2.4).

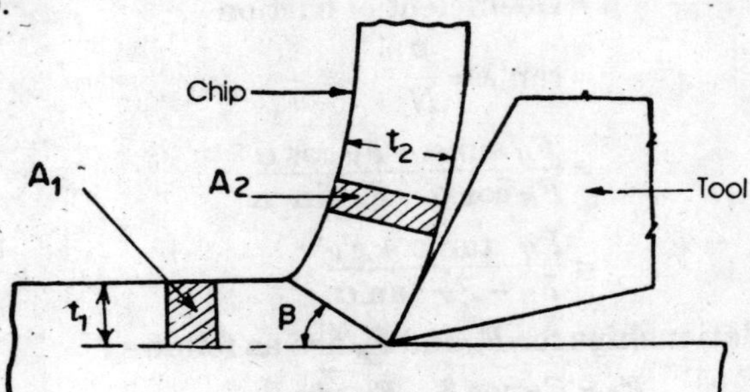

Fig. 2.4.

2.3. Shear Strain

The chip is considered to be consisting of series of plate like elements of thickness Δy and displaced through a distance ΔS relative to each other as shown in Fig. 2.5. Strain is defined as the deformation per unit length.

$$e = \text{Shear strain}$$

$$= \frac{\Delta S}{\Delta y}$$

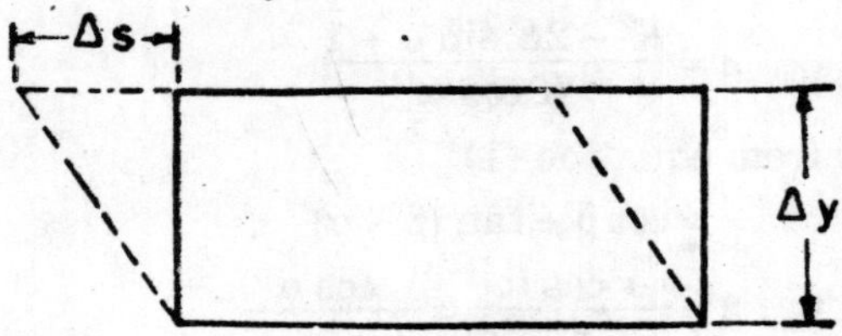

Fig. 2.5.

Fig. 2.6 shows elements of chips in the strain state.

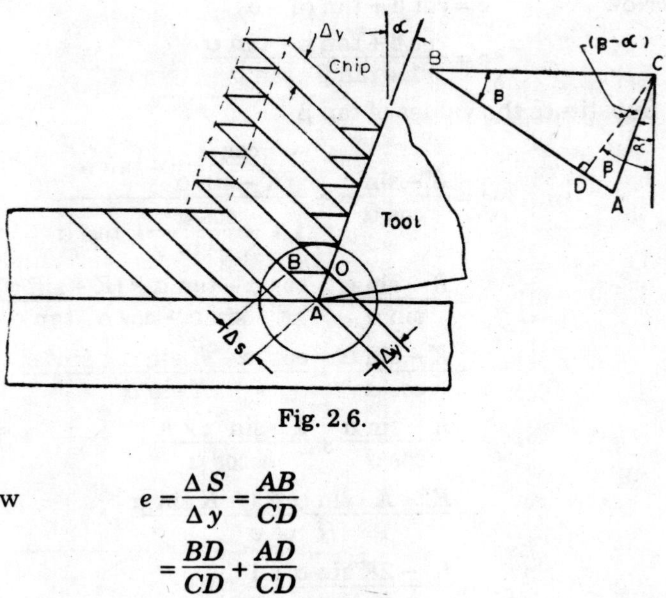

Fig. 2.6.

Now $$e = \frac{\Delta S}{\Delta y} = \frac{AB}{CD}$$

$$= \frac{BD}{CD} + \frac{AD}{CD}$$

$$= \cot \beta + \tan (\beta - \alpha) \quad ....(1)$$

$$= \frac{1}{\tan \beta} + \frac{\tan \beta - \tan \alpha}{1 + \tan \beta \tan \alpha}$$

$$= \frac{1 + \tan^2 \beta}{\tan \beta + \tan^2 \beta \tan \alpha}$$

$$= \frac{\sec^2 \beta}{\tan \beta (1 + \tan \beta \tan \alpha)}$$

$$= \frac{\cos \alpha}{\sin \beta . \cos (\beta - \alpha)}$$

2.3. *(a)* **To prove that**

$$e = \frac{K^2 - 2K \sin \alpha + 1}{K \cos \alpha}$$

We know from equation (1)

$$e = \cot \beta + \tan (\beta - \alpha)$$

$$\tan \beta = \frac{r \cos \alpha}{1 - r \sin\alpha} = \frac{\cos \alpha}{\frac{1}{r} - \sin \alpha}$$

$$= \frac{\cos \alpha}{K - \sin \alpha}$$

Now $\quad e = \cot \beta + \tan (\beta - \alpha)$

$$e = \frac{\cot \beta + \tan \beta - \tan \alpha}{1 + \tan \beta \cdot \tan \alpha}$$

Substitute the values of $\tan \beta$

$$e = \frac{K - \sin \alpha}{\cos \alpha} + \frac{\frac{\cos \alpha}{K - \sin \alpha} - \tan \alpha}{1 + \frac{\cos \alpha}{K - \sin \alpha} \times \tan \alpha}$$

$$= \frac{K - \sin \alpha}{\sin \alpha} + \frac{\cos \alpha - \tan \alpha \times (K - \sin \alpha)}{K - \sin \alpha + \cos \alpha \cdot \tan \alpha}$$

$$= \frac{K - \sin \alpha}{\cos \alpha} + \frac{\cos^2 \alpha - K \sin \sigma + \sin^2 \alpha}{K \sin \alpha}$$

$$e = \frac{K - \sin \alpha}{\cos \alpha} + \frac{1 - \sin \alpha \times K}{K \cos \alpha}$$

$$= \frac{K^2 - K \cdot \sin \alpha + 1 - K \sin \alpha}{H \cos \alpha}$$

$$= \frac{K^2 - 2K \sin \alpha + 1}{K \cos \alpha}$$

where K = Chip reduction coefficient.

2.4. Work Done and Power Required

The work done and power required in metal cutting is calculated as follows :

Let $\quad V$ = Cutting speed (metre /minute)

F_H = Cutting force (kg)

W = Total work done in cutting

$= F_H \times V$ kgm /min

W_1 = Work done in shear.

$= F_S \times V_S$ kg–m /min.

where V_S = Velocity of the chip relative to work in metre / minute

F_S = Shear force in kg.

W_2 = Work done in friction

$= P \times V_C.$ kgm /min.

where

V_C = Velocity of the chip relative to the cutting tool in metre / min.

$$W = W_1 + W_2$$

$$F_H \times V = F_S \times V_S + P \times V_C.$$

$$H.P. = \frac{F_H \times V}{4500}.$$

2.5. Specific Horse Power

Specific horse power means power required to remove unit volume of metal.

Total energy required for unit volume of metal cut is function of the following variables.

(*i*) Work piece material

(*ii*) Friction condition on tool face

(*iii*) Tool sharpness

(*iv*) Cutting speed, feed and depth of cut

(*v*) Rake angle

(*vi*) Clearance angle

(*vii*) Cutting fluid used.

2.6. Machine Tool Efficiency

H.P. used in metal cutting is estimated by measuring the gross horse power (HP_g) and t are horse power (HP_t).

H.P. cutting (HP_c) = $HP_g - Hp_t.$

η = Machine tool efficiency

$$= \frac{HP_c}{HP_g}$$

2.7. Metal Removal Rate (w)

It is the volume of metal removed in unit time. It helps to calculate time required to remove specified quantity of material from the workpiece.

Let, t = Depth of cut in centimetres

f = Feed /revolution in cm.

V = Cutting speed in cm /minute.

$w = t.f.v.\ \text{cm}^3 / \text{min}.$

The metal should be removed by the cutting rapidly to reduce the machining cost. To achieve this the following factors should be considered.

(*i*) The cutting tool should be made up of proper material.

(*ii*) The cutting tool should be properly ground.

(*iii*) Tool should be held rigidly and there should be no vibrations.

(*iv*) Depending upon the rigidity of the machine maximum speed and feed should be used.

The material removed per minute is calculated as indicated in table 2.1 for various operations.

Table 2.1

Operation	*Volume*(cm^3 */min*)
Turning	$f \times t \times V$
Face milling	$B \times t \times T$
Slot milling	$B \times t \times T$
Planing or shaping	$t \times f \times L \times S$

where f = Feed (cm /rev.)

t = Depth of cut in cm.

V = Cutting speed in cm /min

B = Width of cut in cm.

T = Table travel cm /min.

L = Length of work piece in cm.

S = Strokes per minute.

2.8. Ernst-Merchant Theory

According to this theory the relation between rake angle α shear angle β and friction angle γ is as follows.

$$\beta = \frac{\pi}{4} - \frac{\gamma}{2} + \frac{\alpha}{2}$$

(*i*) Shear will take place in a direction in which energy required for shearing is minimum.

(*ii*) Shear stress is maximum at the shear plane and it remains constant.

We have proved that

$$F_H = \frac{F_S \cdot \cos(\gamma - \alpha)}{\cos(\beta + \gamma - \alpha)}$$

Now $F_S = f_S \cdot A_2$

where f_S = Shear stress

A_2 = Area of shear plane $= \frac{b_1 t_1}{\sin \beta}$

$$\therefore \quad F_H = f_S \cdot \frac{b_1 t_1}{\sin \beta} \frac{\cos(\gamma - \alpha)}{\cos(\beta + \gamma - \alpha)}$$

Differentiate w.r.t. β.

$$\frac{dF_H}{d\beta} = -f_S \cdot b_1 t_1 \cos(\gamma - \alpha) \times \left[\frac{\cos\beta \cos(\beta + \gamma - \alpha) - \sin\beta \sin(\beta + \gamma - \alpha)}{\sin^2\beta \cos^2(\beta + \gamma - \alpha)}\right]$$

= 0 in order that β will assume that value which required a minimum force to cut the material

$$\therefore \cos\beta \cos(\beta + \gamma - \alpha) - \sin\beta \sin(\beta + \gamma - \alpha) = 0$$

$$\cos(\beta + \beta + \gamma - \alpha) = 0$$

$$\cos(2\beta + \gamma - \alpha) = 0$$

$$2\beta + \gamma - \alpha = \frac{\pi}{2}$$

$$\beta = \frac{\pi}{4} - \frac{\gamma}{2} + \frac{\alpha}{2}.$$

2.9. Lee and Shaffer's Theory

The theory of Lee and Shaffer was the result of an attempt to apply the plasticity theory to the problem of orthogonal metal cutting. The assumptions made in this theory are follows.

(*i*) The work material ahead of the tool behaves as ideal plastic mass.

(*ii*) There exists a shear plane which separates the chip and workpiece.

(*iii*) No hardening in chip occurs. On the basis of above assumptions the following relationship was obtained.

$$\beta + \lambda - \alpha = \frac{\pi}{4}$$

Lee and Shaffer realised that the above equation could not apply for all values of γ and α such as when γ is $\frac{\pi}{4}$ and α is zero this will give β as zero. Therefore they modified the above equation by including the effect of built up edge by using addition angle θ depending on the size of built up edge and arrived at the following solution.

$$\beta + \gamma - \theta - \alpha = \frac{\pi}{4}.$$

2.10. Velocity Relationship

The velocity relationship in orthogonal cutting are shown in Fig. 2.7. The various velocities are the cutting velocity V, chip velocity V_C and shear velocity V_S. Velocity V_C is the velocity of chip relative to tool and is directed along tool face and V_S is velocity of chip relative to workpiece and is directed along shear plane (Fig. 2.8).

In Fig. 2.8, from right angle triangle OCA

$$AC = OA \sin \beta$$

$$AC = V \sin \beta$$

From right angled triangle BAC.

$$AC = AB \cos (\beta - \alpha)$$

$$AC = V_C \cos (\beta - \alpha) \quad ...(ii)$$

∴ From (*i*) and (*ii*)

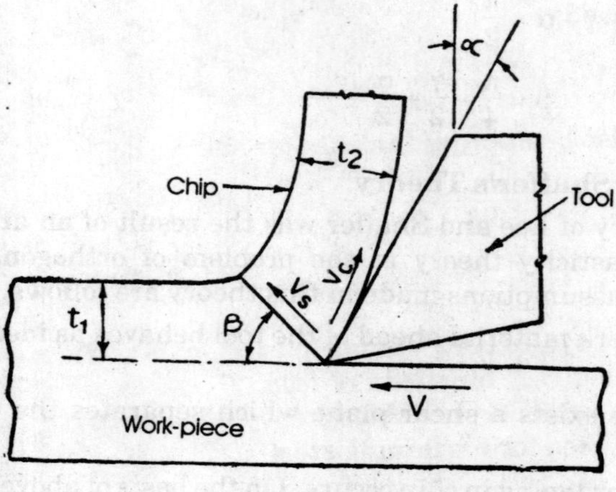

Fig. 2.7.

$$V \sin B = V_C \cos (\beta - \alpha)$$

$$V_C = \frac{V \sin \beta}{\cos (\beta - \alpha)}$$

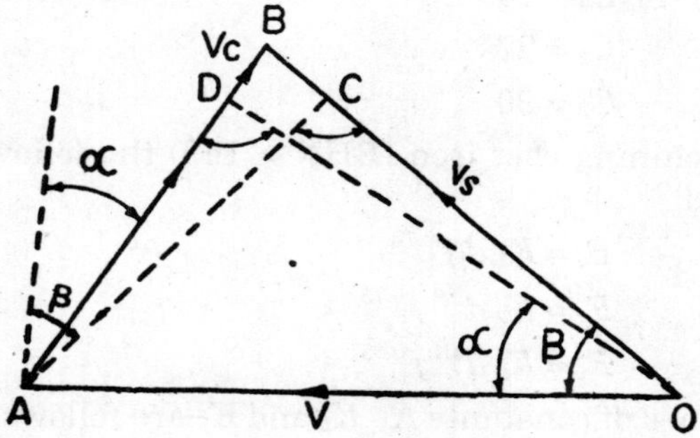

Fig. 2.8.

Again from right angle triangle *ODA*

$$OD = OA \cos \alpha = V \cos \alpha \quad \text{...}(iii)$$

from right angled triangle *ODB*.

$$OD = V_S \cos (\beta - \alpha) \quad \text{...}(iv)$$

∴ From (*iii*) and (*iv*)

$$V \cos \alpha = V_S \cos (\beta - \alpha)$$

$$V_S = \frac{V \cos \alpha}{\cos (\beta - \alpha)}$$

2.10.0. To prove : $V_C = rV$.

We have proved that

$$V_C = \frac{V \cdot \sin \beta}{\cos (\beta - \alpha)}$$

And it has also been proved in chapter one

$$r = \frac{\sin \beta}{\cos (\beta - \alpha)}$$

$$\therefore \quad V_C = \frac{V \cdot \sin \beta}{\cos (\beta - \sigma)} = V \cdot r.$$

2.10.1. Effect of Cutting Variables on Cutting Forces. The cutting forces are direct functions of feed (*f*) and depth of cut (*d*) under conditions of other variables kept constant the following relations may be used for machining steel

$$F_z = C_1 d \cdot f^{0.75}$$

$$F_y = C_2 d^{\,0.9} f^{0.75}$$

$$F_x = C_3 d^{1.2} f^{0.55}$$

For steel having ultimate strength 35 kg/mm² the values of C_1, C_2 and C_3 are as follows.

$$C_1 = 14$$

$$C_2 = 27$$

$$C_3 = 20$$

For machining cast iron (BHN = 150) the following relations may be used.

$$F_z = K_1\, d\, f^{0.78}$$

$$F_y = K_2\, d^{0.9} f^{0.75}$$

$$F_x = K_3\, d^{1.1} f^{0.65}$$

The values of constants K_1, K_2 and K_3 are follows.

$$K_1 = 80$$

$$K_2 = 59$$

$$K_3 = 28.$$

2.11. Improvement of Cutting Efficiency

It is desirable that the metal cutting should be economical.

Cutting efficiency can be improved by following factors.

(*i*) By reducing chip length by means of chip breakers.

(*ii*) By improving surface finish of the tool face by honing or chrome plating.

(*iii*) Increased depth of cut increases the cutting efficiency by a small amount.

(*iv*) By effective removal of heat produced during cutting.

2.12. Requirements made to the Cutting Tool

A tool intended for high production machining should be amply strong and rigid, it should have optimum geometry, be keenly sharpened with a high class finish, producible in manufacture and convenient in use.

2.13. Measurement of Cutting Forces

The cutting forces are measured in order to achieve the following :

(*i*) To determine the power required during cutting process.

(*ii*) To observe the characteristics of workpiece and tool material.

(*iii*) Cutting forces when determined help in proper design of machine tool components.

The cutting forces are generally measured by an instrument called cutting tool dynamometer. There are different designs of dynamometers although their basic principle is same. The general principle used in deflection type cutting tool dynamometer is shown in Fig. 2.8 (A). A stiff member *M* resting on a solid pivot carries a cutting tool at one end and is attached to a frame *N* by means of a leaf spring at the other end. The cutting force F_H deflects the member *M* relative to *N* by an amount depending on the magnitude of F_H and stiffness of spring. The deflection so produced is taken up by the dial gauge which is calibrated to read the magnitude of F_H proportional to deflection. The feed force F_V can be measured by housing the frame in a further solid member so that if deflects in a plane perpendicular to the plane of the given projection.

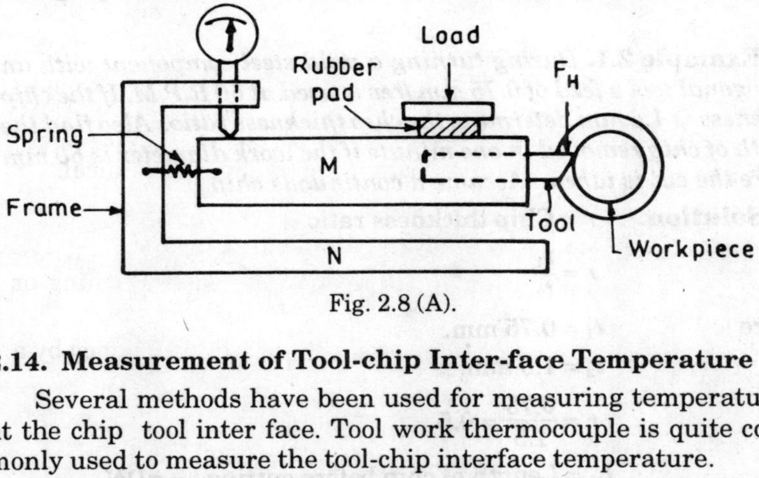

Fig. 2.8 (A).

2.14. Measurement of Tool-chip Inter-face Temperature

Several methods have been used for measuring temperatures at the chip tool inter face. Tool work thermocouple is quite commonly used to measure the tool-chip interface temperature.

In this method the tool-work contact area serves as the hot junction in a thermo-electric circuit and the e.m.f. generated is proportional to its temperature. The e.m.f. developed is measured by a suitable millivoltmeter.

The e.m.f. in the thermoelectric circuit depends only on the difference in temperature between the hot and cold functions. Fig. 2.8 (B) shows the thermocouple technique to measure the tool chip interface tempeature for a work piece fitted on a lathe in which the chip and tool junction constitutes the hot junction while *A* and *B* the cold junction remain at room temperature.

Tool life is more dependent upon the temperature reached at the tool chip interface than the total amount of heat flowing into the tool or work.

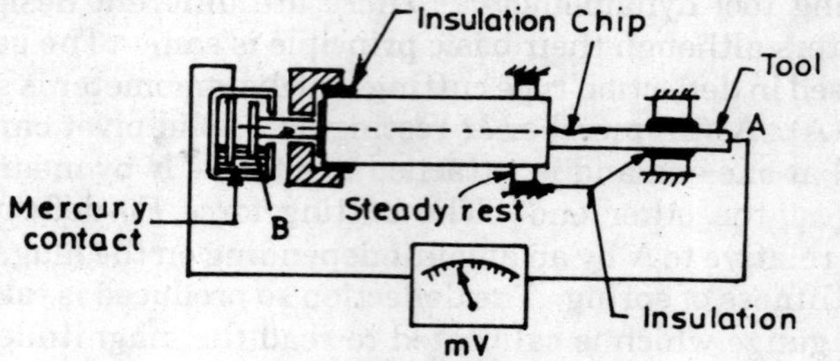

Fig. 2.8. (B)

The rate of tool wear is generally observed to increase with increased tool temperature.

Example 2.1. *During turning a mild steel component with an orthogonal tool a feed of 0.75 mm /rev is used at 50 R.P.M. If the chip thickness is 1.5 mm determine the chip thickness ratio. Also find the length of chip removed in one minute if the work diameter is 50 mm before the cut is taken. Assume a continuous chip.*

Solution. r = Chip thickness ratio

$$r = \frac{t_1}{t_2}$$

where $t_1 = 0.75$ mm.

$t_2 = 1.5$ mm.

$$r = \frac{0.75}{1.5} = 0.5$$

L_1 = Length of chip before cutting. $= \pi DN$

where D = Diameter of work piece = 50 mm.

N = R.P.M = 50.

$L_1 = \pi \times 50 \times 50 = 7850$ mm

L_2 = Length of chip removed per minute.

$$r = \frac{L_2}{L_1}$$

$$0.5 = \frac{L_2}{7850}$$

$L_2 = 3925$ mm. **Ans.**

Example 2.2. *In an orthogonal turning operation*

Cutting speed = 80 m /min

Cutting force = 20 kg.

Feed force = 8 kg.

Back rake angle = 15°

Feed = 0.2 mm /rev.

Chip thickness = 0.4 mm.

Determine the following :

(a) Shear angle.

(b) Work done in shear.

(c) Shear strain.

Solution. r = chip thickness ratio $= t_1/t_2$

where $t_1 = 0.2$ mm

$t_2 = 0.4$ mm

$$r = \frac{0.2}{0.4} = 0.5$$

β = shear angle.

α = rake angle = 15°

$$\tan\beta = \frac{r\cos\alpha}{1 - r\sin\alpha}$$

$$\tan\beta = \frac{0.5\cos 15}{1 - 0.5\sin 15} = 0.55$$

$\beta = 28°$.

F_S = Shear force.

$= F_H \cos\beta - F_V \sin\beta$.

Now F_H = Cutting force = 20 kg.

F_V = Feed force = 8 kg.

$F_S = 20\cos 28 - 8\sin 28$

$= 13.84$ kg.

Now V = Cutting speed = 80 m /min.

$$V_s = \frac{V\cos\alpha}{\cos(\beta - \alpha)}$$

$$= \frac{80\cos 15}{\cos(28 - 15)} = 79 \text{ m /min.}$$

Work done in shear $= F_S \cdot V_S = 13.84 \times 79$

$= 1093$ kg–m /min.

Shear strain $= \cot \beta + \tan(\beta - \alpha)$

$= \cot 28 + \tan (28 - 15)$

$= 1.65.$

Example 2.3. *Calculate the power consumed during cutting of a low carbon steel bar 40 mm diameter if cutting force is 150 kg at 200 R.P.M.*

Solution. F_H = Cutting force

$= 150$ kg.

V = Cutting speed

$$= \frac{\pi DN}{1000} = \frac{\pi \times 40}{10000} \times 200$$

$= 25.12$ m /min.

Work done $= F_H \times V$

$= 150 \times 25.12$ kgm /min.

$$\text{H.P.} = \frac{150 \times 25.12}{4500}$$

$= 0.83.$ **Ans.**

Example 2.4. *Determine the time required to turn a brass component 50 mm diameter and 100 mm long at a cutting speed of 36 m /min. The feed is 0.4 mm/revolution and only one cut is taken.*

Solution. D = Diameter of component.

$= 50$ mm

L = Length

$= 100$ mm

V = Cutting speed

$= 36$ m /min.

f = Feed = 0.4 mm /rev.

N = Spindle speed (R.P.M.)

$$V = \frac{\pi DN}{1000} \text{ m /min.}$$

$$36 = \frac{\pi \cdot 50 \cdot N}{10000}$$

$N = 229$ R.P.M.

$$T = \text{Time required} \quad = \frac{L}{f \cdot N}$$

$$= \frac{100}{0.4 \times 229} \text{ minutes.}$$

$$= \frac{100 \times 60}{0.4 \times 229} = \text{ 65 seconds. } \textbf{Ans.}$$

Example 2.5. *(a) In orthogonal cutting if the feed is 1.25 mm/rev and chip thickness after cutting is 2 mm ; determine the following :*

(i) Chip thickness ratio.

(ii) Shear angle.

The tool bit has a rake angle of 10°

(b) If shear strength = 6000 kg /cm²

Width of cut = 10 mm

Cutting speed = 30m /min.

Coefficient of friction = 0.9

Determine the following :

(i) Shearing force.

(ii) Friction angle.

(iii) Cutting force.

(iv) Horse power at the cutting tool.

Solution.

(*a*) Let r = chip thickness ratio

$$= \frac{t_1}{t_2}$$

where t_1 = Chip thickness before cutting.

t_2 = Chip thickness after cutting.

Now $t_1 = 1.25$ mm.

$t_2 = 2$ mm.

$$r = \frac{1.25}{2} = 0.625$$

Let β = Shear angle

α = Rake angle = 10°

$$\tan \beta = \frac{r \cos \alpha}{1 - r \sin \alpha}$$

$$= \frac{0{\cdot}625 \cos 10}{1 - 0.625 \sin 10}$$

$$= \frac{0.625 \times 0.9848}{1 - 0.625 - 0.1736}$$

$$= 0.65$$

$\beta = 33^o\ 2'$ **Ans.**

(*b*) We know

$$F_S = \frac{f_S \cdot A_1}{\sin \beta}$$

where F_S = Shearing force

f_S = Shear stress

A_1 = Area of chip

= Width of chip × Depth of cut

= 1 cm × 0.125 cm

$$\therefore \quad F_S = \frac{6000 \times (1 \times 0.125)}{\sin 33^o\ 2'}$$

$$= \frac{6000 \times 0.125}{0.545} = 1376 \text{ kg.}$$

Let λ = Friction angle

μ = Coefficient of friction

$\tan \gamma = \mu = 0.9$

$\gamma = 42^o$.

F_H = Cutting force

$$= \frac{F_S \cdot \cos(\gamma - \alpha)}{\cos(\beta + \lambda - \alpha)}$$

$$= \frac{1376 \cos(42 - 10)}{\cos(33' - 2' + 42 - 10)}$$

$$= \frac{1376 \cos 32}{\cos 65^o\ 2'} = 2778 \text{ kg.}$$

H.P. = Horse power at the tool

$$= \frac{F_H \times V}{4500}$$

where V = Cutting speed (metre /min)

$$\text{H.P.} = \frac{2778 \times 30}{4500} = 18.52 \quad \textbf{Ans.}$$

Example 2.6. *In orthogonal cutting of a material the feed force is 80 kg and cutting force is 150 kg. Calculate the following :*

(*i*) *Compression and shear forces on shear plane.*

(*ii*) *Coefficient of friction of the chip on the tool face.*

Take chip thickness ratio as 0.3 and rake angle as 8°.

Solution. We have proved that

F_n = Compressive force on shear plane.

$= F_V \cos\beta + F_H \sin\beta.$

F_S = Shear force on shear plane.

$= F_H \cos\beta - F_V \sin\beta.$

Now $F_H = 150$ kg.

$F_V = 80$ kg.

$\alpha = 8°$

β = Shear angle.

$$\tan\beta = \frac{r\cos\alpha}{1 - r\sin\alpha}$$

$$= \frac{0.3\cos 8}{1 - 0.3\sin 8} = 0.3$$

$\beta = 17°$

$\therefore$ $F_n = F_V \cos\beta + F_H \sin\beta$

$= 80 \cos 17 + 150 \sin 17$

$= 121$ kg. **Ans.**

$F_S = F_H \cos\beta - F_V \sin\beta.$

$= 150 \cos 17 - 80 \sin 17$

$= 119.3$ kg. **Ans.**

μ = Coefficient of friction

$$= \frac{F_H \tan\alpha + F_V}{F_H - F_V \tan\alpha}$$

$$= \frac{150\tan 8 + 80}{150 - 80\tan 8}$$

$= 0.73.$ **Ans.**

Example 2.7. *In orthogonal turning process the feed is 0.25 mm/rev. at 50 R.P.M. The thickness of the chip removed is 0.5 mm.*

(*a*) *What is the chip thickness ratio?*

(*b*) *If the work diameter is 50 mm before the cut is taken, what is the approximate length of the chip removed in one minute. Assume a continuous chip.*

Solution. r = Chip thickness ratio $= t_1/t_2$

t_1 = Chip thickness before cutting
= 0.25 mm.
t_2 = Chip thickness

$$r = \frac{t_1}{t_2}$$

$$= \frac{0.25}{0.5}.$$

= 0.5 **Ans.**

Work diameter, $D = 50$ mm.
= 5 cm.
N = R.P.M.
= 50.
L_1 = Length of chip before cutting

$$= \pi \,.\, D \,.\, N$$

$$= \pi \,.5.\, 50$$

= 785 cm.

L_2 = Length of chip after cutting.

$$r = \frac{L_2}{L_1}$$

$$0.5 = \frac{L_2}{785}$$

$$L_2 = 0.5 \times 785$$

= 392.5 *cm*. **Ans.**

Example 2.8. *A medium carbon steel bar 40 mm diameter is turned on a lathe with a cutting tool having top rake angle 30° and with a cutting speed of 24 mpm (metre per minute). If the cutting force is 200 kg, feed force is 80 kg and feed given to tool is 0.12 mm/rev. length of chip in one revolution = 70 mm, determine the following :*

(*a*) *Shear angle.*

(*b*) *Chip thickness.*

(*c*) *Velocity of chip along the tool face.*

Solution. F_H = Cutting force
= 200 kg.
F_V = Feed force
= 80 kg.

α = Rake angle

$= 30^{\circ}$

f = feed /revolution.

= 0.12 mm /rev.

β = Shear angle.

$$\tan \beta = \frac{r \cos \alpha}{1 - r \sin \alpha}$$

$$= \frac{r \cos 30}{1 - r \sin 30}$$

r = Chip thickness ratio.

$$= \frac{L_2}{L_1}$$

L_1 = Length of chip before cutting.

$= \pi D$

where D = Diameter of workpiece

$= \pi \times 40$ mm

L_2 = Length of chip after cutting

= 70 mm (given).

$$r = \frac{70}{\pi \times 40} = 0.55$$

$$\tan \beta = \frac{0.55 \cos 30}{1 - 0.55 \sin 30}$$

$\beta = 33^{\circ} 6'$. **Ans.**

$$r = \frac{t_1}{t_2}.$$

where t_1 = Chip thickness before cutting.

= feed

t_2 = Chip thickness.

$$r = \frac{\text{Feed /rev.}}{\text{Chip thickness}}$$

$$\text{Chip thickness} = \frac{\text{Feed /rev.}}{r}$$

$$= \frac{0.12}{0.55} = 0.218 \text{ mm. } \textbf{Ans.}$$

V_C = Velocity of chip along the tool face.

$$= \frac{V \sin \beta}{\cos (\beta - \alpha)} = V \times r$$

where V = Cutting speed.

[As we have proved

$$r = \frac{\sin \beta}{\cos (\beta - \alpha)}$$

$$V_c = 24 \times 0.55 = 13.2 \text{ mpm.} \quad \textbf{Ans.}$$

Example 2.9. *To turn a mild steel component the power required is 0.1/c m³/min. The maximum power available at the machine spindle is 5 H.P. If the cutting speed is 35 meter /min and feed rate is 0.25 mm / rev., determine the following :*

(*a*) *Maximum metal removal rate.*

(*b*) *Depth of cut.*

(*c*) *Cutting force.*

(*d*) *Normal pressure on chip.*

Solution. w = Maximum metal removal rate.

$$= \frac{5}{0.1} = 50 \text{ cm}^3 \text{/min.}$$

F_H = Cutting force (kg)

V = Cutting speed (mpm)

$$\frac{F_H \times V}{4500} = \text{Horse power} = 5.$$

$$F_H = \frac{4500 \times 5}{35} = 643 \text{ kg.}$$

t = Depth of cut in cm.

f = Feed in cm. = 0.025 cm/rev.

V = Cutting speed in cm.

$$w = t \times f \times V$$

$$50 = t \times 0.025 \times 35 \times 100$$

$$t = \frac{50}{35 \times 100 \times 0.25} = 0.55 \text{ cm} = 5.5 \text{ mm.}$$

Normal pressure on chip

$$= \frac{F_H}{\text{Chip Area}}$$

$$= \frac{643}{\text{Feed} \times \text{Depth of cut}}$$

$$= \frac{643}{0.25 \times 5.5}$$

$$= 468 \text{ kg /mm}^2 \quad \textbf{Ans.}$$

Example 2.10. *Following observations were made from a metal cutting test carried out on a lathe.*

Cutting force = 180 kg.

Feed = 5 cuts /mm.

Depth of cut = 5 mm.

Cutting speed = 30 mpm.

If overall efficiency of the machine is 70% determine

(*a*) *Normal pressure on chip.*

(*b*) *Power required at the motor to turn the material.*

Solution. F_H = Cutting force

$$= 180 \text{ kg.}$$

$$\text{Feed} = \frac{1}{5} = 0.2 \text{ mm/Rev.}$$

Normal pressure on chip

$$= \frac{F_H}{\text{Cross sectional area of chip}}$$

$$= \frac{180}{5 \times 0.2}$$

$$= 180 \text{ kg /mm}^2.$$

(Cross sectional area of chip

= Depth of cut × Feed per revolution)

Power required for cutting

$$= \frac{F_H \times V}{4500}$$

$$= \frac{183 \times 30}{4500} = 1.2$$

Power required at the motor

$$= \frac{1.2}{0.70} = 1.7 \text{ H.P.} \quad \textbf{Ans.}$$

Example 2.11. *The power required by a lathe when running idle is 300 watts. The power input rises to 2400 watts when an alloy steel is machined on lathe at 120 r.p.m. If the depth of cut is 3.50 mm, feed is 0.2 mm/rev and cutting speed is 24 metre/min. Calculate the following :*

(*a*) *Cutting force and torque at the spindle.*

(*b*) *H.P./cm*^{3}*/min required to cut the material.*

Solution. Power required for cutting

$$= 2400 - 300$$
$$= 2100 \text{ Watts.}$$

H.P. required for cutting

$$= \frac{2100}{735}$$
$$= 2.87$$

T = Torque at the spindle.

N = r.p.m. = 120

$$\text{H.P.} = \frac{2\pi NT}{4500}$$

$$2.87 = \frac{2\pi \times 120 \times T}{4500}$$

$$T = \frac{2.87 \times 4300}{2\pi \times 120} = 17 \text{ kgm}$$

F_H = Cutting force.

V = Cutting speed in metre per minute

= 24 mpm

$$\text{H.P.} = \frac{F_H \times V}{4500}$$

$$2.87 = \frac{F_H \times 24}{4500}$$

$$F_H = \frac{2.87 \times 4500}{24} = 538 \text{ kg.}$$

w = Maximum metal removal rate

$= f \times t \times V$

where f = Feed = 0.2 mm/rev.

= 0.02 cm/rev.

t = Depth of cut.

= 3.5 mm = 0.35 cm

V = Cutting speed

= 24 metre/min

= 2400 cm/min.

$$w = 0.02 \times 0.35 \times 2400 = 16.8 \text{ cm}^3/\text{min.}$$

$$\text{H.P./cm}^3/\text{min} = \frac{2.87}{16.8} = 0.17. \quad \textbf{Ans.}$$

Example 2.12. *During a metal cutting test under orthogonal conditions it was found that cutting force is 110 kg and feed force is*

102 kg when cutting at 165 metre /mint. The rake angle of tool is 10° and shear plane angle was found to be at 19°. Determine the following :

(*i*) *Shear velocity.*

(*ii*) *Chip flow velocity.*

(*iiii*) *Work done per minute in shearing the metal and work done against friction.*

(*iv*) *Show that the work in put is equal to the sum of work done in shearing and against friction.*

Solution. Draw merchant circle diagram (Fig. 2.9).

$F_H = 110$ kg

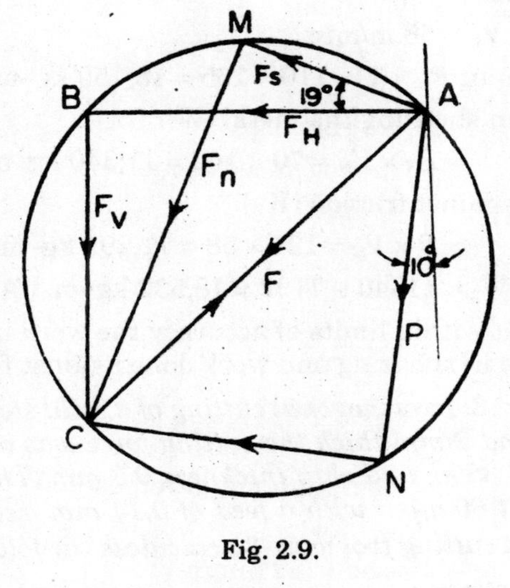

Fig. 2.9.

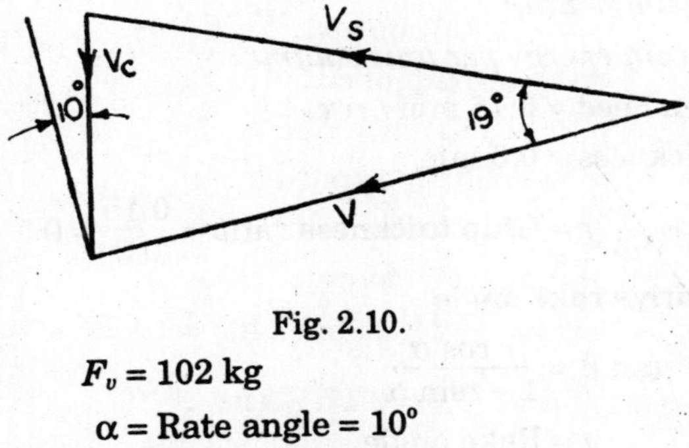

Fig. 2.10.

$F_v = 102$ kg

α = Rate angle = 10°

β = Shear angle = 19°

Take $AB = F_H$ and $BC = F_V$ the two forces being at right angles. Draw a circle with AC diameters.

From the diagram

$$F_S = 70 \text{ kg}$$

$$P = 124 \text{ kg}$$

Now $V = 165$ m/min.

Draw the velocity diagram (Fig. 2.10),

From the diagram

Shear velocity,

$$V_S = 162 \text{ m/min.}$$

Chip flow velocity,

$$V_C = 58 \text{ m/min}$$

(*W*) Work input $F_H \times V = 110 \times 165 = 18{,}150$ kg–m/min

Work done in shearing the metal (W_1)

$$= F_S \times V_H = 70 \times 162 = 11{,}340 \text{ kg–m}$$

Work done against friction (W_2)

$$= P \times V_C = 124 \times 58 = 71{,}292 \text{ kg–m.}$$

$$W_1 + W_2 = 11340 + 7192 = 18{,}532 \text{ kg–m.} \quad \textbf{Ans.}$$

It shows that within limits of accuracy the work input is equal to the work done in shearing and work done against friction.

Example 2.13. *In orthogonal cutting of a mild steel tube of 150 mm diameter and 2 mm thick the cutting force was observed to be 130 kg and feed 35 kg and chip thickness 0.3 mm. The orthogonal cut was taken at 60 mpm with a feed of 0.14 mm /rev. If the back rake angle of the cutting tool was--8°, calculate the following :*

(*a*) *Shear strain,*

(*b*) *Strain energy per unit volume.*

Solution. Feed = 0.15 mm / rev.

Chip thickness = 0.3 mm

$$r = \text{Chip thickness ratio} = \frac{0.15}{0.3} = 0.5$$

For negative rake angle

$$\tan \beta = \frac{r \cos \alpha}{1 + r \sin \alpha}$$

where α = Rake angle

$$\tan \beta = \frac{0.5 \cos 8}{1 + 0.5 \sin 8}$$

$\beta = 26.5°$

Shear strain $= \tan(\beta - \alpha) + \cot \beta$

$= \tan[26.5 - (-8)] + \cot 26.5°$

$\tan 34.5 + \cot 26.5 = 2.68$

Shear stress : $f_s = \dfrac{F_H \cos \beta \sin \beta - F_V \sin^2 \beta}{b_1 \cdot t_1}$

Now $F_H = 130$ kg

$F_V = 35$ kg

$\beta = 26.5°$

$$fs = \frac{130 \cos 26.5 \sin 26.5 - 35 \sin^2 26.5}{2 \times 0.15}$$

$= 145$ kg/mm²

Shear energy per unit volume

= Shear stress × Shear strain

$= 145 \times 2.68$

$= 388.6$ kg / mm². **Ans.**

Example 2.14. *During orthogonal turning operation the following data was obtained.*

Cutting force $(F_z) = 120$ *kg.*

Feed force $(F_x) = 30$ *kg.*

Rake angle = 10°

Feed = 0.2 mm/revolution.

Width of cut = 2.3 mm.

Chip thickness = 0.4 mm

Cutting speed = 120 m /min.

Determine the following :

(*a*) *Chip thickness ratio.*

(*b*) *Shear angle.*

(*c*) *Shear stress.*

Solution. (*a*) r = Chip thickness ratio $= \dfrac{t_1}{t_2}$

t_1 = Chip thickness before cutting

= 0.2 mm.

t_2 = Chip thickness = 0.4 mm

$$r = \frac{0.2}{0.4} = 0.5$$

(*b*) β = Shear angle

α = Back rake angle = 10°

$$\tan \beta = \frac{r \cos \alpha}{1 - r \cos \alpha} = \frac{0.5 \cos 10}{1 - 0.5 \sin 10}$$

$$= \frac{0.5 \times 0.9848}{1 - 0.5 \times 0.1736} = 0.54$$

$$\beta = 28.4^{o}$$

(*c*) F_H = Cutting force = F_z = 120 kg

F_V = Feed force = F_x = 30 kg

$$F_s = F_H \cos \beta - F_v \sin \beta$$

$$= 120 \cos 28.4 - 30 \sin 28.4$$

$$= 120 \times 0.8796 - 30 \times 0.4756 = 91.2 \text{ kg}$$

$$A = \text{Shear area} = \frac{t_1 \times b_1}{\sin \beta}$$

where b_1 = Width of chip

= 2.3 mm

t_1 = 0.2 mm.

$$A = \frac{0.2 \times 2.3}{\sin 28.4} = \frac{0.2 \times 2.3}{0.4756}$$

$$= 0.97 \text{ mm}^2$$

$$f_S = \text{Shear stress} = \frac{F_S}{A} = \frac{91.2}{0.97} = 94 \text{ kg/mm}^2$$

Example 2.15. *During machining of C 20 steel with a triple carbide cutting tool 0-8-6-7-10-70-1 mm ORS shape the following data was obtained.*

Feed = 0.18 mm */revolution.*

Depth of cut = 2 mm

Cutting speed = 120 m/min.

Chip thickness = 0.4 mm.

Determine (a) Chip reduction coefficient

(b) Shear Angle.

Solution. In orthogonal turning

$$K = \text{Chip reduction co-efficient} = \frac{t_2}{f \cdot \sin \phi}$$

where t_2 = Chip thickness = 0.4 mm

f = Feed – 0.18 mm

ϕ = Principle cutting edge angle

= 70°

$$\therefore \quad K = \frac{0.4}{0.18 \times \sin 70} = \frac{0.4}{0.18 \times 0.9397}$$

$$= 2.36$$

(*b*) β = Shear angle

α = Rake angle = 8°

$$\tan \beta = \frac{\cos \alpha}{K - \sin \alpha}$$

$$\tan \beta = \frac{\cos 8}{2.36 - \sin 8}.$$

$$= \frac{0.99}{2.36 - 14} = 0.446$$

$$\beta = 24° - 2'.$$

Example 2.16. *During machining C 20 steel with a carbide cutting tool having a tool geometry given by 0-5-6-6-8-75-1 mm ORS, the following forces have been recorded by a two dimensional dynamometer.*

$$F_z = 130 \text{ kg}$$

$$F_x = 80 \text{ kg}$$

Determine the following :

(*a*) *Radial component of force, F_y*

(*b*) *Frictional force P and normal force N*

(*c*) *Kinetic coefficient of friction, mu.*

Solution. (*a*) In this case ϕ less than 90°.

It is a case of orthogonal system of first kind.

F_x = Feed force = 80 kg.

ϕ = Principal cutting angle = 75°

$$F_x = F_{xy} \sin \phi$$

$$80 = F_{xy} \sin \phi$$

$$F_{xy} = \frac{80}{\sin 75} = \frac{80}{0.9652} = 82.83 \text{ kg.}$$

$$F_y = F_{xy} \cos \phi = 82.83 \times \cos 75$$

$$= 82.83 \times 0.2588 = 21.43 \text{ kg.}$$

(*b*) α = Orthogonal rake angle = 5°

P = Frictional force.

$= F_{xy} \cos \alpha + F_z \sin \alpha.$

$= 82.83 \cos 5 + 130 \sin 5$

$= 82.83 \times 0.9962 + 130 \times 0.0871$

$= 82.5 = 11.3 = 93.8$ kg

N = Normal force

$F_z = F_H$ = Cutting force

$N = F_z \cos \alpha - F_{zy} \sin \alpha$

$= 130 \cos 5 - 82.83 \sin 5$

$= 130 \times 0.9962 - 82.83 \times 0.0871$

$= 129.5 - 7.2 = 136.7$ kg.

(*c*) μ = Kinetic coefficient of friction

$$= \frac{F_{zy} \cos \alpha + F_z \sin \alpha}{F_z \cos \alpha - F_{xy} \sin \alpha}$$

$$= \frac{82.83 \cos 5 - 130 \sin 5}{130 \cos 5 - 82.83 \sin 5}$$

$$= \frac{82.30 \times 0.9962 - 130 \times 0.0871}{130 \times 0.9962 - 82.83 \times 0.0871}$$

$$= \frac{82.5 - 11.3}{129.5 - 7.2} = \frac{71.2}{122.3} = 0.58.$$

Example 2.17. *During machining C 25 steel with 0-10-6-7-8-90-1 mm ORS shaped triple carbide cutting tool, the following observations have been made*

Feed = 0.18 mm/rev.

Depth of cut = 2 mm.

Cutting speed = 150 m /min.

$F_z = 160$ *kg.*

$F_x = 80$ *kg.*

Chip thickness = 0.4 mm.

Determine :

(*i*) *Chip reduction coefficient.*

(*ii*) *Shear force and normal force at shear plane.*

(*iii*) *Kinetic coefficient of friction.*

(*iv*) *Specific energy of friction.*

Solution. (*a*) ϕ = Principal cutting edge angle = 90°

$\lambda = 0.$

It is a case of orthogonal system of second kind

α = Orthogonal rake angle = 10°

K = Chip reduction coefficient

$$= \frac{t_2}{f \cdot \sin\phi}$$

where t_2 = Chip thickness

= 0.4 mm.

f = Feed = 0.18 mm /rev.

$\sin \phi = \sin 90 = 1$

$$K = \frac{0.4}{0.18} = 2.22$$

(*b*) F_S = Shear force = $F_H \cos \beta = F_V \sin \beta$

where F_H = Cutting force = F_z

= 160 kg.

F_V = Feed force

$= F_{xy} = F_x = 80$ kg

β = shear angle

$$\tan \beta = \frac{r \cos \alpha}{1 - r \sin \alpha}$$

r = Chip thickness ratio $= \frac{t_1}{t_2}$

where t_1 = Chip thickness before cutting

= Feed = 0.18 mm

t_2 = Chip thickness after cutting

= 0.4 mm.

$$r = \frac{0.18}{0.4} = 0.45$$

$$\tan \beta = \frac{r \cos \alpha}{1 - r \sin \alpha}$$

$$= \frac{0.45 \cos 10}{1 - 0.45 \sin 10}$$

$$= \frac{0.45 \times 0.9848}{1 - 0.45 \times 1736} = 0.4782$$

$\beta = 25.5°$

$F_s = F_H \cos \beta - F_V \sin \beta$

$= 160 \cos 25.5 - 80 \sin 25.5 = 110$ kg.

F_z = Force normal to shear plane

$= F_V \cos\beta + F_H \sin\beta$

$= 80 \cos 25.5 + 160 \sin 25.5$

$= 140.8$ kg.

(*c*) μ = Kinetic coefficient of friction

$$= \frac{F_H \sin\alpha + F_v \cos\alpha}{F_H \cos\alpha - F_v \sin\alpha}$$

$$= \frac{160 \sin 10 + 80 \cos 10}{160 \cos 10 - 80 \sin 10}$$

$$= \frac{160 \times 0.1736 + 80 \times 0.9848}{160 \times 0.9848 - 80 \times 0.1736} = \frac{106.55}{143.66} = 0.74.$$

(*d*) Specific friction energy (E_f)

$$= \frac{P}{k \cdot b_1 t_1}$$

where b_1 = Width of chip

$$= \frac{d}{\sin\phi} = \frac{2}{1} = 2 \text{ mm.}$$

d being depth of cut.

P = Frictional force

$= F_{xy} \cos\alpha + F_z \sin\alpha$

$= 80 \cos 10 + 160 \sin 10$

$= 80 \times 0.9848 + 160 \times 0.1736$

$= 106.55$ kg.

$$E_f = \frac{106.55}{2.22 \times 2 \times 0.18} = 133.3 \text{ kg/mm}^2.$$

Example 2.18. *A medium steel workpiece is turned on a lathe from 34 mm diameter to 31 mm diameter when depth of cut is 1.5 mm and cutting speed is 50 metre per minute. The lathe has a 5 kW motor whose efficiency is 0.85. If a power of 0.07 kW per cubic centimeter per minute is required for stock removal, find the feed.*

Solution. V = Volume of metal removed

$= f \cdot t \cdot V_1$

where f = feedmm/rev.

t = Depth of cut,

$$= \frac{1.5}{10} \text{ cm.}$$

V_1 = cutting speed

= 50 metre per minute

= 50 × 100 cm per minute

$$V = \frac{f}{10} \times \frac{1.5}{10} \times 50 \times 100$$

$$V = 75 f \text{ cu} \cdot \text{cm /min.} \quad \text{...(1)}$$

Now P = Power of motor

= 5 kW

η = Efficiency of motor

= 0.85

S = Power required for removing one cubic centimeter of material per minute

= 0.07 kW

V = volume of metal removed

$$= \frac{P \times \eta}{S} = \frac{5 \times 0.85}{0.07}$$

$$V = 60.7 \text{ min} \quad \text{...(2)}$$

From (1) and (2)

$$75f = 60.7$$

$$f = 0.81 \text{ mm /rev.}$$ **Ans.**

Example 2.19. *A 90 mm diameter mild steel bar is being turned on a multi tool lathe having six tools at 2 rev. /S. If the depth of cut is 4 mm and feed is 0.3 mm/rev. for all tools determine :*

(*a*) *cutting speed*

(*b*) *total power required.*

Given specific cutting pressure is 1600 N /mm².

Solution. D = Bar diameter = 90 mm

d = Depth of cut

= 4 mm

f = Feed

= 0.3 mm / rev.

N = R.P.S. = 2

$$V = \pi DN = \frac{\pi \times 90 \times 2}{1000}$$
$$= 0.56 \text{ m/s}$$
$$p = \text{Specific cutting pressure}$$
$$= 1600 \text{ N/mm}^2$$
$$= 1.6 \text{ kN/mm}^2$$
$$Z = \text{Number of tools} = 6$$
$$\text{Total power} = Z \times p \times d \times f \times V$$
$$= 6 \times 1.6 \times 4 \times 0.3 \times 0.56 = 6.45 \text{ kW.}$$

Example 2.20. (*a*) *A carbide cutting tool lasted for 100 minutes while machining mild steel work material at a cutting speed of 40 m/min. Determine the tool life if the tool is used for machining mild steel at a 20% higher speed.*

(*b*) *Also calculate the value of cutting speed of the tool is required to machine for 160 minutes without failing. Assume n = 0.26.*

Solution. (*a*) $V_1 = \text{Cutting speed} = 40 \text{ mpm}$

$$T_1 = \text{Tool life} = 100 \text{ minutes}$$
$$V_2 = \text{Cutting speed}$$
$$= 1.2 \times V_1 = 1.2 \times 40 = 48 \text{ mpm.}$$
$$T_2 = \text{Tool life}$$
$$n = 0.26$$
$$V_1 T_1^n = V_2 T_2^n$$
$$40 \times 100^{0.26} = 48 \times T_2^{0.26}$$
$$T_2 = 48.6 \text{ minutes}$$
$$T_3 = \text{Tool life} = 160 \text{ minutes}$$

Now $V_1 T_1^n = V_3 T_3^n$

$$40 \times 100^{0.26} = V_3 \times 160^{0.27}$$
$$V_3 = 33.6 \text{ mpm.}$$

Example 2.21. *In an orthogonal cutting operation on a copper workpiece following data has been obtained.*

Back rake angle = 20°

Chip thickness before cutting = 0.12 *mm.*

Width of chip before cutting = 3.75 *mm.*

Width of chip after cutting = 4.1 *mm.*

Chip length before cutting = 130 *mm.*

Chip length after cutting = 50 *mm.*

Shear stress of work material = 20*kg /mm*^{2}

Coefficient of friction = 0.55

Cutting speed = 30 *mpm.*

Determine the forces and power consumption.

Solution. α = Back rake angle = 20°

$t_1 = 0.12$ = Chip thickness before cutting

t_2 = Chip thickness after cutting

Chip width, $b_1 = 3.75$ mm

$b_2 = 4.1$ mm

Chip Length $(L_1) = 130$ mm

Chip Length $(L_2) = 50$ mm

Now according to volume continuity equation

$$L_1 \cdot b_1 \cdot t_1 = L_2 \cdot b_2 \cdot t_2$$

$$130 \times 3.75 \times t_1 = 50 \times 4.1 \times t_2$$

$$\frac{t_1}{t_2} = 0.42 = r$$

where r =Chip thickness ratio

Now let, β = Shear angle

$$Tan\ \beta = \frac{r \cos \alpha}{1 - r \sin \alpha}$$

$$= \frac{0.42 \times \cos 20}{1 - 0.42 \sin 20}$$

$$\beta = 24°$$

γ = Friction angle of tool face

$$Tan\ \gamma = \mu$$

where μ = coefficient of friction

$$= 0.55$$

$$\gamma = 29\ degrees$$

F_S = Shear force

$$= f_s \times \frac{b_1 t_1}{\sin \beta}$$

where f_S = Shear stress

$$= 20 \text{ kg/ mm}^2$$

(τ is also used as symbol for shear stress)

$$F_s = \frac{20 \times 3.75 \times 0.12}{\sin 24}$$
$$= 22.5 \text{ kg.}$$
$$F_H = \text{Cutting force} = \frac{F_S \times \cos(\gamma - \alpha)}{\cos \theta}$$

where
$$\theta = \beta + \gamma - \alpha$$
$$= 24 + 29 - 20 = 33 \text{ degrees}$$
$$F_H = \frac{22.5 \cos(29 - 20)}{\cos 33} = 26.5 \text{ kg.}$$
$$F_V = \text{Feed force}$$

From Merchant circle diagram
$$\frac{F_V}{F_H} = Tan\,(\gamma - \alpha)$$
$$F_V = F_H \tan(r - \alpha)$$
$$= 26.5 \tan(29 - 20)$$
$$= 4.1 \text{ kg.}$$
$$v = \text{Cutting speed} = 30 \text{ mpm.}$$
$$\text{Power Consumption} = \frac{F_H \times V}{4500} = \frac{26.5 \times 30}{4500} = 0.18 \text{ H.P.}$$

Example 2.22. *During turning a steel rod 80 cm long and 10 cm in dia. on a lathe, with a depth of cut of 5 mm. and the feed of 0.4 mm., the tool life yielded the following equation :*

$$VT^{1.3} = 60$$

The following costs relate to the above operation :

Machine labour cost = Rs. 4 / hr.

Machine burden rate = Rs. 30% of labour

Grinding labour cost = Rs. 5 / hr

Grinding burden rate = 350% of labour

Loading time = 5 min. / part.

Two types of carbide tools were used i.e. Brazed insert and throw away inserts.

For Brazed inserts :

Original cost of tool	*Rs. 25*
Grinding time	*6 minutes*
Tool changing time	*2 minutes*

(One cutting edge/grind, 5 grinds available per tool before rejection plus original cutting edge).

For throw away inserts (Square)

Original cost *Rs. 20*

Tool changing time *0.5 minutes*

Determine which tool is economical ?

Solution.

For Brazed Inserts

$$C_1 = \text{Machine labour cost + Burden cost /min.}$$

$$= \frac{4 + 3 \times 4}{60} = \text{Re.}0.266$$

$$C_2 = \text{Original cost /edge} + \frac{\text{Time}}{\text{grind}}\left(\frac{\text{Labour}}{\text{grind}} + \frac{\text{Burden}}{\text{grind}}\right)$$

$$= \frac{25}{6} + \frac{6\,(4 + 4 \times 3.5)}{60} = \text{Rs.}5.96$$

where Total cutting edges = 5 + 1 = 6

T_m = Tool life for minimum cost.

It is given by the following relation.

$$T_m = \left(\frac{1}{n} - 1\right)\left(\frac{C_1 T + C_2}{C_1}\right)$$

where T = Tool changing time (minutes)

and $n = 0.3$

$$= \left(\frac{1}{0.3} - 1\right) \times \left(\frac{0.266 \times 2 + 4.3}{0.266}\right)$$

$$= 42.38 \text{ minutes}$$

Cutting speed,

$$V = \frac{C}{T_m^n} = \frac{60}{(42.38)\ 0.3} = \text{mpm}$$

$$N = \frac{19.6 \times 100}{\pi \times 10} = 62.4 \text{ rpm.}$$

Therefore

$$S_1 = \text{Loading cost/piece} = \text{loading time} \times C_1$$

$$= 5 \times 0.266 = \text{Rs. } 1.33$$

$$S_2 = \text{Cutting cost/piece} = C_1 \times \frac{\text{length of cut}}{\text{feed} \times \text{rpm}}$$

$$= \frac{0.266 \times 90}{0.04 \times 62.4} = \text{Rs.}9.6$$

S_3 = Tool ginding cost / piece

$= C_1 \times$ tool failure per piece $\times$ Tool changing time

$$= \frac{0.266 \times 90 \times 2}{0.04 \times 62.4 \times 42.38} = \text{Rs.}0.45$$

S_4 = Tool grinding cost/piece = $C_2 \times$ Tool failure/piece.

$$= \frac{5.96 \times 90}{0.04 \times 62.4 \times 42.38} = \text{Rs. } 5.07$$

S = Total cost per piece

$= S_1 + S_2 + S_3 + S_4 = 1.33 + 9.6 + 0.45 + 5.07$

= Rs. 16.45

For Throw Away Inserts

Loading Time / piece = 5 min.

Tool changing time = 0.5 min.

C'_2 Original cost/edge $= \frac{20}{6} = 3.33$

$$T_m = \left(\frac{1}{0.3} - 1\right)\left[\frac{0.5 \times 0.266 + 3.33}{0.266}\right]$$

= 30.4 min.

Now $VT_m^n = C$

$$V = \frac{60}{(30.4)\ 0.3} = 21.6 \text{ M/min.}$$

$$N = \frac{V}{\pi D} = \frac{21.6 \times 100}{3.14 \times 10} = 68.8 \text{ RPM.}$$

R_1 = Loading cost/piece = Loading time $\times C_1$

$= 5 \times 0.266 =$ Rs. 1.3

R_2 = Cutting cost/piece

$$= \frac{0.266 \times 90}{0.04 \times 68.8} = \text{Rs. } 8.7$$

R_3 = Tool changing cost/piece

$$= \frac{0.266 \times 0.5 \times 90}{0.04 \times 68.8 \times 30.4} = \text{Re. } 0.14$$

R_4 = Tool cost/piece

$$= \frac{3.33 \times 90}{0.04 \times 68.8 \times 30.4} = \text{Rs. } 3.58$$

R = Total cost/piece $= R_1 + R_2 + R_3 + R_4$

$= 1.3 + 8.7 + 0.14 + 3.58 =$ Rs. 13.72

As total cost per piece for throw away inserts is less than the total cost for brazed inserts therefore it is economical to use throw away inserts.

Example 2.23. *Calculate the time required to turn a workpiece 140 mm long from diameter 50 mm to 44 mm. The machine is running at 300 RPM and feed is 0.3 mm/rev. Maximum depth of cut is 1.8 mm.*

Solution.

d = Depth of cut = 1.8 mm.

S = Total depth of cut $= \frac{50-44}{2}$

$= \frac{6}{2} = 3$ mm.

n = Number of cuts

$= \frac{S}{d} = \frac{3}{1.8} = 1.7 = 2$ (say)

L = Length of work piece = 140 mm.

f = Feed = 0.3 mm/rev.

N = RPM = 300

T = Machining time $= \frac{L.n}{fN} = \frac{140 \times 2}{0.3 \times 300}$

= 3.1 minutes.

PROBLEMS

2.1. Describe how to calculate the resultant force acting on a single point tool in turning.

2.2. Explain the relationship between various forces in orthogonal cutting.

2.3. Sketch Merchant's circle diagram and explain the different quantities involved.

2.4. (*a*) What are the three velocities of interest in the cutting process.

(*b*) Explain the relationship between cutting velocity and chip-flow velocity and between shear velocity and cutting velocity.

2.5. Write short note on the following :

(*a*) Shear stress in shear plane.

(*b*) Shear strain.

(c) Power required in metal cutting.
(d) Specific horse power.
(e) Machine tool efficiency.
(f) Metal removal rate.
(g) Lee and Shaffer's theory.

2.6. Prove that according to Ernst.

Merchant theory the relation between rake angle (α,) shear angle (β) and friction angle γ is given by

$$\beta = \frac{\pi}{4} - \frac{\gamma}{2} + \frac{\alpha}{2.}$$

2.7. In orthogonal cutting of a mild steel component if the rake angle of tool is 10° and the shear angle is 30°. Calculate the chip thickness ratio.

2.8. (a) In orthogonal cutting of stainless steel depth of cut is 3.125 mm and rake angle of tool is 10° which results in a chip thickness of 4 mm determine the following :

(i) Cutting Ratio.
(ii) Shear Angle.

(b) If Shear Strength = 800 kg /cm²
Width of cut = 12 mm
Cutting speed = 10 m /min.
Coefficient of friction = 0.11.

Determine the following :

(i) Shearing force.
(ii) Friction angle.
(iii) Cutting force.
(iv) Horse power.

2.9. Determine the cutting speed and machining time per cut when the work having 35 mm diameter is rotated at 200 R.P.M. The feed given is 0.2 mm/revolution and length of cut is 60 mm.

[**Ans.** 2.2 m/minute, 1.5 minute]

2.10. Determine the cutting speed (V) and feed (f) to be used for turning a mild steel component with a H.S.S. cutting tool under the following conditions :

Cutting force (F_H) = 280 kg.
Tool life (T) = 270 minutes
Depth of cut (t) = 2.1 mm.

Use the following relationships

$$F_H = 200 f^{3/4}\, t$$

$$V_T^{0.125} \times f^{0.37} \times t^{0.78} = 37$$

Also determine the R.P.M. of the component if the diameter of the component is 30 mm.

2.11. What is the difference between orthogonal system of first kind and second kind.

2.12. Prove that kinetic coefficient of friction (μ) is given by

$$\mu = \frac{F_H \sin \alpha + F_V \cos \alpha}{F_H \cos \alpha - F_V \sin \alpha}$$

where F_H is cutting force and F_V is feed force.

2.13. Prove that dynamic shear strain (*e*) is given by

$$e = \frac{k^2 - 2k \sin \alpha + 1}{k \cdot \cos \alpha}$$

where k is chip reduction coefficient and α is orthogonal rake angle.

2.14. (*a*) Show the merchant's circle diagram of forces and its utility.

(*b*) During machining of C-20 steel with a carbide tool having a shape of 0--(--5)--6--9--8--75--1 mm (ISO) the following force have been measured by a two dimensional electro-mechanical dynamometer :

$P_s = 140$ kg, $P_x = 15$ kg.

Calculate :

(*i*) The radial force, P_y

(*ii*) The friction force, F

(*iii*) The normal force, N

(*iv*) The kinetic co-efficient, μ.

2.15. A soft steel component is to be turned on a lathe from 40 mm diameter to 37 mm diameter when depth of cut is 1.5 mm and cutting speed is 40 m/min. If lathe has a motor of 4 kW whose efficiency is 0.8 find the feed assuming that a power of 0.05 kW is required for removing one cu. cm. of material per minute.

2.16. Write short notes the following :

(*i*) Measurement of cutting forces.

(*ii*) Measurement of tool-chip interface temperature.

2.17. A mild steel bar of 10 cm. diameter is turned with a cutting speed of 4 mpm and feed of 0.28 mm/revolution and depth of cut 3.8 mm. Machine consumes 0.5 kW power when running idle and 2.5 kW when cutting. If shear angle is 20 degrees, determine the following :

(*a*) Shear force

(*b*) Tangential force on tool

(*c*) Force on chip.

3

Machinability

3.1. Machinability

Chips may be cut from some materials with relative case and from others with the greater difficulty. This difference may be attributed to the machinability of the respective materials. Machinability is defined as the ease with which the metal is cut satisfactorily for the purpose intended. In general good machinability is associated with the removal of material with moderate forces, the formation of rather small chips, not excessive tool abrasion and good surface finish. It is commonly observed that high hardness gives poor Machinability because of high temperature power consumption and high tool wear.

Machinability depends upon the following factors :

(*i*) Chemical composition of workpiece material.

(*ii*) Micro-structure of workpiece material.

(*iii*) Physical properties such as tensile strength, ductility and hardness of workpiece material.

(*iv*) Rigidity of tool and work holding devices.

(*v*) Cutting conditions such as cutting speed, feed, etc.

The machinability of plain carbon steels falls steadily as its carbon content rises. Steels up to 300 H.B. hardness do not present great machining difficulty unless large amounts of alloying materials are present .

Fine grained materials take a good surface finish but have an increased resistance to machining. In general good machinability is associated with the removal of material with moderate forces, the formation of rather small chips, not excessive tool abrasion and good surface finish.

It is easier to machine fine grained steel than coarse grained steel and that the addition of small amount of certain elements for example up to 0.1% S or up to 0.2% Pb) can improve the machinability of steel without appreciable changing mechanical properties. Heat resisting steels and super alloys have very poor machinability. Free cutting steels, non ferrous and light alloys can be easily machined at high cutting speeds. A dull cutting tool operating at too small a feed may fail to cut a chip and will work harden the surfaces of the material some of the plastics are much softer than most metals but are more difficult to machine because the abrasive nature of the material results in excessive tool wear. In evaluating the machinability the following criteria may be considered.

(*i*) Rate of metal removal per tool grind.

(*ii*) Tool life between grinds.

(*iii*) Magnitude of cutting forces.

(*iv*) Quality of surface finish.

(*v*) Shape and size of chips.

(*vi*) Temperature during cutting.

(*vii*) Power consumed during machining.

In case of a metal having high machinability.

(*a*) Good surface finish can be produced.

(*b*) Higher cutting speed can be used.

(*c*) Metal removal rate is high.

(*d*) Cutting tool wear is less.

(*e*) There is low power consumption.

3.2. Machinability Index

It is used to compare the machinability of different metals. The rated machinability of two or more metals may vary for different processes of cutting such as heavy turning, light turning, forming, milling etc.

I = Machinability index

V_i = Cutting speed of metal investigated for 20 minutes tool life.

V_s = Cutting speed of a standard steel for 20 minutes tool life.

$$I(\%) = \frac{V_i}{v_s}$$

Free cutting steel having carbon 0.13 (maximum) manganese 0.06 to 1.1 and sulphur 0.08 to 0.03 per cent is taken as standard steel. Its machining index is relatively fixed at 100 per cent, machinability index for some of the materials is shown in Table 3.1.

Table 3.1

Material	*Machinability Index (%)*
Low carbon steel	55-60
Stainless steel	25
Red Brass (Cu = 77 to 80%)	180
Aluminium alloy	390-1500
Magnesium alloy	500-2000

Table 3.1(*a*)

Kind of Steel	*Designation*	*Machinability rating*
Free Cutting Steel	14 Mn 1s14	200
	St 32	160
St. Steels	St 50	125
	St 58	100
	C 14	160
	C 35	125
	C 40	125
Carbon Steels	C 45	100
	C 55	80
	C 85	50
Mn Steel	27 Mn 2	63
Mn-Cr Steel	105 Cr 1 Mn 60	63
Cr-V Steel	50 Cr 1 V 23	50
NI-Cr Steel.	13 NI 9 Cr 80	63

High alloy Cr Steel	07 Cr 13	100
High alloy Cr NI Steel	04 Cr 19 Ni9 Ti	20-40

Table 3.1 (a) indicates machinability rating of some of steels

3.2.1. Effect of Micro Structure on Machining. The high degree of homogeneity decreases the machinability giving tearing, poor finish and build up. Hence the difficulty of machining pure metals such as iron (ferrite) and copper and full solid solutions. Hetrogenous alloy whose components are segregated into bands or excessively large grains is also bad and so arises the bad machinability of wrought steel in which ferrite banding has occured. Hard and soft components uniformly dispersed tend to give good cutting properties. A uniformly heterogeneous structure gives best machining.

3.3. Basic Objectives of Economical Machining

The basic objectives of an efficient and economical machining are as follows :

(*i*) Quick metal removal

(*ii*) Low tool cost

(*iii*) Good surface finish

(*iv*) Minimum idle time of machine tools

(*v*) Less power consumption.

In any machining operation the most important characteristics requiring due considerations are as follows :

(*i*) The life of a tool-workpiece combination

(*ii*) The surface finish produced

(*iii*) The type of chip produced

(*iv*) The power consumed in the formation of chips.

The relative importance of each characteristic depends upon the application.

3.4. Tool Failure

Cutting tools usually reach the end of their useful life either by breaking or by wearing. Breaking is usually caused by overloading or neglect. Tool wear refers to abrasion on the flank below the cutting edge and abrasion of tool face just back of cutting edge.

During cutting the tool should perform satisfactorily. Unsatisfactory performance of the cutting tool indicates tool failure. Tool failure may occur because of failure of the geometry of cutting tool or it results from tool wear. The following drawbacks are observed when the tool failure takes place.

(*i*) The tool ceases to produce the workpiece according to the required dimensions.

(*ii*) The tool gets over heated.

(*iii*) Excessive surface roughness is observed.

(*iv*) Tool failure leads to increased cutting forces and therefore power requirement will be more.

(*v*) Some times a burnishing band will appear on the workpiece if the tool is failing.

It is a judgement decision as to how long a tool should be permitted to operate after preliminary indications, that the tool is beginning to fail. The tool engineer must weigh the factors of the economics of stopping production and regrinding the tool versus allowing it to continue to operate.

Premature failure of cutting tools by mechanical breakage and plastic deformation can be successfully overcome by providing adequate strength toughness and hot hardness in tool materials and by controlling tool geometry. Hardness is essential so that the cutting edge can penetrate into workpiece material. Poor toughness causes breaking of the cutting edge. Heat resistance enables the cutting edge to maintain its hardness when it gets heated due to friction in chip removal.

The failure of tool may be classified in three general ways as follows :

(*i*) Temperature failure

(*ii*) Rupture of tool point

(*iii*) Gradual wear at the tool point.

3.4.1. Temperature failure. Heat produced during metal cutting is mainly responsible for tool failure. When the temperature during cutting becomes very high the tool becomes too soft to function properly and failure ensures. This type of failure occurs quite rapidly, is the frequently accompanied by sparkling and is easily recognised.

The various tool materials can withstand. Various heating temperature (critical temperatures) before they lose the required hardness.

Carbon tool steel	200 to 250°C
High speed steel	560 to 600°C
Cemented carbides	800 to 1000°C

3.4.2. Rupture of Tool point. Because of high hardness required the tip of a cutting tool is mechanically weak and brittle. This type of tool failure is commonly observed in carbide and diamond tipped tools. This failure takes place when the cutting forces exceed the critical value for a given tool when small portions of the cutting edge begin to chip off or the entire tip may break away in one piece. For a given tool material the tendency towards a rupture failure can be diminished either by reducing the causal forces, redirecting them or redesigning the tool to withstand them. Fig. 3.1 show how a redesign of tool from (*a*) to (*b*) redirects the resultant forces *P* so that the tendency for rupture is removed. The forces can also be reduced by increasing the rigidity of tool and workholder.

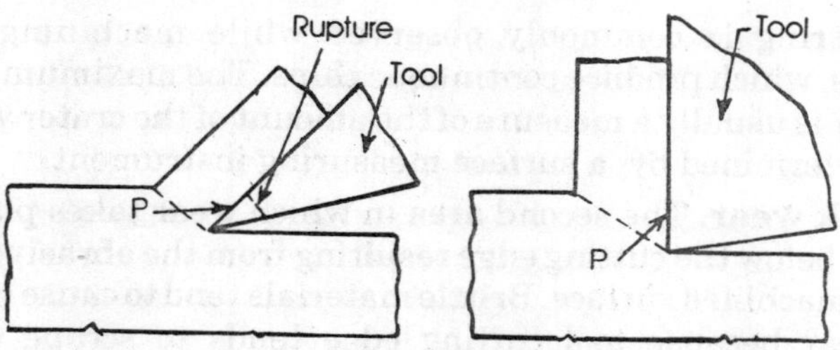

(*a*) (*b*)

Fig. 3.1.

3.4.3. Gradual wear at the tool point. When a tool has been in use for some time, wear becomes evident. In metal cutting main causes of wear are as follows :

(*i*) Adhesion wear

(*ii*) Abrasion wear

(*iii*) Diffusion wear.

Adhesion wear. In metal cutting junctions between the chip and tool materials are formed as part of friction mechanism. When these junctions are fractured small fragment of tool material can be torn out and carried away on the underside of the chip or on the new workpiece surface.

Abrasion wear. This type of wear takes place when hard particles on the under side of the chip pass over the tool face and remove total material by mechanical action.

Diffusion wear. This type of wear takes place due to diffusion process where atoms in a metallic crystal lattice move from a region of high atomic concentration to one of low concentration. During cutting when temperature is quite high at interface of tool and workpiece the atoms move from tool material to work piece material and thus weaken the surface structure of the tool.

3.5.1. Types of wear

The most prevalent type of wear are as follows :

(*i*) Crater wear (*ii*) Flank wear

Crater wear. The major tendency for wear is due to the abrasion between the chip and the face of the tool, a short distance from the cutting edge. This result in a crater being formed in the tool face. The crater is formed on the surface of the tool by the action of chip particles flowing over it because of very high temperature. When cratering becomes excessive the cutting edge may break from the tool.

Cratering is commonly observed while machining ductile materials, which produce continuous chips. The maximum depth of the crater is usually a measure of the amount of the crater wear and can be determined by a surface measuring instrument.

Flank wear. The second area in which wear takes place is on the flank below the cutting edge resulting from the abrasive contact with the machined surface. Brittle materials tend to cause excessive flank wear because tool cutting edge tends to scrape over the machined surface and due to low abrasive action of loose fractured chips on the tool face while the flank is in constant contact with the work.

The worn region at the flank is called wear land. The increased wear land means that frictional heat will cause excessive temperature of the tool at the cutting point and therefore the tool will rapidly loose its hardness and tool failure will take place. Flank wear result

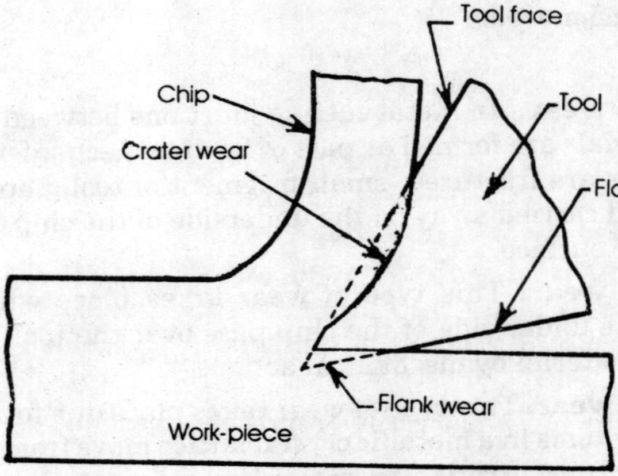

Fig. 3.2.

in a rough machined surface. Fig. 3.2 shows regions of tool wear in metal cutting.

In machining tough (ductile) metals tool wear will proceed in a more complex manner. Flank wear predominates at low cutting speeds when there is no built up edge because of sliding speed being higher on the flank than that of the chip on the tool face.

Whereas in case of heavy chip when pressure on the face is higher a wear crater is formed. Both flank and crater wear take place when feed is more than 0.15 mm/rev. at low and moderate speeds. The dependence of wear on the time of tool operation is expressed by the wear and time curve (Fig. 3.3) that can be divided into three sections.

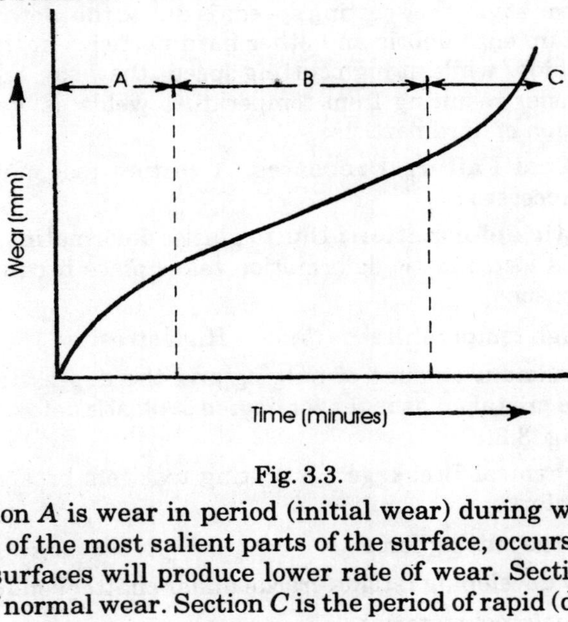

Fig. 3.3.

Section *A* is wear in period (initial wear) during which heavy abrasion of the most salient parts of the surface, occurs. Smoother friction surfaces will produce lower rate of wear. Section *B* is the period of normal wear. Section *C* is the period of rapid (destructive) wear.

Period of rapid wear is not observed with carbide tipped tool because of the high hardness of cemented carbides and very slight reduction in hardness at high temperatures.

The use of cutting fluids, reduces tool wear (especially face wear) because it eases chip formation, reduces friction force on sliding surface and lowers the temperature to which the tool is heated.

The cutting tool wear is thus represented as follows :

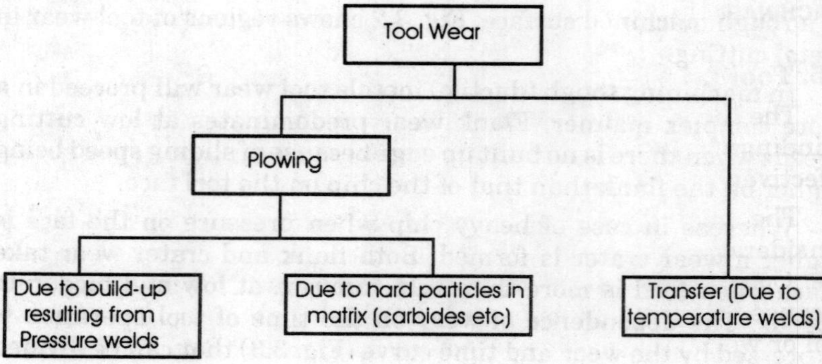

Tool wear at very low cutting speeds is due to the plowing action of the built up edge debris and other hard particles in the matrix such as carbides while at high cutting speeds the wear takes place due to transfer resulting from temperature welds as well as the plowing action of hard particles.

3.5.2. Tool Failure Processes. A cutting tool may fail by following processes :

(*i*) **Plastic deformation :** Due to plastic deformation the form of the tool is lost. Plastic deformation takes place because of the following reasons

(*a*) High temperature (*b*) High stresses

The maximum amount of bulging and the depression of the cutting edge are taken as index for degree of plastic deformation as shown in Fig. 3.3(*a*).

(*ii*) Mechanical Breakage : A cutting tool gets broken due to following factors :

(*a*) Large cutting force

(*b*) By developing fatigue cracks under chatter conditions.

(*c*) Weak tool material.

(*iii*) **Gradual Wear :** It is the result of interaction between the work and the tool material.

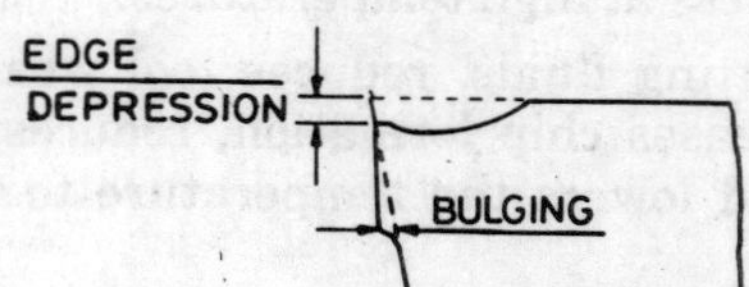

Fig. 3.3(*a*)

3.5. Tool Life

The life is defined as the time elapsed between two successive grindings of the tool. During this period the tool cuts efficiently and effectively.

The cutting tool life is one of the most important economic considerations in metal cutting. The cutting tool should have longer life. Conditions giving a very short tool life will be uneconomical because tool grinding and tool replacement costs will be high. Any tool or work material improvements that increase tool life will be beneficial.

There are number of ways of expressing tool life such as :

(*i*) Volume of metal removed.

(*ii*) Number of work pieces machined.

(*iii*) Time unit.

It is most commonly expressed in minutes. The life of cutting tool is affected by the various factors mentioned below :

1. Machining variables.

   (*i*) Cutting speed.

   (*ii*) Feed.

   (*iii*) Depth of cut.

2. Type of cutting such as continuous and intermittent cutting.

3. Tool geometry.

4. Tool material.

5. Machining conditions.

   (*i*) Temperature of the work and tool.

   (*ii*) Type of cutting fluid used.

6. Properties of material being cut.

   (*i*) Microstructure of workpiece materials.

   (*ii*) Tensile strength and hardness of the material.

   (*iii*) Degree to which the material cold works.

In order that a cutting tool should have long life it is essential that the face of the tool should be as smooth as possible. A blunt tool should not be used as it causes of the following defects.

(*i*) It produces poor surface finish

(*ii*) It produces vibrations during machining

(*iii*) It increases the cutting forces and therefore power consumption is increased.

(*iv*) Tool gets over heated.

Tool life is said to be over when any one or more of following appear.

(*i*) Spoiled cucting edge.

(*ii*) Presence of chatter marks on the workpiece.

(*iii*) Sudden increase in power.

(*iv*) Over heating due to friction.

(*v*) Poor surface finish.

(*vi*) Dimensional unstability.

Expected tool life is as follows :

(*i*) Cast tool steel = 124 minutes.

(*ii*) High speed steel tool = 60 to 120 minutes.

(*iii*) Cemented carbides tool = 420 to 480 minutes.

3.6. Relationship between the Cutting Speed and Tool life

There is a definite relationship between the cutting speed and tool life. The higher the cutting speed the shorter is the tool life.

The relation betwee cutting speed and tool life is given by Taylor formula as follows :

$$VT^n = C$$

where V = cutting speed in metre/min.

T = Tool life in minutes

n = an index closely related to the cutting tool material.

= 0.1 to 0.5 for high speed steel tools.

= 0.2 to 0.4 for tungsten carbide tool.

= 0.4 to 0.6 for ceramic tools.

C = Constant. It is numerically equal to cutting speed that gives a tool life of one minute.

The higher the cutting speed permitted by a tool for the same life, the better its cutting properties and the more productive it will be.

Depending upon the circumstances there is a best economic tool life for every tool. If the cutting duty is made such as to allow the tool to last longer than the best economic time then it is cutting at an efficient rate. On the other hand if its performance is raised to a level such as to cause it to become blunted in less than economic time when undue expense and loss in time are being incurred in the additional sharpening and re-setting necessary.

In tool life testing tools are operated to failure at different cutting speeds and the test results are plotted. In general a parabolic decrease in tool life with increased cutting speeds is obtained (Fig. 3.4).

Such a relationship plots as a straight line on a log-log graph as shown in Fig. 3.5.

Cutting tool life and efficiency can be improved by giving a surface finish of high quality to the cutting edge of the tool.

This is due to the reason that friction between tool and chip is minimised. Roughness of the tool's cutting edge could result in a concentration of stresses which may cause surface cracks and eventual chipping of tool.

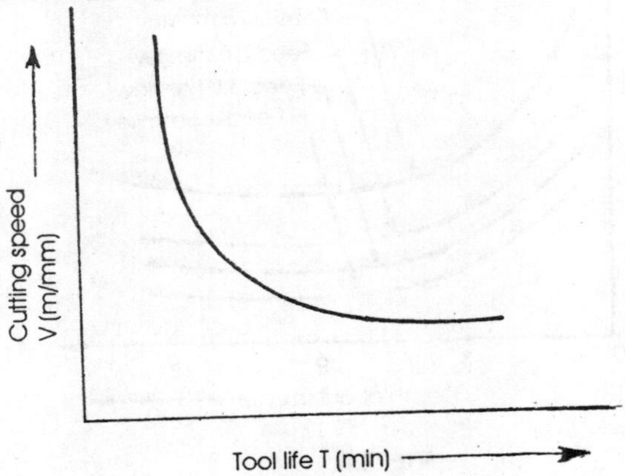

Fig. 3.4.

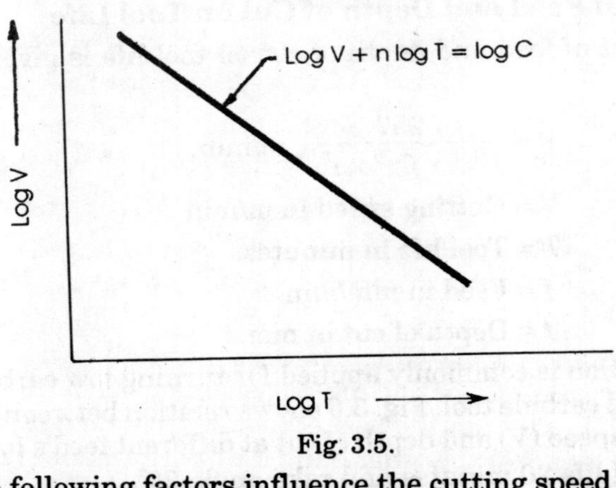

Fig. 3.5.

The following factors influence the cutting speed permitted by a tool.

(*i*) Tool life.

(*ii*) Physico-mechanical properties of metal being machined.

(*iii*) Material of the cutting element of the tool.

(*iv*) Rate of feed and depth of cut.

(*v*) Tool geometry.

(*vi*) Size of the tool shank.

(*vii*) Cutting fluid used.

(*viii*) Maximum permissible amount of wear.

(*ix*) Type of machining process.

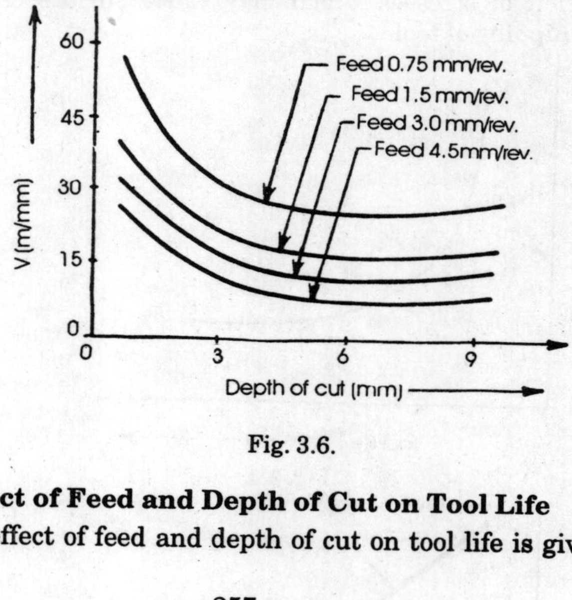

Fig. 3.6.

3.7. Effect of Feed and Depth of Cut on Tool Life

The effect of feed and depth of cut on tool life is given by the formula.

$$V = \frac{257}{T^{0.19} \times f^{0.36} \times t^{0.08}} \text{ m/min.}$$

where V = Cutting speed in m/min.

T = Tool life in minutes.

f = Feed in mm/min.

t = Depth of cut in mm.

This relation is commonly applied for turning low carbon steel by a cemented carbide tool. Fig. 3.6 shows relation between permissible cutting speed (V) and depth of cut at different feed's for H.S.S. tool with tool life 20 minutes and rake angle 20°.

Tool life decreases with increase in feed and depth of cut.

Expected tool life for tools made up of different materials is as follows :

(*i*) Cemented carbides = 240 to 480 minutes.

(*ii*) High speed steel = 60 to 120 minutes.

(*iii*) Cast tool steel = 20 minutes.

Tool life excludes the following points :

(*a*) Removing.

(*b*) Regrinding.

(*c*) Resetting.

The time for the above three operations should be minimum to increase the productive time.

3.7. (*a*) Tool Life in Terms of Metal Removed

During tool wear studies it is convenient to express tool life in terms of metal removed.

For example in case of turning

Let, D = Diameter of workpiece (mm)

N = R.P.M. of workpiece

$V = \text{Surface speed} = \dfrac{\pi DN}{1000}$ m/min.

d = Depth of cut (mm)

f = feed (mm/rev.)

T = Time to tool failure (minutes)

L = Tool life in terms of metal removal unit

Volume removed per revolution

$$= \pi D \cdot df \cdot \text{mm}^3$$

Volume of metal removed per minute

$$= \pi D \cdot df \cdot N \text{ mm}^3/\text{min.}$$

Volume removed in T minutes

$$= \pi D \cdot df \cdot N \cdot T \cdot \text{ mm}^3$$

Thus the volume of metal removed between tool regrinds

$$= \pi D \cdot df \cdot N \cdot T \cdot \text{mm}^3$$

$$\text{or } L = \pi D \cdot df \cdot N \cdot T \cdot \text{mm}^3 = 1000 \cdot V \cdot d \cdot f \cdot T \cdot \text{mm}^3$$

$$= V \cdot d \cdot f \cdot T \cdot \text{cm}^3$$

3.8. Effect of Type of Cutting

Tool life is more in case of continuous cutting as compared to intermittent cutting in which regular impacts on the tool lead to failure much earlier.

3.9. Effect of Tool Material

An ideal tool material is one which removes maximum volume of meterial at all cutting speeds.

For a given cutting speed work material removed by different tool materials in increasing order, is as follows :

(*a*) Cemented oxide,

(*b*) Cemented carbide

(*c*) H.S.S.

3.10. Effect of Tool Geometry on Tool Life

The larger the cutting angle the greater the deformation, heat generation and forces acting on the tool, the more intensive tool wear and shorter the tool life. When cutting angle is reduced (positive rake angle is increased), the cutting forces, deformation and heat generation are reduced and tool life is increased. The more the relief angle of the tool, the less the friction of the tool on the work, the less the tool wear and longer tool life larger values of end cutting edge angle give more life to tool. Similarly a higher values of side cutting edge angle gives longer life to tool. Increase in nose radius improves tool life as the smaller nose radius results in excess stress concentration and greater heat generation. The relationship between cutting speed, tool life (*T*) and nose radius *(r)* is given by $VT^{0.0927} = 331r^{0.244}$ where (*V*) is the cutting speed in feet per minute, (*T*) is the tool life in minutes and *r* is the nose radius in inch.

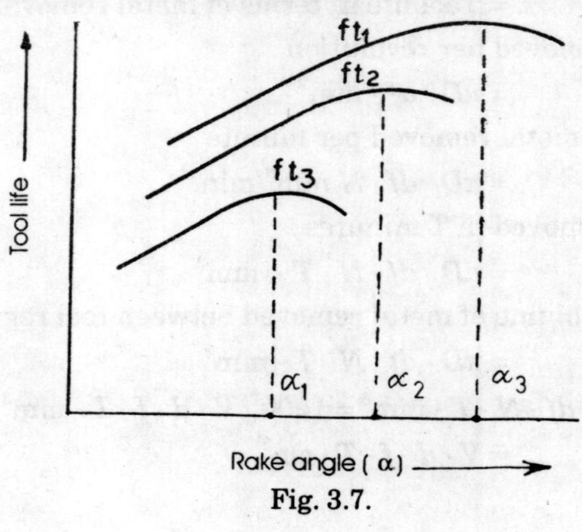

Fig. 3.7.

Fig. 3.7 shows the tool life relationship with positive rake angle.

The optimum value of rake angle (α) is more for smaller values of tensile stress (*ft*), of work material. The tensile stress $ft_3 > ft_2 > ft_1$. The optimum rake angle $\alpha_3 > \alpha_2 > \alpha_1$. The typical relationship between tool life and relief angle is shown in Fig. 3.8.

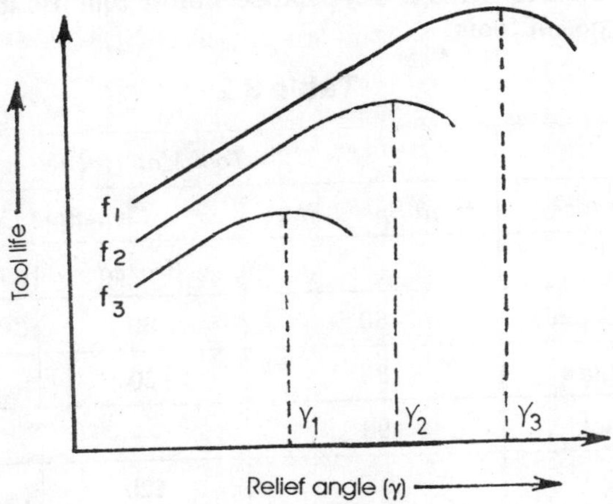

Fig. 3.8.

The greater the relief angle of the tool the less the friction of tool on the work, less tool wear and tool will have longer life. The optimum relief angle for work material at different feed (*f*) is different. Feed $f_3 > f_2 > f_1$ and relief and $\gamma_3 > \gamma_2 > \gamma_1$ angle.

3.11. Effect of Work-piece Material

The microstructure of the work-piece material affects tool life. Hard constituents in the structure result in poor tool life. On the basis of tool life the micro constituents have been placed in the order —Pearlite, Sorbite, Troostite, Bainite and Martansite.

3.12. Effect of Cutting Fluid

Heat produced during metal cutting is carried away from the tool and work by means of cutting fluids. This reduces the coefficient of friction and the cutting temperature. This will help the tool to maintain its hardness and therefore the tool life will be increased.

Cutting fluid which directly controls the amount of heat at the chip tool interface plays an important role in increasing tool life. Schallbroach, Schaumann, and Wallich gave the following formula between tool life and temperature of cutting tool.

$$T\theta^n = C \qquad \text{where} \qquad T = \text{Tool life (minutes)}$$

θ = Temperature at chip tool interface (°C)

n = An exponent. Its value depends on material and shape of cutting tool

C = Constant

Table 3.2 indicates the typical economic tool life in minutes for various types of tools.

Table 3.2

Type of tool	Tool Material		
	High Speed Steel	*Cemented Carbide*	
		Brazed	*Mechinical*
Single point tools	60	30	15
Drills, reamers	30	20	—
Taps and dies	90	—	—
Form tools	120	120	—
Milling cutters	$60 \times K$	$30 \times K$	$15 \times K$

Where factor K for slab, slot or face milling is given by

$$K = \frac{ar \cos\left(1 - \frac{2y}{d}\right)}{360}$$

d = Milling cutter diameter

c = Depth of cut

$w = c = y$.

as indicated in Fig. 3.8 (a) and 3.8 (b).

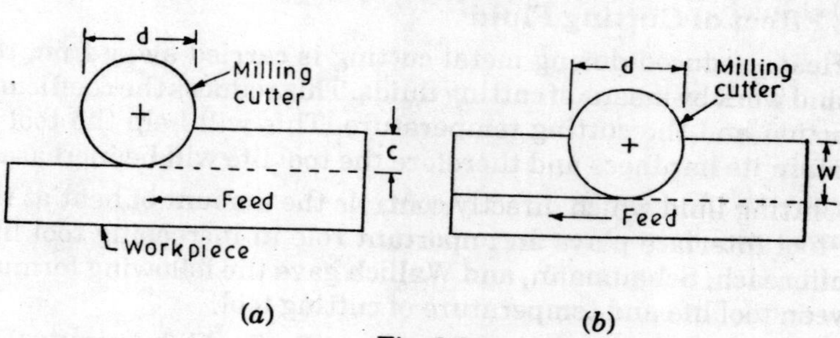

Fig. 3.8

3.13. Tool Grinding

Cutting tools are ground on the off-hand grinding machine.

When grinding carbide tipped tools it is important to ensure than the tool's steel shank does not come into contact with the grinding wheel cemented carbides may be ground with either silicon carbide grinding wheel or diamond impregnated wheels. Although diamond wheels are costly but they cut more effectively and last longer. Diamond impregnated wheels may be vitrified bonded, metal bonded or resinoid bonded. When off-hand grinding vitrified bonded wheels are used mainly for roughing operations whereas for fine grinding operation metal bonded wheels are preferred. Resinoid bonded diamond wheels are quite commonly used for machine grinding of multi-point cutters.

3.14. Cost Analysis

The production of a component involves several machining operations using a variety of machine tools. Production engineering is an economic function. The manufacture of a component must be carried out, at the lowest cost consistent with quality and functional need of product. Production time is defined as the average time taken to produce one component and the production cost is defined as the total average cost of performing the machining operation on a component.

The production cost of a component includes :

(*i*) Cost of material of the work-piece.

(*ii*) Wages of labour

(*iii*) Overhead charges.

3.14.1. Surface Treatment of Tools. Following types of treatments are carried out in order to increase the strength and hardness of cutting tools :

(*i*) Carburising

(*ii*) Nitriding

(*iii*) Finishing

(*iv*) Plating.

Carburising and nitriding are heat treatments processes by which tool surface layers are saturated with carbon and nitrogen respectively. Processes like lapping and superfinishing may be carried out to improve strength. Hardness can be increased to considerable extent by chromium plating using electrolysis process.

Frictional wear of tools can be reduced by the application of very hard low friction layers to tools. These layers are characterised by:

(*i*) high hardness;

(*ii*) low coefficient of friction; (*iii*) high bond strength;

(*iv*) antiweld behaviour ; and

(*v*) resistance to acids and bases.

can be applied to hot and cold working tools and cutting tools. Steel tools are given surface treatment to reduce sliding friction and to increase abrasion resistance by physically and chemically altering the surface of the tool.

The various surface treatment processes are as follows :

(*i*) **Nitriding :** In this surface treatment a surface layer of about 0.025 mm thick that is high in complex iron nitrides can be produced by treating a finished tool in a NaCN-KCN bath at about 1000°F for about 1/2 hour. Surface layer so produced can have hardness up to 1000 Brinell hardness. This surface treatment is generally used for tools taking light cuts such as broaching bits and taps.

(*ii*) **Lapping and Super finishing :** These surface treatment processes produce a fine finish of the order of 1 to 2 microns. Tools with such surface finishes are found to perform better.

(*iii*) **Chromium plating :** By this surface treatment process a layer of about 0.003 mm can be produced on tool surface. The hardness of such layer is estimated to be nearly 800 Brinell.

(*iv*) **Carburising :** By this surface treatment process a high carbon layer of nearly one millimeter thick can be produced by heating the tool surround by charcoal at 1950° C for about 30 minutes. The layer so produced is very hard. However the layer is brittle and the tool performance is not much improved.

(*v*) **Oxidation :** In this surface treatment process the tool is treated in an aqueous bath of NaOH and $NaNO_2$ at 285°F from 5 to 10 minutes. The layer of black Fe_3O_4 so produced is nearly 0.005 mm thick and provides a lower coefficient of friction because the oxide layer can hold oil better than polished surface.

During the last three decades surface enhancement technologies like

(*a*) Chemical vapor deposition (CVD)

(*b*) Physical vapor deposition (PVD)

(*c*) Carbide sputtring etc. have been commonly used.

These processes increase tool life and enhance performance of cutting tools. However these surface treatment methods are quite expensive.

A low cost high performance surface enhancement technology for improving performance and extending the life of cutting tool is Molybdenum Di-Sulphide (MoS_2) spray coating. This coating has a very low coefficient of friction and high wear resistance.

While applying the MoS_2 spray coating following method should be adopted.

(*i*) Surface to which coating is to be applied should be absolutely clean and dry.

Oil and grease films should be removed by slovent cleaning.

(*ii*) Burrs on the cutting edges should be removed.

(*iii*) Apply a single coat of spray from spray bottle uniformly so that the entire cutting portion of the tool is coated.

The film thickness is nearly 2 to 4 microns. Allow the tool to cure MoS_2 film at ambient temperature for about 30 minutes.

(*iv*) Whenever the tool is reground this process should be repeated for recoating of tool.

3.15. Cost per Component

The cost of manufacturing a component is composed of the following elements :

(*i*) Tooling cost

(*ii*) Machining cost

(*iii*) Non-productive cost.

1. **Tooling Cost.** The cost includes the following costs :

(*a*) Cost of tool

(*b*) Tool changing cost

(*c*) Tool sharpening cost.

2. **Machining Cost.** It includes the following costs :

(*a*) Direct labour cost

(*b*) Overhead cost.

Direct labour cost is the cost of direct labour expended for the work done directly on the workpiece. It depends upon the time required for actual machining of the component. The machining time is multiplied by the direct labour rate to obtain this cost.

Overhead cost is the cost of the activities which do not enter directly into the manufacture of the product, but which affect production cost. Overhead cost is composed of the following costs :

(*a*) Indirect labour cost

(*b*) Indirect material cost

(*c*) Fixed cost.

Indirect labour cost includes wages of managers, foremen, supervisors, office staff, and maintenance staff. Indirect material cost includes cost of lubricants, cotton wastes, lighting etc. Fixed cost includes the following :

(*a*) Interest on investment

(*b*) Depreciation

(*c*) Taxes

(*d*) Insurance.

3. **Non-productive Cost.** This cost is related to the activities which are necessary for preparing the machine tool. It is calculated taking into account the time required for the following activities.

(*i*) **Set up time.** It includes the time required to collect all the tools and materials, time required to set these into the machine tool, and make the necessary trial runs and adjustment.

(*ii*) Loading and unloading time.

(*iii*) Time required for inspection and gauging

(*iv*) Time required for fatigue and personal needs.

(*v*) **Down time.** It includes the time required for unpredictable circumstance such as breakdown in machine tool, delay in supply of materials, tool etc.

Many techniques are available to reduce manufacturing costs and increase manufacturing productivity. These measures include using the following :

(*i*) Improved materials, tools and processes.

(*ii*) Automation wherever it improves efficiency.

(*iii*) More effective organisation and factory layout, assembly techniques and material handling.

3.16. Objectives of Machining

Metal cutting is primarily an economic activity. The aim is to remove a particular volume of metal in minimum time or at minimum cost. The basic objectives of efficient and economical machining are as follows :

(*i*) High metal removal rate

(*ii*) Good surface finish

(*iii*) Low tool cost

(*iv*) Minimum idle time of machine tools

(*v*) Less power consumption.

3.17. Choice of Cutting Speed

The metal removal rate (w) is given by

$$w = f \cdot t \cdot V \cdot \text{cm}^3/\text{min}$$

where f = Feed in cm/rev.

t = Depth of cut in cm.

V = Cutting speed in cm/min.

Any increase in cutting speeds for a particular combination of feed and depth of cut will give a directly proportional increase in metal removal rate. This will reduce the machining cost.

But an increase in cutting speed will decrease the tool life and tool and grinding cost will increase. The total cost of machining will be sum of separate costs. Fig. 3.2 shows the variation of costs and cutting speed. The cutting speed corresponding to minimum cost is called economical cutting speed and tool life at this speed is called economical tool life.

The economical cutting speed is found as follows :

Let H = Machining cost/minute

= Labour cost/minute + Overheads / min.

E = Tooling cost

= Cost of changing tool + Cost of regrinding + tool depreciation

S_1 = Cost of machining metal/unit volume of metal cut

S_2 = Cost of servicing tools/unit of volume of metal cut

S = Total cost/unit volume of metal cut = $S_1 + S_2$

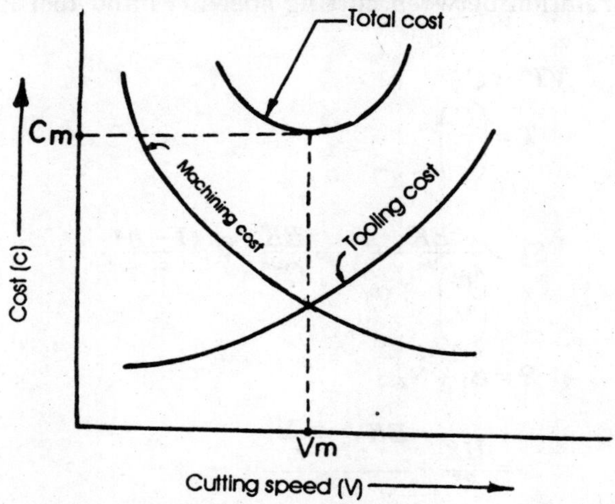

Fig. 3.9.

f = Feed
T = Total life
V = Cutting speed
t = Depth of cut.

Time to machine a unit volume of metal in minutes

$$= \frac{1}{t \cdot f \cdot V}$$

As t and f are constant

Let $\frac{1}{t \cdot f} = K.$

$\therefore$ Time to machine a unit volume of metal in minutes.

$$= \frac{K}{V}$$

where K is constant.

$$\therefore \quad S_1 = H \frac{K}{V}$$

Now number of tool change in $\frac{K}{V}$ minutes

$$= \frac{K}{TV}$$

$$\therefore \quad S_2 = \frac{EK}{TV}$$

As the relation between cutting speed (V) and tool life (T) is given by

$$VT^n = C$$

$$T = \left(\frac{C}{V}\right)^{1/n}$$

$$S_2 = \frac{EK}{\left(\frac{C}{V}\right)^{1/n} \cdot V} = \frac{EK}{C^{1/n}} \cdot V^{\frac{(1-n)}{n}}$$

$$S = S_1 + S_2$$

$$= \frac{HK}{V} + \frac{EKV^{\frac{1-n}{n}}}{C^{1/n}}$$

Differentiating w.r.t. V we get

$$\frac{dS}{dV} = \frac{-HK}{V^2} + \frac{1-n}{n}\frac{EK}{C^{1/n}} V \frac{1-2n}{n}$$

$$= 0 \text{ for the cost to be minimum.}$$

$$\frac{H}{V_2} = \frac{1-n}{n} \cdot \frac{E}{C^{1/n}} \cdot V \frac{1-2n}{n}.$$

$$H = \frac{1-n}{n} \cdot E \cdot \left(\frac{V}{C}\right)^{1/n.} \quad ...(1)$$

Let $$Q = \frac{E}{H}.$$

$$\therefore \quad \frac{1}{Q} = \frac{1-n}{n} \cdot \left(\frac{V}{C}\right)^{1/n}$$

$$V = C \cdot \left[\frac{n}{Q(1-n)}\right]^n$$

This will give the required economical speed at which the cost will be minimum.

From equation (1) $\frac{1}{Q} = \frac{1-n}{n} \times \frac{1}{T}$

as $$\left(\frac{V}{C}\right)^{1/n} = \frac{1}{T}$$

$$\frac{T}{Q} = \frac{1-n}{n} \text{ or } \frac{HT}{E} = \frac{1-n}{n}$$

This will give economic tool life.

3.18. Trends in Conventional Machining (Metal Cutting)

Conventional manufacturing processes have been able to meet major requirements in the field of manufacturing because of the following reasons :

(*i*) due to improvement in cutting tool materials and tool geometry.

(*ii*) due to advent of very powerful strong, rigid and highly automatic machine tools.

(*iii*) due to the introduction of very fast and accurate work-tool handling systems.

(*iv*) integrated computerisation and flexible manufacturing system have added new dimension in machining.

Some or all of the following objectives should be fulfilled during machining by conventional machining methods in addition to basic dimensional requirements with maximum attainable machinability.

(*i*) Minimisation of machining time per component.

(*ii*) Minimisation of production rate.

(*iii*) Minimisation of machining cost per component.

Machining cost can be reduced with following ways :

(A) Reduction of actual cutting time

This is achieved by

(*a*) by using highly powerful, rigid and dynamically stable machine tools.

(*b*) by using machine-fixture-tool work system having high process capability.

(*c*) by using proper tool material and tool geometry.

(*d*) by using sufficiently strong and rigid work and tool holding devices.

(*e*) by using proper cutting fluids.

(*f*) by eliminating vibrations produced during machining.

(*g*) by compounding the processing operations and/or their sub-groups incorporating multi tool and multi spindle working systems.

(B) Reduction of idle time

This can be achieved by

(*a*) reducing the number of idle operations.

(*b*) Mechanisation for flow less and quick handling operations like mounting, setting, indexing, unloading and transfer of blanks and cutting tools.

(*c*) using proper chip control and disposal methods.

(*d*) on-line inspection.

(C) Reduction of tool-change time

This is achieved by

(MIa) using cutting tools of longer life

(*b*) using quick systems for the removal of worn out tools and for setting of new tools.

(D) Reduction of cutting tools cost

This is achieved by

(*a*) using durable cutting tools

(*b*) using in expensive but good quality cutting tools.

(E) Maximisation of profit rate

This is achieved by

(*a*) Minimising machining cost.

(*b*) Minimising rejections through on-line inspection and gauging.

(*c*) Proper replacement of in effective cutting tools.

(*d*) Minimisation of heavy breakdowns.

(*e*) Incorporating proper maintenance schedule for machine tools etc.

Thus higher productivity and overall economy during machining methods can be achieved by using the following :

(*i*) High powerful and rigid machine tools.

(*ii*) Cutting tools of proper materials and strength.

(*iii*) On-line inspection.

(*iv*) Automation of motions, inspections, handling of tools, work piece etc.

Example 3.1. *Determine the optimum cutting speed for an operation carried on a lathe machine using the following operations.*

Tool change time = 4 minutes

Tool regrind time = 3 minutes

Machine running cost = 20 paise per minute

Depreciation tool regrind = Re. 1

The tool life equation is given by

$$VT^n = C$$

Assume $C = 60$

$$n = 1/5.$$

Solution. H = Machining cost = 20 paise/minute

E = Tooling cost

= Tool change cost + Cost of regrinding + Tool depreciation

Tool change cost = 4 × 20 = 80 paise

Tool regrinding cost = 3 × 20 = 60 paise

Tool depreciation = Re. 1

E = Tooling cost = 80 + 60 + 100

= 240 paise

$$Q = \frac{E}{H} = \frac{240}{20} = 12$$

Now V = Optimum cutting speed

$$V = C \times \left[\frac{n}{Q(1-n)}\right]^{n} = 60\left[\frac{0.2}{12(1-0.2)}\right]^{0.2}$$

$$= 26.6 \text{ m / min.} \quad \textbf{Ans.}$$

Example 3.2. *Find the optimum cutting speed and tool life for minimum cost for machining medium carbon steel under the following conditions :*

Cost of operating the machine = 20 paise per minute.

Total cost of tool change = Rs. 8

The cutting speed is 40 metre per min when the tool life is 50 minutes for the depth of cut and feed employed. Assume

n = 0.2 in the relation

$$VT^n = C.$$

Solution. H = Machining cost/minute = 20 paise

E = Tooling cost = Rs. 8

We know $\dfrac{HT}{E} = \dfrac{1-n}{n}$

where T = economic tool life

$n = 0.2$

$$\frac{20 \times T}{8 \times 100} = \frac{1-0.2}{0.2}$$

$$T = 160 \text{ minutes.}$$

Now the cutting speed is 40 metre/min when tool life is 50 minutes.

$$40 \times 50^{0.3} = C = VT^n$$

where V = economic cutting speed and T is economic tool life

$$40 \times 50^{0.2} = V \cdot 160^{0.2}$$

$$V = 30 \text{ metre/min.} \quad \textbf{Ans.}$$

Example 3.3. *Determine the tool cost of a batch of 400 components made on a capstan lathe. Work rate per piece is 5 paise and the direct material cost is 10 paise per piece. Indirect costs are 500% of direct labour cost.*

Solution. N = Number of components = 400

C_1 = Direct cost

= N[Material cost + Labour cost]

$$= \frac{400\,[10+5]}{100} = \text{Rs. } 60$$

$$C_2 = \text{Indirect cost}$$
$$= \frac{500}{100} \times \frac{5 \times 400}{100} = \text{Rs. } 100$$
$$C = \text{Tool cost} + C_1 + C_2$$
$$= 60 + 100 = \textbf{Rs. 160.} \quad \textbf{Ans.}$$

Example 3.4. *A tool will cut for 4 hours before it needs sharpening. Determine the time charged to one cycle if it takes 12 minutes to change the tool and tool can be sharpened 10 times before it is discarded.*

Solution. t = Time charged to one cycle

$$= \frac{T_1 \times T_2}{T}$$

where T_1 = Cutting time

$= 4 \times 60 = 240$ minutes.

T_2 = Tool change time = 12 minutes

T = Tool life = $10 \times 4 = 40$ hours

$= 40 \times 60 = 2400$ minutes

$$t = \frac{T_1 \times T_2}{T} = \frac{240 \times 12}{2400}$$

$= 1.2$ minutes. **Ans.**

Example 3.5. *It is desired to machine 20 castings in two set ups. What is the cost of production if the following data are used.*

Machining time = 15 minutes per casting

Set up time = 20 minutes per set up

Tool sharpening time = 0.5 minute per casting

Tool change time = 0.8 minute per casting

Overhead cost = 15 paise per casting

Fatigue = 15%

Personal need = 5%

Check and *gauging time*

= 12 seconds and 5 checks per casting

Direct labour cost = 5 paise per minute.

Solution. H = Direct labour cost = 5 paise per minute

N = Number of castings = 20.

Tooling cost (C_1) = Tool changing cost + Tool sharpening cost

= (Tool change time + Tool sharpening time) × N.H.

$$= (0.8 + 0.5) \times \frac{20 \times 5}{100} = \text{Rs. } 1.3.$$

Machining cost C_2

= Machining time × N × H + Overhead cost × N

$$= 15 \times 20 \times \frac{5}{100} + \frac{15 \times 20}{100} = \text{Rs. } 18.$$

Set up time = 20 min. per set up × Number of set ups

$$= 20 \times 2 = 40 \text{ minutes.}$$

$$\text{Fatigue time} = \frac{15}{100} \times \text{machining time}$$

$$= \frac{15}{100} \times 15 = 2.25 \text{ minutes.}$$

Time of personal needs

$$= \frac{5}{100} \times \text{machining time}$$

$$= \frac{5}{100} \times 15 = 0.75 \text{ minute.}$$

Checking and gauging time

$$= \frac{12 \times 5}{60} = 1 \text{ minute.}$$

Non productive cost (C_3)

= Set up time cost + Fatigue cost + Cost of personal needs

+ Cost of checking and gauging.

$$C_3 = 40 \times \frac{5}{100} + 2.25 \times 20 \times \frac{5}{100} + 0.75 \times 20 \times \frac{5}{100} + 1 \times 20 \times \frac{5}{100}$$

$$= 2 + 2.25 + 0.75 + 1 = \text{Rs. } 6$$

Total cost, $C = C_1 + C_2 + C_3 = 1.3 + 18 + 6 = \text{Rs. } 25.3.$

Example 3.6. *Determine the cost of manufacturing a component using the following date :*

Initial cost of the machine = Rs. 10,000

Depreciation rate of machine = Rs. 2000 per year

Labour rate = Rs. 3 per hour

Operator and machine overloads = 100%

Number of working days per year = 250

Working hours per day = 8

Machine time = 3 minutes

Non–productive time = 2 minutes

*Tool changing and resetting time = itaic*0.6 min *per component*

Cost of regrinding the tool per component = 7 paise

Total depreciation per component = 6 paise.

Solution. Machine depreciation per minute.

$$= \frac{2000 \times 100}{250 \times 8 \times 60} = 1.66 \text{ paise/min}$$

$$\text{Labour rate} = \frac{3 \times 100}{60} = 5 \text{ paise /min.}$$

Machine and operator overheads = 100%

∴ Machine and operator rate

= 1.66 + 1.66 + 5 + 5 = 13.32 paise/min.

Machining cost = 13.32 × 3 = 39.96 paise

Non productive cost = 13.32 × 2 = 26.64 paise.

Total cost

= Tool changing and resetting cost + Cost of grinding + Tool depreciation

= 0.6 × 13.32 + 7 + 6 = 21 paise.

Total cost

= Machining cost + Non–productive cost + Tooling cost

= 39.26 + 26.64 + 21 = 87.60 paise. **Ans.**

Example 3.7. *Three different methods of production utilising three different grades of labour have been suggested for the manufacture of a component. The manufacturing information is as follows :*

Method	*Machining Time*	Hourly rate	*Tool cost*	*Number of set up per year*	Set up time (Hours)	Hourly Rate for set up
A	*20*	*Rs. 4*	*Nil*	*10*	*2*	*Rs.8*
B	*12*	*Rs.6*	*Rs.240*	*8*	*2.5*	*Rs.6*
C	*9*	MIRs.7	*Rs.960*	*4*	*3*	*Rs.7*

Assuming all time saved can be gainfully used, prepare a graph and show at what quantities methods A and B cease to the most economic.

Solution.

Let C_1 = Total cost per year for method A

C_2 = Total cost per year for method B

C_3 = Total cost per year for method C

n = Number of components produced per year.

Method A

$$C_1 = \text{Tooling cost + Cost of set up + Machining cost}$$

$$= 0 + 10 \times 2 \times 8 + \frac{20}{60} \times 4 \times n$$

$$= \text{Rs. } 160 + \text{ Rs. } 1.33\, n$$

Method B

$$C_2 = \text{Tooling cost + Cost of set ups + Machining cost}$$

$$= 240 + 8 \times 2.5 \times 6 + \frac{12}{60} \times 6 \times n$$

$$= \text{Rs. } 360 + 1.2\, n$$

Method C

$$C_3 = \text{Tooling cost + Cost of set ups + Machining cost}$$

$$= 960 + 4 \times 3 \times 7 + \frac{9}{60} \times 7 \times n$$

$$= \text{Rs. } 1044 + 1.05\, n$$

The break even point between methods A and B occurs when

$$C_1 = C_2$$

$$160 + 1.33n = 360 + 1.2\, n$$

$$n = 1538$$

Now break even point between method B and C occurs when

$$C_2 = C_3$$

$$360 + 1.2n = 1044 + 1.05\, n$$

$$n = 4560.$$

Method A cease to be economic when more than 1538 components are required per year and method B cease to be economic

when more than 4560 components are required. Fig. 3.10 shows cost quantity graph indicating break-even points.

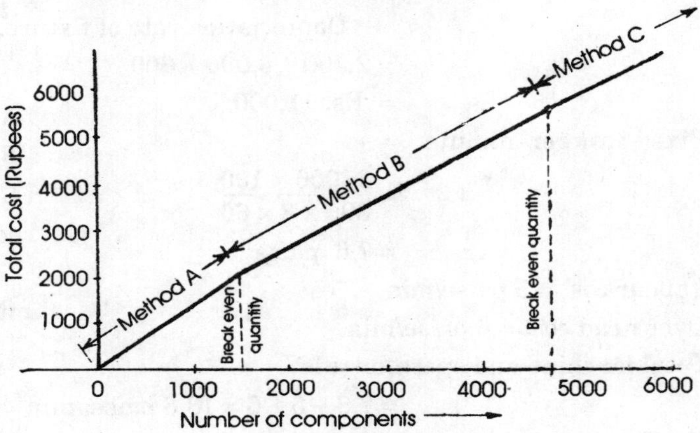

Fig. 3.10.

Example 3.8. *A component is being manufactured by a manufacturing organisation. The manufacturing information is as follows :*

Cost of machine = Rs. 24,000

Depreciation rate of machine = Rs. 2400 per year

Cost of tools consumption = Rs. 80000 per year

Fixture cost = Rs. 3000

Depreciation rate of fixture = 600 per year

Production rate per day = 4 components

Number of working days per year = 300

Working hours per day = 8

Labour cost = 5 paise/min.

Overhead cost = 6 paise /min.

Machining time per component = 70 min.

Tool changing and sharpening time = 10 min.

Handling time = 6 min

Loading and unloading time = 24 min.

Gauging time = 10 min.

Determine the cost of manufacturing.

Solution. Fixed cost per year

= Depreciation rate of machine + Cost of tool consumption

+ Depreciation rate of fixture.

= 2,400 + 8,000 + 600

= Rs. 11,000.

Fixed cost per minute

$$= \frac{11000 \times 100}{300 \times 8 \times 60}$$

= 7.6 paise

Labour cost = 5 paise/min.

Over head cost = 6 paise/min.

Total machine and operator rate

= 7.6 + 5 + 6 = 18.6 paise /min

C = Total cost of manufacturing a component

= Machining cost + Non–productive cost + Tooling cost.

Machining cost = Machining time × 18.6

$$= \frac{70 \times 18.6}{130}$$

= Rs. 13.02

Non productive cost = 18.6 × [Loading and unloading time + Gauging time]

$$= \frac{18.6[24 + 10]}{100} = \text{Rs. } 6.32$$

Tooling cost = [Tool sharpening and changing time + Handling time] 18.6

$$= \frac{[10 + 6] + 18.6}{100} = \text{Rs. } 2.97$$

Total cost of manufacturing a component

= 13.02 + 6.32 + 2.97

= Rs. 22.31. **Ans.**

Example 3.9. *For a cutting tool the tool life is expressed by the equation*

$$VT^n = C$$

In a certain tool test a single point cutting tool had a life of 10 minutes when operating at 240 metre / minute. At what speed should the tool have to be operated in order to a have tool life of 3 hours. Assume n=0.2.

Solution. Tool life is expressed by the equation

$$VT^n = C$$

where $V =$ cutting speed (m/min)

$T =$ Tool life (minutes)

$n = 0.2$

$C =$ constant.

Substituting these values in the given equation, we have

$$240(10)^{0.2} = C$$

$$C = 384$$

when $T = 180$ minutes

$n = 0.2$

$C = 384$

then $VT^n = C$

$$V(180)^{0.2} = 384$$

$\therefore$ $V = 137$ metre/minute. **Ans.**

Example 3.10. *The tool life for a high speed steel (H.S.S.) tool is expressed by the relation $VT^{1/7} = C_1$ and for tungsten carbide (WC) is expressed as $VT^{1/5} = C_2$. If at a speed of 24 metre, per minute the tool life is 128 minutes compare the life of the two tools at a speed of 30 metre / min.*

Solution. For high speed steel tool, $VT^{1/7} = C_1$

$$24 \times 128^{1/7} = C_1$$

$$C_1 = 48$$

For tungsten carbide tool, $24 \times 128^{1/5} = C_2$

$$C_2 = 62$$

when $V = 30$ metres / minute.

Let $T_1 =$ Tool life for high speed steel tool

$T_2 =$ Tool life for tungsten carbide tool.

For high speed steel tool.

$\therefore$ $30 \times T_1^{1/7} = 48$

$$T_1 = 29 \text{ minutes.}$$

For tungsten carbide tool.

$$30 \times T_2^{1/5} = 62$$

$$T_2 = 38 \text{ minutes}$$

$$\therefore \qquad \frac{T_1}{T_2} = \frac{29}{38} = 0.7. \qquad \textbf{Ans.}$$

Example 3.11. *A tool life of 80 minute is obtained at a speed of 30 mpm and 8 minute at 60 m.p.m. Determine the following :*

(a) Tool life equation.

(b) Cutting speed for 4 minute tool life.

Solution. $V_1 = 30$ m.p.m.

$T_1 = 80$ minutes

$V_2 = 60$ m.p.m.

$T_2 = 8$ minutes.

Now the tool life equation is

$$VT^n = C$$

$$V_1T_1^n = V_2T_2^n$$

$$30(80)^n = 60(8)^n$$

$$\frac{300}{60} = \left(\frac{8}{10}\right)^n$$

$$\frac{1}{2} = \left(\frac{1}{10}\right)^n$$

$$n = 0.3$$

$\therefore$ The tool life equation is

$$VT^{0.3} = \text{constant.}$$

Let $V_3 =$ cutting speed

$T_3 =$ Tool life $=$ 4 minutes

$$\therefore \qquad V_1T_1^n = V_3T_3^n$$

$$30(80)^n = V_3(4)^n$$

$$30(80)^{0.3} = V_3(4)^{0.8}$$

$V_3 = 82$ metres /minute. **Ans.**

Example 3.12. *Determine the percentage change in cutting speed required to give 60% reduction in tool life (i.e. to reduce tool life to 2 / 5 of its former value.) The speed / life relationship of cutting tool is given by $VT^n = C$. Take n=0.2.*

Solution. $V_1 =$ cutting speed

$$T_1 = \text{Tool life}$$
$$V_2 = \text{Cutting speed}$$
$$T_2 = \text{Tool life}$$
$$n = 0.2$$
$$V_1 T_1^n = V_2 T_2^n$$
$$\frac{V_1}{V_2} = \left(\frac{T_1}{T_2}\right)^{0.2}$$
$$= \left(\frac{1}{2/5}\right)^{0.2}$$
$$= 1.2$$

Increase in cutting speed

$= 20\%$. **Ans.**

Example 3.13. *The speed life relationship for a tool is given by $VT^{1/3} = 200$ for a given set of conditions and the time taken to change the tool is 6 minutes. Show that operating at a cutting speed of 75 metre per minute gives higher output than operating at either 110 metre / min or 50 metre per minute if other conditions remain unchanged.*

Solution. $VT^{1/3} = 200$

where V = Cutting speed

T = Tool life.

∴ When cutting speed

$V = 50, T = 64$ minutes

$V = 75, T = 18$ minutes

$V = 110, T = 6$ minutes

The average cutting speed at different values of V can be calculated as follows.

Time taken to change the tool is = 6 minutes.

when $V = 50$, Average cutting speed $= \frac{50 \times 64}{64 + 6} = 45.7$ m/min

$V = 75$, Average cutting speed $= \frac{75 \times 18}{18 + 6} = 56.2$ m/min

$V = 110$, Average cutting speed $= \frac{110 \times 6}{6 + 6} = 55$ m/min

Therefore on a time basis 75 metre/minute is the best of the three cutting speeds. **Ans.**

Example 3.14. *The cutting speed and tool life relationship for a tool is given by $VT^n = C$. Where V is the cutting speed in metre per minute and T is tool life in minutes. During machining 18 mm bar on a lathe at a cutting speed of 110 metre per minute the life of tool is found to be 60 minutes. If n=0.2 calculate the speed at which the spindle should be run to give a tool life of 5 hours. If a length of 50 mm per component is machined what is the cutting time per piece and how many pieces can be produced between tool changes. The feed used is 0.15 mm / revolution.*

Solution. V_1 = cutting speed

$= 110$ mpm

$T_1 = 60$ minutes

$T_2 = 300$ minutes

$n = 0.2$

$$V_1 T_1^n = V_2 T_2^n$$

$$V_2 = V_1 \left(\frac{T_1}{T_2}\right)^{0.2}$$

$$= 110\left(\frac{60}{300}\right)^{0.2}$$

$= 80$ metre /min.

Let N = spindle speed

D = diameter of = 1.8 cm.

$$\pi D N = 80$$

$$\pi \times \frac{1.8}{100} \times N = 80$$

$N = 1415$ R.P.M.

f = feed = 0.15 mm /rev

L = length of piece = 50 mm.

Cutting time per piece

$$= \frac{L}{f \times N} = \frac{50}{0.15 \times 1415} \text{ minutes}$$

$$= \frac{50 \times 60}{0.15 \times 1415}$$

$= 14.2$ seconds.

Number of components produced in 5 hours

$$= \frac{5 \times 60 \times 60}{14.2}$$

$$= 1267. \textbf{ Ans.}$$

Example 3.15. *During a tool life cutting test of H.S.S. tool material used to cut a special die steel the following values were obtained.*

Cutting speed V (m/min)	52	50	49	46	42
Tool life (T) (minutes)	3	4	4.9	10.5	30

Use the above values to calculate the constants of the tool life equation $VT^n = C$.

Solution. $VT^n = C$

$$\log V + n \log T = \log C$$

In order to obtain satisfactory results a straight line graph should be plotted. This can be obtained by plotting the equation

$$\log V + n \log T = \log C$$

$$\log V = -n \log T + \log C.$$

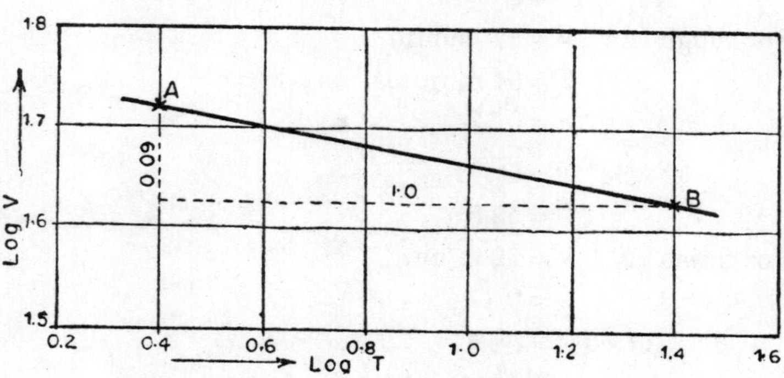

Fig. 3.11.

log V	1.7160	1.6990	1.6902	1.6638	1.6232
log T	0.4771	0.6081	0.6902	1.0212	1.4771

The resulting graph between log V and log T is shown in Fig. 3.11.

To obtain the value of n consider any two points A and B on the graph slope = n = + 0.09

$$\therefore \quad n = 0.09$$

Now $\log V + n \log T = \log C$

$$1.72 + 0.09\,(0.4) = \log C$$

(For point A)

$$\log C = 1.756$$

$$C = 57$$

Therefore the tool life equation is

$$VT^{0.09} = 57. \qquad \textbf{Ans.}$$

Example 3.16. *A tool cutting at 32 m/min has a life of 54 minutes when used for a rough cut. Determine tool life when used for a light finishing cut.*

Given

$$n = 0.124 \text{ for rough cut}$$

$$= 0.1 \text{ for finish cut.}$$

Solution. Tool life equation is given by :

$$VT^n = C$$

For rough cut $\quad V = 32$ m/min

$$T = 54 \text{ minutes.}$$

$$n = 0.124$$

$$\therefore \quad 32 \times 54^{0.124} = C$$

$$C = 52.5$$

For finish cut $\quad V = 32$ m/min

$$n = 0.1$$

$$32 \times T^{0.1} = 52.5$$

$$T = 141 \text{ minutes.} \qquad \textbf{Ans.}$$

Example 3.17. *State the conditions for a cutting tool to give maximum production with minimum maintenance and trouble.*

Solution. A cutting tool will give maximum production with least troubles and maintenance if it satisfies the following conditions.

(*a*) If the tool is made of proper material.

(*b*) If the cutting tool geometry is properly designed.

(*c*) If the tool is properly heat treated.

(*d*) If proper cooling is used during the application of cutting tool.

Example 3.18. *A carbide tool while machining a mild steel workpiece was found to have a life of 1 hour and 40 minutes when cutting at 50 metre per minute. Find the tool life if the tool is to operate at speed 30% higher than previous one. Also calculate the cutting speed if tool is required to have a life of 2 hours and 45 minutes. Assume Taylor's exponent n = 0.28.*

Solution. (*a*) V = Cutting speed = 50 metre /min.

T = Life of cutting tool

= 100 minutes.

$$VT^n = C$$

$$50 \times 100^{0.28} = C \quad ...(1)$$

When speed is increased by 30%

V_1 = Cutting speed

$$= 50 + 50 \times \frac{30}{100}$$

= 65 metre per minute

T_1 = Tool life

$$V_1 T_1^n = C$$

$$65 \times T_1^{0.28} = C \quad ...(2)$$

From (1) and (2) we get

$$50 \times 100^{0.28} = 65 \times T_1^{0.28}$$

T_1 = 39 minutes. **Ans.**

(*b*) T_2 = Tool life

= 165 minutes

V_2 = Cutting speed

$$V_2 T_2^n = C$$

$$V_2 \times 165^{0.28} = C \quad ...(3)$$

From (1) and (3)

$$50 \times 100^{0.28} = V_2 \times 165^{0.28}$$

V_2 = 43.4 metre per minute. **Ans.**

Example 3.19. (*a*) *Define machining time in a lathe operation.* (*b*) *A mild steel pin is of 38 mm diameter and 400 mm length is to* *be turned on a lathe. Determine the turning time to reduce the pin to 36.5 mm is one pass when cutting speed is 30 metres per minute and a feed of 0.7 mm per revolution is used.*

Solution. (*a*) Machining time in a lathe operation is defined as follows :

$$T = \text{machining time for one pass or cut}$$

$$= \frac{L}{f \cdot N}$$

where L = Length of cut, mm

f = Feed, mm /revolution

N = R.P.M. of workpiece.

V = Cutting speed

D = Diameter of workpiece

= 38 mm

$$V = \frac{\pi DN}{1000}$$

$$30 = \frac{\pi \cdot 38 \cdot N}{1000}$$

$$N = 251 \text{ R.P.M.}$$

$$T = \text{Machining time}$$

$$= \frac{L}{f \cdot N}$$

$$= \frac{400}{0.7 \times 251} = 2.27 \text{ minutes.}$$

Example 3.20. *Calculate the time required to drill a 20 mm diameter hole in a workpiece having thickness of 60 mm. The cutting speed is 14 metres per minute and feed is 0.3 mm per revolution. Neglect the length of approach.*

Solution. V = Cutting speed

$$= \frac{\pi DN}{1000}$$

$$14 = \frac{\pi \times 20 \times N}{1000}$$

$$N = 223 \text{ R.P.M.}$$

$$T = \text{Drilling time}$$

$$= \frac{L}{f \cdot N}$$

where L = Thickness of workpiece

$$= \frac{60}{0.3 \times 223} = 0.89 \text{ minutes.}$$

Example 3.21. *(a) During turning operation on a lathe following information was obtained.*

Machine running cost = Rs. 0.5 per min.

Tool regrinding and depreciation cost = Rs. 3.0

Tool change time = 8 minutes

Tool regrind time = 4 minutes

In Taylor's equation

$$n = 0.5$$

$$c = 160$$

Determine the optimum cutting speed.

(b) If 180 components with machined length of 360 mm and 100 mm diameter are to be manufactured determine :

(i) Total cost of machining

(ii) Time required to machine the parts.

Feed may be taken as 0.24 mm / rev.

Solution. Let V_T = Optimum cutting speed

M = Machining cost /minute

= Rs. 0.5

S_1 = Cost of changing tool

= Tool change time × M

= 8 × 0.5 = Rs. 4.0

S_2 = Tool regrind cost

= Tool regrind time × M

= 4 × 0.5 = Rs. 2.0

S_3 = Tool depreciation cost = Rs. 3.0

S = Tooling cost = $S_1 + S_2 + S_3$

= 4 + 2 + 3 = Rs. 9.0

C = 160

n = 0.3

$$R = \frac{S}{M} = \frac{9}{0.5} = 18$$

V_T = Optimum cutting speed

$$= c\left[\frac{n}{R(1-n)}\right]^n$$

$$= 160\left[\frac{0.3}{18(1-0.3)}\right]^{0.3}$$

= 47 metre /minute

(b) N = R.P.M. of spindle

D = Work piece diameter = 100 mm.

V_T = Cutting speed

= 47 metre /min

$$V_T = \pi DN$$

$$47 = \pi \times \frac{100}{1000} \times N$$

$$N = 150$$

f = feed = 0.24 mm /rev.

T_1 = Machining time per component

$= \frac{L}{f \cdot N}$ where L = length to be machined

= 360 mm

$$T_1 = \frac{360}{0.24 \times 150} = 10 \text{ minutes}$$

T = Tool life at cutting speed 47 mpm.

$$V_T^n = c$$

$$47 \times T^{0.3} = 160$$

T = 59 minutes

N_1 = Number of parts /regrind

$$= \frac{T}{T_1} = \frac{59}{10} = 5.9$$

C_1 = Tool change cost per part

$$= \frac{S_1}{N_1} = \frac{2}{5.9} = \text{ Re. } 0.68$$

C_2 = Tool regrind cost per part

$$= \frac{S_2}{N_1} = \frac{2}{5.9} = \text{Re.}0.34$$

$$C_3 = \frac{S_3}{N_1} = \frac{3}{5.9} = \text{Rs. } 0.51$$

$$C_4 = \text{Machining cost per part}$$

$$= M \times T_1 = 0.5 \times 10 = \text{ Rs. } 5.0$$

$$C = \text{Total cost per part} = C_1 + C_2 + C_3 + C_4$$

$$= 0.68 + 0.34 + 0.51 + 5$$

$$= \text{Rs. } 6.53.$$

Total cost of 180 components

$$= 180 \times C = 180 \times 6.53 = \text{Rs. } 1175.$$

$$T_2 = \text{Tool change time per part}$$

$$= \frac{\text{Tool change time}}{\text{N}_1}$$

$$= \frac{8}{5.9} = 1.36 \text{ minutes}$$

$$T_3 = \text{Tool regrind time per part}$$

$$= \frac{\text{Tool regrind time}}{\text{N}_1}$$

$$= \frac{4}{5.9} = 0.68 \text{ minute}$$

$$r = \text{Rate of production per hour}$$

$$= \frac{60}{T_1 + T_2 + T_3}$$

$$= \frac{60}{10 + 1.36 + 0.68} = 4.98$$

Time required for 180 parts

$$= \frac{180}{r} = \frac{180}{4.98} = 36.2 \text{ hours.}$$

PROBLEMS

3.1. **(*a*) What is machinability ? State the factors which come into play while evaluating machinability of any metal.**

(*b*) Define machinability index.

3.2. **(*a*) State the reasons responsible for tool failure.**

(*b*) Explain

(*i*) Crater wear.

(*ii*) Flank wear.

3.3. **(*a*) Define tool life. State the factors which affect tool life ?**

(*b*) Explain the relationship between tool life and cutting speed ?

(*c*) Explain the effect of tool geometry and cutting variables on tool life.

3.4. If $VT^n = C$ is the tool-life equation, calculate the cutting speed that will give a tool life of 1 hour if n =0.2 and C = 90.

3.5. Write short notes on the following :

(*i*) Causes of tool wear.

(*ii*) Tool grinding.

(*iii*) Surface treatments of tools.

3.6. When turning under certain conditions the relationship between cutting speed and tool life could be expressed as $VT^n = C$. In the tool test, a single point tool had a life of 10 minutes when operating at 200 metres/minute. At what speed would the tool have to be operated to have a tool life of 240 minutes. Assume n= 0.2. [**Ans.** 106 m/min]

3.7. A tool cutting at 24 m/min gave a life of 50 minutes between regrinds when operating on rough cuts with medium carbon steel. What will be its probable life when engaged on light finishing cuts. Assume n= 0.125 for rough cutting and n = 0.1 for finishing cuts in the tool life and cutting speed relationship $VT^n = C$.

3.8. Define the following :

(*a*) Direct labour cost.

(*b*) Overhead cost.

(*c*) Fixed cost.

3.9. List the cost items which are classified in the non-machining (non productive) type. Explain each and give example.

3.10. State the basic objectives of efficient and economic machining.

3.11. Derive an expression for the optimum cutting speed at which the cost will be minimum.

3.12. (*a*) Discuss economic tool life.

(*b*) The time required to handle and machine a workpiece is 60 minutes. If the allowance for fatigue is 20% and for personal needs is 5%. Calculate the total time required for each workpiece.

3.13. A company is to manufacture 200 parts per set up and that the job calls for 6 set ups. Calculate the cost of production using the following data :

Machining time = 24 minutes per component.
Non–machining time = 16 minutes per component
Tool sharpening = 2 minutes per component
Set up time = 80 minutes per set up.
Gauging and inspection = 16 seconds and 8 checks per component.
Tool change = 13 minutes
Fatigue = 20%
Personal needs = 4%
Tool life = 12 hours
Direct labour cost = Rs. 3 per hour.

3.14. A batch of 1200 components are to be rough turned to 70 mm diameter for 250 mm of their length using a feed of 0.23 mm per revolution.

The tool life equation is given by

$$VT^{0.26} = 26$$

where V is the cutting speed in metres per second and T is tool life in seconds. If the cost per cutting edge including cost of tool depreciation and cost of resting the cutting edge is rupees six and total machine rate including operator cost is Rs. 62, calculate the following.

(*a*) Tool life to give minimum production costs.

(*b*) Cutting speed that will result in this optimum tool life.

(*c*) Total production time assuming time taken to reset the cutting edge of tool is 40 seconds, time taken to load and unload a components is 50 seconds and initial set up time for the batch is 45 minutes.

(*d*) Total production cost.

3.15. The Taylorian tool life equation for machining C-40 steel with 18-4-1 H.S.S. at a feed of 0.2 mm/min and a depth of cut of 2 mm is given by $VT^n = C$ where n and C are constants depending on cutting conditions and tool work combinations.

The following V and T observations have been noted

Cutting seed (V) m/min	25	36
Tool-life (T) minute	88	20

Calculate the index n and constant C. Hence recommend the cutting speed for a desired tool life of 65 minutes.

3.16. Write short note on the following :

(*i*) Machining time in a lathe operation.

(*ii*) Machining time in drilling.

3.17. Discuss the trends in conventional machining (metal cutting).

4

Cutting Fluids

4.1. Cutting Fluids

During metal cutting heat is generated as a result of the work done. Heat is carried away from the tool and work by means of cutting fluids which at the same time reduce the friction between the tool and chip and between tool and work and also facilitates the chip formation. Cutting, fluids usually in the form of a liquid are applied to the chip formation zone to improve the cutting conditions compared to dry cutting conditions. If sufficient quantity of cutting fluid is properly applied heat can be removed almost as fast as it is generated and the temperature of tool, workpiece and chip can be kept within limit. Cutting fluid is one of the 'important aids to improve production efficiency.'

Most practical cutting fluids have a mineral oil or vegetable oil base the mineral oil being the more widely used.

4.2. Sources of Heat in Metal Cutting

The main factors likely to cause excessive heat during a metal cutting operation are as follows :

(*i*) Cutting speed too high.

(*ii*) Poor surface finish on the cutting face of the tool.

(*iii*) Worn or incorrectly ground cutting tool.

(*iv*) Formation of a built up edge on cutting face of the tool.

(*v*) Friction between tool and work-piece.

4.3. Thermal Aspects of Metal Machining

During metal cutting considerable amount of heat is produced due to the friction between tool and work and plastic shearing of metal in the form of chips. This heat reduces the hardness of the cutting tool, makes it less wear resistant and changes its dimensions. Heat also leads to changes in the dimensions of machined surfaces. These temperature deformations of the tool and work reduce the machining accuracy.

The colour of the chip is frequently noted as a measure of the temperature obtaining at the tool point. A blue temper color on the surface of a chip formed in dry cutting is taken to mean that the tool point is hotter than when an uncolored silvery chip is obtained when cutting with a fluid.

There are three zones at which heat is generated.

(*i*) Shear zone (*ii*) Friction zone

(*iii*) Work tool contact zone.

The heat produced at zone Z_1 (Shear zone) is maximum because of the plastic deformation of metal and practically all of this heat is carried away by the chips. Only a small portion of this heat (5 – 10%) is conducted to the workpiece. The heat is produced at zone Z_2 (Friction zone) due to the friction between moving chip and tool face. In zone Z_3 (work tool contact zone) the heat is generated due to burnishing friction and the heat in this zone goes on increasing with time as the wear land on the tool develops and goes on increasing. From these zones the maximum heat flows to work piece or chip as indicated by arrows (Fig. 4.1). However some heat flows in other directions also. A typical distribution of heat of chips tool and work piece versus cutting speed is shown in Fig. 4.2.

It is observed that distribution of heat in chips, tool and work piece is nearly in the ratio 80 : 10 : 10. When carbide cutting tools are used at speeds about 30 mpm. In Fig. 4.2, V is the cutting speed in metre per minute and Q is total heat.

4.4. Functions of Cutting Fluid

Most machining operations can be carried out advantageously by using a cutting fluid. During metal cutting heat and wear are inevitably produced due to friction and shearing action that takes place as the chip is being formed. Both heat and wear are undesirably in order to obtain a reasonable tool life and good surface finish. One way of improving metal cutting operation is by using a cutting fluid. The cutting fluids can benefit metal cutting in several ways but by far the most important is heat removal. The various functions of a cutting fluid are as follows.

(*i*) It cools the cutting tool and workpiece. The heat produced is carried away by the fluid by supplying adequate quantity of cutting fluid. This makes possible more accurate production and measurement.

(*ii*) It lubricates the cutting tool and thus reduces the coefficient of friction between the chip and tool. This increases tool life.

(*iii*) The use of a cutting fluid result in better surface finish.

(*iv*) As friction gets reduced, the tool forces are also reduced and therefore the power consumption during cutting is also reduced.

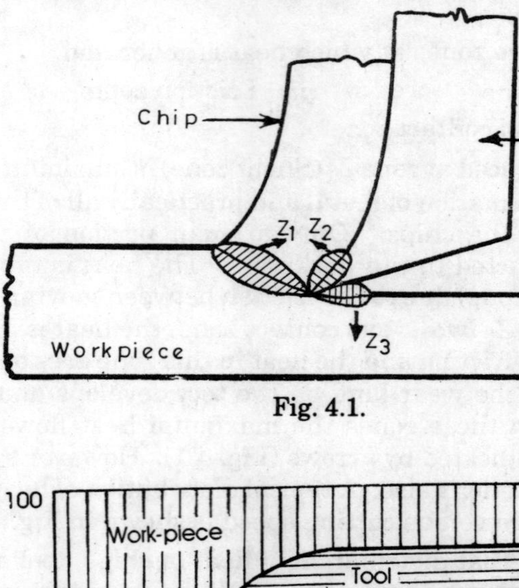

Fig. 4.1.

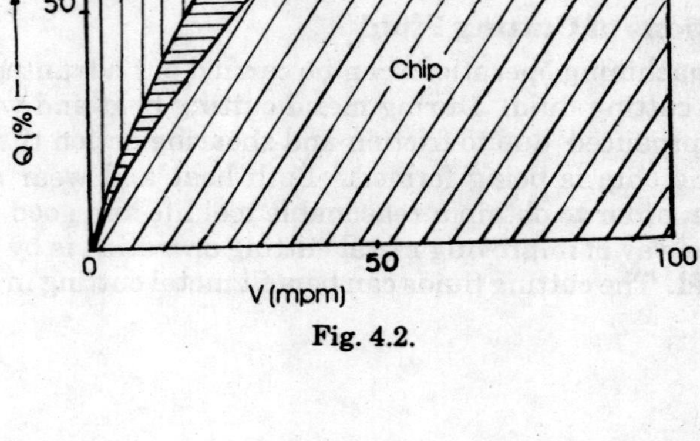

Fig. 4.2.

(*v*) It causes the chips to break up into small pieces.

(*vi*) It washes away the chips from the tool.

(*vii*) It prevents corrosion of work and machine.

(*viii*) Removal of heat from the cutting zone also reduces thermal distortion of the work and permits improved dimensional control.

In performing the above functions the cutting fluid enables the maximum possible cutting speed to be used thus reducing time and cost of production.

4.5. Properties of Cutting Fluid

A cutting fluid should possess the following properties.

(*i*) It should have a high specific heat, high heat conductivity and high film coefficient.

(*ii*) It should possess good lubricating properties to reduce frictional forces and to decrease the power consumption.

(*iii*) It should be odorless.

(*iv*) It should be non-corrosive to work and machine.

(*v*) It should be non-toxic to operating personnel.

(*vi*) It should have low viscosity to permit free flow of the liquid.

(*vii*) It should be stable in use and storage.

(*viii*) It should permit clear view of work which is specially desirable in precision work.

(*ix*) It should be safe particularly with regards to fire and accident hazards.

4.6. Types of Cutting Fluids

One way of improving the metal cutting operation is by using a cutting fluid. Cutting fluids mainly required to carry away heat and swarf are generally based on water. The additions of oils and emulsifying agents serves primarily to inhibit rusting although when the oil concentration is raised some lubrication effects are achieved. A cutting fluid mainly serves two functions.

(*i*) Cooling.

(*ii*) Lubrication

(*iii*) Antiwelding.

Cooling. The cooling function is achieved by supplying an adequate volume of cutting fluid to carry away the heat generated during cutting.

Lubrication. Lubricating the cutting tool reduces the coefficient of friction between chip and tool. This reduces the temperature and tool wear and therefore the cutting process becomes more economical.

All the cutting fluids can be divided into two groups.

(*i*) Water based fluids.

(*ii*) Straight or neat oil based fluids. Many additives are used in conjunction with each of these fluids to accomplish a variety of specific objectives. The most common gaseous cutting fluids are the oxygen and the water vapours in the ordinary atmosphere. In some machining operations are also plays an important role. The best cutting fluid is one that possesses good oiliness in addition to its cooling properties.

Antiwelding. The cutting fluid prevents intimate contact between the surface the chip and tool face. In spite of the lubricating and cooling action of cutting fluids there always exists some metal to metal contact between the tool and the chip and temperature high enough to weld the contacting asperities of the metal. It is prevented by adding compounds of sulphur, chlorine etc. to the cutting fluids. These compounds generate a soapy film which prevents particles of metal from welding.

4.6.1. Water based cutting fluids. Early attempts to improve cooling and lubricating properties of water included the addition of soft soap but there are now oils which have the desired effect and from emulsion and water. These oils are known as soluble oils. Water based cutting fluids are quite commonly used, the most popular being soluble oil (suds or slurry). Soluble oil (1 to 5%) is mixed with water to form an emulsion. This has excellent cooling properties at low cost and there is also some lubricating effect between tool and chip which reduces tool wear. Modern soluble oil contain corrosion inhibitor and a biocide to keep down the growth of bacteria that would otherwise become a health hazard. Less frequently used forms of water based cutting fluids are based on chemical solutions. Soda solutions are often used on grinding operations as it has good flushing action and cooling effect. Water itself is seldom used as it coolant as it causes rust and corrosion.

When water based fluids are used in conjunction with carbide tipped tools a sufficient stream of cutting fluid should be maintained otherwise the tool may be unevenly cooled and the carbide inserts may fail soon by a thermally induced fatigue. Care should be taken that a sufficient flow of fluid is applied at all points of high speed carbide cutters to prevent the temperature at a given point on the cutter from fluctuating appreciably.

4.6.2. Straight or neat oil based cutting fluids. The term straight when applied to lubricants and coolants means undiluted. However most of the oils are not used straight but are mixtures of oils or oil with chemicals such as sulphur and chlorine added to them. Straight or neat oils are classified into following subgroups.

(*i*) Mineral oils.

(*ii*) Straight fatty oils.

(*iii*) Compounded or blended oils.

(*iv*) Sulphurised oils.

(*v*) Chlorinated oils.

1. Mineral oils. Mineral oils are primarily composed of hydro carbons of different structures and molecular weights. These oils are normally used for light machining operations such as turret and capstan lathes and single spindle automatics where free cutting brasses and steels are being machined.

2. Straight fatty oils. The most important variety of straight fatty oils is lard oil. These oils are not stable and rapidly lose their lubricating properties. Neither are they satisfactory coolants as they have a high viscosity. Lard oil is mainly used during thread cutting with taps and dies. These oils are more expensive and less plentiful than mineral oils.

3. Compounded or blended oils. These are mixtures of mineral and fatty oils. The film strength of fatty oils is retained even when diluted with 75% mineral oil. As a result they are much cheaper and more fluid than neat fatty oils. They are suitable for heavier duty operations such as threading on capstan and turret lathes, thread milling and medium capacity automatic lathes.

4. Sulphurised oils. When sulphur (about 5%) is mixed in lard oil it is called sulphurised cutting oil. It is used for heavy duty lathe work, gear cutting and thread grinding.

Extreme pressure (E.P.) cutting oils are mineral oils containing extreme pressure additives like sulphur. Depending on the form in which sulphur is added there are mainly three types of sulphurised E.P. oils :

(*i*) Those containing combined sulphur

(*ii*) Those containing free sulphur.

(*iii*) Those containing both combined are free sulphur.

The first type of E.P. oils are called "In active oils" because they do not stain yellow metals whereas second and third type of E.P. oils mentioned above are called "Active oils" since they stain yellow metals.

5. Chlorinated oils. When chlorine (about 3%) is added in mineral oils it is called chlorinated cutting oil. When both chlorine and sulphur (upto 5%) are present in mineral oil they give the oil and extreme pressure property and are suitable for severe cutting operations on strong and tough materials such as stainless steels and nickel alloys. In broaching operation also these oils are quite commonly used.

4.7. Lubricants

Solid lubricants are employed in a finely divided state and are kept in suspension in the liquid vehicle by means of a depressing agent. Under certain conditions during metal cutting the lubricant reduces the friction on the tool face and thus reduction in power consumption, increase in tool life and improvement in surface finish of the machined surface by reducing the occurrence of a build up edge is achieved. A lubricant used in metal cutting should process the following properties.

(*i*) It should contain suitable reactive ingredients that on reaction with the work material forms a compound of lower shear strength that acts as a boundary lubricant.

(*ii*) It should be sufficiently unstable to be broken down under the temperature and pressure existing at the chip tool interface.

(*iii*) It should have a small molecular size in order to allow rapid diffusion and penetration to the chip tool interface. It should maintain a conventional hydrodynamic film between the chip and the tool face.

Carbon tetrachloride (CCL_4) chloroform ($CHCI_3$), trichloroethane (CH_3CCl_3) and certain other chlorinated hydrocarbons are quite commonly used lubricants when cutting metals at low speeds.

4.8. Selection of a Cutting Fluid

The cutting fluid should be carefully chosen. It is observed that each metal being machined and even each type of machining has its optimum cutting fluid. The selection of a particular type of cutting fluid depends on factors listed below.

(*i*) Cutting speed.

(*ii*) Feed rate.

(*iii*) Depth of cut.

(*iv*) Cutting tool material.

(*v*) Workpiece material.

(*vi*) Velocity of cutting fluid.

(vii) Expected cutting tool life.

(viii) Cost of cutting fluid.

(ix) The life of cutting fluid and loss of cutting fluid during operation.

Low speed and shallow cuts require little cooling or lubrication. A lubricant of considerable oiliness is required while machining tough metals at low speeds and heavy cuts. Shallow cuts at high speeds require good coolants therefore emulsions of soluble and sulphur base cutting oils are frequently employed. A lubricant that excels as a coolant as well as a lubricant is used for heavy cuts at high speeds. Brittle materials like cast iron are often cut without the use of a lubricant although emulsions of soluble oil in water are sometimes used.

Cutting lubricants may be applied by hand from a can, by a gravity feed drops system or by some medium of forced circulation such as centrifugal pump. While using pump care should be taken to filter effectively the lubricant that is returned order to prevent the chips from damaging the pump.

Table 4.1 shows the cutting fluids used during machining for some of workpiece materials.

Table 4.1

Material	*Turning*	*Tapping*	*Drilling*
Cast Iron	Machined dry	Machined Dry or 25% lard oil + 75% mineral oil	Machined dry
Tool and low carbon steels	25% to 70% lard oil mineral oil	20 to 40% lard oil + mineral oil	Soluble oil with 95% water
Alloy steel	25% Sulphur base oil+75% mineral oil	30% lard oil+ 70% mineral oil	Soluble oil with 80% water
Copper	Soluble oil with 90 to 95 % water		
Aluminium	Mineral oil with 10% soluble oil	Lord oil	Soluble oil with 75 to 90%.water

During metal cutting friction must be kept as low as possible to reduce the heat generated. Where the cutting operation is severe and the lubricant can not remove the heat rapidly enough, water soluble oils may be used. When mixed with a high concentration of water, the cooling effect is greatly increased with some lubricating properties retained. These mixtures do not corrode the steel parts with which they come into contact.

Generally following coolants and lubricants may be used for machining different metals.

(*i*) **For steels and wrought iron :** The water soluble oils or sulphur based and mineral oils may be used.

(*ii*) **For aluminium :** The mineral oils and fatty oils or soluble oils may be used.

(*iii*) **For brass, copper, bronze -monel metal and malleable iron :** The soluble oils may be used.

(*iv*) **Cast iron** : It is machined dry.

Lubricating oils are chiefly used to reduce friction and water soluble oils are used chiefly as coolants.

4.9. Cutting Fluid Penetration

The various properties of a cutting fluid which are considered to be essential for the penetration into the capillaries between the chip and tool are as follows :

(*i*) Wetting and spreading.

(*ii*) Surface tension.

(*iii*) Small fat molecules.

The molecules of the fluid should be more attracted to the surface than to each other so that cutting fluid spreads over the surface and wets the surface.

For efficient cooling it is necessary that the fluid penetrates as much as possible to the chip tool interface. Fig. 4.3 shows nature of chip tool interface where the hills and valleys that form a labyrinth of fine capillaries are shown to a greatly increased scale. Surface tension forces in the fluid and the action of pressure difference of one atmosphere due to the tendency to form a vacuous cavity as the tool penetrates the workpiece, will cause the fluid to flow between the capillaries and reach the tool point against the adverse motion of the chip. It would appear unlikely that the fluid can be in the form of a liquid as it penetrates the very fine labyrinth of capillaries. The material is probably carried to a point close to the tool point in the liquid state by capillary forces and is then converted to a vapour upon absorption of some of the heat generated by the cutting process. The vapour could then penetrate the capillaries, physically absorbing on the freshly cut nascent metal as it goes.

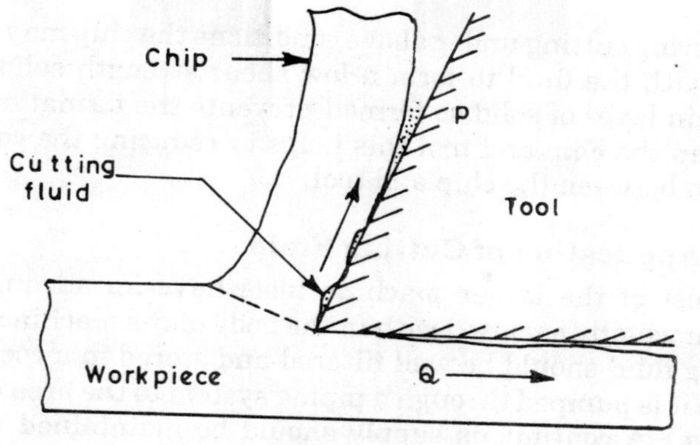

Fig. 4.3.

The field can enter at two pieces one at *P* and the other at *Q* as shown in Fig. 4.3. The motion of the chip across the tool face will tend to prevent fluid from reaching the tool tip from *P* and similarly the motion of the workpiece across the clearance surface of the tool will tend to prevent fluid from entering at *Q*. While the relative velocity of the surfaces at *B* will be more than that at *P* the distance of intimate contact to be traversed at *Q* will usually be much less than that at *P*. The net result is that there will usually be a greater tendency for penetration along the charance surface than along the tool face.

The penetration of the cutting fluid to the tool chip interface becomes difficult at high cutting speeds because of high relative velocity of chip over the cutting face of the tool. This tends to retard the motion of the fluid. In order that a cutting fluid works effectively at higher cutting speed at high velocity stream of fluid is used. Nozzles of 3.3 mm to 0.375 mm diameter are used to obtain high velocity stream of cutting fluid. A fluid of smaller particle size and lower surface tension can enter the voids between tool and chip more readily than a fluid of larger particle size and higher surface tension.

The fluid that finds its way into asperities between chip and tool in the vicinity of tool point is subjected to the following unique combination of conditions.

(*i*) High local temperature.

(*ii*) High local pressure approaching the hardness of the metal cut.

(*iii*) Smooth surface produced.

(*iv*) Highly stressed metal.

During cutting under above conditions the chip may be made to react with the fluid to form a low shear strength solid lubricant. The thin layer of solid so formed prevents the formation of a weld between the chip and tool this helps in reducing the coefficient of friction between the chip and tool.

4.10. Application of Cutting Fluid

Most of the larger machine tools have an adequate coolant system usually enclosed with in the body of the machine itself. The cutting fluid should be well filtered and stored in a cool area from where it is pumped through a piping system to the area of tool work contact. A continuous supply should be maintained at chip tool interface where heat and wear are produced. A intermittent supply of cutting fluid is not desirable because when the supply stops the temperature of the tool quickly rises and when the supply is maintained again it cools the tool which may lead to cracks at the cutting edge. It is preferable to direct a jet of cutting fluid to the cutting area. The stream of cutting fluid should be directed on the point of chip removal (Fig. 4.4) and delivered in a sufficient quantity (8 to 12 and at high speeds up to 20 litres/min.). A high lubricating and cooling effect is obtained if the cutting liquid is mixed with compressed air at a pressure of about 1.5 to 2 kg/cm^2 and supplied through a nozzle, directed at the tool flank. The liquid delivered thus in the atomised state not only reduces friction and facilitates chip formation but removes heat more intensively.

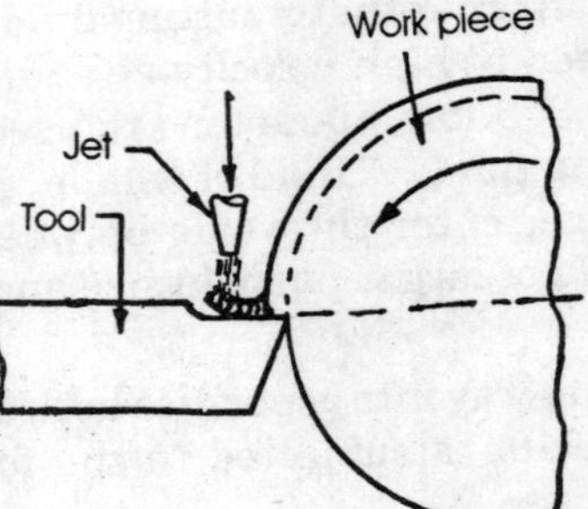

(*a*)

Fig. 4.4.

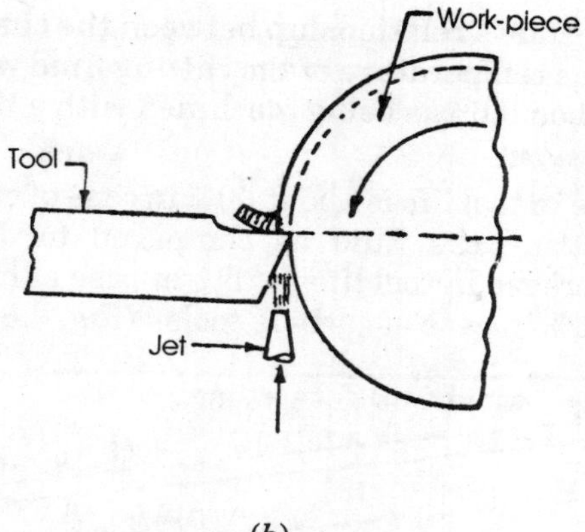

(*b*)
Fig. 4.4.

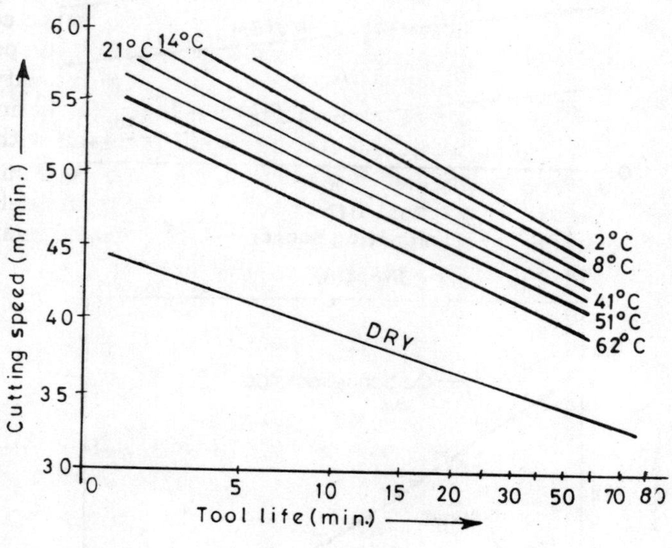

Fig. 4.5.

4.11. Effect of Cutting Fluid on Cutting Speed and Tool Life

Cutting fluids also affect the cutting speed permitted by the cutting tool. The cutting speed can be increased by about 40% in comparison to machining dry if the emulsion cutting fluid is cooled to + 2°C before used. Lower the temperature of the cutting fluid and the farther the curve is from the line representing dry machining the higher the cutting speed permitted by the tool for the same tool life. Fig. 4.5 shows relationship between the cutting speed and tool life at various temperature of the cutting fluid when structural steel having carbon 0.6% is being machined with a high speed steel tool.

The increase in tool life is about 50% in case of carbon tool steel when using cutting the fluid as compared to dry machining. Whereas the increase in tool life is 25% in case of high speed steel tools and 5 to 10% in case of carbide tools. (Fig. 4.6).

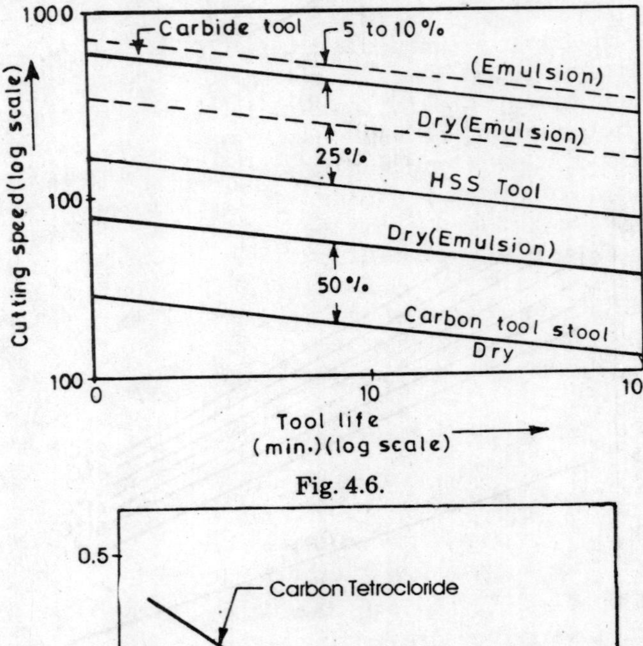

Fig. 4.6.

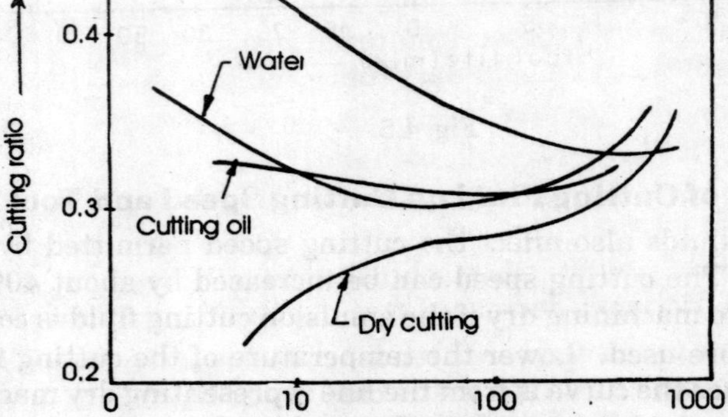

Fig. 4.7.

Tests made by Earnst and Merchant on a variety of cutting fluids shows that use of cutting fluids generally increases the chip thickness ratio (cutting ratio) but that the effect within the normal cutting speed range falls as the cutting speed is increased. A relationship between cutting ratio and cutting speed and various cutting fluids is shown in Fig. 4.7. It is observed from these results that the depth of penetration of cutting fluid into the area of contact where friction occurs falls with the increase in cutting speed.

4.12. Maintenance of Cutting Fluid

One of the important aspect of cutting fluid is its maintenance which is often neglected. From the point of view of both production efficiency and hygenic working conditions it is essential to pay due attention to the quality of water used, preparation of emulsion, concentration control of emulsion, filteration, prevention of tramp oil etc. Poor maintenance of cutting fluids leads to bad odour and bacterial growth thereby spoiling the working environments. For effective and easy maintenance of cutting fluids centralised coolant systems are now finding wider acceptance. It is advisable to exercise greater care on control in disposing of used cutting fluids to preserve the ecology and water resources. Neat oils can be recycled and reused. Emulsions must be slipt into water and oil before they are disposed off.

4.13. Characteristics of a Lubricant

The various characteristics of an efficient lubricant used in metal cutting are as follows as:

(*i*) It should have a small molecular size to allow rapid diffusion and penetration to the chip tool interface.

(*ii*) It should be sufficiently unstable to be broken down under the temperature and pressure existing at the chip tool interface.

(*iii*) The lubricant should have a suitable reactive ingredient which on reaction with the work material forms a compound of lower shear strength that as a boundary lubricant.

The commonly used lubricants are carbon tetrachloride (CCl_4) chloroform ($CHCl_3$) and trichloroethane (CH_3CCl_3).

4.14. Tool Friction

The surface finish of a machined surface is improved when coefficient of friction is decreased.

This is due to the decreased tendency to form a built up edge as the cutting forces and strain in the chip are reduced both of which result when the coefficient of friction is decreased. The coefficient of friction between chip and tool in metal cutting operation may be reduced in the following ways :

(*i*) By using fluids.

(*ii*) By improving surface finish of tool face.

(*iii*) By using free machining additions to steel.

(*iv*) Change of tool material.

(*v*) By increasing cutting speed (some times).

4.15. Effect of Cutting Fluid on Chip Concentration

Surface active cutting fluids greatly affect the chip formation by changing the stressed state in the deformation zone and facilitate disintegration. Fig. 4.8 shows the effect of various surface active cutting fluids in reduction of chip contraction. The various curves are between coefficient of chip contraction. (K) and uncut chip thickness (t_2).

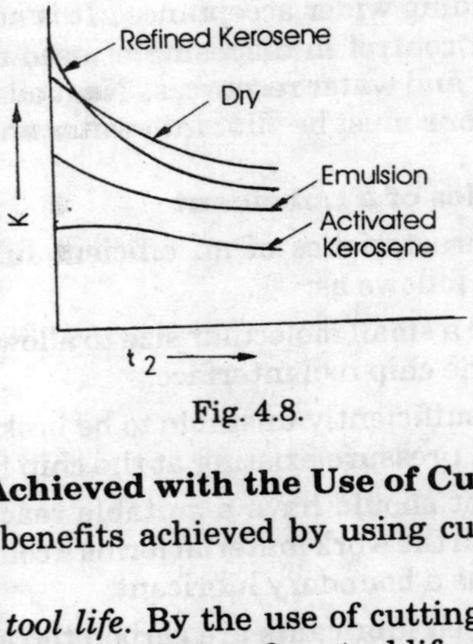

Fig. 4.8.

4.16. Benefits Achieved with the Use of Cutting Fluids

The various benefits achieved by using cutting fluids are as follows :

(*i*) *Increased tool life.* By the use of cutting fluids the cutting temperature is reduced and therefore, tool life gets increased.

(*ii*) *Better surface finish.* By using cutting fluids better surface finish can be obtained.

(*iii*) *Lower tool forces.* By using cutting fluids, the coefficient of friction between chip and tool face is reduced and this reduces the tool forces.

(*iv*) Finished surfaces are protected from corrosion.

(*v*) Better dimensional stability of work piece is obtained.

Example 4.1. *Under certain machining conditions the power required is 0.05 H.P. / cm^3 / min when the cutting speed is 24 metre / minute depth of cut is 6 mm and feed is 0.25 mm / rev. The work is cooled by a flow of 2 kg / min of coolant having a specific heat of 0.82. If 80% of heat produced is taken away by the coolant, calculate the rise in the temperature of coolant.*

Solution. w = Metal removed per minute

= *Feed* × Depth of Cut × Cutting speed

= 0.025 × 0.6 × 24 × 100

= 36cm³/min.

Horse power consumed in cutting

= 0.05 × 36 = 1.8

Heat produced per minute

$$= 1.8 \times 4500 \times \frac{2.34}{10^3} = 19 \text{ kcal.}$$

Heat taken away by the coolant

= 19 × 0.8 = 15.2 kcal.

Let, W = Weight of coolant supplied per minute = 2kg

W × Specific heat × Rise in temperature

= 15.2

∴ Rise in temperature

$$= \frac{15.2}{2 \times 0.82}$$

= 9.3° **C. Ans.**

Example 4.2. *A machining operation is cooled by soluble oil having a specific heat capacity of 2800 J/kg°C flowing at the rate of 50 litres / min. If 12 kW is being absorbed at the cutting point and 85% of the heat generated is taken away by the cooling oil, determine its rise in temperature. (1 litre = 0.9 kg).*

Solution. Assuming all the power to be dissipated as heat at the cutting point we have

Heat generated /min = 12 kW

= 12,000 J × 60 s

= 720,000 joules

Heat taken away by the coolant

= 0.85 × 720,000

= 612,000 joules

Heat taken up by the coolant

$$= \text{Mass} \times \text{Sp. heat} \times \text{Rise in temp.}$$

$$= (50 \times 0.9) \times (2800) \times (\text{Rise in temp.})\ J$$

$$612{,}000 = 50 \times 0.9 \times 2800 \times \text{Rise in temp.}$$

Rise in temperature

$$= 4.9°C.$$ **Ans.**

Example 4.3. *Compare the cooling, lubricating and anti-welding properties of the following cutting fluids :*

(*i*) *Water*

(*ii*) *Mineral oil*

(*iii*) *Fatty oil*

(*iv*) *E.P. cutting oil.*

Solution. The properties are compared are follows :

Cutting fluid	*Cooling properties*	*Lubricating properties*	*Anti-welding properties*
Water	Excellent	Poor	Poor
Mineral oil	Fairly good	Good	Fair
Fatty oil	Fair	Excellent	Fair
E.P. cutting oil	Fair	Good	Excellent

Example 4.4. *During orthogonal cutting of a mild steel work piece the following data was obtained.*

Cutting force = 900 N

Thrust force = 670 N

Cutting speed = 2 m/s

Underformed chip thickness = 0.26 mm

Width of cut = 2.8 mm

Chip thickness ratio (cutting ratio)

= 0.32

Back Rake angle of tool = *zero degree*

Length of contact between chip and tool

= 0.8 mm

Determine (a) Heat generated due to shearing

(*b*) *Maximum temperature along the tool face*

Solution.

$$r = \text{Chip thickness ratio}$$
$$= 0.32$$
$$\alpha = \text{Back rake angle}$$
$$= 0 \text{ degree}$$
$$V = \text{Cutting speed}$$
$$= 2 \text{ m/s}$$
$$F_H = \text{Cutting force}$$
$$= 900 \text{ N}$$
$$F_V = \text{Feed (Thrust) force}$$
$$= 670 \text{ N}$$
$$b = \text{Width of cut}$$
$$= 2.8 \text{ mm} = 0.0028 \text{ m}$$
$$H = \text{Total heat generated during cutting}$$
$$= F_H \times V \quad = 900 \times 2 \quad = 1800 \text{ J/S}$$

H_1 = Rate of heat generated by friction between chip and tool

$$= P \times V_C$$

where V_c = Velocity of chip relative to tool

$$= r \times v$$
$$= 0.32 \times 2$$
$$P = \text{Frictional force}$$
$$= F_V \text{ as rake angle is zero}$$
$$H_1 = 670 \times 0.32 \times 2$$
$$= 428 \text{ J/S}$$
$$H_2 = \text{Heat rate from shearing}$$
$$H = H_1 + H_2$$
$$1800 = 428 + H_2$$
$$H_2 = 1372 \text{ J/S}$$
$$T = T_1 + T_2 + T_3$$

where T = Maximum temperature along tool face

T_1 = Temperature rise of material passing through primary deformation zone.

T_2 = Temperature rise of material passing through the secondary deformation zone.

T_3 = Initial temperature of the workpiece.

R = Thermal Number

L = Length of heat source divided by chip thickness

$$= \frac{L_1}{t_2}$$

where L_1 = Length of contact between chip and tool

$= 0.8$ mm.

$$r = \frac{t_1}{t_2}$$

where t_1 = Undeformed chip thickness = 0.26 mm

t_2 = Chip thickness after cutting

$$t_2 = \frac{t_1}{r} = \frac{0.26}{0.32}$$

$$L = \frac{L_1}{t_2}$$

$$L = \frac{0.8 \times .32}{.26} = 0.98$$

$$R = \frac{\rho \,.\, C \,.\, V \,.\, t_1}{K}$$

where ρ = Density of steel

$= 7200$ kg/m^3 (Assume)

C = Specific heat capacity

$= 500$ J/kg K.

K = Thermal conductivity

$= 43.5$ J/Sm k

$$t_1 = \frac{0.26}{1000} \text{ m} = .00026$$

$$R = 7200 \times 500 \times 2 \times \frac{0.26}{1000} \times \frac{1}{43.5} = 43$$

$$T_1 = \frac{(1-p) \times H_2}{\rho \,.\, C \,.\, v \,.\, t_1 \,.\, b}$$

where p = Proportion of shearing heat conducted into the workpiece

$= 0.1$

$$T_1 = \frac{(1-0.1) \times 1372}{7200 \times 500 \times 2 \times 0.00026 \times 0.0028}$$

$= 235.5$°C.

It is the mean temperature rise in the primary deformation zone and since it is a temperature difference can be expressed in either centigrade (°*C*) or degree Kelvin (°*K*).

T_4 = Average temperature rise of the chip resulting from secondary deformation (Frictional heat source)

$$= \frac{H_1}{\rho \, . \, C \, . \, V. \, t. \, b}$$

$$= \frac{428}{7200 \times 500 \times 2 \times 0.00026 \times 0.0028}$$

$$= \frac{428}{5.24} = 81.7°\text{C}$$

Now $$\frac{R}{L} = \frac{43}{0.98} = 43.87$$

The value of $\frac{T_2}{T_4}$ depends on the values of $\frac{R}{L}$ and width of secondary deformation zone.

A typical value of $\frac{T_2}{T_4} = 4.2$ when $\frac{R}{L} = 43.87$

$$\frac{T_2}{T_4} = 4.2$$

$$T_2 = 4.2 \times T_4$$

$$= 4.2 \times 81.7 = 343°C$$

$$T_3 = \text{Initial temperature of work piece}$$

$$= \text{Room temperature} = 25°C \text{ (say)}$$

$$T = T_1 + T_2 + T_3$$

$$= 235.5 + 343 + 25 = 603.5° \text{ C}$$

PROBLEMS

4.1. (*a*) What are the sources of heat generation in metal cutting ?

(*b*) Show with the aid of a simple sketch the areas of heat generation that occur when using a single point cutting tool on a tathe.

4.2. (*a*) State the functions of a cutting fluid.

(*b*) What are the essential properties of a cutting fluid ?

4.3. Explain the following types of cutting fluids :

(*a*) Water based cutting fluids.

(*b*) Straight or neat oil based cutting fluids.

4.4. Write short notes on the following :

(*a*) Selection of a cutting fluid.

(*b*) Application of cutting fluid.

(*c*) Maintenance of cutting fluids.

4.5. Describe the effect of cutting fluid on cutting speed and tool life.

4.6. Explain the cutting fluid penetration during metal cutting.

4.7. How does a lubricant and cutting fluid differ from each other.

4.8. Describe tool friction.

4.9. (*a*) State the characteristics of a lubricant used in metal cutting.

(*b*) Name the commonly used lubricants.

4.10. Explain the effect of cutting fluids on chip contraction.

4.11. Write short notes on the following :

(*i*) Benefits achieved with the use of cutting fluids.

(*ii*) E.P. cutting oils.

5

Grinding and Surface Finish

5.1. Grinding

It is a metal cutting process, that employs an abrasive tool called grinding wheel. The cutting elements of grinding wheel are grains of abrasive material having high hardness and a high heat resistance. They have sharp edges and are held together by bonding materials. Grinding provides high accuracy and a good surface finish. Therefore it is used as a finishing operation. This process removes comparatively little material usually from 0.25 mm to 0.5 mm. Tolerances as small as 0.0025 mm can be obtained by commercial grinding.

During grinding temperature rises with the increased wear of grains which may lead to distortion of workpiece structural changes and crack formation in the ground surface. Hence an abundant flow of coolant is commonly used in grinding. The coolant also slows down softening of wheel bond which is due to heating.

The various cutting fluids used in grinding steel are as follows:

(*i*) A one per cent solution of soda ash with 0.15 per cent sodium nitrite.

(*ii*) A two per cent aqueous solution of powdered soap.

(*iii*) A 3.5% aqueous solution of a neutral paste type emulsion with an oleinic acid base.

Cast iron and copper are often ground dry. Aluminium is ground by using kerosene with or without the addition of mineral oil as coolant.

The grinding process has certain specific features as follows :

(*i*) As the abrasive grains are some distance apart a grinding wheel has an interrupted cutting edge and not a continuous one as on a milling cutter.

(*ii*) A grinding wheel can be self sharpening during the course of the grinding process.

(*iii*) The process of chip removal by a grain takes place in a very short period.

(*iv*) Due to the pyramidal and rounded shape of the cutting element of the abrasive grains the thickness and width of the uncut chip are inter-related in grinding.

A grinding wheel can be compared to a milling cutter both having the following similarities.

(*i*) Both have a number of cutting edges, each cutting edge having adequate rake and clearance angles.

(*ii*) Each cutting edge is in action only for a short time.

(*iii*) The chip formation process in grinding is similar to cutting by the tooth of a milling cutter. The chip has the same structure and appearance as obtained in milling. Adequate chip space is available for a free cutting action. In the case of a grinding wheel the chip space is available between bonded abrasive particles.

The process of grinding is dependent upon the following inherent properties of the grinding wheel :

(*i*) Type of abrasive

(*ii*) Size and distribution of grits

(*iii*) Amount and type of bond material

(*iv*) Volume of pores relative to that of grits and bonds.

5.2. Abrasive Materials

Materials used as the cutting grains are of two types.

(*a*) Natural abrasives.

(*b*) Artificial or manufactured abrasives.

Natural Abrasives. They include sand stone, diamond, corundum and emery. The principal component of corrundum and emery is natural aluminium oxide (alumina). Corrundum is composed of about 85% aluminium oxide and 15% iron oxide. Emery contains 60% aluminum oxide and 40% iron oxide. The relative abrasive action of each substance depends upon the properties of aluminium oxide.

Diamond abrasive wheels are used extensively for sharpening carbide and ceramic cutting tools. Diamonds are also used for truing and dressing other types of abrasive wheels. Because of their high cost, diamonds are used only when other cheaper abrasives will not produce the desired result.

Artificial Abrasives. They include silicon carbide (SiC) and aluminium oxide (Al_2O_3). Silicon carbide is made by charging an electrical furnace with silica sand, coke, salt and sawdust. A temperature of over 2300°C is maintained for several hours obtained by passing heavy current through the charge and a solid mass of silicon carbide results. After the furnace has cooled the mass of crystals is removed, crushed and graded to various desired sizes. Silicon carbide is very hard (though less than boron carbide and diamond). It has high heat resistance and excellent cutting properties. Two types of silicon carbide is available, namely black and green. The black silicon carbide is of lower quality and contains about 95% SiC. Green silicon carbide is some whât harder and has a high grinding capacity and contains at least 97% SiC.

Green silicon carbide is mainly used for sharpening carbide tipped cutting tools.

Aluminium oxide abrasive is the crystalline form of aluminium oxide (Al_2O_3). It is produced in an arc furnace from bauxite, iron filings and small amount of coke. The mass of aluminium that is formed is crushed and the particles are graded to size. It is softer than silicon carbide but it is considerably tougher and is a more general purpose abrasive. Common trade names for aluminium oxide abrasives are Alundum and Aloxite.

The physical properties of the material to be cut dictate the kind of abrasive to be selected. As a general guide silicon carbide is used for grinding brittle materials and materials of low tensile strength such as cemented carbides, cast iron, ceramics and low tensile strength metals including brass, soft bronze, and copper. Aluminium oxide having less brittle grains is used for tougher and higher strength material such as steel, wrought iron, hardened steel, alloy steel and hard brass and bronze.

In general the physical properties of aluminium oxide compared with silicon carbide are as follows :

(*i*) Silicon carbide is harder than aluminium oxide.

(*ii*) Aluminium oxide can withstand greater stresses than silicon carbide.

(*iii*) Aluminium oxide is more tough than silicon carbide.

(*iv*) Aluminium oxide wheels are generally used for grinding high tensile strength and tough materials whereas silicon carbide wheels are used to grind low tensile strength and non-metallic materials.

5.2.1. Abrasive Grain Size. Abrasive materials are crushed in ball mills and screened for classification into different sizes. The size of abrasive grain required in a grinding wheel depends on the following factors :

(*i*) Amount of material to be removed.

(*ii*) Finish desired.

(*iii*) Hardness of material being ground.

The grit or grain size of an abrasive is denoted by a number representing the number of meshes per inch of the screen through which the grains of crushed abrasives are passed for grinding. The standard grains sizes for grinding wheels are represented in Table 5.1.

Table 5.1

Grit Designation					*Grain Size or Grit Number*		
Coarse	10	12	14	16	20	24	
Medium	30	36	46	54	60		
Fine	80	100	120	150	180		
Very fine	220	240	280	320	400	500	600

The coarser grit will remove the stock at a faster rate and finer finish will require a finer grit.

Sizes from 240 to 600 are designated as flour sizes. These are primarily used for lapping and honing stones.

5.2.2. Bonds. Bonding materials are used as binders to hold the abrasive particles in place. The firmness with which the grains are held in the wheel and the strength of wheel itself in which large centrifugal forces are developed in rotation depend on the bonding material. The bonding material determines whether the wheel is rigid or flexible. It also determines the force that is required to dislodge an abrasive particle from the wheel which plays a major role in the cutting action.

Six types of bonding materials are commonly used.

(*i*) **Vitrified Bond.** Vitrified bond is made of clay and water. The abrasive grains and clay are thoroughly mixed together with sufficient water to make the mixture uniform. The material is formed into a wheel usually by pressing and then these wheels are dried. They then are fired in a kiln which results in the bonding material becoming hard and strong. Vitrified bonds are used most extensively. Vitrified abrasive wheels have a high production capacity, and are moisture proof.

About 75% of grinding wheels have vitrified bonds.

(ii) **Resinoid Bond.** Resinoid bonding is produced by mixing abrasive grains with synthetic resins. Resinoid bonded wheels are strong, elastic and permit high peripheral speeds but are destroyed by alkaline cooling fluids. This can be avoided by impregnating the wheel with paraffin. These wheels normally operate at surface speeds in the region of 300 m/min. They are particularly suitable for use in grinding steel, cast iron and malleable iron castings.

(iii) **Shellac Bond.** Shellac bonded wheels are made by mixing the abrasive grains with shellac in a mixer. After the mixture has been rolled or pressed into desired wheel shapes they are then hardened by baking for several hours at about 160°C. Thin wheels that are strong but possess some elasticity have shellac bond. They can produce high polish and are used in grinding such parts as camshafts and mill rolls.

(iv) **Rubber Bond.** A rubber bond is essentially a mixture of rubber softened by gasoline and sulphur (30%). A rubber bonded wheel has high strength and elasticity and is moisture proof. They are commonly used for snagging work in foundries and for thin cut-off wheels.

(v) **Silicate Bond.** This bond is produced by mixing abrasive grains with silicate of soda (water glass). The mixture is given the desired wheel shape and baked at about 260°C for a day or more. The silicate bonded wheels are soft, comparatively weak and have low production capacity. Such wheels has limited applications.

(vi) **Oxy Chloride Bond.** This bond is produced by mixing abrasive grains with oxide and chloride of magnesium.

Different types of bonds used in grinding are represented by different symbol as shown in table 5.2.

Table 5.2

Types of bond	*Symbol*
Vitrified bond	*V*
Resinoid bond	*B*
Shellac bond	*E*
Rubber bond	*R*
Silicate bond	*S*
Oxy chloride bond	*O*

5.2.3. Grade. Grade or hardness indicates the strength, with which the bonding material holds the abrasive grains in the grinding wheel. The easier a grain is torn out of the bond, the softer the wheel and *vice versa*. The degrees of hardness are specified by the use of latters of the alphabet. Different grades of grinding wheels are shown in table 5.3.

Table 5.3

Soft	A	B	C	D	E	F	G	H		
Medium	I	J	K	L	M	N	O	P		
Hard	Q	R	S	T	U	V	W	X	Y	Z

The grinding wheel of required grade should be selected for each grinding job. The selection of a particular grade of wheel is largely governed by the nature of work, its composition, size and hardness. Hard wheels are used for softer materials and *vice versa*.

5.2.4. Structure. It indicates the spacing between the abrasive grains or in other words density of the wheel. Structure of grinding wheel is designated by a number. The higher the number of wider the spacing. It is observed that the tendency for burns to appear on the ground surface is reduced when a wheel of more open structure is used. Table 5.4 indicates the two types of structure with their numbers.

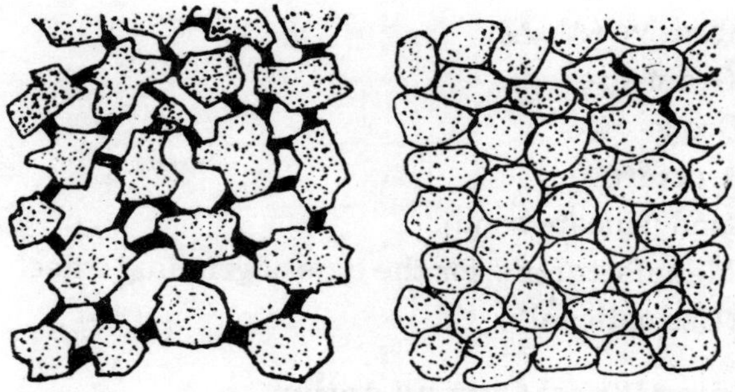

Fig. 5.1.

Fig. 5.1 shows open and dense structure.

Table 5.4.

Structure	*Symbol*
Dense	1 2 3 4 5 6 7 8
Open	9 10 11 12 13 14 15 or more

5.2.5. Marking System of Grinding Wheels. The Indian standards Institution (IS : 551--1954) has specified a standard system of marking the grinding wheels. According to this system the following elements are represented in a definite order :

1. Abrasive
2. Grain size of Grit
3. Grade
4. Structure
5. Bond.

In addition to this manufacturer may add some symbol to indicate the abrasive used.

Apart from the above information diameter of grinding wheel its thickness and bore diameter should also be mentioned.

A grinding wheel with the markings 300 × 30 × 35 W A 36 M 5 S 17 will have the following specifications :

Wheel diameter = 300 mm

Wheel thickness = 30 mm

Bore diameter = 35 mm

W – Manufacture's symbol for abrasive used (Use optional)

A – Abrasive (Al_2O_3)
36 – Grain size
M – Grade
5 – Structure
S – Bond (silicate bond).
17 – Manufacturer's for the type of grinding wheel
(Use optional)

5.3. Grinding Wheel Cutting Action

During cutting action of a grinding wheel the spacing of the abrasive particles and the effect of the bonding material which holds them in the wheel are very important. Each exposed grain constitutes a small cutting edge thus providing a multiplicity of cutting edges, some having positive rake angles and others having negative rake angles. Each cutting edge acts exactly the same as any other cutting edge under similar conditions with chips being formed (Fig. 5.2). As the cutting edges are small therefore the chips produced are also small. Feed and depth of cut should also be small. In order to achieve close tolerances and excellent surface finish large number of cutting edges small depth of cut and small feed should be used.

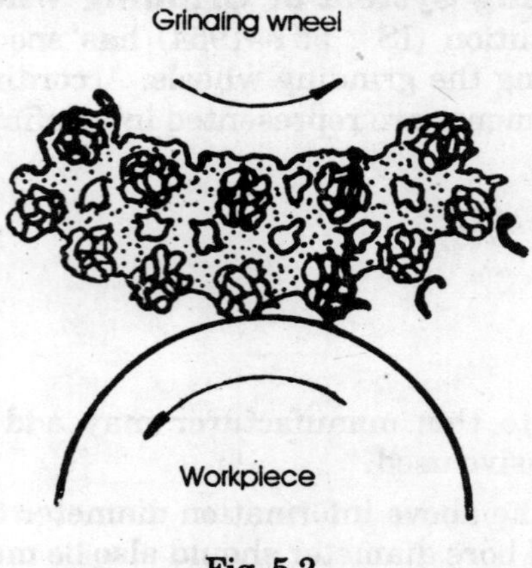

Fig. 5.2.

5.4. Grinding Wheel Selection

In order to achieve optimum results the proper grinding wheel should be selected for a given job. The shape of grinding wheel should be such that it permits proper contact between wheel and the surface to be ground. The size of the grinding machine and the cutting speed for the wheel. The grinding wheel should be of proper abrasive, grain size structure grade and bond. Various factors on which the selection of grinding wheel depends are as follows :

(*i*) Properties of material to be ground such as material, hardness, strength and toughness. Hard dense materials require a relatively soft grade of wheel, hard brittle materials require fine grain or closely spaced abrasives very hard material such as tungsten carbide require widely spaced abrasive wheel to permit rapid release of worm abrasive particles since the material ground is as hard as abrasive. Aluminium oxide wheels are commonly used for materials of high tensile strength, where the materials is neither very brittle nor easily penetrated such as carbon, alloy and high speed steels and wrought iron and tough bronzes. Silicon carbide wheels are used for materials of low tensile strength such as brasses, aluminium, glass and marble.

(*ii*) Amount of material to be removed.

(*iii*) Type of surface finish desired.

(*iv*) Dimensional accuracy required.

(*v*) Rigidity of the grinding machine.

(*vi*) Method and type of grinding.

(*vii*) The area of contact between the work and the wheel.

According to IS : 1249--1958 the following grinding wheels are recommended for different materials :

Table 5.5

Material to be grounded	*Cylindrical grinding*	Surface grinding	Internal grinding
	Specification of grinding wheels.		
Hardened Steel	A 60 LV	A 46 KV	A 24 JV
Soft Steel	A 54 MV	A 46 MV	A 46 JV
Cast Iron	C 46 KV	C 46 JV	C 36 JV

5.5. Shapes of Grinding Wheels

Grinding wheels are manufactured in various standard shapes. Different shapes of grinding wheels are as shown in Fig. 5.3. Straight, recessed on one side and recessed both sides wheels are used primarily for grinding external or internal cylindrical surface and for plain surface grinding. The cylinder shaped wheel is used for producing flat surfaces the grinding being done with the end face of the wheel. Straight cup wheel is used for grinding flat surfaces by traversing the work fast the end or face of the wheel. Flaring cup wheel is used for tool sparpening. Grinding wheels tapered on two sides are used for grinding the gear teeth and threads. Dish type are used for grinding tools saws. Straight grinding wheels can be obtained with a variety of standard faces some of these are shown in Fig. 5.4.

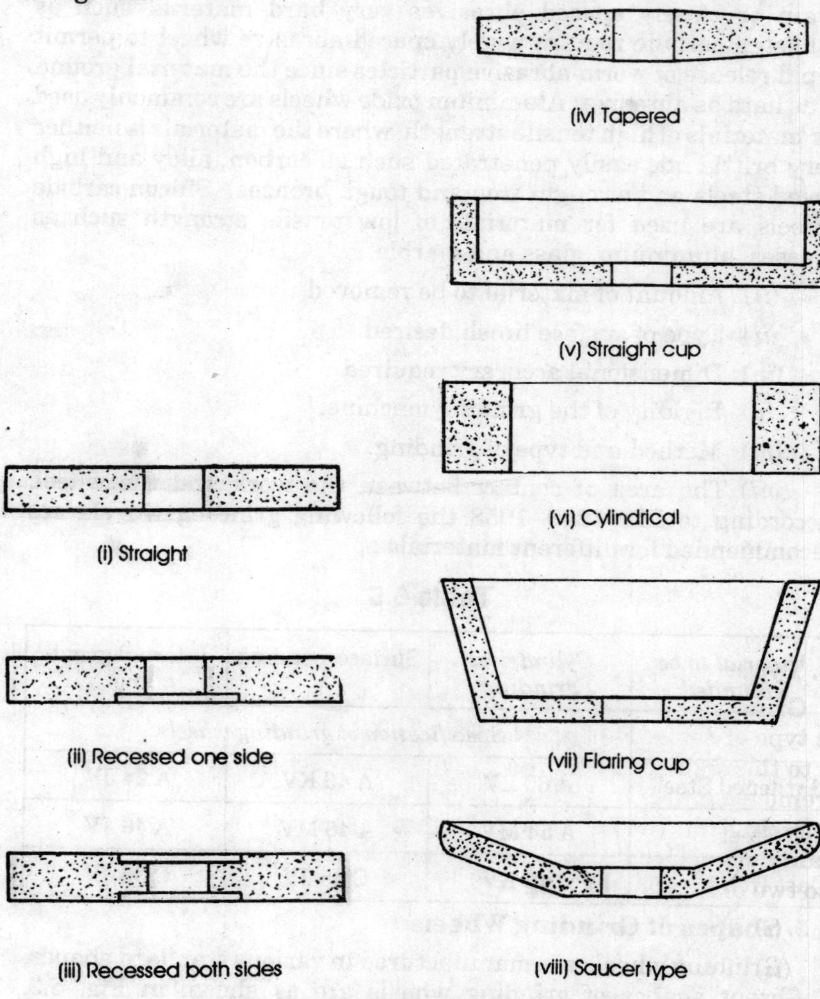

Fig. 5.3. Standard grinding wheel shapes.

5.5.1. Mounted wheels and points. They are small grinding wheels of different shapes. They are attached to metal shanks that can be inserted in the chucks of portable high speed electric motors. Fig. 5.5 shows some mounted wheels and points.

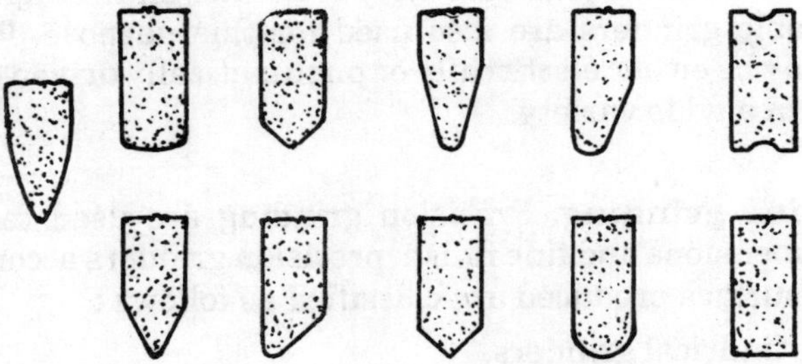

Fig. 5.4. Standard shapes of grinding wheel faces.

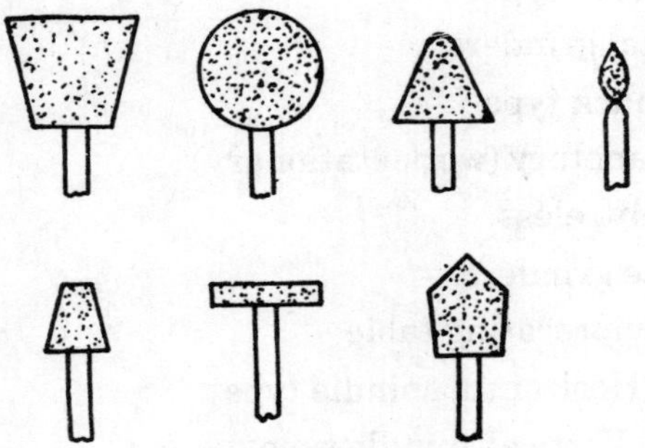

Fig. 5.5. Mounted points.

5.6. Types of Grinding Machines and Processes

Grinding machines can probably be best classified according to the type of surfaces they are used to produce. In order to bring the job to the required shape, size and surface finish the surplus stock is removed either by feeding the job against the revolving wheel or by forcing the revolving wheel against the job. According to the quality of surface finish produced grinding machines are classified into two groups.

(*i*) Rough grinders.

(*ii*) Precision grinders.

Rough Grinders. These grinders are used to produce rough surfaces and the accuracy in dimensions is not high. The various grinders used for rough grinding are swing frame grinders, bench grinder and portable grinder. Pedestal types or swing frame grinders, are usually used for snagging. Snagging is a type of rough grinding that is done in a foundry to remove fins, gates, risers and rough spots from castings preparatory to further machining. Sometimes portable grinders are also used for this purpose. Portable grinders may be either electrically or pneumatically driven and are obtainable in a wide variety.

Precision grinding. Precision grinding are used to obtain accurate dimensions and fine finish, precision grinders according to the type of surface produced are classified as follows :

(*i*) Cylindrical grinders.
- (*a*) Centre type
- (*b*) Centreless
- (*c*) Chuck type.

(*ii*) Internal grinders.
- (*a*) Chuck type
- (*b*) Planetary (work stationary)
- (*c*) Centreless.

(*iii*) Surface grinders.
- (*a*) Reciprocating table
  - (*i*) Horizontal spindle type
  - (*ii*) Vertical spindle type
- (*b*) Rotating table
  - (*i*) Horizontal spindle type
  - (*ii*) Vertical spindle type.

(*iv*) Tool and cutter grinder.
- (*a*) Universal
- (*b*) Special.

Precision grinding machines should be used with care and be operated by shilled personnel. Such machine can be operated economically only if they have high use factor. As these machines are used to produce products that have close dimensional tolerances they must be constructed very accurately. Their frames should be heavy and rigid to assure permanency of alignment. Rotating parts should be accurately balanced to avoid vibration. Spindles should be mounted in very accurate bearings usually of the preloaded ball bearing type. Controls should be provided in order that all movements that determine dimensions of the workpiece can be made with accuracy. The abrasive dust produced during grinding should not enter between the moving parts.

5.6.1. Cylindrical grinders. Centre type cylindrical grinders are quite commonly used to produce external cylindrical surfaces. (Fig. 5.6). It is equipped with head-stock and tail-stock. The workpiece is mounted and rotated between centres. The grinding wheel rotates. Grinding wheel and the workpiece move in the opposite direction at their point of contact. The depth of cut is determined by the infeed of the wheel or workpiece. Provision is made to transverse the workpiece with respect to wheel. In large grinders the wheel is reciprocated because of the massiveness of work. The cylindrical grinder is provided with two tables. The upper table may be swiveled about a centre point for taper grinding. The lower table slides on ways on the bed and provides traverse of the work past the grinding wheel.

In cylindrical grinding two types of grinding is carried out.

(*i*) Traverse grinding

(*ii*) Plunge grinding.

In traverse grinding the work is reciprocated as the wheel feeds to produce cylinders longer than the width of wheel face. In plunge grinding the wheel is fed to the workpiece rotating in a fixed position and grinding is carried out on workpiece in a length equal to or shorter than the width of grinding wheel. This method is used in grinding for relatively short work and especially in form grinding. The output is very high in plunge grinding. Fig. 5.7 shows traverse grinding and plun~e grinding is shown in Fig. 5.8.

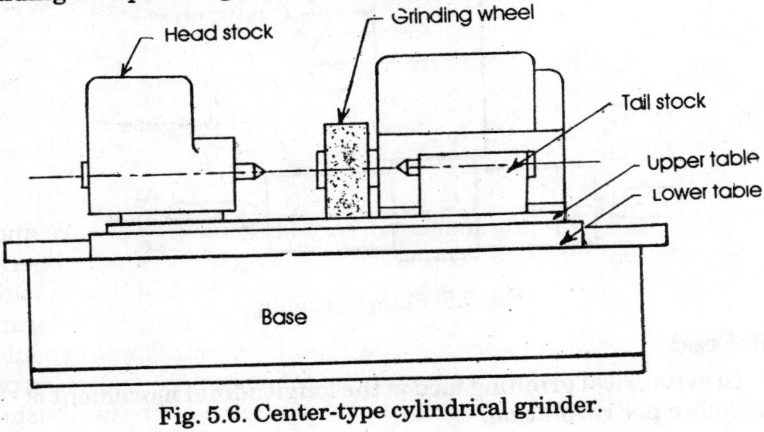

Fig. 5.6. Center-type cylindrical grinder.

5.7. Depth of Cut

It is the thickness of metal removed by the grinding wheel in one traverse stroke (lengthwise).

$$t = \text{Depth of cut}$$

$$= \frac{D_1 - D_2}{2}$$

where D_1 = Diameter of workpiece before grinding

D_2 = Diameter of workpiece after grinding

In finish grinding depth of cut is taken as 0.005 to 0.015 mm per stroke. Other conditions being equal the best surface finish is obtained in grinding with higher speeds of wheel rotation, lower rates of traverse, and smaller depths of cut.

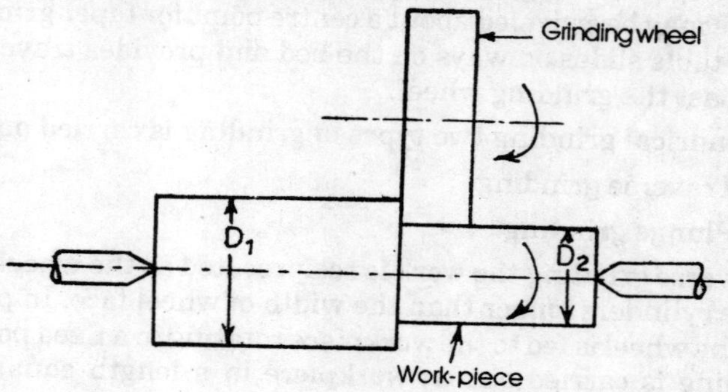

Fig. 5.7. Traverse grinding.

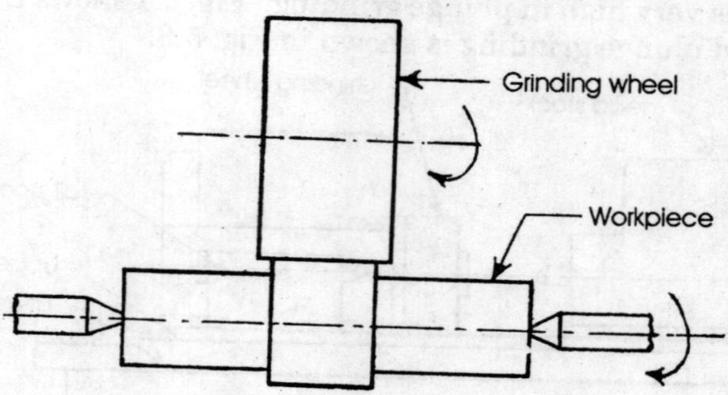

Fig. 5.8. Plunge grinding.

5.8. Feed

In cylindrical grinding feed is the longitudinal movement of the workpiece per revolution.

f = feed in mm per workpiece revolution

$= K_1 B$

where B = Face width of wheel in mm

K_1 = Constant
= 0.4 to 0.6 for finish grinding
= 0.6 to 0.9 for finish grinding

Work table traverse in metre/minute

$$= \frac{f \times N}{1000}$$

where N = Workpiece speed in R.P.M.

5.9. Cutting Speed

It is relative speed of wheel (V_1) and the workpiece. It is expressed in m/sec.

$$V = \text{Cutting speed} = V_1 = \frac{\pi D N_1}{1000 \times 60}$$

where D = Diameter of grinding wheel in mm.
N_1 = Speed of wheel in R.P.M.

5.10. Machining Time

Machining time in traverse cylindrical grinding is given by the formula

$$T = \text{Machining time } = \frac{L \cdot h}{N \cdot ft} \cdot K.$$

where L = Length ground in mm
h = Allowance on each side in mm.
f = Longitudinal feed in mm/rev.
N = R.P.M. of workpiece
t = Depth of cut (Rate of infeed per stroke) in mm
K = Accuracy factor
= 1.1 for rough grinding
= 1.4 for finish grinding.

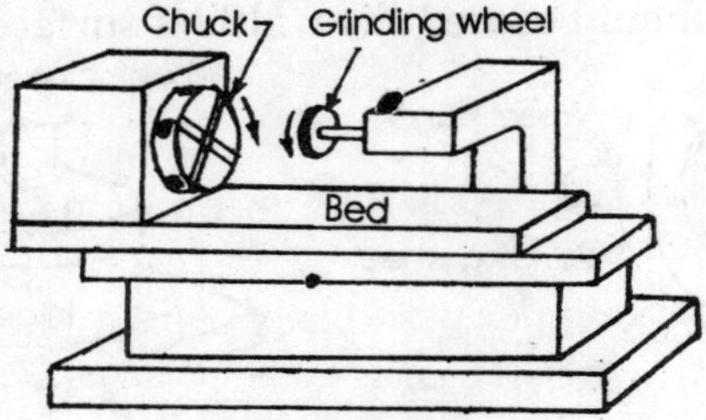

Grinding machine

Fig. 5.9.

Fig. 5.9 shows an internal cylindrical grinder. It uses a chuck to hold the work with the grinding wheel revolving. The table moves from right to left causing the wheel to enter the work and grind its internal surface.

5.11. Surface Grinders

Surface grinding is used mainly to machine flat surfaces. It can be performed either with the periphery of a straight wheel or the face of a cup, cylinder or segmental wheel. A surface grinder uses a magnetic chuck mounted on table to hold the workpieces. There are two basic types of surface grinding machines differing in movement of their tables and the orientation of the grinding wheel spindles.

1. Reciprocating surface grinders
   - (*i*) Horizontal wheel spindle and reciprocating table.
   - (*ii*) Vertical wheel spindle and reciprocating table.
2. Rotary surface grinders
   - (*i*) Horizontal spindle and rotary table.
   - (*ii*) Vertical spindle and rotary table.

5.11.1. Reciprocating table surface grinder. The most common type of surface grinding machine is the one having a reciprocating table and horizontal spindle (Fig. 5.10). The table is mounted on horizontal way and can be reciprocated longitudinally either by hand wheel or by hydraulic powers. Cross feed is given by moving the wheel head in and out. Infeed is controlled by a hand wheel that lowers the grinding wheel towards the work. In such grinders usually the grinding wheel is mounted directly on the motor spindle. The size of the grinder is designated by the dimensions of the working area of table.

Reciprocating table surface grinder with vertical spindle (Fig. 5.11) is primarily used for production type work. In this grinder the wheel diameter should exceed the width of surface to be ground.

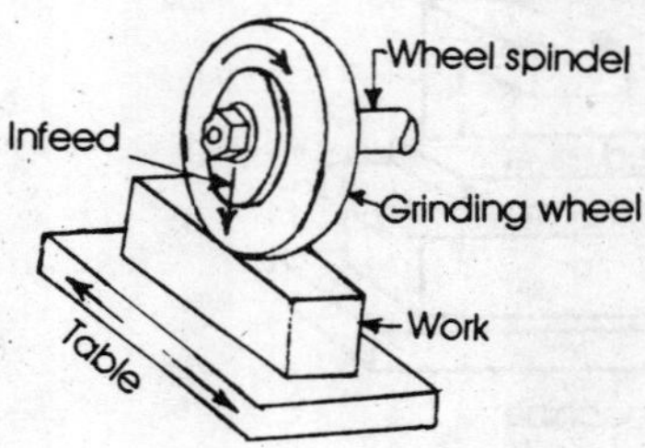

Fig. 5.10.

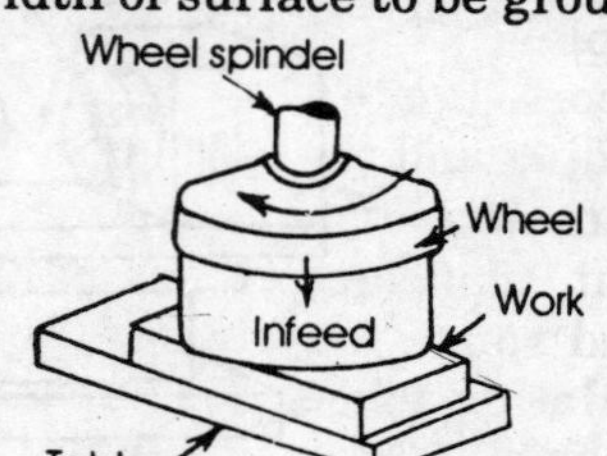

Fig. 5.11.

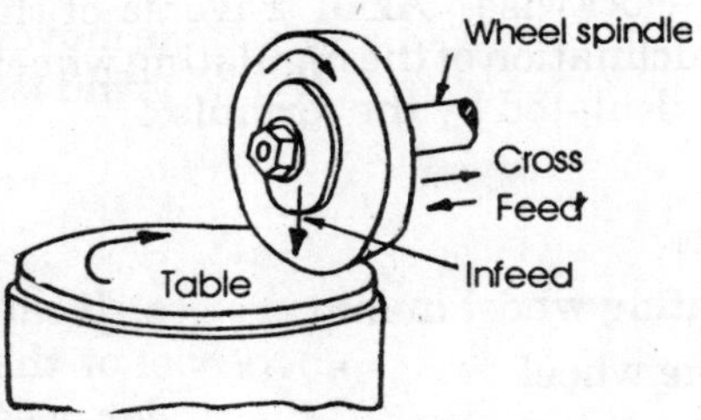

Fig. 5.12.

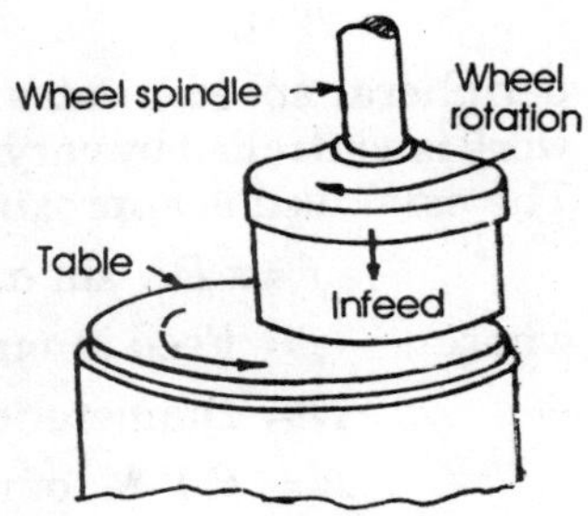

Fig. 5.13.

5.11.2. Rotary table surface grinder. If horizontal spindle rotary table surface grinder (Fig. 5.12) the workpieces are arranged in a circle concentric with the round chuck. The table is made to rotate under revolving wheel both rotating in opposite direction. In vertical spindle rotary table surface grinder (Fig. 5.13) a cup wheel is used. Vertical feed to the wheel is given by moving wheel head.

5.12. Tool and Cutter Grinder

This grinder is used to sharpen cutting tool like milling cutters, drills, hobs, reamers taps and broaches. The depth of cut in this grinder is quite small as the grinding is carried out dry to give the operator a good view. Generally cup and dish shaped grinding wheels are used in this machine. The wheels used are soft and cool cutting. For a carbide tipped tools diamond impregnated wheels are used.

5.13. Centreless Grinding

Centreless grinding makes it possible to grind both external and internal cylindrical surfaces without the necessity of the work piece being mounted between centres in a chuck. The principle of centreless external grinding is shown in Fig. 5.14. In centreless grinding two wheels are used. The larger wheel called grinding wheel operates as regular grinding speeds and does the actual grinding. The small wheel called regulating wheel is mounted at an angle to the plane of grinding wheel. The work with its both ends freely supported on a vee formed by the work rest, rotates between the grinding and the regulating wheels. The grinding wheel is driven by an electric motor and rotates at a maximum surface speed of about 1850 metres per minute. Normally, the regulating wheel speed range may lie within 33 to 130 metres per minute. The regulating wheel does not act as a cutting tool but it is mainly responsible for controlling the speed of rotation and longitudinal motion of the work. The wheels rotate clockwise and the work driven by the regulating wheel and having approximately the same peripheral speed rotates counter-clockwise. Axial traverse of the work is controlled by varying the inclination of the regulating wheel. The axial feed is approximately calculated by the formula :

$$f = \pi DN \sin \alpha.$$

where f = Feed in mm/minute

D = Diameter of regulating wheel in mm.

N = R.P.M. of regulating wheel.

α = Angle of inclination of the regulating wheel.

Centreless grinding is carried out in three different ways :

(*i*) Through feed grinding.

(*ii*) In feed grinding.

(*iii*) End feed grinding.

5.13.1. Through feed grinding. Through feed grinding is normally used for grinding plain cylindrical workpieces. In this process the work is automatically fed through continuously between the grinding wheel and the regulating wheel which have already been set with a particular gap. The grinding starts as soon as the work enters the grinding wheels and grinding of work is complete as soon as it comes out of the wheels. Since the work has to remain outside the wheels before and after grinding operation suitable supports or guides are provided. (Fig. 5.15 *a*).

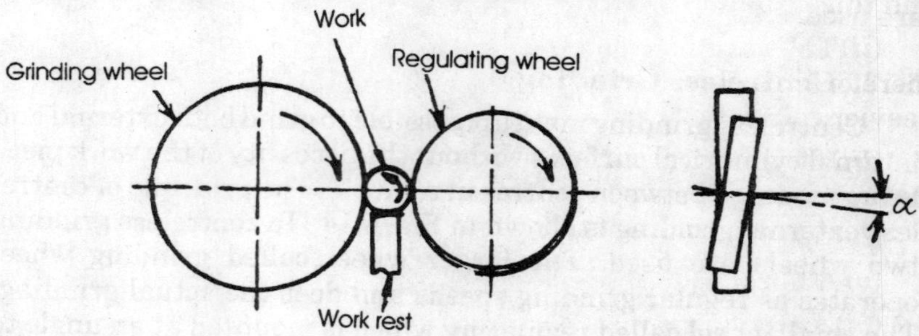

Fig. 5.14.

5.13.2. Infeed Centreless grinding. In this process the work rest and the regulating wheel are retracted so that the work can be put in position and removed when grinding is completed. When the work is in position the regulating wheel is fed inward until the desired diameter is obtained. The work does not move axially as in through feed but is kept supported against an end stop. This arrangement permits multiple diameters and curved parts to be ground. [Fig. 5.15 *b*].

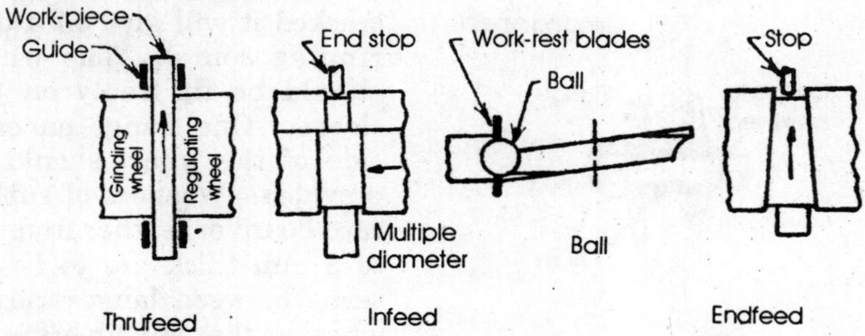

(*a*) (*b*) (*c*)

Fig. 5.15.

5.13.3. End feed centreless grinding. This process is used for grinding taper work. Both the wheels are tapered and thus produce tapered workpieces. In this process the work is feed from one side until it reaches the stop. Fig. 5.15(*c*) shows the work being ground by the end feed method.

5.13.4. Advantages. Various advantages of centreless grinding are as follows :

(*i*) Work chucking and its centring is not required. This saves setting time. Further errors associated with centring are absent and thus grinding allowance can be reduced.

(*ii*) The work-piece is supported rigidly during the operation and therefore no deflection takes place during grinding. This allows heavier cuts to be taken resulting in economical grinding.

(*iii*) It is very rapid process. Frequently it can be made automatic.

(*iv*) Very little skill is required of the operator.

(*v*) A fairly wide range of components can be ground.

(*vi*) Large grinding wheels can be used so that wheel wear is minimised.

(*vii*) Excellent accuracy and fine surface finish can be achieved as there is no distortion of workpiece during grinding.

5.14. Mounting of Grinding Wheel

To ensure efficient and safe operation, the grinding wheel should be firmly clamped on the spindle, properly balanced, tested for strength and reliably enclosed by a guard. Before mounting the wheel should be checked for cracks because they may not be seen.

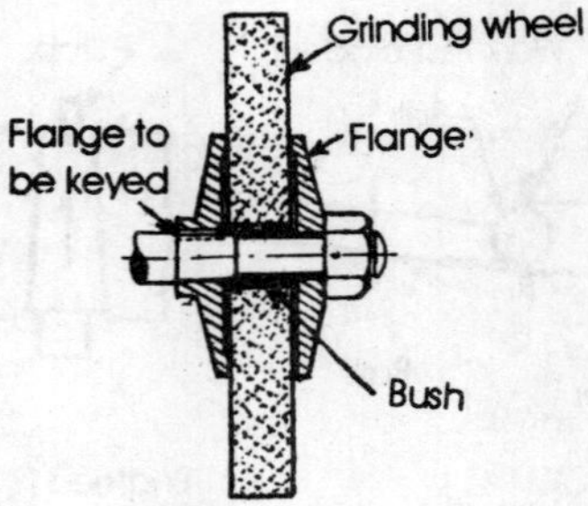

Fig. 5.16.

For this sound the wheel cracks. If the wheel is not cracked it will give off a dull ringing sound. The wheel should be fit freely on the sleeve. One flange on each side of the wheel should be provided. Washers of rubber card board or leather from 0.5 to 3 mm thick are to be inserted between flanges and the wheel so that any unevenness of the wheel surface is balanced and a tight joint is obtained. Both flanges should be of same diameter and flange diameter should be at least equal to the half of the grinding wheel diameter. The nut is then tightened to hold the grinding wheel firmly (Fig. 5.16). To avoid serious accidents the wheel should be enclosed during operation by a safety guard made up of steel. The guard should be sufficiently strong reliably clamped to the grinder and should protect the operator against splashing cutting fluid. When first starting the wheel, the operator should stand aside and allow the wheel to come to the speed before attempting any grinding.

5.15. Dressing and Truing

Grinding wheels must be occasionally dressed or trued to remove dull grains of abrasive and metal particles to resorb the original shape and accuracy of the wheel face.

During grinding operation the grains of the wheel are subjected to wear and the wheel loses its cutting capacity. Along with grain wear another factor that reduces the cut properties of a grinding wheel is the loading of the voids between the grains with the waste material of the grinding process such as sintered metal dust, abrasive grit and particles of bonding material. A worn and loaded wheel ceases to cut properly. This requires sharpening of grinding wheel in order to restore sharp cutting edges and to unload the grinding wheel.

Dressing removes the worn grains and the waste products of grinding. Dressing is carried out by a steel dressing tool consisting of irregularly shaped hardened steel discs that are free to rotate on an axle. The tool is held at an angle against the rotating grinding wheel and moved across its face. The revolving points of the desks remove the foreign particles that have become lodged between the grains and also remove or fracture dulled grains thus producing sharp edges. The other method of dressing is called crush dressing.

In this method a hard steel crushing roll having the same contour as the part to be ground is forced against the grinding wheel while it is revolving usually quite slowly. The crushing action fractures and dislodges some of the abrasive grains thus exposing sharp edges and at the same time imparting a desired shape to the grinding wheel. Dressing may also be carried out by a diamond dresser.

Truing. Truing of grinding wheel is carried out to restore the correct geometric shape of the wheel which has been lost due to non-uniform wear. Truing makes the face of the wheel concentric and the sides plane and parallel. Truing is carried out by means of a diamond dresser. The dresser being held at an angle of 10° to 15° to the wheel face (Fig. 5.17). Diamond wheels are not dressed, they are trued when their shape is no longer sufficiently accurate. Metal bonded diamond wheels are trued with a green silicon carbide dressing stick having a vitrified bond. Fig. 5.18 shows mounted diamonds for truing grinding wheels. During grinding of hard materials the abrasive grains dull more quickly than in grinding soft materials. Therefore wheel for grinding hard materials should lose its grains rapidly. Thus softer grade wheels are used for grinding hard materials and harder grade wheels for soft materials.

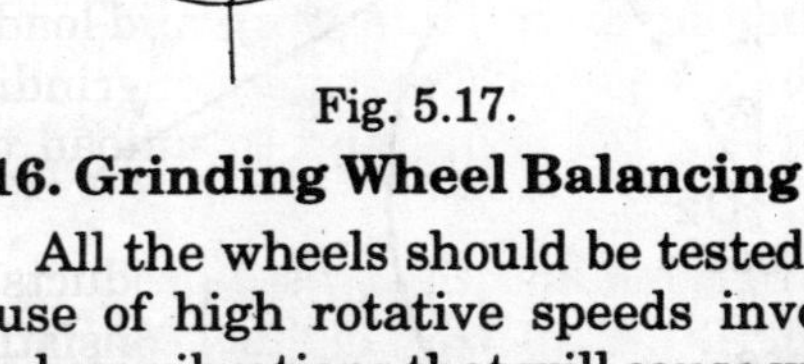

Fig. 5.17.

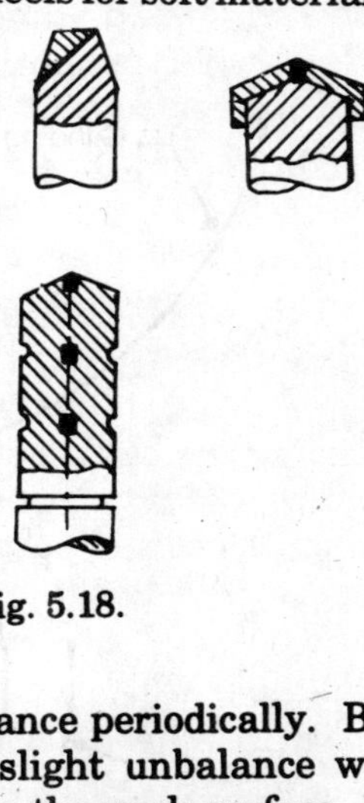

Fig. 5.18.

5.16. Grinding Wheel Balancing

All the wheels should be tested for balance periodically. Because of high rotative speeds involved, a slight unbalance will produce vibrations that will cause waviness in the work surface. In addition unbalance may cause the wheel to break with the probability of serious damage and injury. Balancing is usually done in the static position of wheel by shifting the position of weights on one of the mounting flanges of wheel. Poor balance may be detected by the vibrations set up in the machine, poor finish and difficulty in maintaining size.

5.17. Operating Speeds and Feeds

The surface speeds of grinding wheels are generally high. Table 5.6 shows some typical grinding operations and the average values of wheel surface speeds. The amount of feed for rough grinding varies from 0.025 to 0.1 mm and for finish grinding from 0.005 to 0.01 mm.

Table 5.6

Type of grinding	*Surface speed (metre per min)*
Surface grinding	1200--1800
Cylindrical grinding	1600--1950
Centreless grinding	1500--1800
Tool and cutter grinding	1300--2000
Snagging (Resinoid bonded wheel)	1800--2200

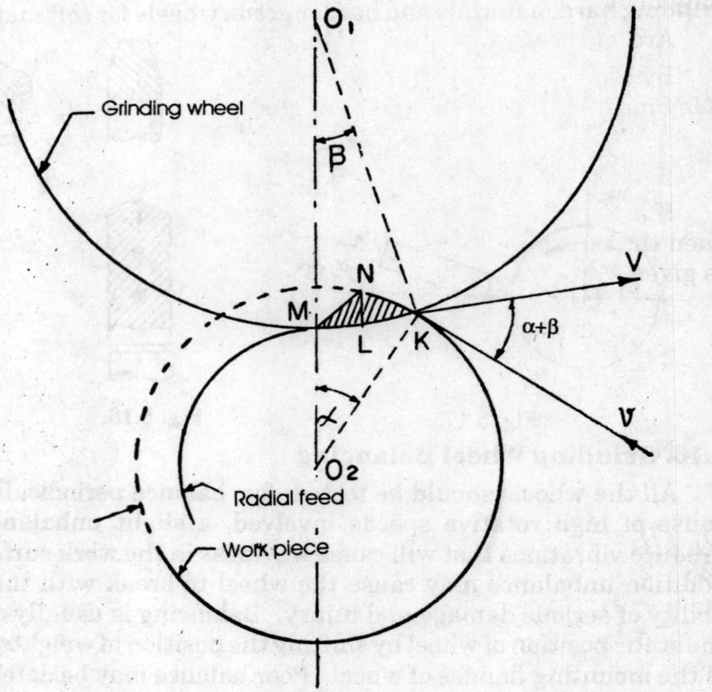

Fig. 5.19.

5.18. Theory of Grinding

During grinding the grinding wheel starts removing the material as soon as it comes in contact with the workpiece. As shown in Fig. 5.19 when an abrasive grain starts to enter the workpiece at K the depth of cut is zero and it increases gradually as the wheel and the work revolve. As usually wheel rotates at higher speed than the work the point of maximum cut depth is almost at the point where the wheel leaves the work. Area KMN is the chip with its maximum thickness of NL.

Let D_1 = Diameter of wheel.

D_2 = Diameter of workpiece.

V = Surface velocity of wheel.

ν = Surface velocity of workpiece.

T = Time takes by a grain on grinding wheel to move from K to M

f = Radial feed.

Arc $KM = V \times T$.

During this time a point on workpiece at A will be able to move only up to N.

Arc $KN = \nu \times T$

By ignoring the very small amount of curvature which occur, KLN may be treated as a right angled triangle, the right angle at L.

$$NL = KN \sin(\alpha + \beta) = \nu\, T \sin(\alpha + \beta).$$

If n = number of grits per unit length of wheel circumference then the maximum chip thickness per grit or grain depth of cut (t) is given by

$$t = \frac{NL}{n(\text{Arc } KM)} = \frac{\nu\, T \sin(\alpha + \beta)}{n \,.\, V \,.\, T}$$

$$= \frac{\nu}{nV} \sin(\alpha + \beta)$$

Now from $\Delta\, O_1 O_2 K$

$$O_1 O_2^2 = O_1K^2 + O_2K^2 - 2\, O_1K \times O_2K \cos\angle O_1KO_2$$

$$\left(\frac{D_1}{2} + \frac{D_2}{2} - f\right)^2 = \left(\frac{D_1}{2}\right)^2 + \left(\frac{D_2}{2}\right)^2$$

$$- 2\,\frac{D_1}{2} \cdot \frac{D_2}{2} \cos\,[180 - (\alpha + \beta)]$$

$$= \left(\frac{D_1}{2}\right)^2 + \left(\frac{D_2}{2}\right)^2 + \frac{D_1 D_2}{2} \cos(\alpha + \beta)$$

Neglecting f_2 as compared to D_1 and D_2 and on simplification, we get

$$\frac{D_1 D_2}{2} - D_1 f - D_2 f = \frac{D_1 D_2}{2} \cos(\alpha + \beta)$$

$$\cos(\alpha + \beta) = 1 - 2f\left[\frac{D_1 + D_2}{D_1 D_2}\right]$$

$$\sin(\alpha + \beta) = \sqrt{1 - \cos^2(\alpha + \beta)}$$

$$= \sqrt{1 - \left[1 - 2f\left(\frac{D_1 + D_2}{D_1 D_2}\right)\right]^2}$$

$$= \sqrt{1 - \left[1 + \left\{2f\left(\frac{D_1 + D_2}{D_1 D_2}\right)\right\}^2 - 2 \times 2f\left(\frac{D_1 + D_2}{D_1 D_2}\right)\right]}$$

Now neglecting $\left\{2f\left(\frac{D_1 + D_2}{D_1 D_2}\right)\right\}^2$, we get

$$\sin(\alpha + \beta) = 2\sqrt{\frac{D_1 + D_2}{D_1 D_2} f}$$

$$\therefore \qquad t = \frac{n}{nV} \sin(\alpha + \beta) = \frac{V}{nV} 2 \cdot \sqrt{\frac{D_1 + D_2}{D_1 D_2} f}$$

$$t = \frac{2v}{nV} \sqrt{\frac{D_1 + D_2}{D_1 D_2 \cdot f}}$$

Let F = Force on individual grits of grinding wheel.

The force F is proportional to the area of the chip formed which is proportional to the square of grain depth of cut

$$F \propto t^2$$

$$\propto \left(\frac{2v}{nV}\right)^2 \frac{D_1 + D_2}{D_1 D_2} \cdot f$$

$$\propto \left(\frac{v}{V}\right)^2 \frac{D_1 + D_2}{D_1 D_2} \cdot f \qquad \text{as} \qquad \frac{2}{n} = \text{Constant.}$$

The above expression shows that the grits will break from the wheel if the force exceeds bond strength and also increase in work speed will be more effective in breaking the grits than increasing the radial feed.

5.19. Grinding Wheel Wear

In the grinding process the grains of abrasive are subject to wear and the grinding wheel losses its cutting capacity.

Fig. 5.20 shows the progress of total grinding wheel wear as measured by the total volume (V_1) of grinding wheel material worn with respect to total volume (V_2) of material ground.

The grinding ratio (R) is defined as follows.

$$R = \frac{C_1}{C_2}$$

where $C_1 =$ Rate of metal removal

$C_2 =$ Rate of wheel wear.

A worn grinding wheel ceases to cut and its cutting capacity can be restored by dressing which may be described as sharpening operation. It is observed that it is sufficient to remove a layer of dulled grains 0.08 mm deep to restore the cutting capacity of a grinding wheel.

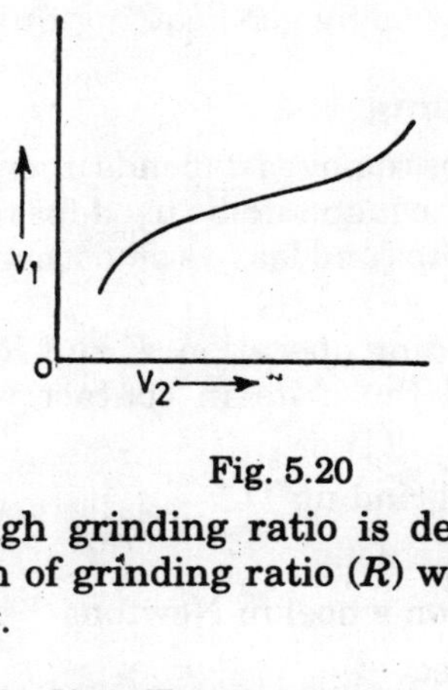

Fig. 5.20

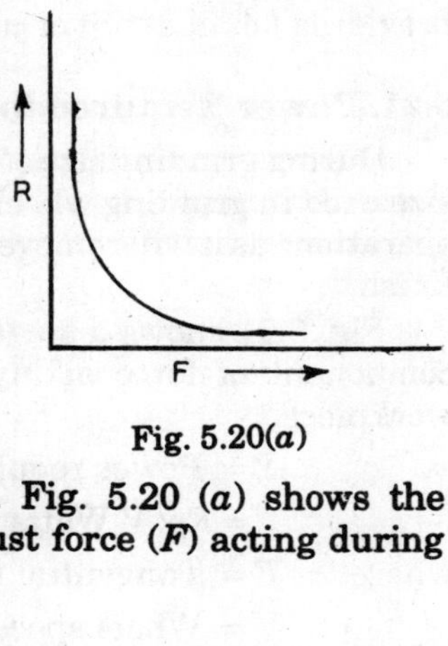

Fig. 5.20(a)

A high grinding ratio is desirable. Fig. 5.20 (a) shows the variation of grinding ratio (R) with thrust force (F) acting during grinding.

5.20. Grinding Temperature

In grinding there is rise in temperature due to the resistance to deformation during shearing of the chips as well as the frictional resistance encountered in the chip tool interface. The temperature changes arising from the grinding process may relate to

(i) The mean grit temperature (T).

(ii) The mean temperature at or just below the ground surface (T_s).

The grit temperature is found as follows :

$$T = \text{A.E.} \sqrt{\frac{V \cdot t}{K \cdot P \cdot C.}}$$

where A = a constant depending on wheel work pair

E = Total specific energy of grinding

V = Surface velocity of grinding wheel

t = Maximum grit depth of cut

K = Thermal conductivity of material

P = Density of job material

C = Specific heat of job material.

The rate of wheel wear depends upon the total grit temperature (T). The surface temperature (T_s) is determined by calculating the shear zone temperature. The severe temperature gradients in the work surface during grinding tend to produce very high residual stresses. Surface damage and residual stresses can be minimised by reducing the time of contact by using higher work speed, by providing small depth of cut and by using good cutting fluid.

5.21. Power Required for Grinding

During grinding size of the chips removed depends upon the grit size used in grinding wheel. A fine grit should be used for finishing operations as it will remove finer chips and leave a smoother surface finish.

Fig. 5.21 shows a surface grinding operation. F and R are the component of force acting on all the grits in contact with the workpiece.

P = Power required for grinding

$= F \times V$ Watts

where F = Tangential force upon wheel in Newtons

V = Wheel speed in m/sec.

H = Power required per mm^3 of metal removed per second

$$= \frac{P}{W} J/mm^3$$

where W = Volume of metal removed per second

$= t \cdot b \times V.$

where t = Depth of cut (mm)

b = Width of cut

v = Work speed (mm /sec).

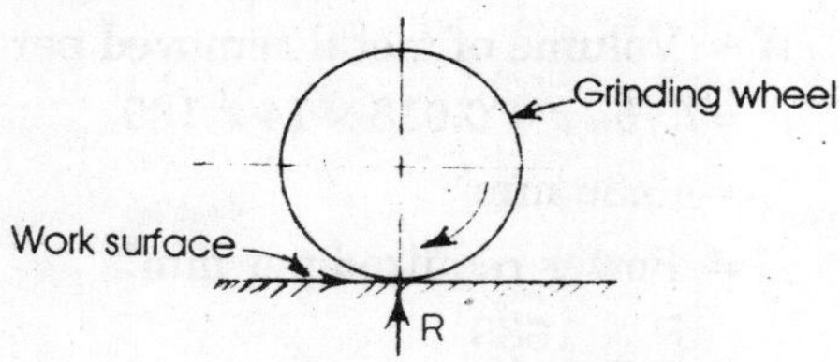

Fig. 5.21.

5.22. Specific Energy for Grinding

The energy per unit volume of metal removed or specific energy for surface or internal or external grinding is given by the following relation

$$E = \frac{HV}{U \cdot b \cdot d}$$

where $E =$ Specific energy
$H =$ Tangential force between grinding wheel and work piece
$V =$ Surface speed of grinding wheel
$U =$ Table speed
$b =$ Width of each cut
$d =$ Wheel depth of cut.

Example 5.1. *Calculate the power required per mm^3 of metal removed per second for a surface grinding operation using the following data.*

Wheel speed $= 20$ *m/s*
Work speed $= 0.18$ *m/s*
Tangential force $= 84$ *N*
Depth of cut $= 0.018$ *mm*
Width of cut $= 14$ *mm*

Solution. $F =$ Tangential force = 84 N
$V =$ Wheel speed
$P =$ Power required
$= F \times V = 84 \times 20 = 1680$ Watts
$t =$ Depth of cut = 0.018 mm.
$b =$ Width of cut = 14 mm
$v =$ Work speed = 0.18 m/sec = 180 mm/sec

$$W = \text{Volume of metal removed per sec}$$
$$= t \cdot b \cdot v = 0.018 \times 14 \times 180$$
$$= 45.36 \text{ mm}^3$$
$$H = \text{Power required per mm}^3$$
$$= \frac{P}{W} = \frac{1680}{45.36}$$
$$= 37 \text{ J/mm}^3.$$

Example 5.2. (*a*) *Define the following*

(*i*) *Abrasive grain size*

(*ii*) *Grade of a grinding wheel.*

(*b*) *During external cylindrical grinding the following observations were made.*

Diameter of work piece = 40 mm

Diameter of grinding wheel = 240 mm

Wheel velocity = 16 m / sec

Work velocity = 14 m / min

Wheel depth of cut = 0.03 mm

Grain are 0.5 mm apart

Calculate grain depth of cut.

Solution. (*a*) **Size of grain.** The size of abrasive grain used in a grinding wheel is designated by a number corresponding to number of openings per unit length in the screen used to size the grain. A number however generally indicates only an average grain size since in sizing the grain a finite number of screen are used.

Grade. The grade of hardness of a grinding wheel indicates the relative strength of the bond which holds the abrasive grains in place. Wheel grade is indicated by letters *A* to *Z*, *A* being the softest wheel and *Z* the hardest. The effective grade of the wheel depends strongly on the speed of wheel and other grinding variables and whether a cutting fluid is used.

(*b*)
$$D_1 = \text{Diameter of grinding wheel} = 240 \text{ mm.}$$
$$D_2 = \text{Diameter of workpiece} = 40 \text{ mm.}$$
$$v = \text{Surface velocity of workpiece}$$
$$= 14 \text{ m/min} = 0.23 \text{ m/sec} = 230 \text{ mm/sec.}$$
$$V = \text{Wheel velocity} = 16 \text{ m/sec.}$$
$$= 16000 \text{ mm/sec.}$$
$$f = \text{Radial feed.}$$

$$= \text{Wheel depth of cut} = 0.03 \text{ mm}$$

$$n = \text{Grit spacing or grains per mm.}$$

$$= \frac{1}{0.5} = 2$$

$$t = \text{Grit depth of cut}$$

$$= \frac{2 \cdot v}{n \cdot V} \sqrt{\frac{D_1 + D_2}{D_1 D_2}} \times f$$

$$= \frac{2 \times 230}{2 \times 16000} \sqrt{\frac{240 + 40}{240 \times 40}} \times 0.03.$$

$$= 0.00043 \text{ mm.}$$

5.23. Surface Finish

The quality of machined surface is characterised by the accuracy of its manufacture in respect to the dimensions specified by the designer. Every machining process leaves its evidence on the surface that has been machined. This evidence is in the form of finely spaced micro irregularities left by the cutting tool. (Fig. 5.22). Each kind of cutting tool leaves its own pattren that can be identified. This pattern is called surface finish or surface roughness. Whenever two machined surfaces come in contact with each other the quality of the mating surfaces plays an important role in the performance and wear of the mating parts. A good surface finish is desirable. Some degrees of roughness which may be extremely small is always present on any surface because of the following reasons.

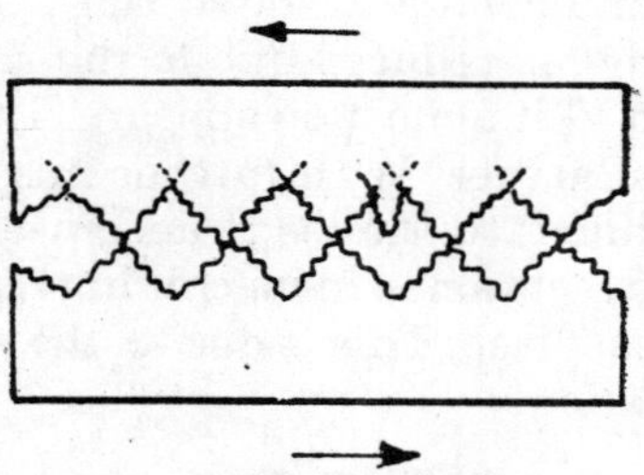

Fig. 5.22.

(*i*) Metals are not absolutely homogeneous. Some portions may be harder than others and may cause the cutting tool to deflect or spring away from the cut surface.

(*ii*) Most metals are of crystalline structure. When metal is cut some of the crystals are sheared through while others are torn loose from the adjoining crystals.

(*iii*) Minute particles or chips may cling to the edge of tool and scratch the surface of the workpiece.

5.24. Factors Affecting Surface Finish

The various factors that contribute to the quality of surface finish are as follows :

1. **Machining variables**

(*a*) Cutting speed.

(*b*) Feed.

(*c*) Depth of the cut.

(*a*) **Effect of cutting speed.** Increase in cutting speed improves the surface finish due to the continuous reduction in built up edge (Fig. 5.23). The curve *A* represents the machining of steels except high alloy grade steels. In the beginning the surface roughness increases when cutting speed changes from V_1 to V_2. This is due to the beginning of built up edge formation which reaches its maximum value at the cutting speed V_2. Then the formation of built up edge is reduced due to the rise in temperature and at cutting speed V_2 it almost disappears. This reduces the height *(H)* of micro irregularities. With further increase in cutting speed the surface roughness continues to decrease. There is almost no hump on the curve *B* obtained in machining high alloy steels, non-ferrous metals and cast iron. This is due to the completed absence of built up edge formation.

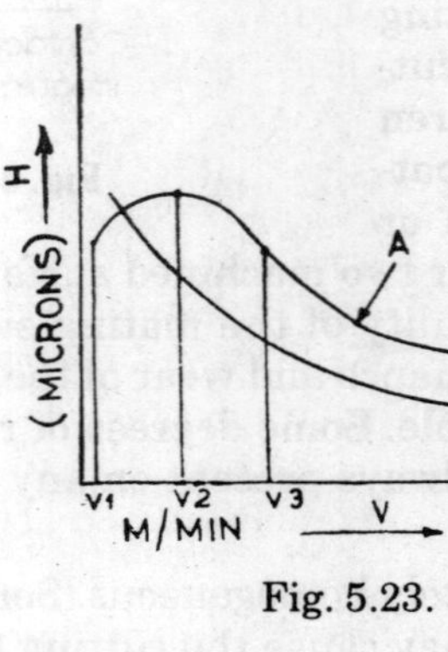

Fig. 5.23.

(*b*) **Effect of feed.** Increase in feed rate deteriorates, surface finish. It is observed that a rate of feed (*f*) in the range from 0.12 to 0.15 mm per revolution has a negligible effect on the height (*H*) of irregularities but further increase in the feed rate increase surface roughness Fig. 5.24 shows the variation of feed with height of micro-irregularities when different cutting fluids are used.

(*c*) **Effect of depth of cut.** Increase in depth of cut deteriorates surface finish.

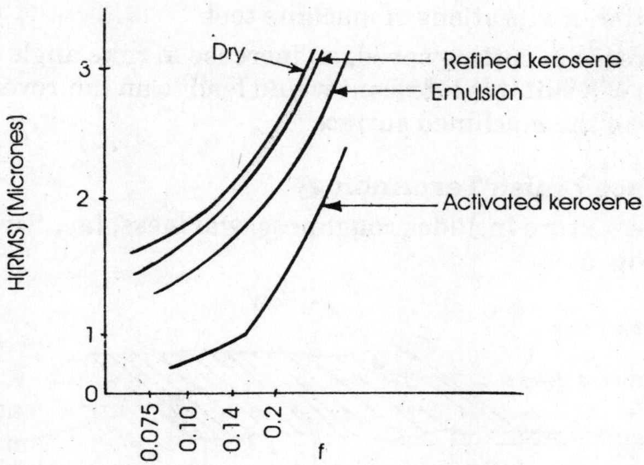

Fig. 5.24.

2. **Tool geometry.** The effect of tool geometry on surface finish is as follows :

(*a*) **Nose radius.** Increase in nose radius improves surface finish. There is an appreciable improvement in surface finish upto 0.3 mm nose radius. Higher value of nose radius produces less improvement in surfaces finish and on the other hand it causes chatter during machining.

(*b*) **Rake angle.** Increase in rake angle of tool improves surface finish.

(*c*) **Relief angle.** An increase in the relief angle adversely affects surface finish but the effect is on the whole small.

(*d*) **Side cutting edge angle.** An increase in side cutting edge angle improves surface finish largely because of the reduced chip thickness but the degree of improvement depends upon the rigidity of the work and its mounting.

(*e*) **Cutting edge.** The height of the micro-irregularities of the cutting edge effects the micro geometry of the machined surface. The jags on the cutting edge are reproduced directly on the ridges of the machined surface, increasing their hight. Therefore cutting edge of the tool should be carefully ground and lapped to reduce the micro-irregularities of the cutting edge.

3. Accuracy of bearings.

4. Method of chip removal.

5. Quality of machine tool.

6. Nature of work material.

7. Chatter or vibrations of machine tool.

An increase in cutting speed, an increase in rake angle and the application of a suitable lubricant would lead to an improvement in the quality of the machined surface.

5.25. Surface Finish Terminology

Surface texture includes roughness, waviness, lay, flaw etc. as shown in Fig. 5.25.

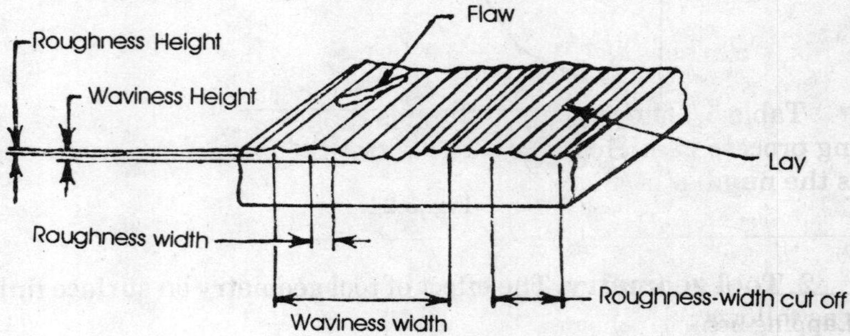

Fig. 5.25.

(*a*) **Roughness.** Roughness consists of surface irregularities which result from the various manufacturing process. These irregularities combine to form surface texture.

(*b*) **Roughness height.** Roughness height is the height of irregularities with reference to an average line. It is measured in millimetres.

The value of roughness height is expressed in two ways.

(*i*) Arithmetical average value or centre line average value.

(*ii*) Root mean square (rms) value.

In most cases the arithmetical average value of roughness height is used. Occasionally the root mean square (rms) value is used.

The rms is obtained by taking the square root of the sum of the squares of *y* measurements divided by the number of

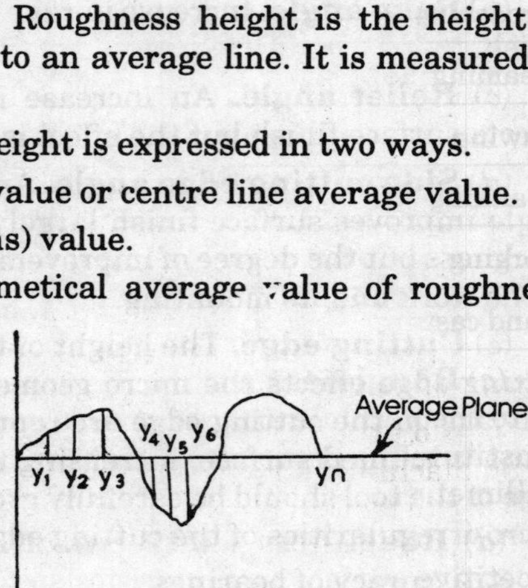

Fig. 5.26.

y measurements. In terms of the measurements indicated in Fig. 5.26 the average and rms values are calculated as follows.

$$\Sigma y_n = y_1 + y_2 + y_3 + \ldots y_n$$

The centre line average (CLA) value or Arithmetical average (AA) height is given by

$$AA = \frac{\Sigma y_n}{n}$$

where n is the total number of vertical measurements.

The r.m.s. (root mean square) value is obtained as follows :

$$\text{r.m.s.} = \sqrt{\frac{y_1^2 + y_2^2 + y_3^2 \ldots y_n^2}{n}}$$

Table 5.7 shows some of the rms ranges for the various machining process in micro inches. The better the surface finish the small is the number of micro inches.

Table 5.7

Process	*rms range* (10^{-6} *inch*)
Lapping honing, polishing	2 – 10
Grinding	5 – 150
Milling, turning, shaping	20 – 300
Drilling	75 – 200
Broaching	10 – 60
Reaming	8 – 50
Sawing	250 – 1000
Blanking	30 – 100
Forging	100 – 400
Sand casting	500 – 1000

(*c*) **Roughness width.** Roughness width is the distance parallel to the normal surface between successive peaks or ridges which constitute the predominate pattern of the roughness. It is stated in millimetres.

(*d*) **Roughness width cut off.** It is the greatest spacing of repetitive surface irregularities so to be included in the measurement of average roughness height. It should always be greater than the roughness width in order to obtain the total roughness height rating. It is expressed in millimetres.

(*e*) **Lay.** It is the direction of predominant surface pattern produced and reflects the machining method.

(*f*) **Waviness.** This refers to the irregularities which are outside the roughness width cut off values. It may be result of work deflecting during machining, working and vibration.

(*g*) **Waviness width.** It is the maximum permitted variation in waviness height. It is measured in millimetres.

(*h*) **Waviness height.** It is the peak to valley distance. It is also expressed in millimetres.

(*i*) **Flaws.** Cracks, scratches and ridges are called flaws. They are not regularly recurring and are imperfections outside the regular pattern of surface texture.

The ISO recommended arithmetical mean roughness values and grade numbers for the specification of surface roughness are indicated in Table 5.8.

Table 5.8

Roughness grade number	*Roughness value* (μm)
N_1	0.005
N_2	0.25
N_3	0.1
N_4	0.2
N_5	0.4
N_6	0.8
N_7	1.6
N_8	3.2
N_9	6.3
N_{10}	12.5
N_{11}	25
N_{12}	50

5.26. Ideal Surface Roughness

The ideal surface roughness represents the best possible finish which may be obtained for a given tool shape and feed and can only be approached if built up edge, chatter, inaccuracies, in machine tool movement etc. are eliminated. Ideal surface finish for the turning operation where a sharp corner tool is used is shown in Fig. 5.27 and where a tool having nose radius is shown in Fig. 5.28.

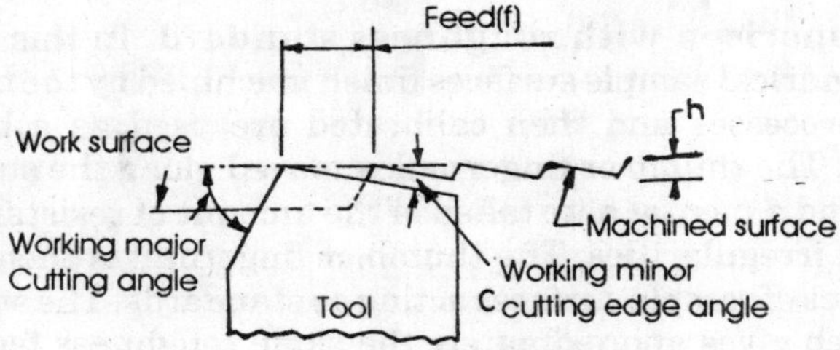

Fig. 5.27.

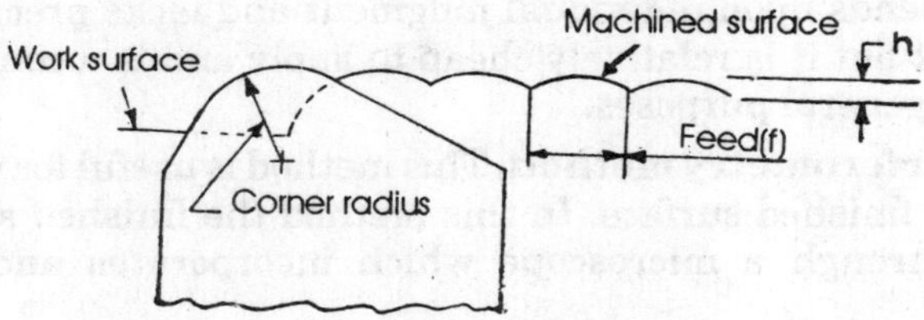

Fig. 5.28.

For a sharp corner tool (Fig. 5.27) the roughness is extremely sensitive to changes in minor cutting edge angle.

Let ξ = Minor cutting edge angle.

θ = Working major cutting edge angle.

f = feed in mm/revolution.

h = Ideal value of surface roughness.

$$= \frac{f}{\cot \theta + \cot \Psi}$$

For a rounded corner tool (Fig. 5.28) the ideal value of surface roughness is given by

$$h = \frac{f^2}{8r}$$

where r = Nose radius in mm.

5.27. Measurement of Surface Roughness

Surface finish is measured by different method using different units of measurement. The commonly used methods are as follows:

(*i*) Comparison with roughness standards.
(*ii*) Interferometry method.
(*iii*) Profilometer.

(1) **Comparison with roughness standard.** In this method flat and cylindrical sample surfaces finish machined by the common workshop processes and then calibrated are used as a basin of comparison. The thumb or fingernail is moved along the surface of workpiece and a mental note taken of the amount of resistance and the depth of irregularities. The thumb or fingernail is then moved across a series of sample surfaces acting as standards. The standard surface which gives approximately the same roughness feeling as that of workpiece indicates the roughness of the workpiece. This method depends upon individual judgment and lacks precision on this account but it is relatively cheap to apply and is a convenient method for general purposes.

(2) **Interferometry method.** This method is useful for viewing very highly finished surface. In this method the finished surfaces are seen through a microscope which incorporates and interferometer.

(3) **Profilometer.** It is used to obtain an enlarged tracing of the surface irregularities. It has a sharp diamond stylus on the end of arm. The stylus is moved across the surface being measured and the stylus follows the contours of irregularities. As the stylus passes over the surface it rises and falls by amounts proportional to surface roughness.

The relative displacement is highly magnified electronically and results presented either as a surface finished graph or as a roughness value. The stylus is required to be slided with respect to a datum set up by the skid (Fig. 5.29).

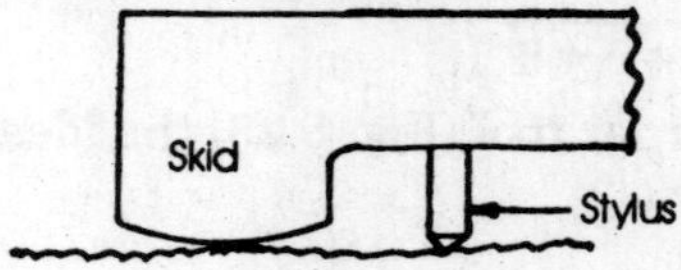

Fig. 5.29

5.28. Surface Finish Representation

Surface finish is either denoted as per IS : 3073-1967 by the symbol ∇ (mean height of the surface irregularities in microns both above and below a mean line) or by (root mean square value. The two systems compare with each other as follows :

Type of finishing operation	*Representation as per IS : 3073-1967*		
	Symbol	*Value in microns*	*Corresponding value in micro inches*
Rough Machining	∇	8-25	250-1000
Fine Machining	∇ ∇	1.6-8	63-250
Grinding Finish	∇ ∇ ∇	0.025-1.6	2-63
Lapping	∇ ∇ ∇ ∇	<0.025	<2

According to Indian standards the surface roughness is expressed in terms of *GLA* value denoted by R_a.

Fig. 5.30 shows representation of surface roughness.

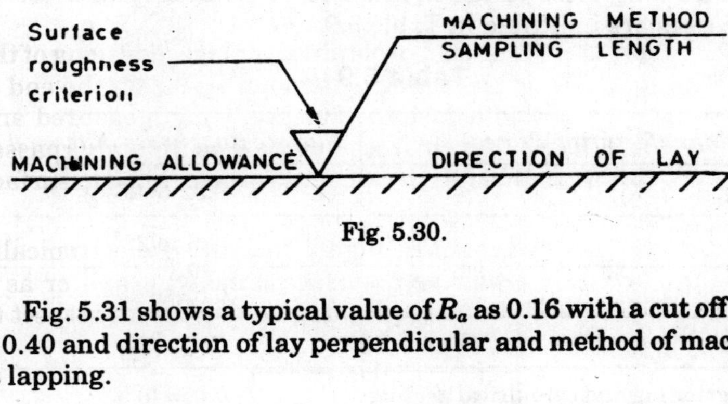

Fig. 5.30.

Fig. 5.31 shows a typical value of R_a as 0.16 with a cut off length of 0.40 and direction of lay perpendicular and method of machining as lapping.

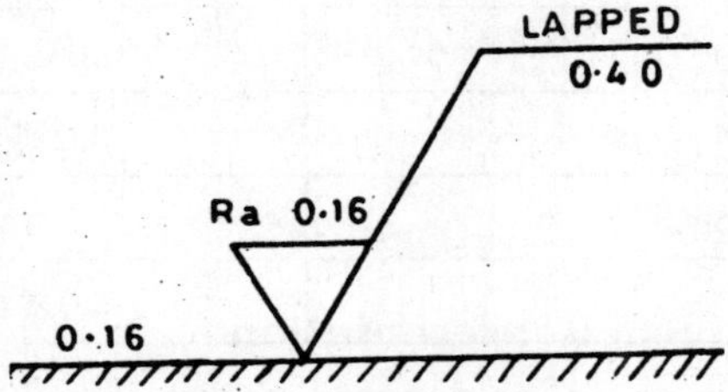

Fig. 5.31.

The direction of lay is represented by the following symbols :

⊥ Lay perpendicular to the line representing the surface to which the symbol is applied.

= Lay parallel to the line representing the surface to which the symbol is applied.

X Lay angular in both directions to the line representing the surface to which the symbol is applied.

R Lay approximately radial relative to the centre of the surface to which the symbol is applied.

M Lay multidirectional.

5.29. Units of Surface Roughness

The following units are generally used :

Micro inch (μ-in) $= 10^{-6}$ inch

Micro (μ-m) meter $= 10^{-6}$ metre = Micron

Nanometres (nm) $= 10^{-9}$ metre (USA/France)

= 0.001 μ– m.

Surface roughness values in microns for different manufacturing processes are indicated in Table 5.9.

Table 5.9

Manufacturing Process	*Surface Roughness (Microns)*
Turning	0.32 to 25
Drilling	1.6 to 22
Milling	0.32 to 25
Shaping	1.6 to 25
Surface grinding and cylindrical griding	0.063 to 5
Lapping	0.012 to 0.016
Honing	0.025 to 0.42
Broaching, reaming	0.4 to 3.2
Boring	0.4 to 6.4

Table 5.10 indicates the Average surface roughness value (Ra) in microns obtainable by different manufacturing methods.

Table 5.10

Manufacturing Mehtod	*Surface Roughness*
Sand casting	6.3 – 12.5
Die casting	0.8 – 3.2
Forging	3.2 – 25
Extrusion	0.8 – 6.3
Rolling	0.8 – 3.2
Flame Cut	25 – 50
Hack Saw Cut	6.3 – 50
Bandsaw, Chipping	3.2 – 50
Filing	1.0 – 12.5
Emery Polish	0.4 – 1.6
Abrasive Belt	0.1 – 6.3
Fibre Wheel brushing	0.2 – 0.8
Cloth buffing	0.05 – 0.1
Shell Milling	3.2 – 25
Drilling	6.3 – 25
Planning & Shaping	1.6 – 12.5
Face Milling	1.6 – 12.5
Turning	1.6 – 12.5
Boring	1.6 – 6.3
Reaming	0.8 – 6.3
Cyl. Grinding	0.4 – 3.2
Centreless Grinding	0.4 – 3.2
Internal Grinding	0.4 – 3.2
Surface Grinding	0.4 – 3.2
Broaching	0.8 – 3.2
Super Finishing	0.1 – 0.4
Honing	0.1 – 0.4
Lapping	0.05 – 0.4

PROBLEMS

5.1. (*a*) What is chatter in machine tools ? (*b*) What are the effects of chatter ?

5.2. Describe the following types of vibrations :
(*a*) Forced vibrations. (*b*) Self-excited vibrations.

5.3. Describe the factors that affect chatter.

5.4. Write short notes on the following :
(*i*) Types of vibratory systems. (*ii*) Elimination of chatter.
(*iii*) Vibration isolation.

5.5. (*a*) What do you understand by surface finish ?
(*b*) Explain the factors which affect the surface finish.

5.6. Define the following :
(*a*) Roughness height.
(*b*) Arithmatical value of surface roughness.
(*c*) R.M.S. value of surface roughness.
(*d*) Roughness width (*e*) Waviness width
(*f*) Waviness height (*g*) Flaw.
(*h*) Lay.

5.7. Discuss the methods of measuring surface roughness.

5.8. Write short notes on the following :
(*a*) Surface finish representation. (*b*) Units of surface roughness.

5.9. Sketch and describe a method to isolate vibrations in a machine tool.

5.10. Write short notes on the following :
(*a*) Vibration measurement in rotating machine tool.
(*b*) Effects of vibrations in machine tool.
(*c*) Causes of vibrations in a machine tool.

5.11. Define the term grinding.

5.12. Describe the various types of abrasives in grinding wheels.

5.13. (*a*) What is a bond ? Name six types of bonds used in grinding wheel manufacture. (*b*) Describe vitrified shellac and resinoid bonds.

5.14. (*a*) What is a grinding wheel ?

(*b*) Differentiate between grains grade and structure of a grinding wheel.

5.15. (*a*) What is the difference between wheel dressing and wheel truing?

(*b*) Sketch two types of mounted diamonds for wheel truing.

5.16. Write short notes on the following :

(*a*) Grinding wheel selection
(*b*) Cutting action of grinding wheel
(*c*) Shapes of grinding wheels
(*d*) Mounted wheels and points.

5.17. Differentiate rough grinder and precision grinder.

5.18. Make a near sketch of centre type cylindrical grinder and explain its operation.

5.19. Make a neat sketch of chuck type internal cylindrical grinder and explain its operation.

5.20. (*a*) What is surface grinding ?

(*b*) Make a neat sketch of horizontal wheel spindle and reciprocating table surface grinder and explain its operation.

5.21. (*a*) What is centreless grinding ?

(*b*) Make a neat sketch of centreless grinder and explain its operation.

(*c*) State the advantages of centreless grinding.

5.22. Write short notes on the following :

(*a*) Mounting of grinding wheel
(*b*) Grinding wheel balancing
(*c*) Marking system of grinding wheel

5.23. Write short notes on the following :

(*a*) Marking system of grinding wheels.
(*b*) Tool and cutter grinder

5.24. Describe the following :

(*a*) Grinding wheel wear
(*b*) Grinding temperature
(*c*) Power required for grinding

5.25. Define the following :

(*i*) Grinding ratio

(*ii*) Specific energy for grinding

5.26. Discuss theory of grinding and derive an expression for chip thickness per grit during grinding.

5.27. Write short notes on the following :

(*i*) Surface finish.

(*ii*) Factors affecting surface finish.

(*iii*) CLA and RMS values of surface finish.

(*iv*) Surface finish representation.

6

Press Tool Design

6.1. Introduction

A press is a machine tool used to shape or cut metal by applying force. There are three different ways of working sheet metal in presses.

(*i*) **Shearing.** In this operation metal is deformed to a shear failure in order to cut various contours from the metallic sheet.

(*ii*) **Bending.** It is a localised deformation within the plastic range.

(*iii*) **Drawing.** In drawing there is a deformation within plastic range involving considerable change of shape.

6.2. Types of Presses

The presses are classified as follows :

(*i*) Based on source of power :

(*a*) Hand press

(*b*) Power press.

(*ii*) Based on type of frame.

(*a*) Pillar press

(*b*) Horn press

(*c*) Inclinable

(*d*) Straight side press.

Presses are exclusively intended for mass production.

(*iii*) Method of actuation of press

(*iv*) Number of slides incorporated

(*v*) Intended use.

The frame of a press is fabricated by casting or by welding, heavy steel plates. Cast frames are quite stable and rigid but expensive. The general classification by frame includes :

(*a*) gap frame

(*b*) straight side.

The gap frame is cut back below the ram to form the shape of letter C. This allows feeding the strip from the side. Gap frames presses are manufactured with solid frames fixed in a vertical or inclined position. The reason for inclining the press is to allow the parts to fall through the open back by gravity. The three position inclinable press is frequently referred to as an open Back Inclinable (O.B.I.) press.

Fig. 6.1*(a)* shows an OBI press. It has the following parts.

(*i*) **Rectangular bed :** It acts as a table to which a bolster plate is mounted.

(*ii*) **Bolster Plate :** It is used for locating and supporting the die assembly.

(*iii*) **Ram :** To ram the punch or upper die assembly is fastened.

(*iv*) **Fly Wheel:** To supply energy to the workpiece.

(*v*) **Knockout :** It is used to eject the workpiece.

(*vi*) **Pitman :** It is used to transfer motion and pressure from the main shaft or eccentric to press slide.

OBI press is quite commonly used for blanking and piercing operations on relatively small workpieces although bending, forming and drawing operations can also be carried out.

The straight side frame press in corporates a slide or ram which travels up and down between two straight sides or housing and is commonly used for heavy and large work.

According to sources of power majority of presses receive their power mechanically or hydraulically. Manually operated presses called hand presses are used for making very small components. Mechanically operated presses use a flywheel driven system to obtain ram movement.

The slide actuation may be achieved by two methods.

(*i*) By using a crank shaft

(*ii*) By using an eccentric.

The number of slides or rams provided on a press depend upon type of operation. A single action press has one slide. A double action press has two slides an inner and an outer. Slide and is quite commonly used for drawing operation.

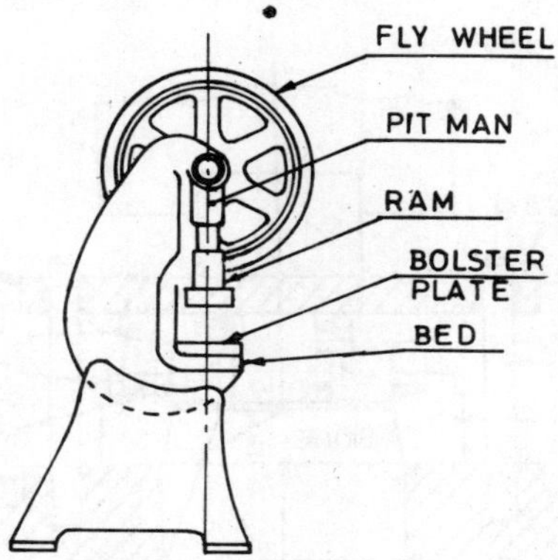

Fig. 6.1. (*a*)

6.3. Selection of Press

Press tool designer has to make proper selection of the type of press to be used and also the kind of press tools to be provided. For example it may be more economical to use a tool which will complete a number of operations at one stroke of the press than to employ a number of cheaper and simpler tools to perform the same work in a series of operations. The design of the tools should be simplest possible and the method of operation the most efficient one. Hydraulic presses are used primarily for forging and coining operations where a comparatively slow stroke is advisable.

While selecting a press the following points should be considered.

(*i*) Force required to cut the metal

(*ii*) Size and type of die

(*iii*) Stroke length

(*iv*) Method of feeding and size of sheet blank

(*v*) Shut height

(*vi*) Type of operation.

6.4. Common Components of a Simple Die

A die is a tool intended to cut or shape thin metals.

Fig. 6.1 shows the various parts of a simple die.

Fig. 6.2 shows a typical two-post die set.

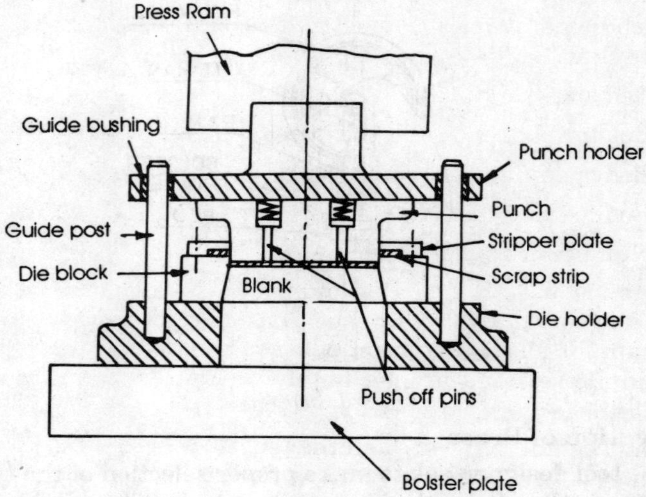

Fig. 6.1.

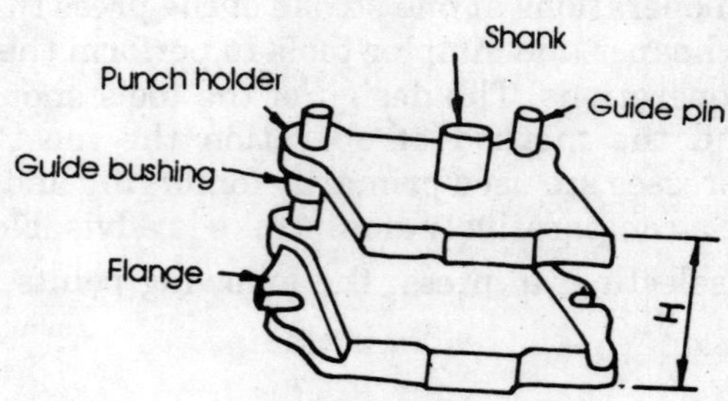

Fig. 6.2.

6.5. Press Features

Some of the features of a press are as follows :

(*i*) *Press tonnage :* It is the force in tonnes that a press can apply safely on work.

(*ii*) *Press stroke :* It is the distance travelled by ram of press during its downward or upward motion. It is expressed in centimetres.

(*iii*) *Die area :* It is the available surface area for mounting punch and die components (press tool) in the press. The die area on the die shoe should be at least 6 mm larger all around the die block.

(*iv*) *Shut height :* It is the distance from the die shoe to the top of the punch holder when the die is in its closed position. Distance *H* indicates shut height in Fig. 6.2.

(*v*) Bed size

(*vi*) Bolster plate size and thickness

(*vii*) Bed opening

(*viii*) Bed to floor height

(*ix*) Number of guide posts.

Die sets are used to hold and aid in the alignment of cutting members. Die sets may have no guide posts at all and rely on the machine ram for alignment or on pilots in the punches. They are called plain die sets and are not highly precision. They may also have shanks or in the very large die sets fasten directly to the ram.

The shut height will establish the length of guide posts which must be at least 12 mm shorter to allow for the reduced shut height due to re-sharpening.

Die holder should be at least 6 mm larger all around than the die block.

Punch forces the sheet strip down and may pierce it or draw it. It takes the assistance of die to do this. Punch holder holds the punch. Generally between the top of punch and punch holder a pressure plate is also introduced to provide some cushioning effect on the top of punch holder there is a shank which is anchored to the press ram. Die holder holds the die block at proper position with respect to the punch. Die holder is clamped to the bolster plate.

Strips of stocks are fed into the die from right, left or front to rear depending upon the method selected.

The punch holder is equipped with an integral round shank which is gripped by a clamp in the press ram. The shank is located in the centre of die space area.

The guide pins and guide posts provide alignment between the die shoe and the punch holder. The guide bushings are mounted in the punch holder and slide over the guide pins. Bushings are available in various lengths, of different materials, removable or press fit, and of plain or ball-bearing type. The flange is a ledge that protrudes from the die shoe to provide a means of clamping the die shoe to the bolster plate of the press. The available surface for mounting punch and die components is called the *die area*. The die area on the die shoe should be at least 6 mm larger all around the die block.

6.6. Types of Dies

Dies are classified by the type of operation performed and by type of construction of die. The various types of dies are as follows

(*i*) *Simple dies* : These dies are designed to perform only one operation such as blanking, piercing, notching, trimming etc.

(*ii*) *Multi-operation dies* : These dies are designed to perform several operations in stroke of ram.

These dies are further classified as follows :

(*a*) Compound dies (*b*) Combination dies

(*c*) Progressive dies.

In compound dies two or more cutting operations such as blanking and piercing can be performed simultaneously in a single stroke at single station.

In combination dies the cutting and forming or drawing operations are combined are carried out in single operation.

Fig. 6.3 shows a compound dies. It is used to produce a workepiece which is pierced and blanked at one station and in one operation. The blanking punch and blanking die opening are mounted in an inverted position.

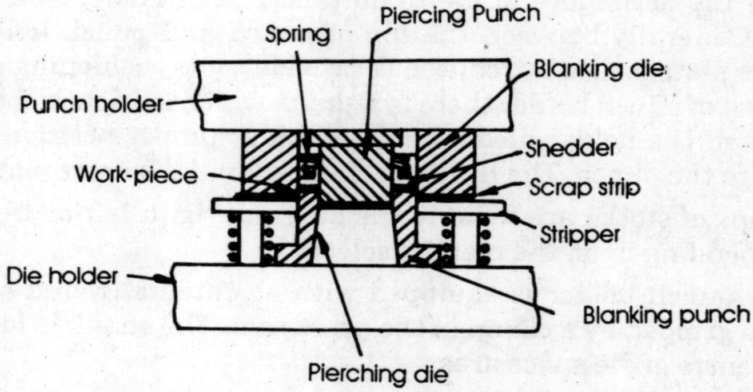

Fig. 6.3.

Compound dies ensure the positional relationship between the various elements of workpiece.

The die sets should be so laid out that the centre of pressure of the blank is central with the shank.

In progressive dies the workpiece moves from one station to another, with separate operations being performed at each station.

All stations work simultaneously and the work piece is retained in stock till it reaches the final station which cuts off the finished piece.

Fig 6.3(*a*) shows a compound die before cutting operation and Fig. 6.3 (*b*) shows the compound die after cutting operation.

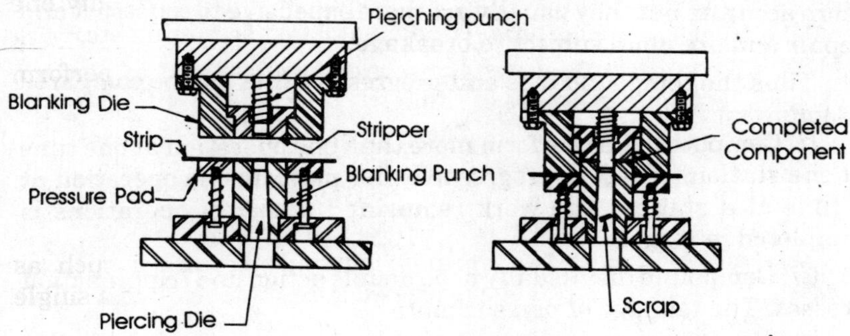

Fig. 6.3. (*a*) Fig. 6.3. (*b*)

Fig. 6.4 shows a progressive die to carry out piercing and blanking operations. The strip moves from piercing to blanking station.

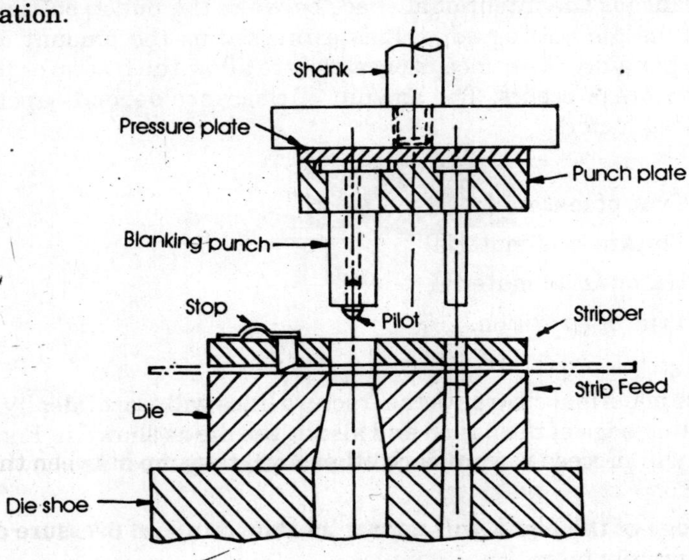

Fig. 6.4.

In progressive die punching is carried out at one station and blanking is carried out at another station. Progressive dies can be used for many variations of piercing, blanking, forming, lancing and so forth. They have the advantage of being fairly simple to construct and are economical to repair because a broken punch or die does not necessitate the replacement of the entire set. However if highly accurate alignment of various operations is required, they are not as satisfactory as compound dies. The compound dies are more accurate but they usually are more expensive to construct and repair and are more subject to breakage.

Thus the compound dies and progressive dies can be compared as follows :

(*i*) Compound dies perform more than one operation at one time at one station. Whereas progressive dies perform one operation at a time at a station. The work requiring number of operations is completed in stages.

(*ii*) Compound dies usually need double action and tripple action presses. The tonnage of press is more.

(*iii*) Compound dies ensure more accurately the position relationship between the various elements of the job.

(*iv*) Progressive dies are simpler in construction.

6.7. Clearance Between Die and Punch

Clearance is the intentional space between the punch cutting edge and the die cutting edge. It is expressed as the amount of clearance per side. Clearance is necessary to allow the fractures to meet when break occurs. The amount of clearance depends upon the following factors :

(*i*) Type of material

(*ii*) Thickness of material

(*iii*) Hardness of material

(*iv*) Type of operation.

In case of normal clearance the fracture lines will start (ideally) at the cutting edge of the punch and also at the die as shown in Fig. 6.5. They will proceed toward each other until they meet as shown in Fig. 6.6.

The edge of the blank will appear as shown in Fig. 6.7. There will be minimum burr.

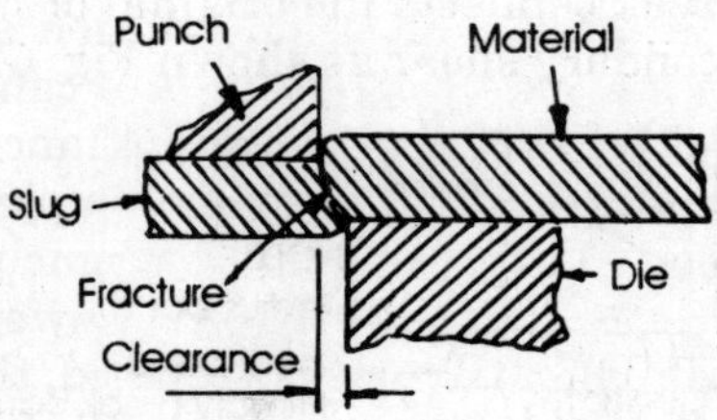

Fig. 6.5.

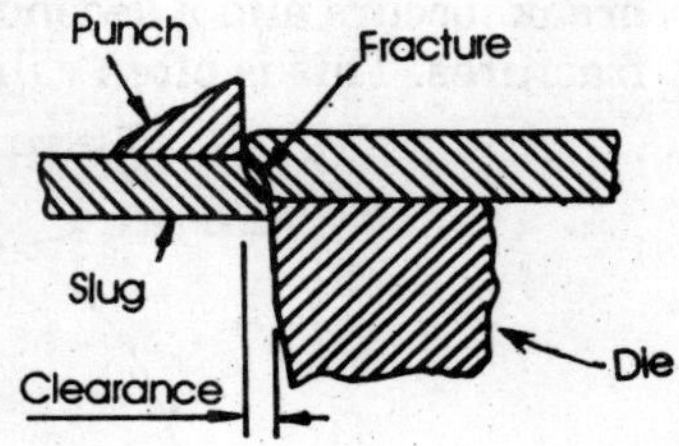

Fig. 6.6.

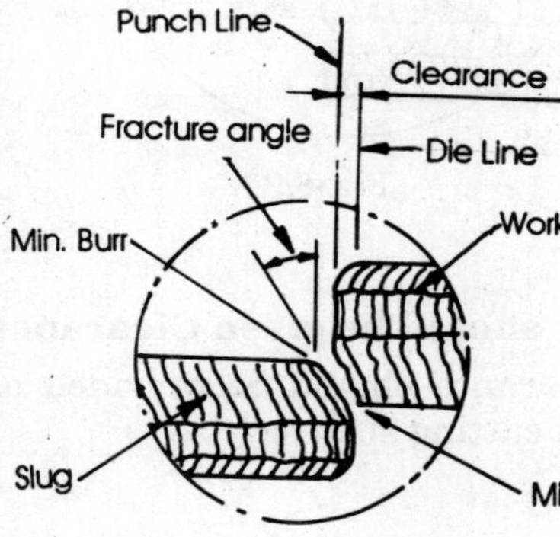

Fig. 6.7.

Excessive clearance allows a large edge radius and excessive plastic deformation. The edge of the material tend to be drawn or pulled in the direction of the working force and the break is not smooth.

Large burrs are present at the break edge (Fig. 6.8).

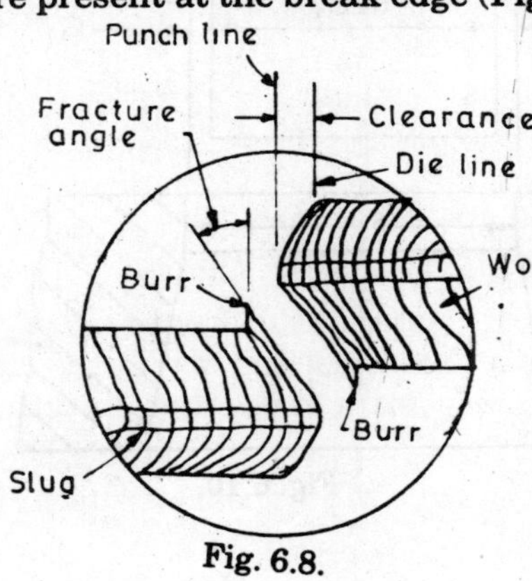

Fig. 6.8.

In sufficient clearance does not allow a clean break. A partial break occurs and a secondary break connects the original or main fractures. This is often called secondary shear as shown Fig. 6.9.

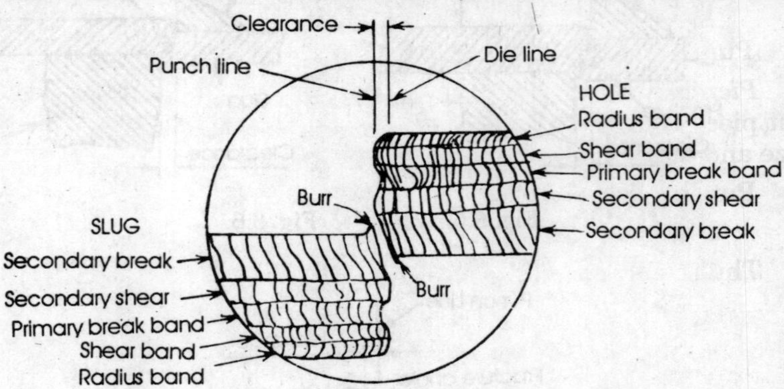

Fig. 6.9

6.8. Which Member should be given Clearance ?

Whether the clearance should be provided on punch or die depends upon type of cutting such as

(*i*) blanking

(*ii*) Piercing.

Blanking. In blanking the cut out piece is the desired part. In this case punch is made smaller in size and the die is made of exact size clearance is thus provided on punch as shown in Fig. 6.10.

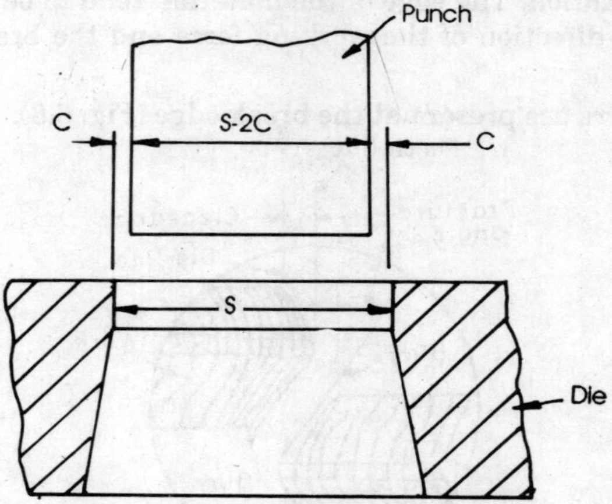

Fig. 6.10.

S = Size of work piece

C = Clearance

Die size = S = Size of work piece

Punch size = S–2C

Piercing : In case of piercing the cut out part is waste and left out piece is of importance. In piercing the punch is made of exact size and die is made of bigger size as shown in Fig. 6.11.

Punch size = size

Die size = size + 2C

Thus clearance is given on die.

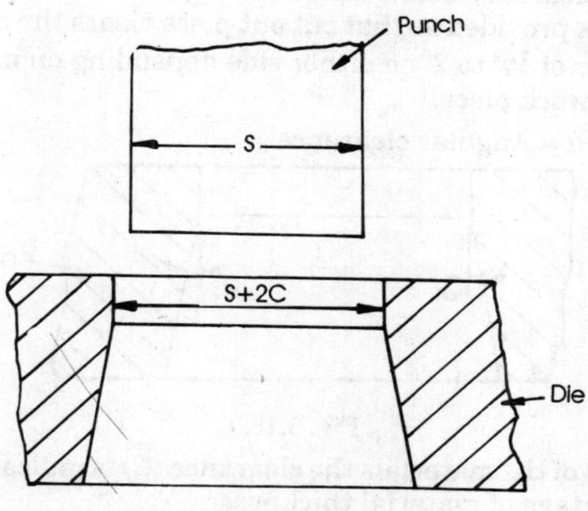

Fig. 6.11.

where C = Clearance

= 3% to 8% of material thickness.

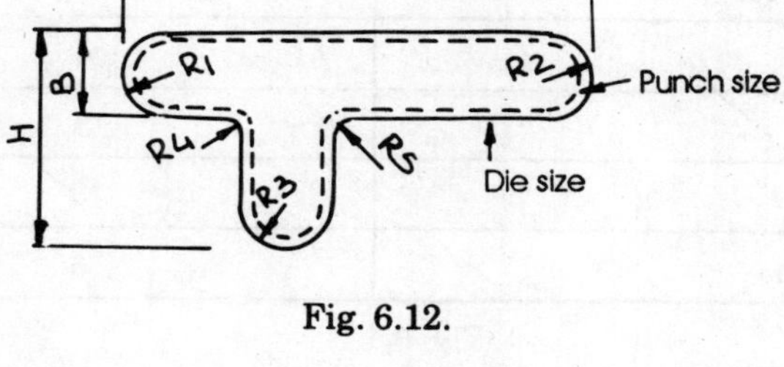

Fig. 6.12.

Hard materials require more clearance than soft materials. To blank a component shown in Fig. 6.12 die will be made of exact size and clearance will be provided on punch as shown by dotted line. The various dimensions on punch will be as follows.

(i) $L - 2C$ (ii) $H - 2C$

(iii) $B - 2C$ (iv) $R_1 - C$

(v) $R_2 - C$ (vi) $R_3 - C$

(vii) $R_4 + C$ (viii) $R_5 + C$.

6.9. Angular Clearance on Die

It is the clearance below the straight portion of die as shown in Fig. 6.13. It is provided so that cut out piece clears the die easily. It is of the order of ½° to 2° on either side depending on material and shape of the work piece.

α = Angular clearance

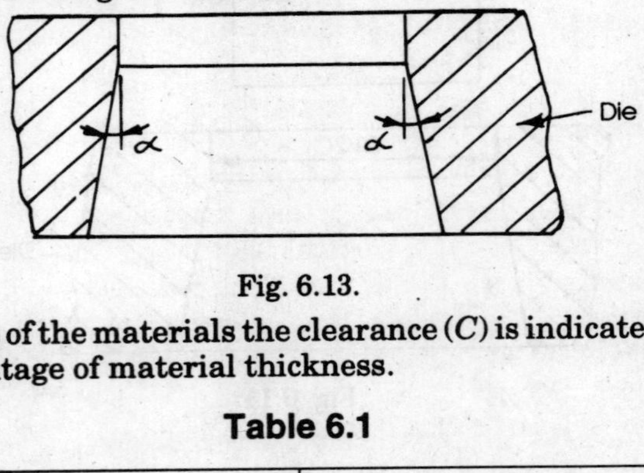

Fig. 6.13.

For some of the materials the clearance (C) is indicated in Table 6.1 as percentage of material thickness.

Table 6.1

Material	*C (%)*
Soft Steel	3
Medium Steel	3.5
Hard Steel	4
Copper	3
Brass	3
Aluminium	6

The general rule for the application of clearances is as follows :

The size of the punch determines the size of pierced hole.

The size of die opening determines the size of the blanked part.

Proper clearance between punch and die :

(*i*) Helps to produce accurate components.

(*ii*) Increase life of tool

(*iii*) Reduces cutting force.

Too small clearances have the following draw backs :

(*i*) Excessive force is required to shear the material

(*ii*) Both punches and dies become blunt, and they have to be ground after short runs.

(*iii*) The burrs on the work piece become predominant.

(*iv*) Blunt cutting edges cause excessive radii on the opposite work surface.

(*v*) The fractured surfaces are rough.

Too excessive clearances also cause burrs along with excessive radii.

6.10. Die Sets

A production die is conventionally constructed upon a die set that consists of a punch holder and die shoe kept in permanent alignment by two or more vertical leader or guide pins. The guide pins are fastened to the die shoe and the punch holder often bushed, slides over them. The die shoe has ledges or bolt slots for fastening it to the bolster plate of the press. The punch holder is bolted to or has its shank clamped in the press ram.

The punch holder and die shoe are of cast iron or semi-steel for ordinary purposes and steel for highest quality. The punches and die block are positioned in a die set so that the resultant of all vertical forces acting during a stroke passes through the center of the ram.

Following information is essential to specify a die set.

(*i*) Diameter of shank or no shank

(*ii*) Overall length and type of guide pins based on

(*a*) Shut height

(*b*) Length of stroke

(*iii*) Type and length of bushing.

(*iv*) Die area.

6.10.1. Types of die sets. There are two types of die sets (*i*) Precision

(*ii*) Commercial.

The major difference between these two types is the closeness of fit between the bushings and the guide pins.

In precision types of die sets the tolerance between the bushings and the guide pins are much closer in order to assure extremely accurate alignment between punches and corresponding holes in die blocks. In general precision die sets are used when the die clearances are low. These are used for cutting operations. Commercial die sets are used for drawing and forming operations.

6.11. Materials for Die Sets

The material used in die sets is cast iron, cast steel, or rolled steel. Cast-iron die sets are lower in cost because of the reduction in necessary machining but are subject to cracking under heavy shock loads. They are primarily used for smaller dies that do not require maximum strength. Cast steel has a greater thoughness and a greater resistance to shock loads. Rolled-steel die sets exhibit maximum toughness and resistance to shock loads and are generally used for larger and special dies. When a large hole is to be machined through the die set for blank removal, a steel die set should be used to increase strength, especially when the die set is placed over a large hole in the bolster plate.

6.12. Types of Die Sets

Die sets are available in different sizes and styles. The commonly used die sets are of following types :

(i) Back-pin die set. In this die set the pins are at the back of set, leaving a clear space for hand feeding blanks for second operations. The good view of moving parts and freedom from obstructing pins and bushings also aids the operator when feeding from left to right.

(ii) Centre-pin type. This set is used when load is too heavy and the feed is from the front. In this guide pins are in alignment with the load along the transverse centre line of the set leaving the front clear but preventing end feeding either by hand or automatically.

(iii) Diagonal pin type. It is used when load is very heavy and feeding is required. In this set one of the pins is placed at the front of set thus avoiding the over hang of the back pin type by having the load in alignment with the pins along a diagonal line and leaving the ends clear for feeding. For round work pieces especially for coming and shaving operations round die sets with pins at the back or along the centre can be used to advantage.

6.12.1. Dowels and screws. Dowels and screws used in blanking and piercing dies should be located diagonally across from each other and as far apart as possible to increase locational accuracy. All dowels and screws should be located at a distance ranging from 1.5 to 2 times their diameter from the component edge. They should be placed near the outer edge of die block as far as possible.

Some of the characteristic features of screws and dowels used are as follows :

(*i*) A minimum of one cap screw and two dowels are necessary to position and hold die component in place. More cap screws may be used for larger components but two and only two dowels should be used for positioning.

(*ii*) Dowels should be located as far apart as possible to increase locational accuracy.

(*iii*) Screws and dowels should be located at 1.5 to 2 times their diameter from the component edge.

(*iv*) The effective thread depth for screws should be 1.5 times to 2 times the screw diameter.

(*v*) Usually 9 to 10 mm screws are used on die components up to 150 mm square. Heavy die components are usually secured. With 12 mm to 16 mm diameter screws.

(*vi*) Dowel and screws diameter should be same.

(*vii*) Cap screws used to secure die blocks should be placed in counter bored holes so that screw head is 3 to 4 mm deeper in the hole. This is provided to allow additional material for die grinding.

6.13. Methods of Punch Support

The punch should be strong enough to withstand stripping forces, should not deflect and should not rotate as a result of cutting action. Deflection of punches may be avoided by making the shank (body) diameter of punch larger than the cutting diameter, as shown in Fig. 6.14.

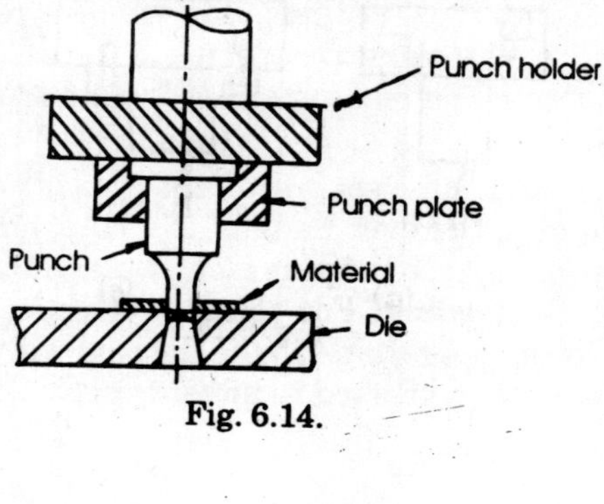

Fig. 6.14.

The punches are usually held in a steel punch plate of the punch holder which is again clamped to the lower end of ram of press.

Fig. 6.15 shows various methods of mounting punches. Punch may be connected to punch plate by screw [Fig. 6.15 *(a)*], the punch may be connected to punch plate by a set screw and is located by two dowel pins. [Fig. 6.15 *(b)*]. The punch is forced in the punch plate [Fig. 6.15 *(c)*] and the top end of the punch is flattened to fit in the counter sunk recess. Set screws may be used to connect punch to the punch plate as shown in [Fig. 6.15 *(d)*] and Fig. 6.15 *(e)*. Punch plates serve to hold, position and in some cases strengthen the punch.

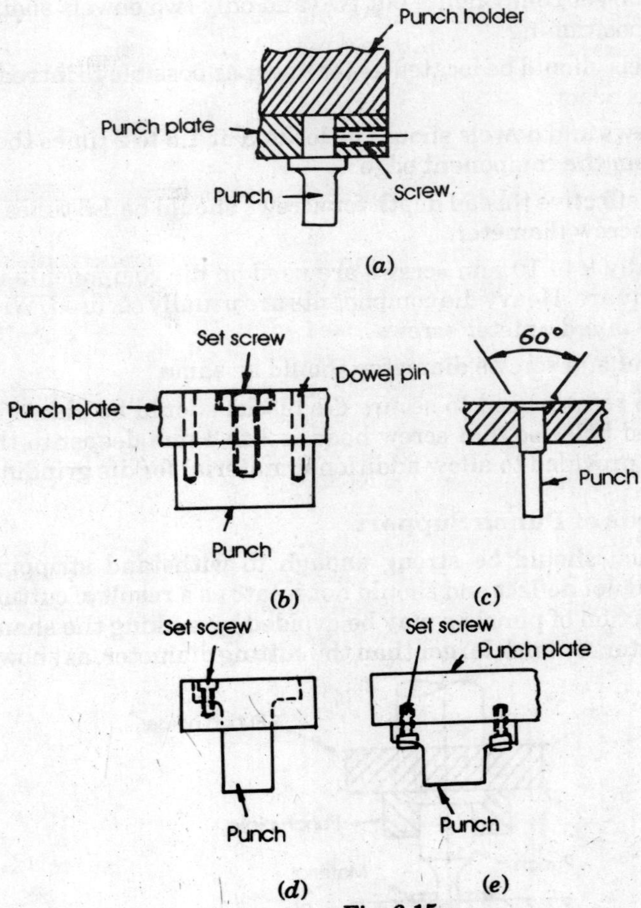

Fig. 6.15.

6.14. Punches Characteristics

The following factors should be considered while designing punches

(*i*) Punches should not defect during use

(*ii*) Punches should be of proper hardness

(*iii*) They should be strong enough to withstand forces

(*iv*) They should not rotate as a result of cutting action.

A large blanking or forming punch usually is made with a flange by which it is bolted and dowled to the punch holder after being aligned with the die block assembly.

The length of the shank of a blanking punch for quantity production should include 3 mm to 6 mm for grinding to re-sharpen it during its life and enough more to reach the die block through the stripper plate and to shear the stock after the punch has been ground down.For stability the width of the flange should not be less than the height of the punch. The nose of a drawing punch should have a smooth radius all around the four to six times the stock thickness.

Piercing punches are pressed in a punch plate and the plate is bolted and doweled to the punch holder.

6.14.1. Punch Holder. It is used to mount the punch either directly or through a back plate and retainer. The upper part of the punch holder is provided with a shank equal in diameter of ram hole. The shank is located in position with a side screw. The dimensions of the punch holder should be about 5 mm larger than the punch. The punch holder varies in thickness from 25 to 75 mm.

6.15. Methods of Die Support

Die may be connected to the die holder by set screw [Fig. 6.16 (*a*)] or set screws and dowel pins may be used to connect die to the die shoe (die holder) as shown in Fig. 6.16 (*b*).

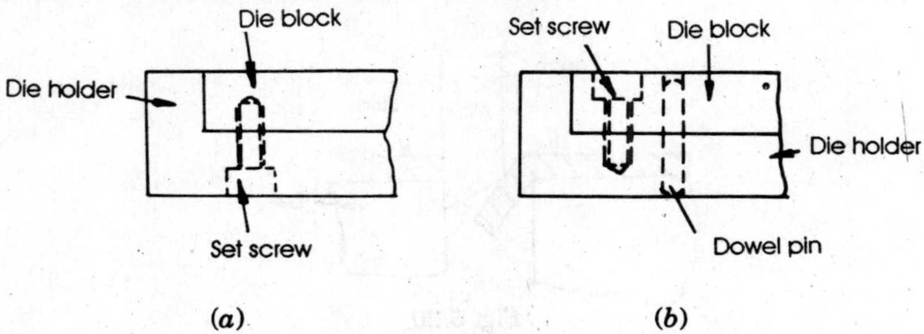

Fig. 6.16.

6.16. Press Work Operations

The commonly used press work operations are as follows :

(i) Blanking : In this operation the cut out part from the material strip is the required component (Fig. 6.17).

(ii) Piercing : In this operation the cut out part from the material strip is waste, hole left in the strip being required (Fig. 6.18).

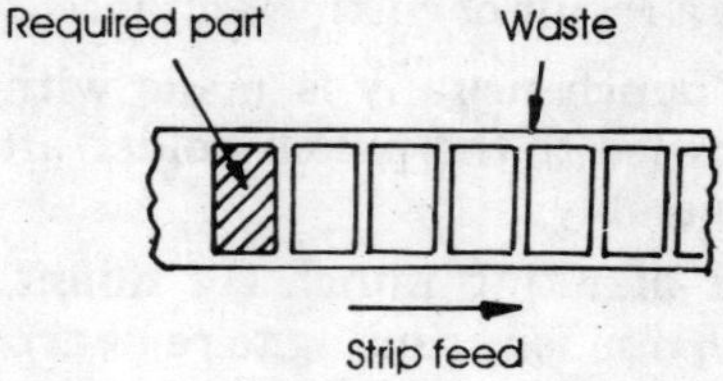

Fig. 6.17.

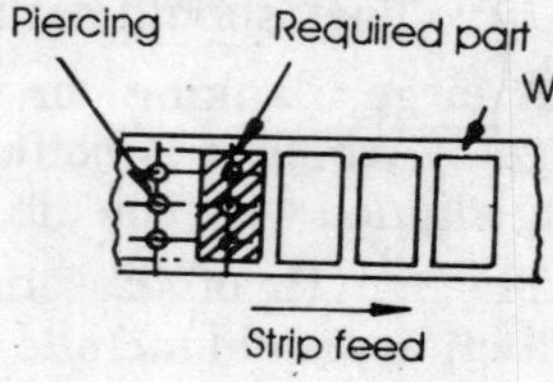

Fig. 6.18.

(iii) Notching : This operation is used to remove small amount of metal from the edges of the metallic strip (Fig. 6.19).

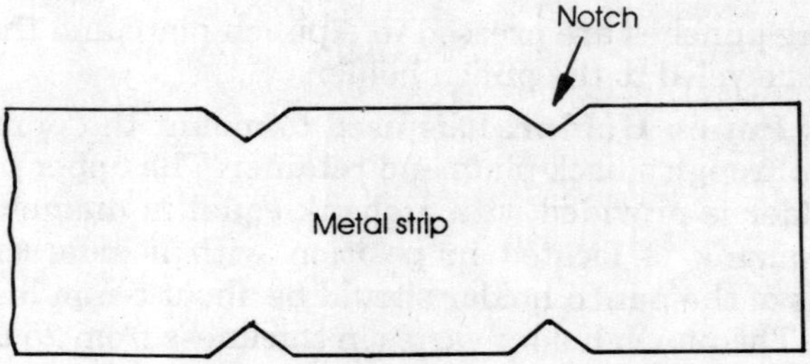

Fig. 6.19.

(iv) Lancing : It is a combined bending and cutting operation. (Fig. 6.20).

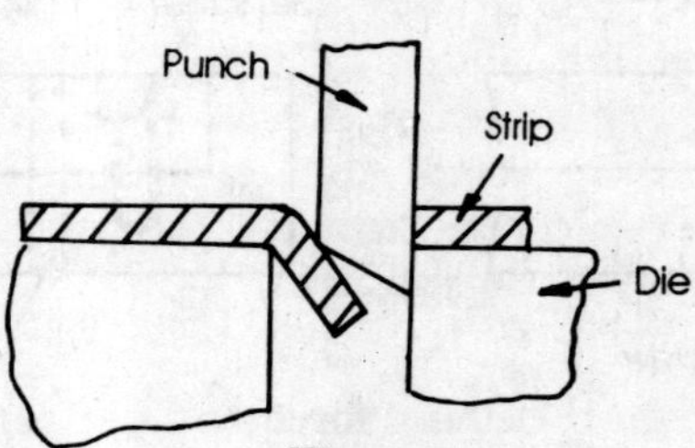

Fig. 6.20.

(v) *Drawing* : It is used to manufacture cup-shaped components.
(vi) *Cutting off*: This operation is used to separate the work material along a straight line in a single line cut (Fig. 6.21).

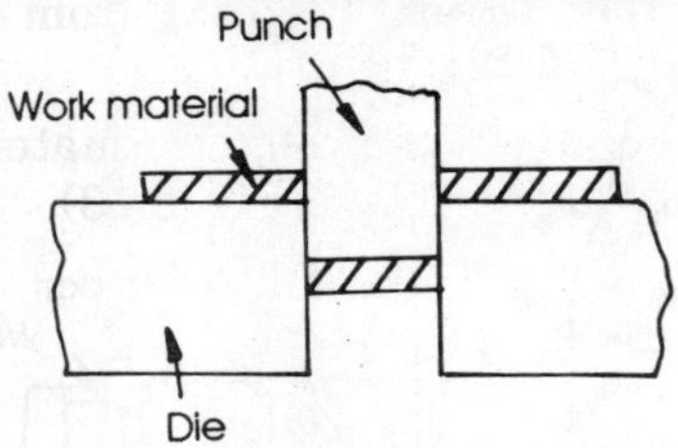

Fig. 6.21.

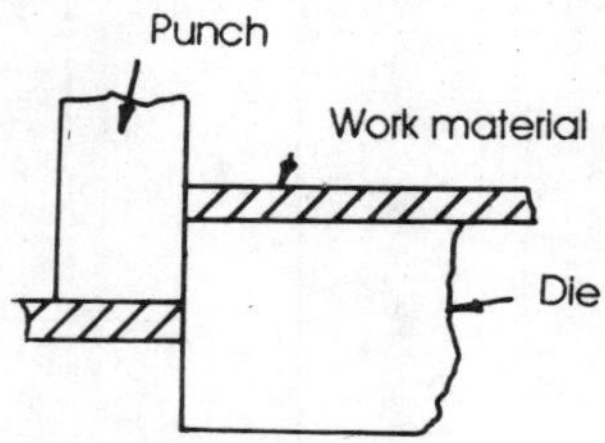

Fig. 6.22.

(vii) *Parting*. This operation is also used to separate the work material but in a double line cut way (Fig. 6.22).

6.17. Cutting Force

Cutting force is a function of the area of the cut edge being sheared at any instant and the shearing strength of the work piece material. Cutting force calculations help in selecting press of proper tonnage (capacity), in order to avoid overloading the press or failure to use it to capacity.

P = Cutting force (tonnes)

$= \pi D t f_S$ for round holes

$= L \cdot t \cdot f_S$ for other contours

where D = Hole diameter (mm)

t = Material thickness (mm).

L = Shear length (mm)

f_S = Ultimate shear strength of material (tonnes / mm^2)

Press capacity is more than the cutting force by about 10 to 20% of cutting force.

Shearing action can be related to cutting force (P) as show in Fig. 6.23. Resistance begins when the punch contacts the stock material. The load builds up rapidly during plastic deformation and continues to increase while penetration is taking place. The load falls away rapidly as the metal ruptures.

Fig. 6.24 shows typical cutting force and per cent penetration graph for blanking operation.

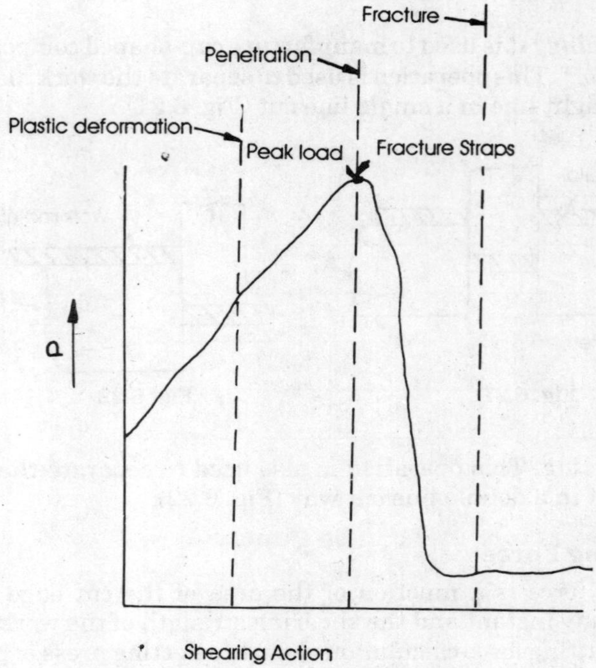

Fig. 6.23.

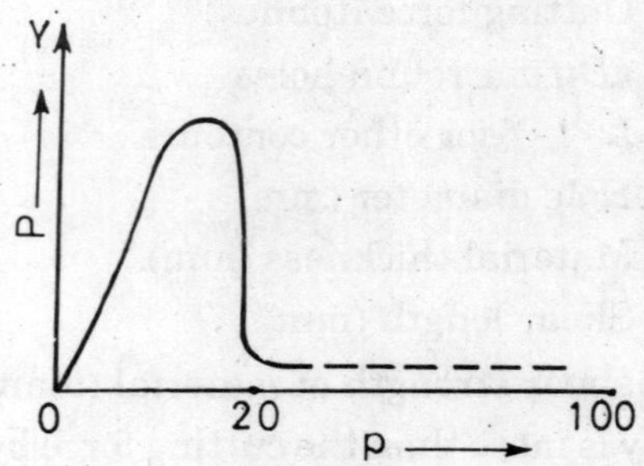

Fig. 6.24.

where P = cutting force (along Y axis)

p = % penetration (along X axis)

Work done = $P \times p \times t$

This is an estimate of course and depends upon the association that maximum punch force is sustained during complete punch penetration of the work metal.

Table 6.2 indicates the percentage penetration (p) for some of the materials.

Table 6.2

Material	*P (%)*
Alluminium alloy	60
Copper	55
Brass	50
Carbon steel	20 to 50
Bronze	25

6.18. Smallest Hole that can be Punched

The punch should have sufficient compressive strength so that it can apply necessary force required during punching :

Let d = Minimum Diameter of hole (mm)

t = Work material thickness (mm)

f_S = ultimate shear strength of work material (italict / mm^2)

f_c = Allowable compressive stress of punch (italict/mm^2)

P = Cutting force = $\pi d t f_S$

F_C = Compressive strength of punch

$$= \frac{\pi}{4} d^2 f_c$$

$$F_c = P$$

$$\frac{\pi}{4} d^2 f_c = \pi d t f_s$$

$$d = \frac{4 t f_s}{f_C}$$

Table 6.3 indicates the strength of some of the common materials.

Table 6.3

Material	*Yield strength* (kg/mm^2)	*Ultimate strength* (kg/mm^2)
Aluminium	15-20	20-40
Steel		
(*i*) Plain carbon	20-40	30-70
(*ii*) Free cutting	-	40-70
(*iii*) Spring steel	150-180	170-240
(*iv*) Low alloy	42-55	60-85
(*v*) High alloy	24-44	55-90
(*vi*) Cast steel	40-85	50-85
Brass	—	30-60
Bakelite	—	4-8
Rubber	—	1-7
Copper	12-18	22-35

The shear force (p) depends on the following factors :

(*i*) Condition of the edges of the cutting element.

(*ii*) Amount of punch die clearances.

(*iii*) Strength of the material of work piece.

(*iv*) Shear speed.

(*v*) Geometric form of the part.

(*vi*) Type and amount of cooling lubricant.

6.19. Die Block Design

The various dimensions of the die block are calculated as follows (see Fig. 6.25) :

(*i*) Dies must be adequately supported on a flat die plate or die plate or die holder (shoe).

(*ii*) Two and only two dowels should be provided in each block or element that requires accurate and permanent positioning. They should be located as far apart as possible for maximum locating effect usually near diagonally opposite corners. Two or more screws should be used depending on the size of die block.

(*iii*) Die block thickness (T) is calculated as follows :

$$T = 15 \text{ mm for } p = 75 \text{ mm}$$
$$= 25 \text{ mm for } p = 75 - 250 \text{ mm}$$
$$= 30 \text{ for larger values of } p.$$

where p = Blanking perimeter.

A grinding allowance up to 3 mm to 5 mm should be added to calculate die thickness. There should be minimum of 30 mm margin around the opening in the die block. Die block should never be thinner than 7 to 10 mm.

(*iv*) For securing the die block to the die holder following rules should be used :

(*a*) On die blocks up to 150 mm square use 10 mm Allen screws and two 10 mm dowel pins.

(*b*) On sections up to 250 mm square use three Allen screws and two dowel pins.

(*c*) For heavier stock and still bigger blocks use screws and pins of 12 mm diameter. Counter bore the die block to accommodate Allen heads at least 3 mm deeper than length of heads to compensate for die sharpening.

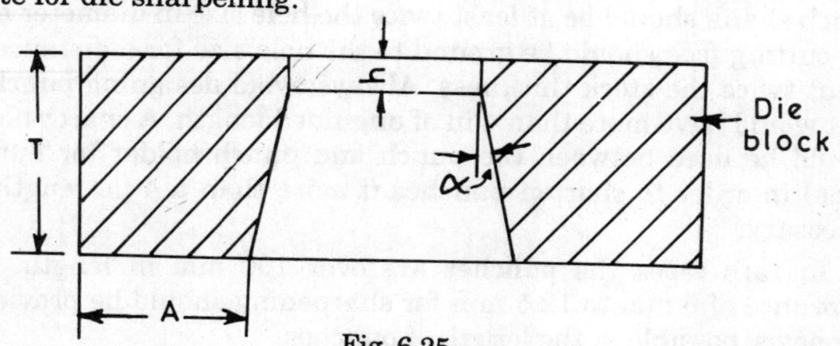

Fig. 6.25.

(*v*) h = Die opening should be straight
= 3 mm

(*vi*) A = Critical distance
= Distance between cutting edge and the die border
= $1.5T - 2T$ for small dies
= $2T - 3T$ for larger dies

(*vii*) α = Angular clearance = ½° to 2°

The overall design of die block depends on

(*a*) Part size and shape

(*b*) Type of die.

Die block is generally made up of cast iron.

6.20. Punch Design

The maximum allowable punch length (L_m) is calculated using the following formula :

$$L_m = \frac{\pi D}{8}\left(\frac{E \cdot D}{f_S \cdot t}\right)^{1/2}$$

where D = Diameter of punched hole

f_S = shear stress

t = Material thickness

E = Modulus of elasticity of punch material

where $\frac{D}{t}$ = 1.1 or higher.

Punch material should have sufficient compressive strength.

Piercing punch should not be smaller in diameter than the thickness of the stock they are to pierce. Where a small unguided puncher must pierce stock thicker than the punch diameter, the punch shank should be at least twice the hole size in diameter and the cutting face should be ground to the hole size for a distance of about twice the stock thickness. Always avoid designing punches that would have more than 4 in of unguided length. A spacer block should be used between the punch and punch holder (or punch plate) in order to shorten punches if more than a 4-in. length is necessary.

In rare cases the punches are over 100 mm in length. An allowance of 6 mm to 12.5 mm for sharpening should be provided whenever possible in the length of punches.

Punch Holder : Punch holder thickness varies between 25 to 75 mm.

Punch Plate : The thickness of punch plate $= 1.5 \times D$

where D = Diameter of punch.

Both punch holder and punch plate are made of cast iron.

While designing a punch following factors should be considered

(*i*) Easier fitting and removal of punch.

(*ii*) Alignment of punch and die.

(*iii*) Adequate provision of screws to overcome stripping force.

(*iv*) Prevention of rotation of punch.

The punch dimensions should be checked for

(*a*) Strength (*b*) Deflection.

6.21. Methods of Reducing Cutting Forces

The cutting forces can be reduced by following methods :

(i) Stepped punches. Punches or groups of punches progressively become shorter by about one stock material thickness as shown in Fig. 6.26.

$$h = t + 0.4 \text{ mm}$$

where t = Material thickness

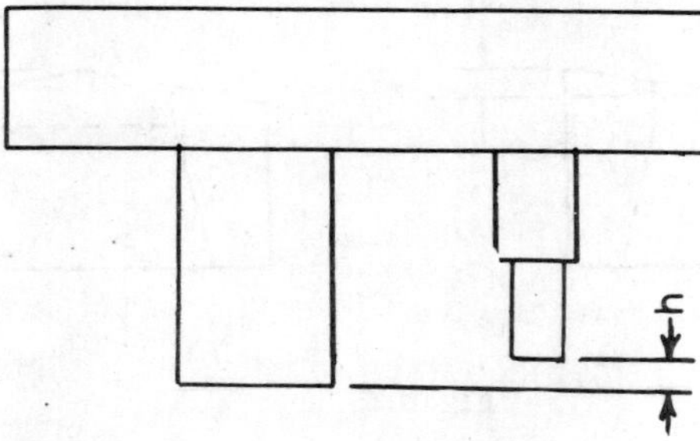

Fig. 6.26.

(ii) Single shear on die or punch. By grinding the face of die (Fig. 6.27) or punch (Fig. 6.28) at a small shear angle with the horizontal. This reduces the area in shear at any one time shear also reduces shock to the press and smoothes out the cutting operation. The shear angle chosen should provide a change in punch length for 1 to $1\frac{1}{2}$ times the stock thickness. Shear that is equal to or greater than the stock thickness is called full shear. Cutting forces can be reduced by about 30 per cent when full shear is used.

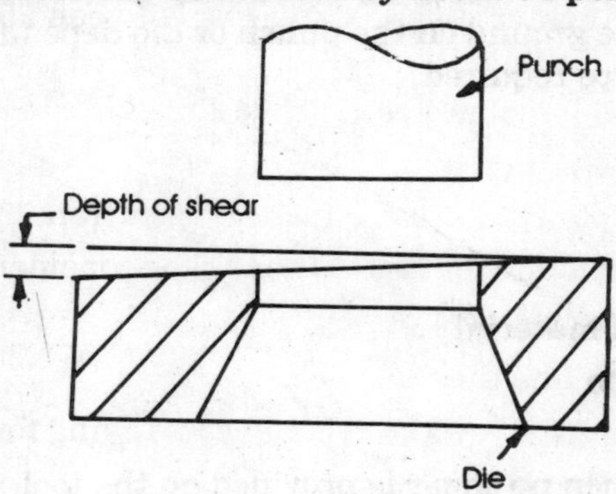

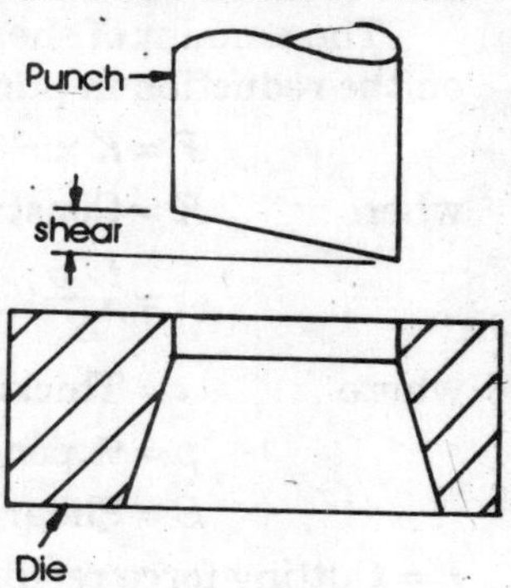

Fig. 6.27. Fig. 6.28.

(iii) Double shear on die or punch. Double shear angle on die (Fig. 6.29) or punch (Fig. 6.30) is preferred over single shear because it does not set up lateral force components.

Shear angle for blanking operation will be on the die number whereas in a piercing operation the shear angle will be on the punch member.

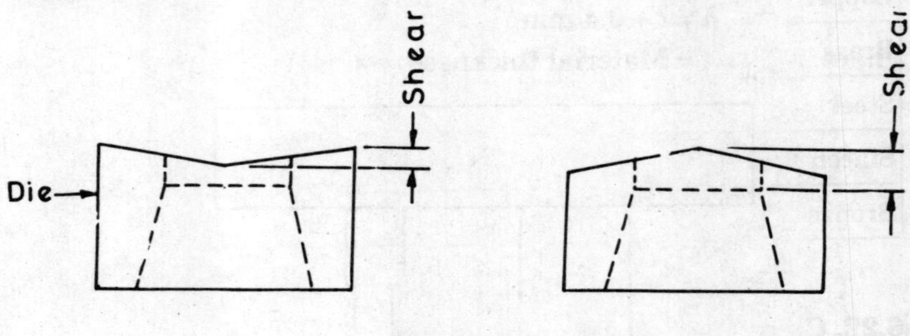

Fig. 6.29.

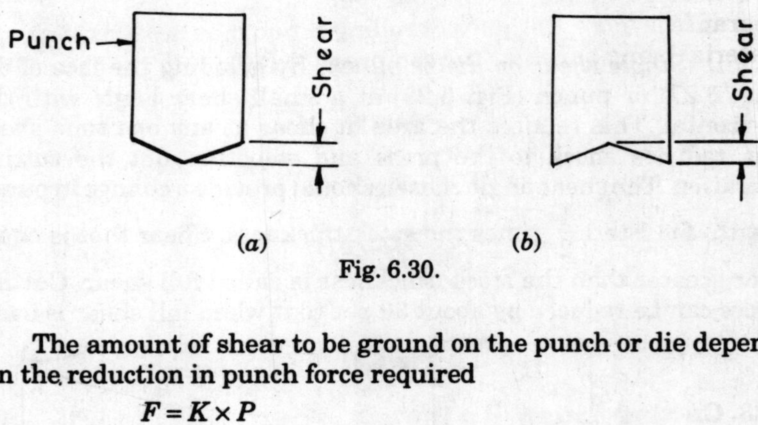

Fig. 6.30.

The amount of shear to be ground on the punch or die depends on the reduction in punch force required

$$F = K \times P$$

where K = Constant

$$= \frac{t \cdot p}{S}$$

where t = Thickness of material

p = % penetration

S = Shear

P = Cutting force required when no shear is provided on the tool.

Table 6.4 indicates the values of per cent penetration (p) for some of the materials.

Table 6.4

Material	*p*
Aluminium alloy	60
Copper	55
Brass	50
Steel	20-50
Silicon steel	30
Bronze	25

6.22. Clearance and Punch Force

The effect of punch to die clearance is shown in Fig. 6.31. If P is the force and R is the perpendicular distance then torque is equal to $P \times R$. Therefore the torque generated will be more if the clearance is more. Torque as a rolling action is as destructive to the material being punch as the compressive load.

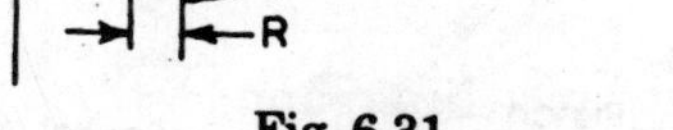

Fig. 6.31.

6.23. Cutting Action in a Die

Fig. 6.32 shows the cutting of metal between die components. It is a shearing process in which the metal is stressed in shear between two cutting edges to the point of fracture (beyond its ultimate strength). In die cutting, when the punch presses the metal which is subjected to different types of stresses at various places as shown in Fig. 6.32. The bottom-most layers of the sheet in die are subjected to tensile stresses and those below the punch are subjected to compressive stresses and this leads to stretching beyond the elastic limit. Further movement of punch leads to plastic deformation, reduction in area and finally fracture starts through clearage planes in the reduced area.

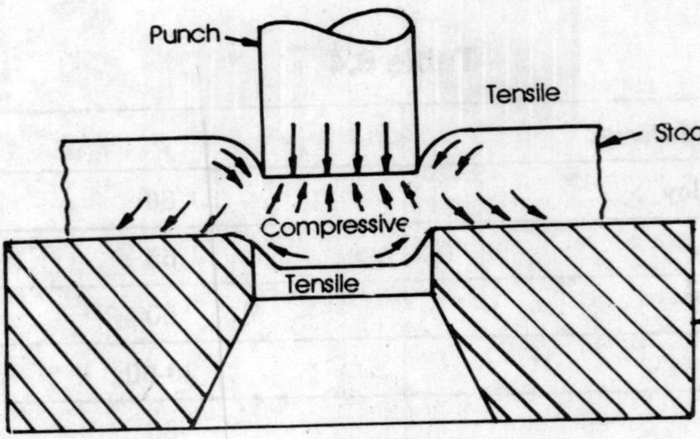

Fig. 6.32.

6.24. Stripper Plate

The function of the stripper plate is to remove the stock from the punch after blanking or piercing operation. There are two types of stripper plate commonly used :

(*i*) Fixed stripper

(*ii*) Spring loaded stripper.

Fixed stripper shown in Fig. 6.33 guides the sheet, strip or workpiece. Spring loaded stripper plate is preferred as it holds the strip in a flat position before the punch contacts the strip. This is necessary where very accurate blanks are needed and when very thin material is to be punched. Fig. 6.34 shows a spring loaded stripper.

The strippers are usually of the same length and width as die block.

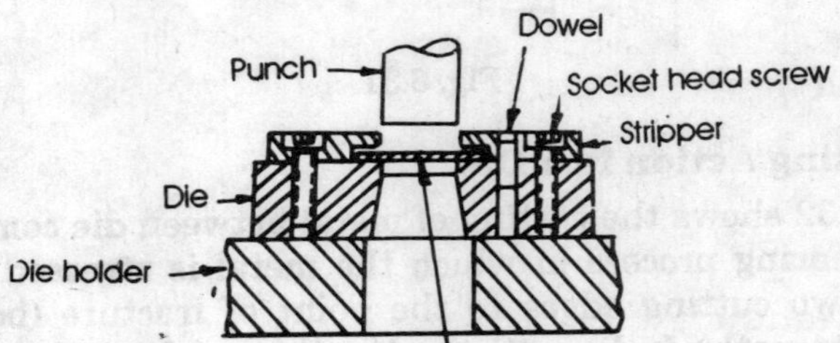

Fig. 6.33.

The stripper thickness should be sufficient to withstand the force required to strip the punch from the stock. The stripper thickness usually varies from 5 to 6 mm. The force required to strip the stock material from the punch called stripping force varies from 5 to 20% of the cutting force.

The punches with polished side walls tends to strip easier than those with rough surfaces. More force is also required to strip punches that are close together.

Selection of stripper depends on

(*i*) Stripping force

(*ii*) Space available.

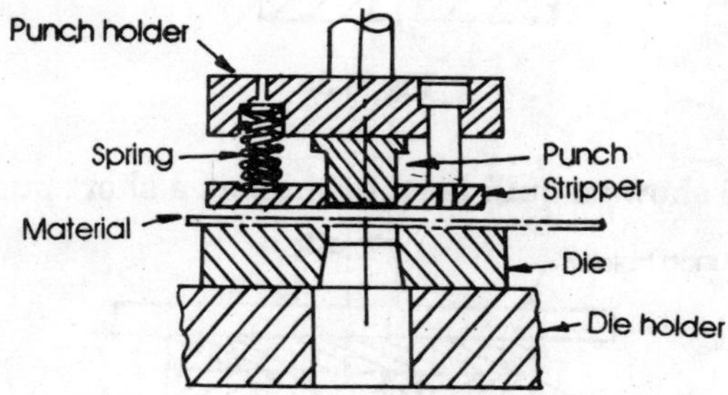

Fig. 6.34.

The force (F) for which springs of spring operated stripper plate is calculated as follows

$$F = 1500\, L \times t$$

where L = cut perimeter (cm)

t = Stock thickness (cm)

Choice of the method of applying springs to the stripper plate depends on the following :

(*i*) Required pressure

(*ii*) Stage limitations

(*iii*) Shape of die

(*iv*) Nature of work.

Fig. 6.35 shows a long thin punch guided through a bushing in the stripper plate. Headless may bushing be used for this purpose. The hardened backing plate should be press fitted into the punch holder. Provisions must be made for removing the plate.

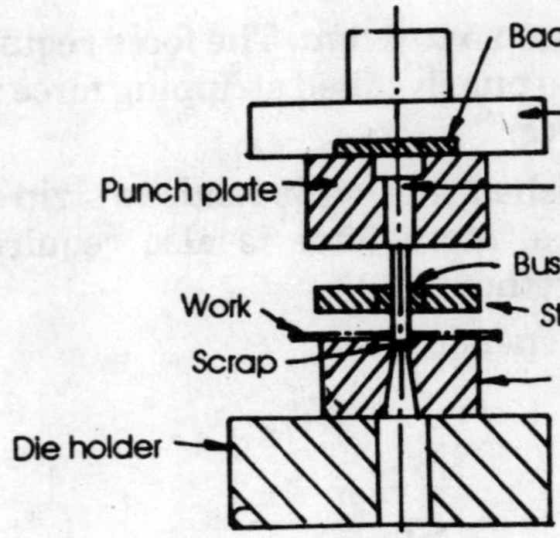

Fig. 6.35.

Fig. 6.36 shows a quill used to support a short punch.

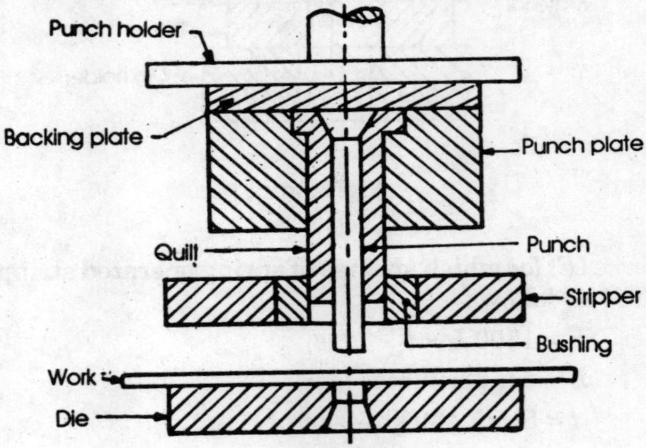

Fig. 6.36.

Some time a spacer is provided to raise the stripper so that there is clearance between the top of the strip and the stripper plate (Fig. 6.37).

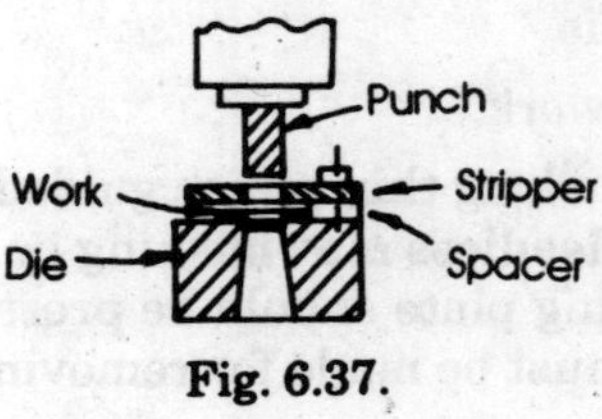

Fig. 6.37.

The clearance between punch and stripper should be 50% of the punch and die.

6.25. Die Springs

Die springs are available in various service grades with corresponding permissible deflections ranging from 25 to 50 per cent of fix length. The selection of die springs depends on the following factors :

(*i*) Stripping force

(*ii*) Space available for spring mounting

(*iii*) Permissible deflection

Based on the deflection the springs may be classified into four load ratings as follows

(*i*) 25% deflection = Extra high pressure (XHP)

(*ii*) 30% deflection = High Pressure (H.P.)

(*iii*) 37% deflection = Medium high pressure (MHP)

(*iv*) 50% deflection = Medium Pressure (MP)

Permissible deflection in die springs is 50 to 25% of free length.

Die springs are designed to resist fatigue failure.

6.26. Die Wear

Punches and dies used for cutting wear out sooner than those used for bending and forming. The various causes of die wear as follows :

(*i*) In sufficient or excessive clearance.

(*ii*) Punches are too close to each other.

(*iii*) Punches and dies are not made of proper materials.

(*iv*) The punches and dies are not properly heart treated.

(*v*) Punches entering too far into the die openings.

(*vi*) Work piece material is too hard.

(*vii*) Punch length is too large as compared to cross-sectional area of the punch.

(*viii*) Stripping action is not proper.

(*ix*) When too many pierces are produced between sharpenings.

(*x*) Die is not properly fitted in the press.

6.27. Trimming Die Design

Trimming is the operation that removes the distorted excess metal from drawn shapes and also provides a smooth edge. While designing trimming dies, the following points should be considered.

1. Die should be such that the part after operation will fall clear or can be removed easily.

2. The material of the cutting edges must be suitable for the purpose.

3. A suitable device should be provided for the accurate location of the part in the die.

4. The extra material (flash) must be easily removed from the punch or die.

5. There should not be any distortion or squeezing of the product during operation.

6.28. Fine Blanking

It is the operation in which the blanked workpieces are characterised by smooth edges and a close wall thickness between pierces holes and the peripheral edge. Generally no further machining operations are necessary to obtain blank or hole edges comparable to machined edges.

Fine blanking press must be of special design because there must be virtually no play between the punch and die and the hold down force may be as high as 2.5 times the blanking tonnage. The material of workpiece to be fine blanked should have high ductility.

The major differences between a fine blanking tool and conventional compound die are as follows :

(*i*) Fine blanking tools should take up forces 1.5 to 2.5 times more than those to which conventional tools are subjected to.

(*ii*) Fine blanking tool has an extremely small cutting clearance between punch and die. It is nearly 0.5% per side of the material thickness as compared to 5 to 10% in conventional press tools.

(*iii*) Due to the extremely close tolerance between punch and die, the guidance and centring of the main punch relative to die plate must be more exact.

(*iv*) In fine blanking edges are sheared bright over complete thickness whereas in conventional blanking edges are sheared up to one third of the thickness and the rest remains fractured.

(*v*) In fine blanking surface finish on sheared edges can be achieved upto 0.6 micron CLA.

6.29. Pilots

The function of a pilot is to position the workpiece or stock strip accurately. When establishing the sequence of operations for progressive dies, piercing operations are carried out first. Advantage is taken of these holes for piloting the blanking punches so that the blank formed is exactly concentric to the pierced hole. This piloting is obtained with the help of pilots secured to the blanking punches. (Fig. 6.38)

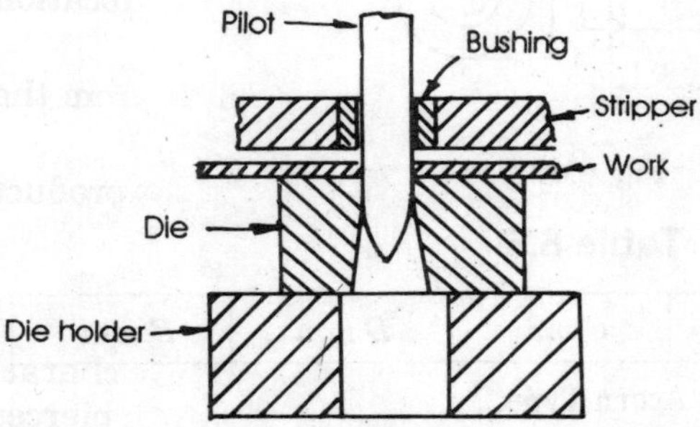

Fig. 6.38.

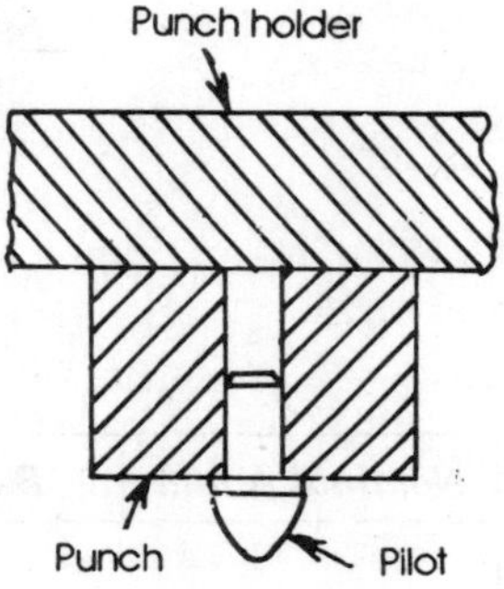

Fig. 6.39.

Pilots are be fitted to the punches by following methods :

(*i*) Press fit pilot (Fig. 6.39).

(*ii*) Threaded shank pilots (Fig. 6.40).

(*iii*) Socket set screw pilots (Fig. 6.41).

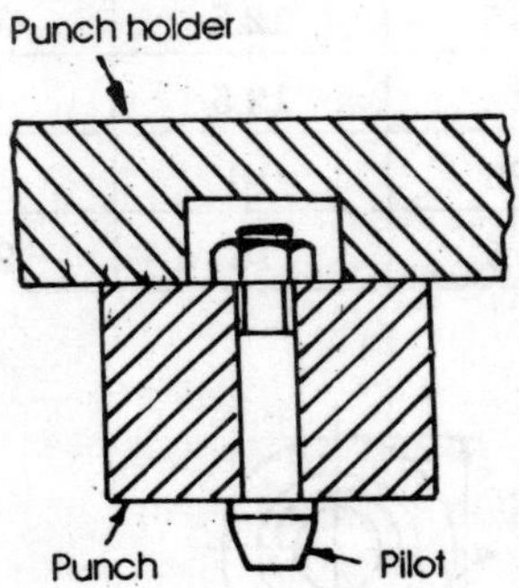

Fig. 6.40.

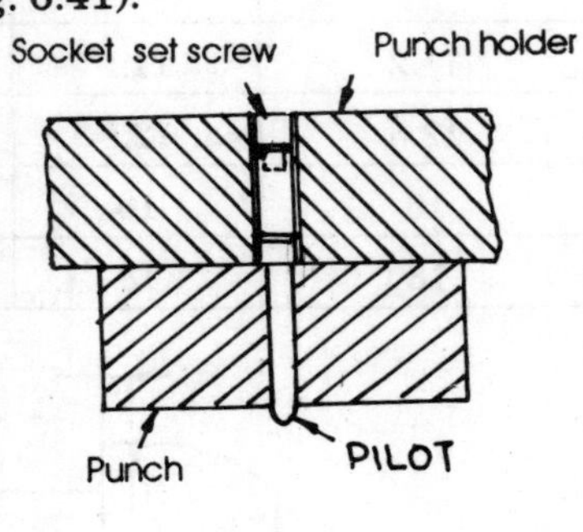

Fig. 6.41.

Press fit pilots are liable to drop out due to friction between the pilot and the pierced hole. They are thus not preferred for high speed work. Fig. 6.42 shows acron type pilot.

Pilots are made of steel heat treated for maximum toughness and to a hardness of Rockwell HRC 56 to HRC 60.

Pilots are of two types :

(*i*) Acorn type (*ii*) Flattened end type.

Fig. 6.42 shows an acorn type pilot. Typical dimensions are indicated in table 6.5.

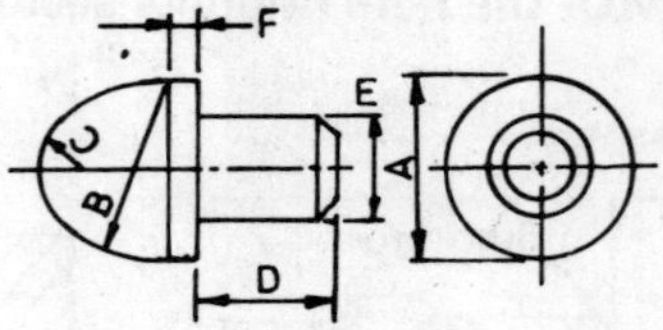

Fig. 6.42.

Table 6.5

Nominal A mm	*B mm*	*C mm*	*D mm*	*E mm*
Acorn Type				
3.15	3.15	0.8	6.3	2.5
4.75	4.75	1.18	6.3	3.15
6.3	6.3	1.6	11.2	4.75
8	8	2	11.2	5.6
9.5	9.5	2.5	12.5	6.3
11.2	11.2	3.15	12.5	7.1
12.5	12.5	4	12.5	8
16	16	4.25	16	9
18	18	4.75	16	9.5

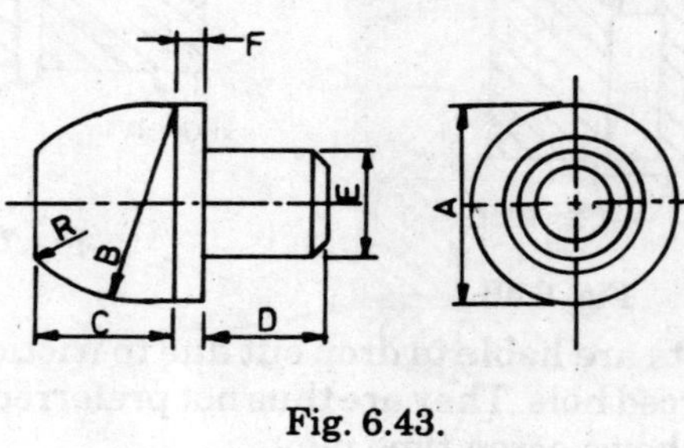

Fig. 6.43.

Fig. 6.43 shows flattened point type pilot. Typical dimensions are indicated in table 6.6.

Table 6.6

A mm	*B mm*	*C mm*	*D mm*	*E mm*
19	19	11.2	16	9.5
22.4	22.4	14	19	11.2
25	25	16	19	12.5
31.5	31.5	19	25	16
35.5	35.5	22.4	25	18
37.5	37.5	25	31.5	19

F = 1.6 mm or thickness of stock whichever is greater.

Punches should be suitably designed to retain the pilot. In general pilot length is at least six millimetre longer than punches in order to ensure the registry is complete before the cutting begins. The pilot should fit in the hole with a close sliding fit.

6.30. Knock out and Shedder

The function of the knock out is to remove the work piece which adhere to the die opening. Fig. 6.44 shows knock out and shedder. The upper end of the knock out registers against the knock out bar of the press which pushes the shedder down so that the work piece is pushed back into the scrap strip or out of the die opening so that it may be ejected. The pinned collar keeps the knock out from dropping out of the punch.

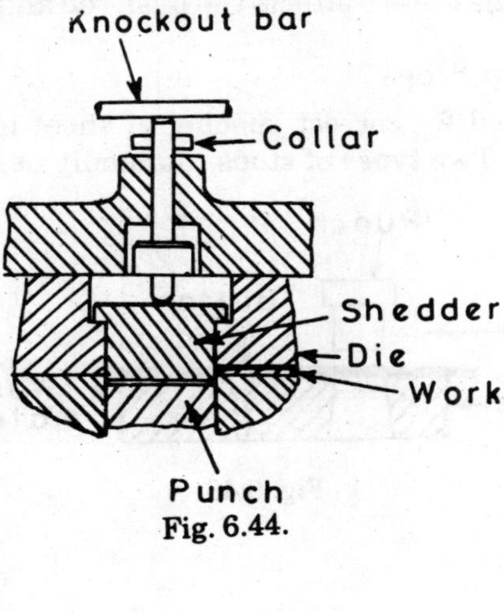

Fig. 6.44.

Fig. 6.45 shows use of knock out and spring stripper. A knock out assembly consists of a plate a push rod and a retaining collar.

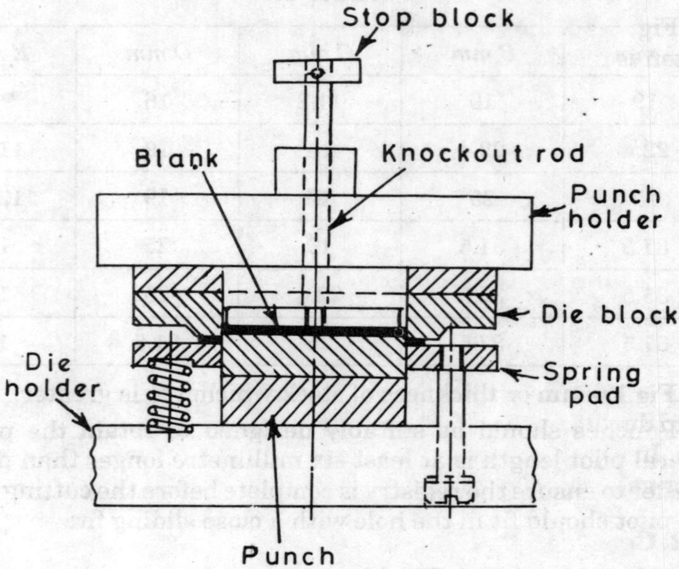

Fig. 6.45.

The plate is a loose fit with the die opening contour and moves upward as the blank is cut. A heavy push rod attached to the plate usually by rivets slides in a hole in the shank of the die set. This rod projects above the shank and a collar retains and limits the stroke of the assembly. Near the upper limit of the ram stroke a knock out bar in the bar in the press contacts the push rod and ejects the blank.

6.31. Stock Strip Stops

Stops are used for correct spacing of sheet metal as it is fed below the punch. Two types of stops commonly used are as follows.

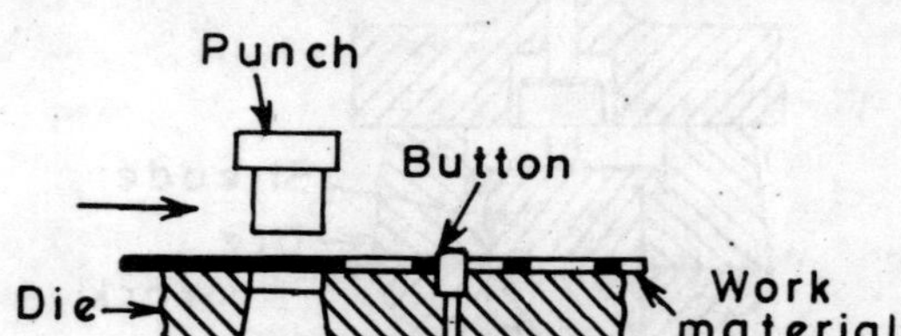

Fig. 6.46.

(*i*) Button type

(*ii*) Lever type.

Fig. 6.46 shows button type stop. In this case a small pin or button is fixed to the die block.

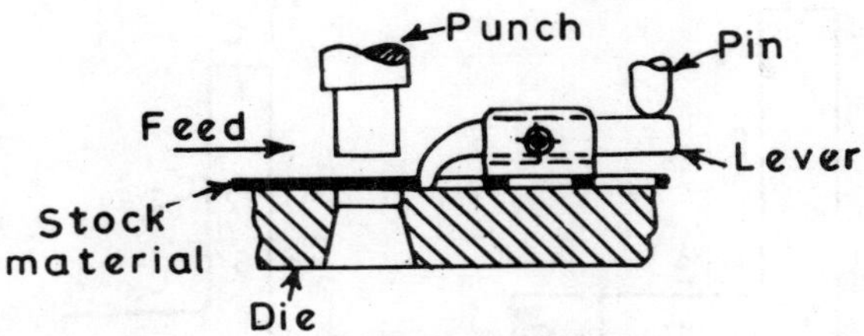

Fig. 6.47.

Fig. 6.47 shows lever type stop. The small end of the lever gets lifted during upward movement of punch leaving the stock material free. In the next instant the stock material is fed forward and the lever gets engaged with the work and locates the work.

6.32. Centre of Pressure

It is the centre of gravity of the line *i.e.* the perimeter of the blank. It is not the centre of gravity of the area. The press tool is so designed that the centre of pressure will lie on the axis of the press ram when the tool is mounted on the press.

Centre of pressure is determined by using the following procedure.

(*i*) Draw the outline of the actual cutting edges.

(*ii*) Draw *XX* and *YY* axes at right angle in convention position.

(*iii*) Divide the cutting edges into line elements such as straight lines, arcs etc. Find the lengths L_1, L_2, L_3, L_4 etc. of these elements.

(*iv*) Mark the centre of gravity of these elements say C_1, C_2, C_3, C_4 etc.

(*v*) Find x_1, y_1 the distances of centre of gravity C_1 from *YY* axis and *XX* axis respectively. Similarly find x_2, y_2 of c_2 and x_3, y_3 of c_3 etc.

(*vi*) Determine distance *X* and *Y* of centre of presure [*c*] from *YY* and *XX* axis as follows :

$$X = \frac{L_1x_1 + L_2x_2 + L_3x_3 + \ldots}{L_1 + L_2 + L_3 + \ldots}$$

$$Y = \frac{L_1y_1 + L_2y_2 + L_3y_3 + \ldots}{L_1 + L_2 + L_3 + \ldots}$$

To determine the centre of pressure of the component shown in Fig. 6.48. Mark the elements 1, 2, 3, 4, 5 and 6 and place the component in *XX* and *YY* axis as shown in Fig. 6.49.

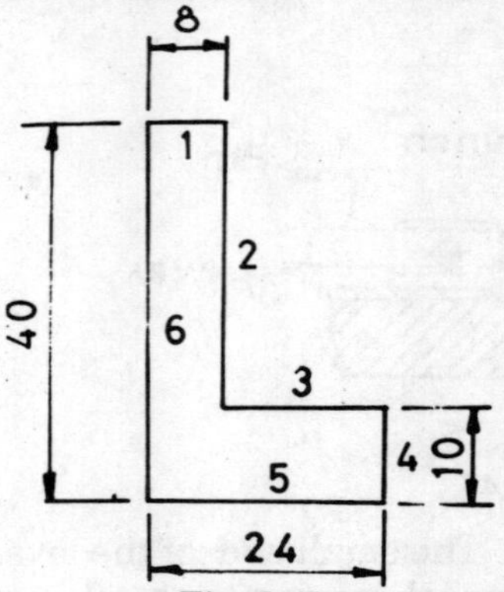

Fig. 6.48.

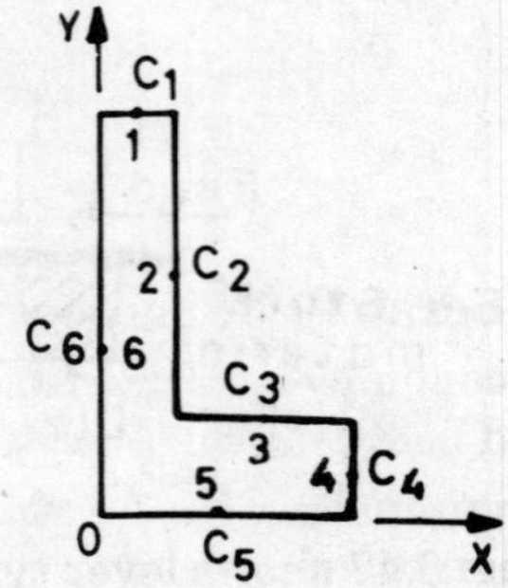

Fig. 6.49.

The lengths of various elements are as follows :

$L_1 = 8 \qquad L_4 = 10$

$L_2 = 30 \qquad L_5 = 24$

$L_3 = 16 \qquad L_6 = 40$

Let $C_1 (x_1 y_1)$, $C_2 (x_2 y_2)$, $C_3 (x_3 y_3)$..... be the centre of gravity of elements 1, 2, 3, ... respectively.

$x_1 = 4$ mm

$y_1 = 40$

$x_2 = 8$

$y_2 = 10 + 15 = 25$

$$x_3 = 8 + \frac{16}{2} = 16 \text{ mm}$$

$y_3 = 10$

$x_4 = 24$

$y_4 = 5$

$x_5 = 12$

$y_5 = 0$

$x_6 = 0$

$y_6 = 20$

Let $C(X,Y)$ be the centre of pressure

$$X = \frac{L_1x_1 + L_2x_2 + L_3x_3 + L_4x_4 + L_5x_5 + L_6x_6}{L_1 + L_2 + L_3 + L_4 + L_5 + L_6}$$

$$= \frac{8 \times 4 + 30 \times 8 + 16 \times 16 + 10 \times 24 + 24 \times 12 + 40 \times 0}{8 + 30 + 16 + 10 + 24 + 40}$$

$$= 8.25 \text{ mm.}$$

$$Y = \frac{L_1y_1 + L_2y_2 + L_3y_3 + L_4y_4 + L_5y_5 + L_6y_6}{L_1 + L_2 + L_3 + L_4 + L_5 + L_6}$$

$$= \frac{8 \times 40 + 30 \times 25 + 16 \times 10 + 10 \times 5 + 24 \times 0 + 40 \times 20}{8 + 30 + 16 + 10 + 24 + 40}$$

$$= 16.25 \text{ mm.}$$

6.33. Scrap Strip Layout

Economical stock utilization is of high importance. The goal should beat least a 75 per cent utilization.

In preparing the layout it should be observed that the distance between the nearest two points of blanks and between the blanks and the edge of strip should in no case be less than the sheet thickness. Fig. 6.50 shows a poor scrap trip lay out because percentage of stock scrapped would be too high whereas Fig. 6.51 shows a better arrangement for conservation of material.

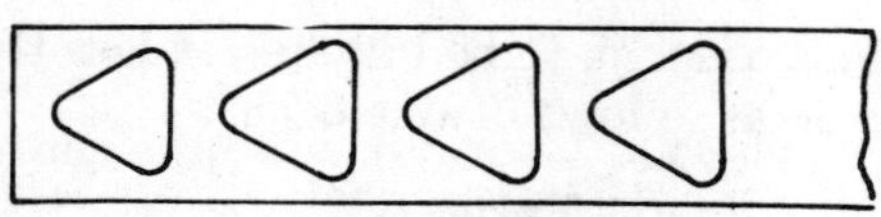

Fig. 6.50.

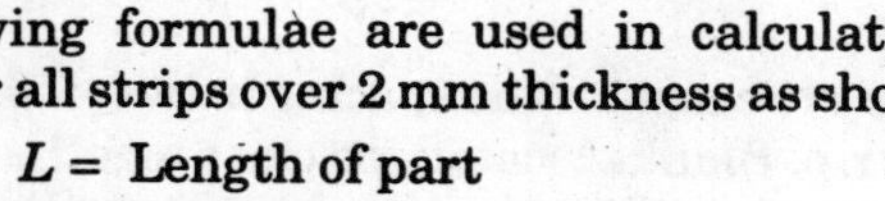

Fig. 6.51.

Strips of standard width should be chosen.

The following formulae are used in calculating scrap strip dimensions for all strips over 2 mm thickness as shown in Fig. 6.25.

L = Length of part

H = Width of part

W = Width of scrap strip

t = Thickness of the material

D = Lead of die

$B = 1\frac{1}{4}t$ when D is less than 60 mm.

$$= 1\frac{1}{2}t \text{ when } D \text{ is 60 mm or more}$$

$$D = L + B$$

where B = Distance between the part and edge of strip.

= Allowance between successive blanks.

N = Number of blanks which can be punched.

$$= \frac{S - B}{D}$$

where S = length of stock

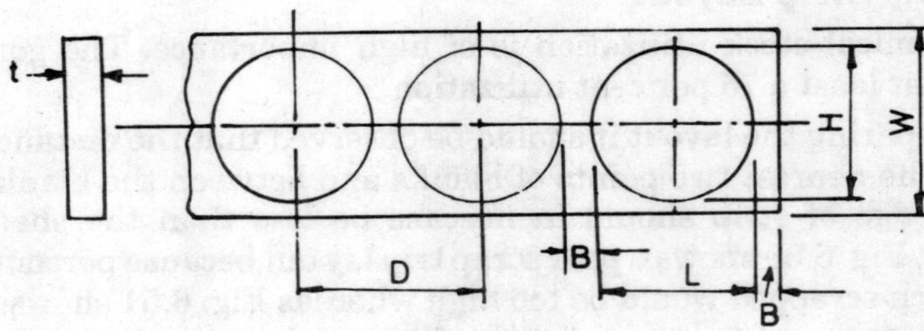

Fig. 6.52.

If the thickness of strip, to be blanked is less than 2 mm then dimension B will be as follows (Table 6.7).

Table 6.7

W (mm)	*B (mm)*
0-75	1.25
75-150	2.25
150-300	2.25
Over 300	2.75

It is necessary to consider the spacing between the blanks when laying out the strip. Blanks located too close together or too close to the edge of strip tend to allow the metal to slip by the cutting edges of the punch and die. The web between the blanks that forms the scrap skelton must be strong enough to withstand the feeding forces especially on a progressive die.

Values of stock allowance B are (when $t > 00.625$ mm) indicated in table 6.8.

Table 6.8

Material Thickness (mm)	*Stock Allowance (B) mm*
0.625 to 0.75	0.75
0.75 to 4.50	t
Over 4.5	4.5

where t = Material thickness.

Values of stock allowance *A* and *B* (Table 6.9), (when t is less than 0.625 mm)

Table 6.9

Material Thickness (mm)	*Stock Allowance (A) mm*		*Stock Allowance (B) mm*	
	Single Pass	*Double Pass*	*Single Pass*	*Double Pass*
0 to 0.75	0.78	1.55	0.78	1.55
0.75 to 1.50	1.55	2.35	1.55	2.35
1.50 to 3.00	2.35	3.10	2.35	3.10
over 3.00	3.10	4.0	3.10	4.0

6.34. Considerations in Press Tool Design

The various points to be considered during press tool design are as follows :

(*i*) All parts which have to withstand heavy forces and repeated blows should be of proper strength.

(*ii*) Tolerances on each part of press tool should be accurate.

(*iii*) There should be safety and ease of use for both operator and setter.

(*iv*) Sufficient space should be available for feeding devices and auxiliary stock devices.

(*v*) Die sets should be made of proper materials.

(*vi*) Thickness of punch-holder and thickness of die shoe should be in line with the strength requirements and allowable press shut height.

(*vii*) Length of guide posts or pins should be specified.

(*viii*) Shank diameter should be specified.

A properly designed punch-die set have the following advantages

(*i*) Alignment of punch and die members.

(*ii*) Improved quality of the part produced.

(*iii*) Minimum set up time.

(*iv*) Good positioning and fastening of work piece.

(*v*) Increased life of punch-die set.

(*vi*) Less maintenance.

6.35. Design Procedure for Blanking Die

The various steps involved in design of blanking die are as follows :

(*i*) Prepare a sketch incorporating all elements of die to be used.

(*ii*) Determine punch and die opening diameters considering whether the operation is blanking or piercing.

(*iii*) Design the die block and select proper die set.

(*iv*) Provide arrangement for fixing the punch in the punch retainer.

(*v*) Provide stock stop.

(*vi*) Prepare following drawings.

(*a*) Sectional front view of punch in position.

(*b*) Bottom view of punch showing position and method of securing punch, dowels, and screws to the punch plate through the back up plate and retainer.

(*c*) Plan of lower portion showing die block, die shoe, stripper, stop pin positions and method of securing each.

(*d*) Side sectional elevation of punch and die assembly.

(*vii*) State type of press and capacity of press.

6.36. Tool Materials

The tool material should be selected carefully in respect of the following properties

(*i*) Wear resistance

(*ii*) Toughness

(*iii*) Resistance to compression and tension

(*iv*) Ability to get hardened.

Usually punches, die plates, and pressure plates are hardened between HRC 55 to HRC 62.

The percentage composition of some of the tool

Steels used for making punches and dies are given in Table 6.8.

Table 6.8

STEEL	*C*	*Mn*	*Si*	*Cr*	*V*	*W*	*Mo*	*Co*
W_1	1.0	—	—	—	—	—	—	—
W_2	1.0	—	—	—	0.25	—	—	—
S_1	0.5	—	—	1.5	—	2.5	—	—
S_2	0.5	—	1.0	—	—	—	0.5	—
O_1	0.9	1.0	—	0.5	—	0.5	—	—
O_2	0.9	1.6						
D_1	1.0			12.0	—	—	1.0	—
D_4	2.25	—	—	12.0	—	—	1.0	—
M_1	0.8	—	—	4.0	1.0	1.5	8.5	—
M_4	1.3	—	—	4.0	4.0	5.5	4.5	
T_1	0.7	—	—	4.0	1.0	18.0	—	—
T_2	0.85	—	—	4.0	2.0	18.0	—	—

W = Water hardened steels

S = Shock resisting tool steels

O = Oil hardened steels

D = High carbon high chromium steels

They combine high wear resistance with deep hardening properties.

M, T = These are general purpose grades of high speed steel.

Example 6.1. ***A steel washer is of 44 mm outer diameter and 22 mm inner hole diameter and is 12 mm thick. If maximum shear stress is 405N / mm² and percentage penetration is 24 find :***

(a) Work done

(b) Shear to be ground on tool if maximum punch force is to be reduced to 0.05 MN.

Solution. ***(a)***

D = Outer diameter of washer = 44 mm.

d = Inside diameter

= 22 mm

t = Thickness of material

= 2 mm.

f = Maximum shear stress

$= 405 \text{ N} / \text{mm}^2$

K = Per cent penetration = 0.24.

S = perimeter be cut

$= \pi(D + d) = \pi(44 + 22)$

= 207.4 mm.

A = Area to be sheared

$= S \times t$

$= 207.4 \times 2$

$= 414.8 \text{ mm}^2$

P = Maximum cutting force

$= A \times f$

$= 414.8 \times 405 = 168000 \text{ N} = 168 \text{ kN}$

= 0.168 MN.

Work done $= P \times k \times t$

$= 168 \times 0.24 \times 2$

= 80.64 kJ

(*b*) F = Reduced force

= 0.05 MN = 50 kN

$P = 168$ *kN*.

No $F = \dfrac{t \cdot p}{S} \times P$

where p = Per cent penetration

= 0.24

t = 2 mm

S = Shear

$$50 = \frac{2 \times 0.24}{S} \times 168$$

S = 1.6 mm.

Example 6.2. *A channel stripper 30 cm long is used for strip stock 60 mm × 3 mm. Calculate :*

(*a*) *Median clearance*

(*b*) *Tunnel height*

(*c*) *Allowable tunnel width.*

Solution. t = Thickness of stock

$= 3$ mm.

(*a*) G = Median clearance

$$= \frac{5t - 0.5t}{2}$$

$= 2.25t = 2.25 \times 3 = 6.75$ mm

Fig 6.53 shows channel stripper

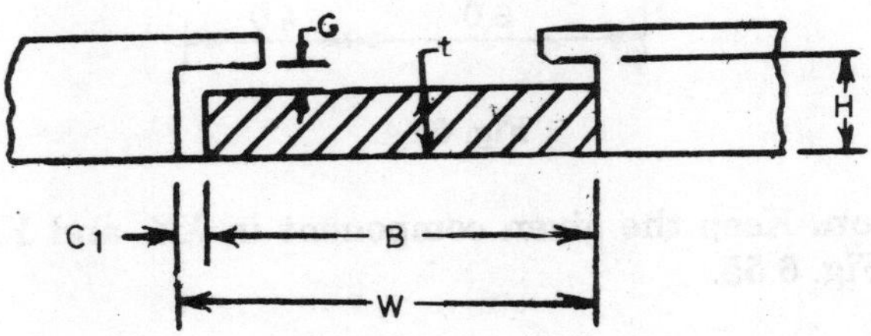

Fig. 6.53.

(*b*) H = Tunnel height

$= t + G$

$= 3 + 6.75 = 9.75$ mm.

(*c*) W = Tunnel width

B = Width of stock

$= 60$ mm

$W = B + C_1$

where C_1 = Clearance width

$= 1$ mm for 30 mm stripper length (assume)

L = stripper length

$= 300$ mm.

$$C_1 = \frac{300}{30} = 10 \text{ mm}$$

$W = B + C_1 = 60 + 10 = 70$ mm

Example 6.3. *Determine centre of pressure of the component shown in Fig. 6.54.*

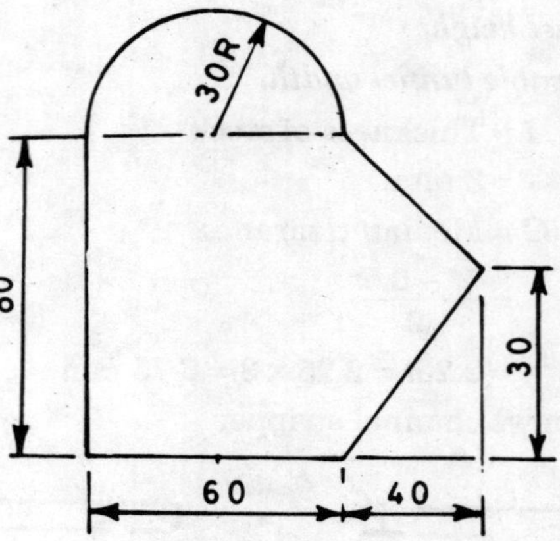

Fig. 6.54.

Solution. Keep the given component in *XX* and *YY* axis as shown in Fig. 6.55.

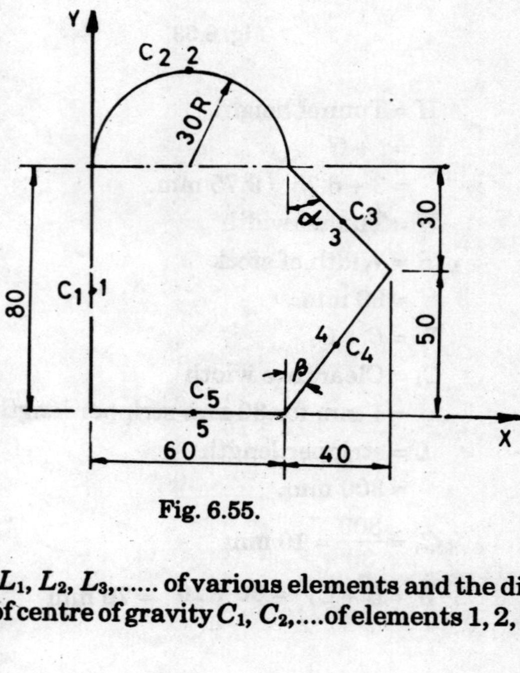

Fig. 6.55.

The lengths L_1, L_2, L_3,...... of various elements and the distances x_1, y_1, x_2, y_2, ... of centre of gravity C_1, C_2,....of elements 1, 2, 3,....etc. are as follows :

Element	*L*	*x*	*y*	*L.x*	*Ly*
1	80	0	40	0	3200
2	94.2	30	99.1	2826	9335.2
3	64	80	55	5120	3520
4	50	80	15	4000	750
5	60	30	0	1800	0
	348.2			13746	16805.2

The values of L_3 and L_4 are *found as follows* :

$$L_3 = \sqrt{40^2 + 50^2}$$

$$= 64 \text{ mm}$$

$$L_4 = \sqrt{40^2 + 30^2}$$

$$= 50 \text{ mm.}$$

$$\tan \alpha = \frac{40}{50} = 0.8$$

$$\alpha = 38.65^\circ$$

$$x_3 = 60 + \frac{64}{2} \sin 38.65$$

$$x_3 = 80 \text{ mm}$$

$$y_3 = 30 + (50 - 32 \cos 38.65) = 55 \text{ mm}$$

$$\tan \beta = \frac{40}{30}$$

$$\beta = 53.12^\circ$$

$$x_4 = 60 + \frac{50}{2} \sin 53.12 = 80 \text{ mm.}$$

$$y_4 = \frac{50}{2} \cos 53.12 = 15$$

$$y_2 = 80 + \frac{2R}{\pi} = 80 + \frac{2 \times 30}{\pi} = 99.1 \text{ mm.}$$

Let X, Y be the distance of centre of pressure *(C)* from Y axis and X axis respectively

$$X = \frac{\Sigma Lx}{\Sigma L} = \frac{13746}{348.2}$$

$$= 39.48 \text{ mm}$$

$$Y = \frac{\Sigma Ly}{\Sigma L} = \frac{16805.2}{348.2}$$

$$= 48.26 \text{ mm.}$$

Example 6.4. *To calculate the centre of pressure of the component shown in Fig. 6.56.*

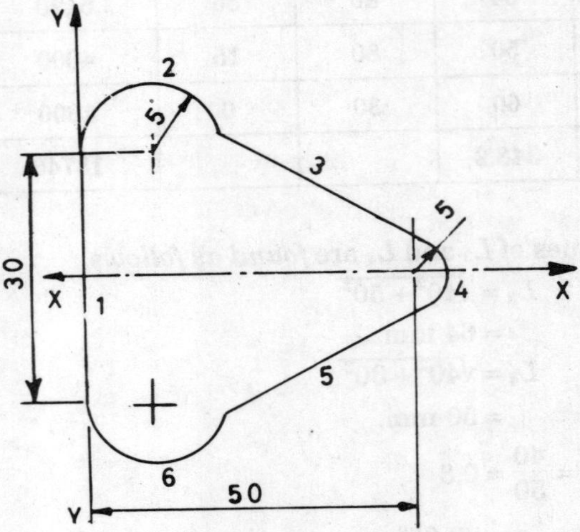

Fig. 6.56.

Solution. As the component is symmetrical about *XX* axis therefore *XX* axis and *YY* axis are chosen as shown.

The elements 1, 2, 3, 4, 5 and 6 have lengths L_1, L_2, L_3, L_4, L_5 and L_6 respectively.

Element	*L*	*x*	*y*	*L.x*	*Ly*
1	30	0	0	0	0
2	15.70	5	$15 + \frac{2 \times 5}{\pi}$ $= 18.19$	78.50	285.58
3	43.24	$10 + \frac{40}{2}$ $= 30$	$\frac{15 + 5}{2}$ $= 10$	1237.20	412.4
4	15.70	$50 + \frac{2 \times 5}{\pi}$	0	835	0

	= 53.18				
5	41.24	30	-10	1237.20	– 412.4
6	15.70	5	-18.19	78.50	– 285.58

The length L_3 of element 3 is given by

$$L_3 = \sqrt{40^2 + 10^2}$$
$$= 41.24 \text{ mm.}$$

In case of semicircular arcs of radius R the C.G. is given by $\frac{2R}{\pi}$ and lies on the line joining the centre of the circle.

The distance X and Y of the centre of pressure from Y axis and X axis respectively are given by

$$X = \frac{\Sigma L_x}{\Sigma L} = \frac{3466.40}{159.58}$$
$$= 21.72 \text{ mm.}$$
$$Y = \frac{\Sigma L_y}{\Sigma L} = 0 \text{ as } \Sigma L_y = 0$$

Example 6.5. *A component shown in Fig. 6.57 is made of C 30 steel. Determine the force required to blank the component if the shear stress of material is 32 kg / mm² and sheet thickness is 1.8 mm.*

Solution.

t = Sheet thickness
= 1.8 mm.

S = Perimeter to be cut

$$= 20 + \pi \times 15 + 5 + 5 + \pi \times 15 + 20 + \frac{\pi \times 15}{2}$$

= 167.75 mm.

f_s = Shear stress = 32 kg/mm²

A = Area to be sheared
$= S \times t$
$= 167.75 \times 1.8$
$= 302 \text{ mm}^2$

P = Blanking force

$= A \times f_s$

$= 302 \times 32 = 9664$ kg

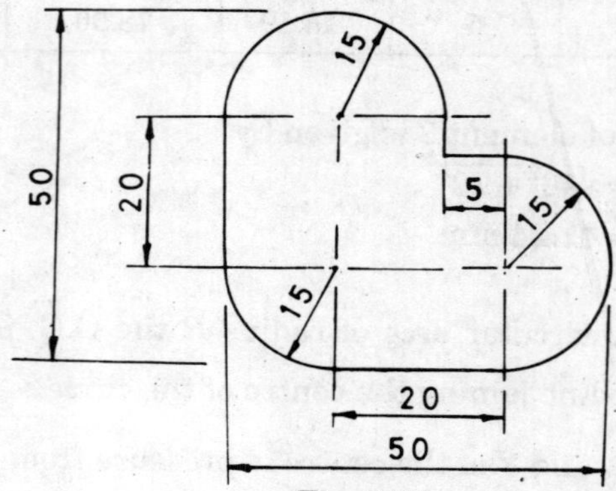

Fig. 6.57.

Example 6.6. *A steel washer of 36 mm outer diameter and 20 mm inside diameter is to be made from 1.2 mm thick sheet in one operation. If the shear stress is 400 N/mm² and percentage penetration is 20% determine :*

(a) Maximum punch force necessary to blank and punch the washer if both punches operate at the same time.

(b) Percentage reduction in punch force if 0.5 mm double shear is ground on the tool.

Solution. (*a*) Washer is shown in Fig. 6.58.

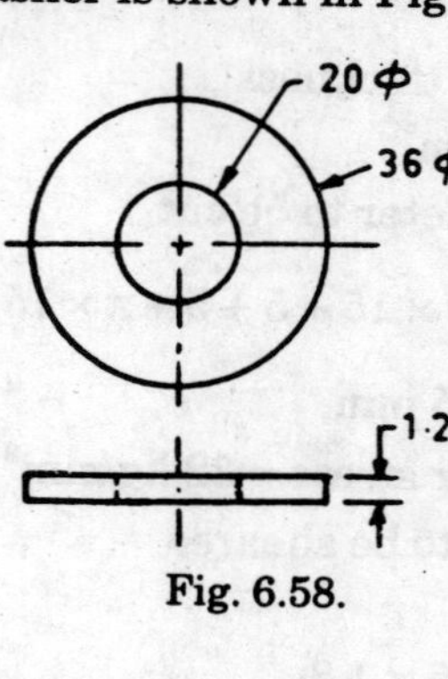

Fig. 6.58.

where
D = outside dia = 36 mm
d = Inside dia = 20 mm
P = Maximum force required to punch
t = Thickness of sheet

$= 1.2$ mm

fs = Shear stress

$= 400$ N / mm^2

A = Area to be sheared $= \pi(D + d) \cdot t$

$P = \pi(D + d) \cdot t \cdot fs$

$= \pi(36 + 20) \times 1.2 \times 400$

$= 84403\ N$

(*b*) F = Reduced force

$$= \frac{k \cdot t}{S} \times P$$

where k = % penetration

$= 0.2$

S = shear

$= 0.5$

$$F = \frac{0.2 \times 1.2}{0.5} \times 84403$$

$= 40513.4$ N.

Example 6.7. *Sketch and design a progressive die to make a steel washer 30 mm outside diameter with 15 mm hole. From 1.6 mm thick steel sheet. The ultimate shear strength of the material is* 32 kg / mm^2.

Solution. The washer will be made on progressive die

(*a*) *Calculate punch and die size*

Fig. 6.59 shows the washer.

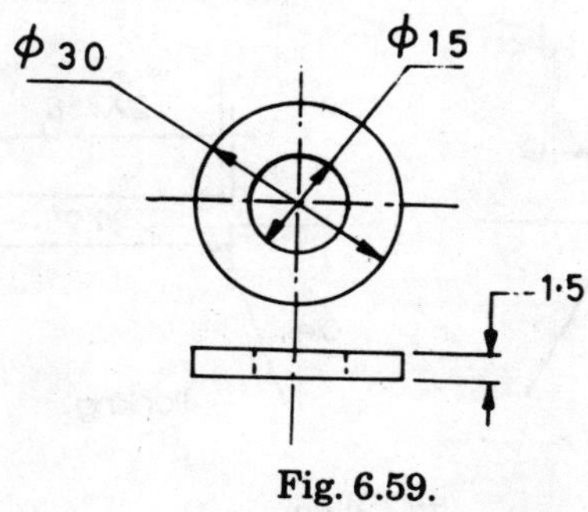

Fig. 6.59.

D = outside diameter $= 30$ mm

d = inside diameter
= 15 mm
t = sheet thickness
= 1.6 mm
A = Area to be sheared
$= \pi(D + d) \cdot t$
$= \pi(30 + 15) \times 1.6 = 226.1 \text{ mm}^2$
f_S = shear stress = 32 kg/mm^2
P = Cutting force
$= A \times f_S = 226.1 \times 32$
= 7235.2 kg = 7.235 tonnes.

Assuming 70% efficiency, Press Capacity

$$= \frac{7.235}{0.7} = 10.335 \text{ tons.}$$

Piercing punch size = size of hole + shrinkage of hole
= 15 + 0.05 = 15.05 mm

C = clearance = 6% of material thickness

Piercing die size = Punch size + 2C

$$= 15.05 + 2 \times \frac{6}{100} \times 1.6$$

$$= 15.05 + 0.192 = 15.242 \text{ mm.}$$

In blanking size of blank is determined by the die size and the washer will expand approximately by 0.05 mm.

Size of blanking die = Blank dia – 0.05
= 30 – 0.05 = 29.95 mm

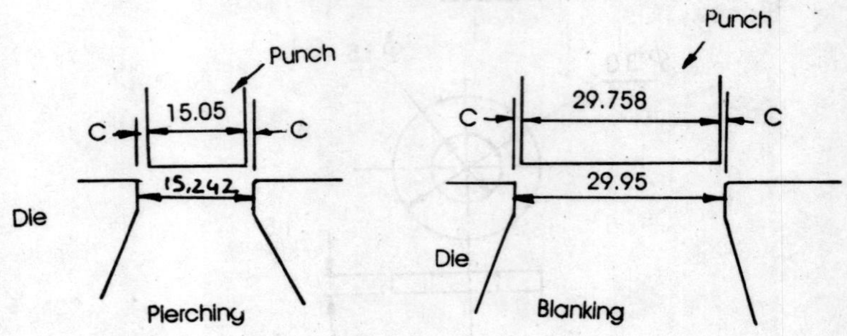

Fig. 6.60.

Size blanking punch = size of blanking die – 2*C*

$$= 29.95 - 2 \times \frac{6}{100} \times 1.6$$

$$= 29.758 \text{ mm.}$$

Dimensions of punches and dies are shown in Fig. 6.60.

(*b*) ***Die block size.*** Fig. 6.61 shows die block

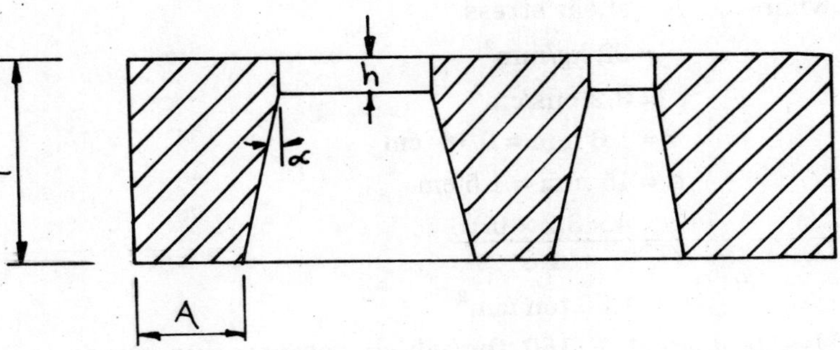

Fig. 6.61.

S = Perimeter = $\pi(D + d)$

$= \pi(30 + 15) = 141.3$ mm.

T = Thickness of die block for 141.3 mm perimeter

= 25 mm

Thickness (T) can also be found by the formula

$T = 25.4 \times P = 25.4 \times 7.235$

= 26.16 mm

Hence T = 26.16 + Grinding allowance

= 26.16 + 5 = 31.16 mm.

A = critical distance

$= 1.5 \times T = 1.5 \times 26.16$

= 37.5 mm

h = Die opening

= 3 mm.

α = Angular clearance

$= 1\frac{1}{2}°$.

The angular clearance allows the blank to drop through the die block without jamming. Die block is made of tool steel such as *T* 160.

(c) Die shoe. The thickness of die shoe or die holder varies from 25 to 75 mm. Let the thickness be 30 mm. The face dimensions of the die shoe are 7 mm larger than the dimensions of the die block at every corner and all around die shoe is made of cast iron.

(d) Punch length :

Let f_c = compressive strength of punch material

Now $$f_c = \frac{4 \cdot f_s \cdot t}{d}$$

where f_s = shear stress

$$= 32 \text{ kg/mm}^2$$

$$= 3.2 \text{tons/cm}^2$$

$$t = 1.6 \text{ mm} = 0.16 \text{ cm}$$

$$d = 15 \text{ mm} = 1.5 \text{ cm.}$$

$$f_c = \frac{4 \times 3.2 \times 0.16}{1.5}$$

$$= 1.36 \text{ ton /cm}^2.$$

Use tool steel T 160 for which compressive stress is 15 ton/cm^2.

L_m = Maximum length of punch

$$= \frac{\pi d}{8} \sqrt{\frac{E \cdot d}{f_s \cdot t}}$$

where E = Young's modulus of elasticity for punch material

$$= 2.1 \times 10^6 \text{ kg/cm}^2 \text{ (assume)}$$

$$= 2.1 \times 10^3 \text{ tons/cm}^2$$

$$L_m = \frac{\pi \times 1.5}{8} \sqrt{\frac{2.1 \times 10^3 \times 1.5}{3.2 \times 0.16}}$$

$$= 45.4 \text{ cm.}$$

However a punch length of about 100 mm length will be enough including a grinding allowance of 10 mm.

Punch plate thickness = $1.5 \times D$

$= 1.5 \times 30 = 45$ mm.

Punch–holder thickness = 35 mm

Both punch plate and punch-holder are made of cast iron.

(e) Shear. For piercing operation shear is applied to the piercing punch and for blanking operation shear is provided on blanking die. Shear = $1.5 \times t = 1.5 \times 0.16 = 0.24$ cm.

Example 6.8. *A steel component 20 mm × 60 mm is to be made from 2 mm thick sheet. Sketch the scrap strip lay out.*

Also determine percentage of stock used.

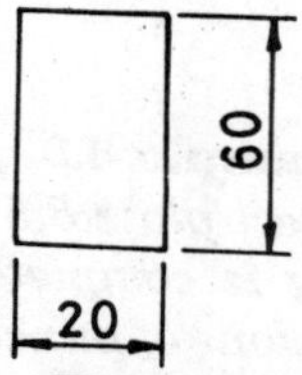

Fig. 6.62.

Solution. *The scrap lay out is shown in Fig. 6.63.*

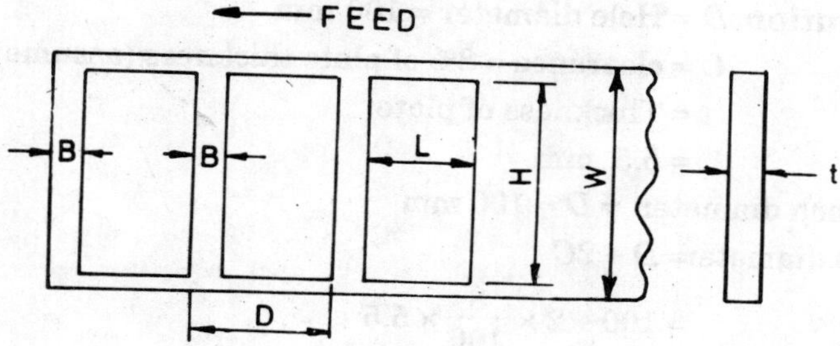

Fig. 6.63.

The various dimensions will be as follows :

t = Thickness of material = 2 mm

L = Length of component = 20 mm.

H = Width of component = 60 mm.

$B = 1.25 \times t = 1.25 \times 2$

$= 2.5$ mm.

$D = L + B = 20 + 2.5$

$= 22.5$ mm.

$W = H + B + B$

$= 60 + 2.5 + 2.5 = 65$ mm.

A = Area of strip used to produce a single blanked part

$= D \times W = 22.5 \times 65$

$= 1462.5 \text{ mm}^2$

a = Area of component

$= L \times H = 20 \times 60 = 1200 \text{ mm}^2$

Percentage of stock used

$$= \frac{a}{A} \times 100$$

$$= \frac{1200}{1462.5} \times 100 = 82\%.$$

Example 6.9. *A hole 100 mm diameter is to be punched in a mild steel plate 5.5 mm thick. With normal clearance on the tools. Cutting is complete at 40% peneteration of punch. Give suitable dimensions of punch and die. The ultimate shear stress for the plate is 3600* kg. / cm^2.

Determine shear angle for the punch in order to bring the work with in the capacity of 10 tonne press.

Solution. D = Hole diameter = 100 mm

C = clearance = 8% of plate thickness (assume)

t = Thickness of plate

= 5.5 mm

Punch diameter = D = 100 mm

Die diameter = $D + 2C$

$$= 100 + 2 \times \frac{8}{100} \times 5.5$$

= 100.88 mm

f_S = Shear stress = 3600 kg/cm^2

A = Area to be sheared

$= \pi Dt$

P = Maximum load on punch

$= A \times f_S = \pi D t f_S$

$$= \frac{\pi \times 100}{10} \times \frac{5.5}{10} \times 3600$$

= 62172 kg.

= 62.172 tonne

F = Reduced force = 10 tonne

W_1 = Work done by punch during shearing stroke when shear is provided

$= F(t \times p + s)$

$= 10(5.5 \times 0.4 + s)$

where p = per cent prenetration

= 0.4

S = Depth of shear on punch as shown in Fig. 6.64

W_2 = Work required to shear hole

$= P \times t \times p = 62.172 \times 5.5 \times 0.4$

Equating the work $10(5.5 \times 0.4 + s) = 62.172 \times 5.5 \times 0.4$

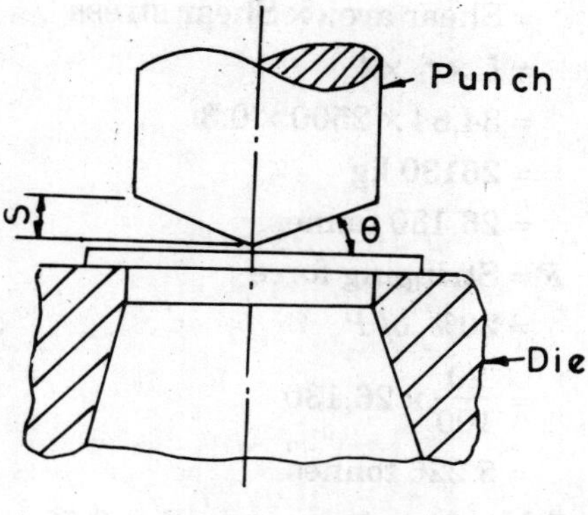

Fig. 6.64.

$$S = 11.4 \text{ mm}$$

$$\tan \theta = \frac{S}{\frac{D}{2}}$$

$$= \frac{11.4}{50} = 0.228$$

$$\theta = 12.84^{\circ}$$

Example 6.10. *Two holes, one 4 cm square and another of 6 cm diameter are to be cut in a metallic sheet 3 mm thick. If shear strength of material is 2500 kg/cm², Determine :*

(a) Cutting force

(b) Stripping force.

Solution. t = Thickness of plate

= 3 mm

= 0.3 cm

d = Hole diameter = 6 cm

b = Side of square hole = 4 cm.

L = Perimeter to be cut

$= \pi d + 4 \times b$

$= \pi \times 6 + 4 \times 4$

= 34.84 cm.

f_s = Shear stress

= 2500 kg/cm²

P = cutting force

$= \text{Shear area} \times \text{Shear stress}$

$= L \times f_S \times t$

$= 34.84 \times 2500 \times 0.3$

$= 26130 \text{ kg}$

$= 26.130 \text{ tonnes.}$

$F = \text{Stripping force}$

$= 20\% \text{ of } P$

$$= \frac{20}{100} \times 26.130$$

$= 5.226 \text{ tonnes.}$

Example 6.11. *A part shown in Fig. 6.65 is to be made from a mild steel sheet 3 mm thick, and 2 m long. Determine :*

(*i*) *Strip layout*

(*ii*) *Number of parts that can be punched from the strip*

(*iii*) *Percentage of stock used.*

(*iv*) *Weight of material needed to produced one blank.*

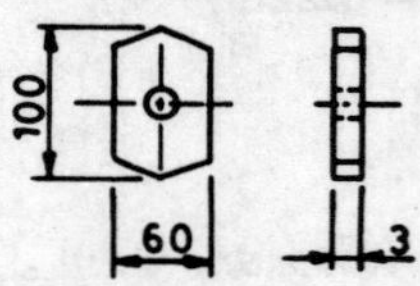

Fig. 6.65.

Solution. Fig. 6.66 shows a typical strip layout.

Let s = Stock length

= 2 m

t = Thickness of sheet = 3 mm

D = Lead of die

L = Length of part = 60

H = Width of part = 100

W = Width of strip

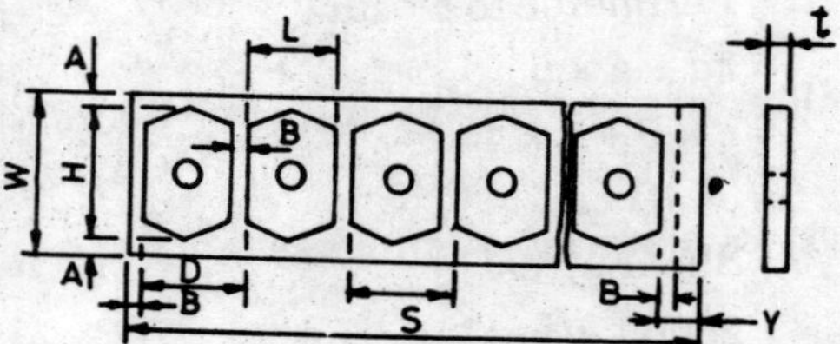

Fig. 6.66

$$A = t + 0.015 \times H$$
$$= 3 + 0.015 \times 100$$
$$= 4.5 \text{ mm.}$$
$$W = H + 2A$$
$$= 100 + 2 \times 4.5$$
$$= 109 \text{ mm.}$$
$$B = t = 3 \text{ mm (From table 6.8).}$$

D = Length of stock to produce one blank

$$= L + B$$
$$= 60 + 3 = 63 \text{ mm.}$$

N = Number of blanks which can be made one length of stock

$$= \frac{S - B}{D} = \frac{2000 - 3}{63}$$
$$= 31.0$$

Y = Scrap remaining at the end of strip

$$= S - (N \times D + B)$$
$$= 2000 - (31 \times 63 + 3)$$
$$= 44 \text{ mm.}$$

$$\% \text{ of stock used} = \frac{a}{A_1} \times 100$$

where a = Area of component

$$= 60 \times 100$$

A_1 = Area of strip used to produce a single blanked part

$$= D \times W$$
$$W = H + A + A$$
$$= 100 + 4.5 + 4.5$$
$$= 109 \text{ mm.}$$
$$\% \text{ Stock used} = \frac{60 \times 100}{63 \times 109} \times 100$$
$$= 87.3\%$$

Weight of material needed to produce one blank

$$= W \times D \times t \times \rho$$

where ρ = Density of material = 0.007 kg/cm^3 (For steel)

$$\text{Weight} = \frac{109}{10} \times \frac{63}{10} \times \frac{3}{10} \times 0.007$$

$$= 0.144 \text{ kg.}$$

Example 6.12. *A steel washer of 28 mm outer diameter and 20 mm inside diameter is to be made from 1.3 mm thick sheet. If the shear stress of the material is 380* N/mm^2. *Calculate the following*

(a) Force required to produce the washer if both punches operate at the same time with no shear. What will be stripping force ?

(b) Force required if only one punch operates at a time (that is the punches are staggered.)

(c) Force needed if in part (b) the punch has a shear of 1.2 mm and penetration is 50%.

Solution. (*a*) D = Outside diameter of washer

= 28 mm.

d = Inside diameter of washer

= 20 mm.

t = Sheet thickness

= 1.3 mm.

f_S = Shear stress in material of washer

= 380 N/mm^2

P = Force required to produced washer

$= \pi(D + d) \times t \times f_S$

$= \pi(28 + 20) \times 1.3 \times 380$

= 74455 Newtons

$$\text{Stripping force} = \frac{12}{100} \times P = 0.12 \times 74455 = 8934.6 \text{ N}$$

(*b*) When one punch operates at a time the punch taking the longest cut will determine the force

P = Force required to produce washer

$\rho = \pi \times D \times t \times f_s = \pi \times 28 \times 1.3 \times 380$

= 43432 N

(*c*) P_1 = Reduced force when shear is provided

$$= \frac{t \cdot p}{S} \times P$$

where S = Shear = 1.2 mm

t = Sheet thickness = 1.3 mm

$$= 50\% = \frac{50}{100} = 0.5$$

$$p = 43342 \text{ N as obtained in part } (b)$$

$$P_1 = \frac{1.3 \times 0.5}{1.2} \times 43432 \quad = 23525 \text{ N.}$$

PROBLEMS

1. What is a press ? Discuss various types of presses.

2. Define the following press operations :

(*i*) Blanking

(*ii*) Piercing

(*iii*) Drawing

(*iv*) Notching

(*v*) Lancing

(*vi*) Parting.

3. What is a die ? Make a neat sketch of a die and discuss the various parts.

4. (*a*)What are various types of dies.

(*b*) Sketch and describe a compound die.

(*c*) Sketch and describe a progressive die.

(*d*) Discuss the difference between a compound die and progressive die.

5. (*a*) What do you understand by clearance between punch and die.

(*b*) Discuss the effect of :

(*i*) Excessive clearance.

(*ii*) Insufficient clearance.

(*c*) State the factors which affect clearance between punch and die.

(*d*) Why angular clearance is provided on die.

6. Write short notes on the following :

(*a*) Die set.

(*b*) Die set materials.

(*c*) Methods of punch support.

(*d*) Methods of die support.

(*e*) Cutting action in die.

7. Describe the method of calculating :

(*a*) Cutting (shearing) force in blanking and punching.

(*b*) Discuss the variation of cutting force with various stages during shearing of metal.

(*c*) Discuss the factors which affect the shearing force.

8. Write short notes on :

(*a*) Die block design.

(*b*) Punch design.

(*c*) Methods of reducing cutting forces.

(*d*) Clearance and punch force.

(*e*) Shut height of a press.

9. What is a stripper plate. Describe various types of stripper plates.

10. Write short notes on following :

(*a*) Stripping force.

(*b*) Die springs.

(*c*) Die wear.

11. What is a pilot ? Sketch and describe various types of pilots.

12. Write short notes on the following :

(*a*) Knock out and shedder

(*b*) Stock strip stops

(*c*) Scrap strip layout.

13. What is centre of pressure ? Describe the method of determining centre of pressure.

14. Find centre of pressure of the object shown in Fig. 6.65.

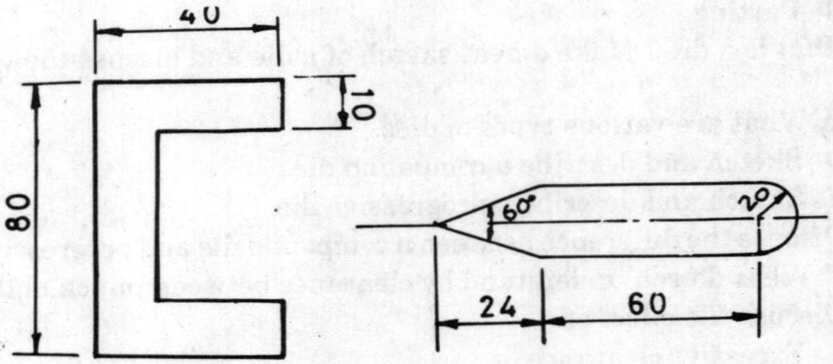

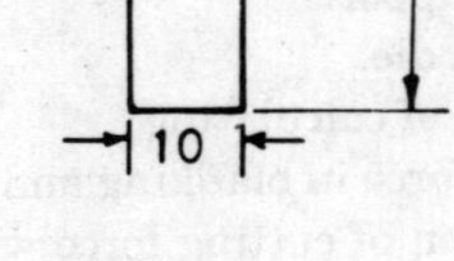

Fig. 6.65a

15. What are various considerations in press tool design. Describe the design procedure for blanking die.

16. Calculate the tonnage required to blank the work piece shown in Fig. 6.66 from M.S. sheet having shear stress 3100 kg/cm^2.

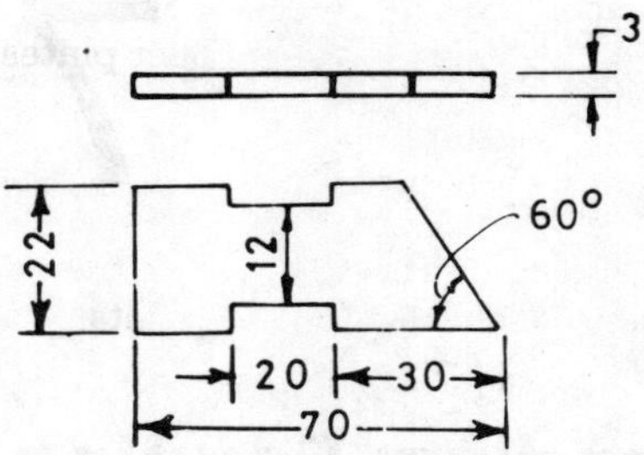

Fig. 6.66.

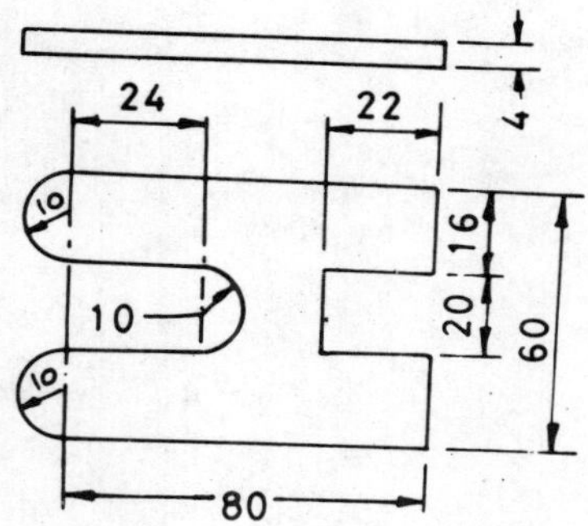

Fig. 6.67.

17. Calculate the press tonnage to blank the component shown in Fig. 6.67 from steel sheet having shear stress 3900 kg/cm^2.

18. Given a scrap strip 2 mm thick lay out as shown in Fig. 6.68 for the 60 mm equilateral triangle, find the following :

(*i*) Values of *A, B, D, H, E, W*.

(*ii*) Number of blanks produced from 3000 mm long strip.

(*iii*) Scrap which remains at the end of each run.

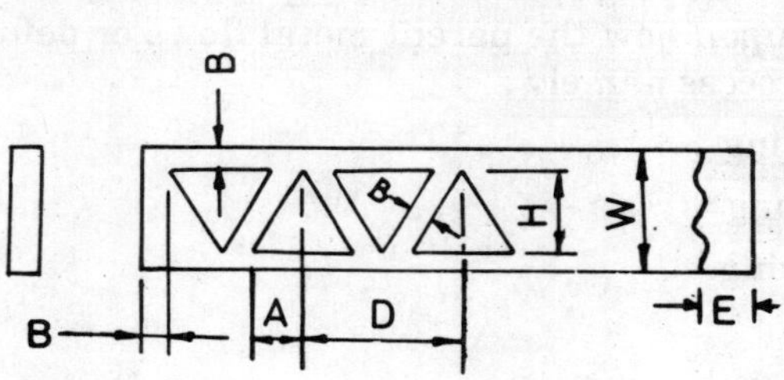

Fig. 6.68.

19. Write short notes on the following :

(*i*) Material for die sets.

(*ii*) Type of die sets.

(*iii*) Fine blanking

(*iv*) Trimming dies.

(*v*) Tool materials.

20. Describe various types of shear which can be applied to a die and or a punch.

7

Bending, Forming and Drawing Dies

7.1. Introduction

Sheet metal shaping operations are generally divided into three groups based upon how the parent metal flows or deforms during the shaping process namely :

(*i*) bending

(*ii*) forming

(*iii*) drawing.

7.2 Bending

In bending the metal flow is uniform along the bend axis with inner surface in compression and outer surface in tension as shown in Fig. 7.1.

The most favourable conditions for bending exist when the axis of the bend is perpendicular to the direction of grains.

Bend angle is the angle included between the two extreme positions of bend radius. It originates at the bend axis. Bend area is the area included between the bend angle. Neutral plane separates the materials.

in compression and tension

$$C = \frac{t}{3} \text{ to } \frac{t}{2}$$

where t = Thickness of material.

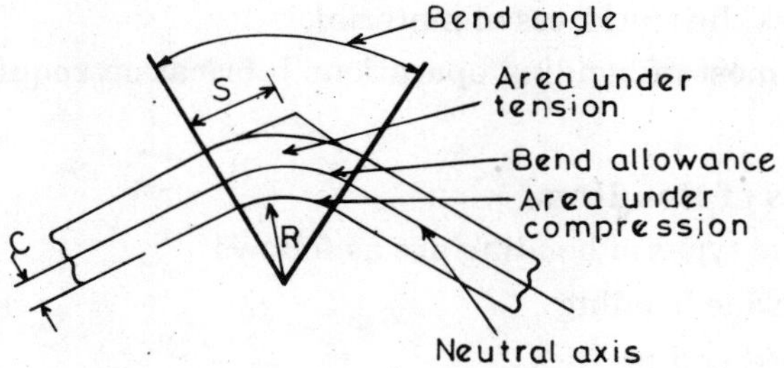

Fig. 7.1

The curved neutral plane of the bend area is called bend allowance.

S = set back

Fig. 7.2 shows typical components produced by bending, forming and drawing.

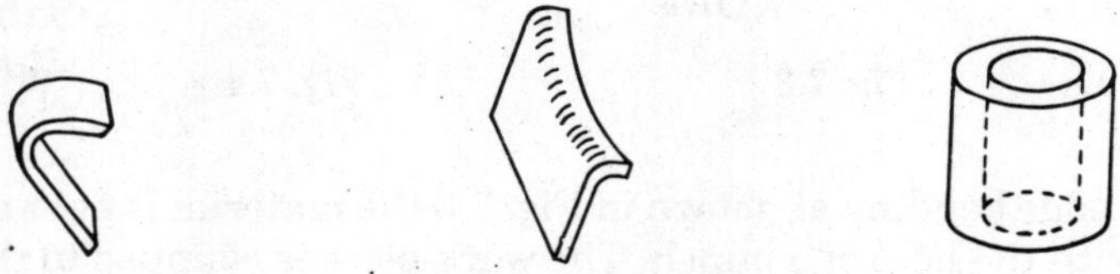

Fig. 7.2

In bending the metal gets distorted plastically within the bend area. Metal towards inner bend surface is under compression and metal towards outer surface is in tension. Thinning of material on tension side of bend is more pronounced than the bulging on the compression side and that is why the neutral plane tends to shift towards the compression side of the bend. Low hardness and high ductility materials can be bent 180° with sharp internal radius without tracture.

Following points are important to be considered during bending

(*i*) Material to be bend should be ductile and strong. It should not be hard.

(*ii*) Bending is smooth if the axis of the bend is perpendicular to the direction of grains.

(*iii*) Spring back phenomenon should be taken care of.

(*iv*) Holes pierced before bending will be distorted if they are close to the bend area. Usually distortion is minimised if the distance between pierced hole and bend line be held to a minimum of 1.5 times the thickness of material.

(*v*) In most of bending operations lubrication required is very less.

7.3. Types of Bending

Various types of bending are as follows :

(*i*) Edge bending

(*ii*) *V*-bending

(*iii*) *U*-bending.

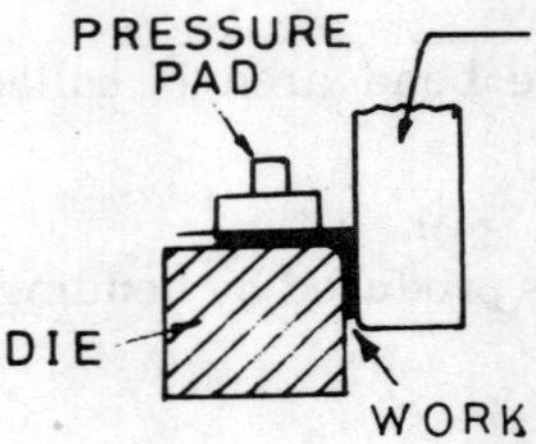

Fig. 7.3

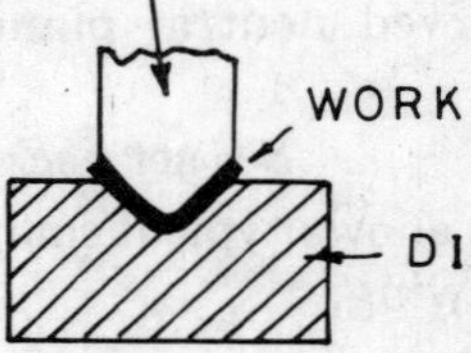

Fig. 7.4

In edge bending as shown in Fig. 7.3 the material is bent at one edge with the help of a punch. The work piece is clamped to the die block by a spring loaded pad. *V* bending also called air bending uses *V* shaped punch to press the work metal (Fig. 7.4) whereas the *U*-bending uses a *U*-shaped punch to give the required shape to the metal (Fig. 7.5).

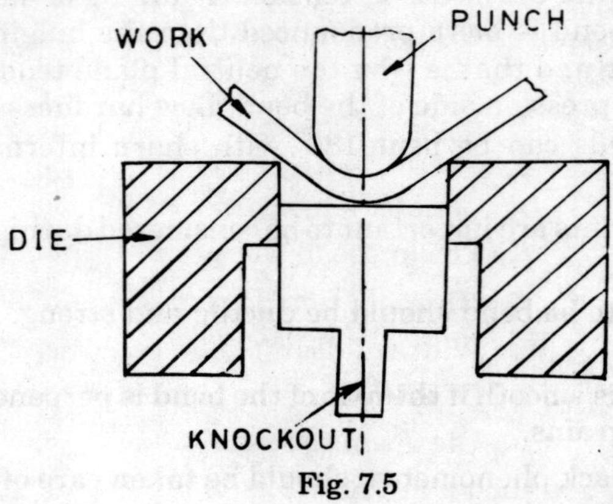

Fig. 7.5

Fig. 7.6 shows components produced by edge bending, *V*-bending and *U*-bending.

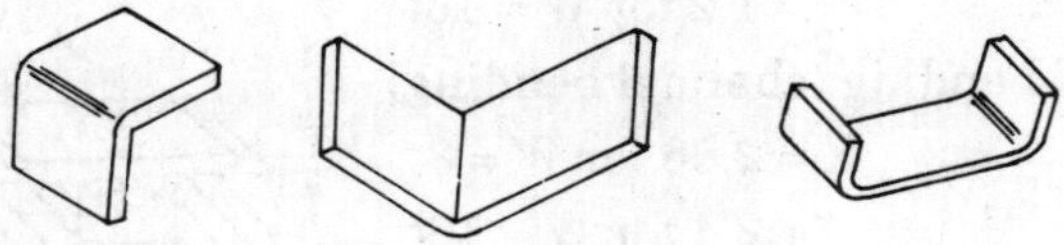

Fig. 7.6

Fig. 7.7 shows a press tool for simple bending operation. The punch presses the metal into die during downward stroke. Bending can be successfully applied to materials which are ductile and strong but no hard.

7.4. Bending Forces

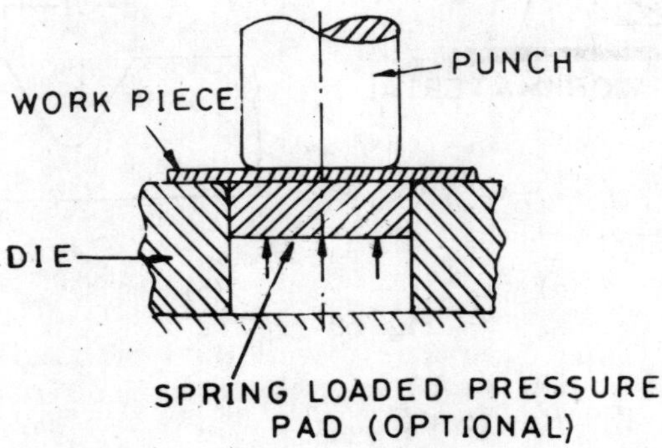

Fig. 7.7

The force required to bend a material is calculated by using the following formula :

$$F_b = \frac{K \cdot L \cdot f \cdot t^2}{W}$$

where L = Contact length of work in cm.

t = Thickness of work material in cm.

f = Ultimate tensile strength in tonnes/cm^2.

W = Width of die (span of beam) in cm.

F_b = Bending force in tonnes.

K = Die opening factor.

L, W and *t* are shown in Fig. 7.8.

For V-bends (air bending)

$$K = 1.33 \text{ for } W = 8t$$
$$= 1.2 \text{ for } W = 16t$$

For U-bending (channel bending)

$$K = 2.66 \text{ for } W = 8t$$
$$= 2.4 \text{ for } W = 16t$$

For edge bending

$$K = 0.67 \text{ for } W = 8t$$
$$= 0.6 \text{ for } W = 16t$$

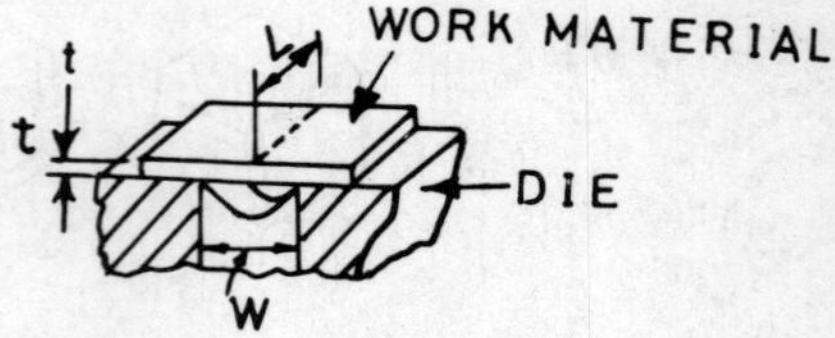

Fig. 7.8

For edge bending the width (W) between contact points on die is determined as follows (See Fig. 7.9)

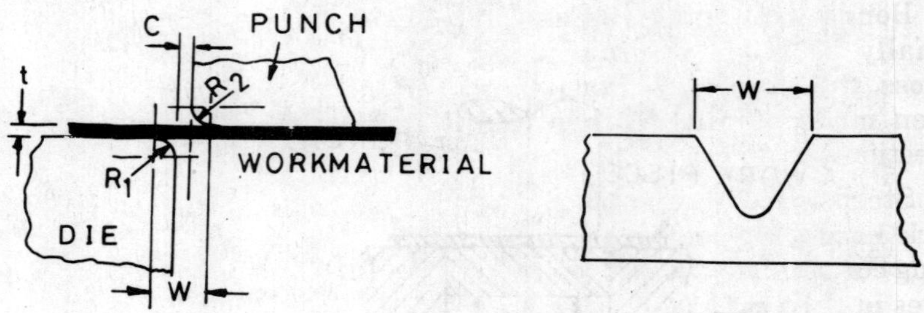

(a) (b)

Fig. 7.9

$$W = R_1 + R_2 + C$$

where R_1 = Die radius

R_2 = Punch radius

t = Thickness of metallic sheet

Clearance $C = t$

$$W = R_1 + R_2 + t.$$

7.5. Bend Allowance

In order to estimate the required flat work piece length to make a bend, calculation of bend allowance is essential.

To make a bend as shown in Fig. 7.10, the length of flat blank is determined as follows :

$$L = L_1 + L_2 + A$$

where L = Length of flat blank required to make the bend

L_1 = Length of bend leg 1

L_2 = Length of bend leg 2

A = Bend allowance

• θ = Bend angle (Angle through which metal is bent)

R = Internal radius of bend

t = Metallic sheet thickness

$$A = \frac{2\pi\theta}{360}(R + Kt)$$

where K = Constant

$= 1/4$ when $R \le t$

$= 1/3$ when $R \le 2t$

$= 1/2$ when $R > 2t$.

Bends with small radius can usually be made when bending across the grain directions than when made parallel to the grain direction.

Steels which are subjected to work hardening may crack while being cut because of burrs or sharp edges in the bent area.

Amount of bending that a material can take is limited by the following factors :

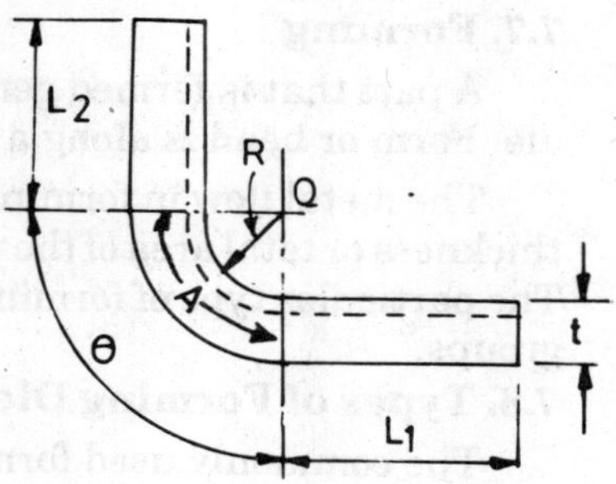

Fig. 7.10

(*i*) Properties of material

(*ii*) Length of bend

(*iii*) Condition of the cut edge at the ends of bend line

(*iv*) Direction of orientation of the axis of the bend to the direction in which material was rolled.

7.6. Spring Back

In bending after the applied force is withdrawn the metal tries to resume its original position causing a decrease in bend angle (as well as an increase in the included angle between bent portions). Such a metal movement is called spring back phenomenon. It is caused by the elastic stresses remaining in the bend area. After bending pressure on metal is released, the elastic stresses are also released, and cause metal movement spring back varies from ½ to 5° in steel whereas in phospher bronze it may be 10—15°.

Spring back depends upon the following factors :

(*i*) Material type

(*ii*) Thickness

(*iii*) Hardness

(*iv*) Bend radius.

A larger bend radius causes greater spring back. Spring back can be prevented by following methods.

(*i*) Over bending can reduce spring back especially in *V*-die air bends.

(*ii*) By coining (squeezing) the metal slightly at the corners in order to relieve elastic stresses. This is sometime referred to as corner setting.

7.7. Forming

A part that is formed generally takes the shape of the punch or die. Form or bend is along a curved axis instead of a straight one.

The metal flow in forming dies is not severe enough to affect the thickness or total area of the workpiece material to any great extent. The particular type of forming operation classifies forming dies into groups.

7.8. Types of Forming Dies

The commonly used forming dies are as follows :

(*i*) Solid form dies

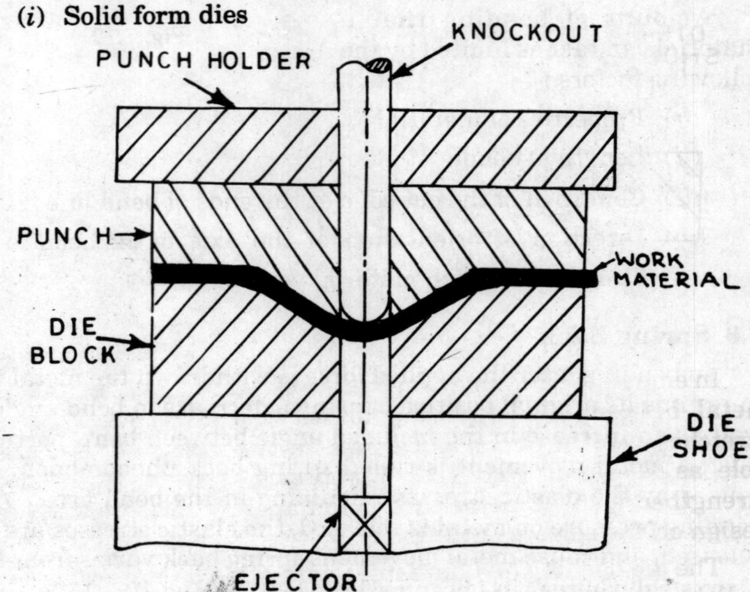

Fig. 7.11

(ii) Pad-type form dies

(iii) Embossing dies

(iv) Coining dies

(v) Bulging dies.

In solid forming dies. The die block is shaped to the matching contour of the work piece. The punch is made from good grade tool steel and shaped to the desired contour of the workpiece. Fig. 7.11 shows solid forming die. This type of die is generally used for forming operations in progressive dies.

Fig. 7.12 shows forming die with pressure pad. This type of die is used where greater accuracy is desired. The pad holds the work in position while it is being worked on. The lip (A) on the pressure pad is about 1½ times the width (B) springs, air cushions or hydraulic cylinders are used to provide the resistance

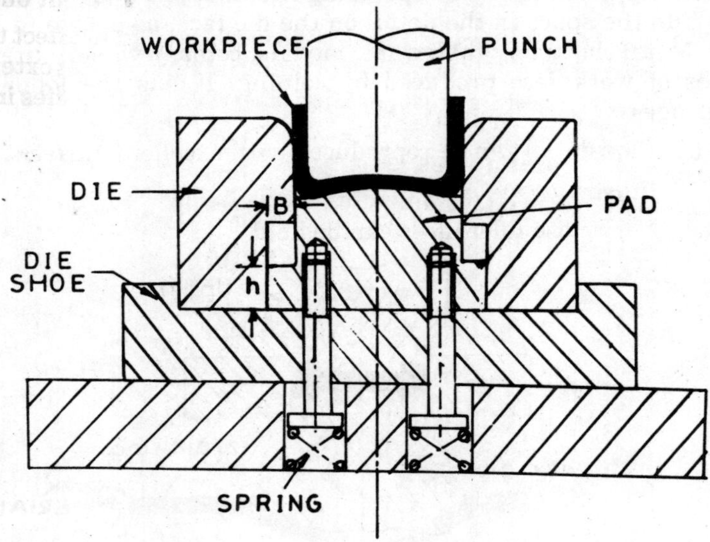

Fig. 7.12

In embossing a shallow surface is formed by displacement of the metal between two opposing mated tool surfaces. The metal stretches over the punch and across the two radius edges of the die hole as shown in Fig. 7.13. Embossing is used to stiffen and strengthen a sheet metal part or to impart a raised or depressed design on the surface of the part.

The die opening has the same width of rib or embossing *W* and a slight radius *R* is added to the edges of the opening to allow the metal to flow freely. The punch is made slightly smaller than the required metal thickness per side so that it does not strike along this area.

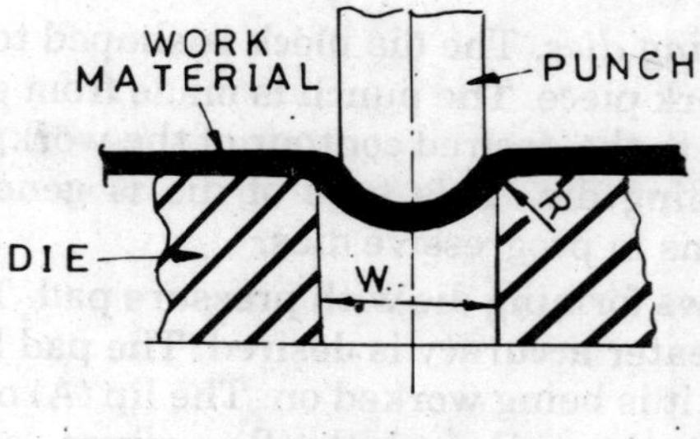

Fig. 7.13

Coining is the process of pressing the metal in a die so that it flows into the space in the detail on the die face, as shown in Fig. 7.14. Metal buttons, tableware, medals, coins, jewellery are examples of workpiece produced by coining. It has the following advantages.

(*i*) Part detail can be reproduced with excellent surface finish.

(*ii*) Very close tolerances can be held.

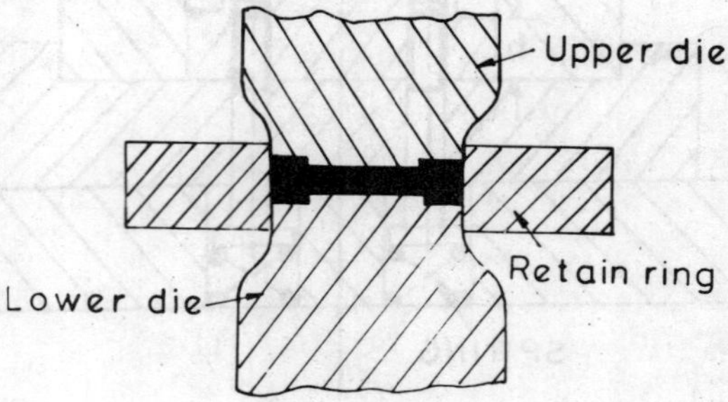

Fig. 7.14

Bulging is an internal forming operation used to expand portions of a drawn shell or tube. In this operation the force is applied from inside the work piece and is transmitted through a medium that will flow and not compress. The commonly used media in bulging are as follows.

(*i*) Rubber
(*ii*) Urethane
(*iii*) Heavy grease
(*iv*) Oil
(*v*) Water.

Rubber and urethane are preferred as a pressure dispersing medium because they are clean and easy to use. Fig. 7.15 shows bulging press tool using rubber as bulging medium.

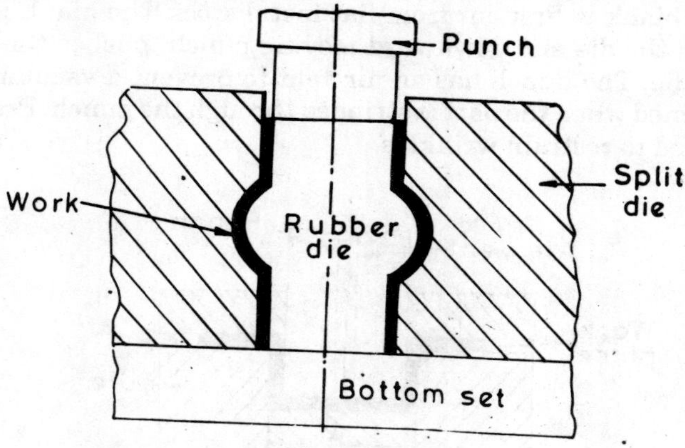

Fig. 7.15

7.9. Drawing

Drawing is an operation of producing cylindrical or box shaped components with straight or tapered sides. During drawing metal is made to flow plastically by applying the required force.

In drawing as the material is pushed through the die opening over a radius, the drawing action causes the shell (work) to hug the punch. This requires a stripping action. As shown in Fig. 7.15(*a*) the pressure pad exerts a force on the lip of the partially drawn shell.

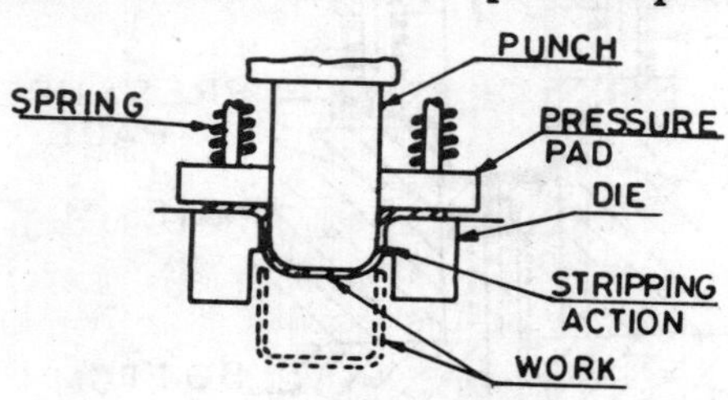

Fig. 7.15(*a*).

This force holds the lip down with a pressure just strong enough to permit the material to slide out from underneath once the punch starts to descend. This makes the metal to flow over the die radius without flopping up.

In drawing the area of the developed blank before drawing should be same as the surface area of the shell after drawing provided the thickness of the material remains unchanged.

7.10. Drawing Dies

A simple drawing die is shown in Fig. 7.16. In drawing the required blank is first cut from flat metal stock.The blank is then placed on the die and downward moving punch pushes the blank into the die. The punch has an air vent to prevent a vacuum from being formed when the part is stripped through the punch. Pressure pad is used to restrain wrinkles.

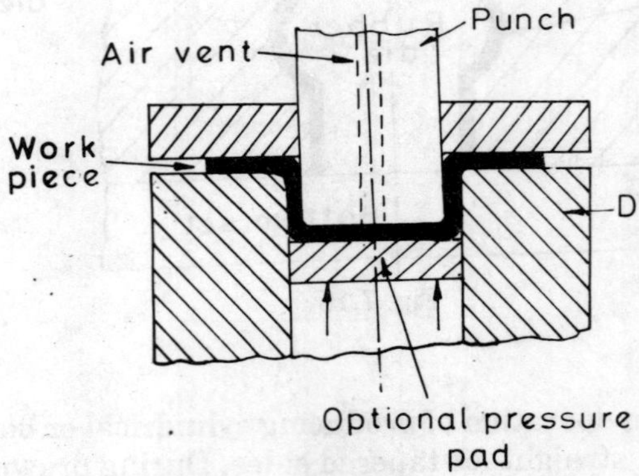

Fig. 7.16

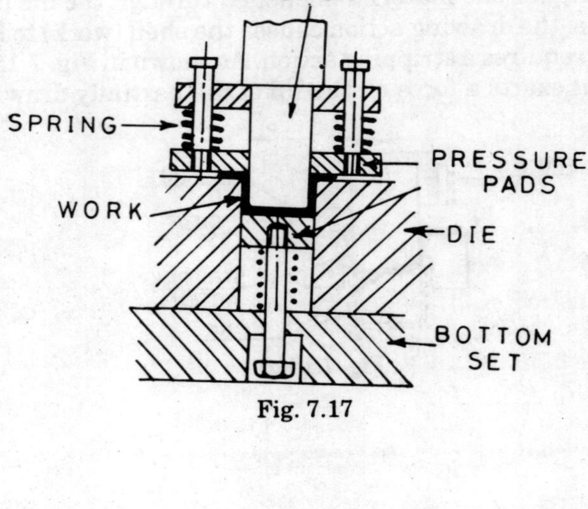

Fig. 7.17

Fig. 7.17 shows a drawing tool to produce a cylindrical cup, the tool using spring loaded pressure pads to hold the work material in position.

In drawing the method by which the blank is held in position is important because successful drawing is somewhat dependent upon the proper control of blank holder pressure.

There are two types of drawing operations

(*i*) Shallow drawing (*ii*) Deep drawing.

In shallow drawing the cup is not deeper than half its diameter. There would be very little thinning of the metal. Deep drawing is the drawing in which cup formed is deeper than half its diameter.

Drawing dies may be

(*i*) Single action dies (*ii*) Double action dies.

Deep drawing may be carried out on single action dies where the pressure on the blank holder is more evenly controlled by a die cushion or pad attached to the bed of the press. Typical construction of such a die is shown in Fig. 7.18. It is an inverted die in which die is attached to the ram and punch and pressure pad are on the lower shoe.

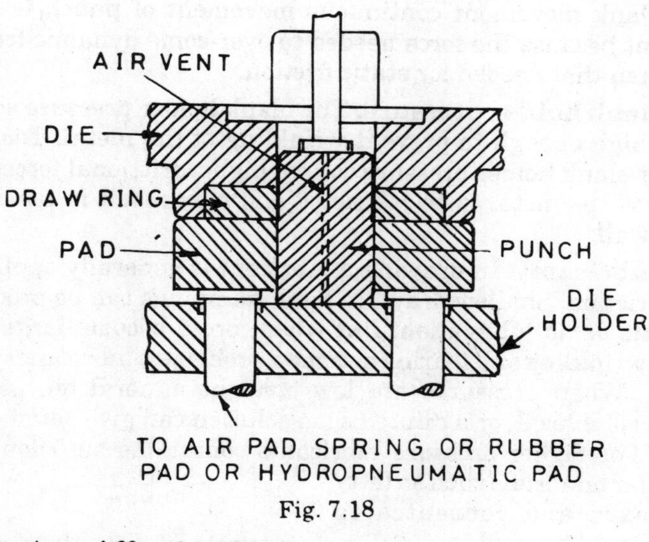

Fig. 7.18

7.11. Factors Affecting Drawing

The various factors that affect the metal flow during drawing are as follows :

(*i*) Type of material

(*ii*) **Ductility**

(*iii*) **Yield strength**

(*iv*) **Force of friction**

(*v*) **Blank holder pressure**

(*vi*) **Lubrication**

(*vii*) **Radius on punch**

(*viii*) **Radius on die**

(*ix*) **Drawing speed**

(*x*) **Die clearance.**

1. Ductility. Ductility is the ability of the metal to under go a change in shape without fracturing. Yield strength is the point at which permanent change of shape occurs in a metal. A low yield strength is desirable so that metal flow can begin easily without tearing near the punch radius.

2. Force of friction. The force of static friction between the work piece and draw die surfaces must be overcome in drawing operation. The force of blank holder adds significantly to the force of static friction. ONce the static friction is over-come by the start of the blank movement continuous movement of punch is quite important because the force needed to over-come dynamic friction is less than that needed for static friction.

3. Blank holder pressure. The blank holder pressure should be only high enough to prevent wrinkling of the metal. Too high values of blank holder pressure causes higher frictional forces and may cause the metal to be restricted and may result in tearing of the cup wall.

4. Lubricants. In drawing a lubricant is generally applied to reduce friction. Shallow draws in light stampings can be produced with little or no lubrication. But when forces become larger and scoring, wrinkling and tearing become a problem, a lubricant should be used. When pressures are low straight mineral oil, general purpose soluble oil, or a diluted soap solution can give satisfactory service. For higher pressure lubricants containing sufficient oiliness (polar materials such as fatty oils, waxes and concentrated soaps) should be used.

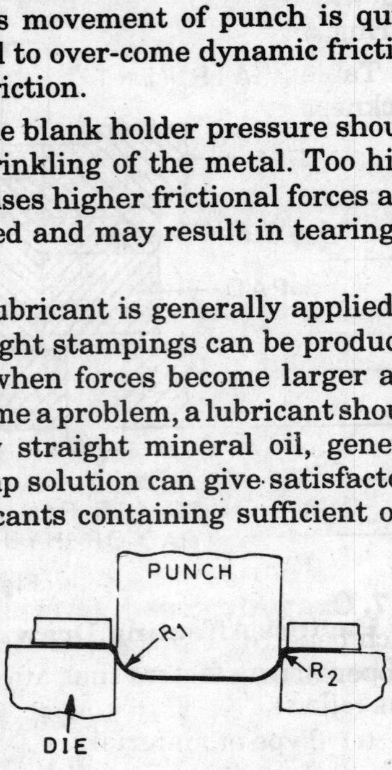

Fig. 7.19

5. Radius on punch. So far radius on punch is concerned a sharper radius will require higher forces when metal is folded around the punch nose and may result in excessive thinning or tearing at the bottom of the cup. The commonly used value of radius on punch (R_1) is as follows :

$$R_1 = 4t \text{ to } 10t$$

where t = Metal thickness.

6. Radius on die. The radius on draw die should be as large as possible to permit full freedom of metal flow as it passes over the radius. Generally,

$$R_2 = \text{Radius on draw die (Fig. 7.19)}$$
$$= 4t.$$

For drawing shallow cups of heavy gauge metals without a blank holder.

$$R_2 = 6t \text{ to } 8t.$$

However if the draw radius is too large the metal will be released by the blank holder too soon and wrinkling will result. On the other hand a too sharp radius will hinder normal flow of metal and will cause uneven thinning of the cup wall with resultant tearing.

Table 7(a) indicates drawing radius for some values of stock thickness.

Table 7(a)

Stock thickness (mm)	*Drawing Radius (mm)*
0.4	1.6
0.8	3.2
1.6	6.3
2	10
2.5	11.2

7. Drawing speed. Drawing speed is the velocity at which the punch penetrates workpiece. It often has a definite effect on drawing operation.

V = Drawing speed
= 10 to 15 mpm for low carbon steel
= 50 to 70 mpm for non–ferrious work material.

When cracking or excessive thinning occurs the drawing speed should be reduced. In general the drawing speed should be less for harder and more ductile materials.

8. Die clearance. Die clearance is the gap left between the punch and die.

$$C = \text{Die clearance}$$
$$= 7 \text{ to } 20\% \text{ of metal thickness.}$$

When clearance is equal to metal thickness or less croning or burnishing of metal will occur near the top of the cup.

7.12. Determining Blank Size

The size of blank for a drawn shell is found as follows .

$$\therefore \quad \frac{\pi}{4} D^2 = \frac{\pi}{4} d^2 + \pi d h.$$

$$\therefore \quad D = \sqrt{d^2 + 4dh} \text{ when } \frac{d}{r} \text{ is 20 or more}$$

$$= \sqrt{d^2 + 4dh} - 0.5\, r \text{ when } \frac{d}{r} \text{ is between 15 and 20}$$

$$= \sqrt{d^2 + 4dh} - r \text{ when } \frac{d}{r} \text{ is between 10 and 15}$$

$$= \sqrt{(d - 2r)^2 + 4d(h - r) + 2\pi r\,(d - 0.7r)}$$

when $\frac{d}{r}$ is below 10.

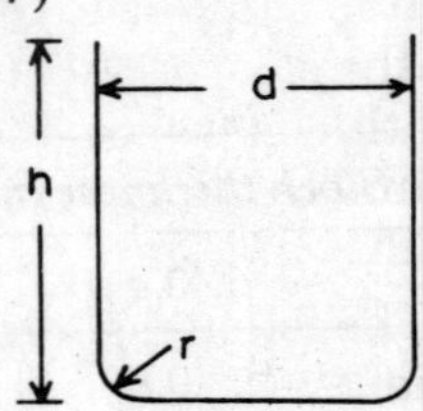

where d = shell diameter
D = Blank diameter
h = shell height
r = corner radius

Fig. 7.20.

as shown in Fig. 7.20.

These formulas give the theoretical blank size which is only an approximation. Extra metal should be added because of

(*i*) Thickening and thinning of metal during drawing.

(*ii*) Non uniformity of materials.

(*iii*) Friction at work-die surface.

(*iv*) Non-uniformity of pressure applied.

(*v*) Condition of deforming tool.

Blank diameter can be calculated by various methods such as :

(*i*) Mathematical

(*ii*) Graphical

(*iii*) Area

(*iv*) Weight.

7.13. Clearance between Punch and Die

Generally enough clearance is left to allow for thickening the metal. The allowance may vary between 7 to 20% of metal thickness. Table 7.0 indicates the values of clearance (C).

C = clearance in per cent of metal thickness.

t = thickness of original blank

Table 7.0

t mm	*First Draw*	*Redraw*	*Sizing Draw*
Upto 0.3	$1.07t - 1.09t$	$1.8 + -1.1t$	$1.04 + -1.05t$
0.3 to 1.25	$1.08t - 1.1t$	$1.09 + -1.12t$	$1.05 + -1.06t$
1.25 – 3	$1.1t - 1.12t$	$1.12 + -1.14t$	$1.07 + -1.09t$
Above 3	$1.12t - 1.14t$	$1.15 + -1.2t$	$1.08 + -1.1t$

7.14. To Calculate Reduction in Wall Thickness

It is possible to reduce wall thickness of drawn shell by controlling the clearance between the punch and die. As a general rule the wall thickness for ductile materials may be reduced by 10% of the original thickness of material, other factor such as type of material, ductility and hardness should also be considered.

The following formulas help to find reduction in wall-thickness of shell

$$h = \frac{h_1 \cdot t_1}{t}$$

where h = mean height of shell

h_1 = Ironed height

t_1 = Ironed thickness

t = original thickness of work material.

The per cent of reduction of a shell may be calculated as follows:

$$\% \text{ reduction } (p) = \frac{(t - t_1)}{t} \times 100$$

Percentage reduction can be calculated by using following formula also

p = percentage reduction

$$= 100\left(1 - \frac{d}{D}\right)$$

where d = Shell outer diameter

D = Blank diameter.

The theoretical maximum percent reduction for first draw is about 50%. It is 30% for second draw and 20% for the third and subsequent draws. Total reduction should not increase from 70 to 75%, when it should be annealed and reduction may start again at the maximum percentage.

7.15. Draw Ratio

Draw ratio is defined as follows :

e = Draw ratio

$$= \frac{h}{d}$$

where h = Shell height.

When draw ratio exceeds 0.625 to 0.75 more than one draw is needed.

7.15.1. Thickness ratio. It is the ratio of thickness (t) of work material and blank diameter.

(D) is called thickness ratio

S = Thickness ratio

$$= \frac{t}{D}.$$

7.16. Drawing Force

To force required to draw a symmetrical cup is calculated as follows :

P = Drawing force

$$= \pi d t \sigma_y \left[\frac{D}{d} - K\right]$$

where d = outside diameter of shell

D = Blank diameter

t = Thickness of metal

σ_y = Yield strength of metal

K = Constant to cover bending and friction.

= 0.6 – 0.7 for ductile materials

F = Total force to be exerted by the press

= Drawing force + Blank holding force + Ironing force.

7.17. Blank Holder Pressure

Blank holder pressure should be only high enough to prevent wrinkling of the metal. Too high values of blank holder pressure causes higher frictional forces and may cause to metal to be restricted and may result in tearing of the cup wall. It varies from very little to a maximum of about ⅓ or more of drawing pressure. It is calculated as follows :

$$Q = \text{Blank holder force} \quad = \frac{\pi}{4}[D^2 - d^2] \times f$$

where f = stress

It depends upon material to be drawn.

D = Blank diameter

d = Shell diameter.

7.18. Redrawing

It is the process of deepening the cup after the first draw.

Redrawing may be obtained by different methods :

(*i*) Direct redrawing

(*ii*) Ironing.

Fig. 7.21 shows stages of deep drawing of a cup and Fig. 7.22 shows the normal form of a redrawing tool where a pressure pad is employed to prevent wrinkling of the work. The throat angle varies from 10 to 15°.

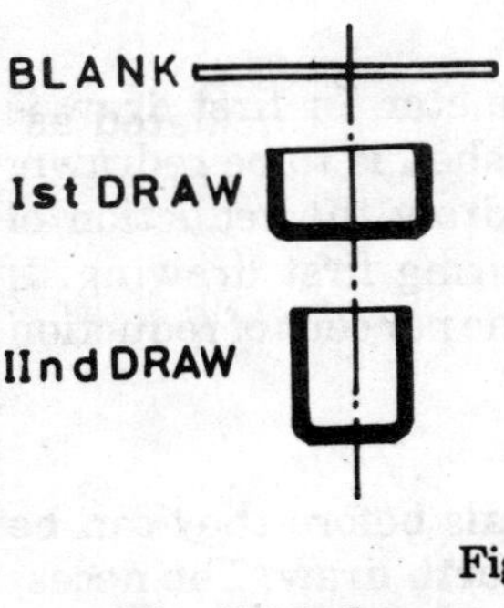

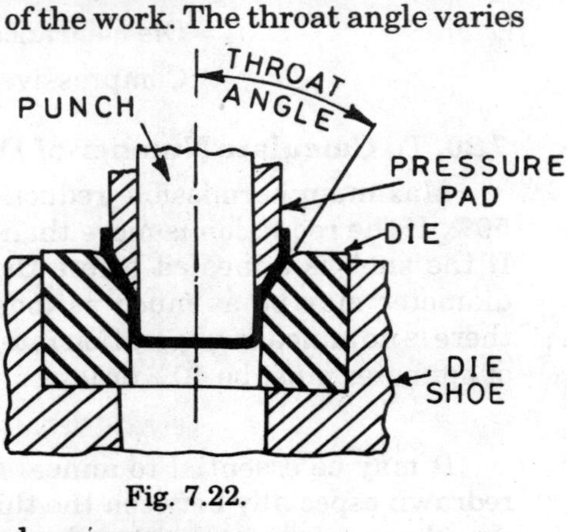

Fig. 7.21. Fig. 7.22.

Fig. 7.23 shows reversed redrawing process.

7.19. Ironing

Ironing reduces wall thickness and consequent lengthening of the cup Annealed cups can be subjected to a wall thickness reduction of about 50%. Fig. 7.24 shows ironing of a cup.

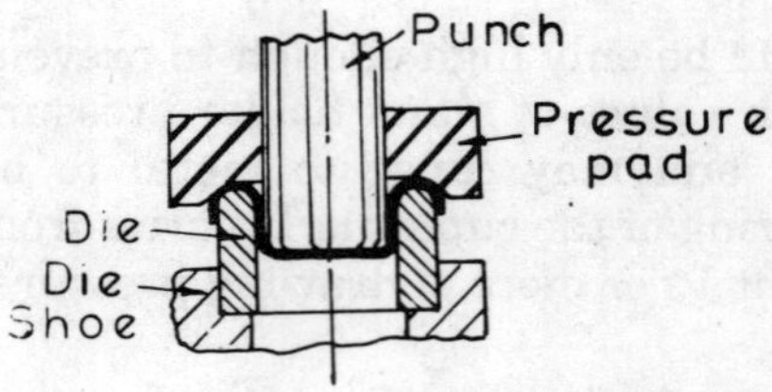

Fig. 7.23.

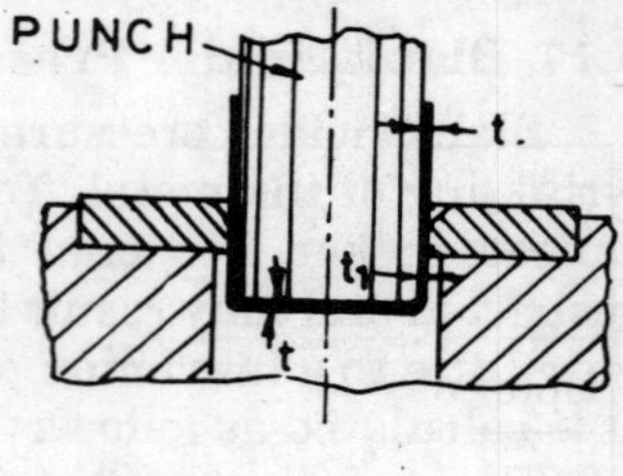

Fig. 7.24.

Let d = Cup diameter

t = Original thickness

t_1 = Reduced thickness

h = height of cup

$$\pi d t h = \pi\, d\, t_1\, h_1$$

$$\frac{t}{t_1} = \frac{h_1}{h}.$$

Ironing force is calculated as follows :

$$F = \pi\, d(t - t_2) \cdot f_C$$

where F = Ironing force

d = Outside diameter of cup

t = Blank thickness

t_2 = Die clearance

f_C = Compressive stress of metal.

7.20. To Calculate Number of Draws

Maximum permissible reduction in diameter for first draw is 50%. If the reduction is more than 50% the shell is to be redrawn. If the shell is annealed before the second draw the reduction of diameter may be as much as took place during first drawing. If there is no annealing operation intervening the per cent of reduction of diameter must be 40% or less.

It may be essential to anneal some metals before they can be redrawn especially between the third and fourth draw. The necessity of annealing depends on the work hardening characteristics of the material. Table 7.1 indicates the possible number of reductions for a given ratio of shell height (h) to diameter (d).

$$e = \frac{h}{d}$$

N = Number of reductions.

Table 7.1

e	*N*	*Reduction %*			
		First Draw	*Second Draw*	*Third Draw*	*Fourth Draw*
Upto 0.75	1	40			
0.75 – 1.5	2	40	25		
1.5 – 3	3	40	25	15	
3 – 4.5	4	40	25	15	10

The number of draws can be calculated as follows :

Let k = Coefficient of drawing or Drawing ratio

$$= \frac{D}{d}$$

where D = Blank diameter

d = Shell diameter

If the coefficient of drawing exceeds 1.5 to 2.0 the cup fails in process due to work hardening and severe deformations. It is desirable to draw the cup or shell in steps.

Fig. 7.25 shows the cup drawn in stages.

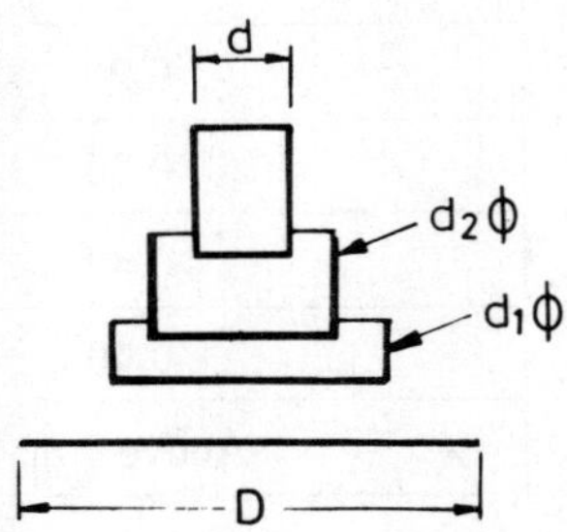

Fig. 7.25.

Let n = Number of stages.

During first draw

d_1 = diameter of shell

$$k_1 = \frac{D}{d_1}$$

During second draw

$$k_2 = \frac{d_1}{d_2}$$

where d_2 = Diameter of shell at end of second draw

In nth draw $k_n = \frac{d_{n-1}}{d_n}$

k = overall drawing ratio

$$= K_1 \cdot K_2 .... K_n$$

$$= \frac{D}{d}$$

Let K_m = Mean draw ratio

$$K = (K_m)^n = \frac{D}{d}$$

$$n \log K_m = \log \frac{D}{d}$$

$$n = \frac{\log D - \log d}{\log K_m}.$$

Table 7.2 indicates the drawing ratio (K) for steel where pressure pad is used.

$$\%S = \text{Thickness ratio} = \frac{t}{D} \times 100.$$

Table 7.2

% S	K
0.15	1.43
0.20	1.54
0.30	1.67
0.40	1.82
0.50	1.91
Above 0.50	2.00

where t = Thickness of work material.

If in between two stages the material gets work hardened the product should be annealed. In repeated operations the drawing ratio (K) should be less than or equal to 1.2. The number of draws usually does not exceed 3 to 4.

7.20. Progressive Dies

These dies have two or more stations. Each station performs an operation on the work piece so that the work piece is completed when the last operation has been accomplished. Operations such as piercing, blanking, forming drawing and cut off can be carried out on progressive dies.

Pierced holes which are to be used as pilots should be punched in the first station and piloted in the second station. Notching stations are usually included in the early stations and backed up with heels if needed.

Drawing operations are usually done in the first or second station bending or forming operations are usually done in the last operation in cooperation with the cut off operation.

7.20.1. Lubricants for drawing. Adequate lubrication lowers the operating forces and helps to prevent pick up of the material on the tools. Table 7.3 indicates the lubricants for drawing and ironing.

Table 7.3

Material	*Drawing Lubricant*	*Ironing*
Aluminium	Graphite and tallow and soaps	Dry Graphite
Brass	Soap lubricants	Graphite and Kaolin
Mild steel	Soaps and Graphite bearing lubricants	Graphite bearing lubricants.

7.21. Design Procedure for a Drawing Die

Following factors should be considered while designing a drawing die :

1. To calculate blank diameter.

2. To calculate number of draws required. Number of draws generally used are up to 4. Total reduction should not increase 70 to 75% when it should be annealed.

3. To calculate the drawing force.

4. To decide clearance between dies and punches.

5. To decide radius of draw die.

6. To determine blank holder pressure venting.

7. To decide venting of punches and bottom forming pads. Venting of punches and bottom forming pressure pads is quite important. Venting allows trapped air to escape and provides passage for lubricants. Further it prevents suction between punch or pad and drawn workpiece or shell.

8. To decide lubricant to be used.

7.22. Drawing Speed

The speed with which drawing operation is carried out depends upon two factors.

(*i*) Type of material

(*ii*) Type of press.

Table 7.4 indicates drawing speed for some of the materials.

Table 7.4

Material	*Drawing speed (m / min)*	
	Single Action	*Double Action*
Steel	18	10 – 16
Copper	45	25
Aluminium	55	30
Brass	65	30
Zinc	45	14

Example 7.1. *Calculate the blank length to make the part shown in Fig. 7.26. Also determine the bending force required if the ultimate tensile strength of material is 3500 kg/cm*^{2}

and die radius is 8 mm. The bend length being 120 cm.

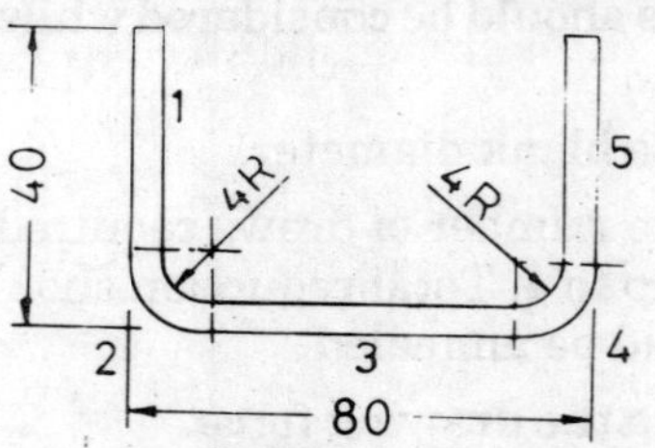

Fig. 7.26

Solution. (*a*) R = Inside radius

$= 4$ mm.

t = Thickness of metal = 2 mm.

L_1 = Length of segment 1

$= 40 - (t + R)$

$= 40 - (2 + 4)$

$= 34$ mm

θ = Bend angle = 90°

Bend Allowance, $L_2 = \dfrac{2\pi\theta}{360}[R + Kt]$

where $K = 1/3$ as $R = 2t$

$$L_2 = \frac{2\pi \times 90}{360}[4 + 1/3 \times 2]$$

$= 7.33$ mm

$L_3 = 80 - [t + t + R + R]$

$= 80 - [2 + 2 + 4 + 4]$

$= 68$ mm

L_4 = Bend allowance

$L_4 = L_2 = 7.33$

L_5 = Length of segment 5

$= L_1$

$= 34$ mm

L = Total blank length

= Length of all segments

$= L_1 + L_2 + L_3 + L_4 + L_5$

$= 34 + 7.33 + 68 + 7.33 + 34$

$= 150.66$ mm

(*b*) t = Sheet thickness

$= 2$ mm $= 0.2$ cm

f = ultimate tensile strength

$= 3500$ kg/cm^2

$R_1 = R_2 = 8$ mm

W = Width of die

$= R_1 + R_2 + C$

where $C = t$

$= 8 + 8 + 2 = 18$ mm

$= 1.8$ cm.

L = Length of part

$= 120$ mm.

$K = 2.66$ for U bending

F_b = Bending force

$$= \frac{K \cdot L \cdot ft^2}{W}$$

$$= \frac{2.66 \times 120 \times 3500 \times 0.2^2}{1.8}$$

$= 24800$ kg

$= 24.8$ tonnes.

Example 7.2. *Calculate the developed length of part shown in Fig. 7.27.*

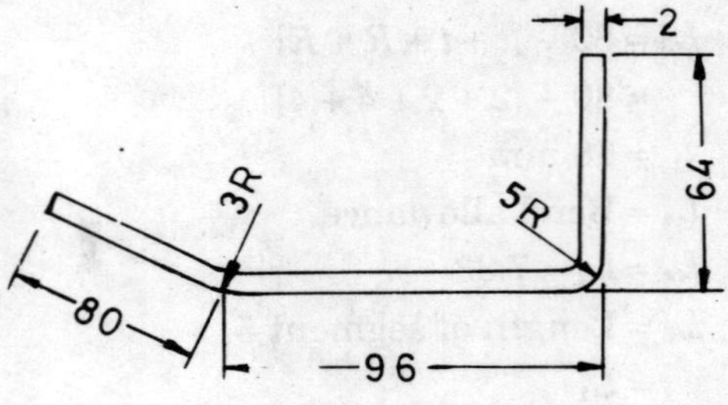

Fig. 7.27

Solution.

As shown in Fig. 7.28

t = Thickness of metallic sheet

= 2 mm

R_1 = Internal radius

$= 5 - t = 5 - 2 = 3$ mm

R_2 = Internal radius

$= 3 - t = 3 - 2 = 1$ mm.

L_1 = Length of leg 1

$= 64 - (t + R_1) = 64 - [2 + 3]$

= 59 mm.

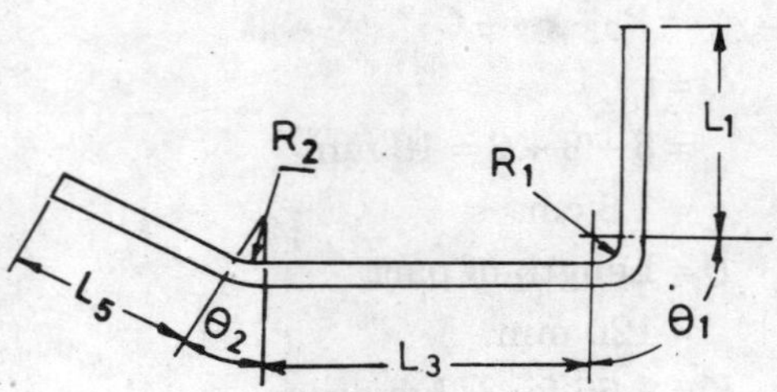

Fig. 7.28.

$\theta_1 = 90°$

L_2 = Length of leg 2

= Bend allowance

$$= \frac{2\pi\theta_1}{360}\left[R_1 + K_1 t\right]$$

where $K_1 = 1/3$ as $R_1 < 2t$

$$= \frac{2\pi \times 90}{360}[3 + 1/3 \times 2]$$

$$= 5.76 \text{ mm.}$$

$$L_3 = 96 - (R_1 + t)$$

$$= 96 - [3 + 2]$$

$$= 91 \text{ mm.}$$

$$\theta_2 = 30^\circ$$

L_4 = Length of leg 4

= Bend allowance

$$= \frac{2\pi\theta_2}{360}\left[R_2 + K_2 \cdot t\right]$$

$$= \frac{2\pi \times 30}{360}[1 + 1/4 \times 2]$$

where $K_2 = 1/4$ as $R_2 < t$

$$= 0.785 \text{ mm.}$$

L_5 = Length of segment 5

= 80 mm.

The developed length is the summation of all these lengths along the neutral bending line

L = Total length 5

$$= L_1 + L_2 + L_3 + L_4 + L_5$$

$$= 59 + 5.76 + 91 + 0.785 + 80$$

$$= 236.54 \text{ mm.}$$

Example 7.3. *Calculate the bending force for a 45° bend of aluminium sheet 1.8 mm thick and 1200 mm long with a die opening 8 times the metal thickness. The bend is to be made by air bending method. The ultimate tensile strength is 3400 kg/cm².*

Solution. t = Sheet thickness

= 1.8 mm = 0.18 cm.

W = Width of die

$$= 8 \times t = 8 \times 1.8 = 14.4 \text{ mm} = 1.44 \text{ cm.}$$

K = Die opening factor

= 1.33 for $W = 8\,t$

L = 1200 mm. = 120 cm.

f = ultimate tensile strength

$$= 3400 \text{ kg/cm}^2$$

$$F_b = \text{Bending load}$$

$$= \frac{K \cdot L \cdot ft^2}{W}$$

$$= \frac{1.33 \times 120 \times 3400 \times 0.18^2}{1.44}$$

$$= 12210 \text{ kg} = 12.21 \text{ tonnes.}$$

Example 7.4. *(a) A 90° bend as shown in Fig. 7.29 (a) is to be made from steel sheet in an air bending type die. The bend length is 30 cm, the stock thickness is 3 mm and beam length is 4 cm. The ultimate tensile strength of stock material is 4000 kg/cm².*

(b) If the bend is to be made by edge bending when die radius and punch radius is 10 mm, find the bending force required.

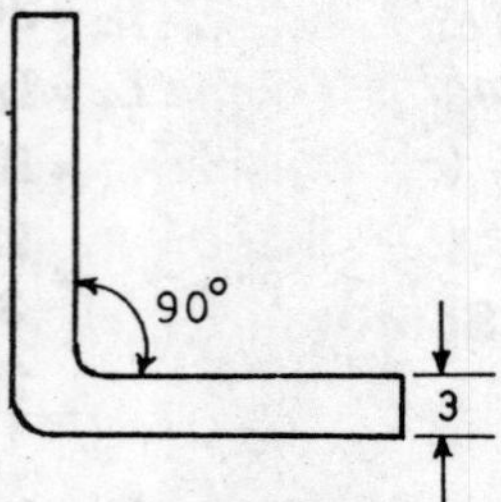

Fig. 7.29.(a)

Solution.

(a)

$$t = \text{Sheet thickness} = 3 \text{ mm} = 0.3 \text{ cm}$$

$$L = \text{Bend length} = 30 \text{ cm}$$

$$W = 4 \text{ cm}$$

$$K = 1.33$$

$$f = \text{ultimate tensile strength}$$

$$= 4000 \text{ kg/cm}^2$$

$$F_B = \text{Bending force}$$

$$= \frac{K \cdot L \cdot ft^2}{W}$$

$$= \frac{1.33 \times 30 \times 4000 \times 0.3^2}{4}$$

$$= 3600 \text{ kg} = 3.6 \text{ tonnes.}$$

(b) For edge bending

$$W = R_1 + R_2 + t$$

Radius, $R_1 = R_2 = 10$ mm

$$R_1 + R_2 = 2 \text{ cm}$$

$$W = 2 + 0.3 = 2.3 \text{ cm.}$$

$$K = 0.67$$

$$F_b = \text{ Bending force} = \frac{K \cdot L \cdot ft^2}{W}$$

$$= \frac{0.67 \times 30 \times 4000 \times 0.3^2}{2.3}$$

$$= 3146 \text{ kg} = 3.146 \text{ tonnes.}$$

Example 7.5. *A drawn steel shell has an outside diameter of 70 mm and is made from 2.4 mm thick sheet having 2300 kg/cm² yield strength. If blank diameter is 136 mm, calculate :*

(*a*) *Dimensions of punch and die*

(*b*) *Drawing force*

Solution. (*a*) d = Punch size = 70 mm

t = Thickness of metal = 2.4mm.

C = Clearance

= 10% of thickness

$$= \frac{10}{100} \times 2.4 = 0.24 \text{ mm.}$$

Die opening size $= d + 2t + 2C = 70 + 2 \times 2.4 + 2 \times 0.24$

= 75.28 mm.

(*b*) $$P = \text{ Drawing force} = \pi dt \cdot \sigma y \left[\frac{D}{d} - K\right]$$

where σ_y = yield strength

= 2300 kg/cm³

K = constant = 0.6 for ductile materials

D = Blank diameter = 136

$$P = \pi \times 7 \times 0.24 \times 2300 \left[\frac{136}{70} - 0.6\right]$$

$$= 16258 \text{ kg} = 16.258 \text{ tonnes.}$$

Example 7.6. *Calculate the blank diameter to make a steel shell shown in Fig. 7.29.*

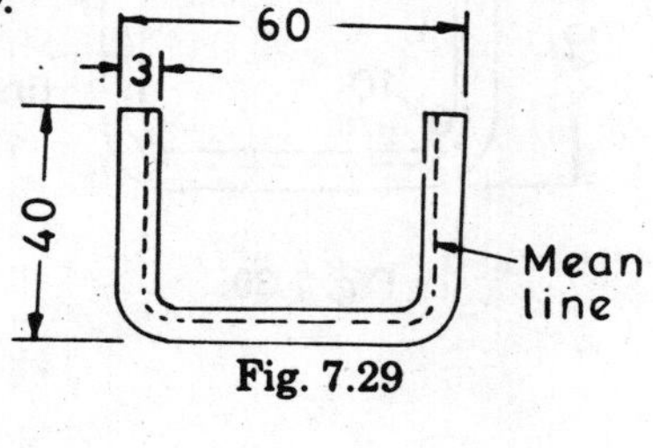

Fig. 7.29

Solution. t = Thickness of metal = 3 mm

d = Mean diameter

$= 60 - t = 60 - 3 = 57$ mm.

h = Mean height

$$= 40 - \frac{t}{2} = 40 - \frac{3}{2}$$

$= 38.5$ mm.

D = Blank diameter

$$= \sqrt{d^2 + 4dh}$$

$$= \sqrt{57^2 + 4 \times 57 \times 38.5}$$

$= 110$ mm.

Example 7.7. *Determine blank diameter to draw a shell as shown in Fig. 7.30.*

Solution. Inside radius = 10 mm.

t = thickness = 3 mm

r = Mean radius

$$= 10 + \frac{t}{2}$$

$$= 10 + \frac{3}{2} = 11.5 \text{ mm}$$

$H = 40$ mm.

To convert the shell to a square corner shell

h = Mean height

$= H - 0.43 \times r$

$= 40 - 0.43 \times 11.5 = 35$ mm.

d = Mean diameter $= 60 - t = 60 - 3 = 57$ mm.

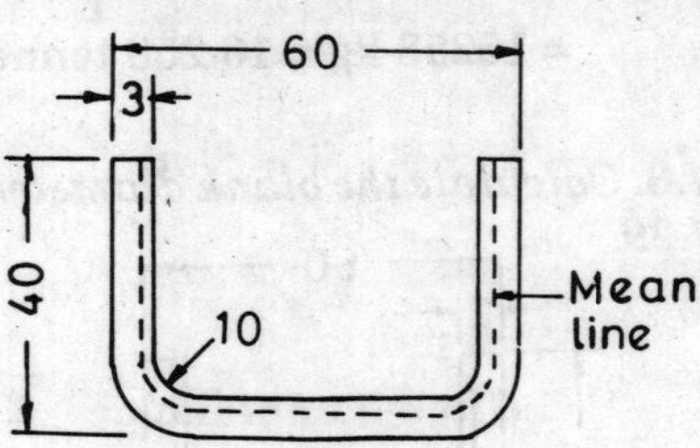

Fig. 7.30

$D =$ Blank diameter

$= \sqrt{d^2 + 4dh} = \sqrt{57^2 + 4 \times 57 \times 35}$

$= 106$ mm.

Example 7.8. *A shell is to have its wall thickness reduced from 1.8 mm by 11%. The new shell will have a new diameter of 40 mm. Determine*

(*a*) *Mean height of the shell*

(*b*) *Shell diameter needed to draw the ironed shell.*

Solution. $t =$ Work material thickness

$= 1.8$ mm

$t_1 =$ Ironed thickness

$$\% \text{ reduction} = \frac{t - t_1}{t} \times 100$$

$$11 = \frac{1.8 - t_1}{1.8} \times 100$$

$t_1 = 1.6$ mm

$h_1 =$ Shell height after ironing

$= 70$ mm.

$h =$ Mean height of shell

$$= \frac{h_1 \cdot t_1}{t}$$

$$= \frac{70 \times 1.6}{1.8} = 62.3 \text{ mm.}$$

(*b*) $d =$ Diameter of shell $= 40$ mm

$D =$ Blank diameter to draw ironed shell

$= \sqrt{d^2 + 4dh}$

$= \sqrt{40^2 + 4 \times 40 \times 62.3} = 107.5$ mm.

Example 7.9. *Calculate blank diameter for a shell as shown in Fig. 7.31.*

Solution. $d =$ Diameter of shell

$= 40$ mm

$d_1 =$ Diameter of flange

$= 60$ mm

$h =$ height of shell $= 50$ mm

$$D = \text{Blank diameter}$$
$$= \sqrt{d_1^2 + 4dh}$$
$$= \sqrt{60^2 + 4 \times 40 \times 50}$$
$$= 107.7 \text{ mm.}$$

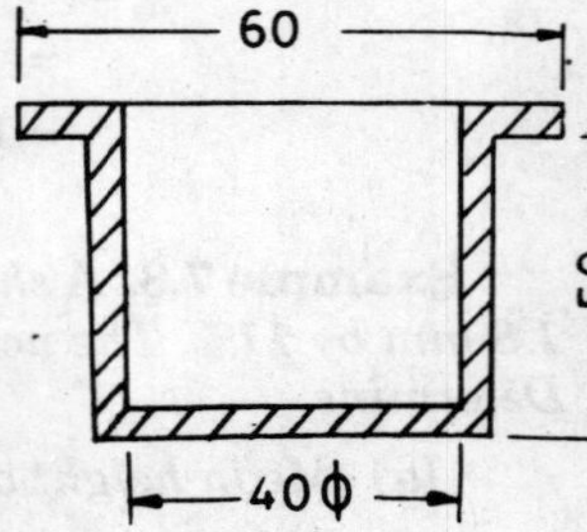

Fig. 7.31.

Example 7.10. *A shell having 32 mm diameter and 108 mm height with a wall thickness of 0.8 mm is to be manufactured from 1.1 mm thick metallic sheet. Calculate the blank diameter.*

Solution. d = Diameter of shell

= 32 mm

h = height of shell

= 108 mm

t = Thickness of metallic sheet

= 1.1 mm

t_1 = Wall thickness = 0.8 mm.

D = Blank diameter

$$= \sqrt{d^2 + 4dh \times \frac{t_1}{t}}$$

$$= \sqrt{32^2 + 4 \times 32 \times 108 \times \frac{0.8}{1.1}}$$

$$= 105.2 \text{ mm.}$$

Example 7.11. *Determine blank diameter to make a tapered shell shown in Fig. 7.32.*

Solution. D_1 = Larger diameter = 80 mm

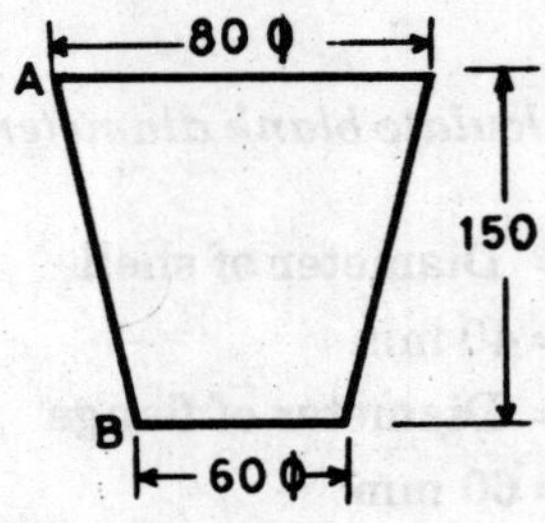

Fig. 7.32

$D_2 =$ Smaller diameter = 60 mm.

$AB = h =$ length of tapered side

$= \sqrt{150^2 + 10^2}$

$= 150.33$ mm

$D =$ Blank diameter

$= \sqrt{2h(D_1 + D_2) + D_2^2}$

$= \sqrt{2 \times 150.33(80 + 60) + 60^2}$

$= 213.76$ mm.

Example 7.12. *A shell shown in Fig. 7.33 is to be drawn from a circular blank. Find the diameter of blank neglecting thickness of material.*

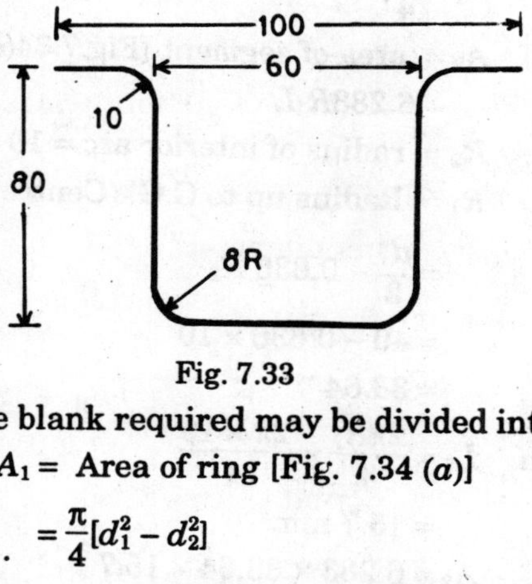

Fig. 7.33

Solution. The blank required may be divided into five areas.

$A_1 =$ Area of ring [Fig. 7.34 (*a*)]

$= \frac{\pi}{4}[d_1^2 - d_2^2]$

where $d_1 =$ Outside diameter of ring = 100 mm

$d_2 =$ Inside diameter of ring

$d_3 =$ Inside diameter of shell = 60 mm

$d_2 = d_3 + 10 + 10 = 60 + 20 = 80$ mm.

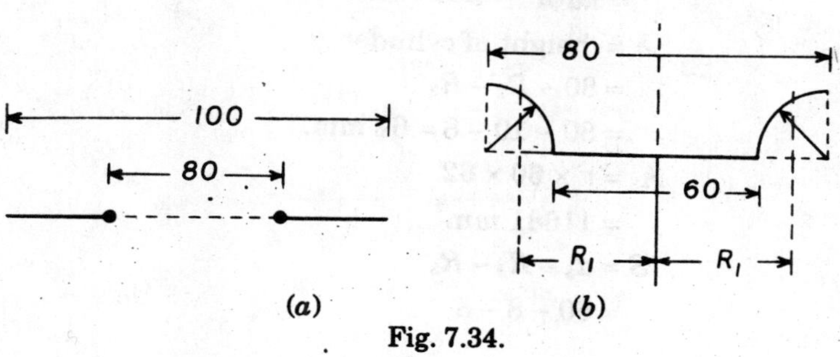

Fig. 7.34.

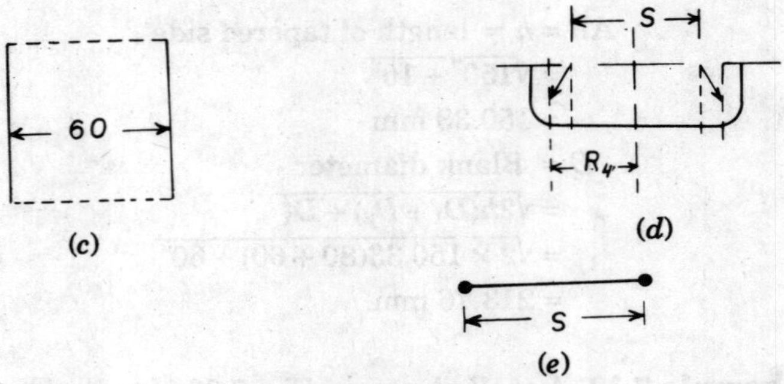

Fig. 7.34

$$A_1 = \frac{\pi}{4}[100^2 - 80^2] = 3600 \text{ mm}^2$$

(b) $A_2 =$ area of segment [Fig.7.34(b)]

$= 6.283 R_1 L$

$R_2 =$ radius of interior arc = 10 mm

where $R_1 =$ Radius up to C.G. (Centre of gravity)

$$= \frac{d^2}{2} - 0.636\, R_2$$

$= 40 - 0.636 \times 10$

$= 33.64$

Arc length $L_2 = \frac{2\pi R_2}{4} = \frac{2\pi \times 10}{4}$

$= 15.7$ mm.

$A_2 = 6.283 \times 33.64 \times 15.7$

$= 3318 \text{ mm}^2$

$R_3 =$ Radius of interior arc = 8 mm²

$A_3 =$ Area of cylinder [Fig. 734 (c)]

$= \pi d_3 h$

where $h =$ height of cylinder

$= 80 - R_2 - R_3$

$= 80 - 10 - 8 = 62$ mm.

$A_3 = \pi \times 60 \times 62$

$= 11681 \text{ mm}^2$

$S = d_3 - R_3 - R_3$

$= 60 - 8 - 8$

$= 44$ mm.

$R_4 =$ Radius upto C.G. of R_3

$$R_4 = \frac{S}{2} + 0.636 \times R_3$$

$$= \frac{44}{2} + 0.636 \times 8$$

$= 27.1$ mm.

$A_4 =$ Area of segment [Fig. 7. 34 (*d*)]

$= 6.283\ R_4 \times L_4$

where $L_4 =$ Length of arc

$$= \frac{2\pi R_3}{4}$$

$$= \frac{2\pi \times 8}{4}$$

$= 12.56$ mm.

If thickness (t) of sheet is to be considered then length of arc (L_4) will be as follows :

$$L_4 = \frac{\pi}{2}\left(R_3 + \frac{t}{3}\right)$$

$$A_4 = 6.283 \times 27.5 \times 12.56$$

$= 2170\ \text{mm}^2$

$A_5 =$ Area of disc [Fig. 7.34 (*e*)]

$$= \frac{\pi}{4} \times S^2 = \frac{\pi}{4} \times 44^2 = 1519\ \text{mm}^2$$

$A =$ Total area

$= A_1 + A_2 + A_3 + A_4 + A_5$

$= 3600 + 3318 + 11681 + 2170 + 1519$

$= 22288\ \text{mm}^2$

$D =$ Blank diameter

$$\frac{\pi}{4} D^2 = A$$

$$\frac{\pi}{4} \times D^2 = 22288$$

$D = 168.5$ mm.

Example 7.13. *A shell shown in Fig. 7.35 has a height of 48 mm and a diameter of 48 mm. The corner radius is 2 mm and work piece* *material is medium carbon steel and is 1 mm thick. Design die for drawing operation.*

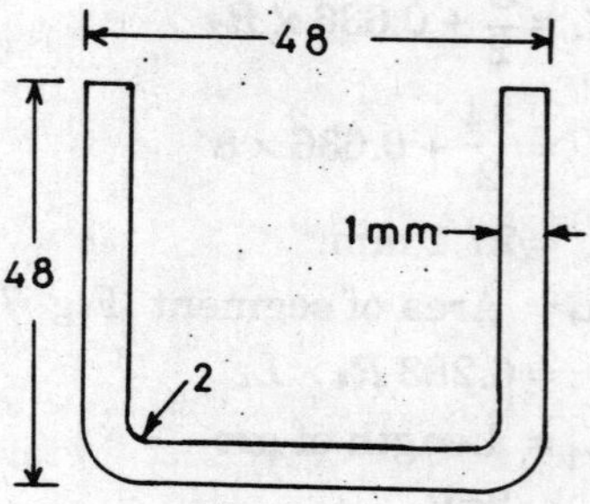

Fig. 7.35.

Solution. (*a*) To find blank diameter

$h =$ height of shell = 48 mm

$d =$ Diameter of shell = 48 mm

$r =$ Radius of corner = 2 mm

$t =$ Thickness of shell material = 1 mm

$$\frac{d}{r} = \frac{48}{2} = 24$$

Then the formula for calculating size of blank will be as follows:

$$D = \sqrt{d^2 + 4dh}$$
$$= \sqrt{48^2 + 4 \times 48 \times 48}$$
$$= 107.3 \text{ mm.}$$

This is the theoretical value of blank size. In order to take into account trimming extra metal of about 3 mm is to be added to blank diameter for each 25 mm of cup diameter.

$$\text{Blank diameter} = D + \frac{3}{25} \times 48$$
$$= 107.3 + 5.7$$
$$= 113 \text{ mm.}$$

(*b*) To find percentage reduction

$p =$ percentage reduction

$$= 100\left(1 - \frac{d}{D}\right) = 100\left(1 - \frac{48}{113}\right)$$

$$= 58\%.$$

Now for one draw the per cent reduction permissible is about 50%. Therefore it is obvious that the cup can not be drawn in one operation.

(c) To find draw number of stages

$$\text{Draw ratio} = \frac{h}{d}$$

$$= \frac{48}{48} = 1$$

As the reduction ratio is more than 0.75 therefore the shell may be drawn in two stages with 40% reduction for first draw and 25% reduction for second draw.

For first draw p = per cent reduction

$$40 = 100\left(1 - \frac{d_1}{D}\right)$$

where D = Blank diameter

$$40 = 100\left(1 - \frac{d_1}{113}\right)$$

$$d_1 = 67.8 \text{ mm.}$$

For second draw (stage)

$$p = 100\left(1 - \frac{d}{d_1}\right)$$

$$= 100\left(1 - \frac{48}{67.8}\right)$$

$$= 29\%.$$

Since per cent reduction is 29% and allowable per cent reduction is 25% therefore the cup should be drawn in three stages.

For second stage

$$p = 100\left[1 - \frac{d_2}{d_1}\right]$$

$$25 = 100\left[1 - \frac{d_2}{678}\right]$$

$$d_2 = 50.85 \text{ mm.}$$

For third stage

$$p = 100\left[1 - \frac{48}{50.85}\right]$$

$$= 6\%.$$

This is within permissible per cent reduction of 15% for third stage.

(*d*) To determine radius on punch and die.

$R_1 =$ Radius on punch

$= 4 \times t = 4 \times 1$

$= 4$ mm.

$R_2 =$ Radius on die

$= 5t = 5 \times 1$

$= 5$ mm.

(*e*) To determine die clearance

$t =$ Thickness = 1 mm.

Die clearance = 1.09 t = 1.09 × 1 = 1.09 mm.(Refer table 7.0).

(*f*) To calculate drawing pressure.

$$P = \pi d t \sigma_y \left[\frac{D}{d} - k\right]$$

$$= \pi \times 4.8 \times 0.1 \times 3600 \left[\frac{11.3}{4.8} - 0.65\right]$$

$= 9224$ kg $= 9.224$ tons.

(*g*) Blank holder pressure

$$(Q) = \frac{1}{3}P$$

$$= \frac{1}{3} \times 9.224$$

$= 3.075$ tonnes.

(*h*) Press capacity

$= P + Q +$ Force of friction

$= 9.224 + 3.075 + 3.075$

$= 15.374$ tonnes.

Example 7.13. *A shell has an outside diameter of 60 mm and is made from mild steel 3 mm thick. Calculate dimensions of punch and die.*

Solution. $d = 60$ mm.

Punch size $d = 60$ mm.

$t =$ thickness = 3 mm

Clearance (C) = 1.12t (Refer table 7.1)

$= 1.12 \times 3$

$= 3.36$ mm.

Die opening size $= d + 2C$

$= 60 + 2 \times 3.36$

$= 66.72$ mm.

Example 7.14. *A cup 80 mm diameter and 70 mm deep is to be drawn from steel sheet of deep drawing quality 0.8 mm thick. The yield stress of the steel is 3200 kg/cm². Determine :*

(*a*) *Blank diameter*

(*b*) *Punch diameter for first draw*

(*c*) *Drawing force.*

Solution. $D =$ Blank diameter

$d =$ Cup diameter

$= 80$ mm.

$h =$ height of cup $= 70$ mm

$$D = \sqrt{d^2 + 4dh}$$

$$= \sqrt{80^2 + 4 \times 80 \times 70}$$

$= 169.7$ mm.

$$\text{Thickness ratio} = \frac{t}{D} \times 100 = \frac{0.8}{169.7} \times 100$$

$= 0.471.$

From table 7.2

$K =$ Drawing ratio $= 1.82$

$$1.82 = \frac{D}{d}$$

$$d = \frac{169.7}{1.82} = 93.24.$$

This gives diameter for first draw.

As the final diameter of cup is to be 80 mm, thus the cup can not be produced by single stage draw.

Let it be drawn in two stages.

Let the percentage reduction in 1st draw be 40%.

$d_1 =$ Diameter after first draw.

$$40 = 100\left[1 - \frac{d_1}{D}\right]$$

$$= 100\left[- \frac{d_1}{169.7}\right]$$

$$d_1 = 101.82.$$

For second draw

$$p = \text{ per cent reduction}$$
$$= 100\left[1 - \frac{d}{d_1}\right]$$
$$= 100\left[1 - \frac{80}{101.82}\right]$$
$$= 21.5\%.$$

This is with in the permissible reduction of 25% for second stage. Hence it is desirable to draw cup in two stages.

$$P = \text{ Drawing force}$$
$$= \pi d t \sigma_y \left[\frac{D}{d} - k\right]$$
$$= \pi \times 8 \times 0.08 \times 3200\left[\frac{169.7}{80} - 0.65\right]$$
$$= 9453 \text{ kg} = 9.453 \text{ tons}.$$

Example 7.15. *A shell of diameter 75 mm and height 200 mm is to be drawn. How many drawing operations would be necessary if there were no annealing operations, intervening. Assume reductions of 50, 40, 30% etc. for each drawing without annealing.*

Solution. D = Blank diameter

d = Shell diameter = 75 mm

h = Height of shell = 200 mm.

$$D = \sqrt{d^2 + 4dh}$$
$$= \sqrt{75^2 + 4 \times 75 \times 200}$$
$$= 256 \text{ mm}$$

d_1 = Diameter after first draw

p_1 = Per cent reduction for first draw = 50%

$$p_1 = 100\left(1 - \frac{d_1}{D}\right)$$

$$50 = 100\left(1 - \frac{d_1}{256}\right)$$

$$d_1 = 128 \text{ mm}.$$

d_2 = Diameter after second draw

p_2 = Per cent reduction for second draw

$$= 40\%$$

$$p_2 = 100\left[1 - \frac{d_2}{d_1}\right]$$

$$40 = 100\left[1 - \frac{d_2}{128}\right]$$

$$d_2 = 77 \text{ mm.}$$

A third draw may be necessary to bring the shell diameter to 75 mm.

The height of the shell may be taken as vertical height only.

In case shell has radii, flanges or bottom etc. then the areas of these segments should be considered and should be subtracted from the area of developed blank. The area remaining will be the area of vertical wall (cylinder).

As the area of a cylinder is the circumference times the height therefore the height may be found by dividing the net area by the circumference.

$$A = \text{ Area of blank} = \frac{\pi}{4} \times D^2$$

$$= \frac{\pi}{4} \times 256^2 = 51445 \text{ mm}^2$$

$$A_1 = \text{ Area of base at first stage}$$

$$= \frac{\pi}{4} \times d_1^2 = \frac{\pi}{4} \times 128^2$$

$$= 12861 \text{ mm}^2$$

$$AV_1 = \text{ Area of vertical cylinder} = A - A_1$$

$$= 51445 - 12861$$

$$= 38584 \text{ mm}^2$$

$$h_1 = \text{ Height of first draw}$$

$$= \frac{AV_1}{\pi d_1} = \frac{38584}{\pi \times 128}$$

$$= 96 \text{ mm.}$$

For second draw

$$A_2 = \text{ Area of base} = \frac{\pi}{4} \times d_2^2$$

$$= \frac{\pi}{4} \times 77^2 = 4654 \text{ mm}^2$$

$$AV_2 = \text{ Area of vertical cylinder}$$

$$= A - A_2 = 51445 - 4654$$

$$= 46791 \text{ mm}^2$$

$$h_2 = \text{Height of second draw}$$

$$= \frac{AV_2}{\pi \times d_2} = \frac{46791}{\pi \times 77}$$

$$= 193.5 \text{ mm}$$

For third draw

$$A_3 = \text{Area of base}$$

$$= \frac{\pi}{4} \times 75^2 = 4415 \text{ mm}^2$$

$$AV_3 = \text{Area of cylinder} = A - A_3$$

$$= 51445 - 4415$$

$$= 47030 \text{ mm}^2$$

$$h_3 = \text{Height of third draw}$$

$$= \frac{AV_3}{\pi \times d} = \frac{47030}{\pi \times 75}$$

$$= 200 \text{ mm.}$$

Thus three drawing operations are needed to draw the shell of 200 mm height.

PROBLEMS

1. What is bending.

2. Define the following

(*i*) Bend allowance (*ii*) Angle of bend

(*iii*) Set back.

3. Describe following types of bending

(*a*) Edge bending (*b*) V-Bending

(*c*) U-Bending

4. Write short notes on the following

(*a*) Bending force

(*b*) Spring back phenomenon in bending

5. What is forming ?

6. Describe following types of forming dies

(*a*) Solid forming (*b*) Pad-type

(*c*) Embossing (*d*) Coining

(*e*) Bulging.

7. What is drawing ? What type of components can be made by drawing operation.

8. Sketch and describe a simple drawing die.

9. Sketch and describe a drawing tool using spring loaded pressure pads.

10. Sketch and describe a deep drawing tool.

11. Discuss the factors affecting drawing.

12. Write short notes on the following :

(*i*) Blank holder pressure

(*ii*) Radius on drawing punch and die

(*iii*) Lubricants used in drawing

(*iv*) Drawing speed

(*v*) Progressive dies

13. Describe the method to determine blank size to manufacture a cup.

14. Write short notes on the following :

(*i*) Clearance between punch and die for drawing operation.

(*ii*) Formula for calculating reduction in wall thickness of a drawn shell.

(*iii*) Drawing ratio

(*iv*) Drawing force

(*v*) Ironing of a cup

15. What is re-drawing. Describe a typical press tool for redraw operation.

16. Derive the formula for calculating number of draws to make a cup.

17. Discuss the procedure for a design of drawing die.

18. Calculate the blank diameters to make the shell shown in Fig. 7.36.

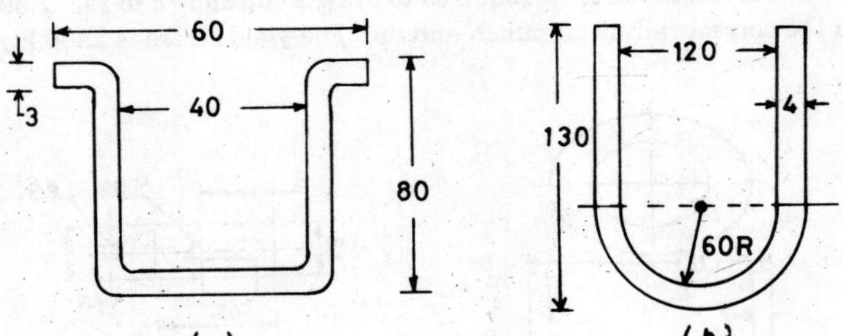

Fig. 7.36

19. Calculate the blank length of the work piece shown in Fig. 7.37.

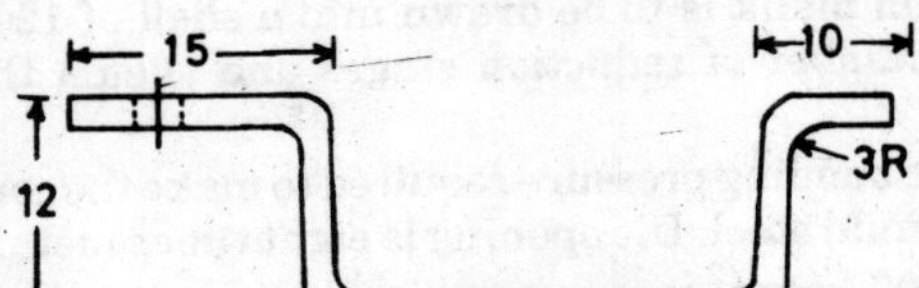

(a)

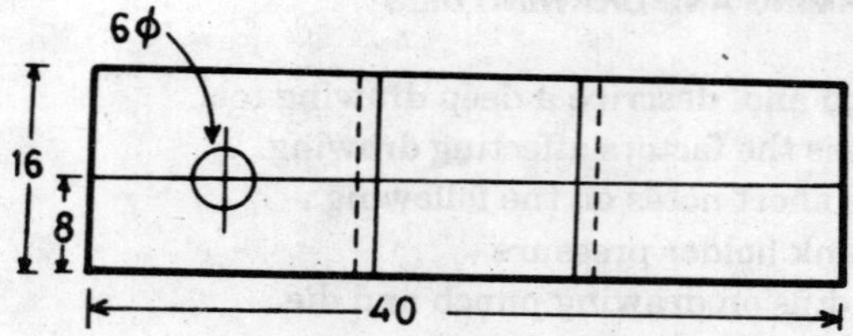

Fig. 7.37 (b)

20. Calculate the bending force required to make the component shown in Fig. 7.38. The ultimate tensile strength of the material is 4200 kg/cm^2.

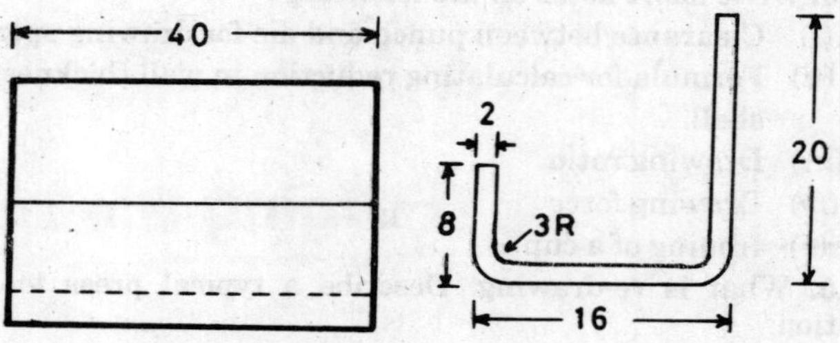

Fig. 7.38

21. Calculate the force required to draw a cup shown in Fig. 7.39. Also find the correct radius on punch and die. The yield stress is 2800 kg/cm^2.

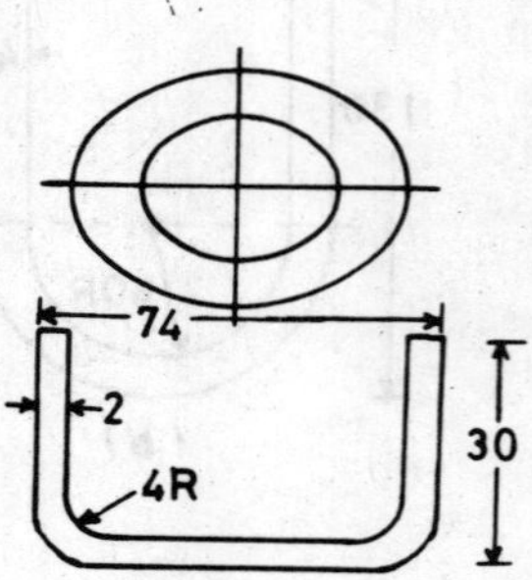

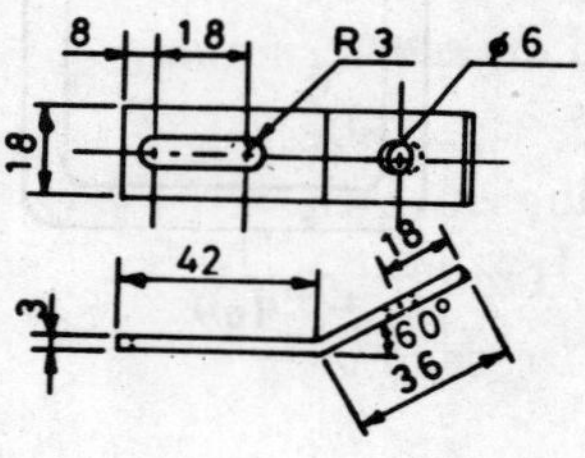

Fig. 7.39 Fig. 7.40

22. A 380 mm blank is to be drawn into a shell of 120 mm diameter. Determine the number of reduction stages and sketch the drawing and redrawing dies.

23. Calculate bending pressure required to make the component shown in Fig. 7.40 form mild steel. Die opening is eight times metal thickness. The yield stress is 3200 kg/cm^2.

8

Forging Die Design

8.1. Introduction

Forging is the process of shaping heated metal by the application of sudden blows or steady pressure and makes use of characteristic of plasticity of the material. A metal such as steel can be shaped in a cold state but the application of heat lowers the yield point and makes permanent deformation easier.

Forging can be divided into two groups.

(*i*) Hand forging

(*ii*) Press forging.

Hand forging or black-smithing is used for small quantity production and for special work whereas machine forging involves the use of dies and is generally used for mass production.

8.2. Forging Temperature

It is the temperature up to which a metal is heated so that it can be forged.

It should be above recrystallisation temperature to avoid work hardening. The suitable forging temperature for some of the metals is indicated in Table 8.1

Table 8.1

Metal	*Forging Temperature* ° (*C*)
Steel	
(*i*) C = 0.2%	1150 – 1200
(*ii*) C = 0.7%	1000 – 1150
Brass, Bronze	600-950
Aluminium and Magnesium alloys	350 – 500

Forging involves the shaping of metal by the application of impact or pressure and the primary difference between the various forging methods is the rate at which the energy is applied to the work piece.The forging hammer has a relatively high rate of deformation while hydraulic press has a relatively slow rate of deformation. The raw material is usually a bar, billet, or blank. Fig. 8.1 shows the typical variation of manufacturing cost per unit (*C*) and the quantity to be manufactured (*Q*) for different methods of manufacturing.

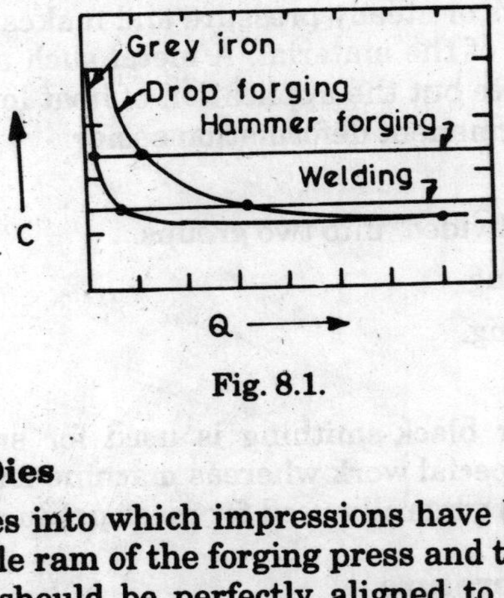

Fig. 8.1.

8.3. Forging Dies

Forging dies into which impressions have been cut are keyed into the movable ram of the forging press and the stationary anvil cap. The dies should be perfectly aligned to produced accurate components. Forging dies are classified as follows :

(1) Based on operations.

(*a*) Drop hammer dies

(*b*) Press dies

(*c*) Up setter dies (*d*) Trimming dies.

Dies used for hammers are called drop hammer dies whereas those for crank type forging presses are called press dies. The dies used for horizontal forging machines are called up setter dies and those used for trimming purpose are called trimming dies.

(2) Based on manufacturing process.

(*a*) Open dies (for flash stampings)

(*b*) Closed dies (for flashless stamping)

Closed dies are of two types

(*i*) Solid (*ii*) Inserted.

In closed dies no flash is formed, whereas an open die forging is the drop forging with the formation of flash. The hardness of dies for open forging is lower than the hardness of impression dies for closed die forging. Fig. 8.2 shows a set of forging dies.

(3) Number of impressions.

Based on number of impression the dies may be

(*a*) Single impression dies

(*b*) Multiple impression dies.

In single impression dies the forging may be completed in just one impression of closed die.

Multiple impression dies contain all the impressions from the preliminary to the finish impression in one set of dies.

(4) Based on parting lines :

(*a*) One parting line dies.

(*b*) Two parting line dies.

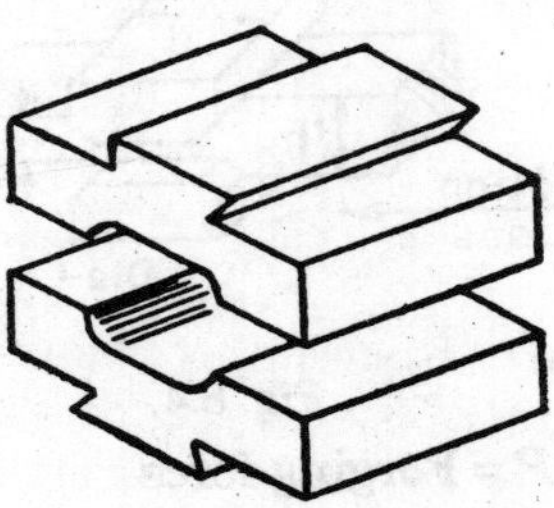

Fig. 8.2.

8.4. Drop Forging

Drop forging is a process used to shape metal in closed dies. Forms are machined into two halves of a closed die set. The metal is heated and under impact the metal becomes plastic and fills the die cavity. Excess metal is trimmed off.

Hot press forging causes a steadily applied pressure instead of an impact force.

Closed die forging is a special form of impression die forging in which metal is deformed in a cavity in such a way that it has no chance to escape or to form flash.

8.5. Forging Die Parts

Fig. 8.3 shows the cross section of a typical die. After forging the component is surrounded by surplus material (flash) which is removed in trimming press.

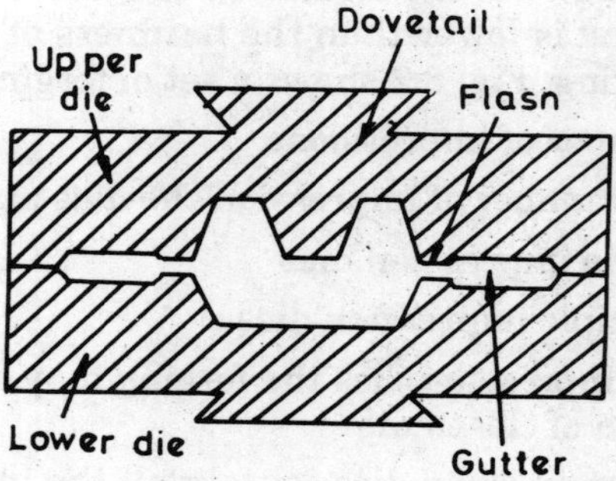

Fig. 8.3.

Fig. 8.4 shows a hot bar forging die which reduces hot billet into a bar by squeezing. The metal gets squeezed between upper and lower die.

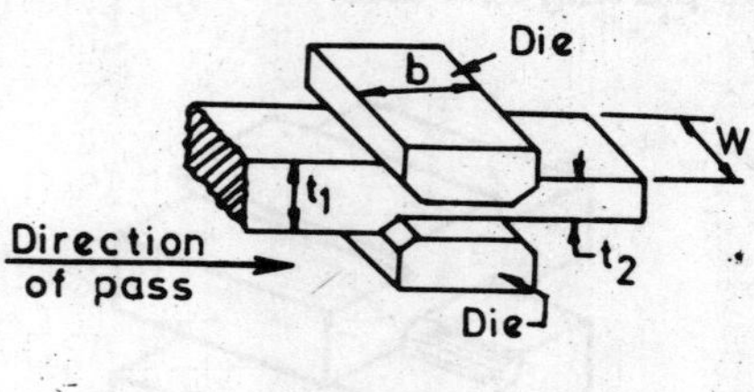

Fig. 8.4.

$$P = \text{Forging force}$$

$$= 2\,bwk\left(1 + \frac{b}{4t^2}\right)$$

where b = width of die

w = width of work

k = shear flow stress (shear stress in the metal at the tool/metal inter face)}

$2k\left(1+\frac{b}{4t^2}\right)$ = Average pressure under the dies

t_1 = Thickness of work before forging.

t_2 = Thickness of work after forging.

In order to avoid distortion the ratio $\frac{w}{t_1}$ should not be more than 1.5. In order that the billet may be properly squeezed.

$\frac{t_1}{b}$ should be less than three.

8.6. Upsetting Forging

Upsetting forging operation is used to increase the cross-sectional area usually be pressing or hammering as shown in Fig. 8.5.

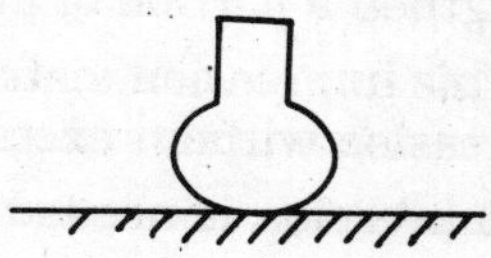

Fig. 8.5.

Upset forging forces the end of a heated bar into a desired shape. The bar is heated, clamped and up set into the die opening as shown in Fig. 8.6.

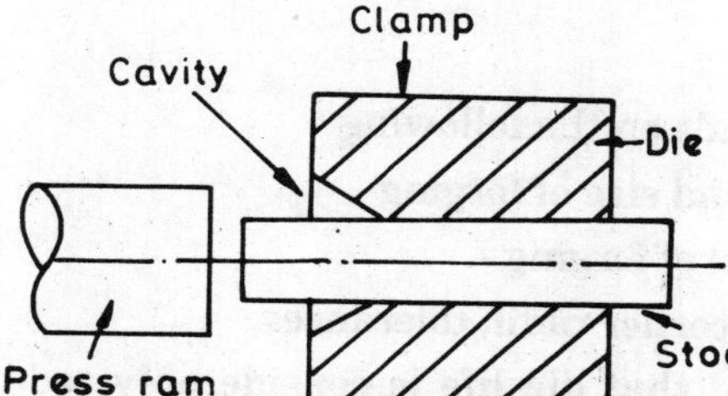

Fig. 8.6.

Fig. 8.7 shows the limitations of the die design for the up setting operation

L = Unsupported length

The unsupported length should not be more than 3 d

where d = Diameter of bar.

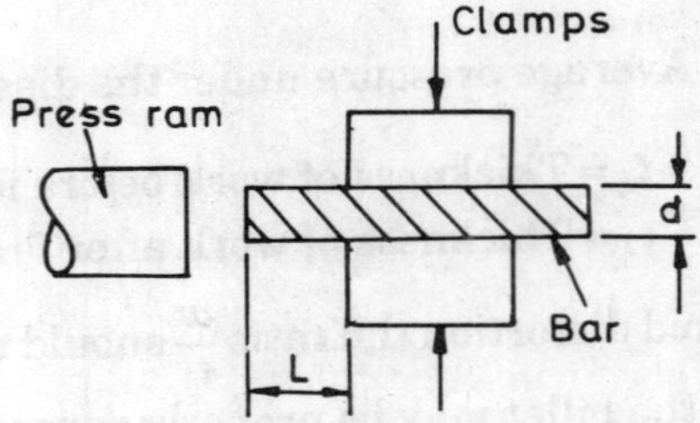

Fig. 8.7.

8.7. Impressions in a Multiple Impression Die

Six types of impressions may be incorporated in a drop forging die for shaping the material progressively from bar form to the finished forging. They are as follows :

(*i*) *Fuller*. This impression in the die is used to reduce the cross-section and to lengthen a portion of forging stock.

(*ii*) *Edge or roller*. This impression distributes the stock so that it will fill the next impression without excessive waste.

(*iii*) *Bender*. This impression is needed when curves or angles are required.

(*iv*) *Blocker*. This impression is of same shape as the finished part. It gives the forging its general shape.

(*v*) *Finisher*. This impression gives the final overall shape to the work piece. It has both gutter and flash impression.

(*vi*) *Cut off*. It cuts the forging from the bar stock.

8.8. Die Life

Die life depends on the following :

(*i*) Shape and size of forging

(*ii*) Material of forging

(*iii*) Fillets, corner radii, tolerances.

It is observed that die life is considerably reduced by sharp fillets, corner radii and close tolerances.

8.9. Trimming

It is the operation of removing flash from a forging. It is done by a hammer or a press and consists of pushing the work through a trimming blade with a punch.

Fig. 8.8 shows a trimming punch and die. A hot trim die is made from unhardened medium carbon alloy steel for heavy trimming jobs and mild steel for light duty service. The cutting edge is built up with stelite, a material which maintains very high hardness characteristics at elevated temperature. Cold trimming dies are also made from tough alloy tool steels which can be hardened up to HRC 52 -- 54, and still maintain their cutting edges.

Hot trim punches are made from medium carbon alloys and hardened to HRC 38 -- 40.

Cold trimming punches are made from tough alloy tool steels and hardened up to HRC 45 - 47.

The punch is made softer so that if it comes in contact with the edge of the trimmer its edge will shear off rather than the trimmer.

$$C = \text{Minimum clearance}$$
$$= 0.375 - 0.5 \text{ mm}$$

Angle $(\alpha) = 5^\circ - 7^\circ$

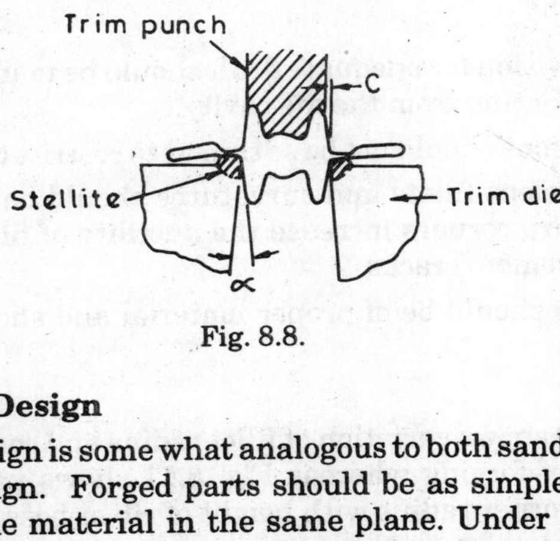

Fig. 8.8.

8.10. Forging Design

Forging design is some what analogous to both sand casting and die casting design. Forged parts should be as simple as possible with most of the material in the same plane. Under cut surfaces should be avoided and deep recesses are undesirable. Forging should be designed to permit plane parting surfaces in the dies.

Drop forgings should be designed with at least 7° of draft since expensive trimming operations may otherwise be required. Drop forgings with deep holes are often made by punching the hole from both sides as shown in Fig. 8.9 to leave a thin flash at the centre which may be removed in a subsequent drilling operation.

For Forgings : Width to thickness ratio of forgings

$$= 3 : 1 \text{ to } 5 : 1$$

While designing parts to be manufactured by forgings the following points should be considered.

(*i*) The parting line of a forging should be in one plane if possible. The parting line should divide the forging about in half.

(*ii*) The direction of fibre flow lines should be kept in mind so that full advantage can be taken of them.

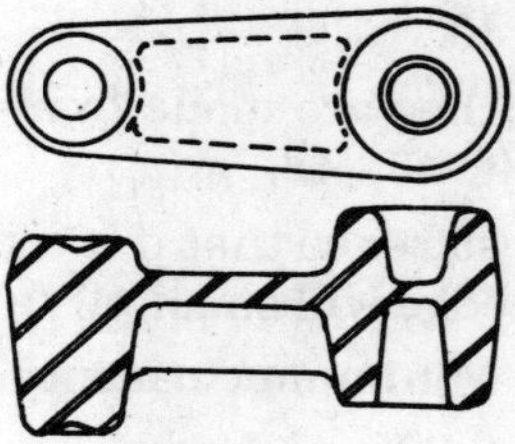

Fig. 8.9.

(*iii*) Provision for adequate draft should be made to permit easy removal of forging from the die cavity.

(*iv*) Sections should not be so thin as to restrict the flow of metal.

(*v*) Sufficient fillets and curvatures should be provided in the forging. Sharp corners increase the ductility of filling die impressions and promote cracks.

(*vi*) Dies should be of proper material and should be properly heat treated.

Fig. 8.10 shows variation of fillet radius and corner radius with weight (w) of forging whereas Fig. 8.11 shows variation of fillet radius and corner radius with height of rib or boss (h).

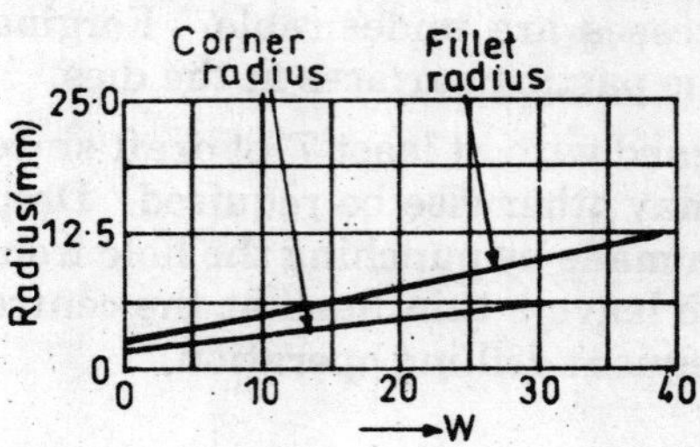

Fig. 8.10.

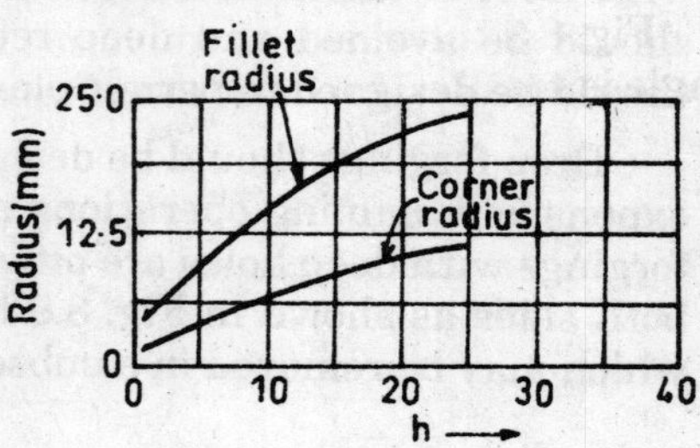

Fig. 8.11.

8.11. Design of Forging Dies

The following considerations are essential while designing forgings dies :

(*i*) *To calculate blank size.* The weight of forging will decide the weight of bar stock taking into account the various losses.

$$W_1 = w + \text{Losses}$$

where W_1 = Weight of stock

w = Net weight of forging.

The various losses considered are as follows :

(*a*) Shear loss = 6% of net weight (w).

(*b*) Sprue loss = 7 -- 8% of w.

(*c*) *Scale loss.* During forging of steel, the steel combines with atmospheric oxygen and forms an oxide which adheres over the forging as scale.

The loss of material is called scale loss.

Scale loss = 6% of w.

(*d*) *Flash loss.* The extra material around the forging is called flash loss.

$$L = \text{Length of stock} = \frac{W}{\rho \times A}$$

where ρ = Density of metal

A = Largest cross–section area.

(*ii*) *Draft angles.* To facilitate the removal of forgings from the die the draft angle is provided.

α = Draft angle for outside faces

$= 5 - 7°$

β = Draft angle for inside faces

$= 7 - 10°$.

Fig. 8.12 shows draft angles on a forging. This shows that draft angle is smaller on outside surfaces than inside surfaces of forging.

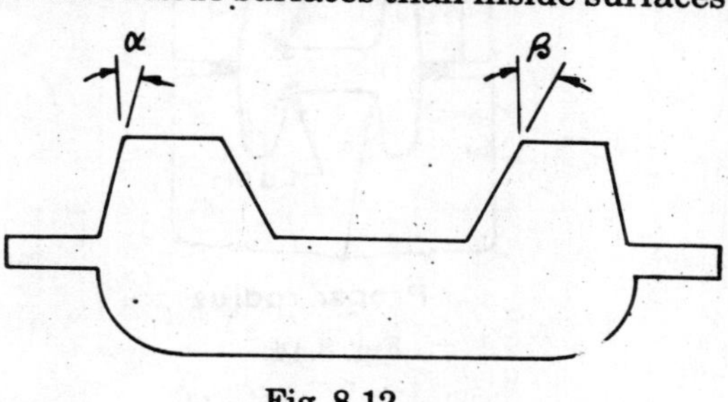

Fig. 8.12.

(*iii*) *Fillet and corner radii.* Rounding of the apex of an internal angle is called a fillet whereas apex of an external angle is corner. Fillet and corner radii are necessary to avoid the formation of forging defects and to prolong die life. Sharp fillet and radii cause more wear and reduce die life. In general, the minimum fillets and corner radii must not be less than 1.5 mm and preferably more.

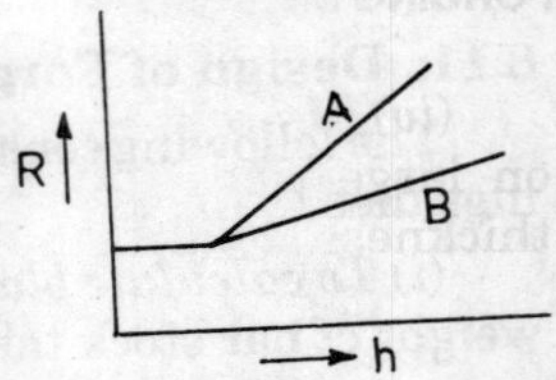

Fig. 8.13.

Fig. 8.13 shows variation of minimum fillet radius (R) with rib height (h). In Fig. 8.13 A is for single die and B for multiple die. Table 8.2 indicates values of corner radius and fillet radius for different weights of forging.

Table 8.2

w(kg)	R_1	R_2
Up to 2.5	1.5	3
2.5 – 5	2.25	4
5 – 15	3	6
15 – 25	4	8

w = Net weight of forging (kg)

R_1 = Radius of corner (mm)

R_2 = Radius of fillet (mm)

Proper and larger radius allow smooth flow of metal wheras small radius produce laps as shown in Fig. 8.14.

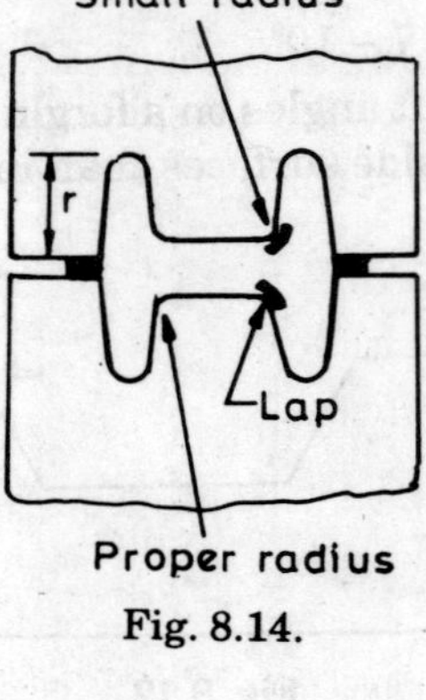

Fig. 8.14.

(*iv*) *Minimum section size.* It is desirable to avoid excess metal on large webs to reduce weight of forging. The minimum web thickness should be nearly 3 mm with a tolerance of ±0.5 mm.

$$t = \text{Web thickness} = \frac{1}{8} \times B$$

where B = Web width

h = Height of rib or web $= 4B$ to $6B$.

(*v*) *Parting lines.* A parting line separates the top and bottom dies parting lines may be of following types :

(*a*) Flat

(*b*) Multi directional.

Fig. 8.15 shows a forging with a flat parting line whereas Fig. 8.16 shows a multi-directional parting line.

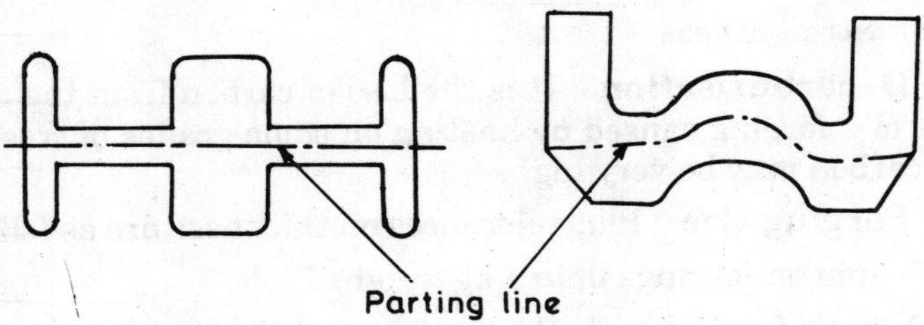

Fig. 8.15. Fig. 8.16.

The shape and location of parting line affect the following :

(*a*) Cost of die

(*b*) Grain flow

(*c*) Trimming

(*d*) Draft.

(*vi*) *Die mismatch.* Misalignment of top and bottom dies is called mismatch. The shift between dies during forging may occur.

(*a*) Side ways (Fig. 8.17) (*b*) End ways (Fig. 8.18).

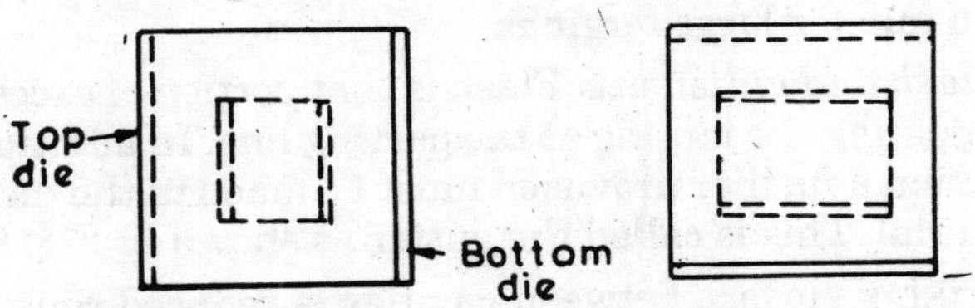

Fig. 8.17 Fig. 8.18

S = shift (mismatch)

= 0.3 mm for forgings upto 5 kg weight

= 0.5 mm for forgings from 5–10 kg weight

A mismatch of 0.125 mm should be added for each additional 5 kg weight of forging.

The dies are laid out with the finish impression as close to the centre of block as possible so that the least amount of shifting can take place as the dies come together.

(vii) Forging tolerance and allowances. A finish allowance is an additional amount of metal added to the surfaces which can not be controlled close enough by forging and must be subsequently machined. Finish allowance depends on the following factors :

(*a*) Shrinkage

(*b*) Mismatch

(*c*) Straightness

(*d*) **Decarburisation.** : It is the loss of carbon from the outer surface of a forging caused by heating on some grades of steel the loss of carbon may be very high.

(*e*) **Forging size** : Plus tolerances on thickness are as follows:

1 mm on forgings upto 1 kg weight

2 m on forgings upto 2 kg weight to 10 kg weight

3 mm from 10 to 20 kg weight

Negative tolerances on thickness are as follows :

0.12 mm upto 1 kg weight of forging

0.5 mm from 2 to 10 kg weight

0.8 mm from 10 to 50 kg weight

Surfaces to be machined should be provided with machining allowance. Machining allowance for steel forgings :

= 1.5 mm per side for small forgings (upto 5 kg)

= 1.5 mm to 3 mm for medium forgings

= 3 to 6 mm for large forgings

(viii) Flash and gutter size. Flash is that portion of excess metal which is adjoining the forging at the parting line. In addition to the flash extension a further provision must be made in the die for any excess material. This is called the gutter as shown in Fig. 8.19.

The striking surface between cavities is reduced considerably by the flashing and guttering of dies.

For steel forgings the flash provided is as indicated in Table 8.3.

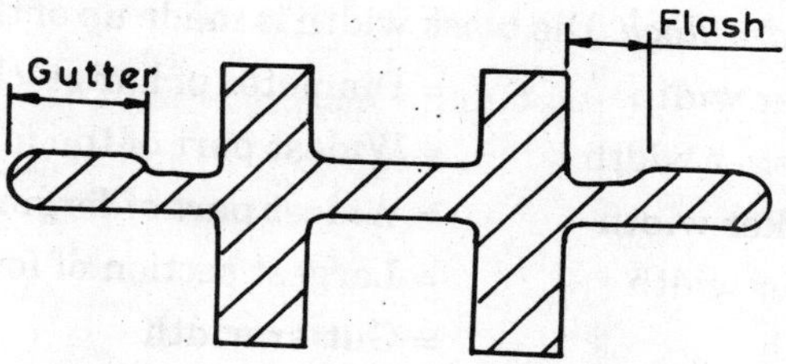

Fig. 8.19.

Table 8.3

D (mm)	t (mm)	b (mm)
0 – 35	1.0	4.0
35 – 50	1.5	6.0
50 – 65	2.0	7.0
65 – 75	2.5	8.0

where D = Diameter

t = Thickness

b = Width.

Depending on weight and size of forging the gutter size is as follows :

h = Depth of gutter

= 3 to 6 mm

B = Width of gutter

= 25 to 45 mm

Provision of fillet radius at sharp corners at the flash line permits ease of metal flow as shown in Fig. 8.20.

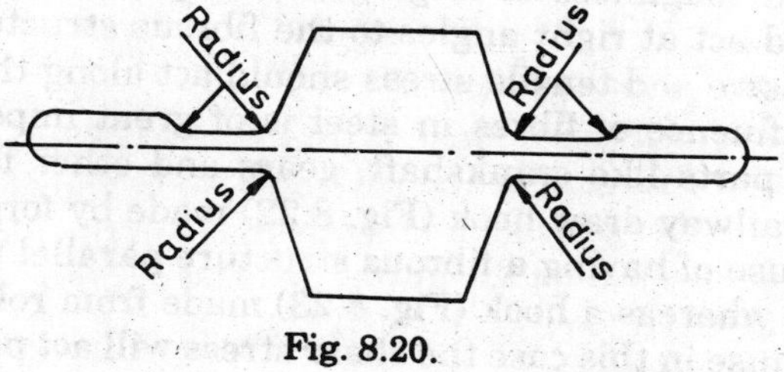

Fig. 8.20.

(*a*) *Size of die block.* Die block width is made up of the following:

(*a*) Fuller width = Diameter of bar stock

(*b*) Finisher width = Widest part of the forging

(*c*) Blocker width = Widest part of forging

(*d*) Edger width = Largest section of forging

(*e*) Flash = Gutter width

(*f*) Bender impression width over all economy must be considered in die designing for the forged part. Dies must be designed to impart the maximum grain flow benefit to the finish machined part.

8.12. Holes and Cavities

Holes and cavities provided in forgings are shown in Fig. 8.21.

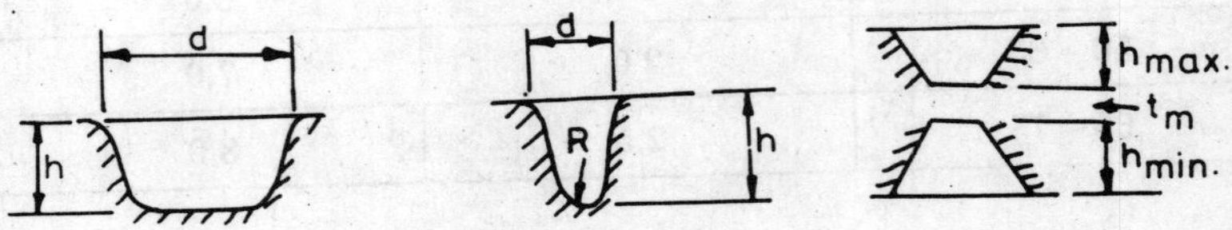

Fig. 8.21.

d = size of diameter

Maximum depth of Cavity (h) = d

= 1.5 d

if a full radius is allowed at the bottom.

8.13. Grain Flow Characteristics

Metals are forged hot because the material will shape more rapidly in this condition and the necessary fibre like flow line structure is obtained. In the fibre like grain flow lies the inherent strength and toughness of forgings. In forged metals the shear stress should act at right angles to the fibrous structure whereas the compressive and tensile stress should act along the directions of fibres. Influence of fibres in steel is of great importance particularly in parts like crankshaft, gears and other forgings. For example a railway draw hook (Fig. 8.22) made by forging is quite strong because of having a fibrous structure parallel to the centre line of hook whereas a hook (Fig. 8.23) made from rolled material is weak because in this case the shear stress will act parallel to the fibres.

Fig. 8.22. Forged

Fig. 8.23. Rolled

Similarly in a forged gear blank (Fig. 8.24) the radial flow grain lines will be obtained. Such gear will have maximum shock resisting properties Fig. 8.25 shows the fibre lines in a forged crank shaft in which the directional qualities of fibre add toughness to the web.

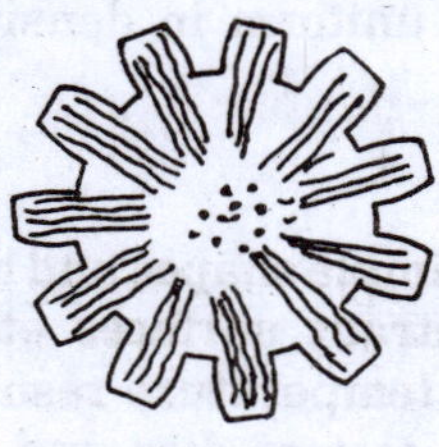

Fig. 8.24.

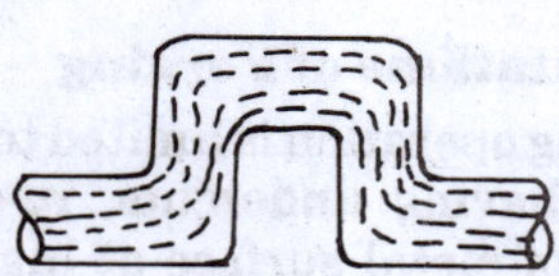

Fig. 8.25.

8.14. Materials of Die Blocks

Carbon steel dies are used when smaller quantity of forgings are to be made whereas alloy steel dies are generally used for large scale production.

Hot piercing dies are made of medium carbon alloy steels and hardened to H.R.C. 36--40 and the punches are made of medium carbon alloy with a stelite facing around the periphery of the punch and on its face.

Hot restriking dies are made from medium carbon alloy steels and hardened to H.R.C. 36--40.

Cold restrike dies are made from a good grade of alloy tool steel hardened to H.R.C. 50--52.

The most commonly used die steels are

(*i*) Chromium-nickel

(*ii*) Chromium-molybdenum

(*iii*) Chromium-titanium

(*iv*) Chromium-tungsten

Die blocks with insert dies are also used. Die blocks may be made of carbon steels whereas inserts only are made of alloy steel. Inserts can be easily replaced when worn out.

Die impressions in die blocks are sunk in the die sinking machines. They are hardened after finishing the impression.

8.15. Advantages of Forging

The various advantages of forging are as follows :

(*i*) Forgings have high strength and offer great resistance to impact and fatique loads.

(*ii*) Forging improves the grain structure of metal and hence its mechanical properties.

(*iii*) Because of intense working flaws are seldom found and workpiece has high reliability.

(*iv*) Forging renders the parts uniform in density as well as dimensions.

8.16. Limitations of Forging

Forging operation is limited to simple shapes and has limitation for parts having undercuts, re-entrant surfaces etc. The rapid oxidation of metal surface at high temperature results in scaling which wears the dies. The initial cost of dies and cost of their maintenance is high.

8.17. Swaging

It is a forging operation in which two halves of a rotating die open and close rapidly while impacting the end of the heated tube or shell. The forging operation may reduce the diameter of the tube or taper the end of the tube as the tube is fed between the dies.

PROBLEMS

1. What is forging ? What is press forging and up-setting forging.
2. What is a forging ? Describe various types of forging dies.
3. Define the following for a forging die with the help of a sketch.
   (*a*) Flash (*b*) Cutter
   (*c*) Draft (*d*) Parting line.
4. Discuss the formula for calculating forging force.
5. Write short notes on the following :
   (*i*) Die life (*ii*) Trimming
   (*iii*) Forging design (*iv*) Upset forging
   (*v*) Swaging.
6. Describe the following types of impressions in multiple impression dies :
   (*i*) Fuller (*ii*) Edger
   (*iii*) Bender (*iv*) Blocker
   (*v*) Finisher (*vi*) Cut off.

7. Explain various steps for the design of forging dies.

8. Describe the grain flow characteristics of metals in forging.

9. Write short notes on the following :

(*a*) Holes and cavities in forgings

(*b*) Materials of die blocks

(*c*) Machining allowance in forging.

10. Discuss the advantages and limitations of forging process.

11. Sketch and design the forging die for making a link shown in (Fig. 8.26) from drop forged steel.

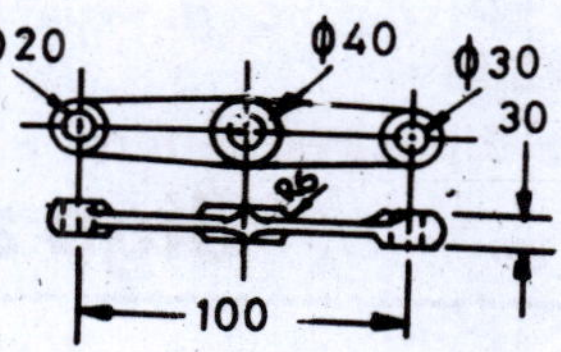

Fig. 8.26

9

Jigs and Fixtures

9.1. Introduction

Jigs and fixtures are designed to hold, support and locate the work pieces to ensure that each part is machined within the specified limits. Use of jigs and fixtures provides a faster and more profitable method of manufacturing in which components can be quickly positioned in the correct relationship to the cutting tool.

9.2. Advantages

The employment of jigs and fixtures has the following advantages :

(*i*) It is an important aspect of work shop engineering for the production of articles in large quantities with a high degree of accuracy and inter-changeability at a competitive cost.

(*ii*) To reduce machining times by eliminating time of handling and setting up of the component parts.

(*iii*) Use of jigs and fixtures ensures the uniformity of finished product.

(*iv*) It facilitates the holding and supporting of the components, to position the component properly and guide the cutters.

(*v*) It becomes possible to accommodate several components at one setting and thus taking advantage of multiple machining.

(*vi*) It makes possible to employ unskilled or semi-skilled machine operators.

9.3. Fixture

It is a device which locates and holds the component for a specific operation. It does not guide the cutting tool.

9.4. Jig

It is a device which is used to hold and position the work piece. In addition it provides some means for guiding the cutting tool.

9.5. Design Principles

The design of jigs and fixtures should be simple and economical. The principal considerations in jig and fixture design are as follows:

(*i*) *Clamping and locating*. The component should be properly clamped and located. The method of location and clamping should be such as to reduce idle time to a minimum.

(*ii*) *Positioning of tool*. The cutting tool should be properly positioned relative to the component.

(*iii*) It should be ensured that the tool can be loaded and unloaded easily.

(*iv*) The workholder or the clamp should be strong enough to resist the cutting forces.

(*v*) Clamps should allow rapid loading and unloading of the components.

(*vi*) Adequate space in the form of channel ways should be provided to enable the metal chips to be blown clear easily.

(*vii*) Adequate arrangements must be made for the supply of coolant to the cutting edges.

(*viii*) Jigs and fixtures should be lighter in weight.

(*ix*) The equipment should be fool proof besides being safe to use.

(*x*) There should be safety of operation.

(*xi*) Tennon strips should be provided for accurate and quick location of the fixture on the machine bed.

9.5.1. Jigs and Fixtures Design Factors

The following are the essential factors which must be considered in designing a jig or a fixture :

1. Study of the component.
2. Study of the type of capacity of the m/c.
3. Study of the locating elements.
4. Study of the loading and unloading arrangement.
5. Study of the clamping arrangement.

The power-driven clamps are operated either by pneumatic or

hydraulic power. The power driven clamps are quick acting, controllable, reliable, and operated without least fatigue to the operator. The power clamps exert high clamping pressure and are employed for gripping heavy workpieces.

The clamps serve the purpose of holding workpieces securely on the jigs or fixtures against the cutting forces. In order to achieve the most efficient clamping, the following operational factors must be considered.

(*i*) The clamping pressure should be exerted on the solid supporting part of the work to prevent distortion.

(*ii*) The clamping pressure should be kept low as far as possible. It should be sufficient to hold the work against the cutting pressure.

(*iii*) The movement of the clamp for loading and unloading purposes should be kept limited.

(*iv*) The clamp should be positively guided to facilitate loading action.

(*v*) The clamp should be simple and fool-proof.

(*vi*) The clamp should be sufficiently robust to avoid bending.

(*vii*) The clamping should be effected by operating a lever, or a knurled knob. The hexagonal headed nuts or bolts should be avoided as far as practicable to eliminate the use of spanners.

(*viii*) The clamps should be case-hardened to prevent wear of the clamping faces.

(*ix*) The clamps should be so arranged on the work to perform as many operations as possible in one setting.

6. Study of clearance between jig and the component.

It is necessary to leave sufficient clearance between the Jig body and the component to accommodate variable sizes of work which are manufactured either by casting or forging.

7. Study of the indexing devices.

8. Study of the tool guiding and setting elements.

9. Study of the fool-proofing arrangement.

It means the designing of Jig and Fixture with such devices so as to make it impossible for an operator to insert a component into a jig or a fixture in any position.

10. Study of ejecting devices.

The jigs and fixtures are designed to eject heavy workpieces mechanically when it is unclamped. This saves time and labour of the operator. The ejection of components are accomplished by wedges, spring loaded or cam actuated plungers.

11. Study of swarf removal arrangement.

The removal of chips from jigs and fixtures can be accomplished by the following methods :

(*i*) By designing the shape of the Jig parts to enable the chips to fall out by gravity.

(*ii*) By undercutting the corners to clear the work.

(*iii*) By using raised supports or buttons for location.

(*iv*) By maintaining marginal clearance between the jig body and the component.

12. To study base or frame construction.

The body and bases of jigs and fixtures are manufactured by any one of the following methods :

(*i*) Machining

(*ii*) Forging and then machining.

(*iii*) Casting.

(*iv*) Fabricating

(*v*) Welding.

13. Tool Guiding and Cutter Setting Arrangement

The cutter is set relative to the work in a fixture by adjustment of the machine or by using the cutter setting block. The tools are guided in Jigs by drill bushes which are fitted on the jig plates. There are three different types of jig bushes : Fixed Bush, Slip Bush, and Linear Bush.

14. Study of rigidity and vibration problems.

15. Study of safety devices.

Jigs and fixtures are designed to assure full safety to the operator.

16. Study of the methods of manufacture of jigs and fixtures.

9.6. Design Steps

While designing jigs and fixtures, following steps may be considered :

(*i*) To inspect the drawing of the component and to note the dimensions to be taken care of.

(*ii*) To decide the sequence of machining operations.

(*iii*) To decide the location system.

(*iv*) To decide the clamping system.

(*v*) To fix the method of positioning the cutting tool relative to the workpiece.

(*vi*) To decide the safety devices to be used.

9.7. Location

The work piece must be accurately located to establish a definite relationship between the cutting tool and some points or surfaces of the workpiece. The locating device should be so designed that each successive work piece when loaded and clamped will occupy the same position in the workholding device. The locating device selected for a given workholding device will mainly depend on nature of work piece and requirements of the metal removing operation.

In the design of jig and fixtures the location of the component is very important aspect as the correct location influences the accuracy of the finished product.

9.8. Basic Rules for Location

The basic rules for locating the component are as follows :

(*i*) Locators should be as spaced as far apart as possible thus using fewer locators and insuring complete contact over the locating surface.

(*ii*) Locators should be positioned to contact the work on a machined surface.

(*iii*) Locators provided should be fool proof *i.e.*, the component can only be loaded into the fixture in the correct position.

(*iv*) Location features should be swarf traps and should have clearance provided where necessary to clear machining burrs.

(*v*) Locating devices should reduce the degrees of freedom to zero with no redundant location feature.

9.9. Clamping

The various forces acting upon the work piece during a machining operation necessitate a means of clamping it in position after it has been correctly located. The method of clamping will depend upon the type of locating device and *vice versa*. The selection of locating and clamping methods and devices will depend upon the machining operation and the configuration of the part.

9.10. Degree of Freedom

A body in space have twelve degrees of freedom *i.e.* it is capable of moving into the space in the twelve different directions as shown in Fig. 9.1.

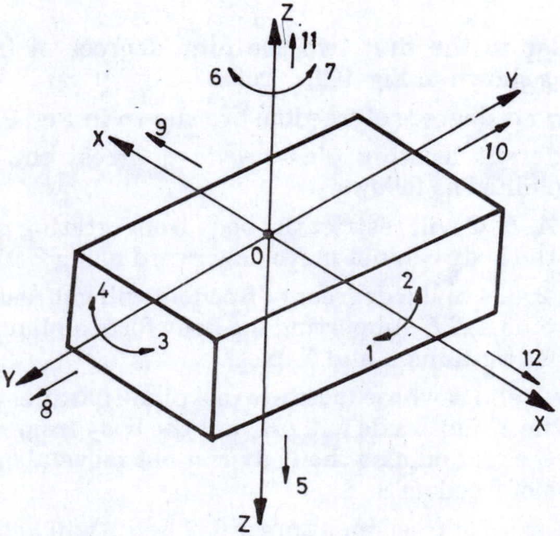

Fig. 9.1.

The body can move in either of two opposed directions along three mutually perpendicular axis and may rotate in either of two opposed directions around each axes clockwise and anti-clockwise. Each direction of movement is considered as one degree of freedom. Thus there are twelve degrees of freedom for any workpiece in space.

9.11. 3—2—1 Principle of Location

3—2—1 principle is also known as six point location principle which is used to constrain or prevent the body from moving in any direction along three axes *XX, YY* and *ZZ*. By providing six locating pins--three in a base plane, two in a vertical plane and one in a plane

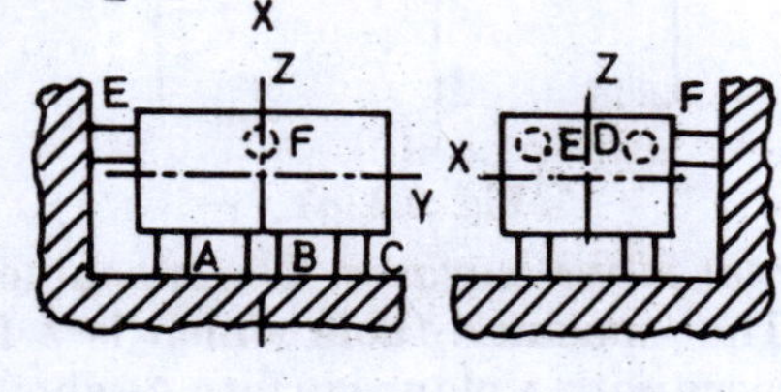

Fig. 9.2.

perpendicular to the first two the nine degrees of freedom are controlled as shown in Fig. 9.2.

The various degrees of freedom are shown in Fig. 9.2.

The different locating pins provided arrest the degrees of freedom explained as follows.

(*i*) Pins *A, B, C* will restrict the body from rotating about *X* and *Y* axes and the body can not move downward along *Z* axis.

Thus 1, 2, 3, 4 and 5 degrees of freedom will get restricted. The faces of the pins *A,B,C* supporting the body form a plane parallel to the plane that contains *X* and *Y* axes.

(*ii*) Pins *D* and *E* whose faces are in a plane parallel to the plane containing the *X* and *Z* axis will prevent the body from rotating the body about *Z* axis and also the body can not move along *Y* axis in the direction of freedom 8.

Thus degrees of freedom number 6, 7 and 8 will get restricted.

(*iii*) Pin *F* will be able to restrict the freedom degree of 9.

(*iv*) Three degrees of freedom 10, 11 and 12 will remain unrestricted. These three degrees of freedom can be restricted by providing three more pins but then the pins will entirely enclose the workpiece which is not desirable and thus the degrees of freedom 10, 11 and 12 may be restricted by means of clamping devices which also may serve to resist the forces generated during metal cutting.

9.12. Choosing a Locating Surfaces

The tool designer should study the workpiece carefully before deciding which surfaces are best suited for locating. The location may be from the following surfaces.

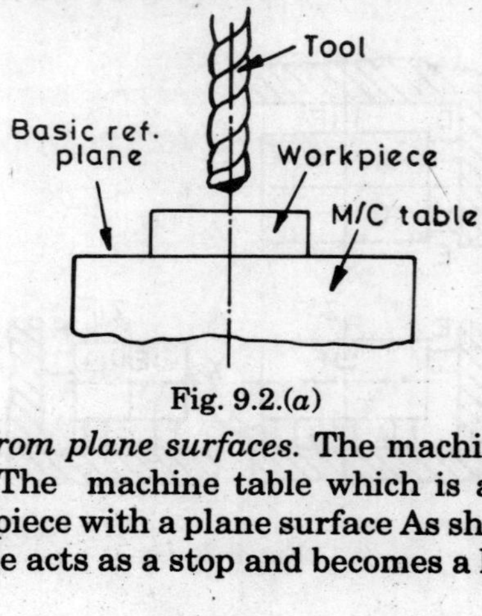

Fig. 9.2.(*a*)

(*i*) *Locating from plane surfaces.* The machine table acts as a reference plane. The machine table which is a flat surface will support the workpiece with a plane surface As shown in Fig. 9.2(*a*). The machine table acts as a stop and becomes a locating surface.

(*ii*) *Locating from circular surfaces.* In this method also the basic reference plane for location is the flat plane of the machine tool table surface. *V*-method is used to locate round workpieces. *V* should be directed in such a way that variations in workpiece size will not affect location as shown in Fig. 9.3.

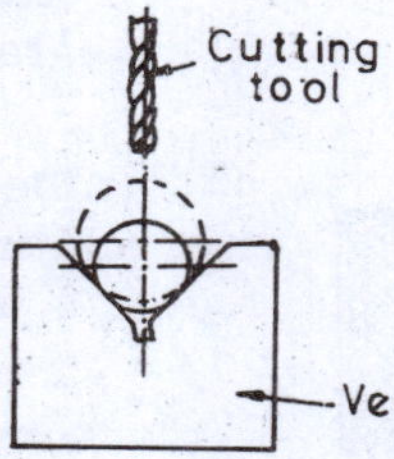

Fig. 9.3.

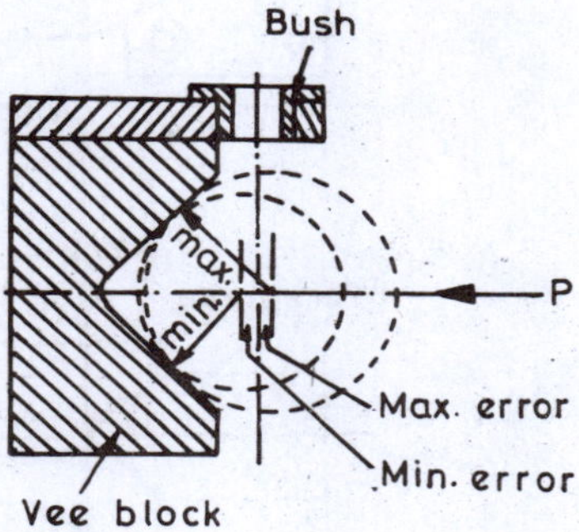

Fig. 9.4.

Fig. 9.4 shows the effect of using *V*-block as a locator where any variation in the diameter of workpiece will produce an off-centre drilling operation which is not preferred.

P indicates clamping force.

(*iii*) *Locating from irregular surfaces.* When the dimensions of the workpiece vary from part to part and further if the surface is rough, the surface is said to an irregular surface. Castings, forgings are typical examples of irregular surfaces. The unevenness of irregular surface allows a maximum of three contact points. It is advisable to use adjustable rest pins or equalisers to compensate for the unevenness of the workpiece surface.

When using Vee locators be sure the locator is positioned to allow for the differences in part sizes as shown in Fig. 9.4(*a*)

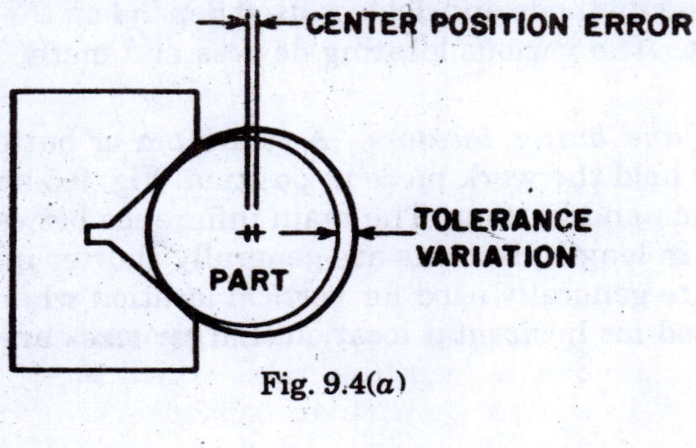

Fig. 9.4(*a*)

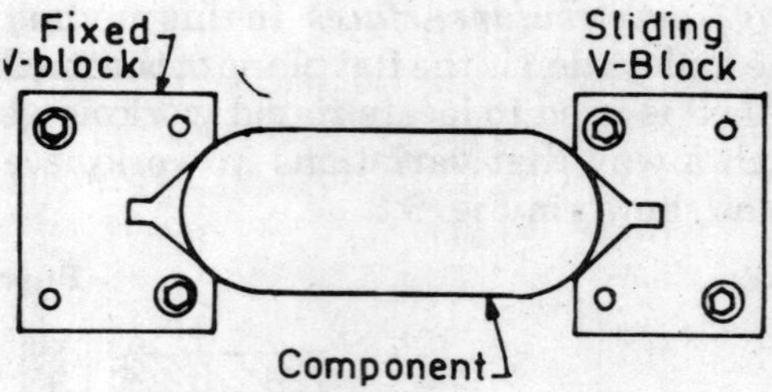

(b)

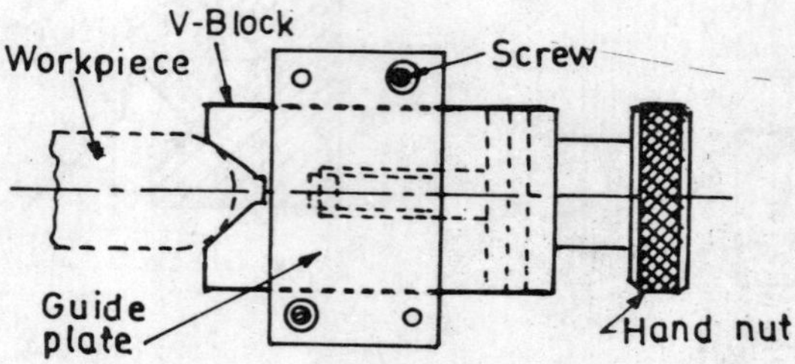

Fig. 9.4(*c*)

Fig. 9.4(*b*) shows use of two V-block locators, one being fixed and other being the sliding V-block. The sliding V-block is secured to the jig body by cap head screw and dowel pins as shown in Fig. 9.4(*c*). All sliding parts should be made of steel which is hardened and ground.

Vee blocks are made of straight carbon steel grade 45 or case hardening steels grade 08 to 20. Very large vee blocks are made of grey CI with hardened steel pads secured by screws to working surfaces Rigid V-blocks with an angle of 90° are most commonly used in jigs and fixtures.

9.13. Locating Methods and Devices

Locating methods and devices used depend on the shape of the component. The various locating devices and methods are as follows:

(*i*) *Pin and button locators.* A round pin or button is used to support or hold the work piece in position. Fig. 9.5 shows various types of pins and buttons. The main difference between pins and buttons is in length. Buttons are generally shorter in length than pins and are generally used for vertical location whereas pins are usually used for horizontal location. Larger sizes are some times referred to as plugs. The locating buttons can be either press fit type or screwed type. The screwed type of locating buttons are used where wear and tear of locating buttons is more and it is to be replaced at quick intervals. However cylindrical fits are best for exact location and not the threads as these cannot align the component properly.

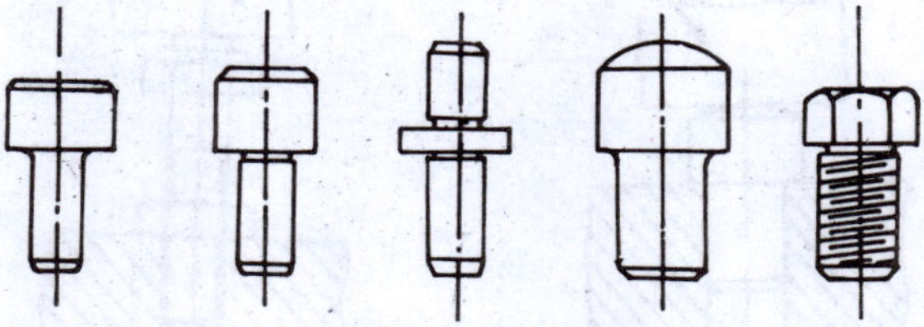

Fig. 9.5.

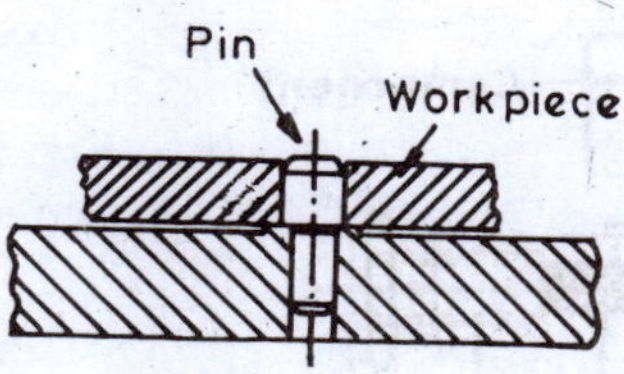

Fig. 9.6.

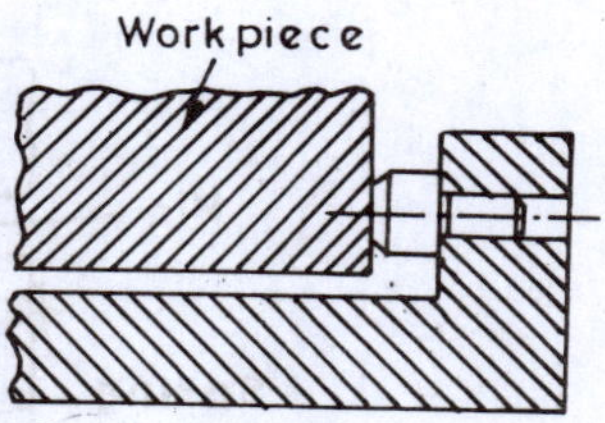

Fig. 9.7.

Fig. 9.6 shows a pin used to locate from a hole produced by previous operation whereas Fig. 9.7 shows used to locate the edge of the work piece (horizontal location).

Fig. 9.8 shows the use of press fit button and screw type button used for locating a component.

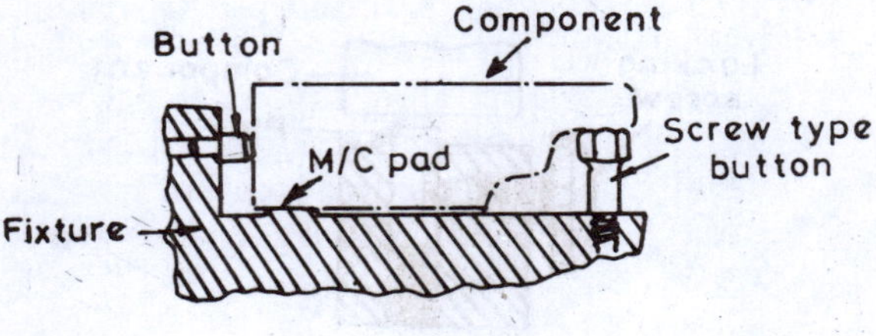

Fig. 9.8.

Fig. 9.9 shows support pins or rest buttons (Fixed type) whereas Fig. 9.10 shows support pins or rest buttons (adjustable type). Adjustable supports are used when the surface is rough or uneven such in cast ports. Fig. 9.11 shows the use of spring loaded jack pin in which the pin is locked.

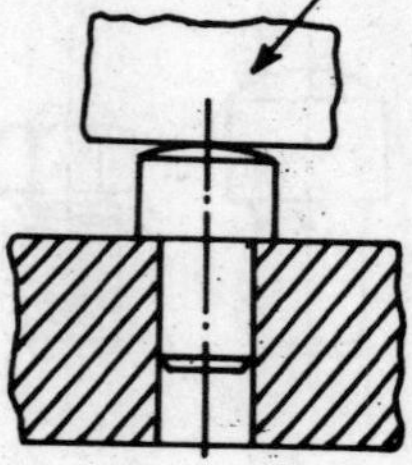

Fig. 9.9.

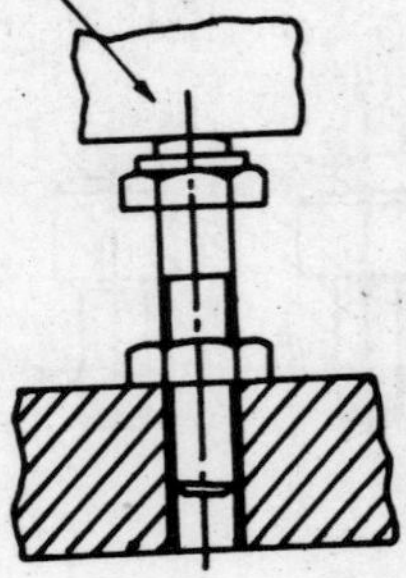

Fig. 9.10.

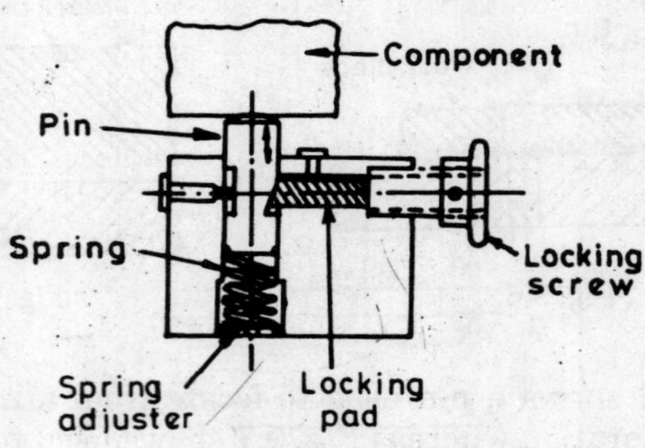

Fig. 9.11.

Another type of jack pin which keeps the supporting pin in position is shown in Fig. 9.12.

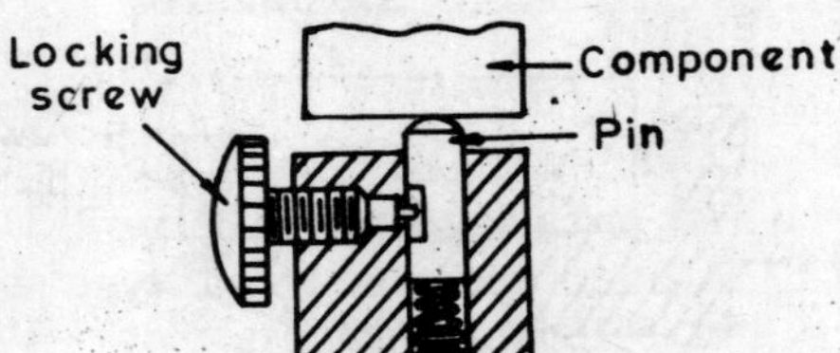

Fig. 9.12.

(*ii*) *Cylindrical locators.* They are quite suitable when fine finished holes are available for positioning purposes. Fig. 9.13 shows plain locating pin whereas plain locating pin with flange is shown in Fig. 9.14. Both of these are used for small holes. For large hole's locating pins shown in Fig. 9.15 are used.

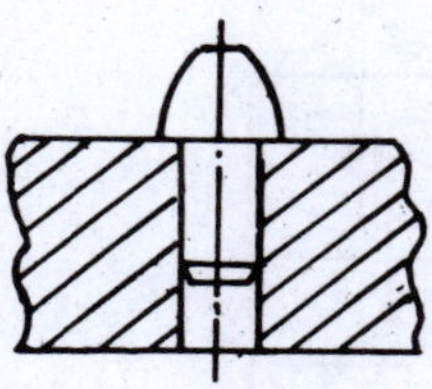

Fig. 9.13.

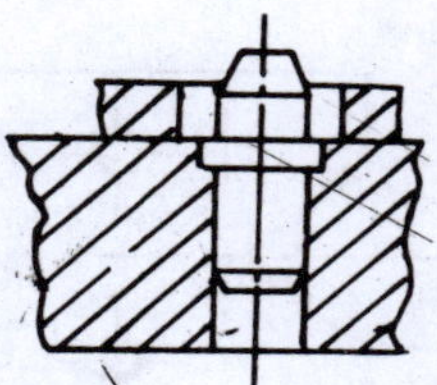

Fig. 9.14.

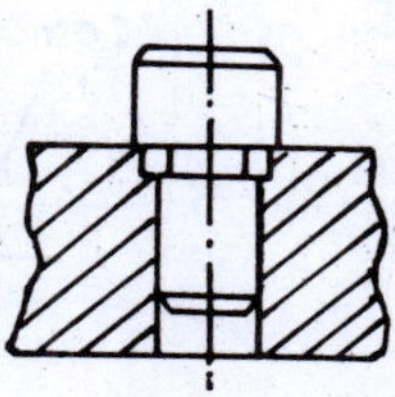

Fig. 9.15.

(*iii*) *Profile locators.* They are used to locate work piece from an external profile or outside edge profile locators may be of (*i*) nesting type (*ii*) V-locators :

(*a*) Fixed type

(*b*) Sliding type

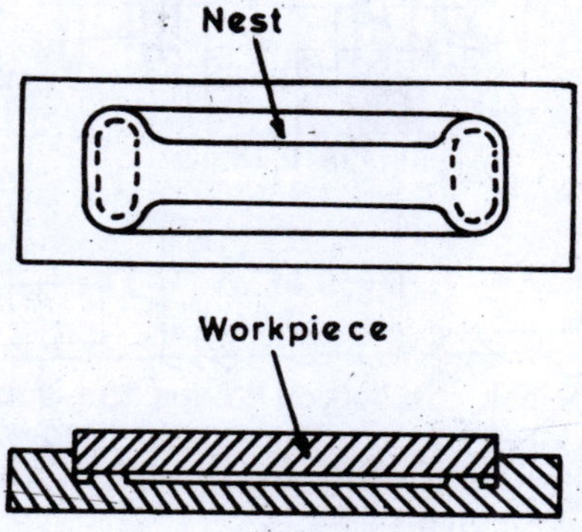

Fig. 9.16.

Fig. 9.16 shows a nest or cavity location. A fixed *V*-type locator is shown in Fig. 9.17. A hand operated screw type sliding *V*-type locator is shown in Fig. 9.18 and a cam operated *V*-type sliding locator is shown in Fig. 9.19.

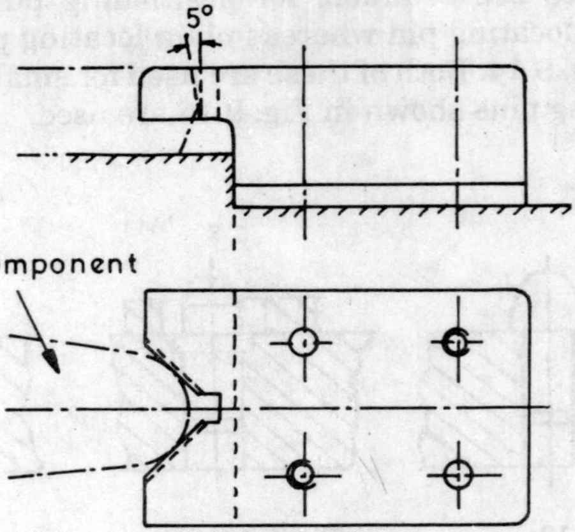

Fig. 9.17.

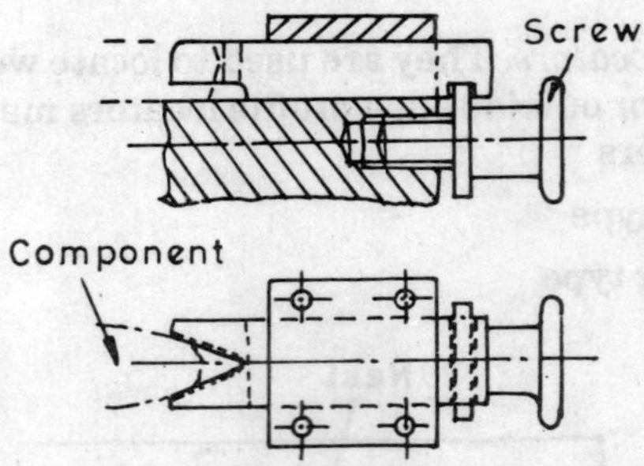

Fig. 9.18.

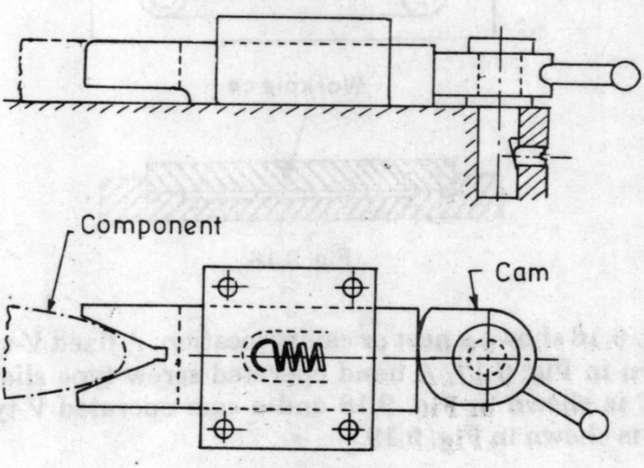

Fig. 9.19.

Fig. 9.19(*a*) shows the use of a *V*-block locator for a cylindrical workpiece for drilling the workpiece from top. An additional pin is provided in the end of the *V*-block to position the hole with reference to length. *V*-block is the primary locator and the adjustable pin is the secondary locator.

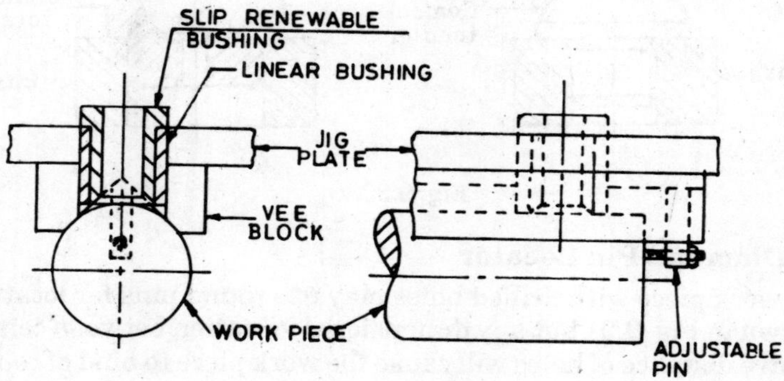

Fig. 9.19(*a*)

(*iv*) *Conical locators.* They are used to locate round work pieces as shown in Fig. 9.20.

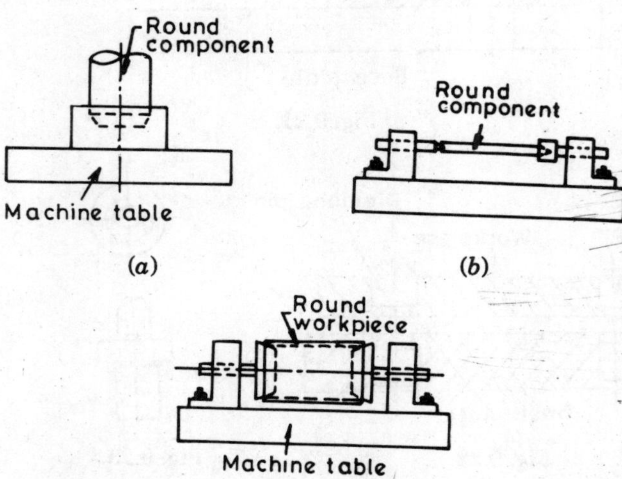

(*a*) (*b*)

(*c*)

Fig. 9.20

Conical locators are used to locate the work piece from a tapered shaft as shwon in Fig. 9.20(*d*) or from a tapered hole as shown in Fig. 9.20(*e*).

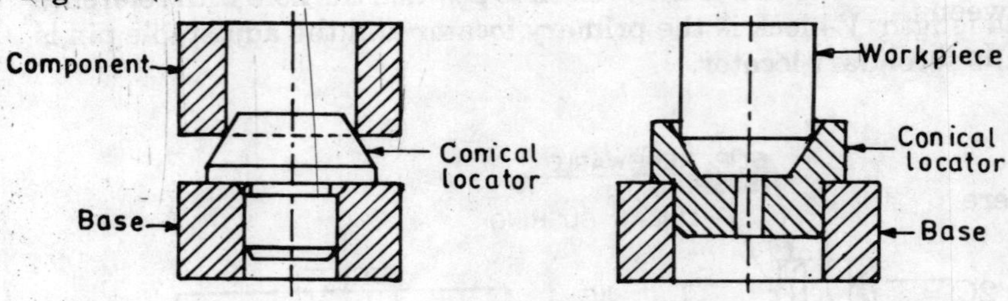

(*d*) (*e*)

Fig. 9.20.

9.14. Diamond Pin Locator

A work piece with drilled holes may use round pins for location as shown in Fig. 9.21 but any dimensional variation between centre to centre distance of holes will cause the work piece to bind of round pins are used. The use of pins of different lengths will overcome binding to a certain extent but more common method used is to use one round pin and one diamond pin as shown in Fig. 9.22.

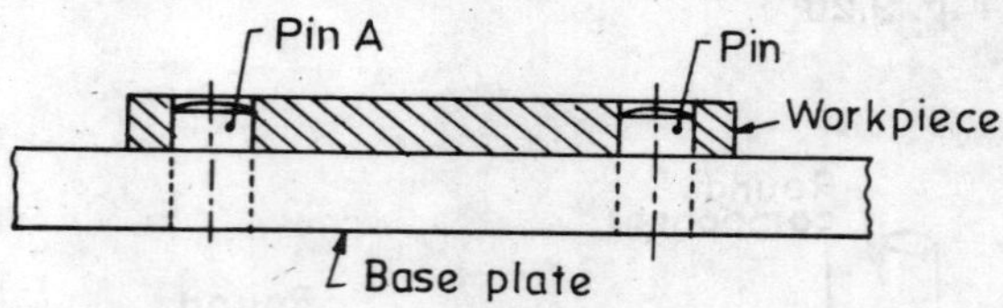

Fig. 9.21.

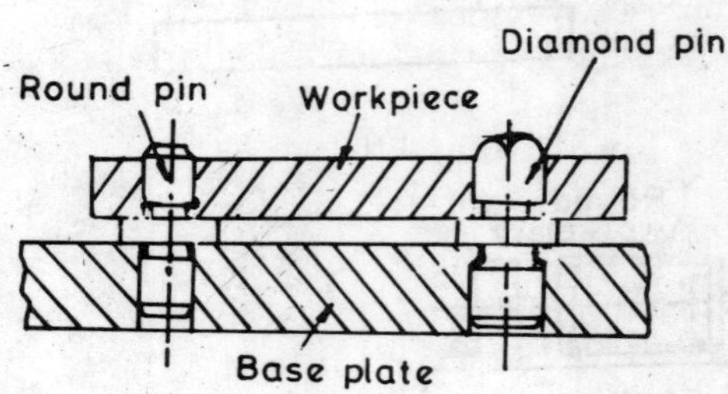

Fig. 9.22.

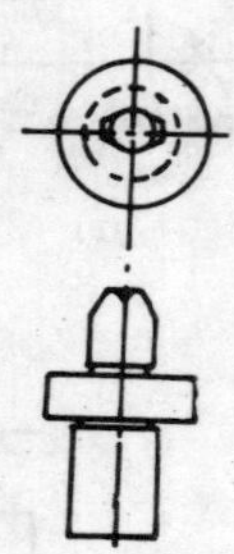

Fig. 9.23.

A typical diamond pin is shown in Fig. 9.23. Diamond pins are relieved on two sides to allow for variation in centre to centre distance of holes. Thus the diamond pin locator enables the positioning of a workpiece on two holes not withstanding some error in distance between their axes.

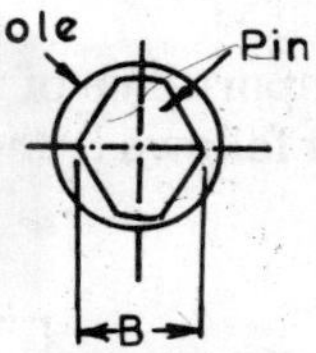

Fig. 9.24

In diamond pin locator as shown in Fig. 9.24.

$$B = \text{Width of diamond pin}$$

$$= \delta_1 + \delta_2 - 2C$$

where δ_1 = Tolerance on work piece

δ_2 = Tolerance on Jig

$2C$ = Diameteral clearance in fitting the work piece on the cylindrical pin.

If $\delta_1 + \delta_2 > 2C$

then diamond pin locator should not be used.

Sometime locator pins are used to pick up a finished hole as shown in Fig. 9.25 or to pick up two previously machined holes as shown in Fig. 9.26. In this case a diamond pin should be used.

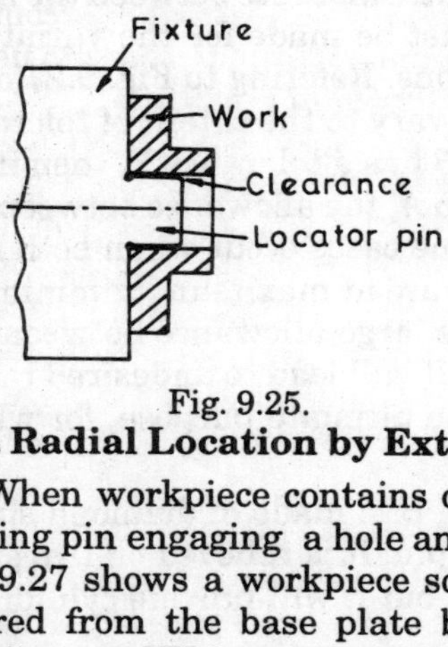

Fig. 9.25.

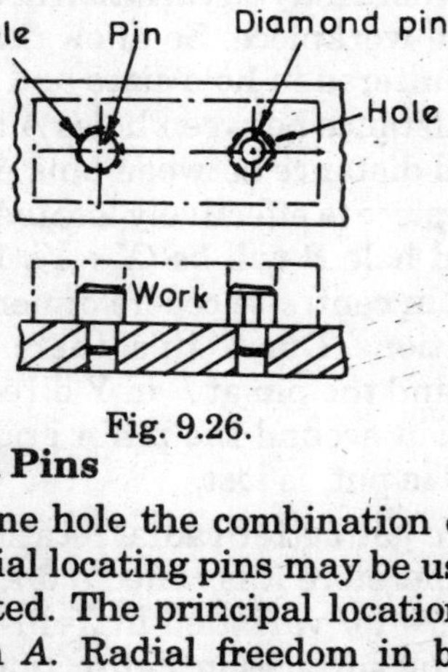

Fig. 9.26.

9.15. Radial Location by External Pins

When workpiece contains only one hole the combination of a locating pin engaging a hole and radial locating pins may be used. Fig. 9.27 shows a workpiece so located. The principal location is secured from the base plate by pin A. Radial freedom in both directions at YY is restricted by two external pins B confining the periphery of the workpiece.

As shown in fig. 9.27(a) when the work piece contains accurate holes that are perpendicular to finished surface, the pins are used for location purpose. Pin A prevents movement in X and Y directions and a diamond pin B is used to prevent rotation of the workpiece about the axis of pin A. The

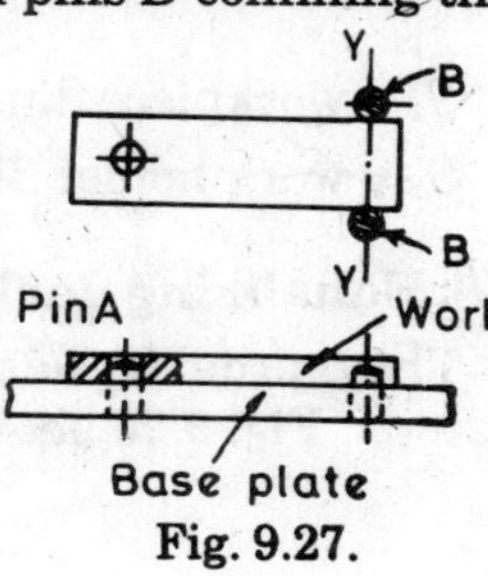

Fig. 9.27.

importance of using a diamond pin for radial location is explained as follows :

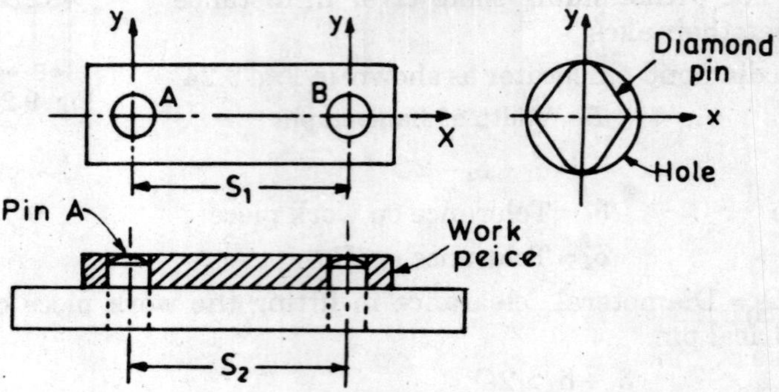

Fig. 9.27(*a*).

The jig or the fixture cannot be made to accurate dimensions. Also there may be variation in the centre distance between the holes in the workpiece. So allowances must be made for the variations encountered in hole sizes and locations. Refering to Fig. 9.27(*a*). If the distance between holes *A* and *B* vary to the extent of tolerance *X* and distance between pins *A* and *B* has a tolerance *Y*, then if the workpiece is effectively located on pin A, the allowance between pin *B* and hole *B* will be $(X + Y)$. Extreme cases occur when both hole and pin centre-to centre dimensions are at maximum or minimum conditions. Due to this, there will be large allowance between the hole and the pin at *B* in *Y*-direction. It will lead to undesired radial rotation around the pin *A* and so the ultimate purpose, for which pin *B* is put, is lost.

To get better radial location, pin *B* is made of diamond shape and therefore it is called a diamond pin. It is relieved on two sides to allow for variation in *X*-direction, but it will provide cylindrical locating surfaces in *Y*-direction.

S_1 = workpiece dimension with tolerance X

S_2 = work holder dimenion with tolerance Y.

9.16. Equalising Jacks

They provide nearly equal contact pressure between the locators. Fig. 9.28 shows a mechanical equalising jack.

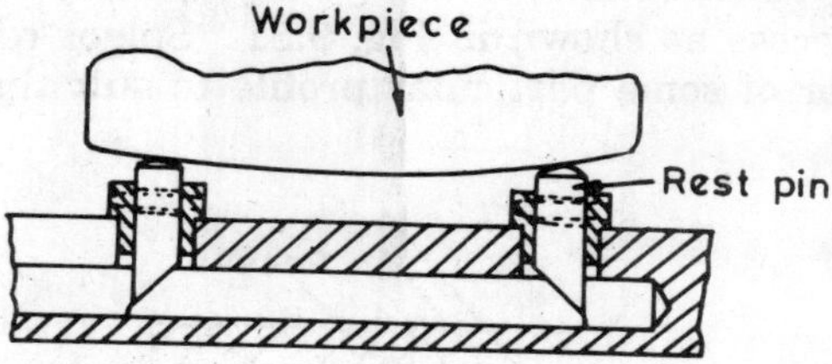

Fig. 9.28.

9.17. Spherical Locating Plugs

Use of spherical locating plugs helps in preventing work piece from sticking because of mis-alignment. This is because of the fact that a sphere has only one dimension and therefore will not bind in a hole no matter which way it is turned. Fig. 9.29 shows a spherical plug locator.

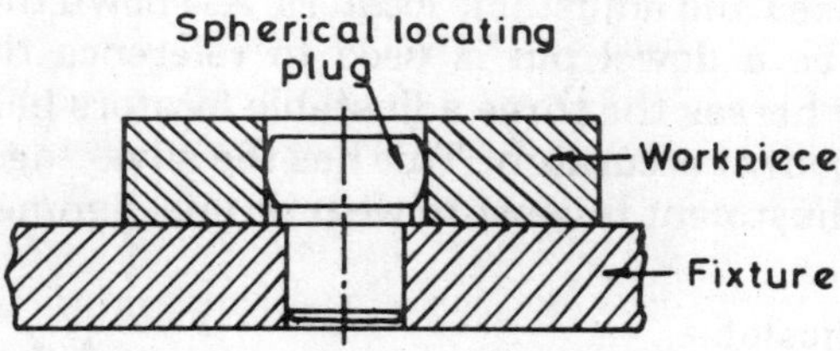

Fig. 9.29.

9.17.1. Location upon a plug or in a spigot recess. A component can be located internally upon a plug as shown in Fig. 9.30. Plugs should not be screwed into the fixture body as a threaded hole will not allow the plug to be positioned in the fixture with sufficient accuracy.

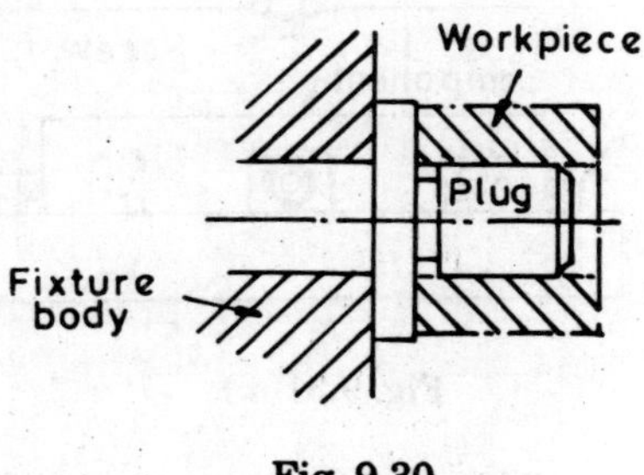

Fig. 9.30.

9.17.2. Recess location. The work piece may be located externally in a recess as shown in Fig. 9.31. Spigot recesses may be cylindrical or of some particular profile to suit the shape of the component.

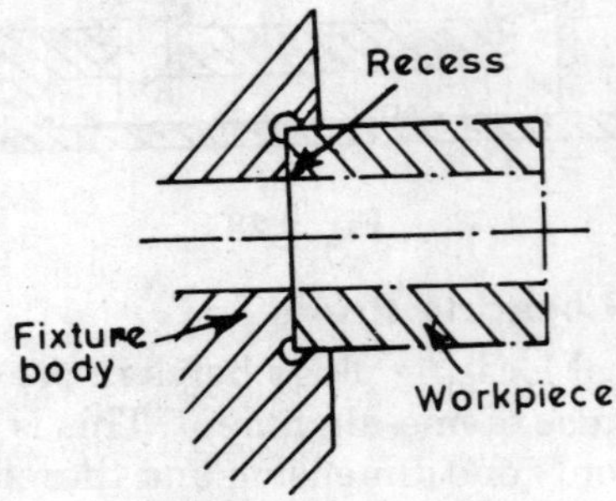

Fig. 9.31.

9.17.2.1. Solid and adjustable locators. Fig. 9.31(*a*) shows use of both fixed and adjustable locators. As shown the fixed locator which may be a dowel pin is used to reference the end of the component whereas the three adjustable locators help in positioning the component accurately. This has the advantage of correcting easily the adjustment because of wear or misalignment.

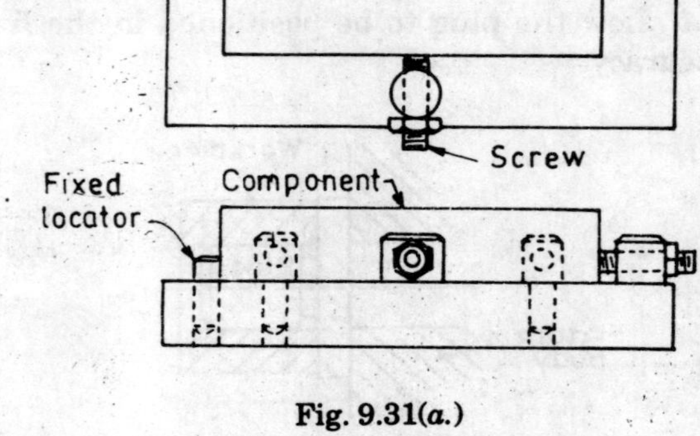

Fig. 9.31(*a*.)

9.18. Fool Proofing

Fool proofing of location system means that the location system provided should be such that it would be difficult for the operator to load the workpiece incorrectly in a fixture. The work piece should be accepted by fixture in one position only. Fig. 9.32 shows a component in which a particular hole to be machined breaks the symmetry of the outline of the component and makes tool proofing necessary. Fool proofing pins have been denoted by *P*.

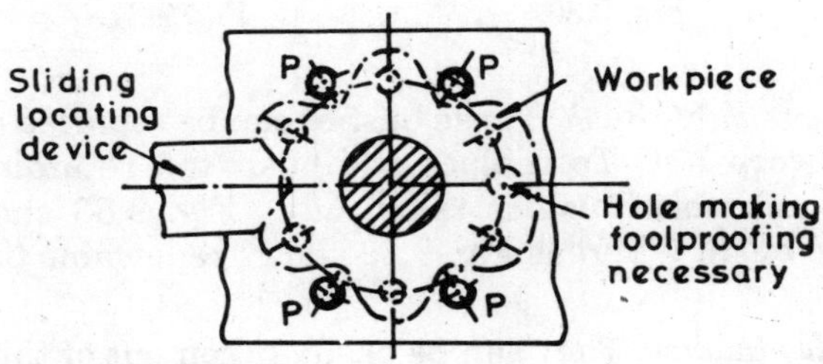

Fig. 9.32.

9.19. Jig Bushes

Cutting tools like drills, reamers and counterboring cutters are located and guided by jig bushes. They are fitted into that portion of the jig known as the bush plate. Drill bushes are hardened and ground to exact size. They are subjected to wear because of action of chips. Therefore consideration should be given to the necessity of replacing the bushings in the design of jig. Drill bushes are made of mild steel and case hardened.

Drill bushes may be classified as follows :

(*i*) *Fixed bushes* : (*a*) Plain type (*b*) Head type.

Fig. 9.33 shows a plain type bush and Fig. 9.34 shows headed type bush. These bushings are pressed directly in the jig body and are intended to remain in the jig until they wear out. Fig. 9.35 shows plain type and head type bushing fitted into the jig plate.

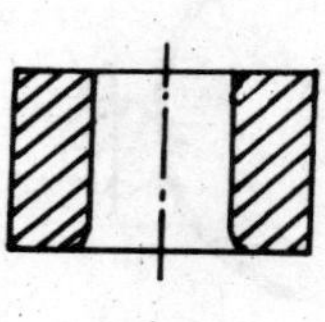

Fig. 9.33.

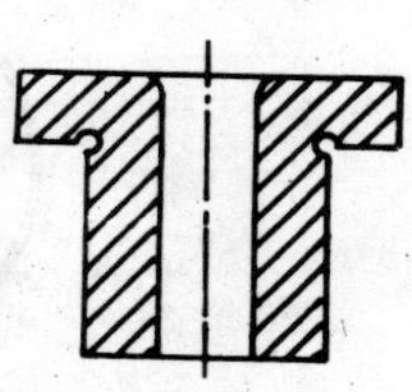

Fig. 9.34.

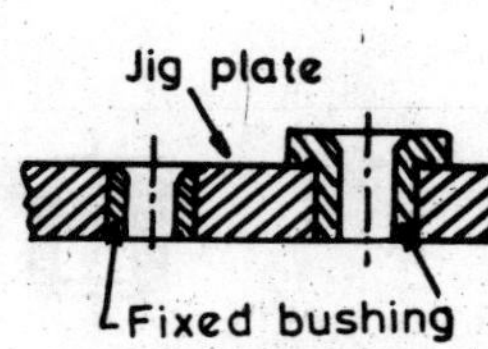

Fig. 9.35.

(*ii*) *Liner bushes.* Liner bushes are also press fitted and are used to act as hardened guide for both renewable and slip bushes.

Fig. 9.36 shows plain type liner and Fig. 9.37 shows head type liner bush.

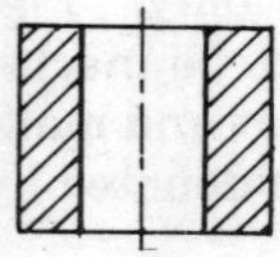

Fig. 9.36.

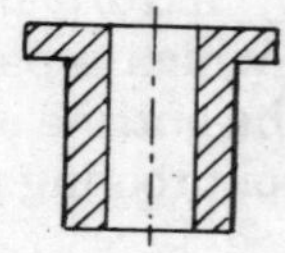

Fig. 9.37.

(*iii*) *Renewable bush.* These bushes can be replaced easily when they get worn out. To replace the bush the retaining screw is removed and worn bush is taken out. Fig. 9.38 shows a fixed renewable bush. Whereas Fig. 9.39 shows renewable bush in position.

(*iv*) *Slip bushes.* They can be easily taken out of the liner bush without opening the retaining screw. The head of the bush is knurled and by rotating the head counter clockwise until the through slot coincides with the screw head and then pulling upward the bush can be removed. They are used to guide various sized tools. They are available in several inside diameter sizes for each outside diameter size. Therefore the bushing may be used, removed and a larger inside diameter bushing may be used. Fig. 9.40 shows a slip bushing while Fig. 9.41 shows slip bush fitted in fixture.

Fig. 9.38.

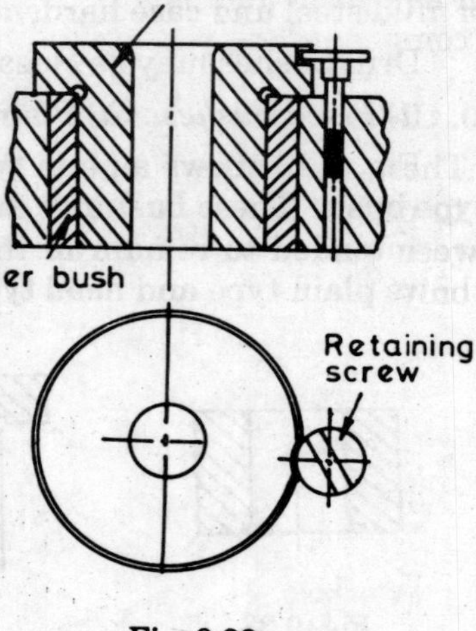

Fig. 9.39.

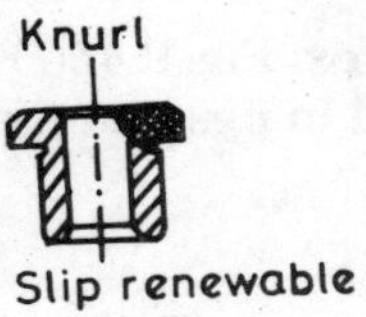

Fig. 9.40.

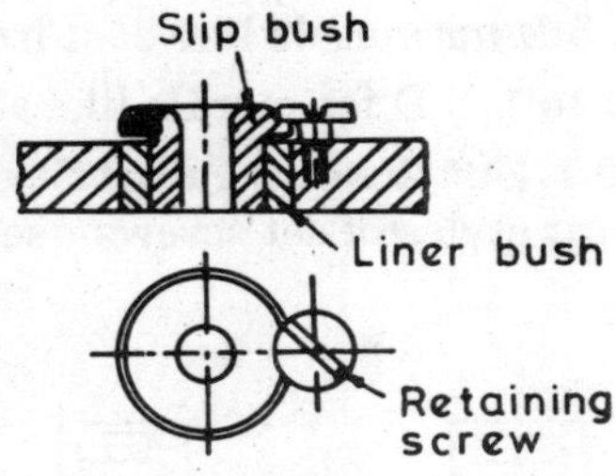

Fig. 9.41.

(*v*) *Screw or clamping bushes.* They are used where work piece is also to be clamped such as when a light work piece is to be drilled. They have external threads. Due to rapid wear of threads these bushes are not preferred for accurate work. (See Fig. 9.42).

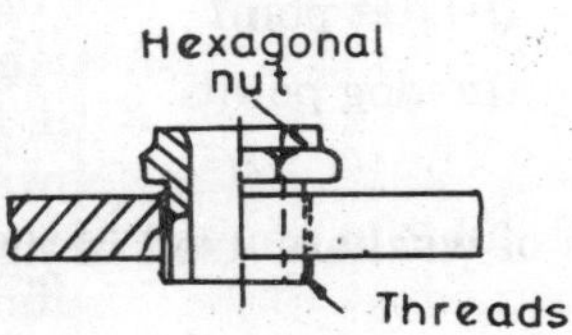

Fig. 9.42.

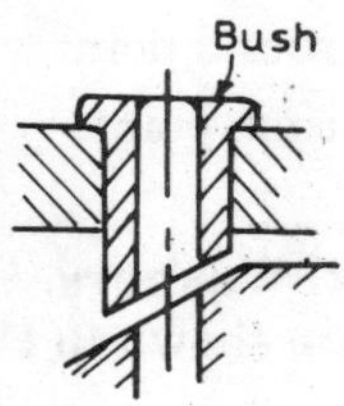

Fig. 9.43.

(*vi*) *Special bushes.* These bushes are used for special operations such as bottom of a bushes requires shaping to suit the profile of the component to prevent deflection of tool as shown in Fig. 9.43.

9.20. Clearance between Workpiece and Bushing

There should be proper clearance between workpiece and bushing to permit the removal of chips. Fig. 9.44 shows no clearance between bushing and workpiece used for maximum precision drilling only. Clearance may be provided as shown in Fig. 9.45.

Fig. 9.44.

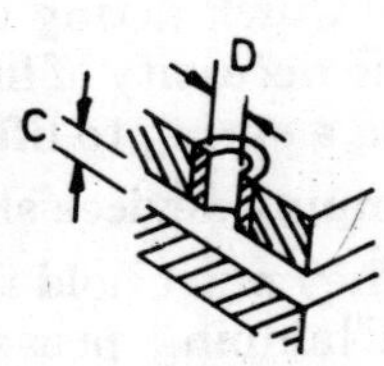

Fig. 9.45.

C = Clearance between work piece and chip.

= 0.5 D for metals like cast iron which produce small chips.

= D to 1. 5 D for metals like steels which produce long chips.

9.20.1. Set Screws Point Styles. Fig. 9.45(*I*) shows commonly used point styles of set screws used in jigs and fixtures. They are :

Fig. 9.45(*I*)

(*i*) round point (*ii*) flat point

(*iii*) cone point (*iv*) dog point.

9.20.2. Washers. Common types of washers used in jigs and fixtures are shown in Fig. **9.45(*II*)**

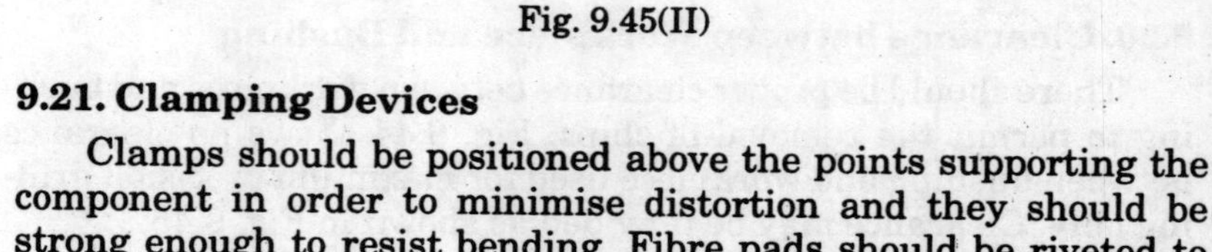

Fig. 9.45(II)

9.21. Clamping Devices

Clamps should be positioned above the points supporting the component in order to minimise distortion and they should be strong enough to resist bending. Fibre pads should be riveted to clamp faces where metallic contact with the work would cause damage. Quick acting clamps should be used whenever possible. Avoid the necessity of lifting a clamp by hand if the job can be done by fitting a spring to lift it.

Clamping devices should fulfill the following requirements :

(*i*) They must hold the workpiece rigidly against all disturbing forces. Clamping pressure should only be enough to hold the workpiece against the locators. The locators should resist bulk of thrust. The clamping force should be applied at points where the workpiece has the support of the solid metal of fixture body.

(*ii*) Clamps should be positioned such that they do not interfere with the operation of machine or tool and enable the operator to work easily and safely.

(*iii*) Clamping devices must be quick acting so that the time required for loading and unloading the workpiece is as short as possible.

(*iv*) The clamps while holding the work piece should not damage it.

(*v*) The clamping devices are subjected to vibrations, chatter or heavy cutting pressure and therefore should not get distorted or loosen during use.

Fig. 9.4 (a) shows various methods of clamping workpiece using T-bolt.

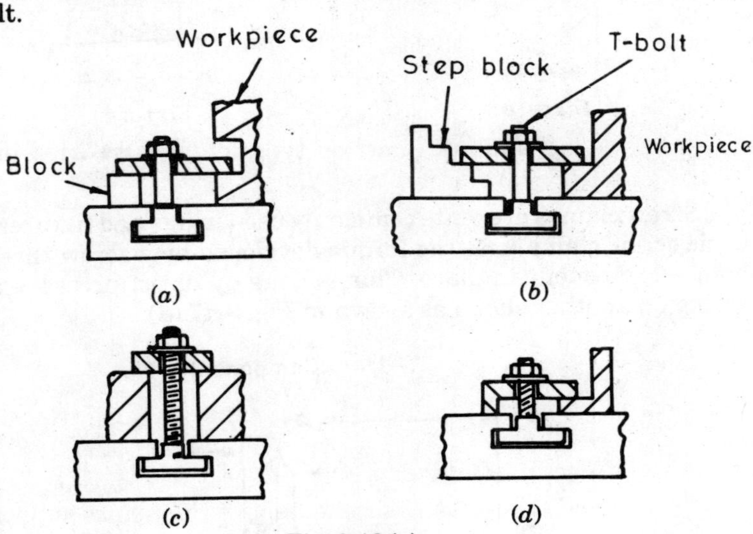

Fig. 9.46 (*a*)

9.22. Clamping Force

Clamping force is the force required to hold a component against the locators. It depends on the following factors :

(*i*) Tool forces being applied.

(*ii*) The method of positioning the component.

Clamps should always contact the workpiece at the most rigid point. This prevents the clamping force from bending or damaging the workpiece.

The clamps should be so positioned that they do not interfere with the operation of the tool or machine and the operator can work easily and safely.

9.23. Types of Clamping Devices

Various types of clamping devices are as follows :

(*i*) *Screw clamps.* These are simple clamps and make use of threaded rod equipped with some method of tightening. Fig. 9.46 and Fig. 9.47 show screw clamps.

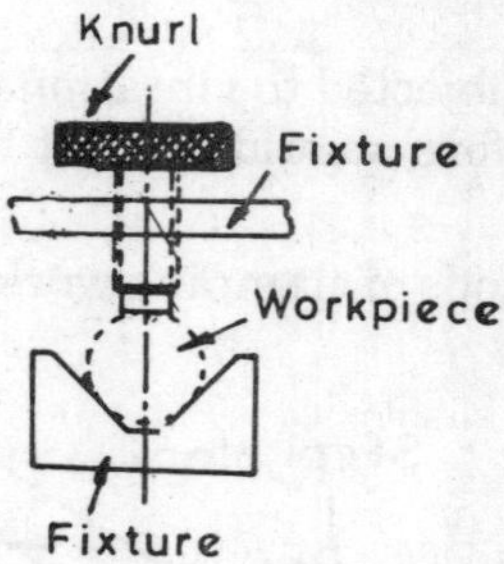

Fig. 9.46.

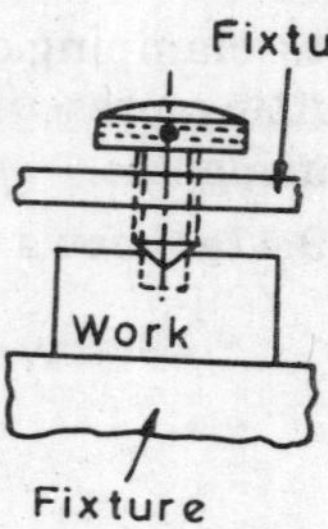

Fig. 9.47.

Screw clamps are quite commonly used in jigs and fixtures. The basic screw clamp uses the torque developed by a screw thread to hold a component in place. This is done by direct pressure or by acting on another clamp as shown in Fig. 9.47 (*a*).

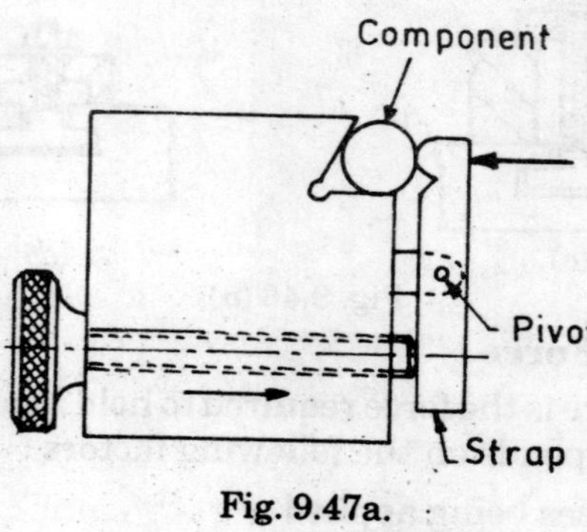

Fig. 9.47a.

Table 9.1(*a*) indicates average holding force for screws of different sizes.

Table 9.1(*a*)

Screw size	*Holding Force* (Newtons)
M6	700
M8	1100
M10	1650
M12	3100
M16	4900
M20	7100

(*ii*) *C-Clamps.* These are quick-acting clamps. The component can be easily removed. The locking nut can release or lock the clamp in about one turn only. Fig. 9.48 shows a free *C*-clamp whereas a captive *C*-clamp is shown in Fig. 9.49.

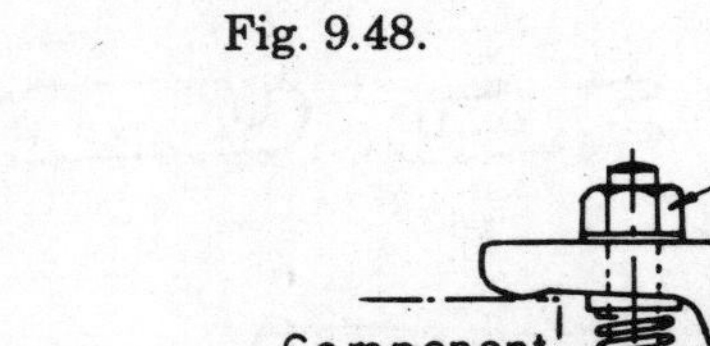

Fig. 9.48.

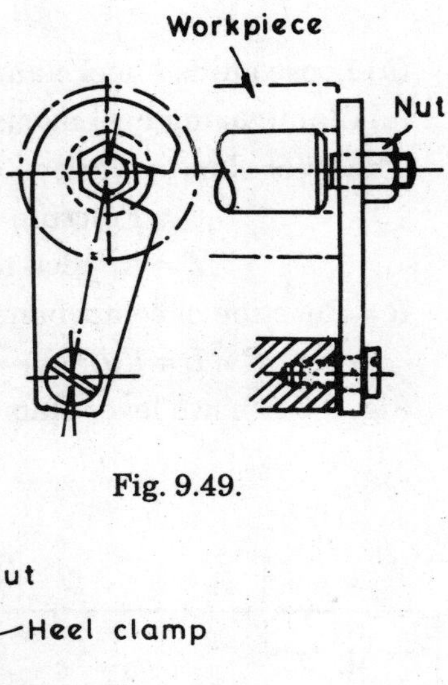

Fig. 9.49.

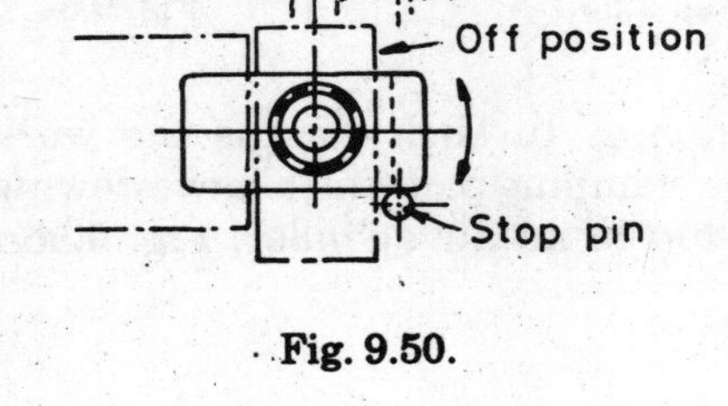

Fig. 9.50.

(*iii*) *Strap or lever clamps.* In these clamps as the nut is unscrewed the spring pushes the clamp upwards. The clamp has a longitudinal slot so that it can be pushed clear of the work.

There are three types of lever clamps.

(*a*) Solid heel clamp (Fig. 9.50)

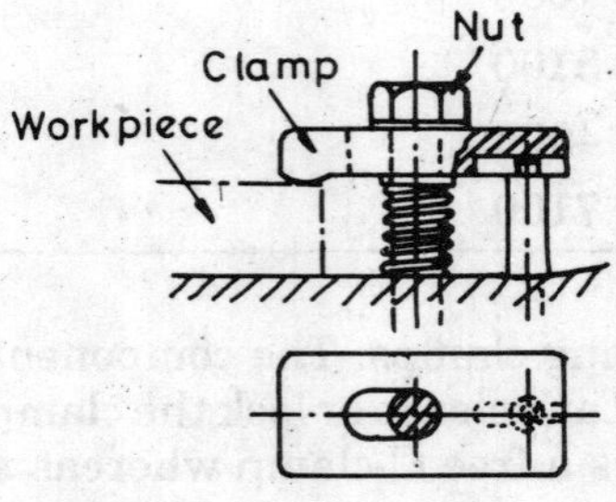

Fig. 9.51.

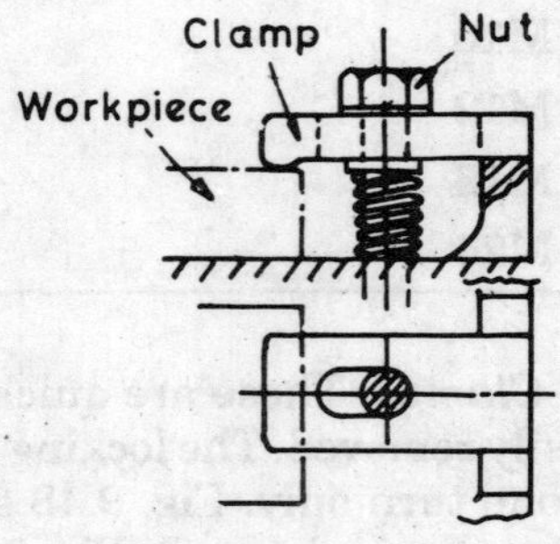

Fig. 9.52.

(*b*) Loose guided heel clamp (Fig. 9.51).

(*c*) Clamp using heel in casting (Fig. 9.52).

The lever clamps work on general principal shown in Fig. 9.53.

C = Fulcrum

F = Applied force

R = Reaction of component to the clamping force.

$$R \times L = F(L - x)$$

Fig. 9.54 shows lever clamps called straps commonly used.

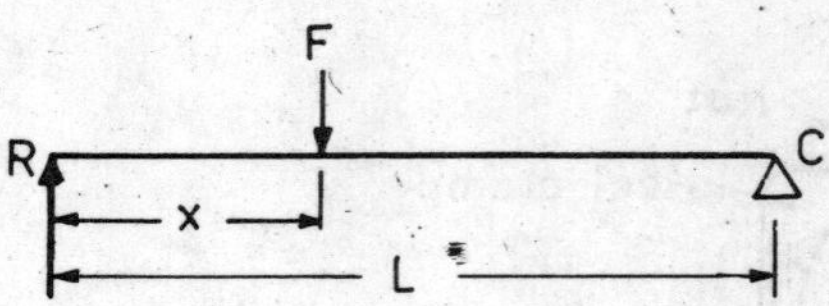

Fig. 9.53.

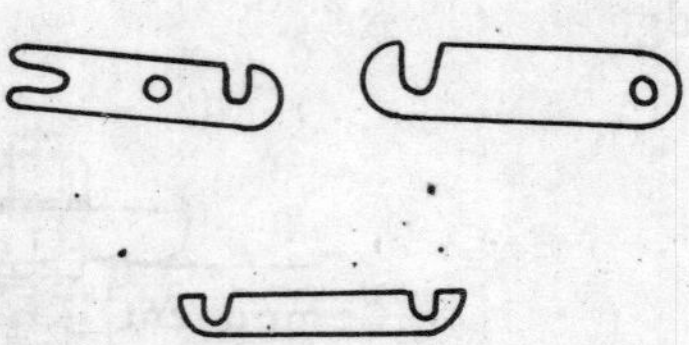

Fig. 9.54.

(*iv*) *Toggle clamps.* In such clamps the work piece is held securely under the clamping pad which move downward by forward motion of the piston in an air cylinder. Fig. 9.55 shows a toggle clamp.

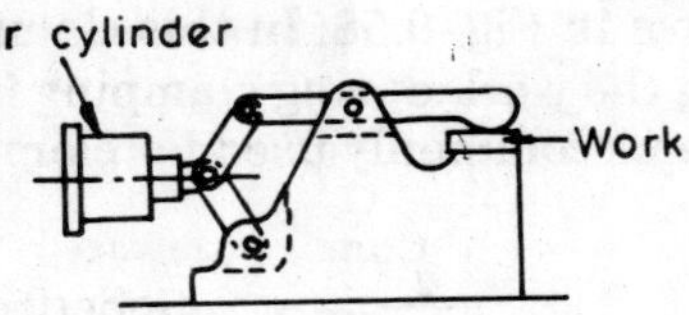

Fig. 9.55.

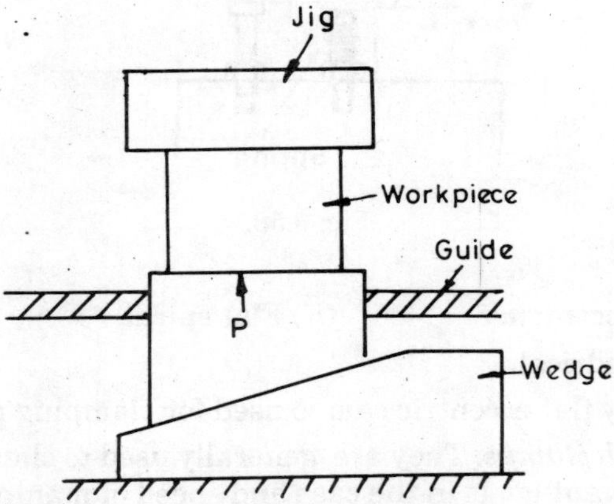

Fig. 9.56.

(*v*) *Wedge clamp.* Fig. 9.56 shows a wedge clamp. The horizontal movement of wedge causes upward vertical clamping force (*P*) on the workpiece. Wedges having angle of 1–4° are self-holding type and generally hold the workpiece without additional attachments. But wedges with larger angles need another holding device such as cam or screw to hold the wedge and workpiece in position.

Fig. 9.57 shows a wedge clamp in which wedge is used to force the wedge end of clamp upward which causes the clamping action.

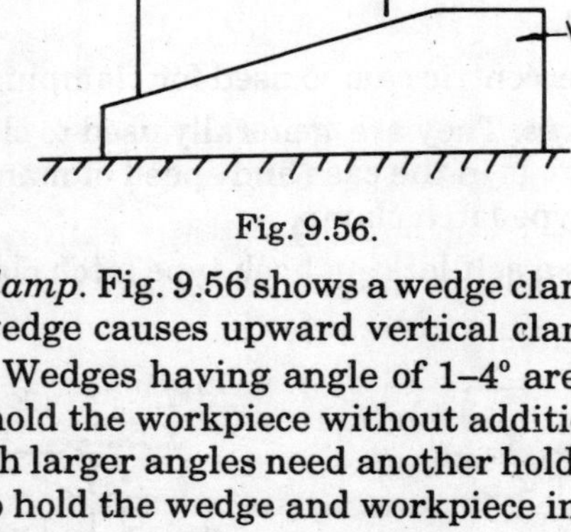

Fig. 9.57.

(*vi*) *Cam operated clamps.* These are quick acting clamps and the workpiece can be quickly placed in position by the fast movement of cam as shown in Fig. 9.58. In this clamp the possibility of loosening or shifting the work during clamping is decreased. There are three types of cams commonly used for clamps :

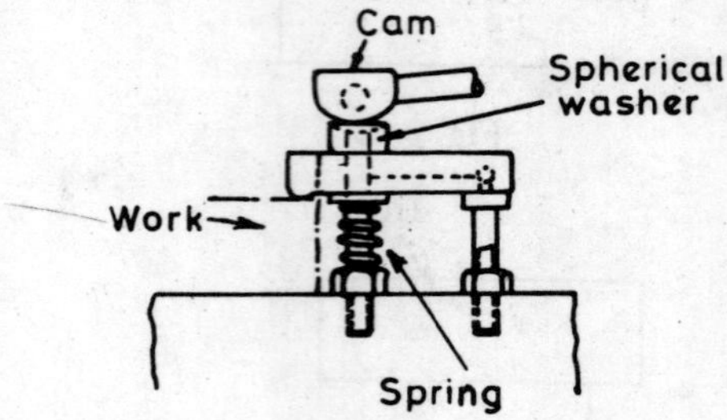

Fig. 9.58.

(*i*) Flat eccentric (*ii*) Flat spiral

(*iii*) Cylindrical.

Generally flat eccentric cam is used for clamping purposes.

(*vii*) *Latch clamps.* They are generally used to clamp light jobs. The main advantage is in the case and speed of manipulation. Fig. 9.59 shows a cam type latch clamp.

Fig. 9.60 shows a self-locking hook type latch clamp.

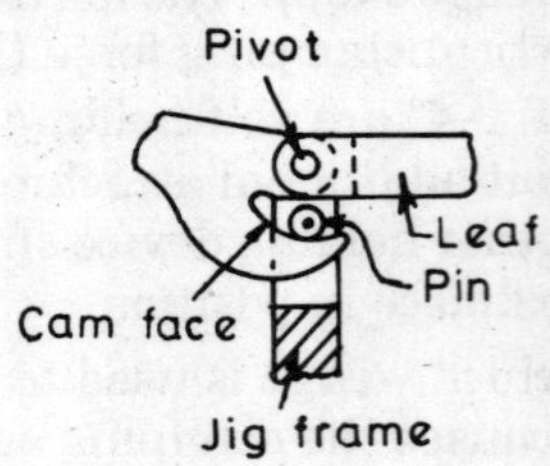

Fig. 9.59.

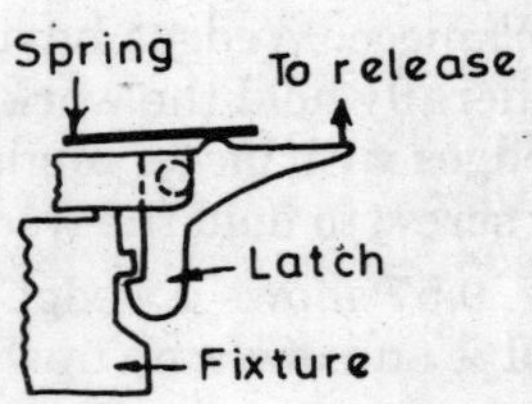

Fig. 9.60.

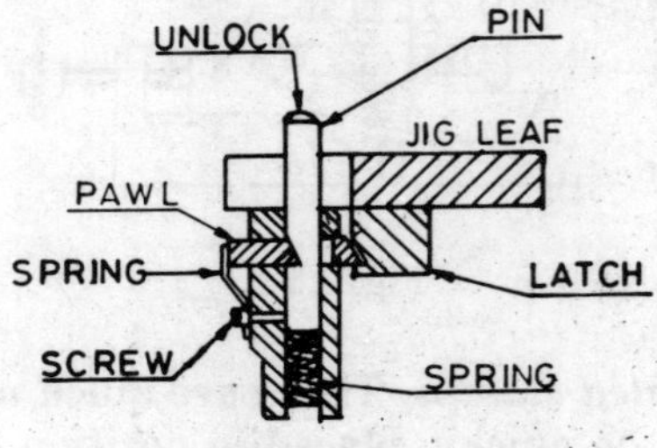

Fig. 9.60(*a*)

Fig. 9.60(*a*) shows a pin type self- locking latch which is very rapid in action. The operator can open the jig with one hand by pushing down on the pin as he raises the leaf.

(*viii*) *Swing clamp.* Fig. 9.61 shows a swing clamp. When locking screw is loosened and the clamp assembly is revolved through 90° the workpiece can be removed.

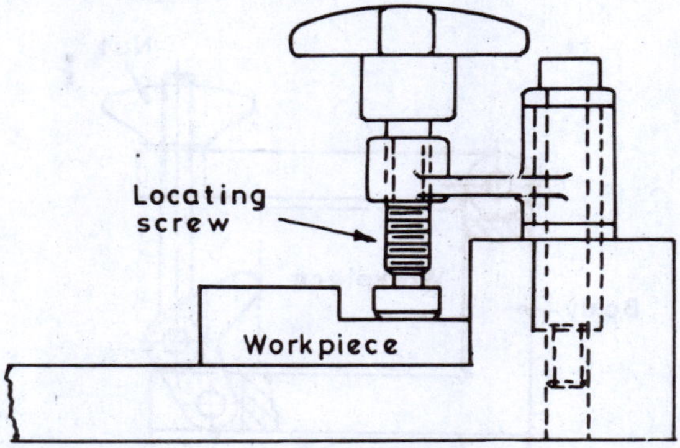

Fig. 9.61.

(*ix*) *Power operated clamps.* They have better control of clamping pressure. They may use hydraulic power or pneumatic power.

Fig. 9.62 shows a typical power clamping device. Pneumatic and hydraulic clamping is usually justified when production requirements are high. The energy expended by the operator is very small and the force exerted is even and uniform.

Fig. 9.62.

(*x*) *Quick acting nut.* The clearance hole is machined at an angle (θ)

$$\theta = 3 \text{ to } 7^\circ$$

when the nut is assembled it is inclined to the clearance hole axis and passes over the male thread. Fig. 9.63 shows a quick acting nut.

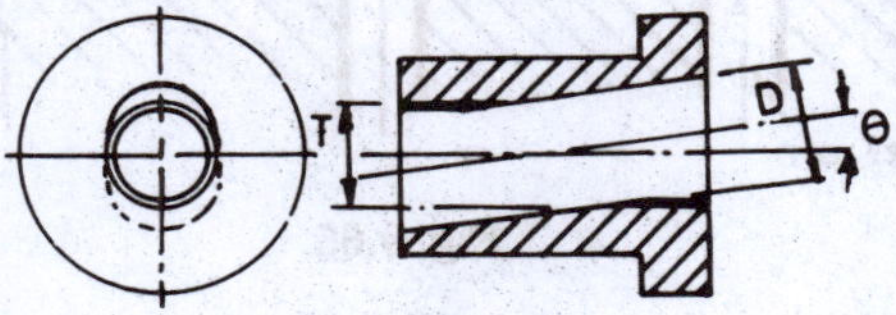

Fig. 9.63.

The nut is so made that it is from two to three thread diameters in length and has the hole slightly larger than the outside diameter of the thread

$$D > T$$

(xi) Two way clamp. This clamp shown in Fig. 9.64 has a quick release action. When nut is released the clamp becomes loose.

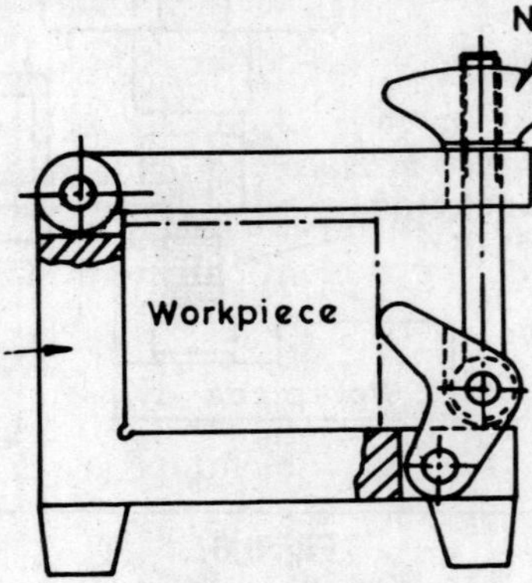

Fig. 9.64.

(xii) Bridge clamp. Fig. 9.65 shows a bridge clamp. When nut is unscrewed the spring pushes the clamp upwards.

M.A. = Mechanical Advantage = L/S. Distance B should not be greater than distance S.

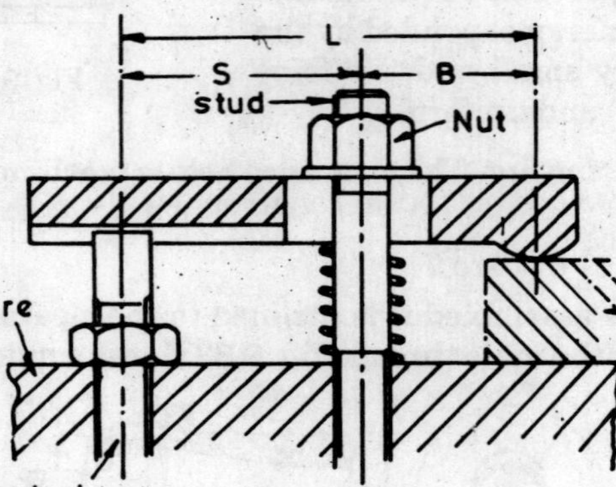

Fig. 9.65.

9.24. Locating and Clamping Surfaces

In order to decide the locating and clamping surfaces of the component drawing should be studied to find the best surfaces to locate and clamp the part. The order of preference is as follows :

(*i*) Holes.

(*ii*) Two machined surfaces which form a right angle.

(*iii*) One machined and one unmachined surface which form a right angle.

(*iv*) Two unmachined surfaces which form a right angle.

The prime requirement for a locating surface is repeatability. The parts must be positioned identically within the tolerance limits part after part.

9.25. Cams used in Clamps

Various types of cams used in clamps are as follows :

(*i*) Flat single cam [Fig. 9.66 (*a*).]

(*ii*) Single cam [Fig. 9.66(*b*).]

(*iii*) Double cam [Fig. 9.66 (*c*).]

S = RISE

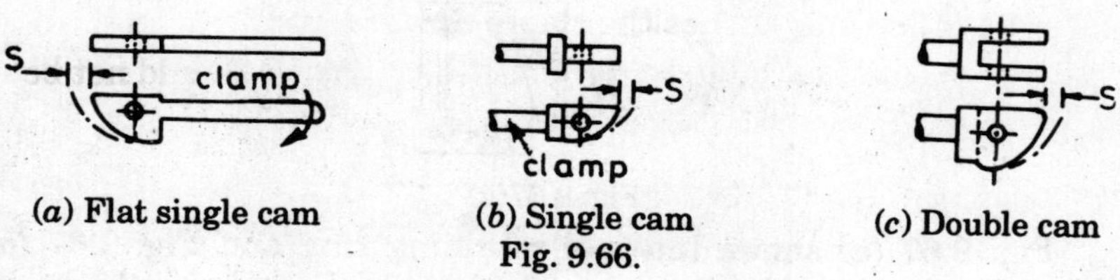

(*a*) Flat single cam (*b*) Single cam (*c*) Double cam

Fig. 9.66.

Fig. 9.67 shows a typical cam construction. Table 9.1 indicates the sizes of such cam.

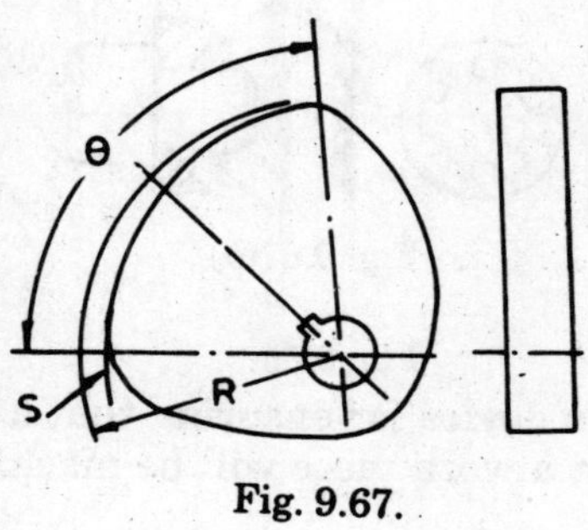

Fig. 9.67.

θ = Cam angle = 72°

R = Base circle radius

S = Rise

Table 9.1

S (mm)	R (mm)
3.97	29.37
5.16	37.8
7.94	56.36
10.32	72.2
11.12	77

9.25.1. Retaining Rings. Retaining rings is a fastener that can save many hours of work. It provides necessary strength to most tooling equipment. Retaining rings are of two types

(*i*) Internal retaining rings.

(*ii*) External retaining rings.

Fig. 9.67(*a*)

Fig. 9.67 *(a)* shows internal retaining ring and Fig. 9.67 *(b)* shows external retaining rings. These rings have been shown in assembled position also.

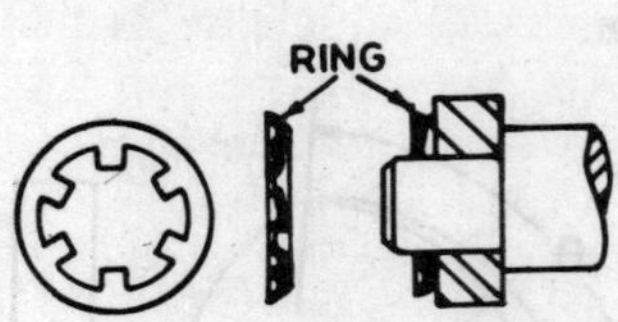

Fig. 9.67(*b*)

9.26. Drilling Jigs

A drilling jig is a device for ensuring that a hole to be drilled, tapped or reamed in a work piece will be machined in the proper place. Jig is used to guide the drill into the proper place. Drill is guided by bushings. Jigs makes it possible to drill, ream and tap holes at much greater speeds and with greater accuracy than when the holes are produced by conventional hand methods. Another advantage is that skilled operators are not required when jigs are used. A jig basically consists of a clamping device to hold the work piece in position under hardened steel bushing through which the drill passes during drilling operation. Drill jig should be such that the work piece can be quickly inserted and quickly removed after the machining operation has been performed. The hole pattern should be within the required tolerances on each part. The locating points on a drilling jig should be designed in such a way that it is impossible to load the work piece in correctly.

Locators subjected to wear should be easily replaceable and should be made of hardened tool steel. Standard rest button [Fig. 9.68*(a)*], spherical radius locator button, [Fig. 9.68 *(b)*] and rest pad [Fig. 9.68*(c)*] commonly used in jigs are shown in Fig. 9.68.

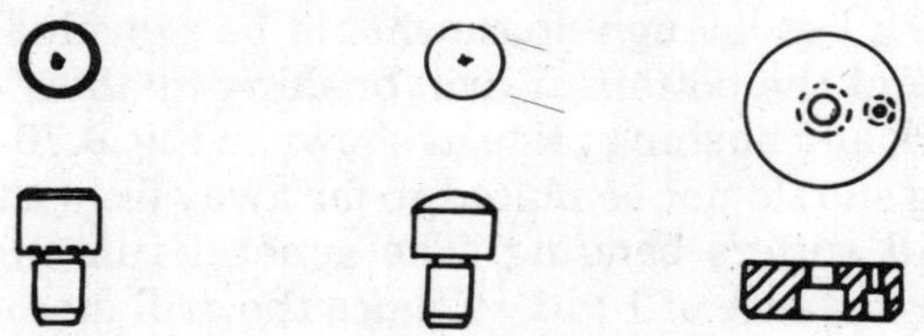

(a) *(b)* *(c)*

Fig. 9.68.

Method of locating and clamping should be easy and quick to reduce the idle time to minimum. Provisions should be made for the coolant to get to the drill and for escape of the coolant.

A drill jig should stand on four feet (or legs) rather than on a flat surface. Jig feet may be built into the body or added separately. Fig. 9.69*(a)* shows rest button type and Fig. 9.69*(b)* shows flat jig feet. Fig.[9.69*(c)*] shows a jig foot cast integral with the body of jig.

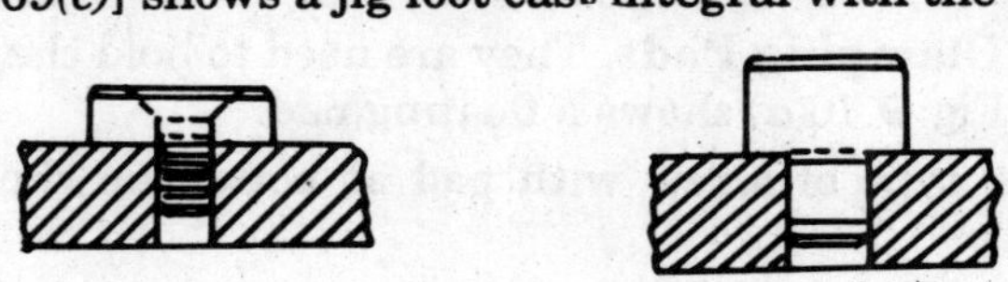

(a) Rest button *(b)* Flat jig feet

Fig. 9.69.

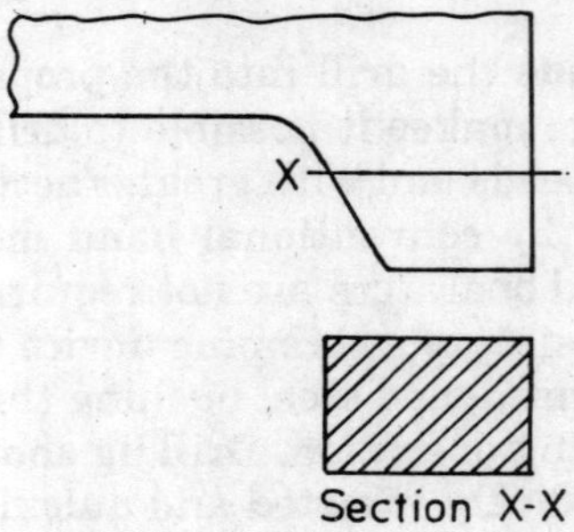

Fig. 9.69 (c)

The body of jig has two common forms of construction :

(*i*) Built up : (*a*) Using dowels and screws for fabricating the members.

(*b*) Fabricating by welding.

(*ii*) Cast iron bodies.

In drilling jigs enough space should be provided between the work piece and the bottom of drill bushing to allow chips to pass between work and bushing plate as shown in Fig. 9.70. However the drill bushing should not be placed so far away from the work piece that the drill suffers bending. The general rule is to place the bushing at a distance of 1 to 1 ½ times the drill diameter from the work piece surface.

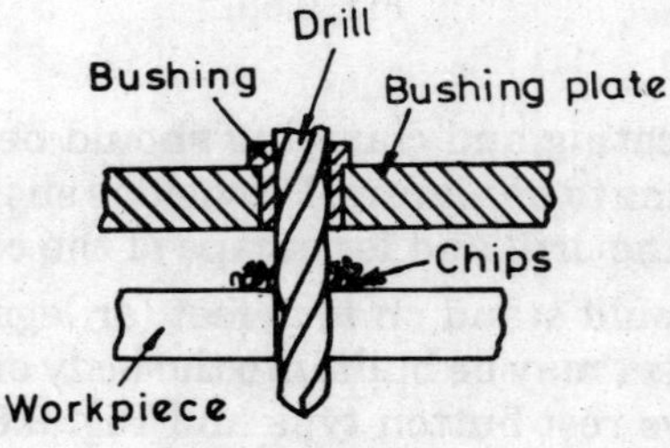

Fig. 9.70.

9.26.1. Clamping Pads. They are used to hold the work piece in position Fig. 9.70(*a*) shows a floating pad.

Another type of screw with pad at bottom is shown in Fig. 9.70(*b*).

9.27. Accessories

In jigs and fixtures the various accessories used are as follows:

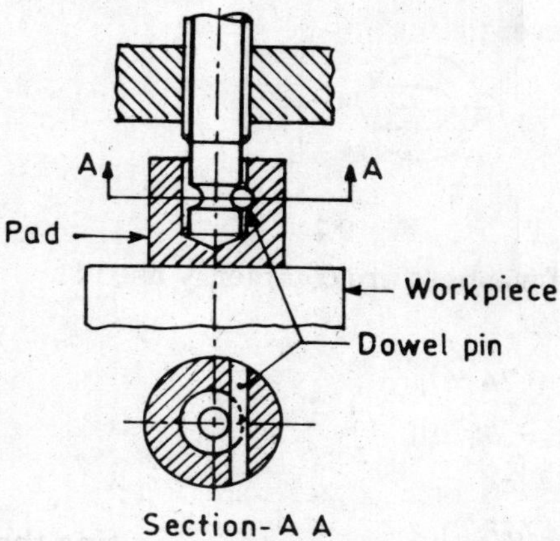

Fig. 9.70(*a*)

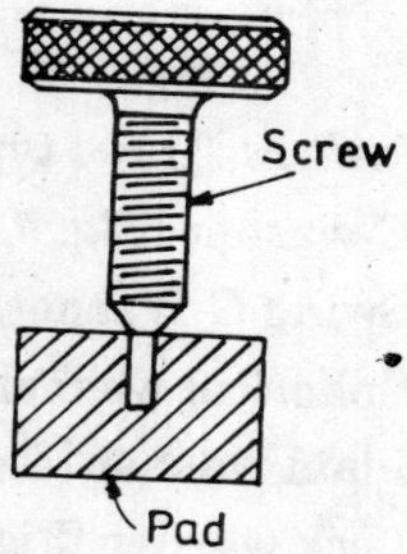

Fig. 9.70(*b*).

(*i*) *Screws.* Fig. 9.71 *(a)* shows a screw used to clamp or hold work when light pressures are required. Whereas the screw shown in Fig. 9.71 *(b)* is used to apply medium clamping pressure.

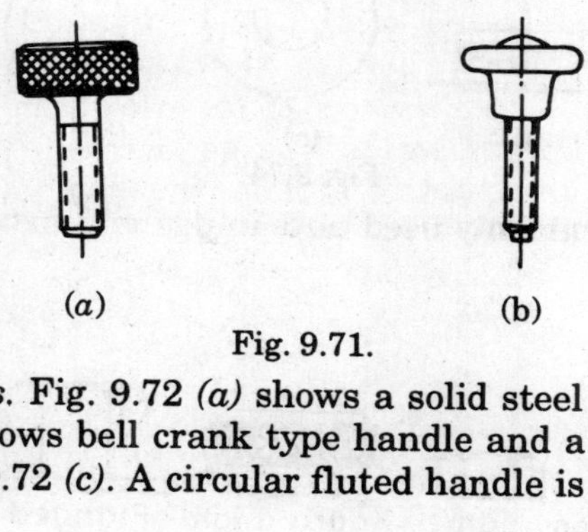

(*a*) (b)

Fig. 9.71.

(*ii*) *Handles.* Fig. 9.72 *(a)* shows a solid steel handle whereas Fig. 9.72 *(b)* shows bell crank type handle and a speed handle is shown in Fig. 9.72 *(c)*. A circular fluted handle is shown Fig. 9.72 *(d)*.

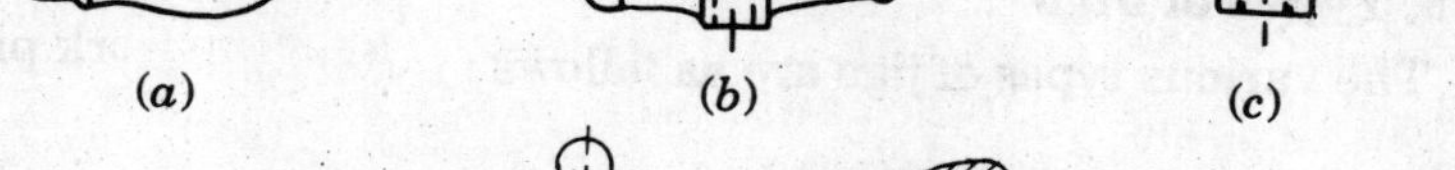

(*a*) (*b*) (*c*)

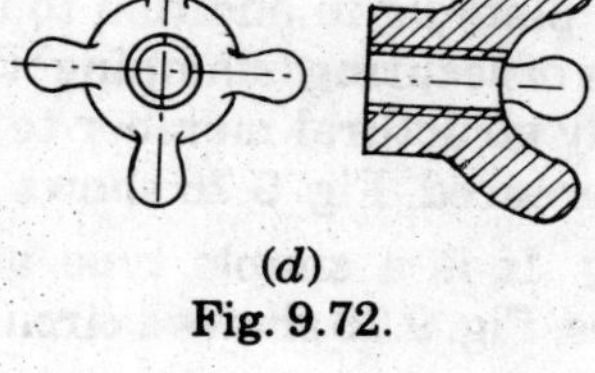

(*d*)

Fig. 9.72.

Fig. 9.73 shows a two ball lever :

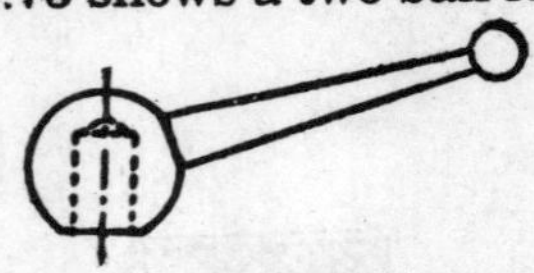

Fig. 9.73.

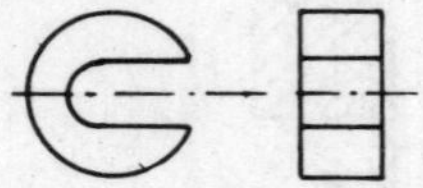

Fig. 9.74.

(iii) Washers Three types of washers are commonly used :

(*a*) *C*-washer [Fig. 9.74]

(*b*) Swing *C*-Washer [Fig. 9.74 *(a)*]

(*c*) Spherical washer [Fig. 9.74 *(b)*]

(*d*) Plain washer [Fig. 9.74 *(c)*]

(*e*) Lock washer [Fig. 9.74 *(d)*]

(*f*) Internal star [Fig. 9.74 *(e)*.]

(*iv*) Bushings

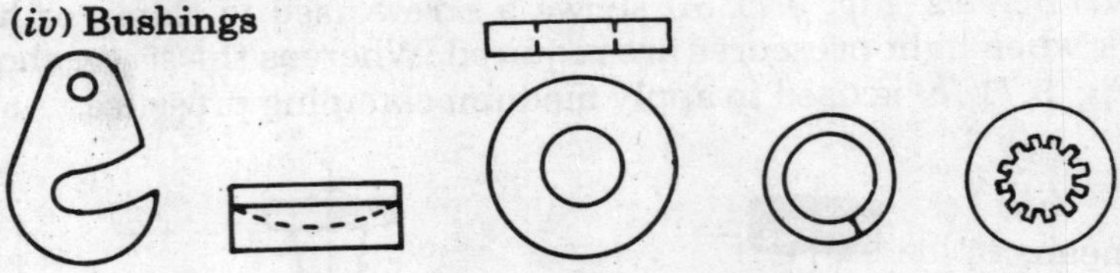

(*a*) (*b*) (*c*) (*d*) (*e*)

Fig. 9.74.

(*v*) *Nuts.* Commonly used nuts in jigs and fixtures are shown in Fig. 9.74(*f*).

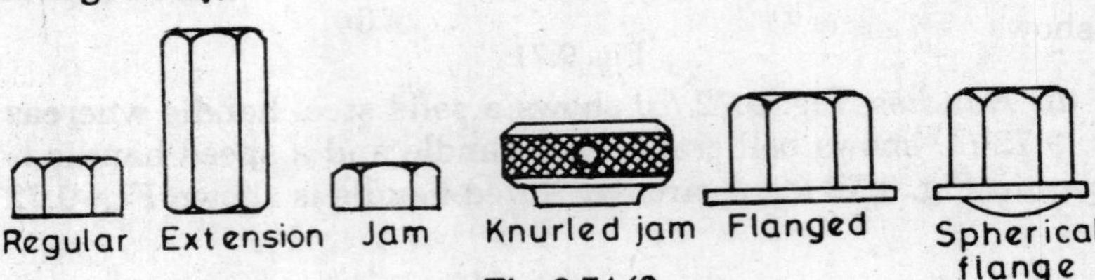

Fig. 9.74 (f)

9.28. Types of Jigs

The various types of jigs are as follows :

(*i*) *Plate Jig.* The plate jig in addition to location function also in corporates a means of securing (clamping) the work piece. It uses a flat plate as its only structural member to which all the details are attached and referenced. Fig. 9.75 shows a plate jig.

(*ii*) *Template Jig.* It is a simple type used for locating hole pattern on workpieces. Fig. 9.76 shows a circular plate template jig.

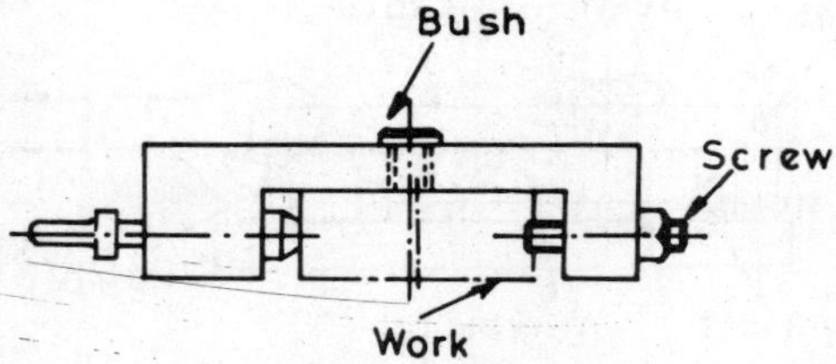

Fig. 9.75.

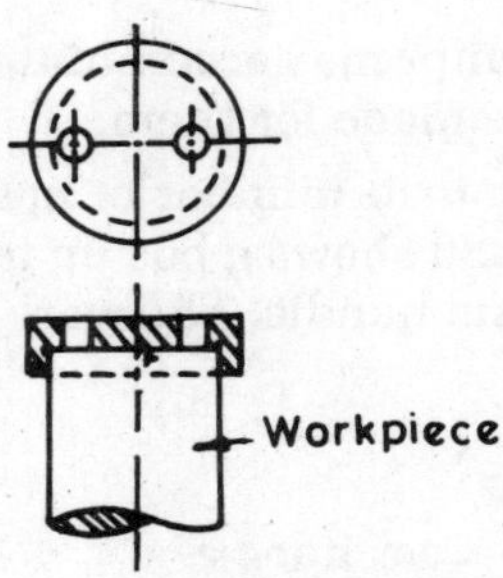

Fig. 9.76.

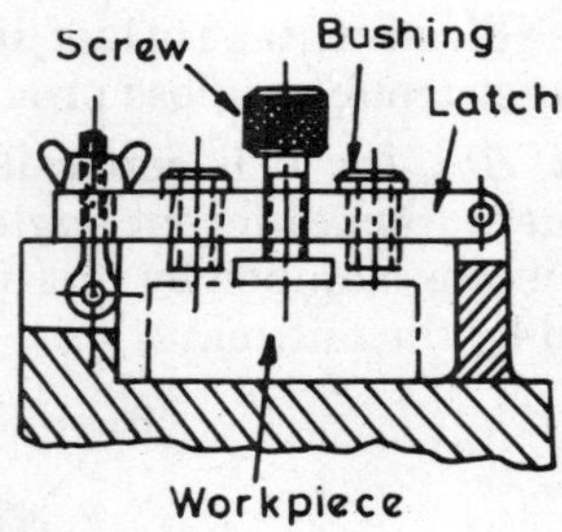

Fig. 9.77.

(*iii*) *Latch type Jig*. In this jig a pivoted latch provides an easy means of loading and unloading the workpiece. Fig. 9.77 shows a latch type jig.

(*iv*) *Channel Jig*. This jig provides better stability and support for the workpiece. The workpiece is mounted against the top and one side of the jig while it is clamped from the other side. Fig. 9.78 shows a channel jig.

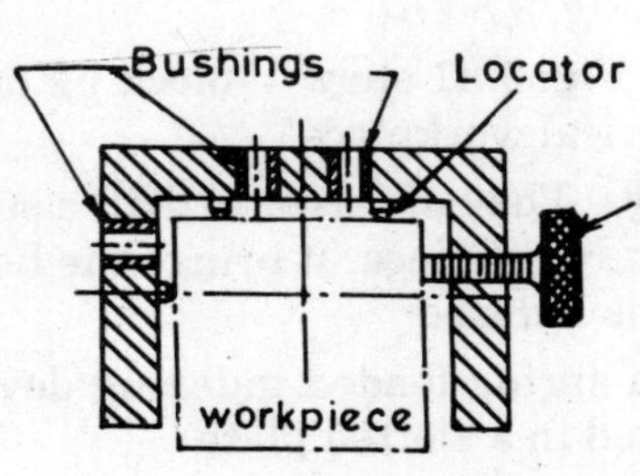

Fig. 9.78.

(*v*) *Leaf Jig*. In this jig (Fig. 9.79) leaf carrying the bushing can be swing to load and unload quickly the workpiece. The leaf can be locked by means of cam operated latch. Leaf jigs are quite suitable for complicated workpieces with irregular contours. Holes may be drilled in more than one place.

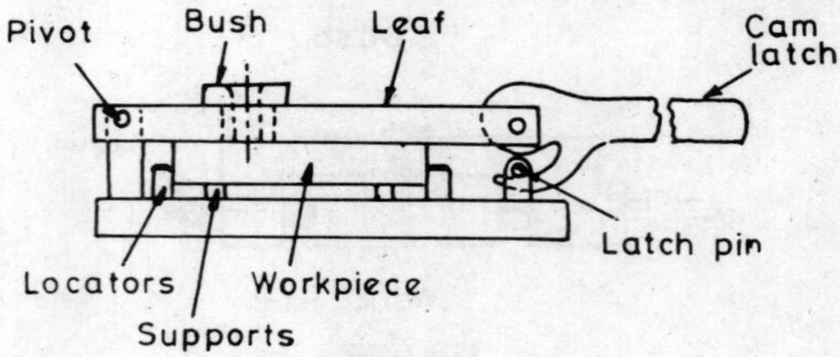

Fig. 9.79.

The disadvantage of leaf jig is that chips may accumulate in side and cause trouble unless provisions are made for them.

(*vi*) *Box Jig.* It is generally used to drill number of holes on a workpiece from different angles. Fig. 9.80 shows a box jig in which workpiece is clamped by rotating the cam handle. The workpiece is located by the button.

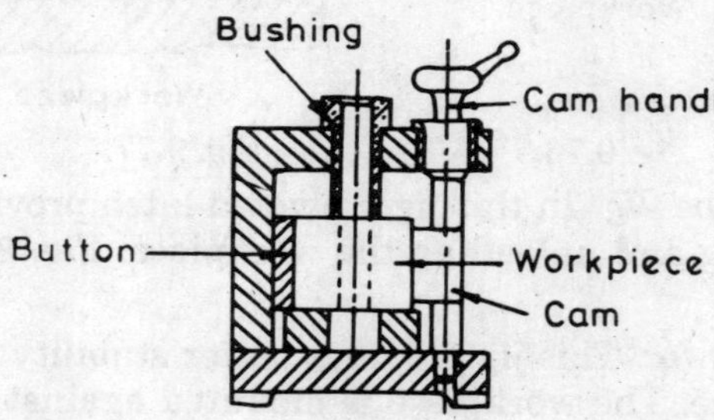

Fig. 9.80.

Fig. 9.80(*a*) shows a typical box jig to drill 4-holes in the component shown in Fig. 9.80(*b*).

(*vii*) *V-Block Jig.* Fig. 9.81 show *V*-block jig used to drill holes in cylindrical or spherical workpiece.

(*viii*) *Indexing Jigs.* They are used to drill a series of holes in a circle on the face of the workpiece. It brings the hole portion under the drill each time it is indexed.

Fig. 9.82 shows a spring loaded indexing device in which the indexing pin is engaged in a slotted plate.

Fig. 9.83 shows an indexing jig in which indexing is achieved by using a reference plate and a plunger.

(*ix*) *Commercial drill Jig.* Fig. 9.84 shows a commercial drilling jig. It can be used for drilling and counter boring operations. As shown the workpiece is a bearing cap and is clamped between adapter plate and pin when handle is brought down. The jig has a base which is integral with two vertical column guides.

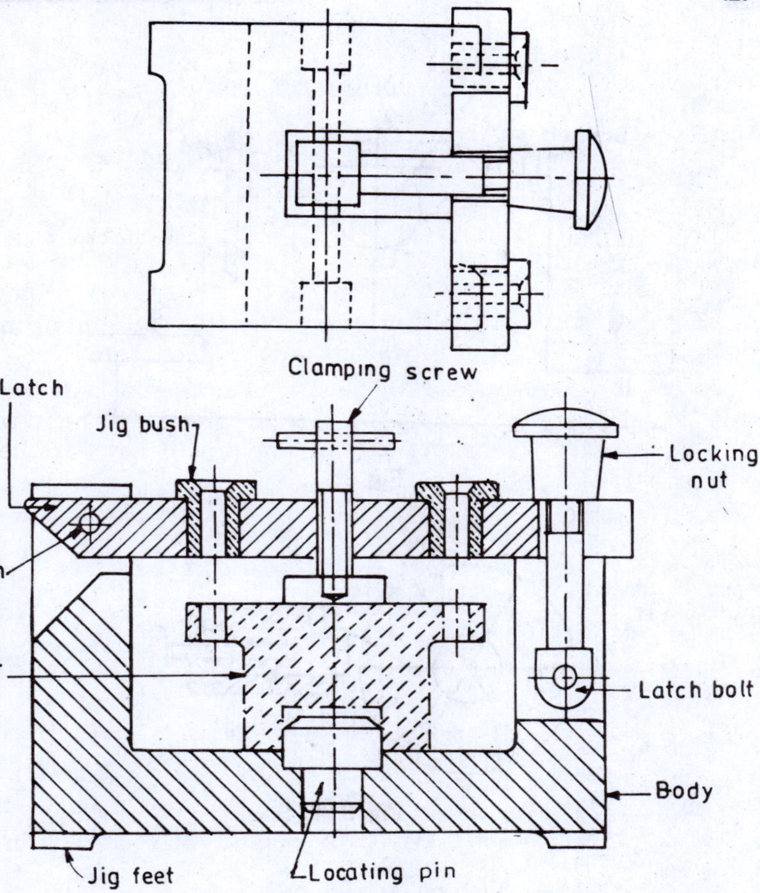

Fig. 9.80 (*a*).

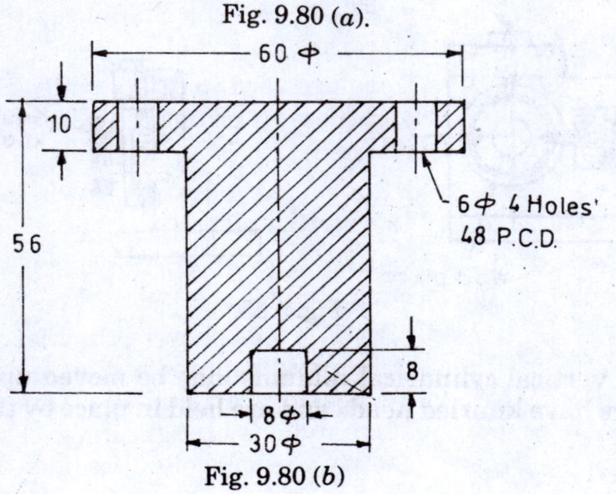

Fig. 9.80 (*b*)

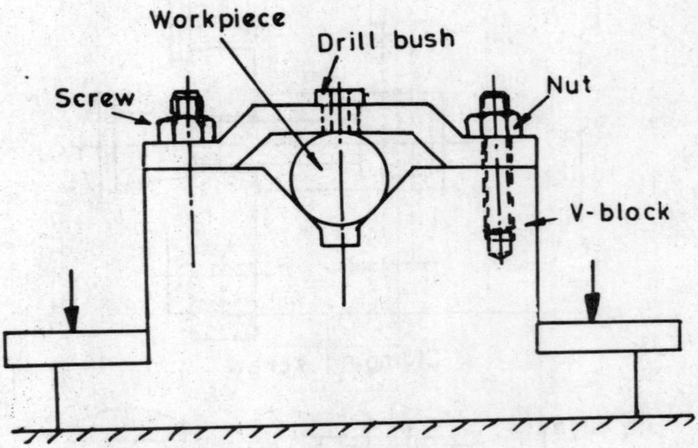

Fig. 9.81.

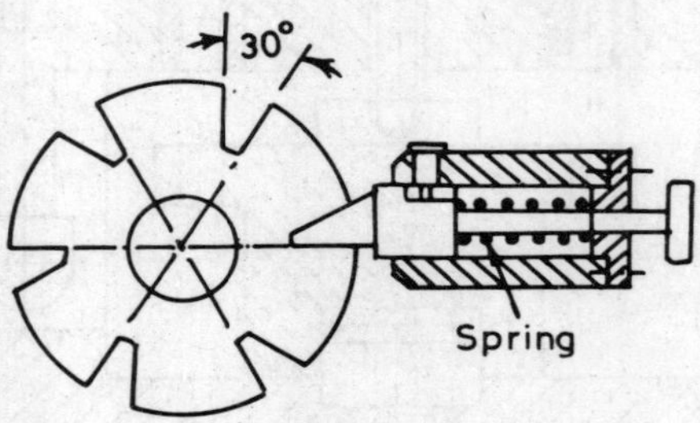

Fig. 9.82.

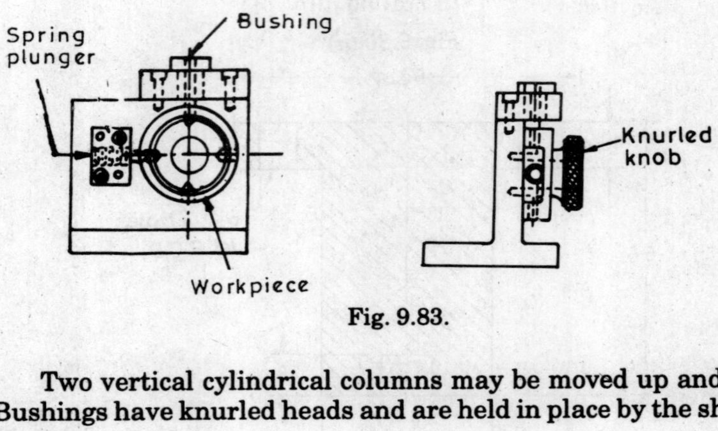

Fig. 9.83.

Two vertical cylindrical columns may be moved up and down. Bushings have knurled heads and are held in place by the shoulder screws.

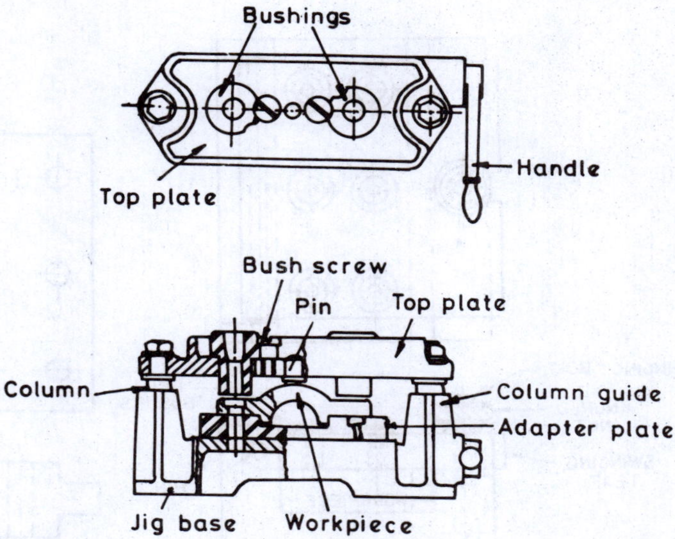

Fig. 9.84.

(x) *Angle plate Jig*. These jigs are used to drill holes in the work piece at some angle.

Fig. 9.85 shows an angle plate jig.

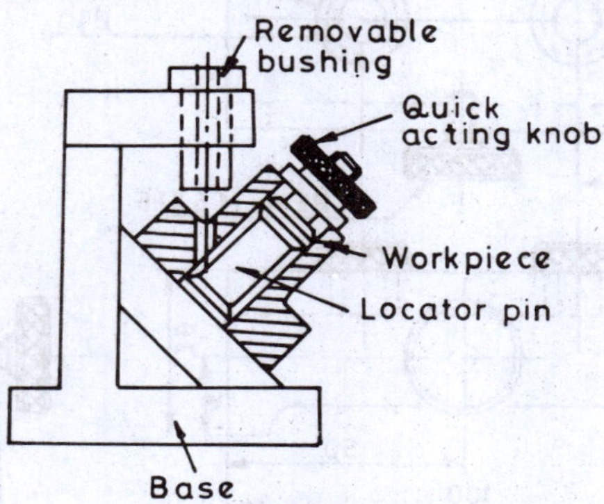

Fig. 9.85.

9.28. Leaf Jig

Fig. 9.85(*a*) shows a swinging leaf jig for drilling holes in the component shown in Fig. 9.85(*b*)

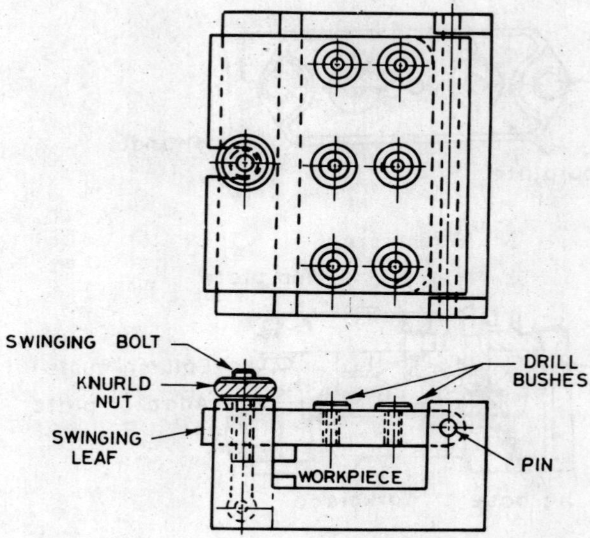

Fig. 9.85(*a*).

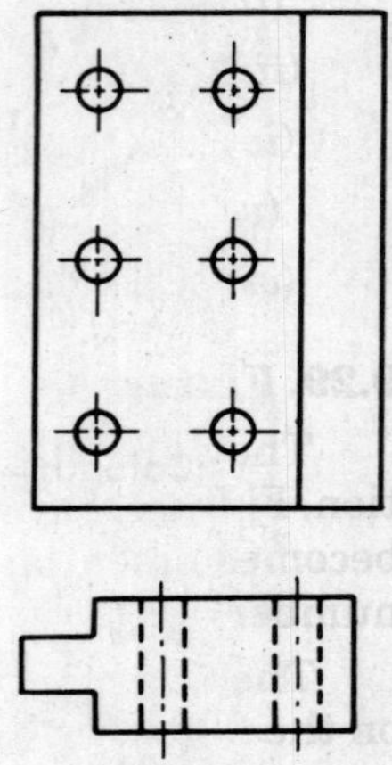

Fig. 9.85(*b*).

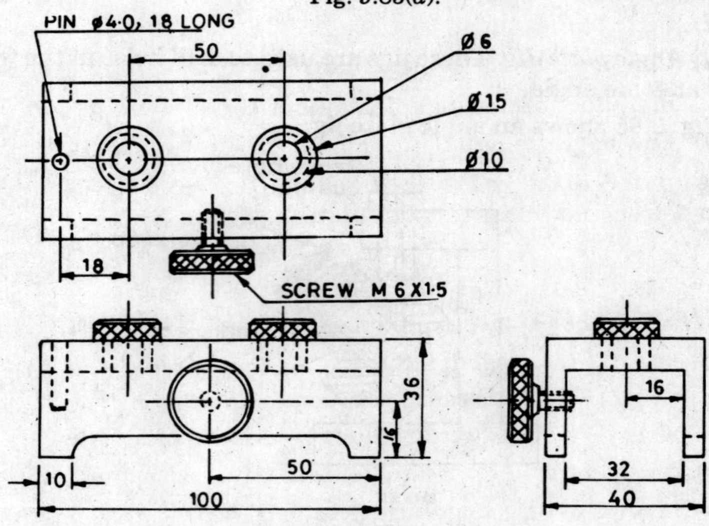

Fig. 9.85(*c*)

9.28.1. Assembly tool drawing. It shows the entire tool in its completed form with all parts in their proper places indicating all dimensions.

Fig. 9.85 *(c)* shows a channel drilling jig assembly with typical dimensions.

9.28.2. Selection of a Jig

Selection of a jig depends upon the following factors :

(i) Type of work

(ii) Scale of production

(iii) Type of machining operation

(iv) Method of locating and clamping

(v) Loading and unloading time should be minimum

(vi) Cost of jig.

9.29. Fixtures

They are used to hold a work-piece during machining operation. Fixture is always fixed to the machine bench. The use of fixture becomes essential when components to be produced are in larger number.

The economic aspects of the use of a fixture can be considered on the following basis :

(i) Cost of fixture should be low.

(ii) Fixture life should be more.

(iii) Components for which fixture is to be used are to be manufactured in sufficient quantity per year.

(iv) Low operating cost.

The number of pieces (N) to be manufactured per year to break even on a proposed fixture are calculated as follows

$$N = \frac{C \times k + S \times R}{E(1 + D)}$$

where N = Number of pieces produced per year

C = Cost of fixture

S = Difference between unamortised and scrap value of old fixture

R = Yearly interest on capital (expressed as a decimal)

E = Savings in direct operating cost per piece

D = Percentage of burden (expressed as a decimal).

$$K = R + U + T + \frac{1}{A}$$

where U = Yearly percentage of cost for up keep (Expressed as a decimal)

T = Yearly percentage of cost for taxes, insurance etc.

A = Years required for amortising the cost of the fixture out of savings

Fixtures are bolted to the machine table. Whenever necessary tenon blocks screwed to the under side of the fixture can be used to locate the fixture on the machine table in the correct position as shown in Fig. 9.86.

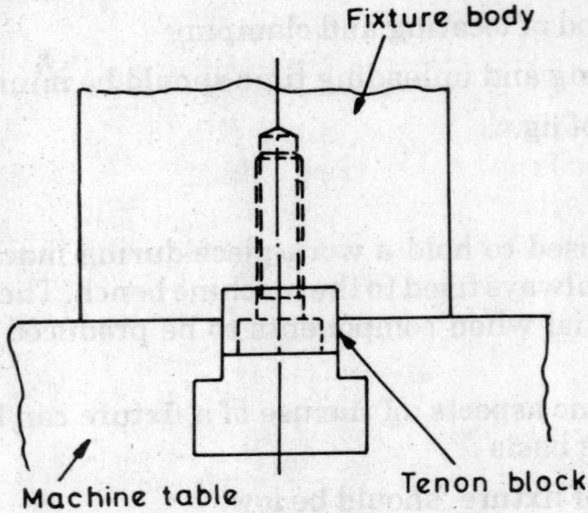

Fig. 9.86

9.29.1 Jigs and Fixture Bodies. Jigs and fixture bodies provide a rigid base for mounting the locators, supports, clamps and for holding the workpiece. The bodies may be

(*i*) Cast bodies

(*ii*) Welded bodies

(*iii*) Built up bodies

Cast bodies made of cast iron or aluminium are quite commonly used welded bodies are more costly built up bodies may be made of steel, aluminium and have the advantages like adaptability, design versatility, ease of modification and short lead time.

9.30. Milling Fixtures

A milling fixture is used to hold the work piece in correct relation to the cutter. The fixture is attached to the milling machine table by means of *T*-bolts or hold down clamps.

Milling fixture consists of following parts :

(*i*) Base

(*ii*) Clamps

(*iii*) Rest blocks or nest

(*iv*) Locating points

(*v*) *T*-Bolts

(*vi*) Gaging surfaces

The base of milling fixture consists of a base plate which has flat and accurate under surface and forms the main body on which various components are mounted. This surface mates with the surface of the milling machine table and forms the reference plane with respect to the mill feed movements. The base is provided with slots for the purpose of clamping the fixture to the mill table. The clamping devices used should be extremely rigid, clamps must not loosen by vibrations caused by interrupted cutting of milling cutter. Rest blocks provide support to the work piece.

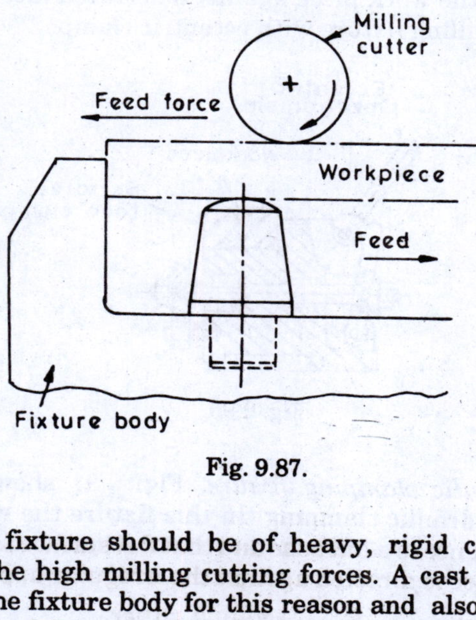

Fig. 9.87.

Milling fixture should be of heavy, rigid construction to withstand the high milling cutting forces. A cast iron casting is chosen for the fixture body for this reason and also because it has the property of damping the vibrations during milling operation. Fig. 9.87 shows work piece resting against the solid face of fixture body to resist the considerable feed force of the milling operation.

9.31. Types of Milling Fixtures

Various types of milling fixtures are as follows.

(*i*) *String or line milling fixtures.* In this fixture number of components are strung behind each other in a line. The fixture moves relative to the cutters as shown in Fig. 9.88 and Fig. 9.89.

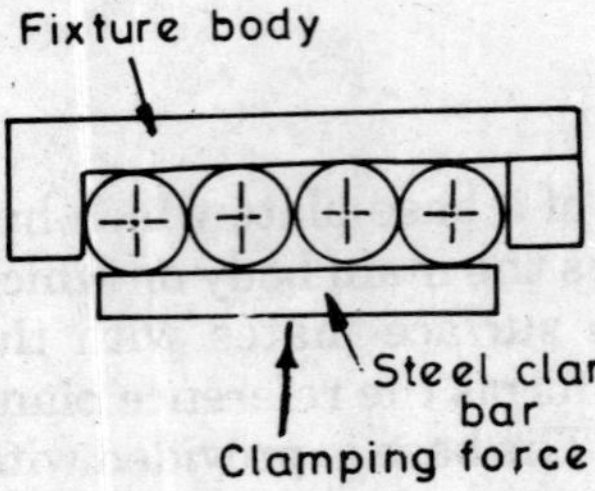

Fig. 9.88.

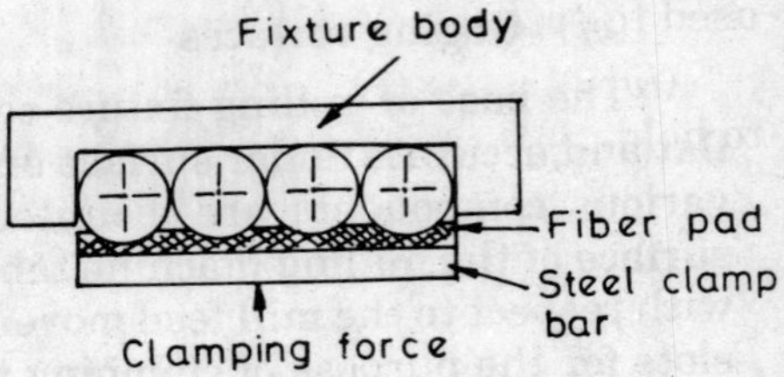

Fig. 9.89.

(*ii*) *Eccentric clamp Fixture.* In this fixture an eccentric clamp is used to hold the work piece against a serrated face clamp. Fig. 9.90 shows a milling fixture with eccentric clamp.

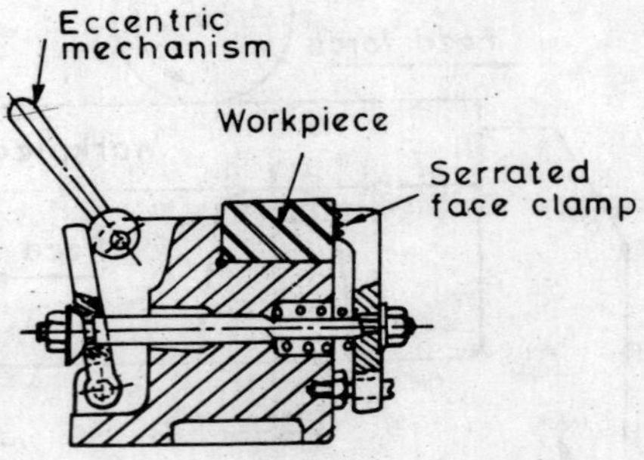

Fig. 9.90.

(*iii*) *Hydraulic clamping fixture.* Fig. 9.91 shows a milling fixture with hydraulic clamping. In this fixture the work piece is located by reference to a flat base and that flat surfaces of a key-way. The holding force is directed against the irregular upper surface of

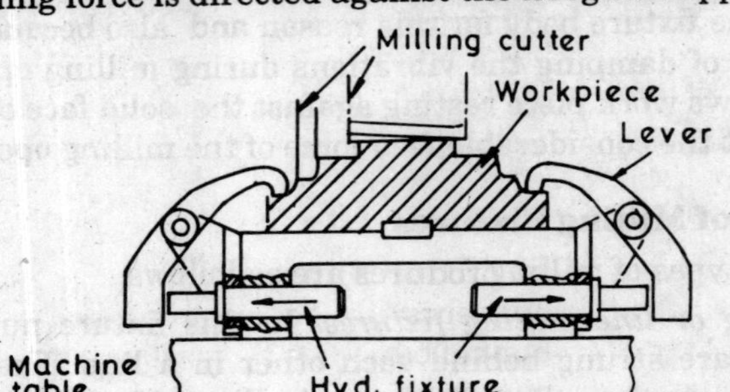

Fig. 9.91.

the works piece. Hydraulic force is applied by means of pistons is used to operate clamping levers.

(*iv*) *Spring type fixture.* Fig. 9.92 shows a spring operated fixture to hold the work-piece in position by means of a screw clamp.

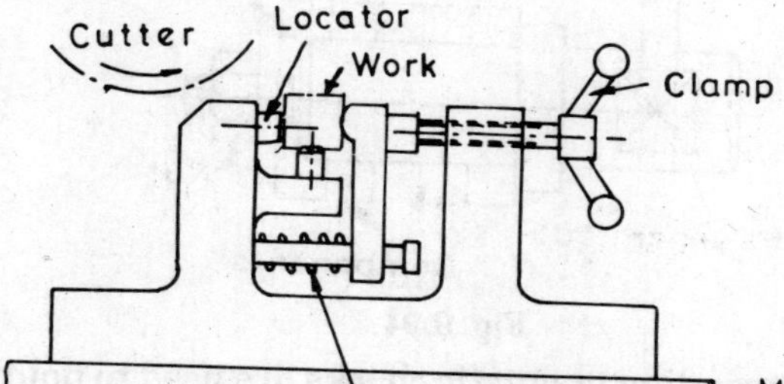

Fig. 9.92.

(*v*) *Clamp type fixture.* Fig. 9.93 shows a milling fixture for cutting key slots in circular shafts. Clamp is used to keep the work piece in position.

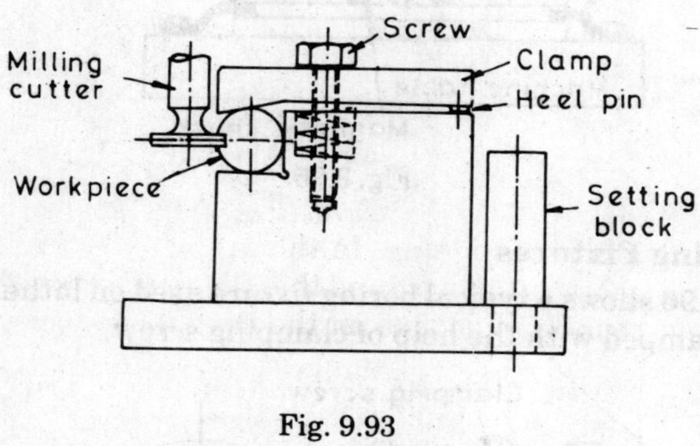

Fig. 9.93

9.32. Grinding Fixtures

Fig. 9.94 shows a plain production type cylindrical grinding mandrel. A number of components can be mounted on the arbor which is ground to the low limit of bore. The C - washer is used with a nut for clamping. A driving peg is driven into the shank of the mandrel. Spanner flats allow the mandrel to be gripped when the clamping nut is being tightened.

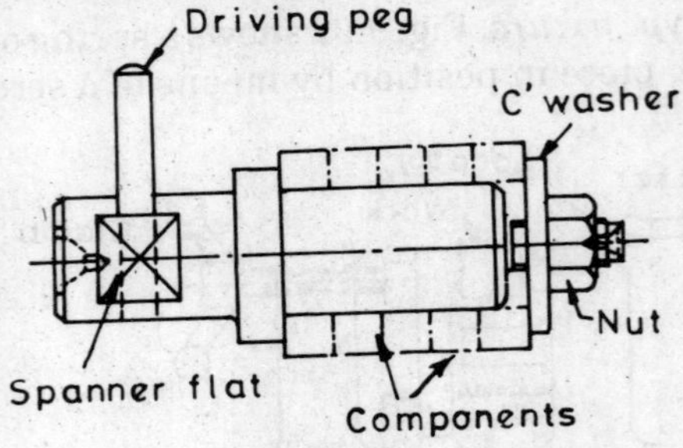

Fig. 9.94.

For surface grinding magnetic checks are used to hold the work pieces directly or to hold a fixture which holds the work pieces. Vices may be held by the magnetic chuck. Fig. 9.95 shows a magnetic chuck commonly used for holding work pieces during surface grinding.

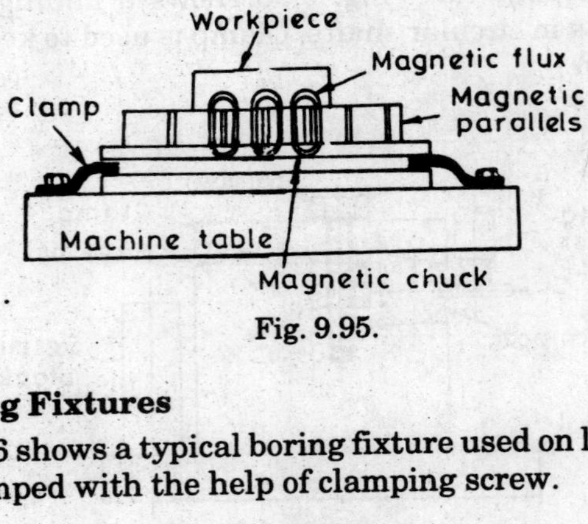

Fig. 9.95.

9.33. Boring Fixtures

Fig. 9.96 shows a typical boring fixture used on lathe. The work piece is clamped with the help of clamping screw.

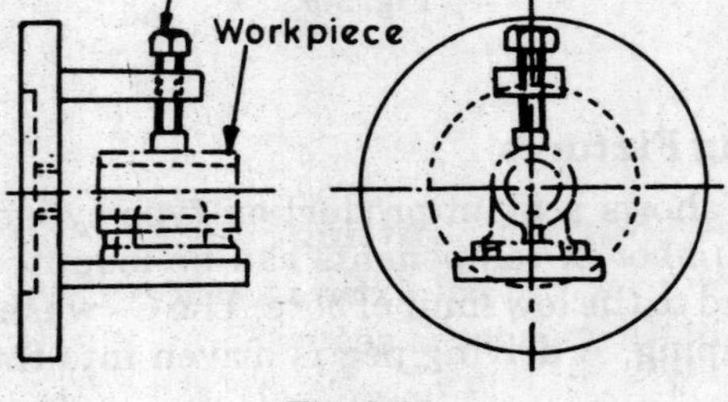

Fig. 9.96.

Fig. 9.97 shows a face plate boring fixture. An angle plate P is clamped to the face plate of the lathe with the seat of the angle plate located at the correct distance from the centre line of the lathe spindle. A balancing counter weight (K) is used to balance approximately the over hung angle and the work is bored by employing a single point boring tool. Clamping bolts (B) are used for clamping purpose.

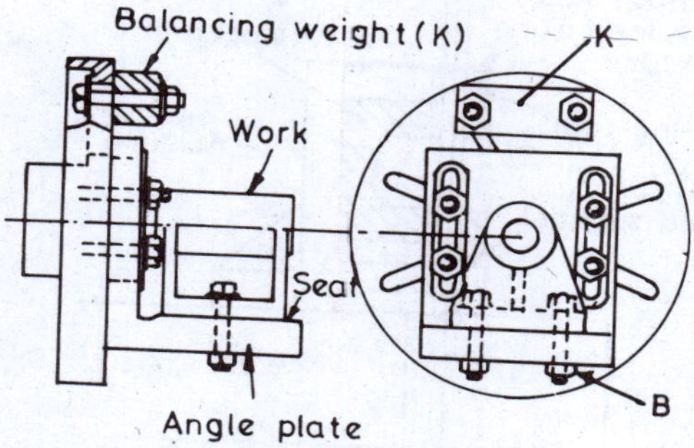

Fig. 9.97

Fig. 9.98 shows a boring fixture in which the work piece is used as a support for the boring bar. Bushings are inserted in previously bored holes.

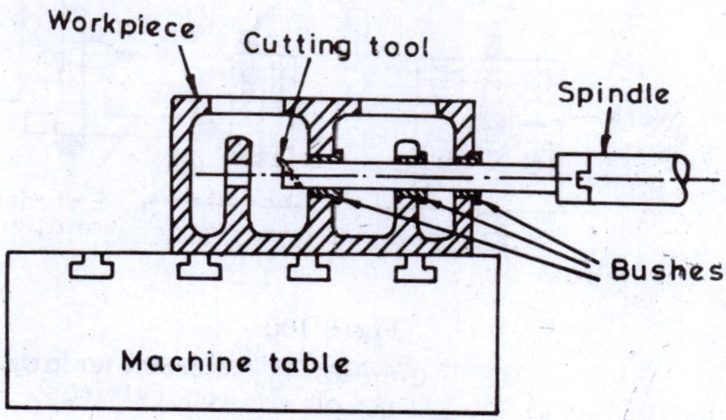

Fig. 9.98

Fig. 9.99 shows a fixture for line boring operation using end support mounted in fixture. The fixture holds the workpiece in correct position relative to the boring bar.

9.34. Fixture for Key Way Cutting

Fig. 9.100 shows a typical fixture for cutting internal keyways on a shaper. The work piece is seated in a V-block that is part of the fixture and clamped in place by screw. The fixture is bolted to the shaper table by T-bolts.

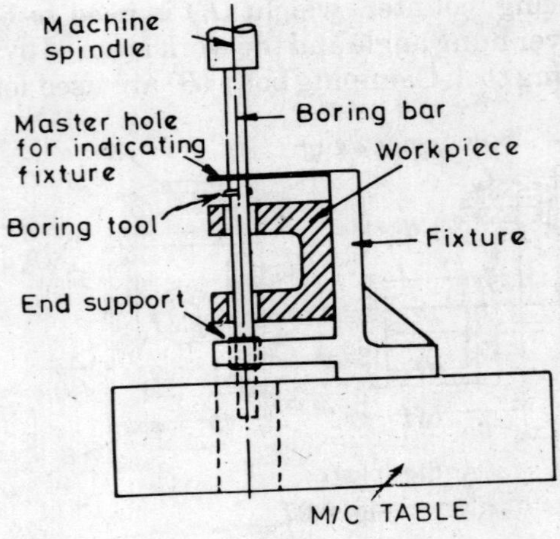

Fig. 9.99

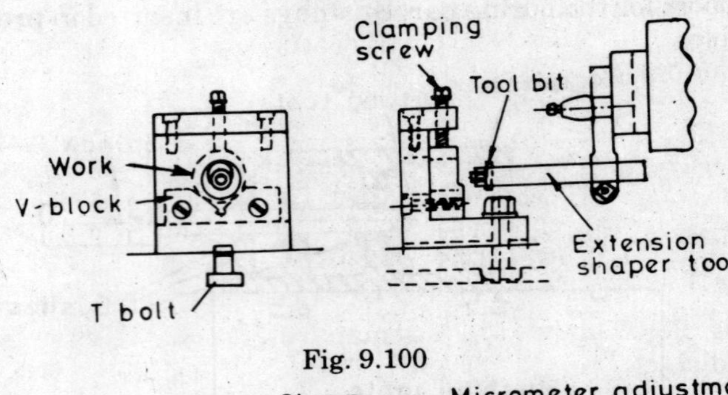

Fig. 9.100

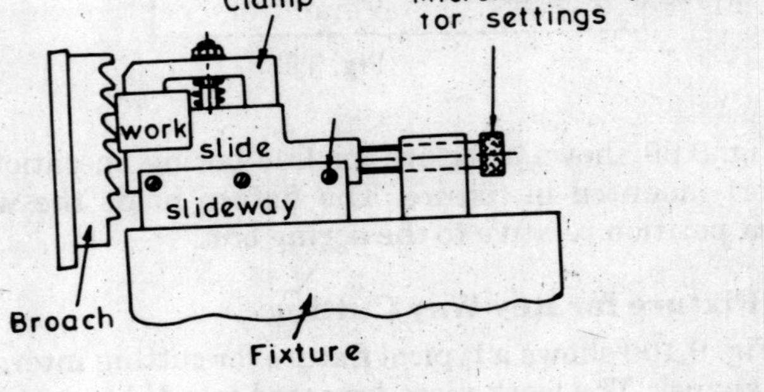

Fig. 9.101

9.35. Broaching Fixture

Fig. 9.101 shows a surface broaching fixture. The work piece is clamped using a clamping bolt.

9.35.1. Multi purpose Tooling. To carry out more than one machining operation multipurpose tools can be designed. Fig. 9.101 *(a)* shows a drill jig/milling fixture for the completed part shown in Fig. 9.101 *(b)*.

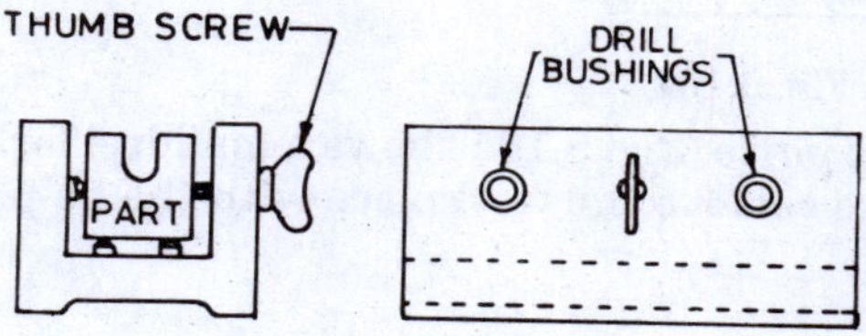

Fig. 9.101 (*a*)

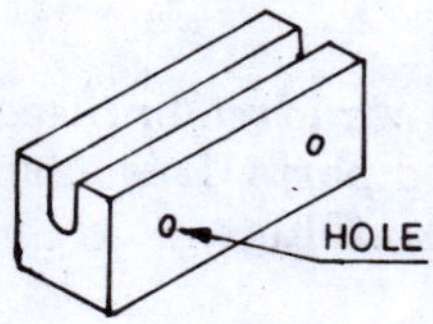

Fig. 9.101 (*b*)

9.36. Lathe Mandrels

They are used to support work pieces having holes. Various types of mandrels used are as follows :

(*i*) *Plain mandrel or solid mandrel.* It has a slight taper to permit it to be pressed into hollow workpiece. The taper provided is 0.004 to 0.006 inch per foot.

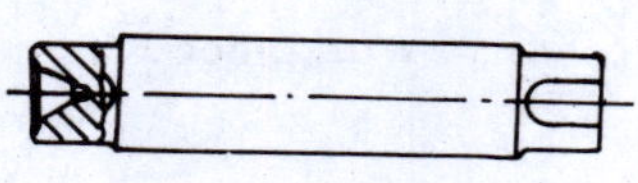

Fig. 9.102.

Fig. 9.102 shows a plain mandrel. It is made of hardened and ground steel.

Fig. 9.103 shows a plain mandrel mounted between centres.

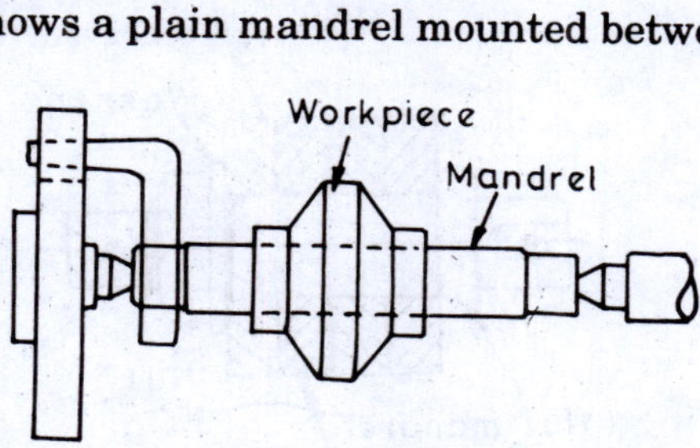

Fig. 9.103

(*ii*) *Expanding type mandrel.* It is sufficiently tapered (Fig. 9.104). So that it will expand the sleeve to permit it to grip the work piece. There are generally several sizes of sleeves for each mandrel.

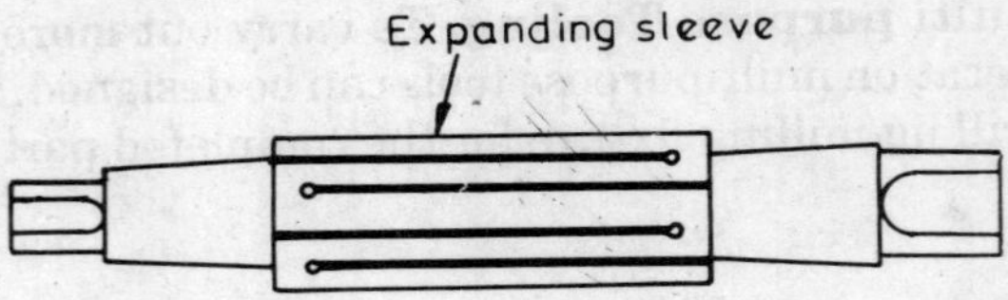

Fig. 9.104

(*iii*) *Mandrel for threaded parts.* Fig. 9.105 shows a mandrel for threaded parts. It is easier to remove the workpiece with the help of knock off lugs.

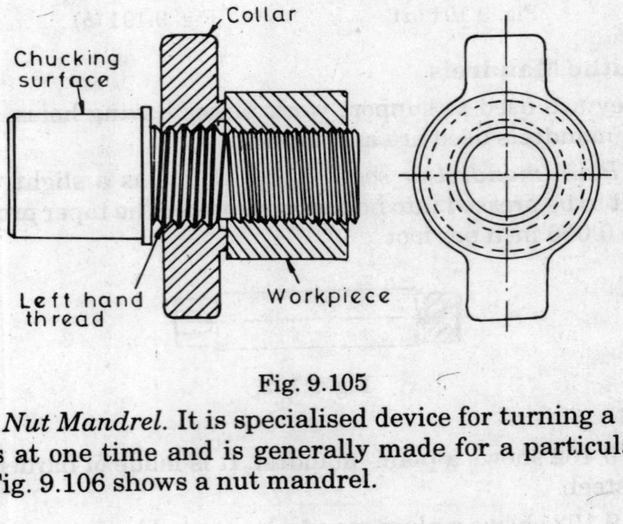

Fig. 9.105

(*iv*) *Nut Mandrel.* It is specialised device for turning a number of parts at one time and is generally made for a particular work piece. Fig. 9.106 shows a nut mandrel.

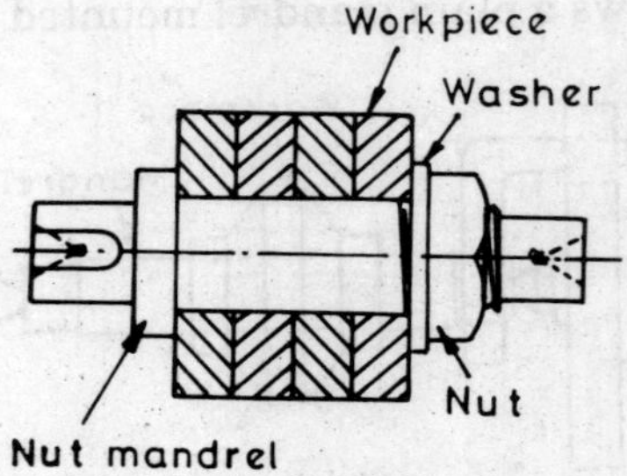

Fig. 9.106

9.37. Nesting Fixture for Brazing. Fig. 9.106 (a) shows a nesting fixture in which two work piece and brazing ring have been placed.

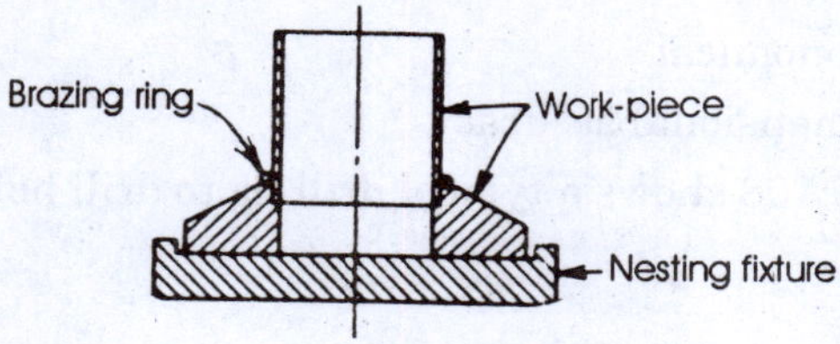

Fig. 9.106(*a*)

Example 9.1. (*a*) *State the initial characteristics for proper design of jigs and fixture.*

(*b*) *Sketch a suitable drilling jig for producing holes in the component shown in Fig. 9.107.*

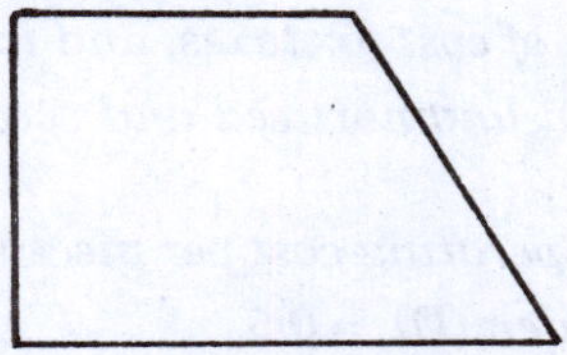

Fig. 9.107.

Solution. *(a)* For proper design of jigs and fixture the essential characteristics are as follows :

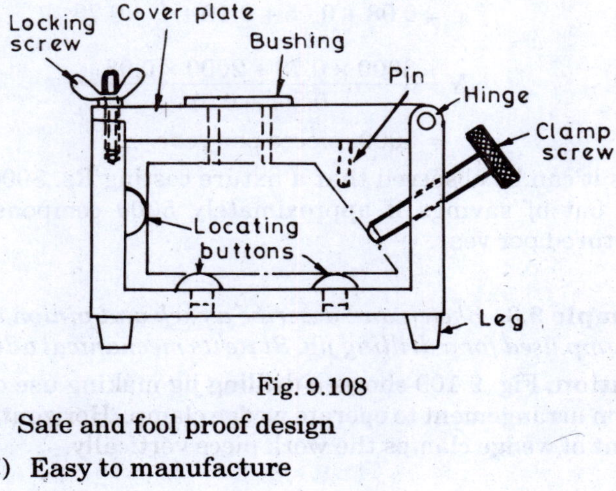

Fig. 9.108

(*i*) Safe and fool proof design

(*ii*) Easy to manufacture

(*iii*) Ease to handling

(*iv*) Ruggedness

(*v*) Adaptability

(*vi*) Economical

(*vii*) Dimensional accuracy.

(*b*) Fig. 9.108 shows a typical drill jig to drill holes in the given component.

Example 9.2. *Determine the number of pieces that should be produced using a fixture for following details*

Cost of fixture (C) = Rs. 8000

Years of amortising the cost of fixture (A) =2

Rate of interest on capital (R) = 8% = 0.08

Yearly percentage of cost for up keep (U) = 0.05

Yearly percentage of cost for taxes, and insurance (T) = 0.10

Difference between unamortised and scrap value of old fixture (S) = Rs. 2000

Saving in direct operating cost per piece (E) = Rs. 0.8

Percentage of burden (D) = 0.5

Solution.
$$N = \frac{C \times K + S \times R}{E\ (1 + D)}$$

where
$$K = R + U + T + \frac{1}{A}$$

$$= 0.08 + 0.05 + 0.10 + \frac{1}{2} = 0.73$$

$$N = \frac{8000 \times 0.73 + 2000 \times 0.08}{0.8(1 + 0.5)}$$

$$= 5000 \text{ pieces per year.}$$

Thus it can be observed that a fixture costing Rs. 8000 can be paid for out of savings if approximately 5000 components are manufactured per year.

Example 9.3. *Sketch and describe a rack and pinion operated wedge clamp used for a drilling jig. State its mechanical advantage.*

Solution. Fig. 9.109 shows a drilling jig making use of a rack and pinion arrangement to operate wedge clamp. Horizontal linear movement of wedge clamps the work piece vertically.

Let h = Work movement

θ = Lever movement

P = Effort

F = Clamping force.

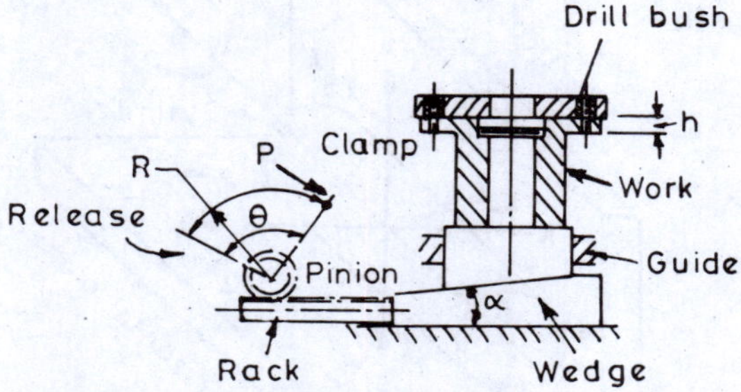

Fig. 9.109.

α = Wedge angle

R = Lever radius

D = Pitch circle diameter of pinion

$$\theta = \frac{360\, h}{\pi D \tan\alpha}$$

$$P = \frac{FD \tan \alpha}{2R}$$ assuming 100% efficiency for the mechanism.

$$\text{M.A. (Mechanical advantage)} = \frac{F}{P}.$$

Example 9.4. *Sketch and describe a fixture to support a rough casting.*

Solution. Fig. 9.110 shows a fixture to support a rough casting. Adjustable locators have been provided to position the casting. Fixture body is a cast construction.

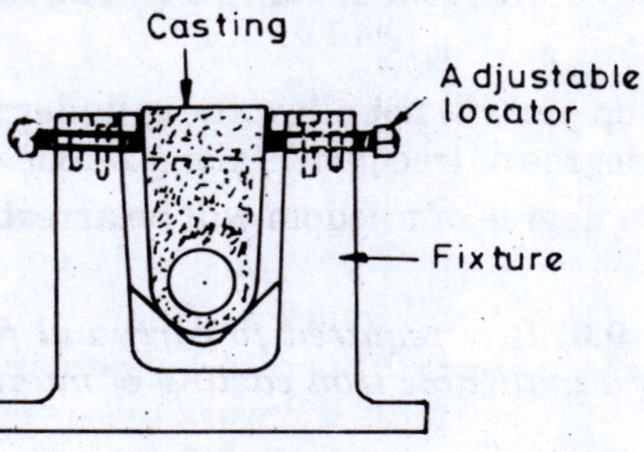

Fig. 9.110.

Example 9.5. *Determine the degrees of freedom arrested by V locator with a stop pin of a cylindrical workpiece shown in Fig. 9.111.*

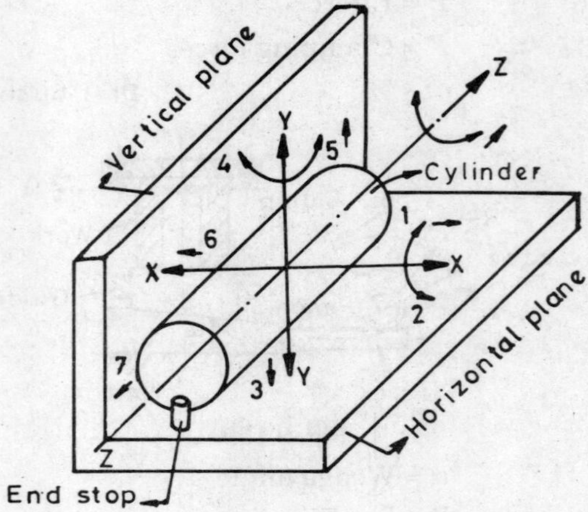

Fig. 9.111.

Solution. The cylindrical has 12 degrees of freedom.

The *V*-locator with stop pin will arrest seven degrees of freedom explained as follows :

(*i*) The horizontal base plane is parallel to *X* and *Z* axis. It will restrict the movement of the cylinder from rotating about *X* axis and downward translatory movement along *Y* axis. Thus degree of freedom 1, 2 and 3 will be restricted.

(*ii*) The vertical plane which is parallel to *Y* and *Z* axis will not allow the cylinder to have rotary motion about *Y* axis and to have translatory motion along, *X* axis leftward in the direction of freedom 6. Thus degrees of freedom 4, 5 and 6 will be restricted.

(*iii*) The stop pin will not allow the cylinder to have translatory motion along degree of freedom 7, along *Z*-axis.

Thus seven degree of freedom will be arrested.

Example 9.6. *It is required to carry out face milling on two flange faces of a malleable iron casting of manifold shown in Fig. 9.112.*

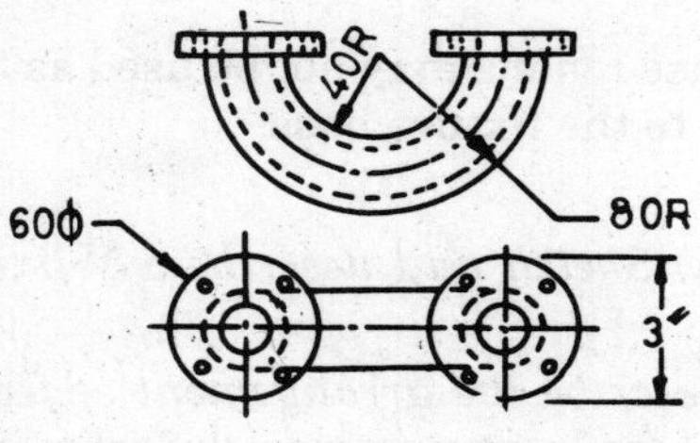

Fig. 9.112.

Prepare a design study for single piece loading showing the location method based on the six point location principle, and the clamping points.

Solution. Face milling can be carried out on vertical milling machine with the flange faces horizontal.

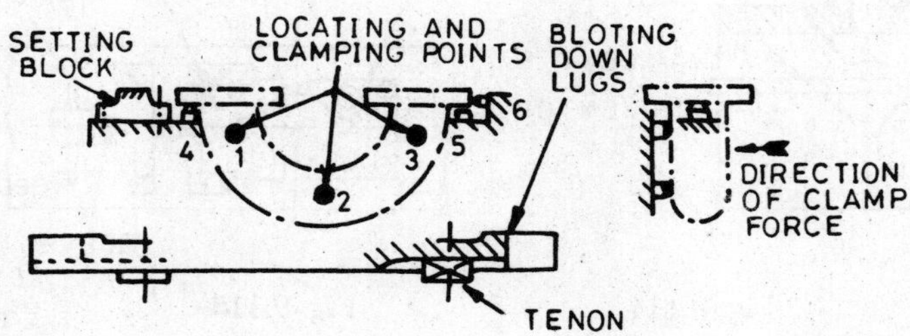

Fig. 9.113.

(*a*) **Location points.** (*i*) Location will be taken from the pipe and since it has a cast surface three point location (points, 1, 2, 3) must be used.

(*ii*) To keep the flanges horizontal two location points 4 and 5 should be provided.

(*iii*) End movement of manifold must be prevented by a single point 6.

(*b*) **Clamping points.** Clamping force must be applied on positively supported surfaces *i.e.* directly above the location points. Locating points 4 and 5 cannot be used because the surfaces to be machined are above these locating points. Therefore locating points 1 and 3 will be the choice. Suitable clamping devices can be used as shown in Fig. 9.113. Tenons are usually essential for milling fixtures but in this case tenons may not be used as the face milling need only be parallel to the fixture base.

Example 9.7. (*a*) *Sketch and describe a V-fixture to locate a round workpiece.*

(*b*) *Sketch and describe the arrangement of fixed and sliding V-blocks arrangement for locating a round workpiece.*

Solution. (*a*) Fig. 9.114 shows a *V*-fixture for locating a round workpiece. Any variation in workpiece size will not affect the centre line accuracy.

(*b*) Fig. 9.115 shows a typical fixed and sliding *V* locator for locating a round workpiece.

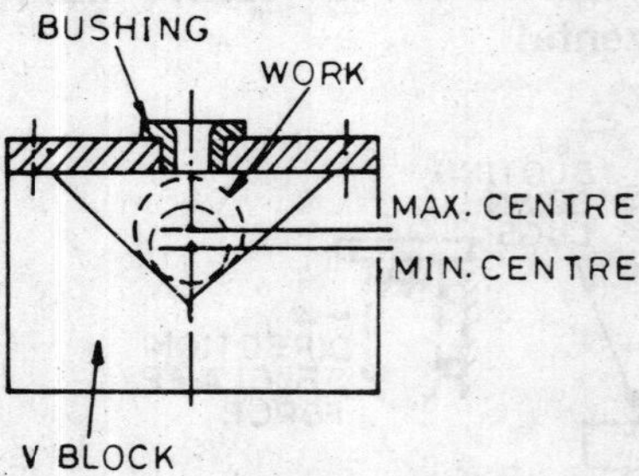

Fig. 9.114.

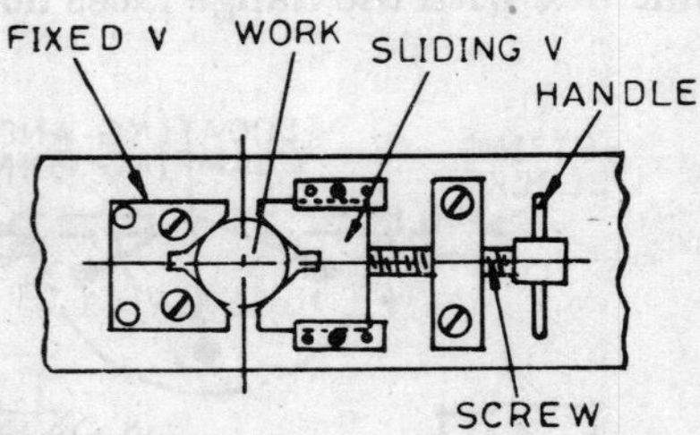

Fig. 9.115.

Example 9.8. (*a*) *Sketch and describe a sliding and fixed V-block arrangement for locating a lever shown in Fig. 9.116.*

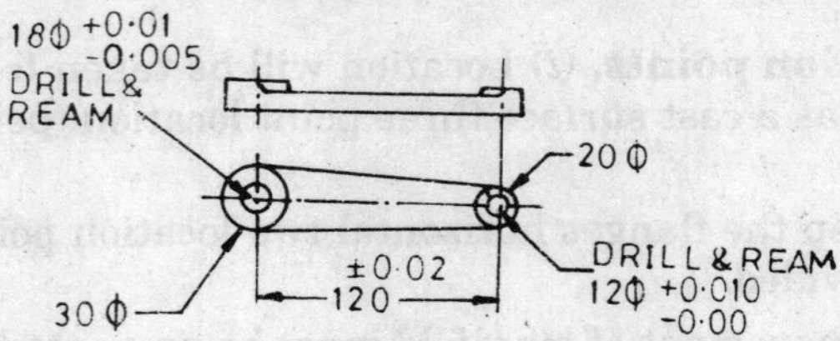

Fig. 9.116.

(*b*) *Sketch the location of lever on two plugs.*

Solution. (*a*) A fixed and sliding Vee block arrangement to locate the given lever is shown in Fig. 9.117.

(*b*) Fig. 9.118 shows location of lever upon two plugs. Two completely round location plugs would allow much less variation in the hole centres thus providing a very precise form of location.

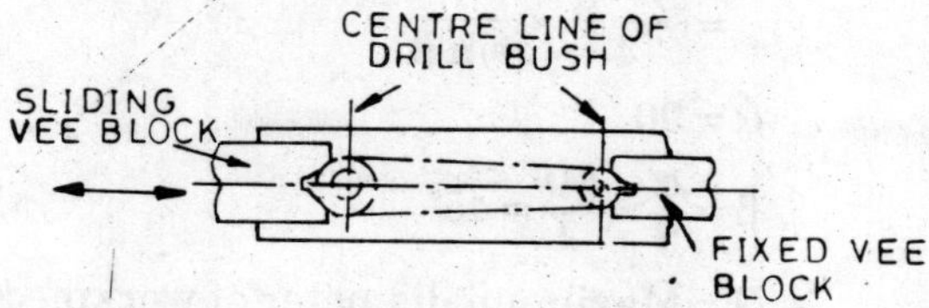

Fig. 9.117.

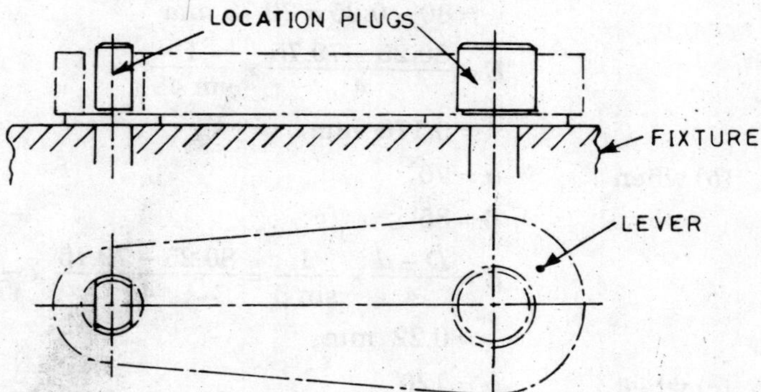

Fig. 9.118.

Example 9.9. *A hole is to be drilled in a 80 mm diameter rod which has a tolerance of ±0.25 mm. V-block fixture is to be used. Determine the possible variations from the centre line of the drill bushing when*

(*a*) 90° *V-block is used.*

(*b*) 70° *V-block is used.*

(*c*) 120° *V-block is used.*

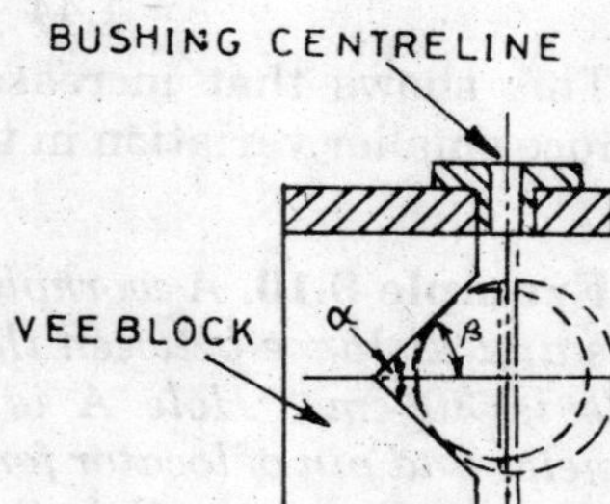

Fig. 9.119.

Sketch the fixture :

Solution. (*a*) Fig. 9.119 shows a *V*-block fixture

Let α = Included angle of *V*–block

Angle $\beta = \dfrac{\alpha}{2}$

E = Variation from the centre line of bushing

$$= \frac{D-d}{4} \times \frac{1}{\sin \beta}$$

$$\alpha = 90$$

$$\beta = \frac{\alpha}{2} = \frac{90}{2} = 45^\circ$$

D = Maximum diameter of workpiece

$= 80 + 0.25 = 80.25$ mm

d = Minimum diameter of workpiece

$= 80 - 0.25 = 79.75$ mm

$$E = \frac{80.25 - 79.75}{4} \times \frac{1}{\sin 45}$$

$= 0.176$ mm.

(*b*) when $\alpha = 70^\circ$

$$\beta = 35^\circ$$

$$E = \frac{D-d}{4} \times \frac{1}{\sin \beta} = \frac{80.25 - 79.75}{4} \times \frac{1}{\sin 35}$$

$= 0.22$ mm.

(*c*) when $\alpha = 120^\circ$

$$\beta = 60^\circ$$

$$E = \frac{D-d}{4} \times \frac{1}{\sin \beta} = \frac{80.25 - 79.75}{4} \times \frac{1}{\sin 60}$$

$= 1.44$ mm.

This shows that increase is included angle of *V*-block will produce smaller variation in the location.

Example 9.10. *A workpiece has two holes and distance between the centres of holes is 30 cm. Hole A is of 50 mm diameter and pin of locator for hole A is of 49.998 mm diameter. Hole B is of 44 mm diameter and pin B is of 43.998 mm diameter. Find the maximum possible angular error when the workpiece is placed in the fixture.*

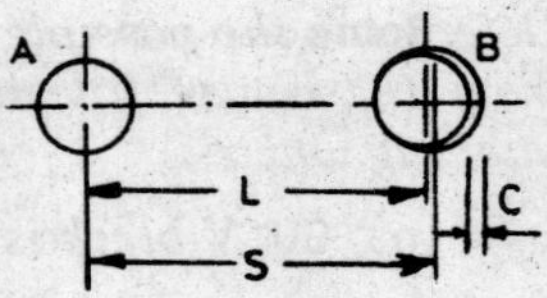

Fig. 9.120

Solution. The holes are shown in Fig. 9.120.

Let D_1 = Diameter of hole A

$= 50$ mm

D_2 = Diameter of hole B $= 44$ mm

$$d_1 = \text{Diameter of pin at } A$$
$$= 49.8 \text{ mm}$$
$$d_2 = \text{Diameter of pin at } B$$
$$= 43.8 \text{ mm}$$
$$L = \text{Centre distance between holes}$$
$$= 300 \text{ mm}$$
$$\alpha = \text{Angular error}$$
$$\tan\alpha = \frac{(D_1 + D_2) - (d_1 + d_2)}{L}$$
$$= \frac{(50 + 44) - (44.8 + 43.8)}{300}$$
$$= 0.0013$$
$$\alpha = 0^\circ - 48'$$

Example 9.11. (*a*) *Sketch and describe a location method to drill a hole in a cast or forged boss of a component.*

(*b*) *Sketch and describe correct application of vee location for a cylindrical workpiece.*

Solution. (*a*) Fig. 9.121 shows a concentric location for cast or forged bosses in which a hole is to be drilled. A cone is used to locate the boss Co-axial with the drill bush.

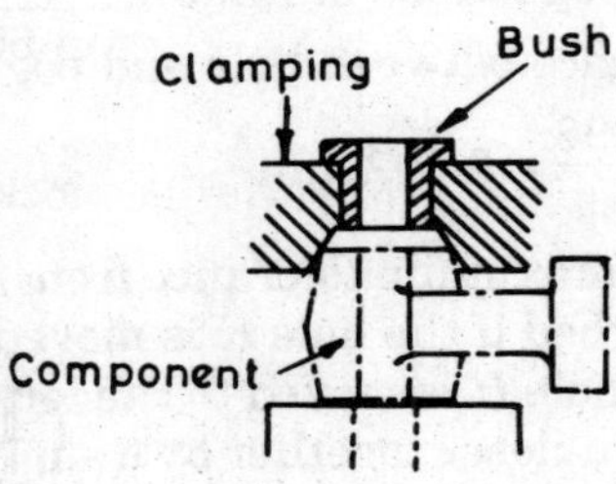

Fig. 9.121

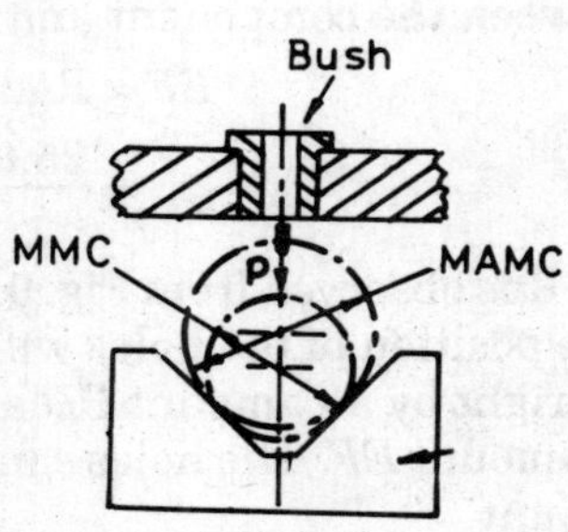

Fig. 9.122.

(*b*) Fig. 9.122 shows correct application of vee-location in which variations in workpiece diameter do not affect the position of drilled hole relative to the component centre line. The workpiece is positively supported against cutting and clamping force (*P*). MMC indicates minimum metal condition and MAMC indicates maximum metal condition.

Example 9.12. *The two location plugs in a milling fixture are 24.996 and 24.995 mm diameter, one being milled to 7.6 mm across flats. If the holes of the component which fit on the location pegs are reamed to 25.000 and 25.002 mm diameter. Calculate the maximum pitch variation which can be permitted when producing the holes in the component.*

Solution. Fig. 9.123 shows hole *H* and peg

Hole *H* size is 25.000 and 25.002 mm.

Peg size is 24.996 and 24.995 mm.

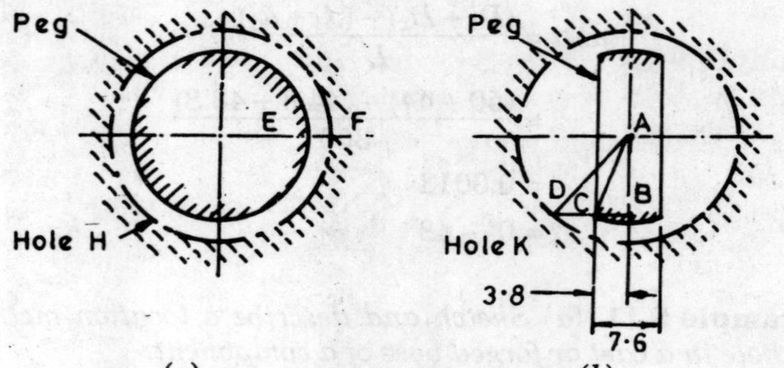

Fig. 9.123.

when Minimum Metal Condition (MMC) occurs *i.e.* when hole is 25.000 mm in diameter (Low limit of hole) and the location peg 24.996 mm in diameter (High limit of Shaft) then the clearance between the component and location peg will be minimum.

$$EF = \text{Radial clearance between hole and peg}$$

$$= \frac{25.000 - 24.996}{2} = 0.002 \text{ mm}$$

It is observed from Fig. 9.124 that maximum tolerance from the true position of the holes will be absorbed if the hole *K* is moved to the right by an amount *CD* and if the hole *H* is moved to the left by an amount *EF*. The holes can also move closer together by a similar amount.

$$x = \text{Total tolerance on pitch of holes}$$

$$= \pm(CD + EF)$$

$$CD = BD - BC$$

$$= \sqrt{[AD^2 - AB^2]} - BC$$

$$= \sqrt{[AD^2 - (AC - BC^2)]} - BC$$

$$= \sqrt{[AD^2 + (AC + BC)(AC - BC)]} - BC$$

$$= \sqrt{12.5^2 - \left[\left(\frac{24.996}{2} + \frac{7.6}{4}\right)\left(\frac{24.996}{2} - \frac{7.6}{2}\right)\right]} - \frac{7.9}{2}$$

$$= 0.006 \text{ mm.}$$

$$x = \text{Total tolerance on pitch of holes}$$

$$= \pm(CD + EF)$$

$$= \pm(0.006 + 0.002)$$

$$= \pm 0.008 \text{ mm.}$$

Example 9.13. *Sketch and describe a typical turning fixture with location from the workpiece profile.*

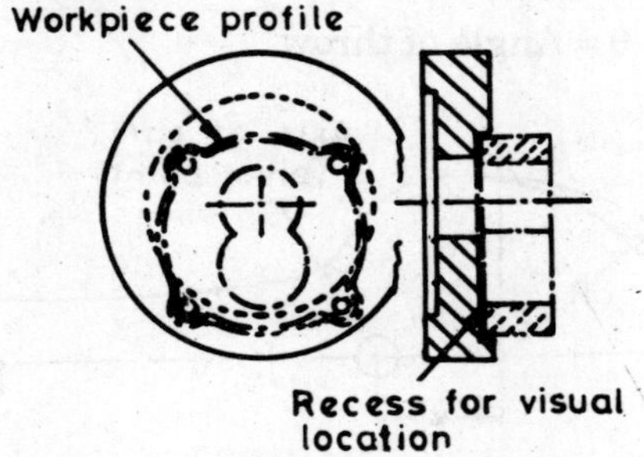

Fig. 9.124.

Solution. To provide a machinist with the means for visually setting a workpiece with an irregular profile in a symmetrical position in a jig, a profile plate or recess may be used as shown in Fig. 9.124.

Example 9.14. *Define and describe the following for cam in a cam operated clamping device.*

(*i*) *Rise*

(*ii*) *Throw*

(*iii*) *Eccentricity.*

Explain the working of eccentric and spiral cam. How each type is constructed.

Solution.

(*i*) *Rise.* It is the amount of movement perpendicular to the cam face which takes place when cam is moved through the arc of engagement or throw.

(*ii*) *Throw.* It is the cam rotation through a specified arc.

(*iii*) *Eccentricity.* It is the distance between centre line of pivot point and the centre of radius required to actuate the cam.

Fig. 9.125 shows an eccentric cam. It is constructed first by drawing the pivot point. The eccentric centre is then offset by the amount calculated and finally required radius is drawn using the eccentric point as the centre.

$$e = \frac{x}{1 - \cos \theta}$$

where e = Eccentricity

x = Rise

θ = Angle of throw

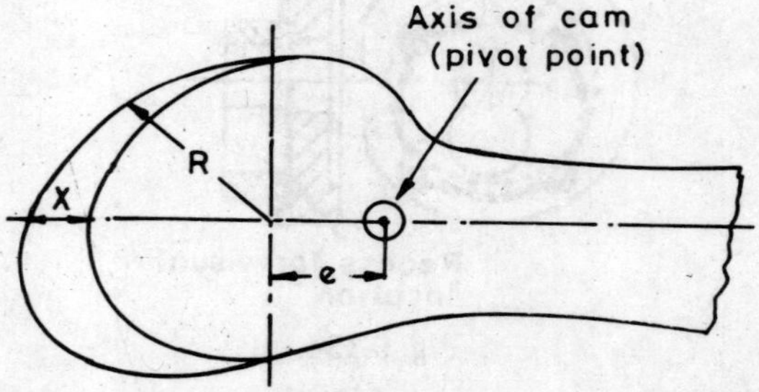

Fig. 9.125.

$$R = e\left(\cos \theta + \frac{\sin \theta}{\mu}\right)$$

where R = Radius required to actuate the cam

μ = Coefficient of friction.

The value of μ is generally taken as 0.10.

Rise in a spiral cam depends on length of throw and radius of base circle.

$$x = \text{Rise (mm)} = 0.001 \times R_1 \times \theta$$

where R_1 = Base circle radius (mm)

θ = Throw in degrees.

The spiral cam is generated from the base circle. The outer and inner circles represent the limits of cam rise. Usually there should be 0.025 mm rise per 25 mm of radius per degree of throw. Cam throw is usually 60 – 90 degrees. An additional 5 to 10 degrees should be added to each end of throw angle as shown in Fig. 9.126.

Total throw angle $= 90 + 2 \times 5$

$= 100^\circ$

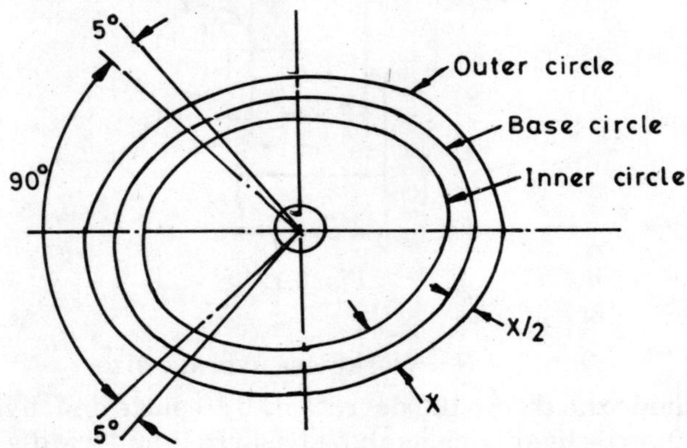

Fig. 9.126.

In spiral cam first base circle is drawn and then inner and outer circles are drawn. The limits of throw are then marked.

x = Rise.

Example 9.15. *In a cam operated clamping device the cam has a base circle of 60 mm diameter and total rise takes place through 100 degrees. The middle of the rise is to clamp the average block size. Design the cam.*

Solution. θ = Throw = 100 degrees

R_1 = Base circle radius $= \frac{60}{2} = 30$ mm

x = Rise in mm

$= 0.001 \times R_1 \times \theta$

$= 0.001 \times 30 \times 100$

$= 3$ mm.

Half of the rise is above the base circle and half below the base circle as shown in Fig. 9.127.

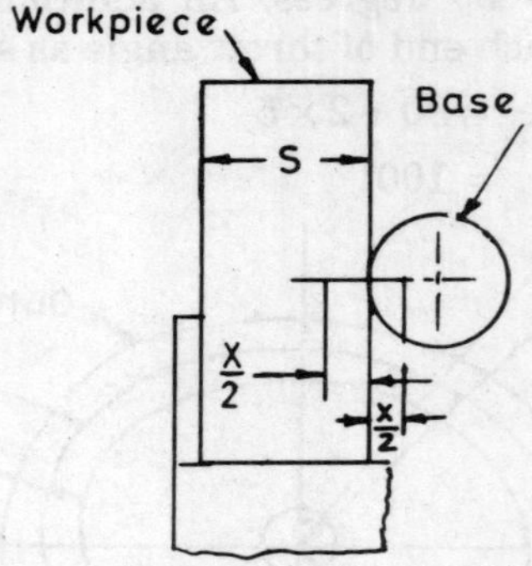

Fig. 9.127.

S = Workpiece average size

Divide the throw 100 degrees into 10 parts and divide rise also into 10 parts, five divisions above base circle and five divisions below the base circle.

From centre O draw arcs to obtain the intersection points. The intersections are joined to obtain cam surface as shown in Fig. 9.128.

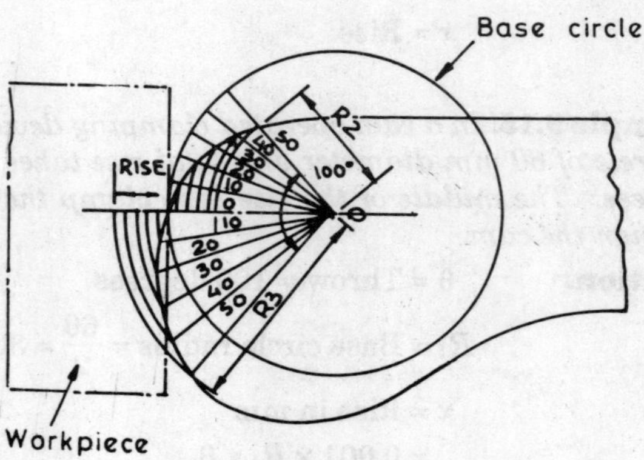

Fig. 9.128.

Example 9.16. ***In a strap clamp shown in Fig. 9.129 the bolt is halfway between the pivot point (C) and the workpiece. The distance between pivot point and workpiece is 150 mm and bolt diameter is 15 mm.***

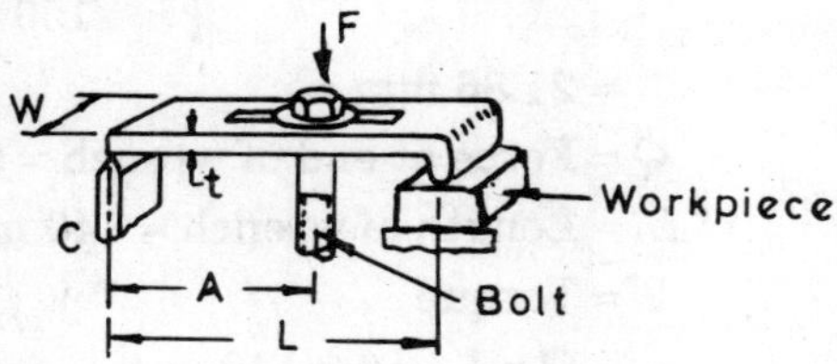

Fig. 9.129.

Determine the following :

(a) Width of strap (b) Thickness of strap

(c) If an open end wrench 140 mm long is used to tighten the bolt by applying a force of 6 kg at the end of wrench find the load an bolt.

(d) Force on workpiece.

Solution. As shown in Fig. 9.130.

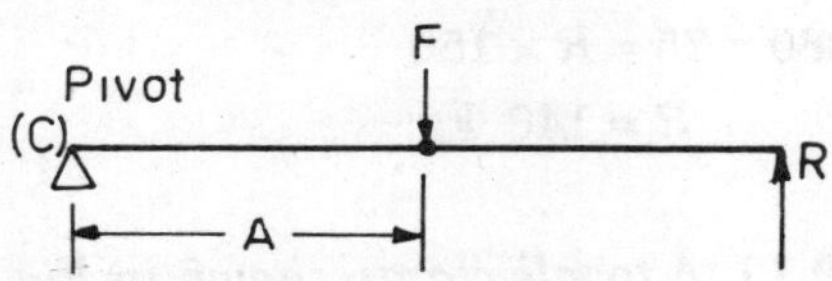

Fig. 9.130.

L = Distance between workpiece and pivot

= 150 mm

A = Distance of bolt centre to pivot point

$= \frac{L}{2} = \frac{150}{2}$

= 75 mm.

d = Bolt diameter

= 15 mm

(*a*) W = Width of strap

= 2.3 d + 1.5mm

= 2.3 × 15 + 1.5

= 36 mm

(*b*) t = Thickness of clamp

$$= \sqrt{0.85d \times A\left(1 - \frac{A}{L}\right)}$$

$$= \sqrt{0.85 \times 15 \times 75\left(1 - \frac{75}{150}\right)}$$

$= 21.86$ mm

(c) Q = Force at end of wrench = 6 kg.

L_1 = Length of wrench = 140 mm.

T = Torque

$= Q \times L_1 = 6 \times 140$

$= 840$ kg. mm

F = Force on bolt

$$= \frac{5T}{d} = \frac{5 \times 840}{15}$$

$= 280$ kg.

(d) R = Force at workpiece

Taking moments about pivot

$$F \times A = R \times L$$

$$280 \times 75 = R \times 150$$

$$R = 140 \text{ kg.}$$

Example 9.17. *A toggle clamp shown in Fig. 9.131 is required to deliver a force of 200 kg to the work piece in a fixture. Determine*

(a) *Diameter of pin*

(b) *Input force.*

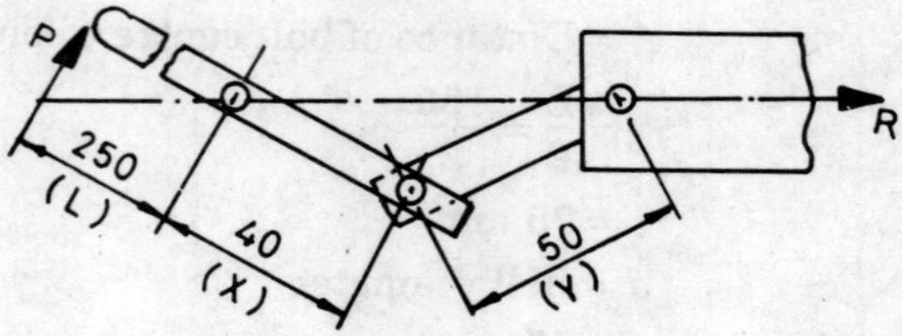

Fig. 9.131

Given : Allowable shear stress in pin is 400 kg/cm² and co-efficient of friction is 0.2.

Solution. f_s = Shear stress = 400 kg/cm^2

(a) P = Input force.

R = Output force = 200 kg.

μ = Coefficient of friction = 0.2

$$d = \text{Diameter of pin}$$

$$= 2\sqrt{\frac{\mu \cdot R}{f_s}}$$

$$= 2\sqrt{\frac{0.2 \times 200}{400}}$$

$$= 0.64 \text{ cm.}$$

$$= 6.4 \text{ cm.}$$

(*b*) $P = \text{Input force}$

$$= 4.\mu.d.R.\left(\frac{x+y}{L \times y}\right)$$

where $x = 40$ mm

$y = 50$ mm

$L = 250$ mm

$d = 6.4$ mm

$$P = 4 \times 0.2 \times 6.4 \times 200\left(\frac{40+50}{50 \times 250}\right)$$

$$= 7.38 \text{ kg.}$$

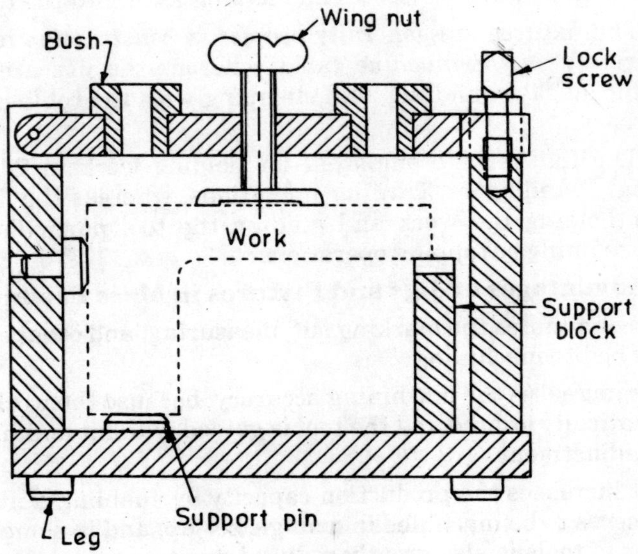

Fig. 9.132

Example 9.18. *Sketch and describe a drilling jig for drilling holes in an angle plate.*

Solution. Fig. 9.132 shows a typical drilling jig for drilling holes in an angle plate.

Example 9.19. (*a*) *State the difference between jig and fixture*

(*b*) *State advantages of using jigs and fixtures in mass production.*

(*a*) **Jig**. A jig may be defined as a device which holds and locates a workpiece and guides and controls one or more cutting tools. The holding of the work and guiding of the tool are such that they are located in true positions relative to each other.

Fixture. It may be defined as a device which holds and locates a workpiece during an inspection or for a manufacturing operation. The fixture does NOT guide the tool.

Difference betwen Jigs & Fixtures

The following are the fundamental differences between a Jig and a fixture :

(1) A fixture holds and positions the work but does not guide the tool, whereas a jig holds, locates and as well as guides the tool.

(2) The fixtures are generally *heavier in construction* and are *bolted rigidly on the machine* table, whereas the jigs are made lighter for quicker handling, and clamping with the table is often unnecessary.

(3) The fixtures are employed for holding work in 'Milling', 'Grinding' 'Planning' or 'Turning' operations, whereas the jigs are used for holding the work and guiding the tool particularly in drilling, reaming or tapping operations.

(*b*) **Advantages of Jigs and Fixtures in Mass Production:**

(1) It eliminates the marking out, measuring, and other setting mehtods before machining.

(2) It increases the machining accuracy, because the workpiece is automatically located and the tool is guided without making any manual adjustment.

(3) It increases the production capacity by enabling a number of workpieces to be machined in a single set-up, and in some cases a number of tools is also greatly reduced due to quick setting and locating of the work. The speed, feed and depth of cut for machining can be increased due to high clamping rigidity of jigs and fixtures.

(4) It reduces the operator's labour and consequent fatigue.

(5) It enables semi-skilled operator to perform the operations as setting operation of the tool and the work are mechanised. This saves labour cost.

(6) The cost of quality control of the finished products is reduced.

Example 9.20. (*Sketch and describe (i) screw clamp (ii) Cam clamp (iii) Strap clamp.*

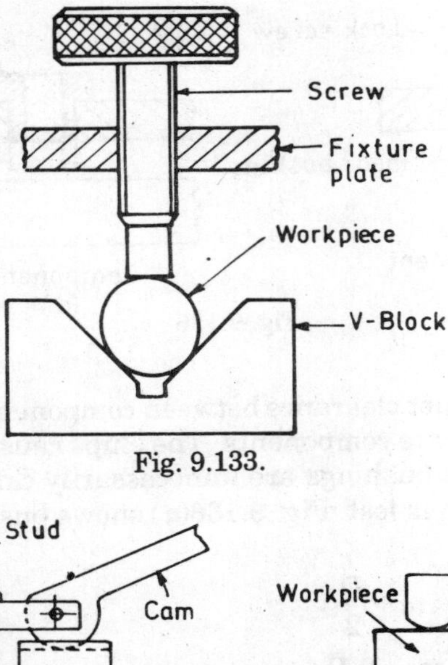

Fig. 9.133.

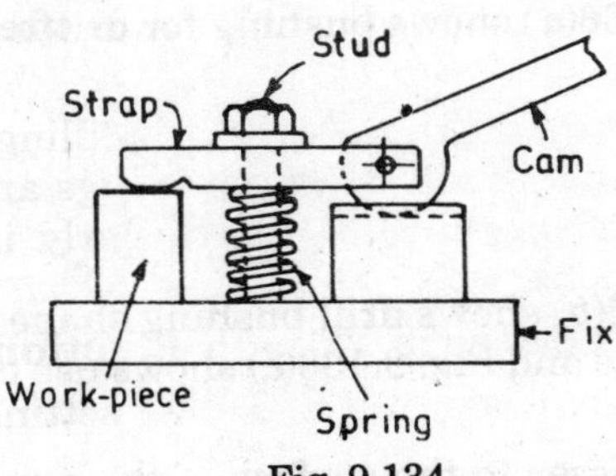

Fig. 9.134.

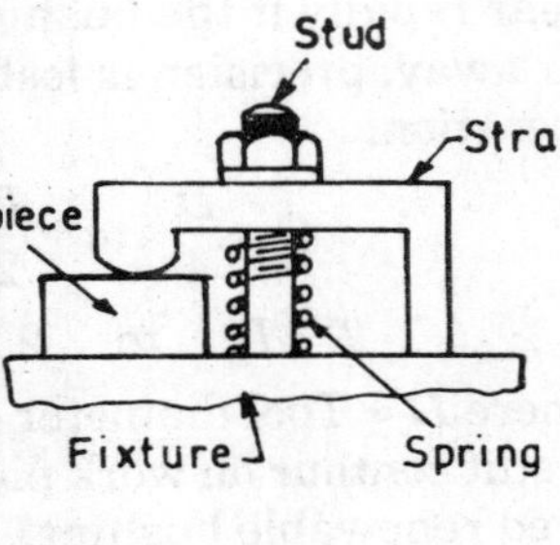

Fig. 9.135.

Solution. Fig. 9.133 shows a screw clamp. In this clamp a screw is used to hold the work piece in position. In cam clamp (Fig. 9.134) a cam is used to hold a strap in position. Which further holds the work piece in position. In strap clamp (Fig. 9.135) the strap operated by a stud and spring arrangement applies the necessary clamping force on the work piece.

Example 9.21. *Discuss four types of Drill Bushes.*

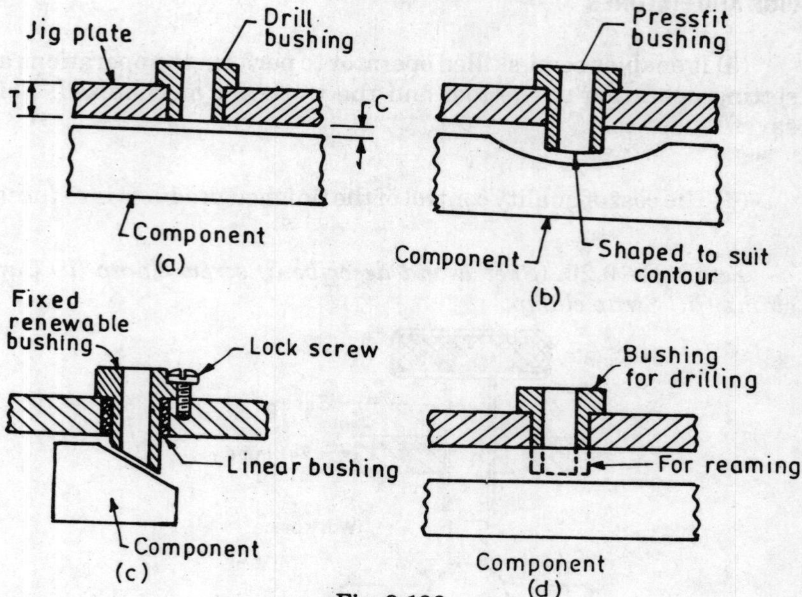

Fig. 9.136

Solution. Proper clearance between component and drill bushing produces accurate components. The chips cause the bushing to wear repidly if the bushings are unnecessarily close. If placed too far away, precision is lost. Fig. 9.136(*a*) shows bushing for drilling operation.

$$C = \frac{D}{4} \quad \text{to} \quad \frac{D}{2}$$

$$T = D \quad \text{to} \quad 2D$$

where D = Tool diameter Fig. 9.136(*b*) shows drill bushing shaped to suit contour on work piece surface and Fig. 9.136(*c*) shows use of fixed renewable bushing.

Bushing for reaming is more closer to the surface of the component [Fig. 9.136(*d*)].

Example 9.22. *(a) Sketch and describe a typical angle plate jig.*

(b) Describe two types of clamping methods for jigs.

Solution. (*a*) Fig. 9.137 shows an angle plate jig the body is of unequal T-shape made from cast iron. The jig plate is made from cast flat stock. The parts should be doweled and screwed together with the locator fastened.

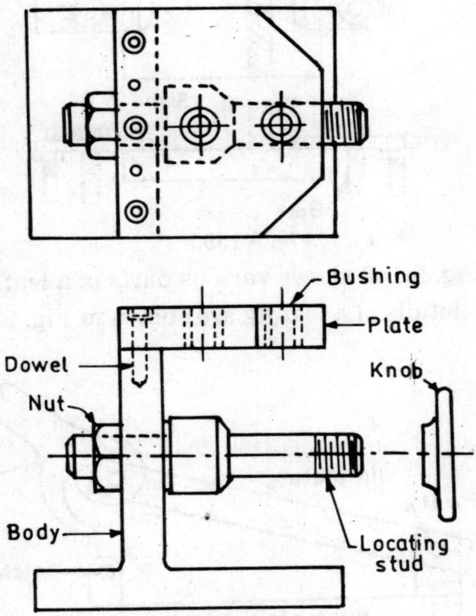

Fig. 9.137.

(*b*) The jig may be clamped to the machine either by slot and T-bolts as shown in Fig. 9.138 or by means of strap clamp as shown in Fig. 9.139.

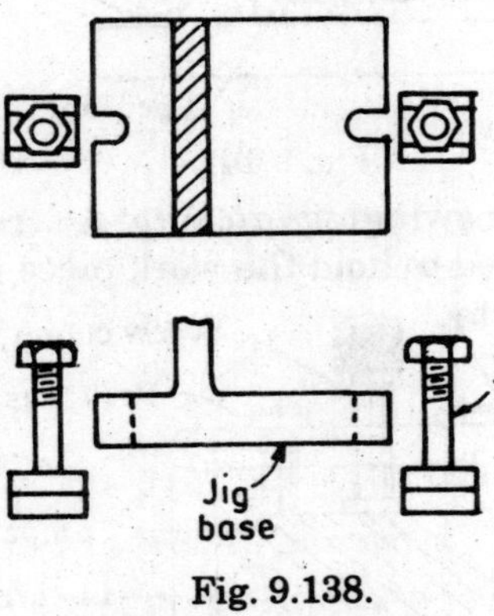

Fig. 9.138.

Example 9.23. *Sketch and describe a typical Leaf Jig and Latch Jig.*

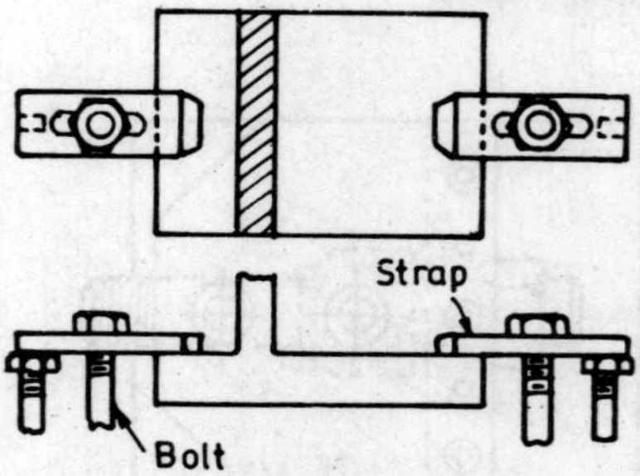

Fig. 9.139.

Solution. Fig. 9.140 shows various parts of a leaf jig. Positioning details of a leaf jig are shown in Fig. 9.141.

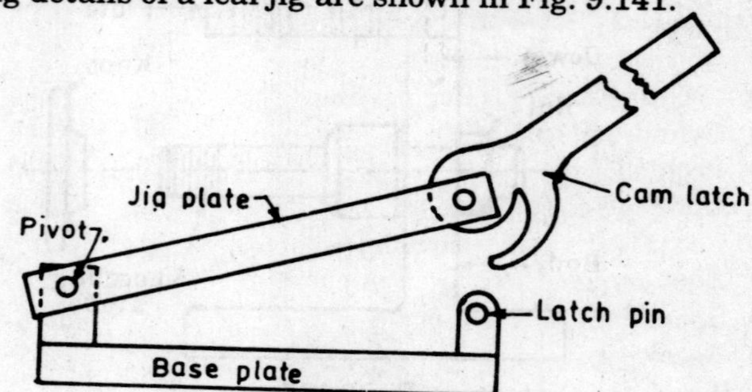

Fig. 9.140.

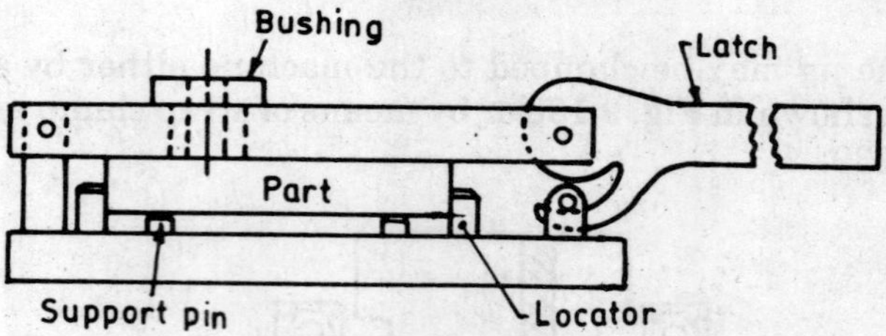

Fig. 9.141.

Fig. 9.142 shows a swinging *latch jig*. A screw clamp with pad at bottom has been used to hold the work piece in position.

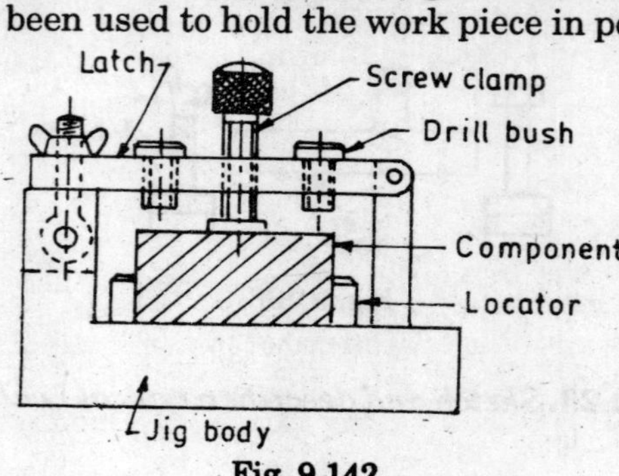

Fig. 9.142.

PROBLEMS

1. (*a*) Define Jig and fixture.

(*b*) State the advantages of using jigs and fixtures during machining.

2. Describe the design principles for jig and fixture.

3. (*a*) What is location ?

(*b*) Describe 3-2-1 principle of location.

(*c*) State the basic rules for location.

4. What is clamping ? Describe any five types of clamping devices.

5. Write short notes on the following :

(*i*) Clamping force

(*ii*) Degrees of freedom

6. Write a short notes on the following

(*a*) Choosing a locating surface

(*b*) Locating methods and devices

(*c*) Cylindrical locators

(*d*) Profile locators

(*e*) Diamond pin locator

(*f*) Radial location by external pins

(*g*) Equalising jacks

(*h*) Spherical locating plugs

(*i*) Recess locators.

7. (*a*) What is the function of jig bushes

(*b*) Describe various types of jig bushes

8. Write a short notes on the following :

(*a*) Cams used in clamps

(*b*) Clearance between work piece and bushing

(*c*) Wedge clamp.

9. What is a drilling jig. What are the requirements of a drilling jig.

10. Describe various types of drilling jigs.

11. Write short notes on the following

(*a*) Accessories of jigs and fixtures

(*b*) Nut mandrel.

(*c*) Mandrel for threaded parts.

12. What is fixture. Describe following types of fixtures

(*a*) Milling fixtures

(*b*) Grinding fixture

(*c*) Boring fixture

(*d*) Fixture for key way cutting

(*e*) Broaching fixture

(*f*) Lathe mandrels.

13. Discuss two advantages achieved over other methods if pneumatic or hydraulic devices are used to actuate clamps.

14. Sketch and describe a milling fixture for a mild steel component shown in Fig. 9.143.

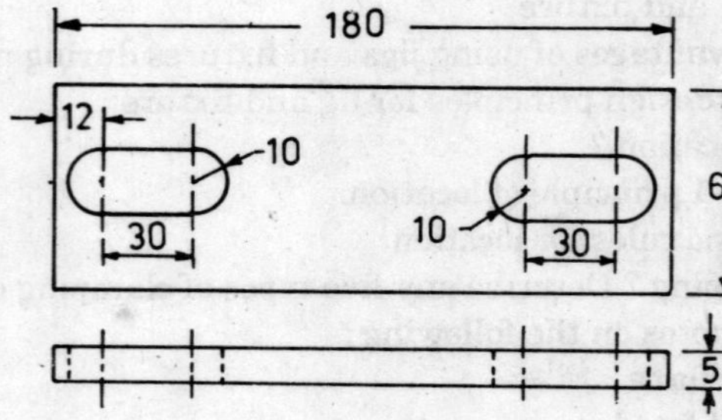

Fig. 9.143.

15. State four operational factors considered to achieve most efficient clamping.

16. Write a short notes on the following :

(*a*) Retaining rings.

(*b*) Jig and fixture bodies.

(*c*) Nesting fixture for brazing.

(*d*) Multipurpose tooling.

(*e*) Angle plate jig.

10

Process Planning and Cost Estimation

10.1. Process Planning

Development of a product is carried out in two distinct functions:

(*i*) Product design (*ii*) Process design.

Product design is aimed at determining the size and shape of product that will give satisfactory performance for an adequate life whereas the process design function includes developing methods of manufacturing the product so that it can be produced at competitive price.

10.2. Aims of Process Planning

Aims of process planning are as follows :

(*i*) To choose economical methods of manufacturing a product.

(*ii*) To determine the sequence of operations to be performed during manufacturing of product.

(*iii*) To prepare a material list for all the components of the product.

(*iv*) To determine the machine tools to be used.

(*v*) To determine the type of cutting tools, jigs, fixtures, dies etc., to be used.

(*vi*) To determine the stages of inspection and types of inspecting tools and gauges.

(*vii*) To determine type of labour to be used.

(*viii*) To determine the set up time and standard time for each operation and fix up rate of payments.

(*ix*) To determine what parts to be manufactured and what parts of the product to be purchased.

(*x*) To determine the estimated cost of the product.

10.3. Process Planning Sheet

It is the planning department which is primarily responsible for determining how the various components are to be made. Process planning sheet indicates the following information :

(*i*) Drawing of the component.

(*ii*) Material and weight of the component.

(*iii*) Description and number of operations and their sequence.

(*iv*) Type of machine tools to be used.

(*v*) Type of jigs, fixtures, cutting tools and gauges.

Process Planning Sheet

Sheet No. ...... *Drawn By*	*Date* ....
1. Product	6. Net weight ....
2. Part Name	7. Blank size ....
3. Part No.	8. Lot size ....
4. Material	9. Sketch ....
5. Gross weight	10. Sketch No. ....

Operation Number	*Operation description*	*Shop*	*Machine Tool*	*Tools*	*Jigs and Fixtures*	*Gauges*	*Time Analysis*	*Labour Cost*

Fig. 10.1

(*vi*) Elements of standard time such as :
(*a*) Setting time (*b*) Handling time (*c*) Machining time.

(*vii*) Cutting speed, feed.

(*viii*) Job rating of the worker for each operation.

Fig. 10.1 shows a typical process planning sheet.

10.4. Production Control Chart

Machines and labour should be coordinated in order to achieve completion of work in all stages of manufacture. Fig. 10.2 indicates a typical production control chart.

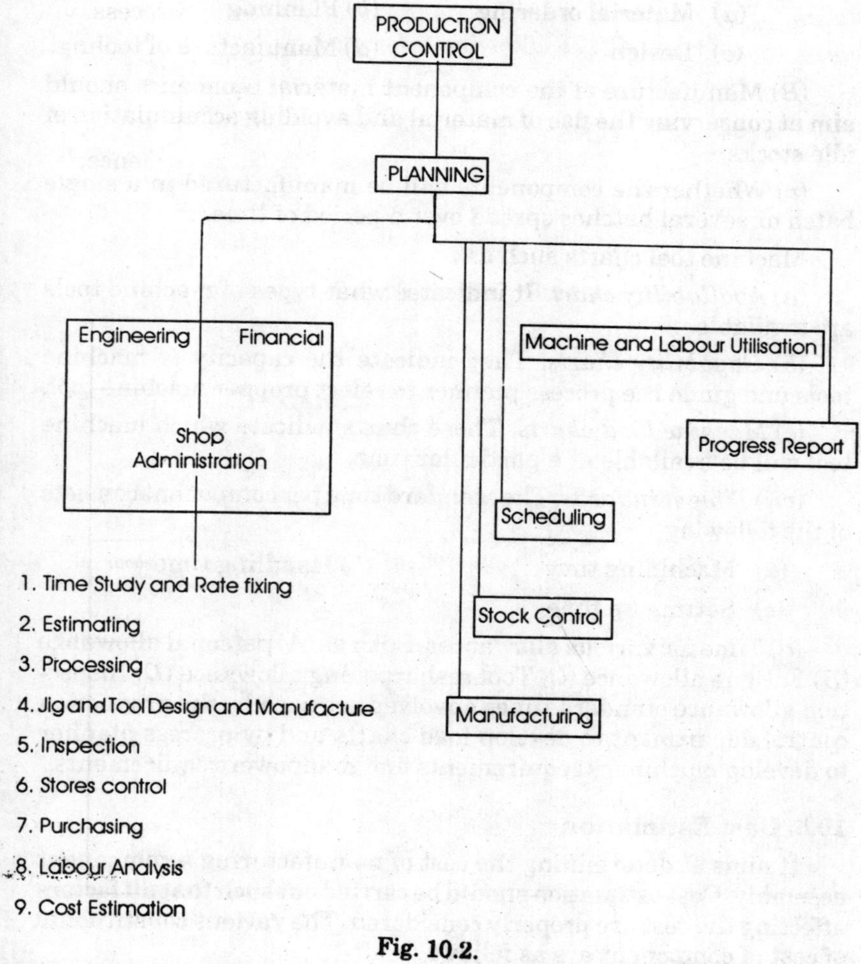

Fig. 10.2.

The chart shows the various stages of planning during manufacturing of products.

10.4.1. General factors in production planning. When planning the production of manufacturing components, following points should be considered:

(*i*) Types of machine tools available.

(*ii*) What form and size of raw material is most economical for a given component.

(*iii*) Number of components to be produced.

(*iv*) Time available for :

(*A*) Preparation :

(*a*) Material ordering (*b*) Planning

(*c*) Design (*d*) Manufacture of tooling.

(*B*) Manufacture of the component material economics should aim at conserving the use of material and avoiding accumulation of idle stocks.

(*v*) Whether the components will be manufactured in a single batch or several batches spread over a period of time.

Machine tool charts such as :

(*a*) *Availability chart.* It indicates what types of machine tools are available.

(*b*) *Capability charts.* They indicate the capacity of machine tools and guide the process planner to select propper machine tool.

(*c*) *Machine load charts.* These charts indicate which machine tool will be available at a particular time.

(*vii*) *Time standards.* The standard time per component consists of the following.

(*a*) Machining time (*b*) Handling time

(*c*) Setting up time

(*d*) Time for various allowances. Such as (*A*) personal allowance (*B*) Fatigue allowance (*C*) Tool resharpening allowance (*D*) Inspection allowance standard times envolved are used by the production control department to develop load charts and by process planner to develop machinery requirements and manpower requirements.

10.5. Cost Estimation

It aims at determining the cost of manufacturing a component assembly. Cost estimation should be carried out such that all factors affecting the cost are properly considered. The various constituents of cost of component are as follows :

(*i*) Machining cost

(*ii*) Tooling cost

(*iii*) Non productive cost. These costs have been described in Chapter 3.

(*iv*) Material cost

(*v*) Indirect expense

(*a*) Factory expense

(*b*) Administrative expense

(*c*) Selling expense.

10.6. Cost of a Casting

Costs incurred with cast iron castings are as follows :

(*i*) Time taken for making pattern

(*ii*) Cost of pattern material

(*iii*) Time taken for producing casting

(*iv*) Cost of material for casting

(*v*) Machining time.

10.7. Cost of Welded Construction

Costs incurred with welded construction are as follows :

(*i*) Cost of material such as :

(*a*) Weld material

(*b*) Construction material.

(*ii*) Time taken for

(*a*) Preparation

(*b*) Welding.

(*iii*) Time taken for machining the welded parts

The over all cost of welded construction is less than casting.

10.8. Set up Time and Economical Lot Size

Set up time is allocated to a particular lot size on the basis of past experience. The economic lot size yields the lowest cost for each unit to be produced. The number of set ups needed for a component is a function of economic lot size. Economic lot size indicates cost of

(*i*) set up

(*ii*) tooling

(*iii*) handling

(*iv*) carrying charge.

$$L = \text{Economic lot size}$$

$$= 5\sqrt{\frac{N \times S}{F \times C}}$$

where N = Pieces used per month

S = Set up cost in rupees

F = Carrying charge factor (%)

The carrying charge factor (F) takes into account the following:

(*i*) Interest (*ii*) Taxes

(*iii*) Storage (*iv*) Obsolescence

(*v*) Insurance

The value of F varies between 5 to 30%

C = Cost per Component in rupees

t = Hours permitted for each set up

$$= \frac{LS}{N}.$$

10.9. Standardisation as an Economic Factor

The principle that standard parts should be used whenever possible should be in the fore front of the minds of all engineers concerned with design. Standardisation is an important consideration during manufacturing and while deciding about the tooling equipment.

Various advantages of standardisation are as follows :

(*i*) It improves production planning.

(*ii*) Standardisation of the tooling equipment helps to keep the production costs down.

(*iii*) It increases productive efficiency.

(*iv*) It leads to quantitative reduction of special equipment including tooling equipment.

10.10. Using Special Equipment

During manufacturing of a component the cutting equipment like machine tools, cutting tools, jigs, fixture etc. should be used as far as possible. However, in case special equipment is required during manufacturing then it is desireable to manufacture a particular minimum number of component to justify the cost of special equipment.

N = Minimum number of components to be produced

$$= \frac{C}{(E - S)}$$

where C = Cost of special equipment

E = Machining cost of component using existing equipment

S = Machining cost of component using special equipment.

10.11. Work Handling and Machine Manipulation Time

The work handling and machine manipulation time should be minimum. The elements involved in handling and machine manipulation are as follows :

(*i*) Initial setting up of machine

(*ii*) Manipulation of machine during operation

(*a*) Winding cross slide by hand

(*b*) Gear changing.

(*iii*) Loading and unloading of component

(*iv*) Measuring and gauging

(*v*) Changing and re-setting tools.

In addition to the above items allowances are made for :

(*a*) Contingencies (*b*) Fatigue

(*c*) Personal reasons.

The magnitude of these allowances will depend on the demands made on operator by whom the work is being performed.

Table 10.1 indicates handling and manipulation times for a plain milling machine.

Table 10.1

Element	*Time (seconds)*
Switch motor on/off	5
Start/stop spindle	3
Engage/Disengage feed	4
Change spindle speed	6
Change feed rate	5
Approach component to cutter	6
Wind table slide	6
Cross slide	12

Table 10.2 indicates handling and machine manipulation times for a capstan lathe.

Table 10.2

Element	*Time (seconds)*
Load/unload in self centring chuck	30
Feed bar to stop-self centring chuck	15
Feed bar to stop-collet	8
Load/unload in collet (per component)	6
Start stop spindle	2
Change speed	3
Change feed	4
Index tool post, advance to work piece, set to mark, return	8
Index turret, clamp advance to workpiece, return, unclamp	5
Wind saddle	3
Wind cross slide	5

10.12. Tooling Allowances

Time allowances per component for tooling may be calculated as follows

$T =$ Total cutting time per component (minutes)

$M =$ Average tool life per tool (minutes)

$N =$ Number of tools in set-up

$t =$ Average time to reset one tool (minutes)

$S =$ Total tool life

$= M \times N$ (minutes)

$Z =$ Number of components for a complete set of tool changes

$$= \frac{S}{T} = \frac{M \times N}{T}$$

$A =$ Allowance per component per tool

$$= \frac{t}{Z} = \frac{t \times T}{M \times N}$$

$$B = \text{Allowance/component for } N \text{ tools}$$
$$= A \times N$$
$$= \frac{t \times T}{M \times N} \times N$$
$$= \frac{t \times T}{M} \text{ minutes.}$$

10.13. Process Cost Comparison

During process planning various manufacturing methods should be compared in order to select an economical manufacturing method. One way of comparing two manufacturing methods A and B is as follows :

N = Total number of components to be produced

x = Number of components for which the unit costs will be equal for each of two compared methods A and B (Break even point)

T_1 = Total tool cost for method A

P_1 = Unit tool process cost for method A

T_2 = Total tool cost for method B

P_2 = Unit tool process cost for method B

C_1 = Total unit cost for method A

C_2 = Total unit cost for method B

$$x = \frac{T_1 - T_2}{P_2 - P_1}$$

$$C_1 = \frac{P_1 N + T_1}{N}$$

$$C_2 = \frac{P_2 N + T_2}{N}.$$

10.14. Labour Expenses

Labour is the single most expensive factor in manufacturing. If labour expenses can be reduced overall production costs will get reduced.

Jigs and fixture help to achieve the following :

(*i*) To reduce machining time

(*ii*) To reduce need for skilled labour

The unskilled labour can produce accurate components at a reduced wage rate.

The labour cost can be calculated as follows :

C = Labour cost

$$= \frac{N}{H} \times R$$

where $N =$ Lot size

$H =$ Parts made per hour

$R =$ Wage rate per hour.

10.15. Grouping of Machining Operations

Various criteria to be considered while grouping machining operations are as follows :

(*i*) *Size of order.* The number of components to be produced will determine to a large extent how much can be spent on the following:

(*a*) Tools

(*b*) Fixtures

(*c*) Special machines.

The processor should keep in mind the following of new equipment is to be purchased for machining.

(*a*) Cost of labour

(*b*) Cost of tooling set up and tear down

(*c*) Maintenance cost.

(*ii*) *Rate of production.* Rate of production is an important factor to be considered while writing process sheet. Production schedules and commitments to the customer must be met.

(*iii*) *Size of work piece.* Depending on size of workpiece. The various operations should be combined is such a way that it should be easier to move the work piece from one machine to the other machine.

(*iv*) *Machines available.* The process or should know the following details of various machines available.

(*a*) Operations which can be performed on machines available

(*b*) Power rating of machines

(*c*) Size of work piece that can be handled by various machines

(*d*) Precision

(*e*) Dependability.

(*v*) *Nature of surfaces to be machined.* A surface which is controlled by close tolerances may be need to be machined independently whereas adjacent surfaces may be machined in oil set up.

Example 10.1. *A steel casting shown in Fig. 10.3 is to be machined at pads AB and CD, using milling and broaching using following data.*

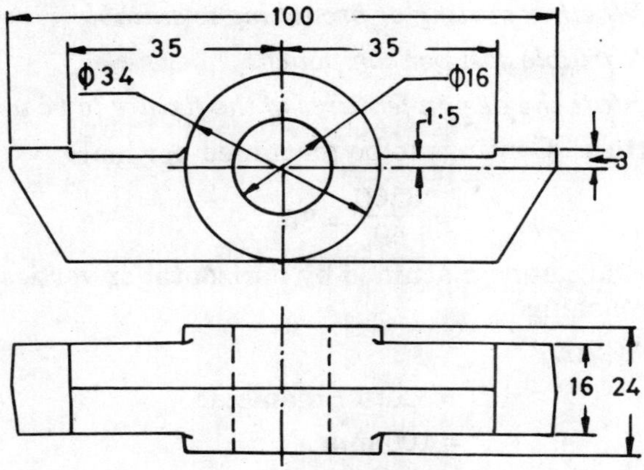

Fig. 10.3.

	Milling	*Broaching*
Tooling cost	*Rs. 8000*	*Rs. 9000*
Material cost per component	*Rs. 6.0*	*Rs. 6.0*
Operating labour cost	*Rs. 8/h*	*Rs. 8/h*
Standard time/component	*0.8 min*	*0.9 min*
Setting up labour cost	*Rs. 18/h*	*Rs. 18/h*
Setting up time	*2h*	*4h*
Machine over heads	*300% of operating labour cost*	*500% operating labour cost*

Milling cutter diameter = 100 *mm*

Number of teeth on cutter = 12

Depth of cut = 4 *mm.*

Feed = 0.08*mm/tooth*

Milling cutter speed = 30 *m/min*

Broaching speed = 0.06 *m/s*

Cut per tooth for broaching = 0.025 *mm*

3200 castings are to be producing per week of 40 hours.

Determine :

(*a*) *Whether milling or broaching is suitable*

(*b*) *Variable cost per component*

(*c*) *State the design features of the fixture to be used.*

Solution. Castings to be machined per hour

$$= \frac{3200}{40} = 80$$

The pads can be machined by horizontal or vertical milling or surface broaching.

(*a*) *Milling*

$D =$ Cutter diameter

$= 100$ mm

$T =$ Number of teeth

$= 12$

$t =$ Depth of cut

$= 4$ mm.

As shown in Fig. 10.4

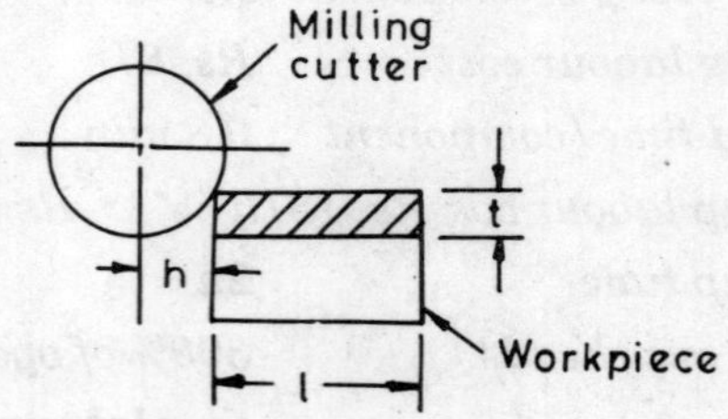

Fig. 10.4.

$h =$ Approach

$= \sqrt{t(D - t)}$

$= \sqrt{4(100 - 4)} = 19.6$ mm

$l =$ Length of workpiece

$= 16$ mm.

$L =$ Total cutter travel

$= h + l +$ over run of cutter

$= 19.6 + 16 + 5 = 40.6$ mm.

$V =$ Milling cutter speed = 30 m/min

$f =$ feed

$= 0.08$ mm/tooth

$= 0.08 \times T$ mm/rev.

$= 0.08 \times 12 = 0.96$ mm/rev.

$N =$ R.P.M. of cutter

$$V = \frac{\pi DN}{1000}$$

$$30 = \pi \times \frac{100}{1000} \times N$$

$$N = 95.54$$

$T =$ Machining time

$$= \frac{L}{f \times N} = \frac{40.6}{0.96 \times 95.54}$$

$= 0.44$ minutes $= 27$ seconds

$T_1 =$ Total time

$=$ Machining time + Allowances time

$= 27 + 20 = 47$ seconds $= 0.78$ minute

$$\text{Output per hour} = \frac{60}{0.78} = 77.$$

Although this quantity is below the desired output but two castings can be machined at a time as shown in Fig. 10.5.

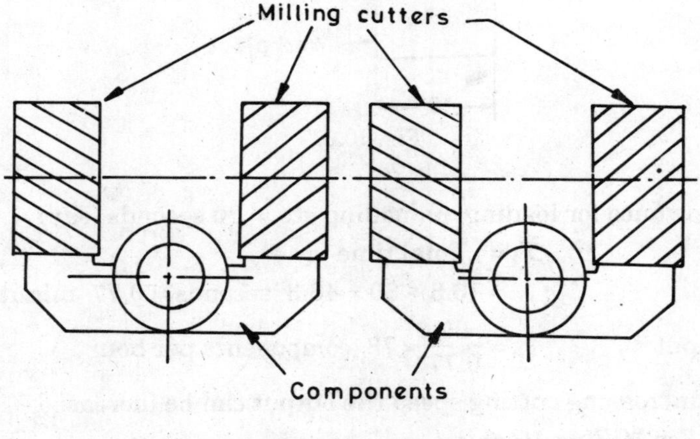

Fig. 10.5.

Broaching :

$L =$ Length to be broached = 16 mm.

$p =$ pitch $= 1.5\sqrt{16} = 6$ mm.

$d =$ Depth of cut = 4 mm.

$h =$ rise per tooth (cut per tooth) = 0.025 mm.

$Z_1 =$ Number of teeth

$$= \frac{d}{h} = \frac{4}{0.025} = 160$$

$L_1 =$ Length of cutting portion required

$= Z_1 \times p = 160 \times 6 = 960$ mm.

$L_2 =$ Total length $= L_1 + L_2 = 960 + 16 = 976$ mm.

$V =$ Cutting speed = 0.06 m/s

$T =$ Machining time

$$= \frac{L_2}{V} = \frac{976}{1000} \times \frac{1}{0.06}$$

= 16.3 seconds.

Fig. 10.6 shows broaching of component.

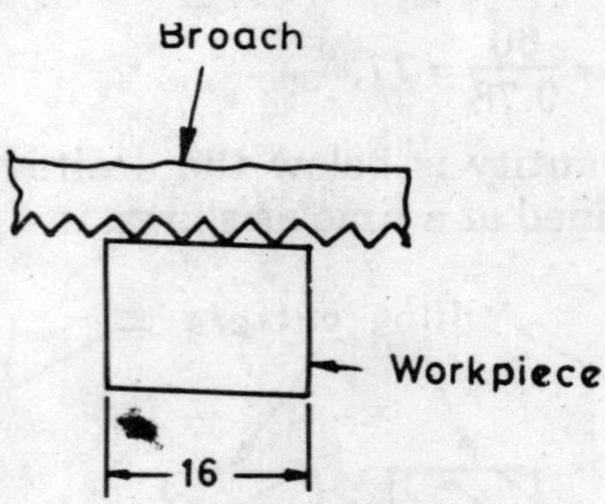

Fig. 10.6.

Allowance for loading, unloading etc. = 30 seconds (say)

$T_1 =$ Total time

= 16.3 + 30 = 46.3 seconds = 0.77 minute

output $= \frac{60}{0.77} = 78$ components per hour

By increasing cutting speed the output can be increased.

(*b*) *For Milling Machine*

$C =$ Over heads per hour

$$= \frac{300}{100} \times \text{ operating labour cost}$$

$$= \frac{300}{100} \times 8 = \text{Rs. } 24$$

C_2 = Setting up cost = Time × labour rate

$= 2 \times 18 = \text{Rs. } 36$

C_3 = Fixed cost

$= \text{Tooling cost} + C_2 + C_1 \times 2$

$= 8000 + 36 + 48 = \text{Rs. } 8084$

C_4 = Operating labour cost

= Operating labour rate × Machining time

$$= 8 \times \frac{0.8}{60} = \text{Rs. } 0.011$$

C_5 = Material cost per component

= Rs. 6

C_6 = Overheads for machining time

$$= 24 \times \frac{0.8}{60} = \text{Rs. } 6$$

C_7 = Variable cost per component

$= C_4 + C_5 + C_6$

$= 0.011 + 6 + 0.32 = \text{Rs. } 6.33.$

(c) *For broaching machine*

C_1 = Over heads per hour

$$= \frac{500}{100} \times \text{operating labour cost}$$

$$= \frac{500}{100} \times 8 = \text{Rs. } 40$$

C_2 = Setting up cost

= Time × Setting up labour cost

$= 4 \times 18 = \text{Rs. } 72$

C_3 = Fixed cost

$= \text{Tooling cost} + C_2 + C_1 \times 4$

$= 9000 + 72 + 40 \times 4$

= Rs. 9232

C_4 = Operating labour cost

= Operating labour rate × Time

$$= 8 \times \frac{0.9}{60} = 0.012$$

C_5 = Material cost per component = Rs. 6

C_6 = Overheads for machining time

$$= 40 \times \frac{0.9}{60} = \text{Rs. } 0.6$$

C_7 = Variable cost per component

$$= C_4 + C_5 + C_6 = 0.012 + 6 + 0.6 = \text{Rs. } 6.612.$$

As both fixed and variable costs of the broaching process are little higher than for the milling process therefore it is obvious that the milling process may be used for machining of given casting.

(*c*) Having decided upon the milling process the design features of the fixture will be as follows :

(*i*) Location

(*ii*) Machine capacity

(*iii*) Clamping

(*iv*) Tool setting

(*v*) Out line of construction of fixture

(*vi*) Operator safety.

Example 10.2. *Determine the minimum cost batch size for producing an assembly costing Rs. 1500. Which is sold at the rate of 1200 per year. Rate of interest per annum for articles in stock is 10%. Setting up and general preparation costs are Rs. 900 per batch. Assume 300 working days per year.*

Solution. N = Number of days per year = 300

R = Rate of consumption of product per day

$$= \frac{1200}{300} = 4$$

I = Cost of interest on articles in stock per unit time

(cost per unit/unit time)

$$= \frac{10}{100} \times 1500 \times \frac{1}{300} = \text{Rs. } 0.5$$

P = Preparation cost = Rs. 900

Economical batch size

$$= \sqrt{\frac{2RP}{I}}$$

$$= \sqrt{\frac{2 \times 4 \times 900}{0.5}} = 120 \text{ Assemblies.}$$

Example 10.3. *A component can be produced with equal facility on either a capstan lathe or a single spindle automatic lathe with the following informations available.*

	Capstan lathe	*Automatic lathe*
Tooling cost	*Rs. 60.00*	*Rs. 60.00*
Cost of cams		*Rs.300.00*
Material cost / component	*Rs. 4.00*	*Rs. 4.00*
Operating labour cost	*Rs. 8.0 / h*	*Rs. 5.0 / h*
Cycle time / component	*4 min.*	*2 min.*
Setting up labour cost	*Rs. 12.0 / h*	*Rs. 12.0 / h*
Setting up time	*1 hour*	*6 hour*
Machine overheads (setting and operating)	*Rs. 18.00 / h*	*Rs. 40.0 / h*

Determine :

(*a*) *Fixed cost*

(*b*) *Variable cost*

(*c*) *Break even quantity*

Solution. For Capstan lathe

C_F = Fixed cost

C_1 = Tooling cost

C_2 = Setting up cost

C_3 = Over heads

$C_F = C_1 + C_2 + C_3$

$= 60 + 12 \times 1 + 18 \times 1 =$ Rs. 90.00

C_V = Variable cost/Component

C_4 = Labour cost

= Operating labour cost/h × Time

$= 8 \times \frac{4}{60} =$ Rs. 0.53

C_5 = Material cost/component

= Rs. 4.00

C_6 = Overheads

$$= \text{Overheads/h} \times \text{Time}$$

$$= 18 \times \frac{4}{60} = \text{Rs. } 1.2$$

$$C_V = C_4 + C_5 + C_6$$

$$= 0.53 + 4 + 1.2 = \text{Rs. } 5.73.$$

For automatic lathe

$$C_1 = \text{Tooling cost}$$

$$= \text{Rs. } 60.00$$

$$C_2 = \text{Setting up cost}$$

$$= 12 \times 6 = \text{Rs. } 72$$

$$C_3 = \text{Over heads} = 40 \times 6 = \text{Rs. } 240$$

Cam cost = Rs. 300.00

$$C_F = \text{Fixed cost}$$

$$= C_1 + C_2 + C_3 + \text{ Cam cost}$$

$$= 60 + 72 + 240 + 300 = \text{Rs. } 672.00$$

$$C_4 = \text{Labour cost}$$

$$= 5 \times \frac{2}{60} = \text{Rs. } 0.16$$

$$C_5 = \text{Material cost/Component} = \text{Rs. } 4.00$$

$$C_6 = \text{Overhead} = \text{Overhead/h} \times \text{time}$$

$$= 40 \times \frac{2}{60} = 1.33$$

$$C_V = \text{Variable cost per component}$$

$$= C_4 + C_5 + C_6$$

$$= 0.16 + 4 + 1.33 = \text{Rs. } 5.49.$$

The break even quantity (Q_E) can be found as follows :

Let x = Number of components to be produced

C_C = Total cost of producing x components an capstan lathe

$$= C_F + C_V \times x$$

$$= 90 + 5.73 \times x$$

For automatic lathe

$$C_C = C_F + C_V \times x$$

$$= 672 + 5.49 \times x$$

when $x = Q_E$ then total costs for each machine should be equal

$$90 + 5.73x = 672 + 5.49x$$

$$x = 2425.$$

Example 10.4. *In a company 1200 parts are used in assembly department per month. The cost of each part is Rs. 11.00 and cost of each set up is Rs. 60.00 per lot.*

Determine :

(*a*) *Economic lot size*

(*b*) *Set up hours permitted for each lot*

Carrying charge factor is 20%.

Solution. (*a*) L = Economic lot size

N = Pieces used per month = 1200

S = Set up cost = Rs. 60.00

F = Carrying charge factor = 20% = 0.2

C = Cost per component = Rs. 11.00

$$L = 5\sqrt{\frac{N \times S}{F \times C}} = 5\sqrt{\frac{1200 \times 60}{0.2 \times 11}}$$

= 904 Components.

(*b*) t = Hours permitted for each set up

$$= \frac{LS}{N} = \frac{904 \times 60}{1200}$$

= 45.2 hours.

Example 10.5. *Determine the minimum number of components to be produced to justify use of special equipment for manufacturing the components using following data.*

Cost of special equipment = Rs. 2000

Machining cost of component using existing equipment = Rs. 12.00

Machining cost of component using special equipment = Rs. 2.00.

Solution.

N = Minimum number of components to be produced

$$= \frac{C}{E - S}$$

where C = Cost of special equipment = Rs. 2000

E = Machining cost of component using existing equipment = Rs. 12.00

S = Machining cost of component using special equipment = Rs. 2.00

$$N = \frac{2000}{12 - 2} = 200.$$

Example 10.6. *Two manufacturing methods A and B suggested for manufacturing a component are to be compared with following information.*

Total tool cost for method A = Rs. 8000

Unit tool process cost for method A = Rs. 10

Total tool cost for method B = Rs. 2000

Unit tool process cost for method B = Rs. 18

Total number of parts to be produced in a single run = 500

Determine :

(*a*) *Quantity of components at break even point*

(*b*) *Total unit cost for method A and B.*

Solution. $N = 500$

T_1 = Rs. 8000

P_1 = Rs. 10

T_2 = Total tool cost for method B

= Rs. 2000

P_2 = Unit tool process cost for method B

= Rs. 18

x = Quantity of components at break even point.

= Number of parts for which the unit costs will be equal for method A and method B

$$= \frac{T_1 - T_2}{P_2 - P_1}$$

$$= \frac{8000 - 2000}{18 - 10}$$

= 750 components.

C_1 = Total unit cost for methods A

$$= \frac{P_1 N + T_1}{N}$$

$$= \frac{10 \times 500 + 8000}{500}$$

= Rs. 28.00

C_2 = Total unit cost for method B

$$= \frac{P_2N + T_2}{N}$$

$$= \frac{18 \times 500 + 2000}{500} = \text{Rs. } 22.00.$$

Example 10.7. *Determine the allowance per component for tool changes on a turret lathe using the following conditions.*

(a) Total cutting time / component = 10 min

Average tool life = 48 minutes

Number of tools = 8

Average time to reset 1 tool = 12 minutes.

(b) As above but with combined tooling set on 8 tool positions and using a total of 12 tools.

Solution. (*a*) B = Allowance per component

$$= \frac{t \times T}{M}$$

where T = Total cutting time per component

= 10 min

t = Average time to reset one tool = 12 minute.

M = Average tool life

= 48 minutes

$$B = \frac{12 \times 10}{48}$$

= 2.5 minutes.

(*b*) N_1 = Number of tools = 8

N_2 = Number of tools in second stage = 12

B = Tool allowance per component

$$= \frac{t \times T}{M} \times \frac{N_2}{N_1}$$

$$= \frac{12 \times 10}{48} \times \frac{12}{8}$$

= 3.75 minutes.

Example 10.8. *The cost of a new machine is Rs. 50,000. The scrap value of the machine is estimated to be Rs. 6000. The annual maintenance cost of the machine is Rs. 900. Assuming straight line rising cost of repairs determine the economical life of machine.*

Solution.

C = Cost of machine

= Rs. 50,000

S = Scrap value

= Rs. 6000

M = Annual maintenance cost

= $Rs.$ 900.

N = Number of years of economic repair life

$$= \sqrt{\frac{2(C - S}{M}}$$

$$= \sqrt{\frac{2(50000 - 6000)}{900}}$$

= 9.88 years.

Example 10.9. *Four thousand parts are to be milled using a fixture capable to produce 50 parts per hour. What is the cost of labour if the machine operator earns Rs. 8 per hour.*

Solution. N = Lost size = 4000

H = Parts per hour = 50

R = Wage rate per hour = 8

C = Cost of labour

$$= \frac{N}{H} \times R$$

$$= \frac{4000}{50} \times 8$$

= Rs. 640.

Example 10.10. *Determine the cost per component for a milling operation for 6000 components if the fixture cost is Rs. 4000 and labour cost is Rs. 32000.*

Solution. C = Cost per component

C_1 = Fixture cost = Rs. 4000

C_2 = Labour cost

= Rs. 32000

N = Number of components = 6000

$$C = \frac{C_1 + C_2}{N}$$

$$= \frac{32000 + 4000}{6000} = \frac{36000}{6000} = \text{Rs. } 6.$$

Example 10.11. *Describe the various types of costs of engineering products.*

Solution. The cost of engineering products can broadly be grouped as follows :

(*a*) Direct costs (*b*) Indirect costs

Direct costs are the costs of material and labour. Indirect costs or overhead costs can be sub-divided as under :

(*i*) Works overheads such as wages of works superintendents, foremen, inspectors, storekeepers etc. and costs of depreciation of machines, costs of cutting oil, cost of heating lighting etc.

(*ii*) Office overheads such as cost of wages of all office staff, postage, legal expenses etc.

(*iii*) Sales overheads such as cost of sales staff, advertising etc.

Costs may be more conveniently grouped as follows :

(*a*) Fixed costs

(*b*) Variable costs

Fixed costs includes depreciation cost, interests, cost of tooling, setting up etc.

Variable cost includes directs labour cost, material cost and part of indirect costs which will vary as production varies.

Example 10.12. *What is the cost per part of a machining operation for 6000 parts when a fixture costs Rs. 2000 and labour expenses are Rs. 24 per part.*

Solution. N = Lot size = 6000

C_1 = Cost of fixture = Rs. 2000

C_2 = Cost of labour = 24 × 6000

= Rs. 144000

C = Total cost = $C_1 + C_2$

C = 2000 + 144000 = 146000

Cost per component

$$= \frac{C}{N}$$

$$= \frac{146000}{6000} = \text{Rs. } 24.33$$

Example 10.13. *A flange plate adaptor costs Rs. 9 per part to drill without a jig and Rs. 4 per part when a drill jig is used. If the jig cost is Rs. 5000, how much the jig will save over for production of 1200 parts.*

Solution. S = Saving

N = Lot size = 1200

C_1 = Cost per part without jig = Rs. 9.

C_2 = Cost per part using jig = Rs. 4

C = Jig cost = Rs. 5000

$$S = N(C_1 - C_2) - C$$

$$= 1200\,(9 - 4) - 5000$$

$$= \text{Rs. } 1000 \quad \textbf{Ans.}$$

PROBLEMS

1. What is process planning. Discuss aims of process planning.

2. Write short notes on the following :

(*i*) Process planning sheet

(*ii*) Production of machining operations

(*iii*) Grouping of machining operations

(*iii*) Cost estimation of a component.

3. Discuss work handling and machine manipulation.

4. Write short notes on the following :

(*i*) Use of special equipment in machining.

(*ii*) Set up time and economical lot size.

(*iii*) Standardisation as an economic factor.

(*iv*) Cost of a casting.

(*v*) Cost of welded construction

(*vi*) Tooling allowances

(*vii*) Labour expenses.

5. Discuss process cost comparison.

11

Boring Tool and Sawing Tool

11.1 Boring Tool and Sawing Tool

Boring : It is the operation of enlarging the diameter of a drilled hole. In boring operation either boring bar is fixed and the workpiece moves into the bar (Fig 11.1) or the workpiece is fixed and the boring bar moves into the workpiece (Fig. 11.2).

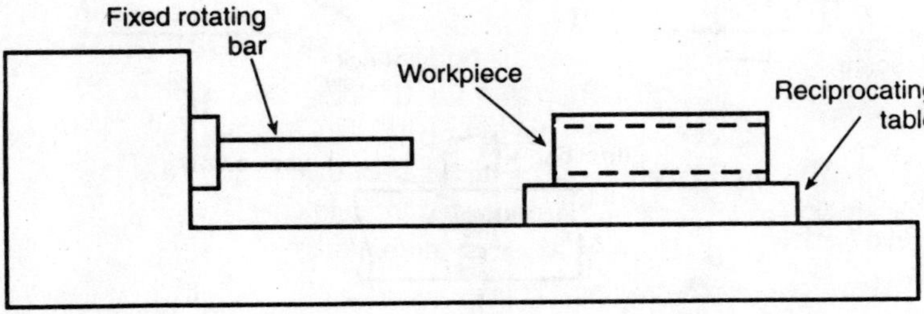

Fig. 11.1

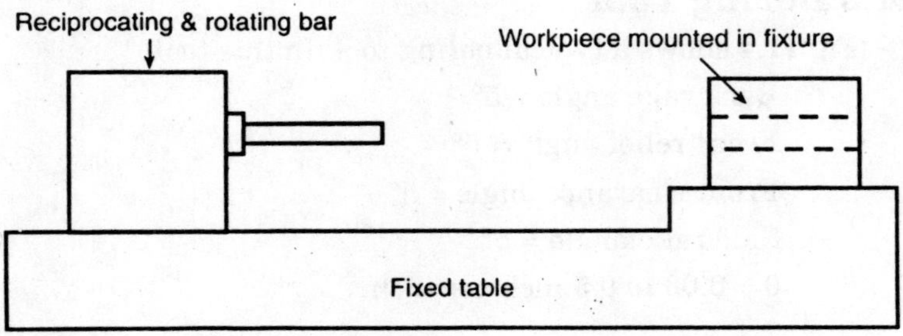

Fig. 11.2

Boring bars are classified as follows:

(*i*) Stub bar (*ii*) Single piloted bar

(*iii*) Double pilot bar

Stub bars are commonly used for boring short holes, as in jig-boring operations. They are also used to bore blind holes that do not permit the extension of a bar through the work. Boring fixtures for stub bars serve to hold the work in the correct relation to the bar. Multiple holes are bored by moving either the work or boring bar.

Boring fixtures are divided into two general classes. In one,the fixture guides the boring bar,as in drill jigs; in the other, the fixture holds the work in the proper relation to the bar, as in mill fixtures. The particular class of boring fixture to be used depends upon the type of boring bar,the type of boring machine,or both.

11.2 Boring Bars

A boring bar holds the tool. Fig 11.3 shows various types of boring bar's for mounting single point tools.

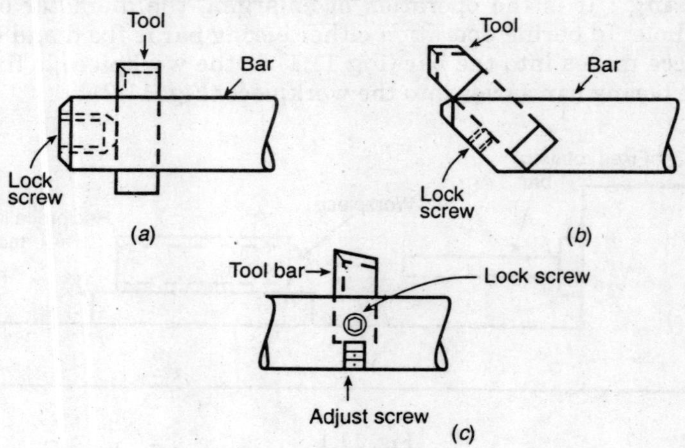

Fig. 11.3.

11.3 Boring Tool

Fig 11.4 shows a typical boring tool. In this tool,

Back rake angle = 5°

Front relief angle = 5°

Front clearance angle = 5°

Side rake angle = 5°

θ = 0.03 to 0.5 inch per inch.

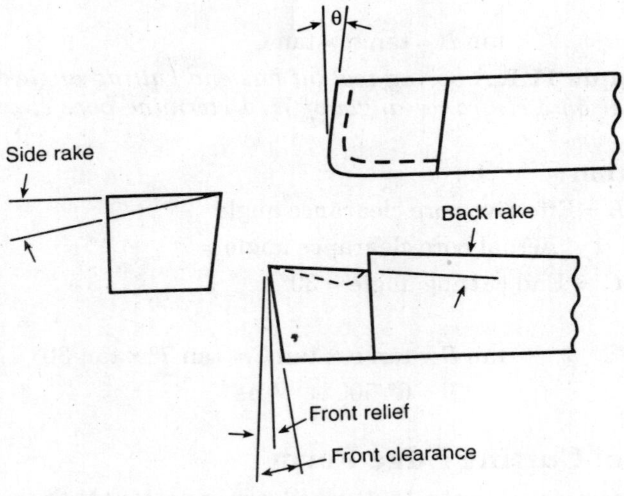

Fig 11.4

Fig. 11.5 shows a boring tool bit with various angles, tool bit may be made of high speed steel or cemented carbide.

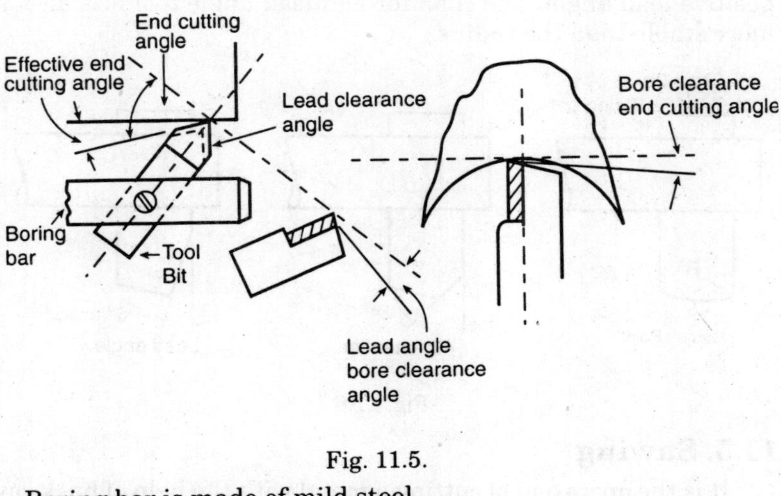

Fig. 11.5.

Boring bar is made of mild steel.

Let B = Effective bore clearance angle

α = Actual bore clearance angle

C = End cutting angle

Then

$$\tan B = \tan \alpha \times \tan C$$

Example 11.1. *A boring tool bit has end cutting angle of 30° and actual bore clearance angle of 7°. Determine bore clearance angle.*

Solution :

Let, B = Effective bore clearance angle

α = Actual bore clearance angle = 7°

C = End cutting angle = 30°

Now,

$$\tan B = \tan \alpha \times \tan C = \tan 7° \times \tan 30°$$

$$B = 6°\text{-}50'. \quad \textbf{Ans.}$$

11.4 Tool Cutting Edge Form

The geometry of the tool cutting edge is important to the cutting operation. Once a satisfactory grind is established, it should be duplicated as accurately as possible. In Fig 11.6 shows three types of cutting tips. The radius tip is the standard grind. If this produces chatter, or poor finish than it should be changed to a chamfer or positive lead angle. The chamfer and lead angle tool bits also are more stable than the radius.

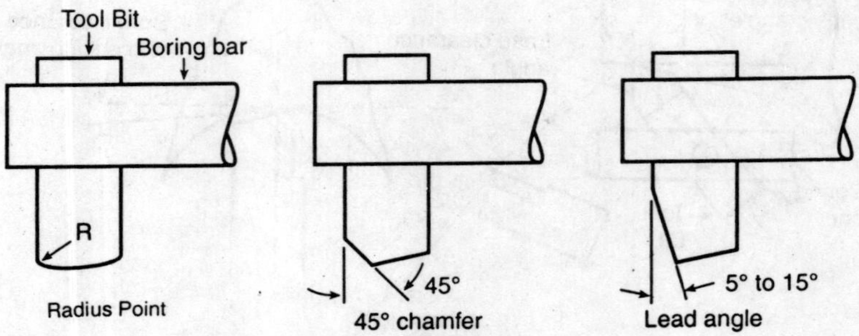

Fig. 11.6.

11.5. Sawing

It is the operation of cutting a metal with the help of hack saw. A hand hack saw has the following main parts as shown. in Fig 11.7.

(*i*) Handle (*ii*) Frame

(*iii*) Blade (*iv*) Wing nut

11.6 Blade

Frame may be solid or adjustable. Blade is usually made of high speed steel.

Blade has number of teeth an its length. A hack saw blade is classified by the number of teeth per inch as follows.

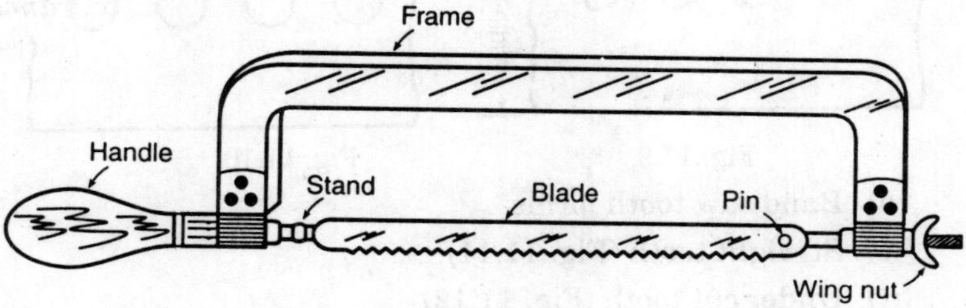

Fig. 11.7

(*i*) A general purpose blade has 16—18 teeth her 25 mm.

(*ii*) A coarse blade has 14—18 teeth per 25 mm

(*iii*) A fine blade has 20—30 teeth per 25 mm

Fig. 11.8 shows tooth pitch.

θ = Angle of blade to the cut = 30°

r = Rate of sawing should be 40—50 strokes per minute.

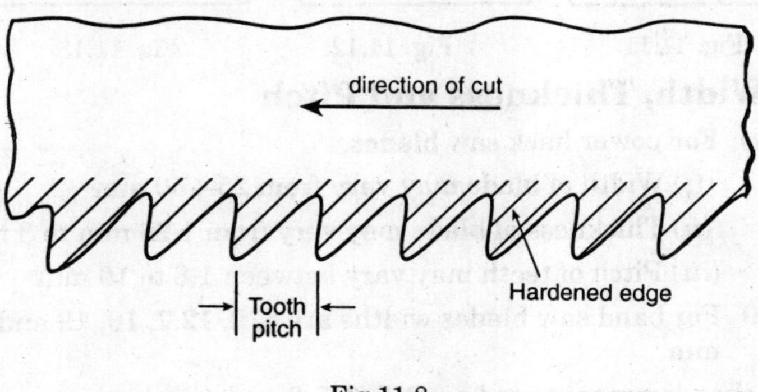

Fig 11.8.

11.7 Tooth Form

The teeth provided on the blade are of the following types

(*a*) For power saw blades

(*i*) Straight tooth (Fig. 11.9)

(*ii*) Under cut tooth (Fig. 11.10)

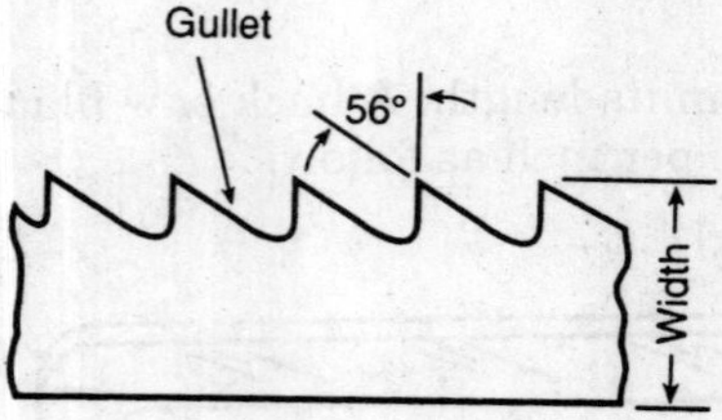

Fig. 11.9.

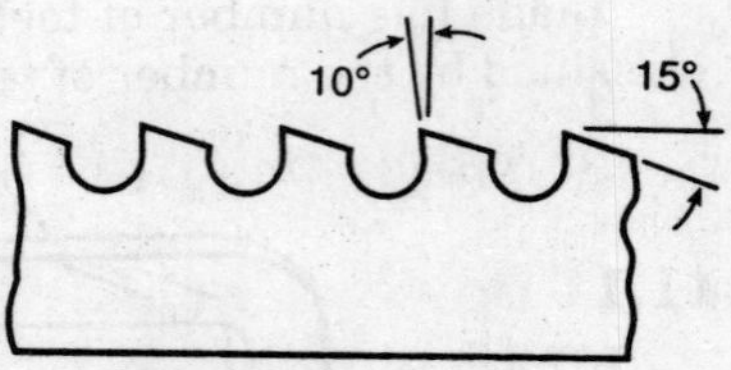

Fig. 11.10.

(*b*) Band saw tooth forms

(*i*) Straight tooth (Fig. 11.11)

(*ii*) Under cut tooth (Fig. 11.12)

(*iii*) Skip teeth (Fig 11.13)

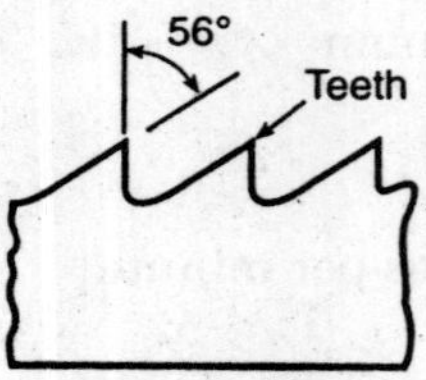

Fig. 11.11.

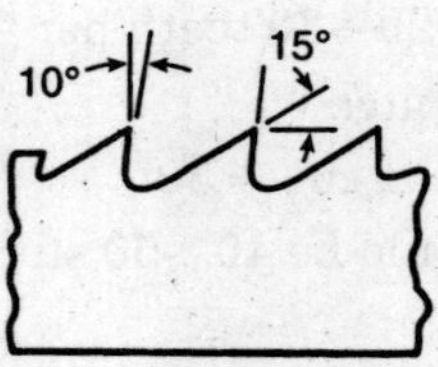

Fig. 11.12.

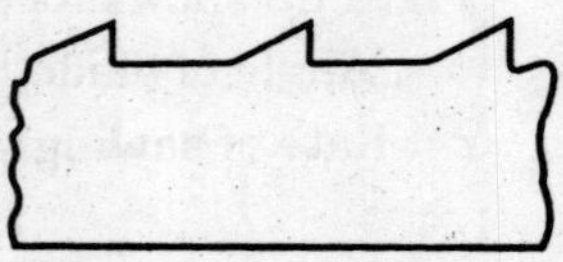

Fig. 11.13.

11.8 Width, Thickness and Pitch

(*a*) For power hack saw **blades**:

(*i*) Width of blade may vary from 25—50 mm

(*ii*) Thickness of blade may very from 1.25 mm to 3 mm

(*iii*) Pitch of teeth may vary between 1.8 to 10 mm

(*b*) For band saw blades widths are 6, 9, 12.7, 16, 18 and 25 mm.

Pitches commonly used are 1.5, 2.5, 3 and 4 mm.

11.9 Types of Hack-Saws

(*a*) Reciprocating saw

(*i*) Manual hacksaw (*ii*) Power hacksaw

(*b*) Band saw

(*i*) Vertical cut off (*ii*) Horizontal cut off

(*c*) Circular saw.

11.10 Basic Features of Hacksaw Blades

They are as follows.

(i) Material
(ii) Tooth form
(iii) Tooth spacing
(iv) Tooth set
(v) Blade Thickness.

11.11 Power Hacksaw

It has a motor driven attachment which moves the hacksaw blade to and fro. According to Indian standards. (IS 2594 - 1964), for power hack saw

(i) Length of blade = 300 to 600 mm
(ii) Width of blade = 20 mm to 50 mm
(iii) Thickness = 0.8 mm to 2.5 mm of blade
(iv) Pitch of teeth = 1.4 to 6.3 mm.

11.12 Position of Teeth

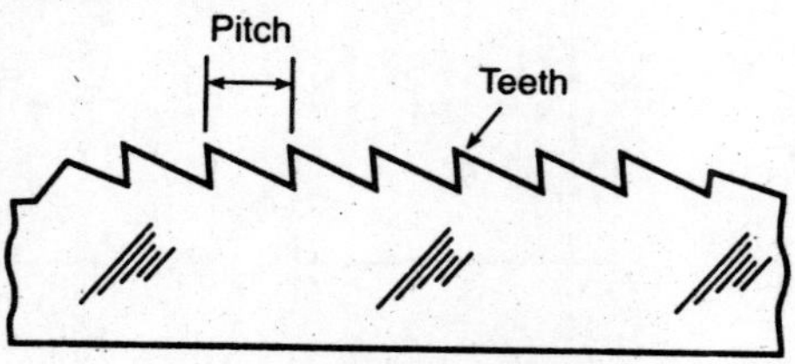

(a) Pitch

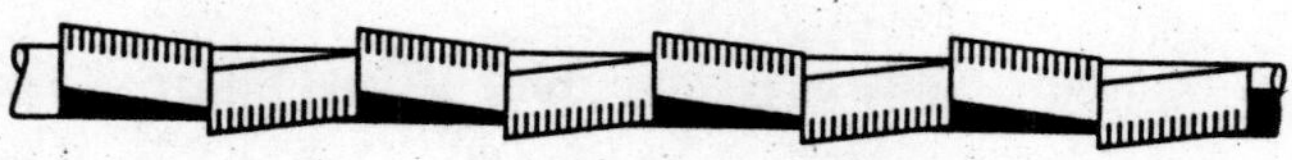

(b) Set of teeth

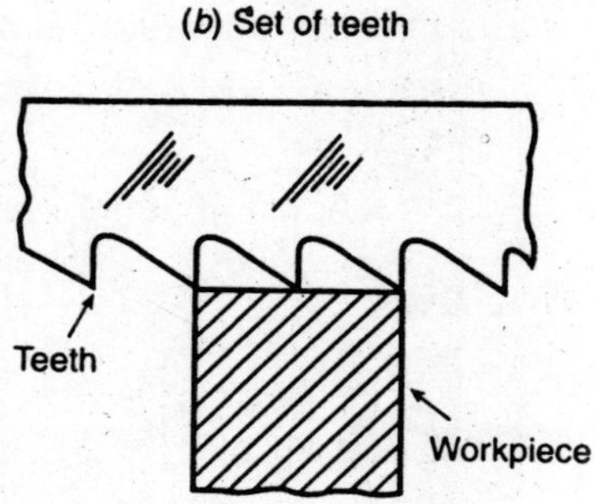

(c) Teeth in contact

Fig. 11.14.

Fig. 11.14 shows position of teeth, indicating

(*i*) pitch of teeth

(*ii*) set of teeth

(*iii*) teeth in contact with the workpiece.

Problems

1. What is boring
2. Sketch three types of boring bars.
3. Sketch a boring tool and name the angles.
4. Sketch a boring tool tip and name the angles.
5. Sketch the shapes of boring tool cutting edge.
6. What is sawing, sketch a hand hack saw and name its parts.
7. Sketch and explain blade tooth shapes.
8. Name types of hack saws and their applications.
9. State basic features of hack saw blades.

12

Taps & Dies

12.1 Tapping

A tap is used for cutting internal threads in a hole.

12.2 Parts of a Tap

The various parts of a tap are shown in Fig. 12.1. The taps are usually made of high speed steel and are properly hardened.

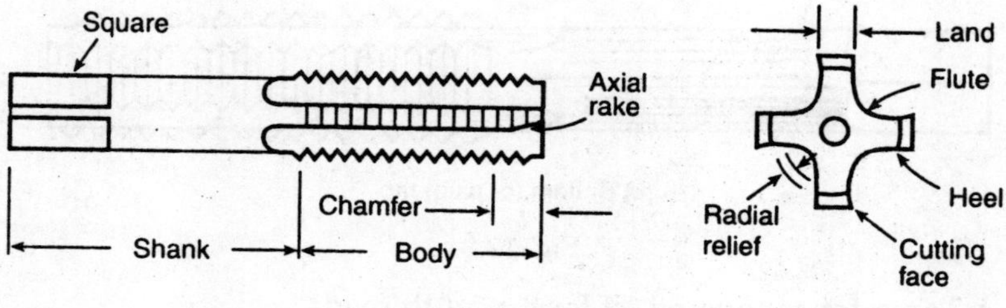

Fig. 12.1

12.3 Types of Taps

A tap is provided with cutting edges and hardened so that when it is screwed into a hole it cuts the metal. The shank of tap is left plain and the end is squared to accomodate the tap wrench shown in Fig. 12.2. The wrench is adjustable. The taps are usually made in sets of three to cut a particular size. These three taps are called:

(*i*) taper tap

(*ii*) second tap

(*iii*) bottom tap (plug tap)

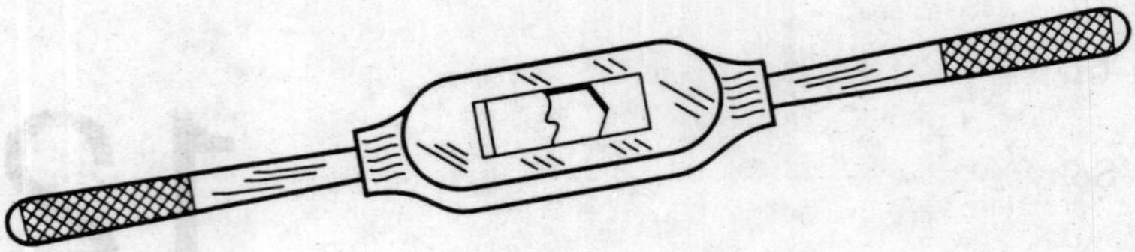

Fig. 12.2

These are shown in Fig. 12.3.

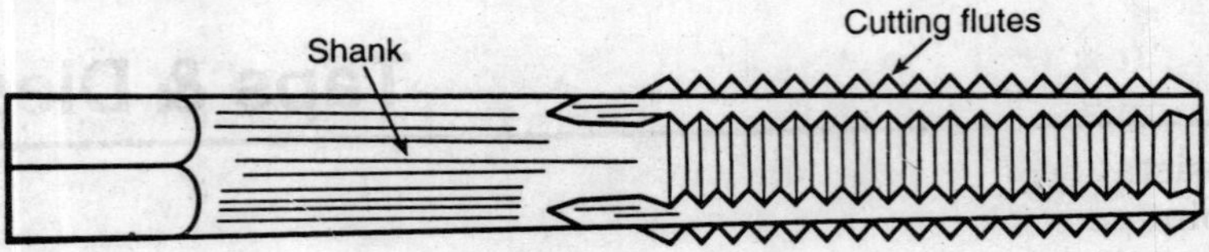

(*a*) Taper tap

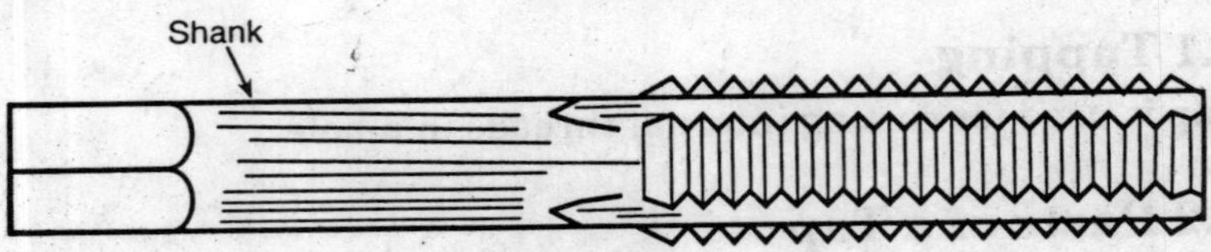

(*b*) Second tap

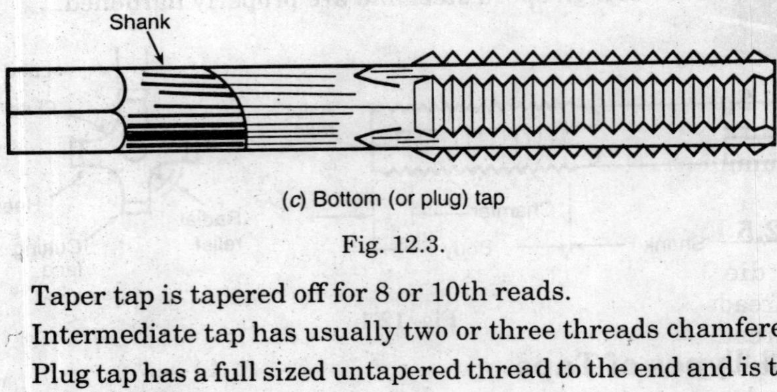

(*c*) Bottom (or plug) tap

Fig. 12.3.

Taper tap is tapered off for 8 or 10th reads.

Intermediate tap has usually two or three threads chamfered.

Plug tap has a full sized untapered thread to the end and is the main finishing tap.

12.4 Use of Taps

For tapping following procedure is adopted :

(*i*) Drill a hole into the work piece. Tapping size $= D - 2 \times h$

where D = Outside diameter

$\boldsymbol{h}$ **= Depth** of thread = 0.64 × pitch of thread (*ii*) Move taper tap into the workpiece with the tap wrench.

(*iii*) Except cast iron cutting fluid, soluble oil paraffin etc. should be used.

Soluble oil is used for

(*a*) Steel, (*b*) Brass and (*c*) Copper

Paraffin is used for aluminium.

(*iv*) After every half turn the tap should be reversed to clear the threads

(*v*) Then use second tap and plug tap.

When the end of the tap reaches the bottom of the hole, some resistance will be felt and no further force should be used at this point as the tap may be broken or the thread spoiled. Remove the taper tap and take the second one down as far as it will go and finally threads are cut at the bottom of the hole with a plug tap.

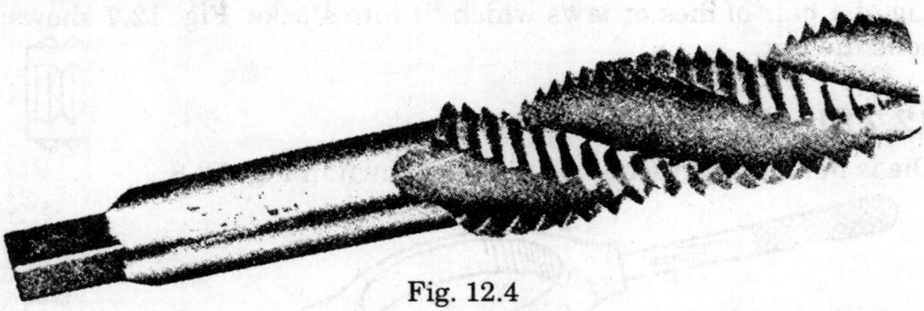

Fig. 12.4

Spiral fluted taps as shown in Fig. 12.4 have a helix similar to as in a twist drill. This tap can easily cut stainless steel, copper and aluminium.

12.5 Die

A die is used to cut external threads on bolts, pipes etc. The threads may be right hand or of left hand nature. A die is usually made of high quality steel and properly heat treated. Fig. 12.5 shows a die.

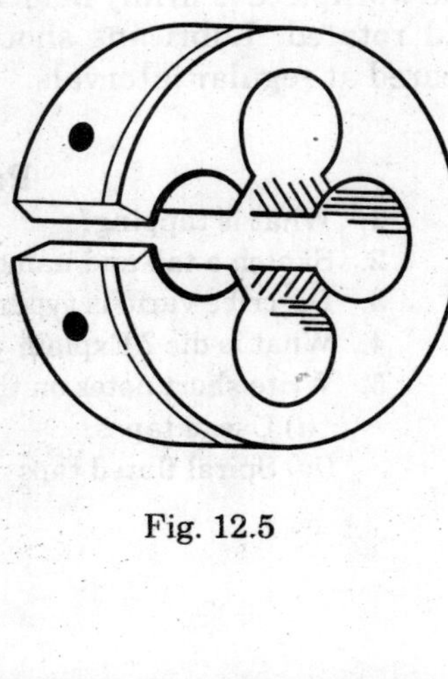

Fig. 12.5

12.6 Types of Dies

Various types of dies are as follows:

(*i*) Button dies or split dies

(*ii*) Half dies (*iii*) Solid die nut.

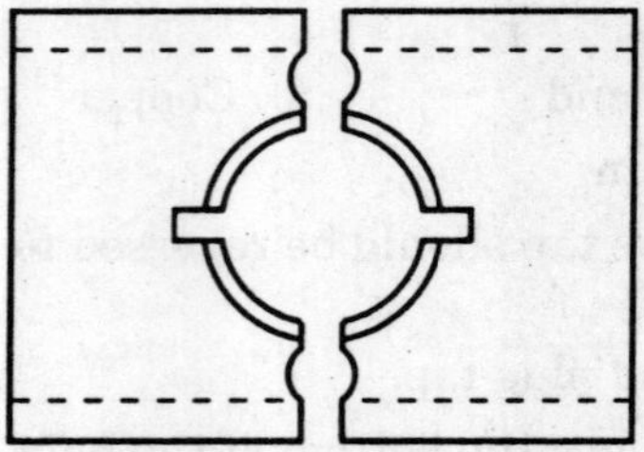

Fig. 12.6

Fig. 12.7

Button die allows a limited amount of adjustment. Half dies have the advantage of taking smaller cuts and the solid die nut is used to repair a damaged thread. Fig. 12.6 shows half dies consisting of a pair of dies or jaws which fit into stocks. Fig. 12.7 shows solid die nut.

12.7 Stock

Die is held in and turned by a stock shown in Fig. 12.8.

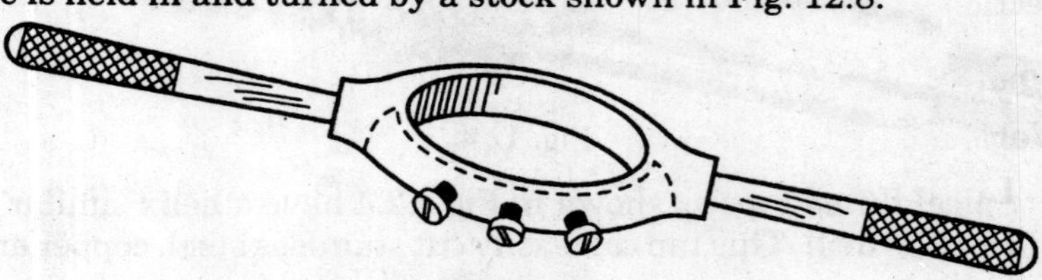

Fig. 12.8

12.8 Using dies

The workpiece is firmly held in vice and the die is held in die stock and rotated. Lubricant should be used and threads should be cleared at regular intervals.

Problems

1. What is tapping?
2. Sketch a tap and name its parts.
3. Describe various types of taps.
4. What is die ? Explain various type of dies.
5. Write short notes on the following.
   (*i*) Use of tapes, (*ii*) use of dies, (*iii*) Die stock
   (*iv*) Spiral fluted taps (*v*) Tap wrench.

13

Gauges

13.0 Introduction

Gauges are used to check a part against a pre-set standard size every part manufactured should meet a standard for size and shape in order to perform its design function properly. Gauges can check the various dimensions of a component quickly and accurately. Basically there are three types of gauges (*i*) Work-shop gauges, (*ii*) Inspection gauges and (*iii*) Master gauges.

13.1 Types of Gauges

Various types of gauges are as follows :

1. Limit gauges :

(*a*) Plug gauges

(*b*) Snap gauges

(*c*) Ring gauges

13.1.1. Plug Gauges

Fig. 13.1 shows a plain cylindrical plug gauge. It is used to check the size of a hole. It has two ends called Go end and No Go end.

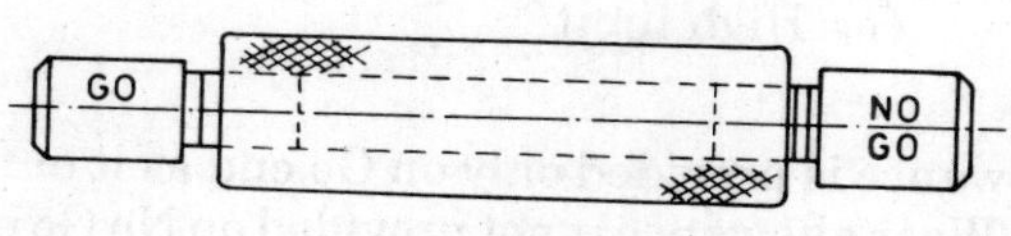

Fig. 13.1

The Go end should pass through the hole in the component whereas No Go end should not pass through the hole as shown in Fig. 13.2.

No Go end is smaller than Go end. Go and No Go ends are called gauging members of the plug gauge.

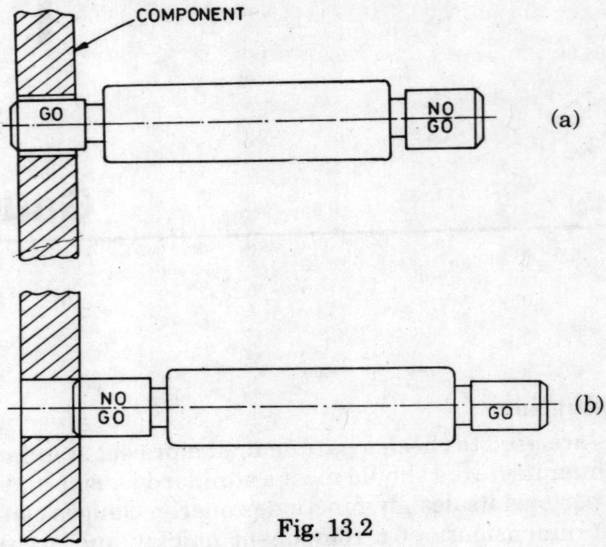

Fig. 13.2

The size of Go end and No Go end is determined as follows :

$$D = \text{Go end diameter (new)}$$

$$= (K + Z) \pm \frac{H}{2}$$

where k = Low limit

Z = Wear allowance

$\frac{H}{2}$ = Manufacturing allowance

D_1 = No Go end diameter

$$= G \pm \frac{H}{2}$$

where G = High limit

Wear allowance is provided only on Go end as it enters the hole continuously. Wear allowance is not provided on No Go end. In order to increase the wear resistance of plug gauges they are chrome plated. The gauges are hardened and ground and lapped.

The advantage of chrome plating is that when finally the 'Go' end wears it can be readily renewed by plating and brought to original dimensions by grinding and lapping.

Wear allowance is usually taken equal to 5 to 15% of work tolerance. Gauging elements of the gauge may be made from OHNS steel or EN-31. The usual hardness is HRC55 to HRC60.

Tolerance may be specified on the gauge as shown in Fig. 13.3.

Reference temperature for gauging is 20°C.

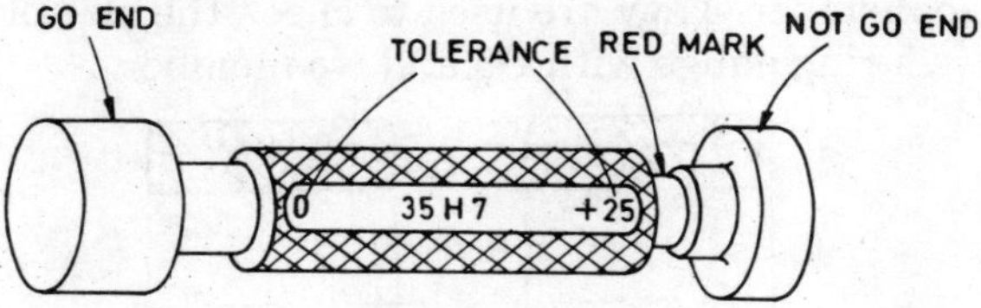

Fig. 13.3

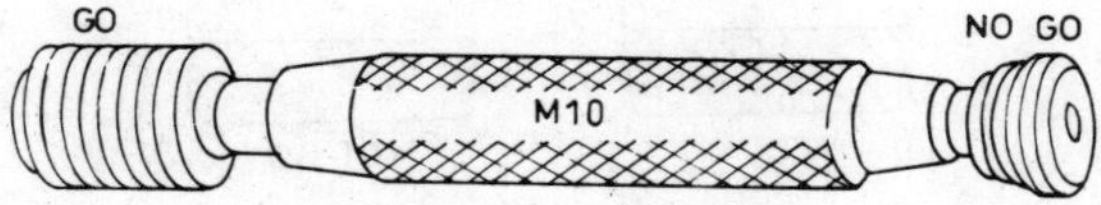

Fig. 13.4. Shows a threaded plug gauge.

13.1.2. Snap Gauge

It is used to measure the diameter of a shaft. Fig. 13.5 shows a C-shaped snap gauge having two button anvils.

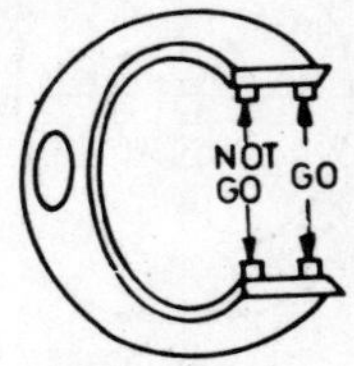

Fig. 13.5

The size of Go end and No GO end are determined as follows:

G = High limit

K = Low limit

$\frac{H}{2}$ = Manufacturing tolerance

Z_1 = Distance between centre of tolerance zone of new go gauge and go work piece limit

Y_1 = Wear allowance

α_1 = Safety zone provided for compensating measuring uncertainties of gauges

$$\text{Go gauge (new) size} = (G - Z_1) \pm \frac{H}{2}$$

Go gauge (worn out) size $= G + Y_1 - \alpha_1$

No go gauge $= K + \alpha_1 \pm \dfrac{H}{2}$

13.1.3. Ring gauge

Ring gauges are usually used in pairs consisting of Go member and No Go member. They are used to check the size of shafts. Fig. 13.6 shows a ring gauge with Go and No member.

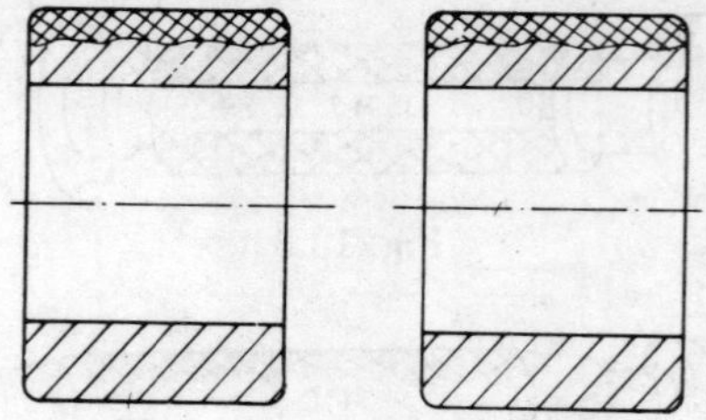

Fig. 13.6.

2. Receiver gauge.

It is used to check both inside and out side diameter of a ring. Fig. 13.7 shows a receiver gauge.

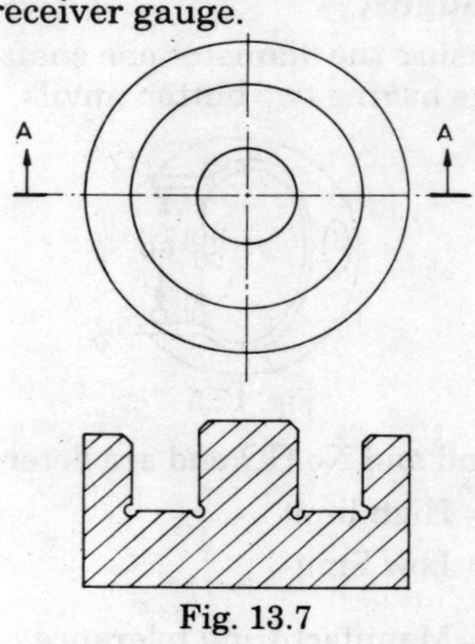

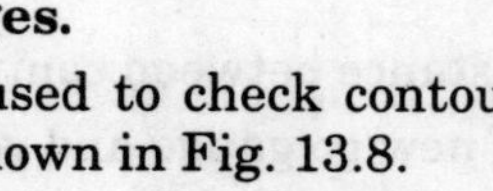

Fig. 13.7

3. Template gauges.

They are mainly used to check contour forms such as radii, angles or threads as shown in Fig. 13.8.

Template gauges compare a surface against a master of the exact shape. When used, they can easily detect any variation from the desired form.

4. Flush Pin gauge.

It is mostly used as depth indicator.

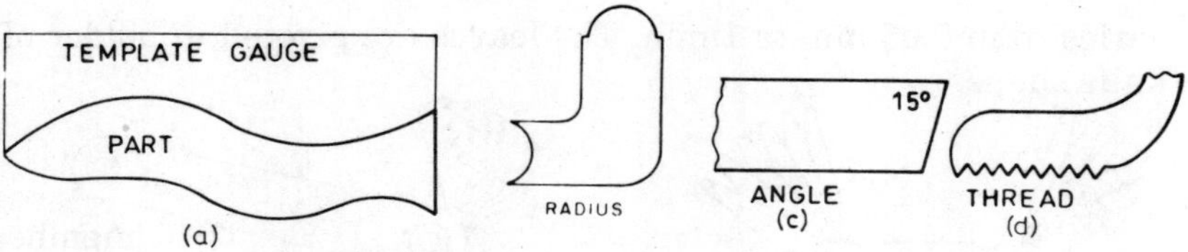

Fig. 13.8

A pin or rod is used to check the relationship of a surface to the top of the gauge. Figure 13.9 shows the top edge of the part resting against the under-side of the gauge, and the pin checking the depth of the slot. If the slot is too shallow, the pin will not drop in far enough. If the slot is too deep, it will drop too far.

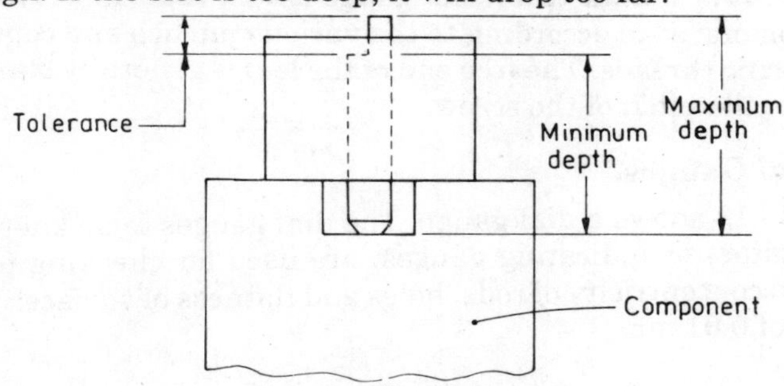

Fig. 13.9

The limits are set by two ground surfaces and determination is made by passing the finger and over the edge of the pin. It is a relatively simple gauge to use and is more accurate than the plate gauge.

5. Radius or Fillet Gauge

Fig. 13.10 shows a radius gauge. It is used to check the radii of curvature of concave or convex surfaces. It consists of a number of steel blades having standard radii ground and lapped on the ends and sides.

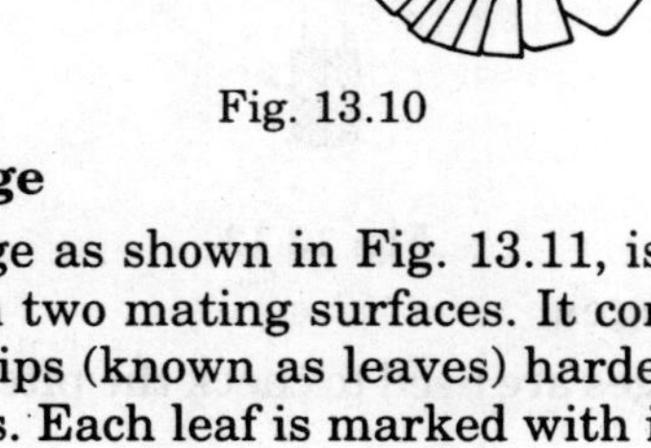

Fig. 13.10

6. Feeler Gauge

The feeler gauge as shown in Fig. 13.11, is used to check the clearances between two mating surfaces. It consists of a series of thin steel sheet strips (known as leaves) hardened and ground to various thicknesses. Each leaf is marked with its thickness which varies from 0.05 mm to 1 mm. The leaves are pivoted in holder of knife shape.

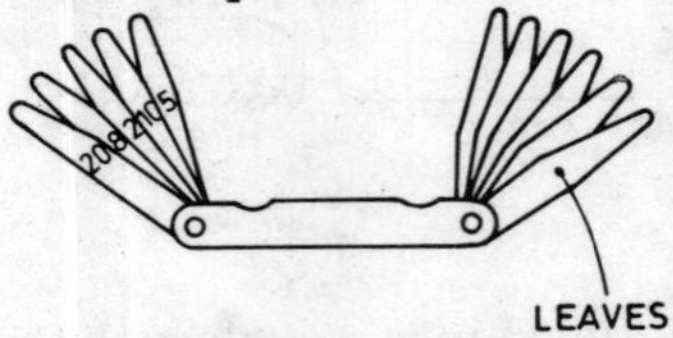

Fig. 13.11

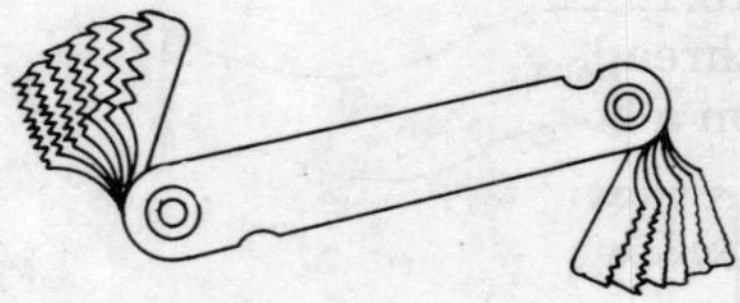

Fig. 13.12. Screw pitch gauge.

7. Screw Pitch Gauge.

Fig. 13.12 shows screw pitch gauge. It is used to check the pitch of a screw. It is similar to a feeler gauge except that the leaves are notched on one edge according to the various pitches and contours of the specific threads. The free end of the leaf is generally stamped to indicate the pitch of the screw.

8. Dial Gauges.

Fig. 13.13 shows a dial gauge. The dial gauges (also known as dial indicators or indicating gauges) are used for checking parallelism and concentricity of rods, holes and flatness of surfaces to an accuracy of 0.01 mm.

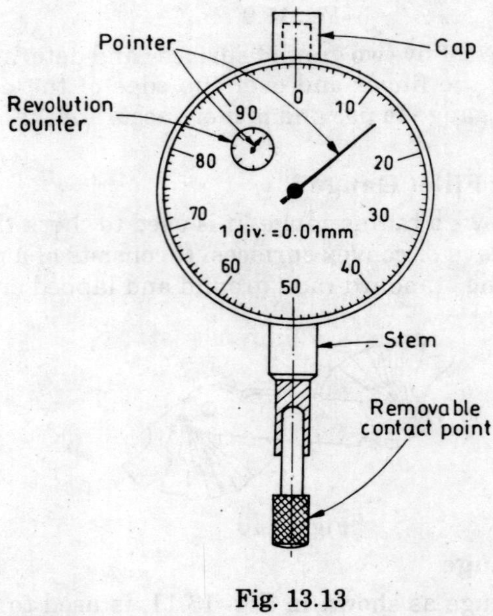

Fig. 13.13

9. Thread Gauges.

The thread gauges are used to check the pitch diameter of screw threads.

Fig. 13.14 shows external limit thread gauge whereas. Fig. 13.15 shows internal thread gauge. It is a plug gauge to check threads in a nut. External thread gauge is used to check the threads on a bolt.

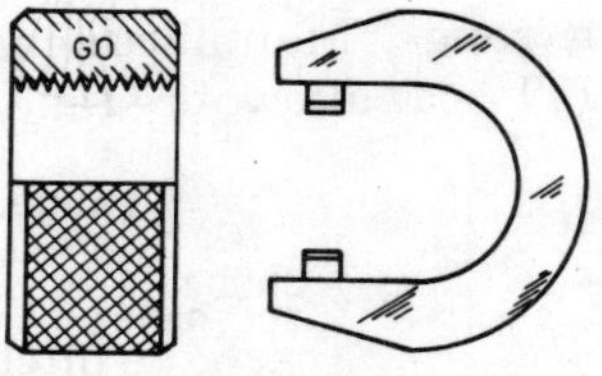

Fig. 13.14

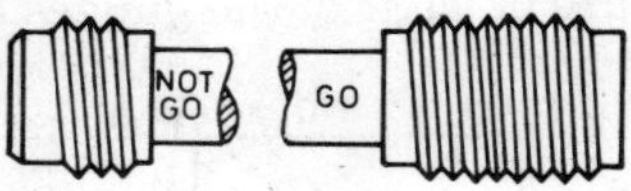

Fig. 13.15

13.2 Taylor's Principle

It states that Go gauge should check all related dimensions simultaneously whereas No Go gauge should check only one dimension at a time.

For example, a hole in a plate can have the following errors.

(*i*) Dimensional error

(*ii*) Circularity error

(*iii*) Strengthness error.

According to Taylor's principle, a single Go gauge should check all the above errors simultaneously whereas separate No Go gauges should be used to check each error.

13.3 Maximum Metal Condition (M.M.C.)

It refers to the condition of hole or shaft when maximum material is left on *i.e.* high limit of shaft and low limit of hole.

13.4 Minimum Metal Condition (M.M.C.)

If refers to the condition of hole or shaft when minimum material is left on. Such as low limit of shaft and high limit of hole as shown in Fig. 13.16.

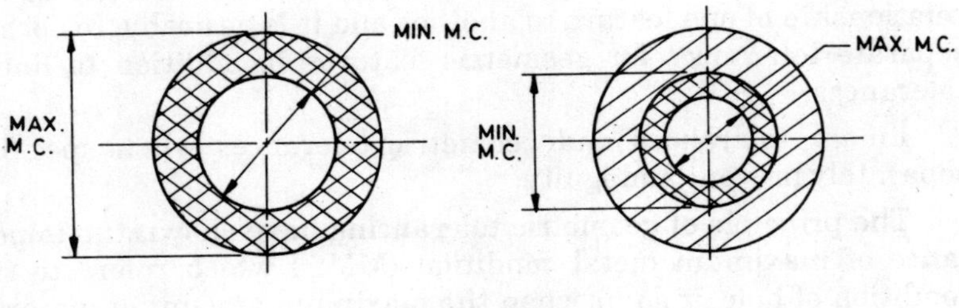

Fig. 13.16

13.5 Allowances

Gauges should be provided with (*a*) Manufacturing tolerance (*b*) Wear allowance

Manufacturing tolerance is disposed opposite to the direction of wear as shown in Fig. 13.17 for a plug gauge. Manufacturing tolerance is nearly 10% of work tolerance (T) wear allowance takes care of wear of the gauges during use.

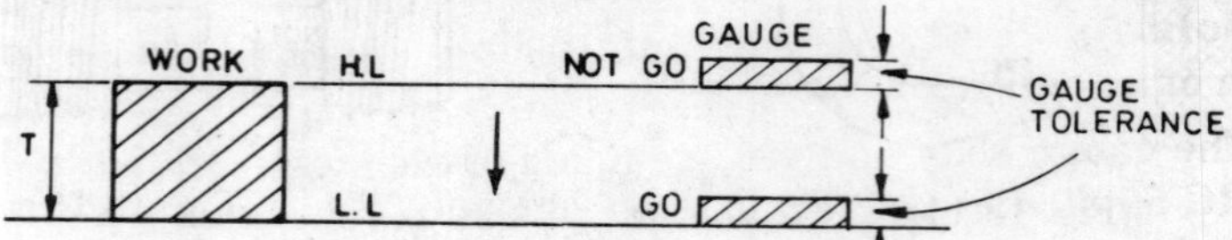

Fig. 13.17

13.6 Inspection Fixtures

There are two general types of inspection fixtures :

1. Gauging fixture 2. Measuring fixture.

Gauging fixtures are used to check a part against a present standard size. Measuring fixtures can indicate exactly where and how much part is out of tolerance.

While measuring fixtures are useful, they are often too fragile for shop use and must remain in the inspection room. Gauging fixtures, however, are built tougher and can normally be used in the shop.

13.7 Geometric Tolerances

Geometric features of a component such as :

(*i*) Strengthness (*ii*) Flatness

(*iii*) Parallelism (*iv*) Squareness

(*v*) Angularity (*vi*) Concentricity

must be considered and specified and must be controlled.

Geometric tolerance are concerned with the accuracy of the relationship of one feature to another and it is desirable to specify separate tolerances for geometric features in addition to linear tolerances.

Linear tolerances and geometric tolerances when specified separately prevent ambiguity.

The principle of geometric tolerancing have shown the importance of maximum metal condition (MMC) which refers to the condition of hole or shaft when the maximum amount of material is left on *i.e.* high limit shaft and low limit hole.

It is always these limits which critically affect inter-changeability of parts.

Example 13.1. *Design and sketch a flush pin gauge to measure a hole depth of* 100 ± 0.2 *in a mild steel work piece shown in Fig. 13.18.*

Solution. Fig. 13.19 shows a flush pin gauge to measure the depth of hole in the workpiece.

The gauge body and pin are made of die steel with a hardness of HRC 55-60. Grub screw is made of C30 plain carbon steel.

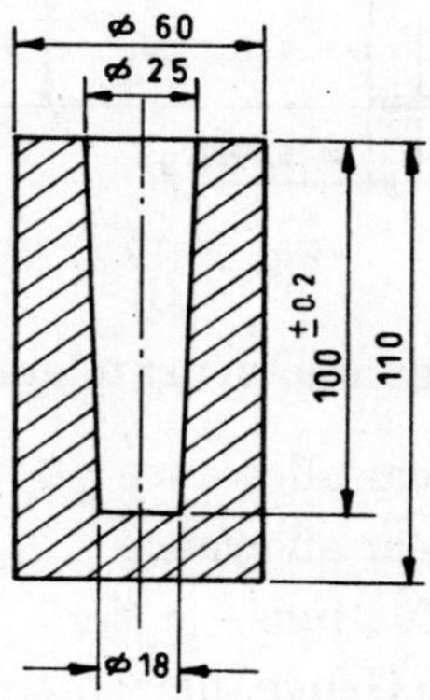

Fig. 13.18

Example 13.2. *Design and sketch a plug gauge to measure a hole of diameter* $40^{\pm 0.02}_{\pm 0.01}$.

Solution.

$$
\begin{aligned}
\text{Basic size} &= 40 \text{ mm} \\
&= 40.01 \text{ mm} \\
K &= \text{Low limit (L.L.)} \\
G &= \text{High limit (H.L.)} \\
&= 40.02 \text{ mm} \\
T &= \text{Work tolerance} \\
&= \text{H.L.} - \text{L.L.} \\
&= 40.02 - 40.01 = 0.01
\end{aligned}
$$

From table 13.1 for gauge tolerance for checking holes for $T = 0.01$ and basic size 40 mm.

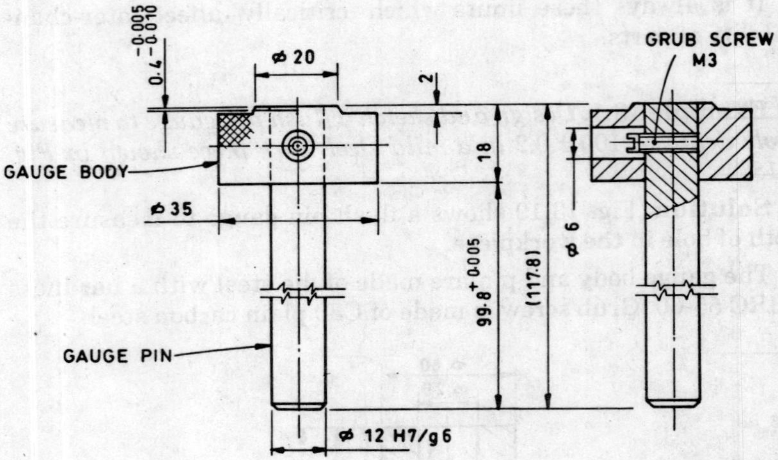

Fig. 13.19

$$\frac{H}{2} = \text{Manufacturing tolerance} = 0.002 \text{ mm}$$

$$Y = \text{Wear allowance} = 0$$

$$Z = \text{Wear allowance}$$
$$= 0.011 \text{ mm}$$

$$D = \text{Go Gauge (new) diameter}$$
$$= (K + Z) \pm \frac{H}{2}$$
$$= (40.01 + 0.011) \pm 0.0.002$$
$$= 40.021 \pm 0.002 \text{ mm}$$

Go gauge (work out) = K – Y

$$= 40.01 - 0$$
$$= 40.01 \text{ mm}$$

$$D_1 = \text{No go gauge diameter}$$
$$= G \pm \frac{H}{2}$$
$$= 40.02 \pm 0.002$$

Fig. 13.20 shows a plug gauge with typical dimensions.

Table 13.1. Gauge Tolerance for Checking Holes
(All dimensions are in microns)

Nominal size, mm		*Symbol*	*Work Tolerance Grades*						
Over	*upto & includ*		6	7	8	9	10	11	12
–	3	T	6	10	14	25	40	60	100
		H/2	0.6	1	1	1	1	2	2
		y	1	1.5	3	0	0	0	0
		Z	1	1.5	2	5	5	10	10
3	6	T	8	12	18	30	48	75	120
		H/2	0.75	1.25	1.25	1.25	1.25	2.5	2.5
		y	1	1.5	3	0	0	0	0
		Z	1.5	2	3	6	6	12	12
6	10	T	9	15	22	36	58	90	150
		H/2	0.75	1.25	1.25	1.25	1.25	3	3
		$H_2/2$	0.75	0.75	0.75	0.75	0.75	2	2
		y	1	1.5	3	0	0	0	0
		Z	1.5	2	3	7	7	14	14
10	18	T	11	18	27	43	70	110	180
		H/2	1	1.5	1.5	1.5	1.5	4	4
		$H_2/2$	1	1	1	1	1	2.5	2.5
		y	1.5	2	4	0	0	0	0
		Z	2	2.5	4	8	8	16	16
18	30	T	13	21	33	52	84	130	210
		H/2	1.25	2	2	2	2	4.5	4.5
		$H_2/2$	1.25	1.25	1.25	1.25	1.25	3	3
		y	1.5	3	4	0	0	0	0
		Z	2	3	5	9	9	19	19
30	50	T	16	25	39	62	100	160	250
		H/2	1.25	2	2	2	2	5.5	5.5
		$H_2/2$	1.25	1.25	1.25	1.25	1.25	3.5	3.5
		y	2	3	5	0	0	0	0
		Z	2.5	3.5	6	11	11	22	22

Material of gauge : T 215 Cr 12
Hardness : HRC 55 – 60
Material of body : C60

Example 13.3. *Design and sketch a snap gauge to check shaft of diameter* $270^{-0.05}$

Solution.

G = High limit = 270 mm
K = Low limit = 270 – 0.05 = 269.95 mm

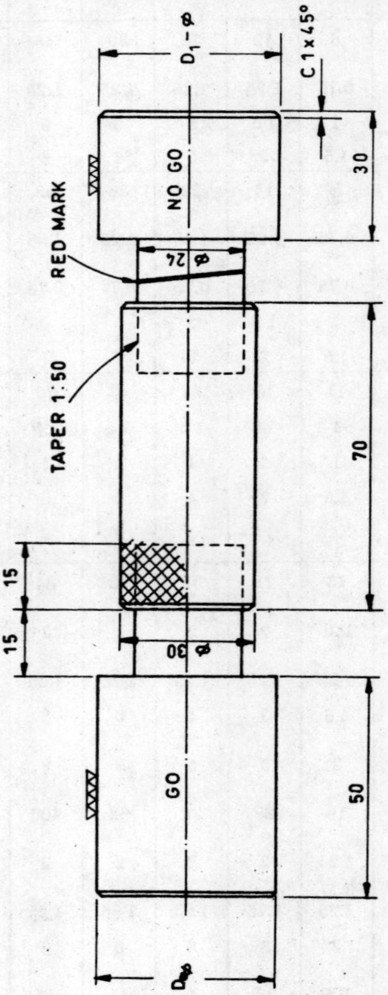

Fig. 13.20

$$T = \text{Work tolerance} = H.L. - L.L.$$
$$= 270 - 269.95 = 0.05$$

Form table 13.2, $\frac{H}{2}$ = Manufacturing tolerance= 0.006 mm

$$Y_1 = 0.006 \text{ mm}$$
$$Z_1 = 0.008 \text{ mm}$$
$$\alpha_1 = 0.003 \text{ mm}$$

Go gauge new size $= (G - Z_1) \pm \frac{H}{2}$

$$= (270 - 0.008) \pm 0.006 = 269.992 \pm 0.006 \text{ mm}$$

Go gauge worm out size $= G + Y_1 - \alpha_1$

$$= 270 + 0.006 - 0.003 = 270.003 \text{ mm}$$

No Go gauge size $= K + \alpha_1 \pm \frac{H}{2}$

$$= 269.95 + 0.003 \pm 0.006$$
$$= 269.953 \pm 0.006 \text{ mm}$$

Fig. 13.21 shows a snap gauge.

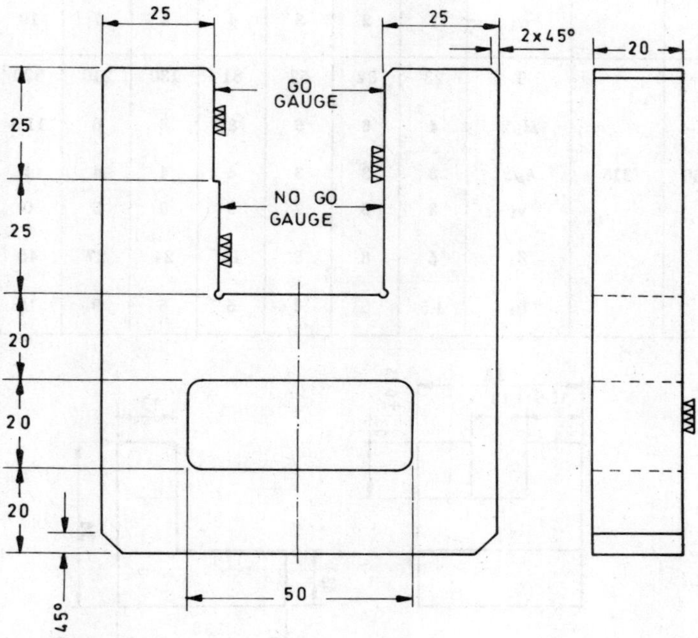

Fig. 13.21

Table 13.2 Gauge Tolerance for Checking Shafts

(All dimensions in microns)

Nominal size, mm		*Symbol*	*Work Tolerance Grades*							
Over	*upto & includ*		5	6	7	8	9	10	11	12
120	180	T	18	25	40	63	100	160	250	400
		$H_1/2$	2.5	4	4	6	6	6	9	9
		$H_p/2$	1.75	1.75	1.75	2.5	2.5	2.5	2.5	2.5
		y_1	3	4	4	6	0	0	0	0
		Z_1	3	6	6	9	18	18	32	32
180	250	T	20	29	46	72	115	185	290	460
		$H_1/2$	3.5	5	5	7	7	7	10	10
		$H_p/2$	2.25	2.25	2.25	3.5	3.5	3.5	3.5	3.5
		y_1	3	5	6	7	0	0	0	0
		Z_1	4	7	7	12	21	24	40	45
		α_1	1	2	3	4	4	7	10	15
250	315	T	23	32	52	81	130	210	320	520
		$H_1/2$	4	6	6	8	8	8	11.5	11.5
		$h_p/2$	3	3	3	4	4	4	4	4
		y_1	3	6	7	9	0	0	0	0
		Z_1	5	8	8	14	24	27	45	50
		α_1	1.5	3	4	6	6	9	15	20

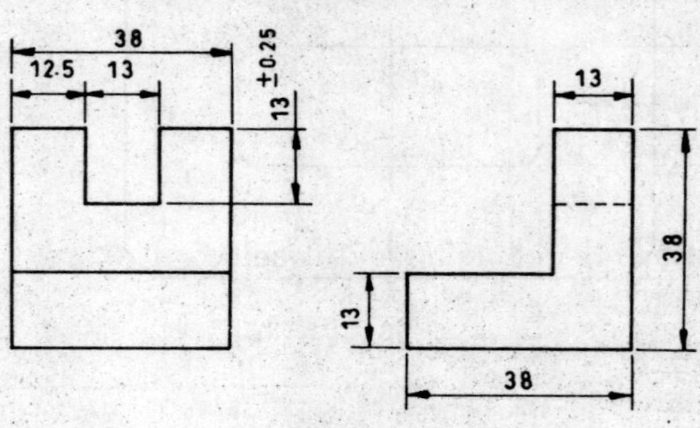

Fig. 13.22

Example 13.4. *Draw and design a flush pin gauge to measure a depth of slot* $13^{\pm .25}$ *mm in a mild steel component shown in Fig. 13.22.*

Solution. Fig 13.23 shows the flush pin gauge to check the depth of slot.

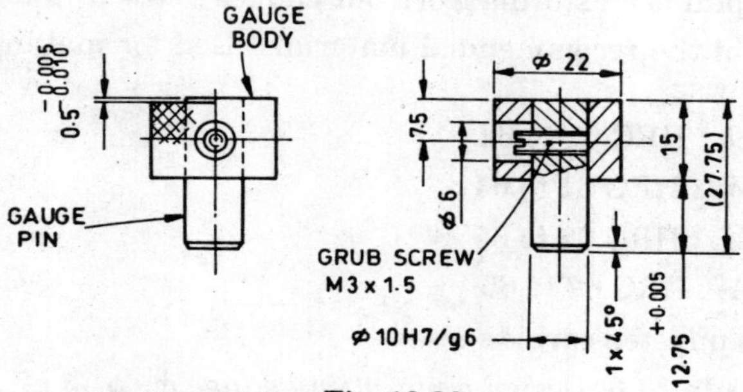

Fig. 13.23

Example 13.5.

(*a*) *State the main purposes of gauging.*

(*b*) *State factors which affect selection of materials used for making gauges.*

Solution.

(*a*) Gauges are used mainly (*i*) to control the dimensions of a component within the prescribed limits.

(*ii*) to reject components which are outside the given limits.

Gauges are designed to check one of the following seven basic elements of workpiece geometry.

(*i*) Distance

(*ii*) Flatness

(*iii*) Parallelism

(*iv*) Perpendicularity

(*v*) Angularity

(*vi*) Concentricity

(*vii*) Surface texture

(*b*) Following factors affect the selection of materials used for making gauges.

(*i*) Tolerance to be checked

(*ii*) Number of components to be checked

(*iii*) Composition and hardness of material

(*iv*) Complexity of workpiece to be gauged

(*v*) Cost of the material

(*vi*) Wear resistance of the material.

Chromium plating of gauges increases the wear resistance. It is also helpful for restoring worn out gauges to the original size.

Some of the recommended materials used for making gauges are as follows :

(*i*) O_2 : HRC 61 to 64

(*ii*) W_1 : HRC 61 to 64

(*iii*) M_2 : HRC 62 to 65

(*iv*) A_2 : HRC 62 to 65

(*v*) Tungsten carbide

Example 13.6. *Design a plain ring gauge for ϕ 35 k7 shaft.*

Solution. Fig. 13.24 shows a go and no go ring gauge. Ring gauges are made in pairs.

$$35\,k7 = 35^{+0.027}_{+0.002}$$

K = Low limit = 35.002 mm

G = High limit = 35.027

T = Work tolerance = $G - K$

$$= 35.027 - 35.002 = 0.025$$

From table 13.3.

For $T = 0.025$ mm

$\frac{H}{2}$ = Manufacturing tolerance

$$= 0.002 \text{ mm}$$

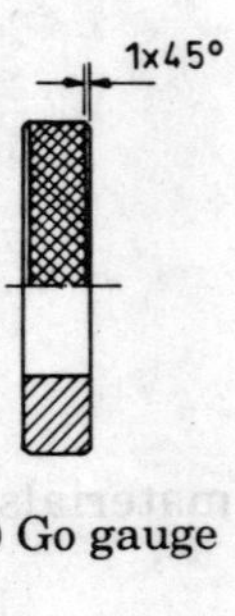

(*a*) Go gauge

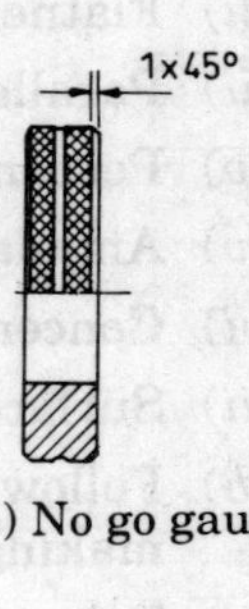

(*b*) No go gauge

Fig. 13.24

$$Y_1 = 0.003$$

$$Z_1 = 0.0035 \text{ mm}$$

Table 13.3. Gauge to lerauce for checking shafts (All values are in microns)

Nominal mm	*Sizes*		*Work Tolerance Grades*																
Over	Up to & Incl.	Symbols	5	6		7	8	9		10	11		12	13		14	15		16
–	3	T	4	6		10	12	25		40	60		100	140		250	400		600
		$H_1/2$	0–6		1		1–5		1–5			2			5			5	
		$H_p/2$	0–4		0–4		0–6		0–6			0–6			1			1	
		Y_1	1		1–5		3		0			0			0			0	
		Z_1	1		1–5		2		5			10			20			40	
3	6	$H_1/2$	0–75		1–25		2		2			2–5			6			6	
		$H_p/2$	0–5		0–5		0–75		0–75			0–75			1–25			1–25	
		Y_1	1		1–5		3		0			0			0			0	
		Z_1	1		2		3		6			12			24			48	
6	10	T	6	9		15	22	36		58	90		150	220		360	580		90
		$H_1/2$	0.75		1–25		2		2			13			7–5			7–5	
		$H_p/2$	0–5		0–5		0–75		0–75			0–75			1–25			1–25	
		Y_1	1		1–5		3		0			0			0			0	
		Z_1	1		2		3		7			14			28			56	
10	18	T	8	11		18	27	43		70	110		180	270		430	700		110
		$H_1/2$	1		1–5		2–5		2–5			4			9			9	
		$H_p/2$	0–6		0–6		1		1			1			1–5			1–5	
		Y_1	1–5		2		4		0			0			0			0	
		Z_1	1–5		2–5		4			8			16			32		64	

Table 13.3. (Contd...)

Nominal mm	*Sizes*		*Work Tolerance Grades*																
Over	Up to & Incl.	Symbols	5	6		7	8	9		10	11		12	13		14	15		16
18	30	T	9	13		21	33	52		84	130		210	330		520	840		130
		$H_1/2$	1–25		2		3		3			4–5			10–5			10–5	
		$H_p/2$	0–75		0–75		1–25		1–25			1–25			10–5			10–5	
		Y_1	2		3		4		0			0			0			0	
		Z_1	1–5		3		5		9			19			36			72	
30	50	$H_1/2$	1–25		2		3–5		3–5			5–5			12–5			12–5	
		$H_p/2$	0–75		0–75		1–25		1–25			1–25			2			2	
		Y_1	2		3		5		0			0			0			0	
		Z_1	2		3–5		6		11			22			42			80	
50	80	$H_1/2$	1–5		2–5		4		4			6–5			15			15	
		$H_p/2$	1		1		1–5		1–5			1–5			2–5			2.5	
		Y_1	2		3		5		0			0			0			0	
		Z_1	2		4		5		0			20			48			80	

$$\text{Go gauge new diameter} = (G - Z_1) \pm \frac{H}{2}$$

$$= (35.027 - 0.0035) \pm 0.002$$

$$\text{No go gauge} = K \pm \frac{H}{2}$$

$$= 35.002 \pm 0.002$$

Material : OHNS

Hardness : 60-62 HRC

For a ring gauge wear allowance is given in the opposite direction of its wear that is its initial dimension will be smaller than nominal Go limit dimension.

Wear allowance ranges between 5 to 20% of workpiece tolerance, higher percentages used for closely tolerated workpieces.

Example. 13.7. *To design a centre distance gauge to measure a centre distance of 52 mm between two holes in a M.S. component. The two holes have a diameter of* ϕ 15 *H*9 *and* ϕ 14 *H*10.

Solution. Fig. 13.25 shows the component and Fig. 13.26 shows the gauge. The gauge has

(*i*) Pin A

(*ii*) Pin B

(*iii*) Base plate

Pin *A* is of diameter $\phi\ 14.9^{-0.005}$ and pin *B* is of diameter $\phi\ 13.9^{-0.005}$. Pin *A* and Pin *B* are 24 mm long.

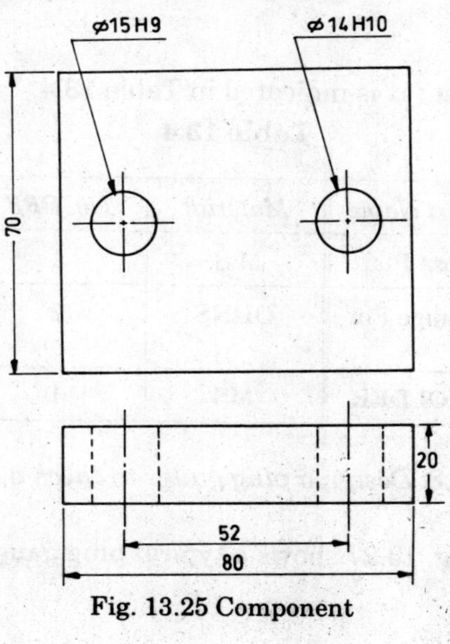

Fig. 13.25 Component

The centre distance (C.D.) between pins in gauge will be as :

$$CD = 52 \pm 0.005$$

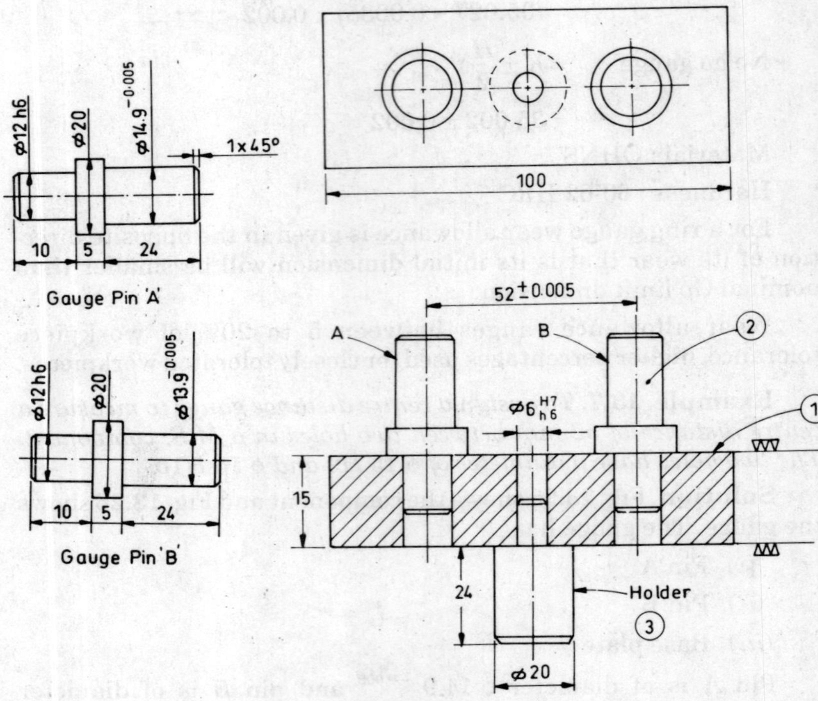

Fig. 13.26

Material List : It is indicated in Table 13.4.

Table 13.4

S.No.	*Part Name*	*Material*	*No. OFF*	*REMARKS*
1	Base Plate	M.S.	1	—
2	Gauge Pin	OHNS	2	Hardness 55-60 HRC
3	HOLDER	MS	1	—

Example 13.8. *Design a plug gauge to check a hole of diameter $180^{+0.25}$.*

Solution. Fig. 13.27 shows a typical plug gauge

G = High limit (H.L.)

$= 180.25$ mm

k = Low limit (L.L.)

$= 180$ mm.

T = Work tolerance

$= H.L - L.L.$

$= 0.25$

From table for gauge tolerance for checking holes.

$$\frac{H}{2} = 0.009$$

$$Y = 0$$

$$Z = 0.032$$

For go gauge

$$D = \text{Diameter} = (K + Z) \pm \frac{H}{2}$$

$$= (180 + 0.032) \pm 0.009 \text{ mm}$$

For no go gauge

$$D = \text{Diameter} = G \pm \frac{H}{2}$$

$$= 180.25 \pm 0.009$$

Other dimensions may be taken as follows :

d = Inside diameter of plug

$= 150$ mm

d_1 = Shank diameter

$= 20$ mm

$l_1 = 20$ mm

$l_2 = 40$ mm

$l_3 = 25$ mm

$L = 120$ mm

$W = 20$ mm

Screw = $M6 \times 1$

Material :

Plug : OHNS, 60–62 HRC

Shank : C35 Steel

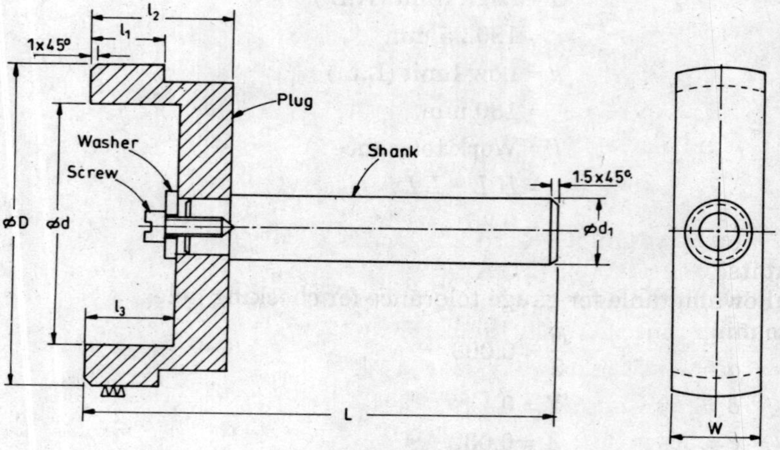

Fig. 13.27

Example 13.9

(*a*) *Sketch and explain a pilot plug gauge.*

(*b*) *Sketch and describe a taper plug gauge.*

(*c*) *Sketch and designate the parts of a snap-gauge.*

Solution.

(*a*) **Pitot plug gauge :** Fig. 13.28 shows a pilot plug gauge. The gauge has a small chamber, then a narrow ring or pilot having the same diameter as that of a gauge followed by a groove and the main body of the gauge.

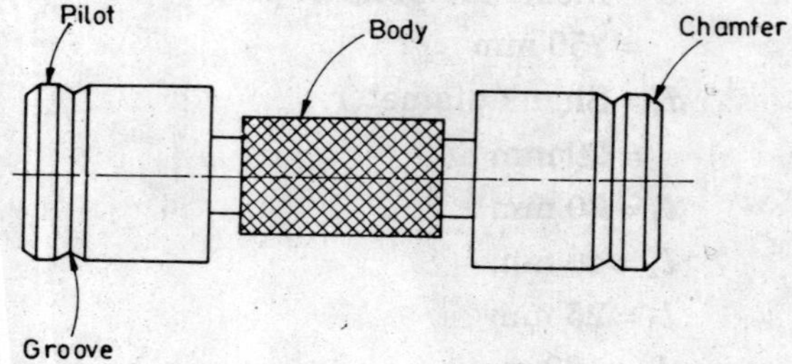

Fig. 13.28

(*b*) **Taper plug gauge :** Fig. 13.29 shows a taper plug gauge. It is used to check the taper and size of tapered cylindrical hole such as in drill sleeve and machine tool spindles.

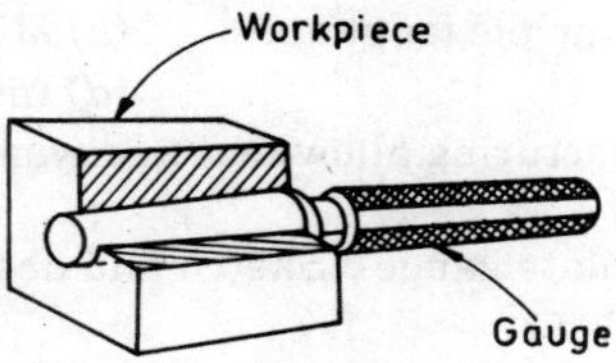

Fig. 13.29

(*c*) Snap gauge : Fig. 13.30 shows a snap gauge. It has two jaws at its two ends. One jaw is marked Go and corresponds to maximum allowable diameter. The other jaw is marked No Go and corresponds to minimum allowable diameter.

a = maximum size go side

b = minimum size no go side

c = actual size of the shaft.

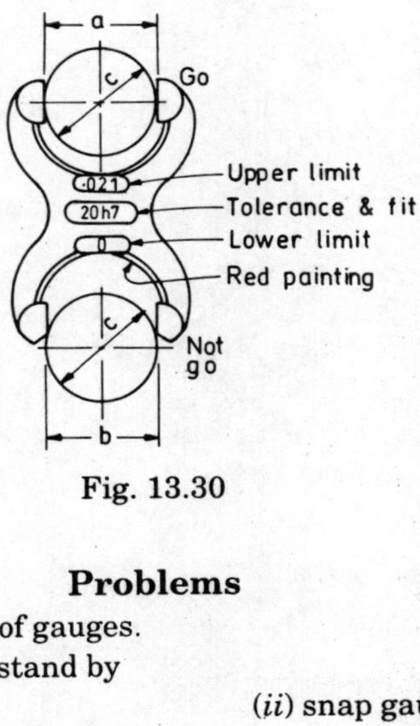

Fig. 13.30

Problems

1. State the purposes of gauges.
2. What do you understand by
   (*i*) plug gauges (*ii*) snap gauges
   (*iii*) ring gauges
3. Discuss the design of
   (*i*) plug gauge (*ii*) flush pin gauge
   (*iii*) snap gauge
4. Sketch and design a plug gauge to check hole of size 42 H_7
5. Sketch and design a shaft snap gauge to check the shaft of diameter $32g^6$.
6. Sketch and design a flush pain gauge to check hole of 5ϕ and depth $15^{\pm 0.3}$ mm in a cylinder of 10ϕ and 60 mm long.
7. Write short notes on the following :

(*a*) Taylor's principle for gauges (*b*) MMC
(*c*) Min M.C. (*d*) Inspection fixtures

8. Discuss manufacturing allowance and wear allowance provided in gauges.
9. What is a template gauge ? Sketch and describe the following template gauges :
   (*i*) Radius gauge (*ii*) Thread gauge
   (*iii*) Angle gauge
10. Sketch and describe the following types of gauges :
   (*i*) Flush pin gauge (*ii*) Radius gauge
   (*iii*) Feeler gauge (*iv*) Screw pitch gauge
11. Write short notes on the following :
   (*i*) Dial gauge (*ii*) Thread gauge

14

Moulds and Dies

14.1 Introduction

The components made from plastics are shaped by the process of moulding in metal moulds. From manufacturing view point the moulds have mainly two parts.

(*i*) cavity and core

(*ii*) remainder of the mould. This is commonly referred to as bolster work.

Cavity is the female portion of the mould which generally gives the external shape to the part to be moulded.

Core is the male portion of the mould. It gives internal shape to the part being produced.

Fig. 14.1 shows movable core and Fig. 14.2 shows stationary core.

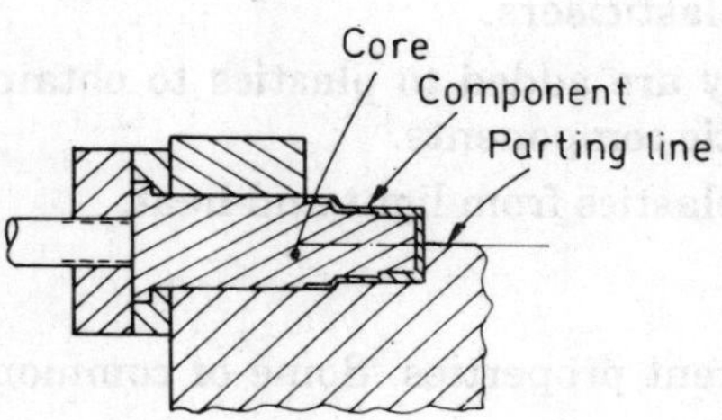

Fig. 14.1 Movable Core.

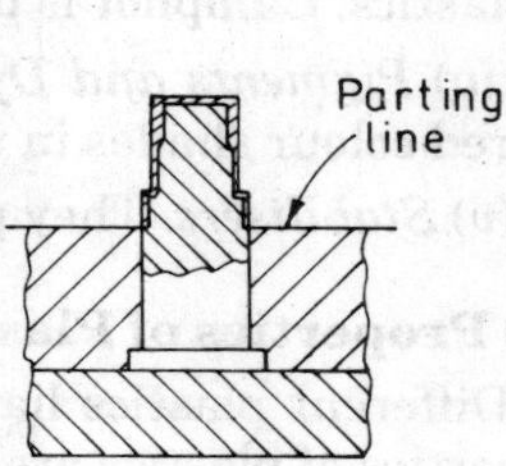

Fig. 14.2 Stationary Core.

Stationary cores are generally satisfactory only when the axis of the hole to be formed is at right angles to the parting line of the die.

14.2 Plastics.

Plastics are the organic materials which can be moulded into various shapes through the application of heat and pressure. They are prepared from natural and synthetic resins. Natural resins include shellac, wax, wood resins and amber etc. Synthetic resins are prepared by the recurring chemical reaction of a simple organic compound. The molecules of simple organic compound combine and form a high molecular weight composition.

Resin is the substitute word usually used in place of plastic synthetic resins are of two types namely : (*i*) Thermosets, (*ii*) Thermoplastics.

14.2.1. Terms and definitions.

(*i*) *Monomer, polymer, polymerisation.* Monomer is a substance consisting of short molecules. They link together to form long molecules called polymers. The process in which indefinite repitition of original molecules called monomers of synthetic resins combine together and give rise to polymers is called polymerisation.

(*ii*) *Fillers.* Fillers are added to plastics to reduce the consumption of plastics and to give certain specific properties to plastics. They are usually in the form of minute particles or long fibres. The commonly used fillers are wood, flour, paper pulp, asbestos and mica. Asbestos when added makes the plastics resistant to heat and electricity.

(*iii*) *Plasticisers.* These materials are added to plastics to improve toughness, plasticity and flexibility so that the moulding of plastics becomes easy. These materials also counteract the brittleness of moulded parts. Plasticisers are generally added to thermoplastics. Camphor is used as plasticisers.

(*iv*) *Pigments and Dyes.* They are added to plastics to obtain desired colour shades in the plastic components.

(*v*) *Stabilisers.* They protect plastics from light and heat.

14.3 Properties of Plastics.

Different plastics have different properties. Some of common properties of plastics are as follows :

(*i*) Light weight combined with adequate strength.

(*ii*) Easy to mould into different shapes.

(*iii*) They have low thermal conductivity and provide good insulation to heat.

(*iv*) They have good resistance to corrosion.

(*v*) They have good resistance to most of the chemicals.

(*vi*) They can be easily produced in different colours.

(*vii*) They are good electrical insulators.

(*viii*) As compared to metals they have better resistance to shock and vibration.

14.4 Types of Plastics.

Plastics are of two types :

1. *Thermo plastics*

(*i*) Cellulose derivatives

(*ii*) Polyhydrocarbons, such as polyethylene polystrene, polypropylene

(*iii*) Vinyl polymers

(*iv*) Linear polyesters.

2. *Thermosetting plastics*

(*i*) Formaldehyde resins

(*ii*) Epoxy resins

(*iii*) Silicon resins

(*iv*) Polyester resins.

14.5 Thermosetting Plastics.

These plastics after heating and pressing acquire a permanent shape and do not soften on reheating. They are thus more suitable for high temperature application than thermoplastic materials. They undergo chemical change during moulding. They are brittle and require some filler to make them hard and tough. As compared to thermo-plastics, thermosetting plastics are stronger and cheaper. Their scrap can not be reused.

The thermo-setting plastics, because of their resistance to melting and to solvents have a very wide use. Â typical application is in lacquers to be employed as protective lining in chemical reaction vessel.

14.5.1 Types of Thermosetting Plastics. Thermo-setting resins include the following :

(*i*) Phenol formaldehyde (*ii*) Phenol furfural

(*iii*) Urea formaldehyde (*iv*) Melamine formal dehyde

(*v*) Polyesters

(*vi*) Silicons

(*i*) **Phenol Formaldehyde.** It is obtained by mixing phenol and formaldehyde. It is also known as Bakelite. It has high resistance to heat, water and electricity. It has high mechanical strength and hardness. It is used for electric, plugs, switches radio cabinets, tooling, forming dies, gears and bearings, cameras, ash trays, air plane parts, and brake linings. It has good resistance to alcohol oil, greases and to weak acids and alkalis.

(*ii*) **Phenol Furfural.** It is obtained from husks of rice, sugar-cane refuse, oats shells etc. It is dark coloured and has good resistance to moisture and electricity. It can be easily mould. It has high strength and durability. It is used for making brake linings and electrical components. It has better moisture resistance than phenol formaldehyde plastics.

(*iii*) **Urea Formaldehyde.** It is obtained by mixing urea and formaldehyde. It is light coloured plastic and has high resistance to oil, water, weak acids and alkalis. It is used for making clock cases, buttons, electric switches and plugs, lighting fittings, toilet seats etc. It has good resistance to most solvents and common chemicals.

(*iv*) **Melamine Formaldehyde.** It is obtained by the condensation of melamine and formaldehyde. It is hard and has high resistance to moisture and heat. It has excellent electrical properties. It is mainly used for circuit breakers switch panels and lamp reflectors.

(*v*) **Polysters.** They have high dielectric strength and good colourability. They are mainly used for aircraft parts and car bodies.

(*vi*) **Silicones.** They are water repellent and can withstand high temperatures up to about 260°C. They are used as an additive to oils, waxes, rubbers etc.

14.6 Thermo Plastics.

These plastics become hard during moulding and cooling but can be softened on reheating and can be remoulded. The thermoplastic materials are injection molded and compression moulding method is seldom used. They can be moulded from powder form at relatively low temperatures (100°C) by comparatively small pressures.

14.6.1 Types of Thermo-plastics. Thermoplastic resins are as follows :

(*i*) **Cellulose nitrate.** It is obtained by treating purified cotton linters with a mixture of nitric acid and sulphuric acid. It is highly inflammable and tough. It is used for toys, combs, handles and coverings, brushes, spectacle frames, toilet goods, shoes, and type writer keys.

(*ii*) **Cellulose acetate.** Cellulose acetate is prepared by the action of acetic acid on cellulose. As compared to cellulose nitrate it is superior in moldability and resistance to flame but it is inferior to cellulose nitrate in resistance to moisture. It is tough and durable. It has good impact strength. It provides good electric insulation. It is used for extruded sheets, tubes, toilet articles, coatings, photographic films, lamp shades radio cabinets, buttons and buckles.

(*iii*) **Ethylcellulose.** It exhibits toughness and good resistance to chemicals. It is mainly used for forming dies, coatings, tool handles, and telephones. It has good resistance to acids and alkalis.

(*iv*) **Cellulose acetate butyrate.** It is made by treating cellulose with both acetic acid and butyric acid. It can be easily machined and moulded. It is resistant to most of the house hold chemicals but is adversely affected by alcohol and strong alkalis.

It processes high resistance to impact. It is tough and absorbs less moisture. It is used for helmets, coatings insulating tapes, machinery guards, special purposes hoses, instrument panels, pens, furniture.

(*v*) **Polythene.** It is wax like material and is chemically inert to most liquids. It has high electrical resistivity and is very tough. It is used as an electrical insulating material.

(*vi*) **P.V.C. (Polyvinyl chloride).** It is a rubber like material and is non inflammable. It is widely used as an insulating cover on electrical cables, gloves conveyor belting, toys, dolls, special purpose hose and tubing. It has good resistance to acids, alkalis and most common chemicals.

(*iv*) **Teflon.** It is a wax like material. It has high electrical resistance and a very low coefficient of friction. It does not absorb water and is resistant to chemicals. It is used for electrical insulation and for gaskets.

Cellulose propionate. It has better heat resistance than cellulose acetate. It is easily machined and moulded. It is used for pens and pencils and telephone hand sets.

(*vii*) **A.B.S. (Acrylonitrile-butadrinl-styrene)**

It is strong, crack resistant and can be made in many colors.

Its trade name is kralastic. It is used for portable hairdryers, cases for portable appliances, radio & TV cabinets.

14.7 Plastic processing methods.

Plastic components can be made by one or more of the following methods. Selection of method depends upon the shape of the component and the type of plastic used. The plastic processing methods are of two types :

(*i*) Casting.

(*ii*) Moulding.

14.8 Casting.

This method is similar to metal casting. It consists in heating the plastic and pouring the liquid plastic into mould.

After curing for definite period of time the components (castings) are knocked out of mould. This process is slow and is suitable for small production.

14.9 Moulding.

Moulding is the most commonly used method for plastic fabrication. In this method shaping of plastics is achieved under pressure and temperature.

The basic principle in moulding is that the plastic material becomes fluid under the influence of heat and pressure and the material is forced into an opening in the mould to obtain the desired shape.

The various moulding processes are as follows.

(*i*) Compression moulding.

(*ii*) Injection moulding.

(*iii*) Extrusion moulding.

(*iv*) Transfer moulding.

(*v*) Blow moulding.

14.9.1 Compression moulding.

In this process plastic powder is placed in a heated mould. Fig. 14.3 It is compressed into the required shape by a punch. The moulded part is knocked out after some time. This method is quite suitable for thermosetting plastics.

14.9.2 Injection moulding.

In this process (Fig. 14.4) the plastic powder is filled in the hopper. It is then pushed forward by ram. The plastic powder is heated in heating cylinder and it is then forced into mould. After some time when the plastic has been cooled in the mould, the mould is opened and the moulded part is knocked out. This process is commonly used for components made of thermoplastics.

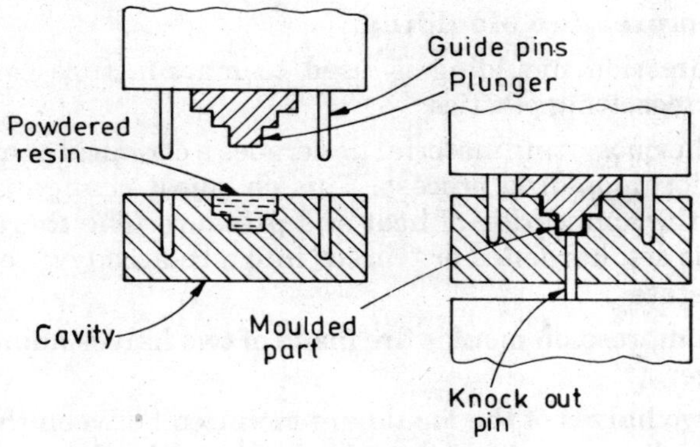

Fig. 14.3 Compression moulding.

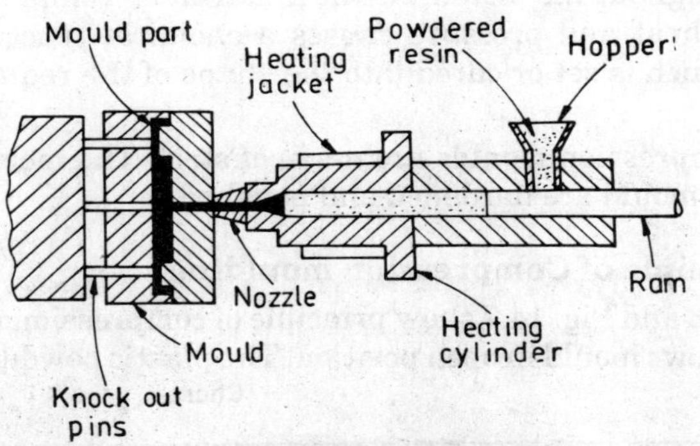

Fig. 14.4 Injection moulding.

14.9.3. Extrusion moulding.

In this process Fig. 14.5 plastic powder is filled into the hopper. The plastic powder is fed into heating chamber by means of a feed screw. Hot material is then extruded through a die of a requisite shape. This process is quite suitable for thermoplastic. It is used to make plastic conduits, rods, and sheets, etc.

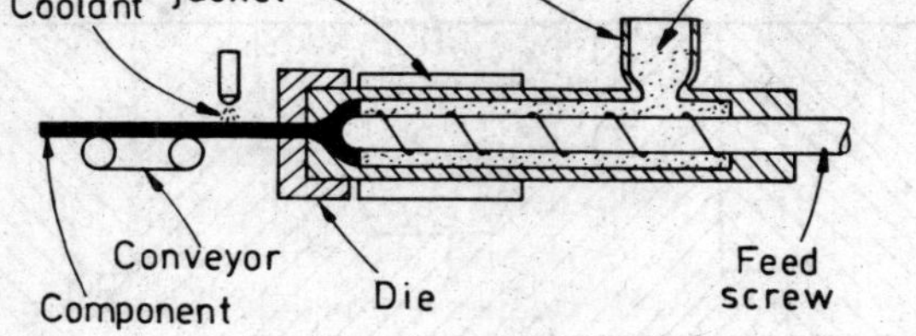

Fig. 14.5.

14.10 Compression Moulding

Compression moulding is used to manufacture components from thermosetting plastics.

The thermosetting material undergoes a chemical change in the compression moulding process. This chemical change is brought about by the application of heat and pressure. The thermosetting material is set, hardened or "cured" into a relatively insoluble and infusible state.

The compression moulds are made of two halves namely cavity and plonger.

The two halves of the mould are mounted between the platens of a hydraulic press. The material is placed in the cavity of the heated mould in the form of a powder or perform. As the two halves of the mould are closed by the press, the plunger causes the material to flow throughout the mould. As the material is "compressed" into shape, the heat and pressure causes a chemical reaction in the material which is set or cured into the shape of the required piece part.

The compression moulds are made of steel. The moulding sections of the mould are hardened and polished.

14.11 Principle of Compression moulding.

Fig. 14.6 and Fig. 14.7 show principle of compression moulding. Fig. 14.6 shows mould in open position. The plastic powder is placed

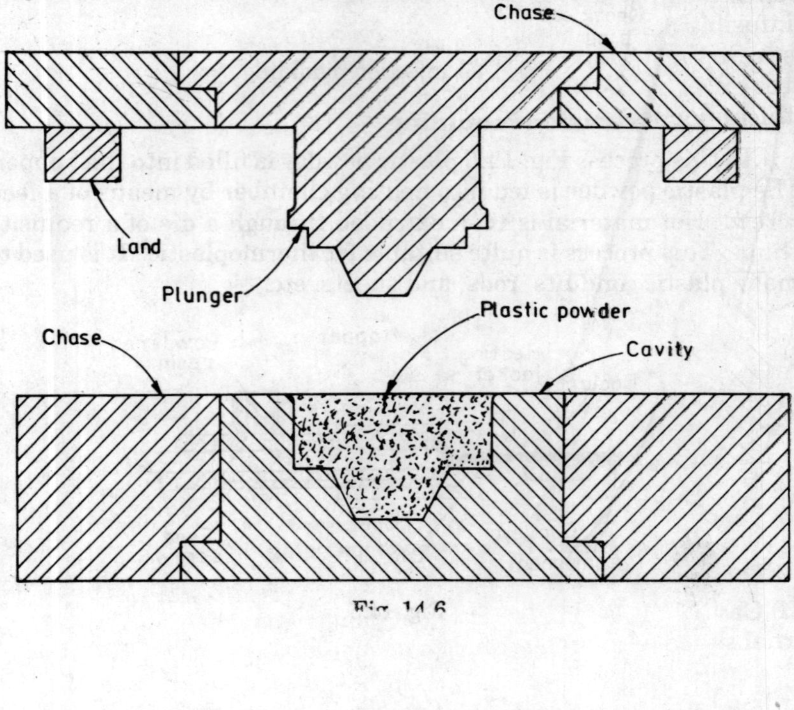

Fig. 14.6

in the space provided in cavity Fig. 14.7 shows the mould in closed position in which the plunger compresses the plastic powder and converts it into desired shape. The upper part containing plunger remains stationary where as lower part containing cavity moves up to close the mould.

The mould is held in closed position under pressure long enough to cure the material.

(Fig. 14.7) After the component has been made the lower part moves downward and then component is removed.

Some of the parts made by compression moulding process are as follows.

(*i*) Electrical switchgear

(*ii*) Dishware such as (*a*) plates (*b*) dishes (*c*) cups

(*iii*) Camstor timer for dryers

(*iv*) Housing industry such as sanitary tubs, stall, showers

(*v*) Wiring devices

(*vi*) Bottle caps

(*vii*) Vacuum assist brake parts.

Compression moulding may be used with a wide range of thermoset moulding compounds. A thermoset requires heat to first soften or plasticize the material, then to cause polymerization into an infusible mass. Pressure, which is required to flow or move the plasticated material before setting into all portions of the mould, causes excess material to flow out over the land areas so that a thin fin thickness is obtained.

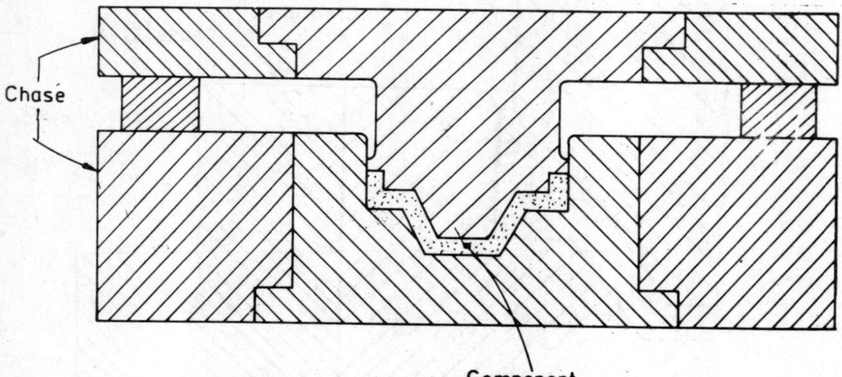

Fig. 14.7 Compression moulding.

14.12 Terms and definitions

(*i*) **Cavity :** It is female section of mould which gives generally external shape to the component to be moulded.

(*ii*) **Plunger :** It is the male portion of the mould. It forces the material into the opening in the cavity. It gives the internal shape to the part being moulded. In injection moulding, the plunger is often referred to as the core.

(*iii*) **Platen :** Platen constitute the flat surfaces of the moulding press onto which the two halves of the mould are mounted. Generally positioned horizontally on compression presses, and vertically on injection machines.

(*iv*) **Land :** It is the horizontal surface. It is used to limit the stroke of the press.

(*v*) **Chase :** These are the steel plates which are used to hold cavities and plungers.

(*vi*) **Flash :** In compression positive mould there is very little clearance between the plunger and the cavity wall. In the positive mould, almost all the pressure is exerted on the material and very little material is allowed to escape, as shown in Figure 0.125. The clearance between the plunger and cavity varies between 0.038 mm to 0.125 mm per side, depending on the size of the mould and the material to be moulded. The amount of material that escapes through the clearance between the plunger and cavity is called flash. The flash is formed vertically on the type mould shown. The thickness and position of this flash depends on the design of the mould, type of material being moulded, and accuracy of the mould.

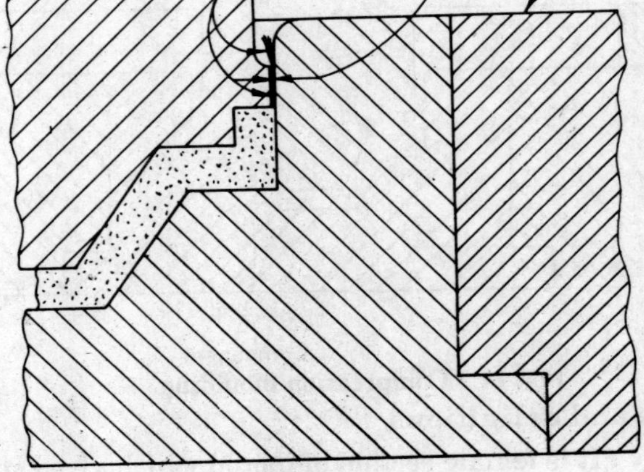

Fig. 14.8.

Flash is removed by filing, sanding, and tumbling. Flash and clearance is shown in Fig. 14.8.

(*vii*) Well : It is the space provided in the cavity block for the uncured moulding powder or perform.

(*viii*) Draft : It is the angle or taker provided on the wall of the cavity and on the plunger so the piece part can be removed from the mould. A minimum of 1/2 degree per side is recommended.

Fig. 14.9 shows draft angle and well.

$$\theta = \text{Draft angle}$$

$$H = well$$

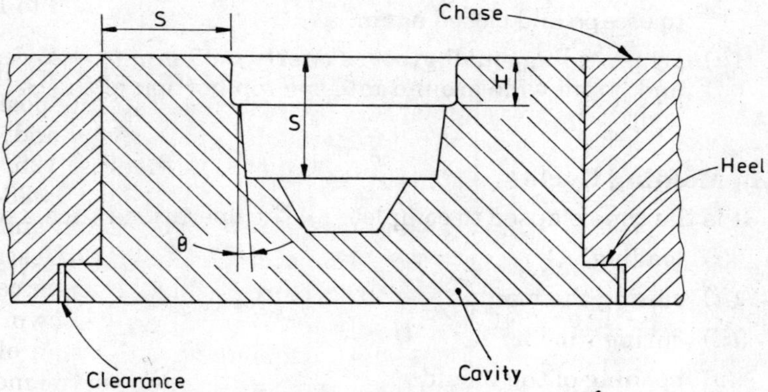

Fig. 14.9.

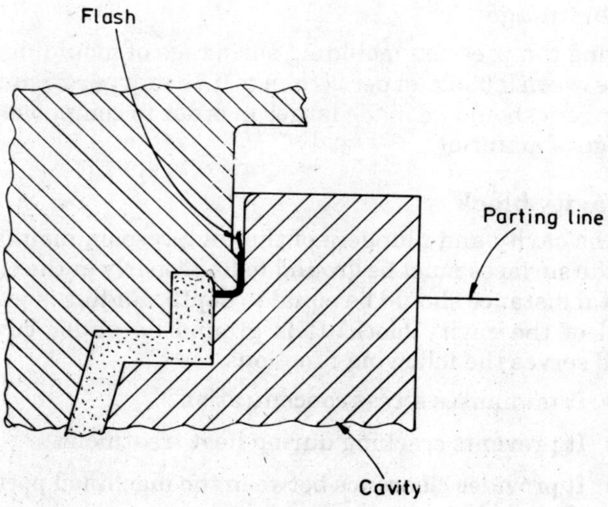

Fig. 14.10.

The horizontal distance (S) should be equal to depth (S) so that cavity does not distort under moulding pressure.

Parting Line. It is the line at which two halves of the mould namely cavity and plunger meet as shown in Fig. 14.10.

14.13 Venting

In compression moulding process gases are formed as the chemical reaction takes place in the material some of the methods to get rid of the gases are as follows.

(*i*) To allow the mould to breathe that is the mould is closed and then opened again for about 3 mm to allow the gases to escape and closed again.

(*ii*) By providing small grooves nearly 0.05 mm to 0.25 deep and 3 mm wide ground into the top portion of the cavity wall.

14.14 Molding Cycle

It is the time elapsed to complete all the operations such as

(*i*) loading

(*ii*) closing the mould

(*iii*) curing time

(*iv*) opening of the mould

(*v*) cleaning the mould for next loading of the material

14.15 Shrinkage

During compression moulding shrinkage of moulding material varies between 0.038 mm per 25 mm to 0.75 mm per 25 mm cavities and plungers should be made larger in order to compensate for the shrinkage of material.

14.16 Cavity block

As the cavity and plungers of the compression mould are hardened, the surfaces must be ground to fit properly in the chase. The horizontal distance should be equal to depth. Radius is provided at the heel of the cavity block. It is ground as under cut. Radius provided serves the following functions.

(*i*) It minimises stress concentration.

(*ii*) It prevents cracking during heat treatment.

(*iii*) It provides clearance between the machined pocket in the chase and cavity block.

14.17 Factors affecting compression moulding

Important factors which influence compression moulding are as follows.

(*i*) Temperature

(*ii*) Pressure

(*iii*) Cure time

Pressure required to mould a particular component depends on following :

(*a*) Flow characteristics of the material

(*b*) Cavity depth

(*c*) Prosected area of the component

The recommended pressure for material with no preheat is given by.

P = Recommented pressure

= 20 to 300 kg/cm of projected area.

Preheating material in the range of (90 – 120°C) may result in a 50% reduction in pressure required cure time is the time elapsed when movement of the press stops until the pressure on the moulded part is released.

T = cure time

= 1 to 2 minutes for smaller and thin walled components

= 10 to 15 minutes for components with thick sections

Temperature for moulding of thermosetting plastics varies from 150°C to 200°C. Too high temperature causes blisters and burn spots on the finished components.

Temperature is affected by other factors like

(*i*) geometry of moulded part

(*ii*) type of mould

(*iii*) whether loose powder or preheated powder is used

14.18 Types of moulds.

Depending upon the size of components to be made and production requirement, there and three types of compression

(*i*) Hand moulds

(*ii*) Semi-automatic moulds

(*iii*) Automatic moulds.

Hand moulds are used for making limited number of small parts. In this mould the material is put into the cavities and the two halves of the mould are assembled and placed between the platens of the press. After the press has been closed and the parts moulded the mould is removed from the press and the parts ejected from the mould on a conveniently located bench.

Hand moulds weigh nearly 10 to 12 kg semi-automatic moulds are mounted onto the platens of the press by clamps.

The mould is loaded with material and the two halves close. After the pieces have been moulded, some sort of ejection mechanism pushes the parts out of the cavity or off the plunger.

Automatic moulds are similar to semi automatic moulds but because of the following additional advantages of automatic moulds as compared to semi-automatic moulds, the automatic moulds are used for mass production of components.

(*i*) use of combination of loading devices and timing devices.

(*ii*) positive ejector systems

(*iii*) provision of safety devices micro switches

(*iv*) use of quick cleaning apparatus

(*v*) use of sweeps

(*vi*) these moulds do not need operator once the mould has been set up for a production run.

Compression moulds according to number of cavities provided are classified as follows.

(*i*) Single cavity moulds

(*ii*) Multi cavity moulds

Single cavity moulds produce one component in each cycle. They are particularly suitable for making larger components. Multi cavity moulds are used for making large number of components per cycle.

Multi cavity moulds are of following types

(*a*) Identical cavity moulds : They contain a separate (*i*) cavity (*ii*) plunger and (*iii*) loading well for each component.

(*b*) Sub-cavity mould or gang mould : Such moulds contain common (*i*) well or loading chamber and (*ii*) plunger

In these moulds number of identical parts can be made. Sub-cavity mould is commonly used for making small parts.

n = Number of cavities in multiple cavity moulds

= 2 to 48.

The number of cavities provided depend on.

(*i*) Size of component to be made

(*ii*) Size of press

(*iii*) Force entered by the press

(*iv*) Ease of loading

(*v*) Ejection system

In compression moulds an external land is provided to keep the plunger 0.05 to 0.125 mm from land surface.

This clearance between the land surface and the plunger forms a thin fin a flash between the cavities which breaks off easily.

It is desireable to keep the land area between the cavities to be minimum. So that enough moulding pressure gets applied on the component. If land area between cavities is too large then much of moulding pressure will be wasted on moulding the flash resulting in component produced of low density.

It is suggested that

A = Molding area (minimum)

$$= 3\,A_L$$

where, A_L = Land area

Fig. 14.11 shows various features of gang mould for producing number of identical parts. This mould is also called sub cavity mould. It the land area between cavities is too large much of the moulding pressure is wasted an moulding the flash. This results imparts produced of low density.

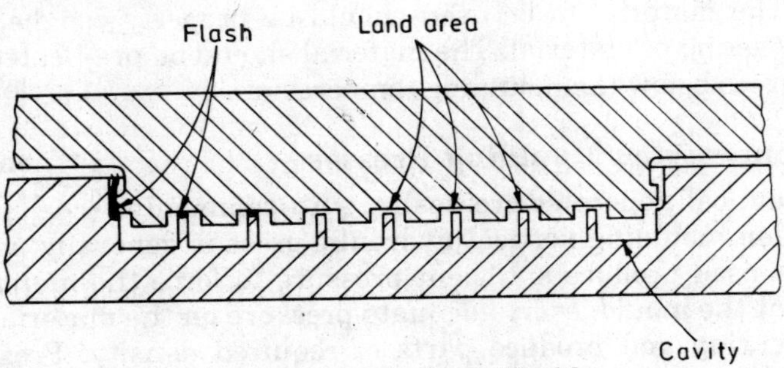

Fig. 14.11 Gang Mould.

Another type of mould is called. Split wedge mould or split cavity mould. This mould is particularly useful for making components having under cuts such as spool shaped components. The cavity is constructured in two or more sections.

14.19 Methods of heating

In compression moulding the mouldings are cured by heat and pressure. Heating serves the following purposes :

(*i*) It softens the material so that it can easily flow under pressure to any desired shape.

(*ii*) It brings about the necessary chemical change or polymerise it into its hard infusible finished state.

There are two methods commonly used in heating press platens and moulds using thermosetting materials.

(*i*) Steam (*ii*) Electricity

Using steam for heating is economical whereas electric heating is preferred because of

(*i*) cleanliness

(*ii*) lower maintenance cost

Figure shows heating of a semi automatic type mould using strip heating elements an insulating layer of asbestos is placed between the press plateu and strip heaters so that heat will not dissipate into press parts. All electrical heating elements should be thermostatically controlled by the use of thermocouples, rheostat etc. Some time compression moulds and transfer moulds are heated by steam channels which are drilled into various parts of the mould base.

14.20 Loading of Moulds

The thermo setting materials used in compression moulds range in size from a fine granulated powder to approximately mesh size 16. The material to be used should be properly weighed to prevent wasting of material. The material should be pre-heated to a few degrees below the moulding temperature.

14.21 Compression Moulding Presses

Hydraulically operated presses are quite commonly used during compression moulding vertical hydraulic press is generally used. The press used produce sufficient pressure to force the material throughout the mould, exert adequate pressure on the material to promote curing and produce parts of required density. Presses having as high as 4000 tons capacity are used.

14.22 Cure Time Variables

The time required to harden thermosetting materials to partial or complete polymerisation is called cure time. Many compounds produce parts that are hard enough, blister tree and apparently cured. Yet the polymerisation of the resin system is not complete and a post bake cycle may be required to optimise properties. Various variable affecting cure time are as follows :

1. **Temperature :** To achieve the minimum cure time the material must be at the maximum temperature when it is loaded into the moulds. The process engineer must determine this temperature to produce high-quality parts.

2. **Mold Temperature :** The process engineer must have knowledge of the recommended mould temperature for each type of material. He must arrive at the maximum mould temperature and cycle that will produce high-quality parts at the shortest overall cycle.

3. **Material Type** : General purpose materials having woodflour, cotton flock, cellulose, paper, and so on offer the greatest moulding latitudes. Adjustments of preheat temperature, plasticity, and mould temperature must be studied to obtain the optimum mould cycle.

4. **Cross-Sectional Area** : The cross-sectional area or wall thickness will determine the cure time required to produce the part. A cross section up to about 2-3 mm thick will cure in a matter of seconds, whereas increased wall sections may require minutes. Parts having thicknesses or cross-sectional areas in excess of 9.5-13 mm may be difficult to mould by compression when endeavoring to establish minimum cure cycles ; transfer or injection methods of moulding might be better.

14.23 Types of Presses

The different types of press are used to produce parts by compression moulding.

1. **Manual or Semiautomatic Presses :** The conventional press is of vertical design having upward or downward closing action. Hydraulic fluid or air is the pressure medium, and the clamp tonnage may be obtained by hydraulic rams or toggle clamps. Production presses range from 50 to 500 tons ($4.4 \times 10^5 - 4.4 \times 10^6$).

2. **Automatic Presses :** Automatic presses were introduced in the early 1930s and are self-contained. Recent presses have solid-state electrical controls for sequential control of the cycle. They are of the conventional vertical design and are available from the small air-toggle 25-ton (2.2×10^5 N) to 300-ton (2.2×10^5 N) capacity. They have such added features as material loading mechanisms and unloading trays or devices.

3. **Automatic-Rotary Presses :** These presses are quite commonly used recent developments in press design, preheating methods, and other areas have made them a factor to be considered in high-production parts. They are available having individual

vertical stations mounted in a complete circle, and may contain 6, 10, 20, or 30 stations. Clamp tonnage is generated by hydraulic fluid and may develop 3, 5, 18, or 40 tons per station. Part size is limited by the clamp tonnage available. Parts may have top knockout only. Automatic-rotary presses are ideal for small parts having shallow draw, diameters not in excess of 76 mm and rectangular parts having projected area of 77-97 cm^2.

Some of the components manufactured by this press are as follows

(*i*) Switches

(*ii*) Times

(*iii*) Home circuit breakers

14.24 Material Charge

The thermoset material must be deposited in the mould cavity from an outside source, either manually or automatically. It is recommended that the material be preheated to the optimum temperature to produce high-quality parts. The preheating will reduce cure time, reduce pressure, and improve finish and overall quality, and reduce mould maintenance costs.

14.25 Moulds Design

There are five main design of compression moulds.

1. Flash type

2. Fully Positive. A fully positive, or direct positive, mould is used only for large deep draw parts where maximum density is required. If very bulky, long fabric-or glass-filled compounds are specified, adequate loading space can be provided. Such moulds are usually limited to single cavity production.

3. Landed Positive. Multicavity moulds may use the landed positive design. Escapements are incorporated on the plunger to permit maximum density with uniform height from cavity to cavity.

4. Semipositive Horizontal Flash. The semipositive horizontal flash design is well suited for automatic moulds.

5. Semipositive Vertical Flash. The semipositive vertical flash method is used where no visual flash line scar is permitted on moulded parts.

14.26 Advantages of Compression Moulding

1. Best method for holding close tolerances.

2. Lower mould shrinkage as compared to transfer or injection moulding such as 0.0015-0.002 in./in.
3. Uniform mould shrinkage due to uniform flow pattern of material.
4. More uniform density of moulded parts is achieved.
5. Because of more uniform fill of cavity there are no strains in moulded part.
6. Venting of mould may be needed, but not to the extent required in transfer or injection moulding.
7. Quite useful for shallow draw parts.
8. Improved impact strength, since no degradation of fibers during flow.
9. Generally, flash scrap lower than transfer or injection moulding is obtained.
10. On shallow draw parts, maximum number of cavities per bed area due to less moulding pressure, and without the necessity of long runner systems and sprue or plunger locations.
11. Large parts having large projected areas, deep draw, and weights can readily be moulded.
12. Semipositive or landed full positive moulds can be used.
13. Generally compression moulds are less costly to construct than transfer or injection moulds.
14. Part cost and tooling costs may be more economical than moulding by transfer or injection moulding.

14.27 Disadvantages of Compression Moulding

1. It is difficult to make components with under cuts or side draws.
2. Rates of cure for more wall thickness are longer than transfer or injection moulding.
3. Molded in holes are limited to depths of 2.5 times diameter.

14.28 Wall Thickness

The commonly used wall thickness of components made from thermosetting material is indicated in table 14.1.

Table 14.1

Material	*Small parts*		*General parts*		*Large parts*	
	in.	*mm*	*in.*	*mm*	*in.*	*mm*
Phenolic	0.062-0.125	1.575-3.175	0.093-0.187	2.36-4.75	0.187-1.00	4.75-25.4
Urea	0.062-0.125	1.575-3.175	0.093-0.187	2.36-4.75	0.187-0.375	4.75-9.52
Melamine	0.062-0.125	1.575-3.175	0.093-0.187	2.36-4.75	0.187-0.375	4.75-9.52
DAP	0.045-0.093	1.143-2.362	0.078-0.156	1.98-3.96	0.125-0.375	3.175-9.52
Alkyd	0.078-0.125	1.98-3.175	0.100-0.187	2.54-4.75	0.187-0.500	4.75-12.7
Polyester						
Granular	0.078-0.125	1.98-3.175	0.100-0.187	2.54-4.75	0.187-0.500	4.75-12.7
Bulk moulding compound	0.045-0.093	1.143-2.362	0.078-0.156	1.98-3.96	0.125-0.375	3.175-9.52
Sheet moulding compound	0.062-0.093	1.575-2.362	0.093-0.187	2.36-4.75	0.187-0.375	4.75-9.52

14.29 Injection Moulding

Introduction : It is used to make components from thermoplastics. The thermoplastics undergo only a physical change in their. Structure when they are heated to a fluid state and then cooled to harden. In this process the material is heated to a molten stage and this material is then forced into cavities of a closed cool mould where the material becomes sets into the desired shape.

Various advantages of injection moulding are as follows :

(*i*) Part made by this method possess very little or no flash. This eliminates secondary operations such as

(*a*) sanding

(*b*) filing

(*c*) tumbling

(*ii*) There is shorter moulding cycle as compared to compression moulding. This increases production rates

(*iii*) There is no wastage of material scrap and incompletely moulded components can be remoulded.

(*iv*) This is more efficient and economical method of making components.

14.30 Principle of Injection Moulding

The injection moulding system consists of three main components :

(*i*) mould

(*ii*) Plasticising system

(*iii*) System for mould clamping

The principle of injection moulding is shown in Fig. 14.12.

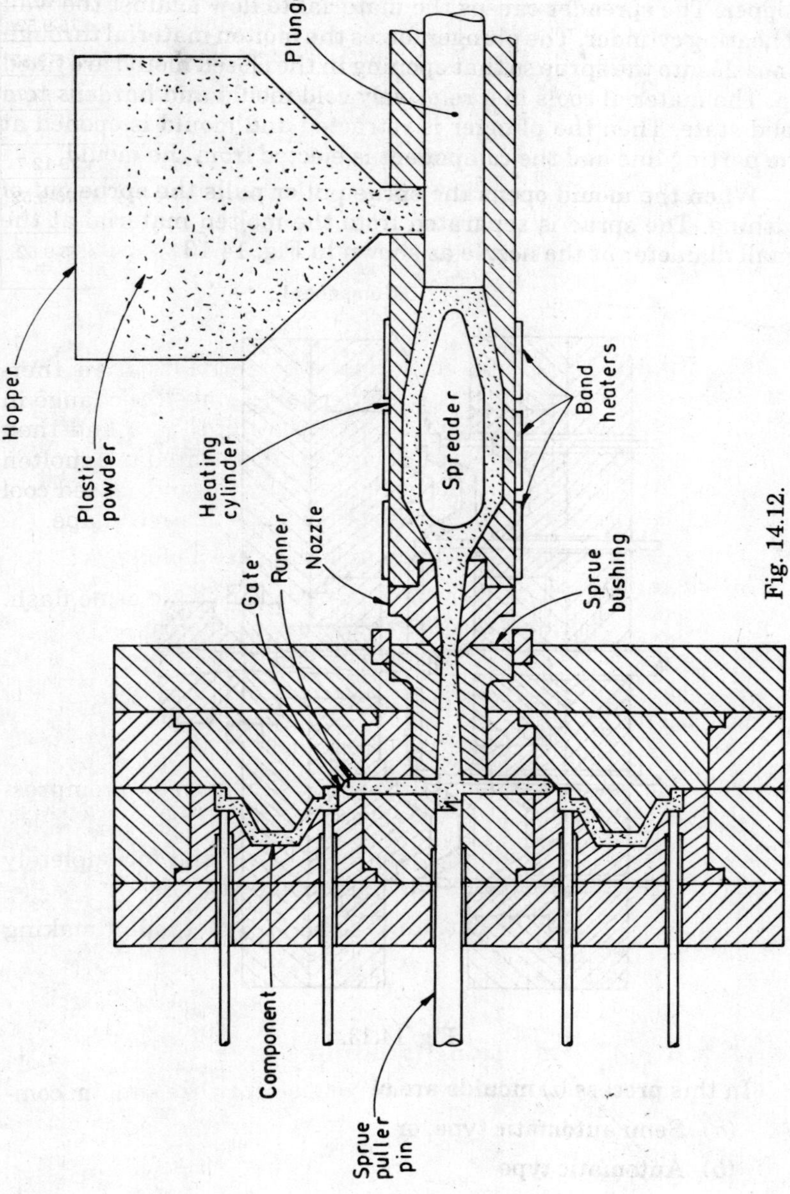

Fig. 14.12.

Injection moulding consists of forcing the liquid plastic into a closed mould. The mould has been shown inclosed position after a shot has been made. Shot is a term used to describe the total amount of material that has been injected into the mould in one cycle including component to be made, runner, gates and sprues. In this process the material in the form of powder or pellet is placed in the hopper. The spreader causes the material to flow against the wall of heating cylinder. The plunger forces the molten material through a nozzle into the sprue so that opening in the closed mould are filled up. The material cools in a relatively cold mould and hardens to a solid state. Then the plunger is retracted and mould is opened at the parting line and the component is ejected from the mould.

When the mould opens the sprue puller pulls the sprue out of bushing. The sprue is separated from the molten material at the small diameter at the nozzle as shown in Fig. 14.13.

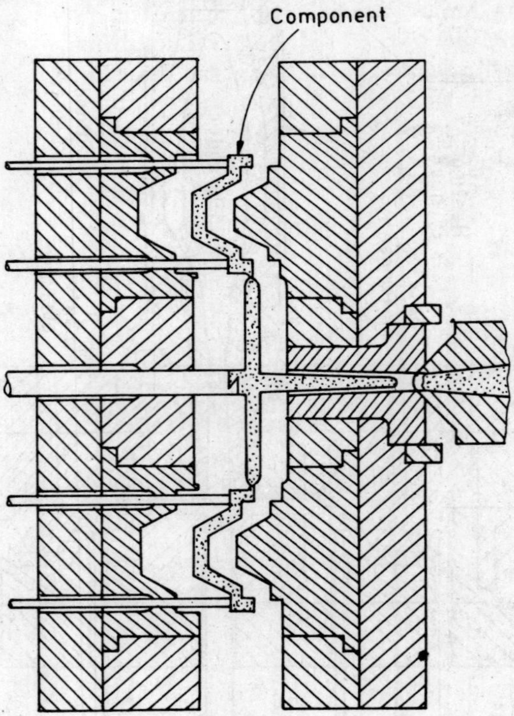

Fig. 14.13.

In this process (*i*) moulds are of

(*a*) Semi automatic type, or

(*b*) Automatic type

(*ii*) moulds are made in single or multiple cavity depending on

(*a*) size of component to be made

(*b*) size of press.

(*iii*) a variety of ejector systems which are generally integral part of the mould are used to eject the components, from the mould.

(*iv*) The two halves of the mould are mounted on the plates or platens one of which is fixed and other movable usually by a hydraulic system.

The hydraulic system is programmed so that a plunger (ram) brings the mould halves together at a decreasing speed allowing the mould halves to come together gently.

Figure 14.14 shows the variation of pressure in the mould during filling for a typical cycle. Since the plastic contracts on cooling as a result of the shrinkage on solidification (if the plastic is semicrystalline) and thermal contraction, the moulding pressure must be sufficiently high to pack enough material into the mould to counteract this decrease in volume. It should be noted that the plastic is quite viscous, and filling does not occur instantaneously.

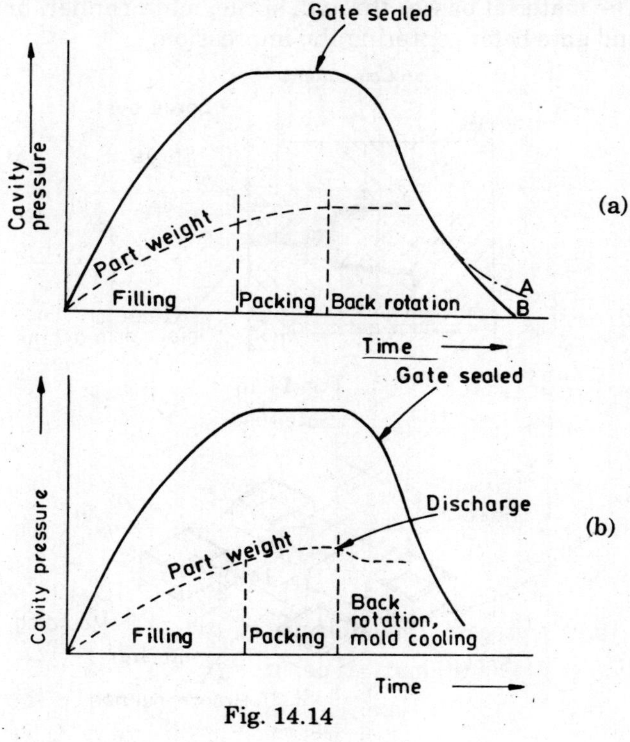

Fig. 14.14

The weight of the moulded part continues to increase during this holding period while packing continues, until the entrance to the mould (the gate) freezes shut. This packing is necessary to prevent voids in the center of the part as a result of solidification shrinkage, to minimize sink marks near heavy sections, and to assure that air within the mould has had time to escape so that mould filling can be complete.

As shown in Fig. 14.14 the mould cavity pressure variation with time. (*a*) Gate seals during packing ; (*b*) gate seals later. Discharge occurs back through the gate.

Injection moulding has been applied to thermoplastics and thermosets, foamed parts, and has been modified to yield the reaction injection moulding (RIM) process, in which the two components of a thermosetting resin system are simultaneously injected and polymerize rapidly within the mould. Most injection moulding is however performed on thermoplastics.

14.31 Feed System

Feed system consists of :

(*i*) Sprue (*ii*) runner (*iii*) gate.

The material passes through sprue, main runner, branch runner and gate before entering the impression.

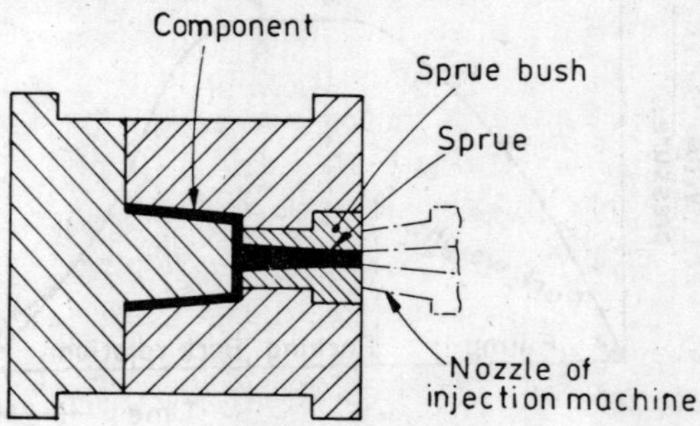

Fig. 14.15

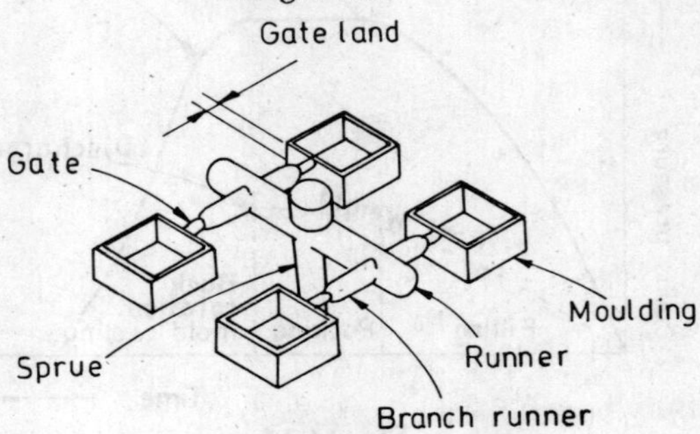

Fig. 14.16.

Fig. 14.15 shows a typical feed system for a single impression mould.

Fig. 14.16 shows a typical feed system for a four impression mould.

It is desireable to keep the distance that material has to travel to minimum to reduce.

(*i*) pressure loss (*ii*) heat loss.

The runner is a channel machined into the mould plate to connect the sprue with the entrance (gate) to the impression. In the basic two-plate mould the runner is positioned on the parting surface while on more complex designs the runner may be positioned below the parting surface.

14.32 Runner layout

The layout of runner system depends on the following factors

(*i*) Number of impressions (*ii*) Shape of component

(*iii*) Type of mould such as two plate or multiplate mould.

(*iv*) Type of gate.

While designing runner layout it should be observed that

(*i*) runner length should be kept to a minimum to reduce pressure losses.

(*ii*) runner should be balanced which means the distance plastic material travels from sprue to gate should be same for each moulding in order to ensure that all impressions will get filled up uniformly and interruption provided the gate lands and gate areas are identical.

Fig. 14.17 shows a radial runner arrangement to fill up four cavities.

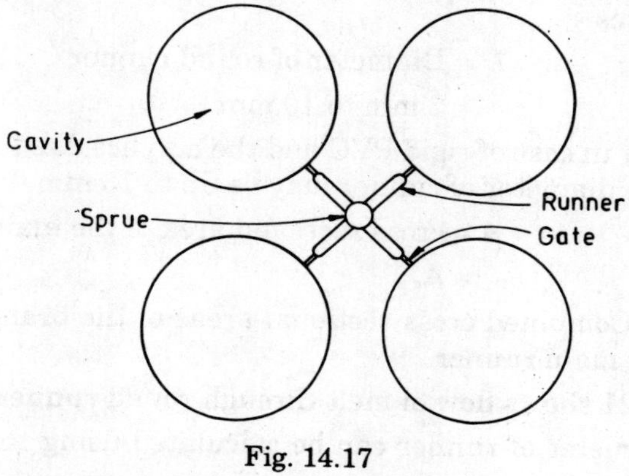

Fig. 14.17

Runners may be of following shapes.

(*i*) Round (Fig 14.18)

(*ii*) Trapezoidial (Fig. 14.19)

(*iii*) Hexagonal (Fig. 14.20)

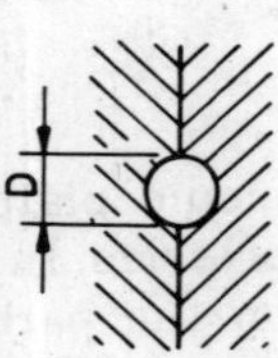

Fig. 14.18.

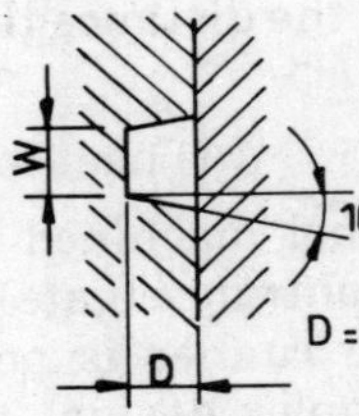

Fig. 14.19.

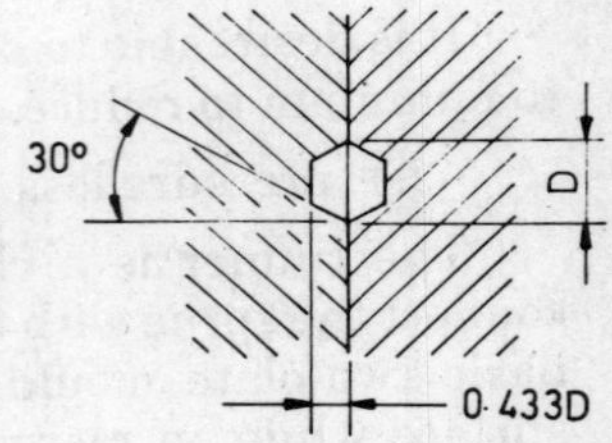

Fig. 14.20.

The hexagonal runner is basically a double trapezoidal runner, where the two halves of the trapezium meet at the parting surface. The cross-sectional area of this runner type is about 82% of that of the corresponding round runner.

14.33 Size of Runner

While deciding the size of runner following factors should be considered.

(*i*) Volume of moulding

(*ii*) Type of material to be used for moulding

(*iii*) Wall section of moulding

(*iv*) Distance of impression from the main runner or sprue

(*v*) Runner cooling considerations

The cross sectional area of the runner should be sufficient to permit the melt to pass through and fill the impression before runner freezes

$$D = \text{Diameter of round runner}$$
$$= 2 \text{ mm to } 10 \text{ mm}$$

However in case of rigid PVC and the acrylics due to their high viscosity the diameter of runner may be up to 13 mm.

$$A = \text{cross sectional area of the main runner}$$
$$= A_c$$

where A_c = Combined cross sectional areas of the branch runners being fed by main runner.

Fig. 14.21 shows flow of melt through round runner.

The diameter of runner can be calculated using the following formula.

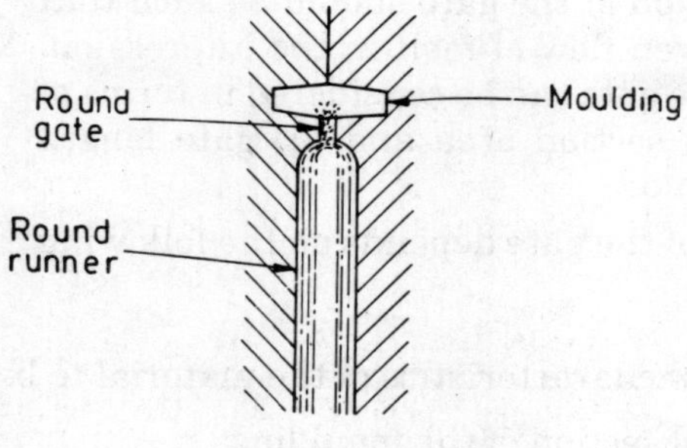

Fig. 14.21

$$D = \frac{\sqrt{W} \times \sqrt[4]{L}}{3.7}$$

where D = Runner diameter in mm

W = weight of moulding in grams

L = Height of runner in mm

14.34 Sprue puller

Fig. 14.22 shows a sprue puller. A pin point gate has been used to feed the part.

H = 0.75 to 1 mm

S = 0.75 plus 10° per side

θ = 2 to 3° per side

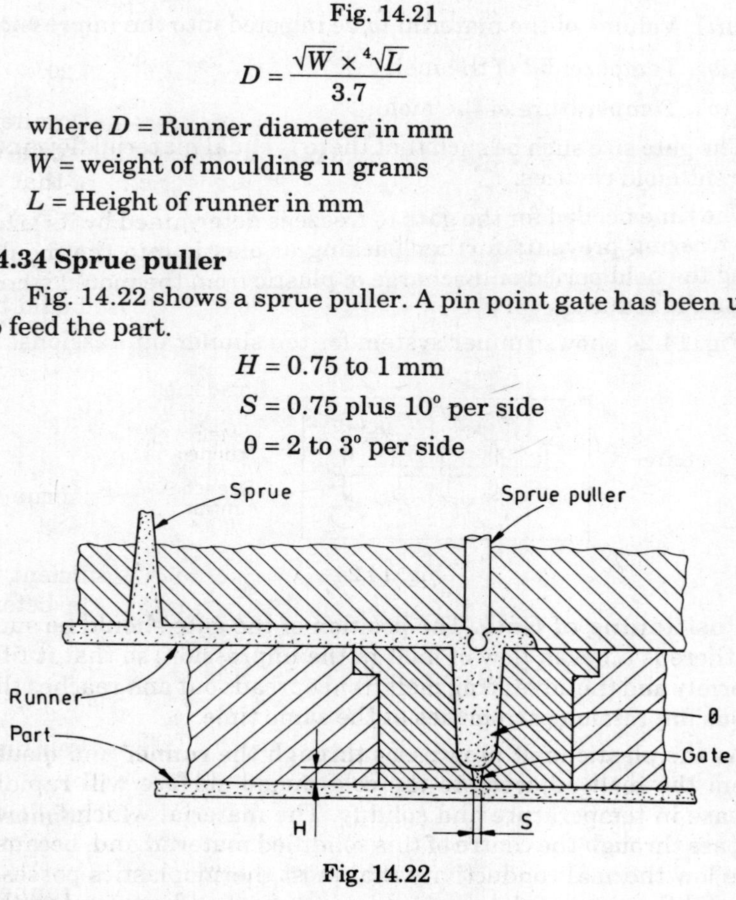

Fig. 14.22

14.35 Gate

Gate is a channel or orifice connecting runner with the impression. Fig. 14.23 shows edge gating of a cup shaped moulding.

The position of the gate should be such that there is an even flow of melt in the impression. The size of the gate can be considered in terms of (*i*) gate cross section area and (*ii*) gate length called gate land.

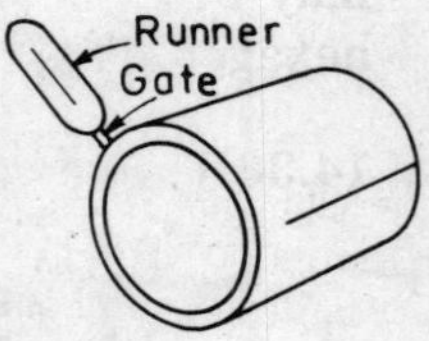

Fig. 14.23

The size of the gate depends on the following factors

(*i*) Flow characteristics of the material to be molded.

(*ii*) Wall section of the moulding

(*iii*) Volume of the material to be injected into the impression

(*iv*) Tempezoidal of the melt

(*v*) Temperature of the mold.

The gate size such be such that there is equal material flow into different mold cavities.

The time needed for the gate to freeze is determined by its size. Gate freezing prevents further packing of plastic into the mould during the hold period or discharge of plastic from the mould when pressure is reduced.

Fig. 14.24 shows runner system for ten similar impressions.

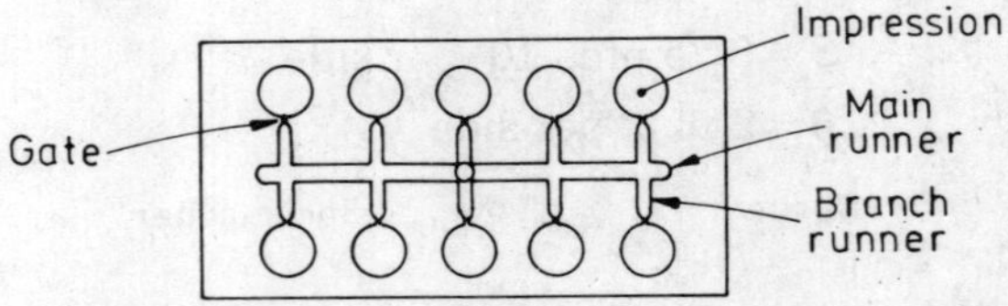

Fig. 14.24

Positioning of Gate. The position of the gate should be such that there is an even flow of melt in the impression, so that it fills uniformly and the advancing melt front spreads out and reaches the various impression extremities at the same time.

As the plastic melt progresses through the runner and mould system the melt adjacent to the cold mould surface will rapidly decrease in temperature and solidify. The material which follows will pass through the centre of this solidified material and, because of the low thermal conductivity that most thermoplastics possess, the solidified material acts as an insulation and maintains the temperature of the central melt flow region. Ideally, the gate should therefore be positioned in line with the centre of the runner to receive the material from the central flow stream. This condition may be achieved with the fully round runner and also with the hexagonal runner.

14.36 Types of gates

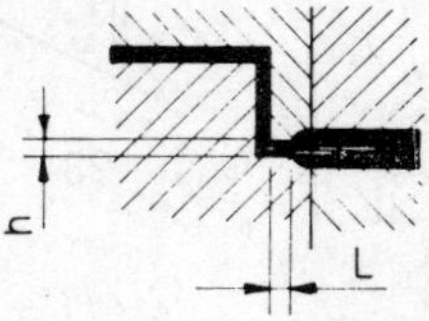

Fig. 14.25

The commonly used gates are of following types

(*i*) *Rectangular edge gate* :- This is the commonly used gate and is in the form of a rectangular channel machined in one mould plate to connect the runner to the impression. Fig. 14.25 shows a typical rectangular gate

L = Length

W = Width

h = depth

The depth of gate is given by

$$h = n.t.$$

where h = Depth of gate (mm)

t = wall thickness (mm)

n = Material constant

= 0.6 for polythene, polystyrene

= 0.7 for polyacetal, polycarbonate and for polypropylene

= 0.8 for cellulose acetate, nylon

= 0.9 for PVC

The minimum depth of gate control the time for which the gate remains open. This gate open time should be sufficient for the material to reach the entremities of the impression

W = width of gate in mm

$$= \frac{n\sqrt{A}}{30}$$

where A = surface area of cavity in mm^2

n = material constant

(*ii*) *Sprue gate* :- In this material is fed from sprue

(*iii*) *Over lap gate*

(*iv*) *Diaphragm gate*

(*v*) *Ring gate*

(*vi*) *Pin gate*

(*vii*) *Fan gate*

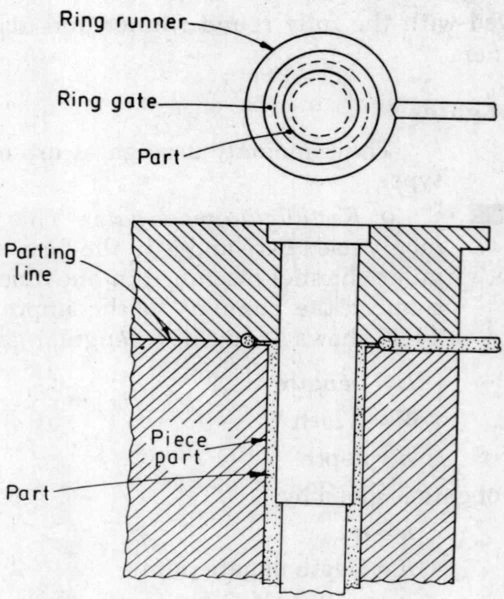

Fig. 14.26

(*viii*) *Film gate*

(*ix*) *Round edge gate*

14.37 Parts of ejector plate

Fig. 14.27 shows ejector plate assembly. It consists of the following

(*i*) Ejector plate (*ii*) Ejector rod

(*iii*) Retaining plate (*iv*) Ejector rod bush

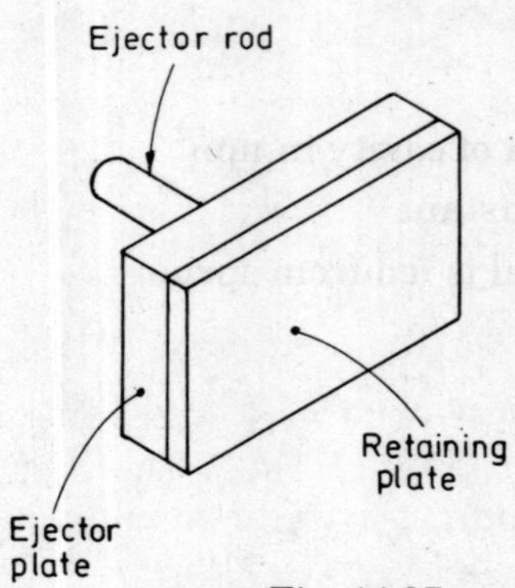

Fig. 14.27

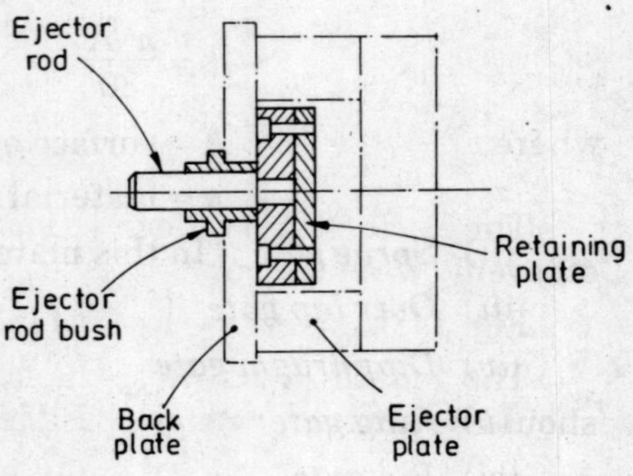

Fig. 14.28.

Fig. 14.28 shows ejector plate in position.

Ejector plate assembly is that part of the mould in which ejector element is attached one end of ejector rod is threaded and is screwed into the ejector plate.

14.38 Ejection methods

Depending on the shape and size of the moulding the various ejection methods are as follows :

(*i*) Pin ejection	(*ii*) Sleeve ejection
(*iii*) Bar ejection	(*iv*) Blade ejection
(*v*) Air ejection	(*vi*) Stripper plate ejection.

Facilities are provided on the injection machine for automatic actuation of an ejector system, and this is situated behind the moving platen. Because of this, the mould's ejector system will be most effectively operated if placed in the moving half of the mould, *i.e.* the half attached to the moving platen.

Pin ejection method :- This is the simplest method of ejecting the moulding. Moulding is ejected by the application of a force by a steel rod called ejector pin.

Fig. 14.29 shows a typical shouldered pin. The ejector pin is headed to facilitate its attachment to the ejector plate assembly. The location of the ejector pin elements and number of ejector pins used depends on shape and size of the component.

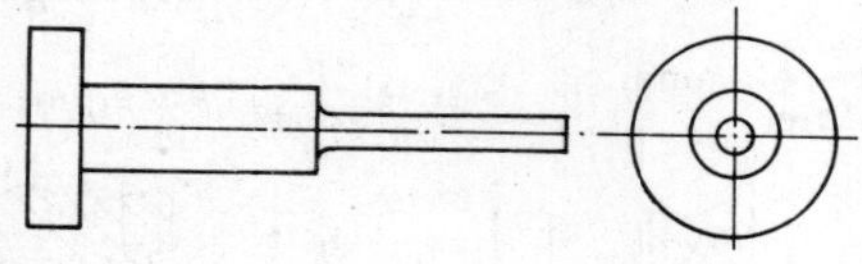

Fig. 14.29

The ejector pin should be so located that the moulding is pushed off evenly from the core.

Fig. 14.30 shows removal of moulding using number of pins.

The length of smallest diameter portion of the stepped pin should be kept ar short as possible.

A = Length in contact with the mould plate

= $5d$ to $6d$ (To be kept minimum)

B = Ejector stroke

C = Length of clearance diameter hole in the mould plate

d = Diameter of pin

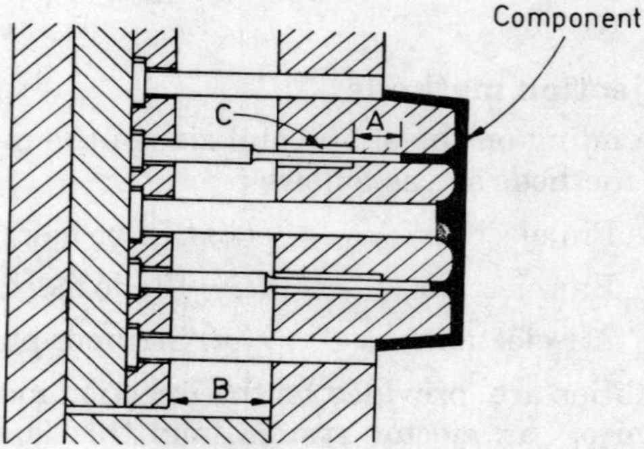

Fig. 14.30

Sleeve ejection :- In this method the moulding is ejected by means of a hollow ejector pin (see Fig. 14.30*a*) called a *Sleeve*.

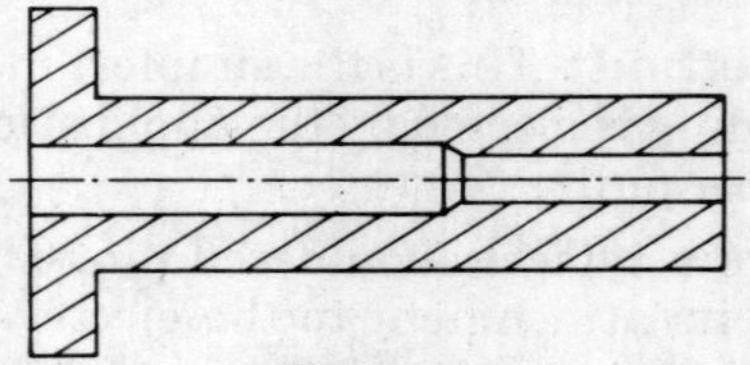

Fig. 14.30(*a*)

Fig. 14.31 shows sleeve ejection method. This method has the advantage that the force is applied to a relatively large surface area.

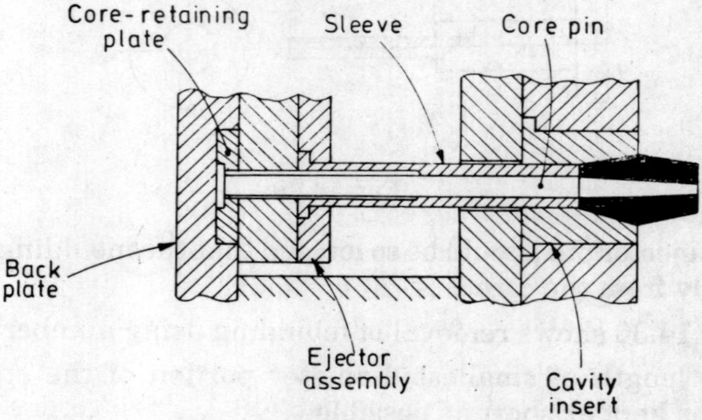

Fig. 14.31

Blade ejection : This method of ejection is particularly suitable to eject slender parts such as ribs and other projections. A blade is basically a rectangular ejector pin as shown in Fig. 14.32. The rectangular blade ejector is accomodated in a complementary shaped hole in the mould plate. Fig. 14.33 shows blade ejection method.

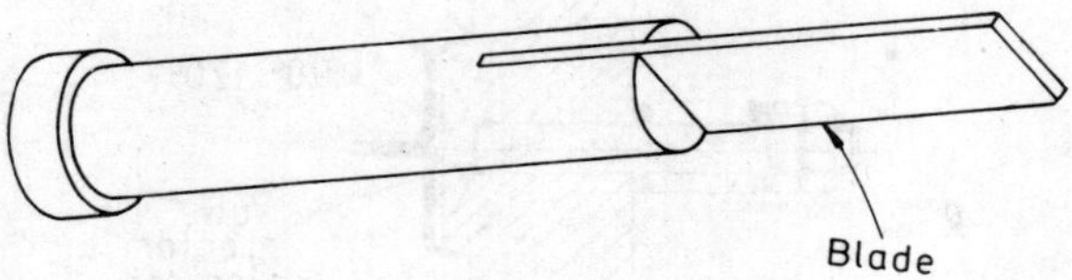

Fig. 14.32

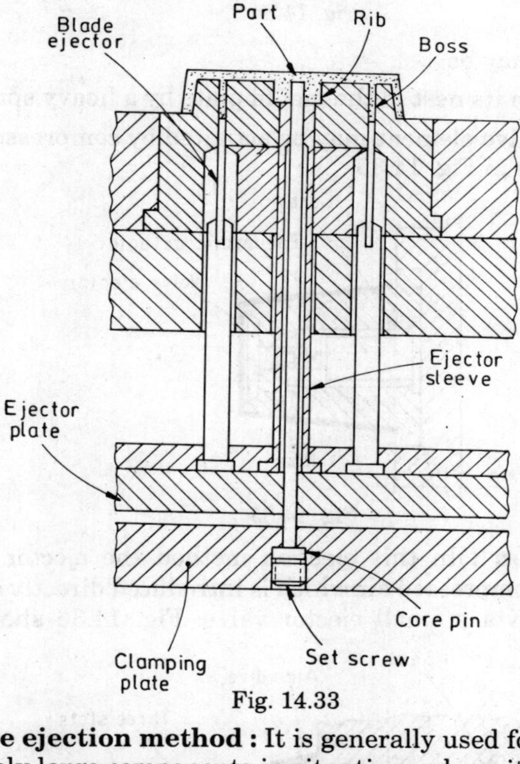

Fig. 14.33

Valve ejection method : It is generally used for the ejection of relatively large components in situations where it is difficult to use standard parting surface pins. The valve ejector element is basically a large diameter ejector pin.

The valve-type ejector element is designed to apply the ejector force on to the inside surface of the moulding. The ejector elements consists of a valve type head which is seated in a nest machined into the core.

Material of valve-type ejector element = Nickel-chromium steel suitably heat treated.

In operation, when the mould opens, the shank of the valve ejector element is arrested by the actuator rod of the injection machine and the moulding is ejected.

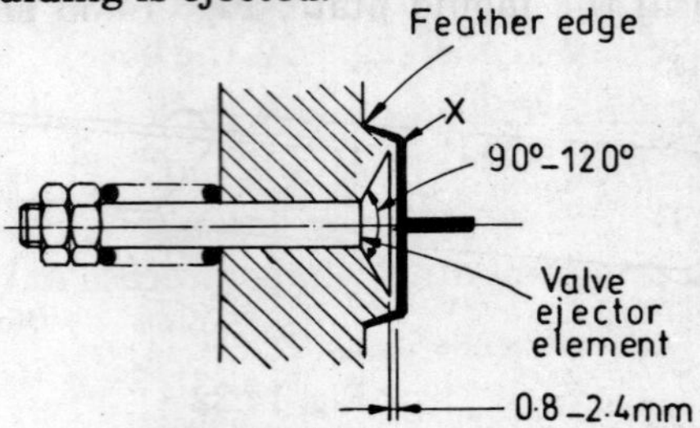

Fig. 14.34

The valve may be

(*a*) held in its nest in the mould plate by a heavy spring, or

(*b*) the valve element may be actuated by compressed air as shown in Fig. 14.35.

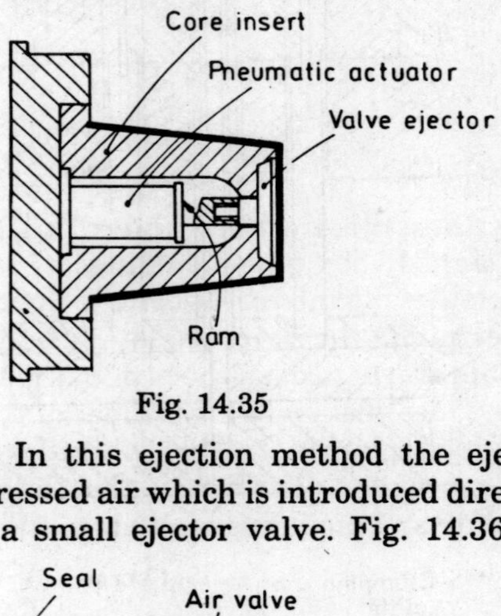

Fig. 14.35

Air ejection : In this ejection method the ejector force is provided by a compressed air which is introduced directly on to the moulding face via a small ejector valve. Fig. 14.36 shows com-

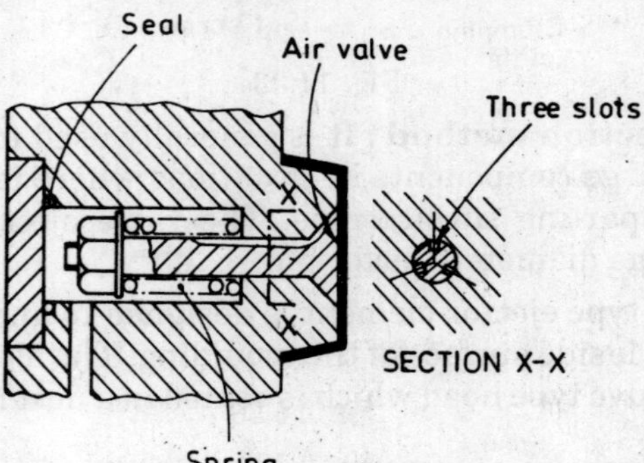

Fig. 14.36

pressed air ejection which uses three slots provided into the shank of the valve. These slots act as passage way for air.

Stripper Bar ejection method :- In this method the ejector element is caused to push against the bottom edge of the moulding.

It is particularly suitable for the ejection of the thin wall box type moulding.

Fig. 14.37 shows stripper bar assembly. The stripper bar is fitted into a complimentary shaped recess in the mould plate.

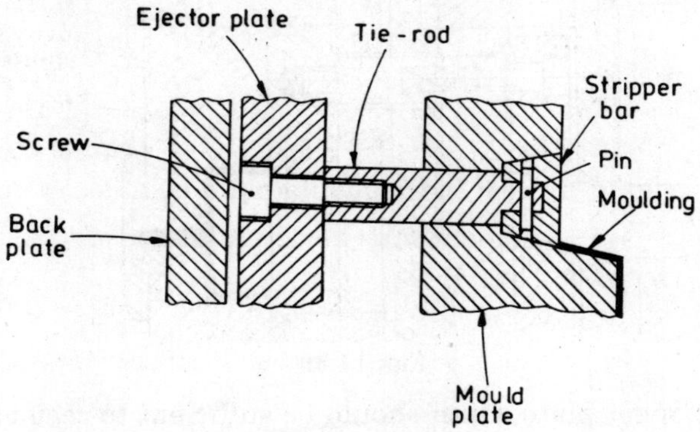

Fig. 14.37

Stripper plate ejection method :- This method is generally used to eject circular box type mouldings as shown in Fig. 14.38. The stripper plate is mounted between the cavity plate and the core plate. The aperture in the stripper plate is a sliding fit on the core. When the mould starts to open the stripper plate moves back with the core plate. Once the moulding is clear of the cavity, the movement of the stripper plate is arrested, while the core plate continues the rearward movement. The core is thereby withdrawn through the stripper plate and moulding ejected.

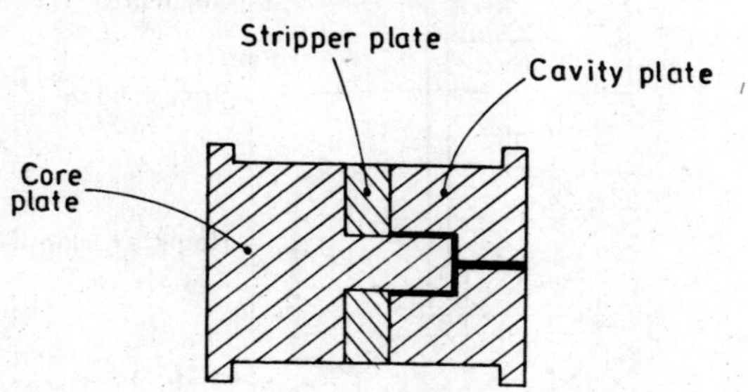

Fig. 14.38

Fig. 14.39 shows a part section through a typical stripper plate mould. In this mould the stripper plate is mounted on guide pillars which are fitted in the core plate. The apertures in the stripper plate, through which the core and the guide pillars pass, are all bushed. The cavity mould plate is of conventional design.

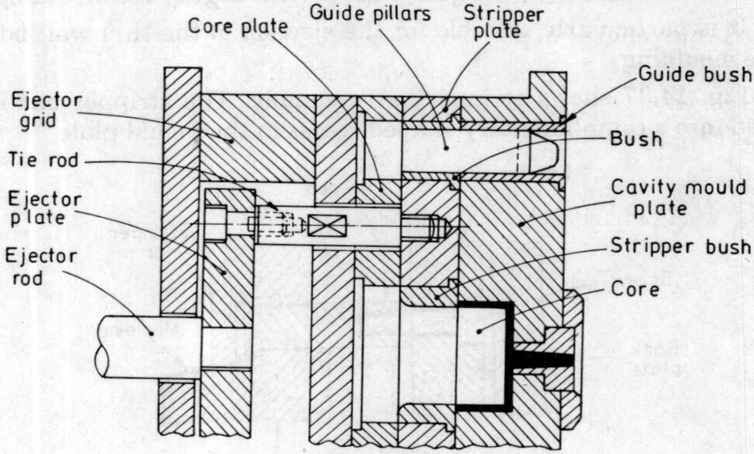

Fig. 14.39

The stripper plate depth should be sufficient to resist bending forces applied to the plate as the moulding is ejected.

14.39 Locating ring for mould

Locating ring also called register ring is used to locate the mould in its correct position on the injection machine platen as shown in Fig. 14.40. The locating ring is a flat circular member fitted on to the front face of the mould.

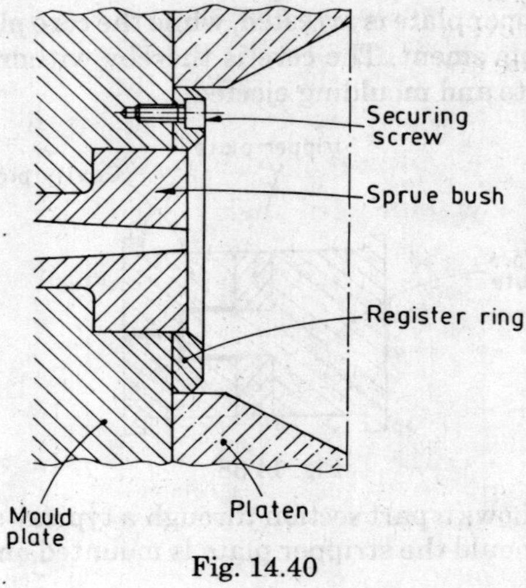

Fig. 14.40

14.40 Guide pillars

They are used to

(*i*) allign the two mould halves

(*ii*) prevent the mould from being assembled in the wrong way that is a guide pillar acts as a locating pin.

$D = d + 7$ mm where d = working diameter

n = Number of pillar

= 2 to 4.

Fig. 14.41 shows a typical guide pillar.

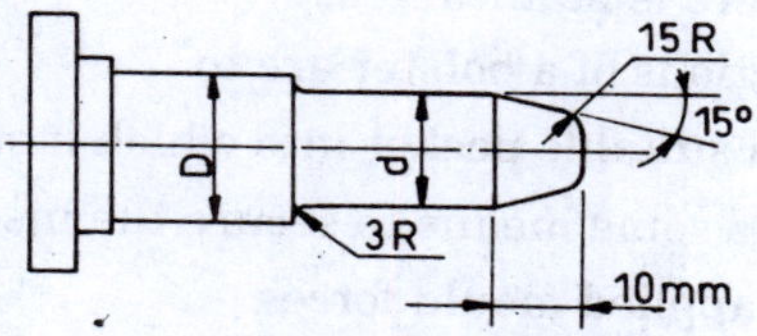

Fig. 14.41

14.41 Guide bush

It is incorporated in the mould to provide a suitable wear-resisting working surface for the guide pillar and to permit replacement in the event of wear or damage.

It is made from C 30 plain carbon steel and case hardened. Fig. 14.42 shows a typical guide bush.

14.42 Sprue bush

It is that part of the mould in which sprue is formed. It provides a suitable aperture through which the material can travel on its way to the impressions or to the start of the runner system in multi-impression moulds.

Fig. 14.43 shows a typical shape of sprue bush.

α = Included angle = 3 to 5°

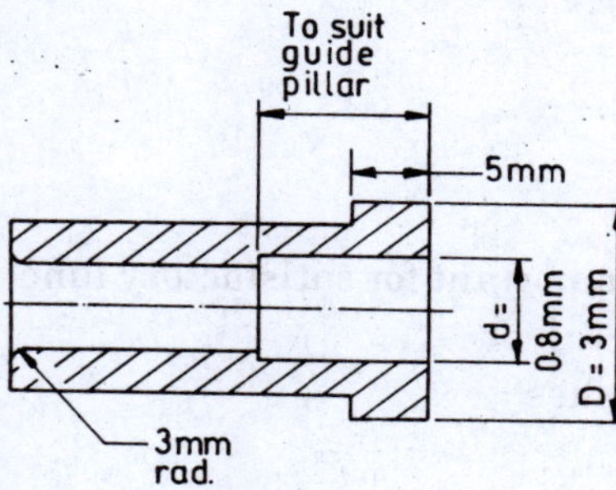

Fig. 14.42

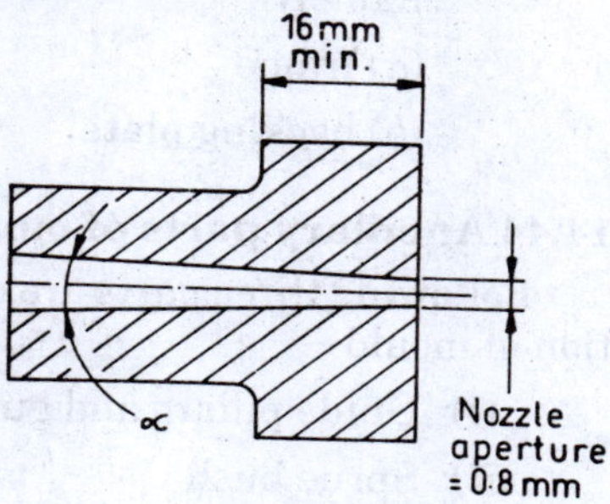

Fig. 14.43

Fig. 14.44 shows fitting of guide pillar and guide bush to two plate mould.

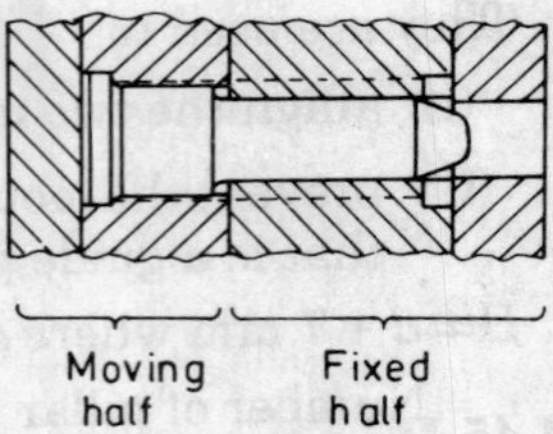

Fig. 14.44

14.43 Bolsters

When it is desired to incorporate cavity and core into the mould as inserts, they must be securely retained in the mould. This is achieved by fitting the inserts into a bolster which when fitted with suitable guiding arrangements ensures that alignment of the cavity and core is maintained.

The main functions of a bolster are to

(*i*) provide a suitable pocket into which insert can be fitted

(*ii*) to provide some means to secure the insert

(*iii*) to resist applied mould forces

Various types of bolster are as follows.

(*i*) Solid bolster :- Fig 14.44 shows a solid bolster. It is useful for both rectangular and circular inserts

(*ii*) Strip type bolster

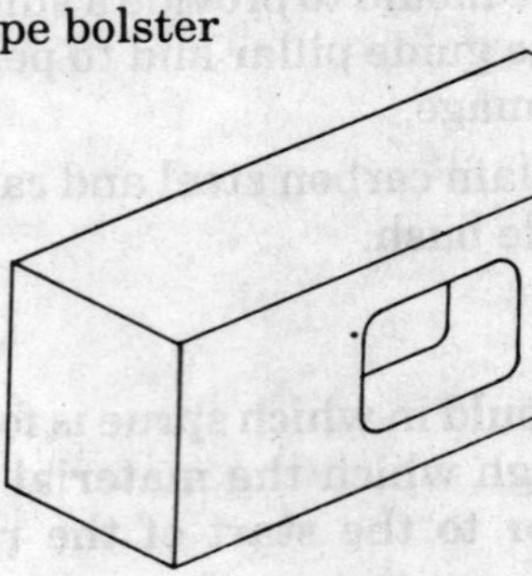

Fig. 14.45

(*iii*) Frame type bolster :— This bolster consists of two parts namely

(*a*) frame

(*b*) backing plate.

14.44 Ancillary parts of mould

Following three parts are quite important for satisfactory function of mould

(*i*) Guide pillars and guide bushes

(*ii*) Sprue bush

(*iii*) Register ring

These parts ensure that

(*i*) two mould halves remain in correct alignment

(*ii*) path for the plastic material is provided from the machine nozzle to mould face correctly

(*iii*) mould is accurately position on the machine

14.45 Mould Cavities and Cores

In general core is incorporated in the moving half and cavity in the fixed half. The cavity and core can be incorporated into the mould by two methods namely

(*i*) Integer method

(*ii*) Insert method

Fig. 14.46 shows integer type moulds.

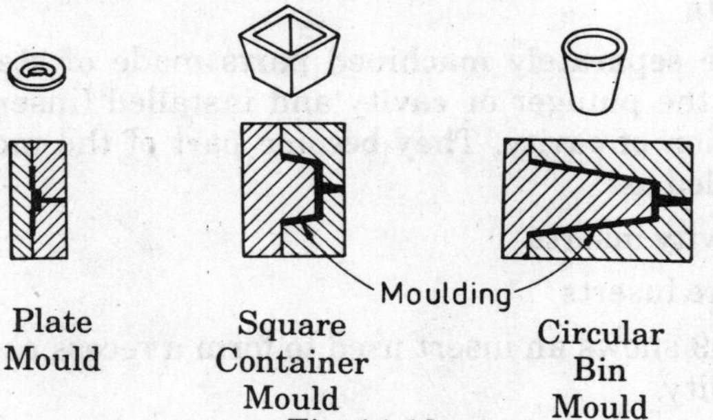

Fig. 14.46

14.46 Attachment of mould to platen

There are two methods of attaching mould to the platen of injection moulding machine

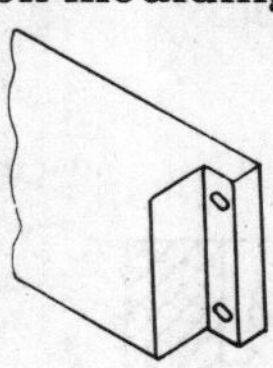

Fig. 14.47

1. Direct bolting method :- In this method bolts are used to directly secure the mould to the platen. Fig. 14.47 shows a typical arrangement in which front plate incorporates a projection which extends beyond the remainder of the mould half. Holes are provided in this portion so that bolts can be inserted into these holes.

2. In direct bolting method :- In this method the mould is attached to the machine by means of a clamp plate as shown in Fig. 14.48. Indirect bolting consists of three parts namely

(*i*) clamp plate

(*ii*) bolt

(*iii*) packing piece.

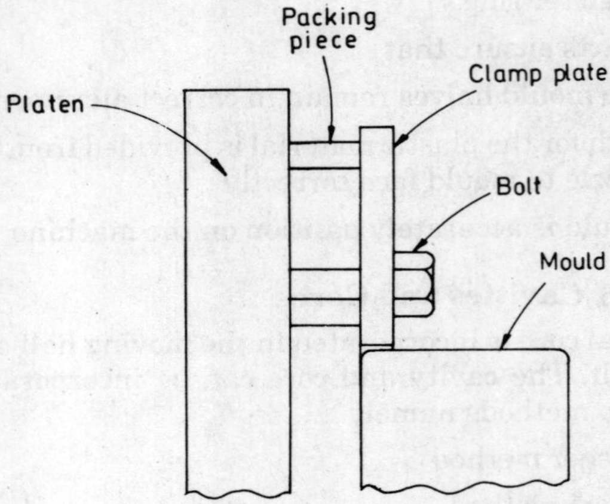

Fig. 14.48

14.47 Inserts

They are separately machined parts made of steel or same material as the plunger or cavity and installed (inserted) in the proper position of cavity. They become part of the molding unit. They are called as

(*a*) Cavity inserts

(*b*) Core inserts

Fig. 14.49 shows an insert used to form a recess at the bottom of a deep cavity.

Fig. 14.50 shows how an insert is used in producing sharp corners at the cavity wall and narrow slots.

Fig. 14.51 shows a typical core pin insert used in a cavity or a plunger.

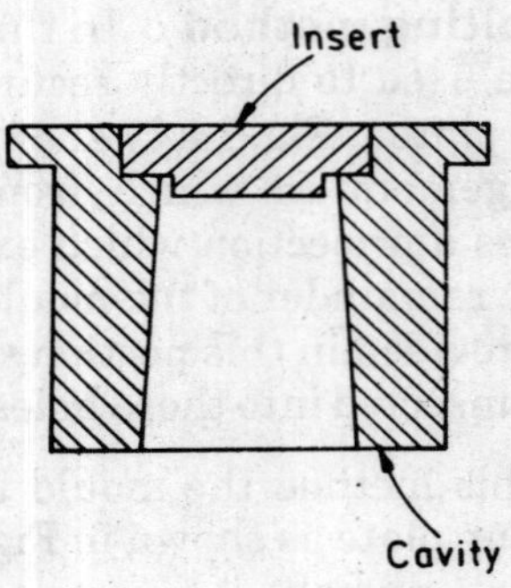

Fig. 14.49

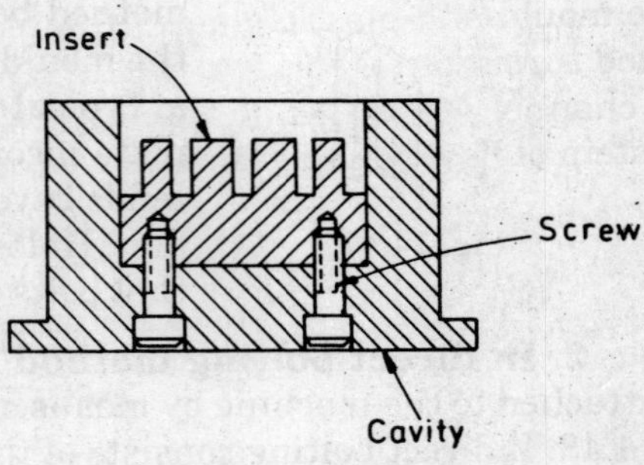

Fig. 14.50

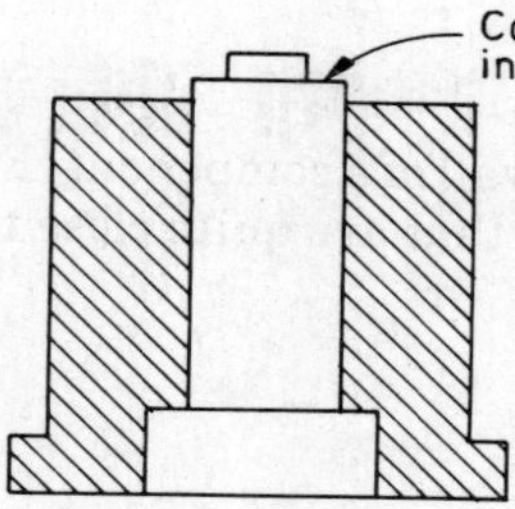

Fig. 14.51

14.48 Mould filling

The filling of the mould by molten polymer proceeds rather slowly. Typical mould cavities take nearly 2 seconds to 30 seconds to get filled up.

14.49 Venting

It is desireable to provide vents in the mould to allow air and other gases to escape freely.

The vent is normally a shallow slot not more than 0.05 mm deep by 3 mm wide machined in the land.

14.50 Mould Cooling

The operating temperature of a mould depends on the following factors

(*i*) Type of plastic material

(*ii*) Wall section of the moulding

(*iii*) Length of flow within the impression

(*iv*) Length of feed system.

The molten plastic must be cooled rapidly to harden plastic, to yield minimum production time. Water cooling channels in the mould provide the required cooling. The lower the mould temperature, the faster the cycle time ; but the mould temperature also affects the mechanical properties of the completed part, since more rapid cooling increases residual stress and molecular orientation.

While the melt flows more freely in a hot mould, a greater cooling period is required before the solidified moulding can be ejected. To maintain the required temperature differential between the mould and plastic material water or some other fluid is circulated through the holes or channels within the mould. These holes or channels are called flow ways or water ways and the complete system of flow ways is called the circuit.

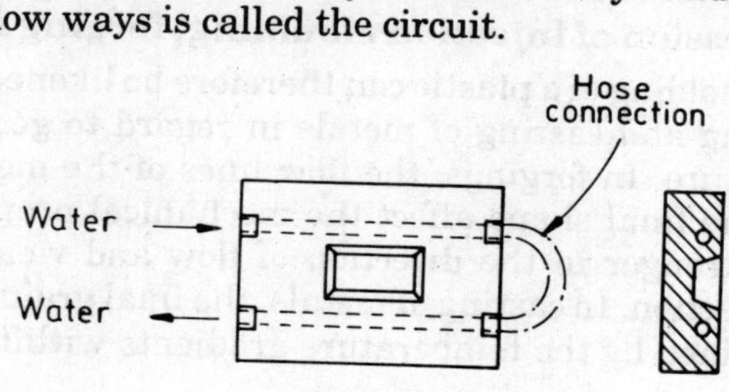

Fig. 14.52

Fig. 14.52 shows integer cavity plate cooling system using water circulated through holes.

14.51 Distance between holes

When holes are to be cast near the side wall of a component (Fig. 14.53) or if one or more holes are to be cast that are quite close the side wall as shown in Fig. 14.54.

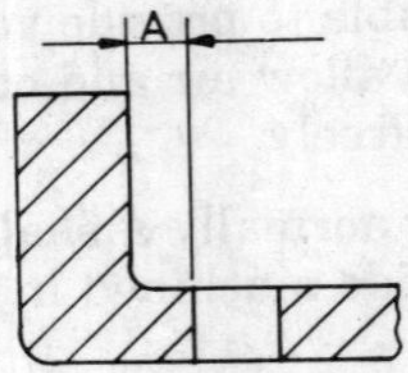

Fig. 14.53

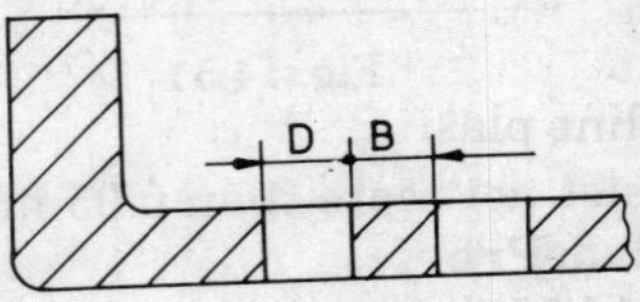

Fig. 14.54

Table 14.2

Diameter of hole, D	*Minimum to side wall, A*	*Minimum between holes, B*
mm	*mm*	*mm*
1.58	1.58	1.58
3.17	2.38	2.38
4.76	3.17	3.17
6.35	3.17	3.96
9.52	3.96	4.76
12.70	4.76	5.55

There are limitations to the distance between holes or side wall as indicated in Table 14.2.

14.52 Compression of Injection moulding, forging and casting

Injection molding of a plastic can therefore be likened to a cross between forging and casting of metals in regard to generation of internal structure. In forgings, the flow lines of the metal as it is deformed to the final shape affect the mechanical properties, the metal being stronger in the direction of flow and weaker in the transverse direction. In casting of metals, the final grain configuration is determined by the temperature gradients within the mold.

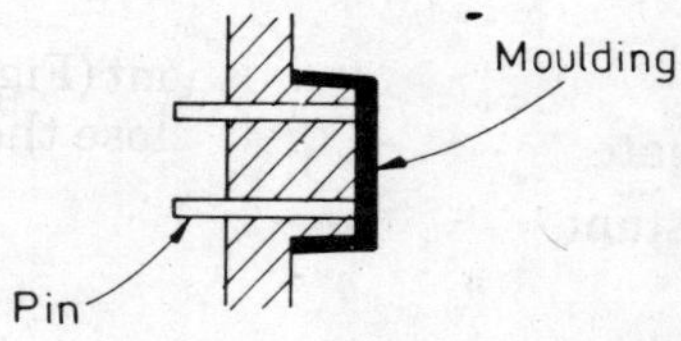

Fig. 14.55

tion is determined by the temperature gradients within the mould. Similar results occur in injection moulding of plastics, in which the flow of the material results in orientations of the molecules in the flow direction, which therefore develop into the stronger direction within an anisotropic material. Mold wall thermal gradients determine the size and orientation of crystallites forming in semicrystalline plastics.

Problem 14.1 : *Is it desireable to eject box type moulding (Fig. 14.55) by moulding face pins.*

Solution. It is not desireable to eject box type moulding with moulding face pins as this will spoil the base of the moulding as shown in Fig. 14.55.

Problem 14.2 *Sketch two typical mouldings which can be sleeve ejected.*

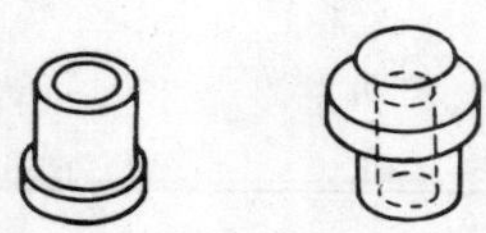

(*a*) (*b*)

Fig. 14.56

Solution :- Fig. 14.56 shows two typical mouldings that can be ejected by sleeve ejection method.

Problem 14.3 *What is ejector grid. Name the alternative designs.*

Solution

Ejector Grid. It is that part of the mould which supports the mould plate and provides a space into which the ejector plate assembly can be fitted and operated. The grid normally consists of a back plate on to which is mounted a number of conveniently shaped 'support blocks'.

There are three alternative designs :-

(*i*) The in-line ejector grid

(*ii*) The frame-type ejector grid

(*iii*) The circular support block grid.

In-Line Ejector Grid. This consists of two rectangular support blocks mounted on a back plate.

Problem 14.4 *Calculate the diameter of a round gate which is used to feed a cylindrical component of 60 mm diameter and 90 mm length. The wall section thickness is 0.7 and material of component is polythene.*

Solution.

d = Diameter of gate

r = Material constant

= 0.6

C = Constant depending on wall thickness

= 0.178 (From Table 14.3)

D_1 = Diameter of component = 60 mm

L = Length of component = 90 mm

A = Surface area of cavity

$$= \Pi D_L + \frac{\Pi}{4} \times D^2 = \Pi \times 60 \times 90 + \frac{\Pi \times 60^2}{4}$$

$$= 19782 \text{ mm}^2$$

Table 14.3

t	C
0.75	0.178
1	0.206
1.25	0.23
1.5	1.24
2	0.29
2.25	0.31

where t = wall thickness in mm

d = Diameter of round gate

$$= \text{n.c.} \sqrt[4]{A} = 0.6 \times 0.178 \sqrt[4]{19782}$$

$$= 1.26 \text{ mm.}$$

Problem 14.5 *Sketch a typical mould indicating sprue bush, register ring guide pillars and guide bushes.*

Solution. Fig. 14.57 shows the various parts of a mould such as

(*i*) Sprue bush (*ii*) register ring

(*iii*) guide prillars

(*iv*) guide bushes

(*v*) fixed half and moving half.

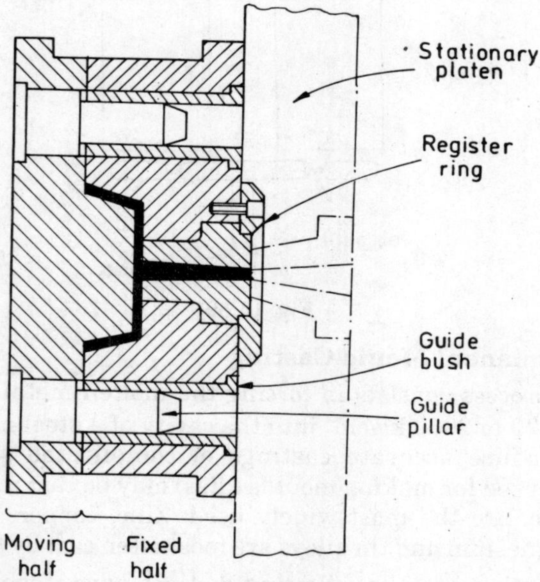

Fig. 14.57

Problem 14.6 *Sketch a typical (a) multiple runner and gating system (b) Tab gate.*

Solution. Fig. 14.58 shows the use of a multiple runner and gating system to fill a deep cavity through a hole in the part to be produced,

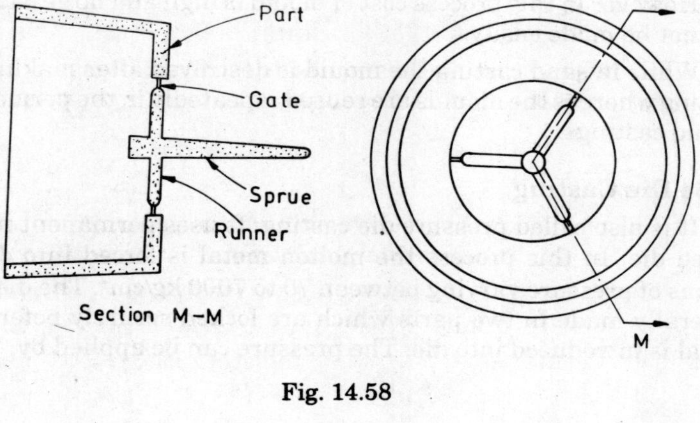

Fig. 14.58

Fig. 14.59 shows a tab gate arrangement.

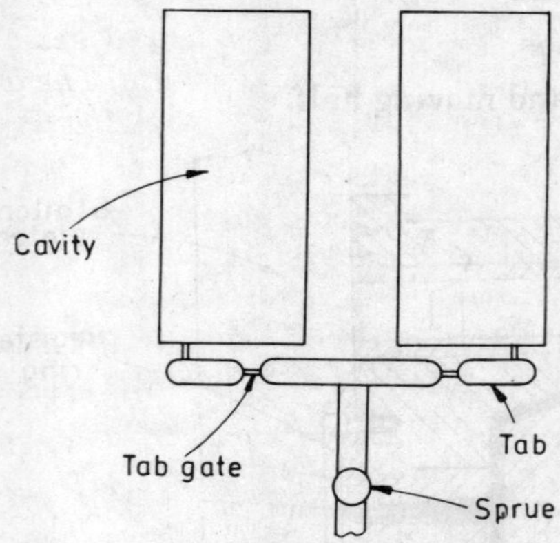

Fig. 14.59

14.53 Permanent Mould Casting

This process consists in forcing the molten metal under high pressure (20 to 2000 kg/cm^2 into the cavity of a steel mould or die. It can produce accurate castings of complicated shapes. The materials used for making moulds (dies) may be cast iron although alloy steels are the most widely used. Zinc, copper, aluminium, Lead, magnesium and tin alloys are most often cast by this process.

Die casting has the following distinct advantages over sand mould casting :

1. Close dimensional tolerance
2. Castings of complicated shapes can be easily produced.
3. Better surface finish.
4. Greater mechanical strength of parts made.
5. Quite suitable for mass production.

However in this process cost of mould is high and large castings can not be made easily.

While in sand casting the mould is destroyed after making the casting whereas the moulds are reused repeatedly in the permanent mould castings.

14.54 Die Casting

It is also called pressure die casting. It uses permanent mould called die. In this process the molten metal is forced into die by means of pressure varying between 70 to 7000 kg/cm^2. The dies are generally made in two parts which are locked securely before the metal is introduced into die. The pressure can be applied by, (*i*) hydraulically operated piston

or (*ii*) compressed air

The die casting machines commonly used for die casting are of two types :

Die castings are made of six principal base alloys : tin, lead, zinc, copper, aluminium, and magnesium. Of these, zinc, aluminium, and magnesium, in that order, account for the major tonnage. Zinc is used for many structural parts in the automotive, electric-appliance, and business-machine industries because of its low cost, ease of casting, and ability to take a good finish ; most of the chromium-plated parts on a modern automobile are zinc die castings. Aluminium is increasing rapidly in popularity, due in large part to a decreasing price trend in the cost of the raw material : it is light in weight, has better dimensional stability than zinc, is a good electrical conductor, and have good corrosion resistance. Magnesium is used primarily because of light weight.

Vents, ranging in depth from 0.015 mm to 0.04 mm in are incorporated in the die to allow air that is displaced by the molten metal to escape from the die impression. Failure to provide suitable venting may result in unsound castings. Many methods of venting are available, and the die designer must determine the method and the extent of venting required depending on from the size, contour, and section of the casting.

14.55 Requirements of success die casting

The three main requirements to produce sound and economical die castings.

1. A smoothly working casting mechanism, properly designed to hold and operate a die under pressure.
2. A properly designed die.
3. Suitable material to be cast.

14.56 Ribs and fillets

Ribs and generous radii 3 mm to 6 mm add to the strength and stiffness of die cast parts. They help in reducing distortion that might occur when parts cool and ejected.

On heavy bosses and overhanging projection ribs add stiffness and act as feeders in filling such sections in the die. Fig 14.60 shows ribs and fillet provided on a component.

The aims of providing ribs in die casting can be summed up as follows.

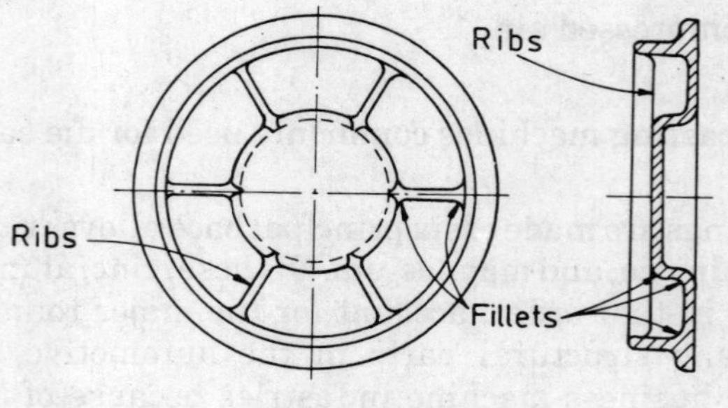

Fig. 14.60

1. To increase strength and stiffness.
2. To decrease warpage.
3. To facilitate the flow of molten metal into die cavities.
4. It is usually advantageous to add ribs to deep bosses or heavy metal sections, tying such sections to the main body of the casting. The ribs then act as gates or feeders and aid materially in filling these sections in the die.

14.57 Die Steels

The steels used for die casting dies should be of high quality and free from defects especially in the area where the die cavity will be located.

Die steels should posses the following characteristics.

1. Good machinability.
2. Structural soundness and uniformity.
3. High resistance to heat.
4. Sufficient strength and hardness to resist deformation in service.
5. High thermal conductivity.
6. Sufficient toughness to resist cleavage cracking.
7. Low coefficient of thermal expansion
8. High resistance to the erosive and washing action of the die casting alloy.

Die steels for die-casting aluminium and magnesium must be of an especially high grade because of the high melting points of these alloys. One of these types that is often used has a nominal composition of 0.40 per cent carbon, 0.40 per cent manganese, 1.00 per cent silicon, 5.25 per cent chromium, 1.00 per cent molybdenum, and 1.00 per cent vanadium.

The usual chemical composition of die steels may be as follows

	Percent
Carbon	0.37 to 0.42
Silicon	0.85 to 1.10
Manganese	0.20 to 0.50
Chromium	5.00 to 5.50
Vanadium	0.90 to 1.10
Molybdenum	1.00 to 1.25
Sulfur	Not over 0.03
Phosphorus	Not over 0.03

14.58 Die Casting Machines

The commonly used die casting machines are as follows

1. Hot chamber die casting machine
2. Cold chamber machine

1. **Hot chamber die casting machine.** This machine has two types of arrangements.

(*a*) Sub merged plunger type die casting machine

(*b*) Direct air pressure die casting machine

It is mainly used for low melting point alloys and metals like zinc, lead etc.

Fig. 14.61 shows submerged plunger type hot chamber die-casting machine. In this machine the molten metal from the metal container is forced inside the die with the help of a plunger submerged in the molten metal and operated hydraulically. The plunger moves inside the cylinder having a hole in its bottom. When the plunger moves up, the molten metal comes up and fills the cylinder which is then forced into the die cavity through the nozzle in the goose-neck of the container in the down stroke of the plunger.

The goose neck type metal container always remains immersed in the metal pot. The die is made in two parts.

(*i*) Stationary die platen

(*ii*) Movable die platen. The movements of the plunger and the movable die platen are synchronised such that when metal is being forced, the two die halves are in match and on solidification when plunger is moving up, the movable die platen moves away and the casting is removed.

The molten metal is forced into the die cavity at a pressure of 70 to 150 kg/cm^2.

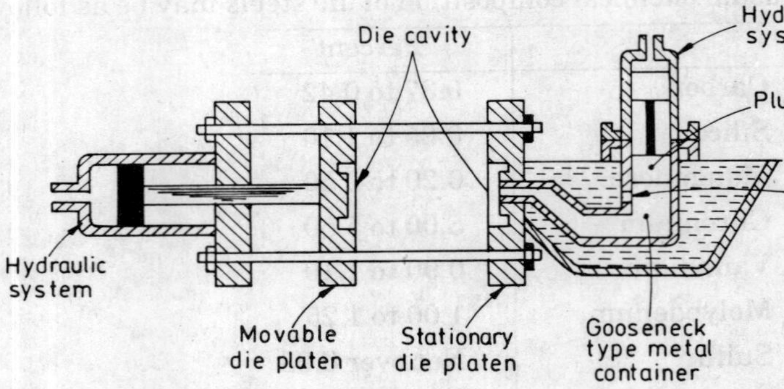

Fig. 14.61

Fig. 14.62 shows direct air pressure die casting machine principle. In this machine compressed air is used to force metal inside the die cavity.

The goose-neck container is operated by a lifting mechanism. Initially it is submerged in the molten metal and is filled by gravity.

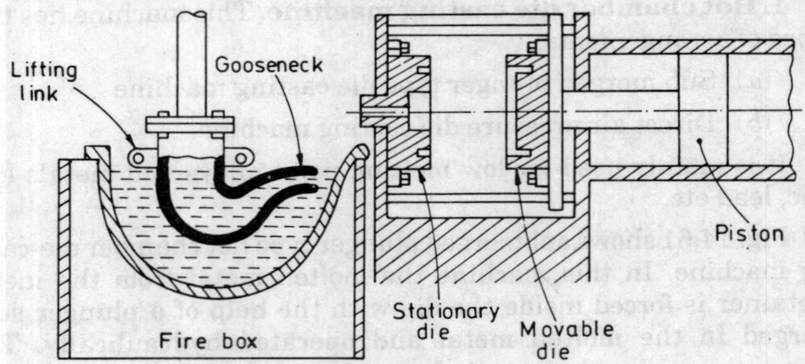

Fig. 14.62. (*a*)

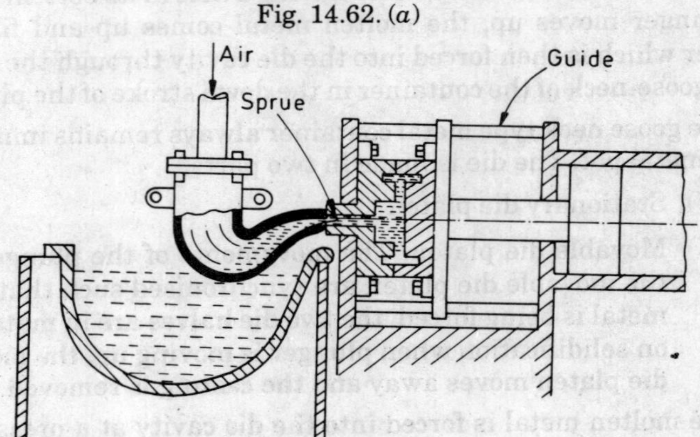

Fig. 14.62 (*b*)

Then it is raised so as to bring the nozzle in contact with the die opening and is locked in that position. Compressed air then forces the metal into the die and pressure is maintained till solidification. When the metal gets solidified the goose neck is lowered and casting is removed. The compressed air pressure used is about 40 kg/cm^2.

Fig. 14.63 shows a details of a submerged plunger machine for die casting process. These machines are generally hydraulically operated and are equipped with automatic cycling controls and safety devices.

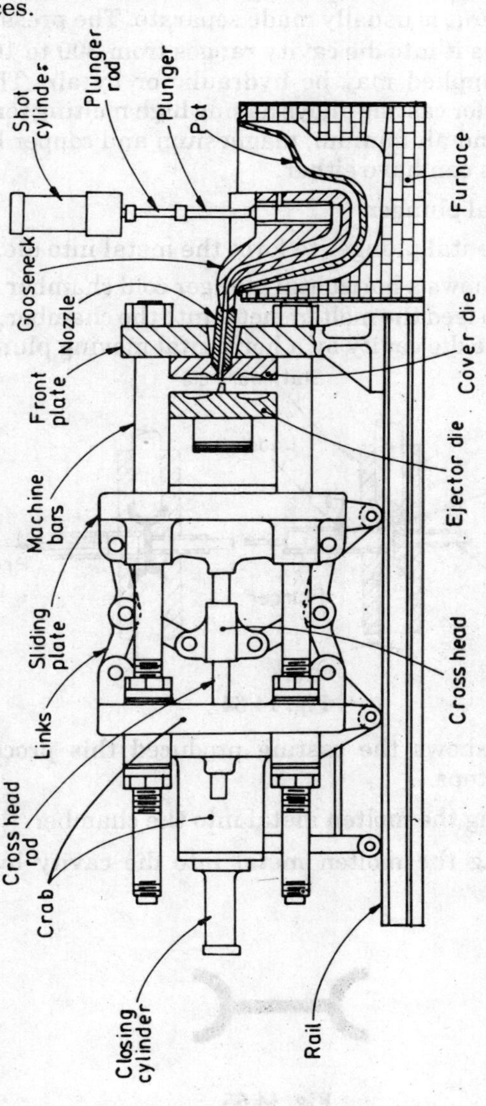

Fig. 14.63.

First, the gooseneck is lowered into the molten alloy. The compressed-air connection to the lid is opened to the atmosphere by means of a valve. This allows the metal to flow into the gooseneck through the spout. The gooseneck is then mechanically lifted from the melting pot, thus allowing the surplus metal to drain from the spout. It is tilted backward slightly to prevent drip, and continuation of the stroke brings the spout into contact with the die orifice, where it is locked in position.

2. **Cold chamber die casting machine.** In this machine the metal melting unit is usually made separate. The pressure applied on metal to force it into die cavity ranges from 300 to 1600 kg/cm^2. The pressure applied may be hydraulic or by air. This is quite commonly used for casting alloys having high melting temperatures such as brass and aluminium, magnesium and copper base alloys. These machines can have either.

(*i*) vertical plunger

or (*ii*) horizontal plunger to force the metal into die.

Fig. 14.64 shows a horizontal plunger cold chamber machine. A saddle is used to feed the molten metal into the chamber. This metal is forced into the die cavity by a horizontal moving plunger.

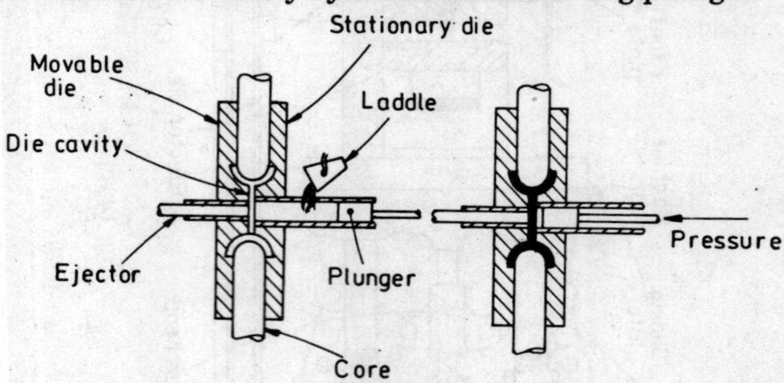

Fig. 14.64.

Fig. 14.65 shows the casting produced this process mainly consist of four steps.

1. Pouring the molten metal into the chamber.
2. Forcing the molten metal into die cavity by means of plunger.

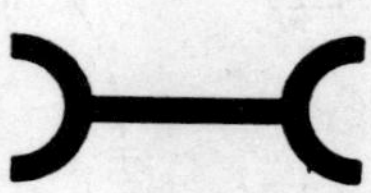

Fig. 14.65.

3. Withdrawing of cores after metal gets solidified.
4. Opening the dies and removing the casting automatically by means of ejector.

Fig. 14.66 shows details of a cold chamber machine for die casting. This machine has largely replaced the gooseneck machine in commercial production. Injection pressure. It is operated by

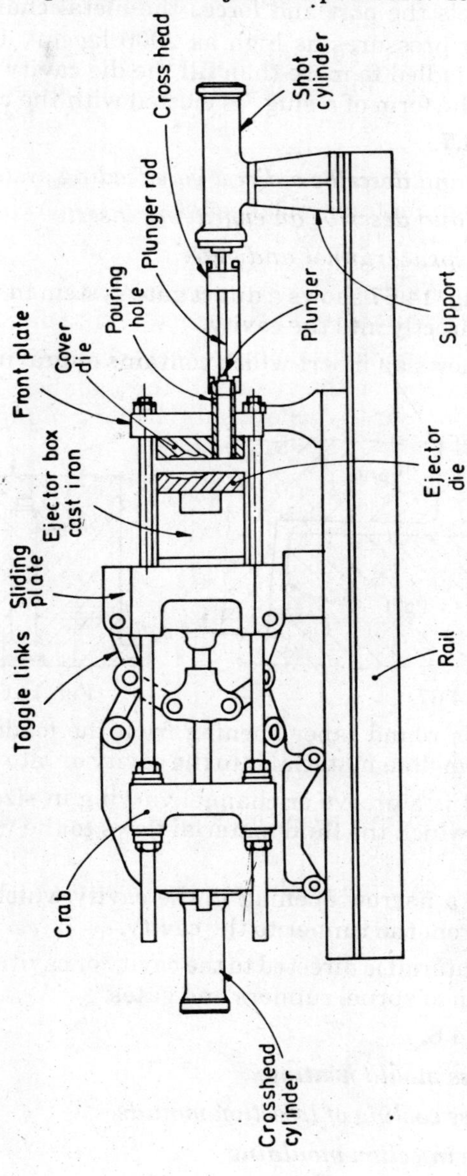

Fig. 14.66

hydraulic pressure as high as 2000 kg/cm^2 can be produced by this machine.

The cold-chamber machine uses a hydraulically operated plunger to force molten metal into the die. The metal is first poured into the cold chamber by a ladle that holds enough metal for several die fillings. Immediately after the pouring operation, the plunger is advanced ; it seals the port and forces the metal charge into the locked die under pressures as high as 2000 kg/cm^2. In all cases, enough metal is ladled to more than fill the die cavity ; the excess metal, being in the form of a slug, is ejected with the casting.

Example 14.7.

(*a*) *Sketch and describe a direct gate feeding system.*

(*b*) *Sketch and describe an engraving insert.*

(*c*) *Define sprue, runner and gate.*

Solution. Fig. 14.67 shows a direct gate system in which sprue feeds material directly into the cavity.

Fig. 14.68 shows an insert which contains engraving.

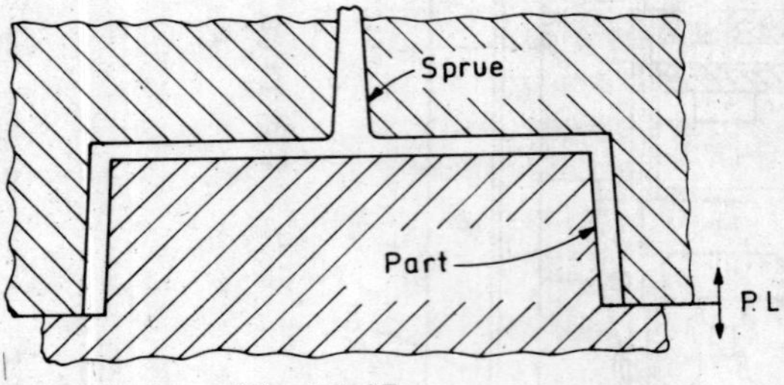

Fig. 14.67

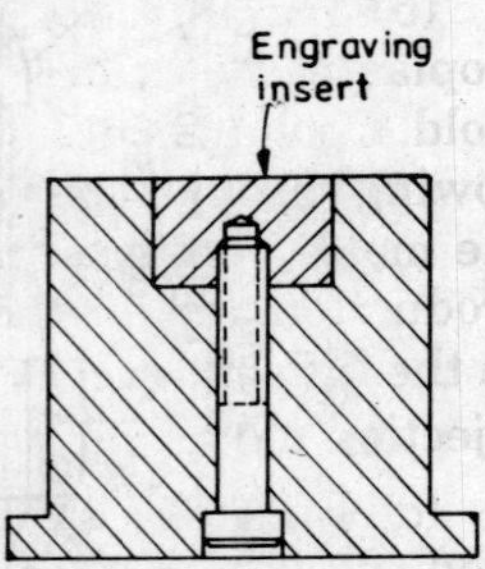

Fig. 14.68

Sprue : It is round taper opening from the loading chamber which feeds the molten material into the cavity or into the runners.

Runner : It is a groove or channel varying in size, shape and length through which the fluid material flows to the vicinity of the cavity.

Gate : It is a narrow opening in the cavity which carries the fluid material from the runner to the cavity.

The fluid material is directed to the cavity or cavities by a sprue or a combination of sprue, runners and gates.

Example 14.8.

(*a*) *Discuss mould heating.*

(*b*) *Discuss cooling of injection moulds.*

(*c*) *Define injection moulding.*

Solution.

(*a*) Moulds may be heated electrically or by using steam.

Besides being heated electrically, many compression and transfer molds are heated by steam. The steam is directed through the mold by a series of steam channels drilled into the various parts of the mold. Steam channels are drilled into cavity and core plates, clamping plates, support plates, etc. Steam channels should be so located as to heat the material in the molding area as uniformly as possible. Practical, channels are drilled so that they follow the contour of the piece part. It is recommended that steam channels be kept approximately two to three times the diameter of the drilled channel away from any molding surface.

For smaller molds, steam channels are drilled about 60 mm between centers and 15 mm in diameter, with 10 mm pipe thread for plugs or fittings for the intake and outlet of the steam.

On larger molds, the channels are drilled about 100 mm betweeen centers and 18 mm in diameter, with 12 mm pipe thread at the ends of the hole.

(*b*) The injection molds are cooled in order to have the thermoplastic material harden or set after it has been forced into the mold. Cooling is accomplished by a continuous circulation of water flowing through channels which are drilled into various portions of the mold. Temperatures must be carefully controlled for efficient production and for the prevention of stresses, strains, blisters, etc. on the finished piece part. The temperture of the water used to cool injection molds varies from 75° to 135°F.

(*c*) Injection molding is the most common process for part production in the plastics industry, as the process can produce parts of great complexity in shape in thermoplastic and thermosets. Part size can vary tremendously depending on the capacity of the unit ; small knobs to automobile door liners are routinely produced.

Example 14.9.

(*a*) *Discuss the position of flash in a mould.*

(*b*) *Sketch a feed system for multi-impression mould.*

(*c*) *State the purpose of using insert in die cast part.*

Solution.

(*a*) When flash is liable to develop it is important that mould design should be such that flash is in line of draw whenever the component has side element (see Fig. 14.69).

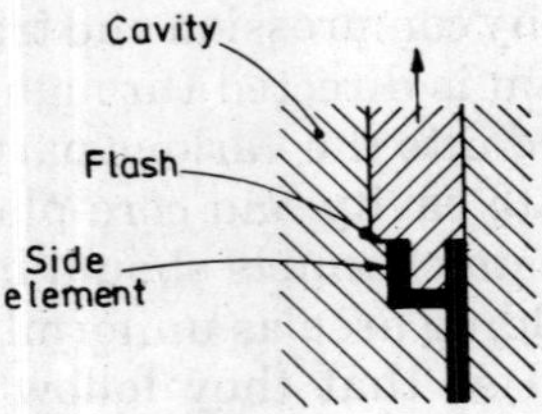

Fig. 14.69

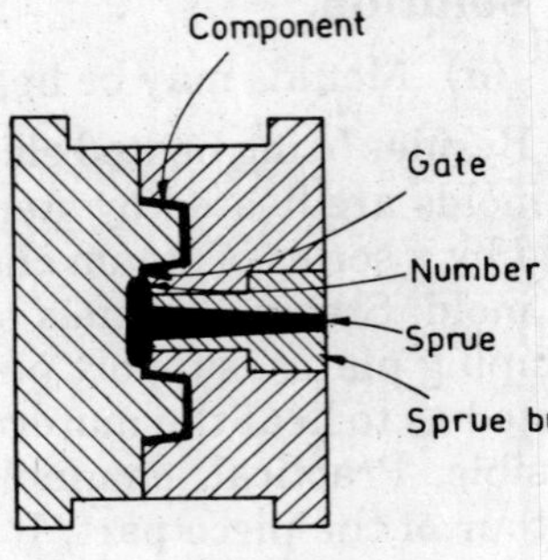

Fig. 14.70

(*b*) Fig. 14.70 shows a feeding system through a runner and gate the feeding system for a multi impression mould.

(*c*) Inserts are separately fabricated parts that are cast in and become an integral part of the casting. Important and necessary reasons for using inserts are as follows.

(*i*) To provide means for joining the die casting to other mating parts during assembly. They thus obviate the necessity of bolting, pinning, screwing, or welding individual pieces to the casting after it comes from the casting machine.

(*ii*) To impart to the die casting certain properties that are not inherent in the cast metal. Examples are inserts used for additional mechanical strength, hardness, corrosion resistance, arc and spark resistance, spring resiliency, magnetism, or as a base for soldering.

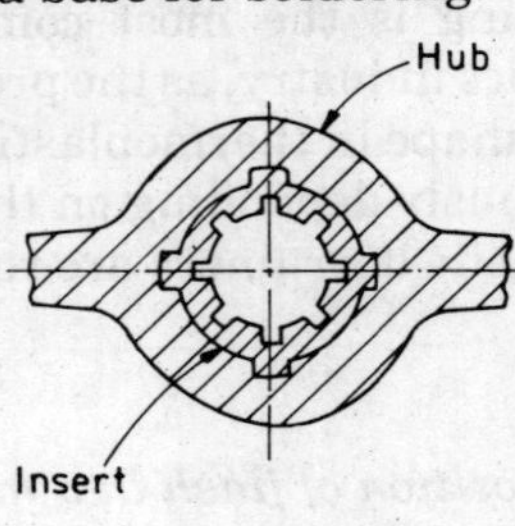

Fig. 14.71

Fig. 14.71 shows how in a die-cast hub a hardened steel or bronze insert is cast in place and secured against both radial and end thrust by means of the four lugs located around the outside of the insert. In casting, the insert is placed over a splined core in the die.

Example 14.10. *Discuss typical copper base die casting alloys.*

Solution. The copper base diecasting alloys are used for small and medium sized parts that are subjected to wear in service.

Although the corrosion resistance of brass die castings is excellent, they usually are not applied for decorative purposes because the protective oxide film that forms on the surface detracts from its appearance, and because plated or colored zinc or aluminium die castings usually are less costly. However, brass die-casting alloys have excellent characteristics and high strength.

Table 14.4 indicates chemical composition of standard. Copper base (brass) die casting alloys.

Table 14.4

Metal	*Composition, per cent*		
	Alloy type A	*Alloy type B*	*Alloy type C*
Copper	57.0 min	63.0 to 67.0	80.0 to 83.0
Silicon	0.25 max	0.75 to 1.25	3.75 to 4.25
Lead	1.50 max	0.25 max	0.15 max
Tin	1.50 max	0.25 max	0.25 max
Manganese	0.25 max	0.15 max	0.15 max
Aluminum	0.25 max	0.15 max	0.15 max
Iron	0.25 max	0.15 max	0.15 max
Magnesium	....	0.01 max	0.01 max
Other elements	0.50 max	0.50 max	0.25 max
Zinc	30.0 min	Remainder	Remainder

σ = The ultimate tensile strength

= 3000 kg/cm^2 for alloy type *A*

= 4000 kg/cm^2 for alloy type *B*

= 6000 kg/cm^2 for alloy type *C*

Brinell hardness = 120 for alloy type *A*

= 130 for alloy type *B*

= 170 for alloy type *C*

Alloy *A* is a general-purpose low-cost brass composition that has wide limits as to impurities. Alloy *B* is a higher purity alloy having good castability and good mechanical properties in the die-cast state. Alloy *C* is harder and has better physical properties than alloy *B* and consequently finds considerable use where resistance to wear is an important requirement.

Example 14.11. *Describe the following*

(*a*) *Mould alignment*

(*b*) *Transfer moulding*

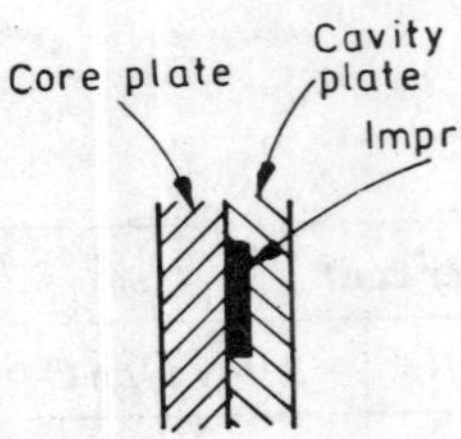

Fig. 14.72

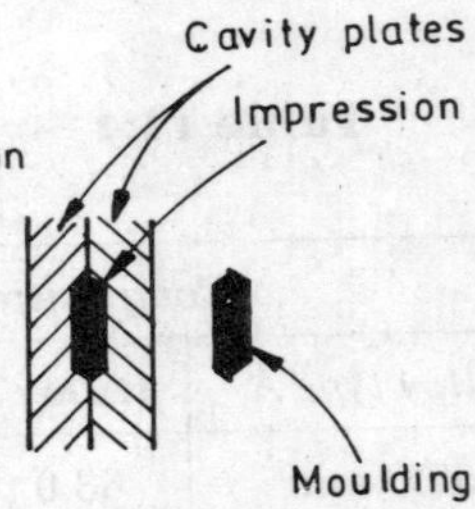

Fig. 14.73

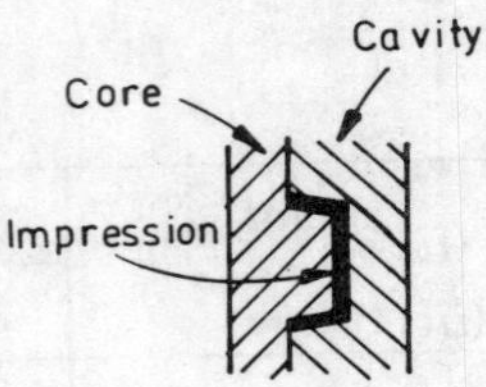

Fig. 14.74

Solution. It should be ensured that both halves of the mould are kept in proper alignment when the mould is closed.

As shown in Fig. 14.72 when impression is in one mould plate, only nominal alignment between mould plates is required whereas when impression is formed by both mould plates (Fig. 14.72) accurate alignment is essential. In case cavity and core form the impression as shown in Fig. 14.73 alignment is must be accurate in order to produce moulding with equally thick walls.

(*b*) **Transfer molding.** It is another method of molding thermosetting materials. In this method the material is not placed in the cavity as in compression molds but is heated in a loading chamber and enters the closed mold in a fluid state by the action of a plunger or hydraulic cylinder. The fluid material is directed to the cavity by a sprue or combination of sprue, runners and gates. Pressures is kept on the material until the part is cured.

Transfer molds are of semi-automatic type. They are of two types :

(*i*) Pot transfer mold

(*ii*) Plunger transfer mold.

Pot and plunger are made of tool steel. Advantages of transfer molding are as follows.

(*i*) There is shorter molding cycle than compression molding.

(*ii*) Closer tolerance can be achieved.

(*iii*) It can more easily mold thin wall sections.

(*iv*) Material flows better around intricate protrusions and inserts.

(*v*) There is less strain on small core pins.

Example 14.12. *Discuss the characteristics of die steels.*

Solution. Characteristics of die steels.

The steels used for making die casting dies should have following characteristics.

(*i*) Structural soundness and uniformity : The die casting dies should be made of highest quality tool steel. The steel should be free from segregated impurities, crackes, seams, scale and other defects.

(*ii*) Good machinability

(*iii*) High resistance to heat

(*iv*) High strength hardness, and resistance to deformation

(*v*) Sufficient toughness to resist cleavage cracking

(*vi*) High thermal conductivity

(*vii*) Low coefficient of thermal expansion.

Example 14.13. *Name and discuss the various types of*

(*a*) *Compression molds.*

(*b*) *Compression molding presses.*

Solution.

(*a*) The compression molds are of following types.

(*i*) Hand mold

(*ii*) Semi-automatic mold

(*iii*) Fully automatic mold.

Hand mold production is limited to

(*i*) small parts

(*ii*) short runs

or (*iii*) prototype work

Semi-automatic molds are self contained units security mounted in a conventional compression press. Fully automatic compression molds are of special design and are constructed to be adapted to a completely automatic compression press.

(*b*) **Compression molding presses :** They are usually hydraulically operated presses. The most common type of press used for compression molding is the vertical hydraulic press.

A press should (*i*) produce sufficient pressure to force the material throughout the mold (*ii*) enert adequate pressure on the material to promote curing (*iii*) produce parts of required density.

Example 14.14. *Name the various parts of a compression mold.*

Solution. The main parts of a compression mold are as follows:

1. Cavity block
2. Heaters.
3. Core (Punch or force)
4. Landing bars
5. Back plate
6. Ejector pins.

Fig. 14.75

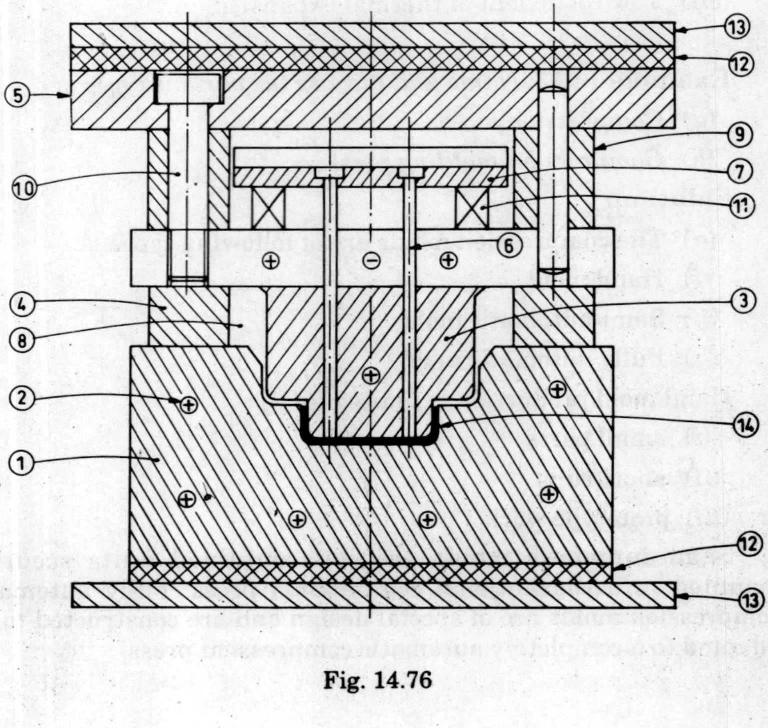

Fig. 14.76

7. Ejector Assembly.
8 Loading chamber or Cavity well
9. Guide pillars and bushings
10. Dowels and Allen screws
11. Springs
12. Asbestos sheet
13. Mild steel (M.S.) sheet
14. Component

Fig. 14.75 shows a component for which a compression mold is shown in Fig. 14.76.

Problems

1. What is a mould ? Name its parts.
2. Discuss various types of plastics.
3. Define following terms
   (*a*) Manomer (*b*) Filler
   (*c*) Plasticiser (*d*) Stabilizers
4. Sketch and describe the following methods of moulding
   (*a*) Compression moulding
   (*b*) Injection moulding
   (*c*) Extrusion moulding
5. Describe the following
   (*a*) Cavity (*b*) Plunger
   (*c*) Platen (*d*) Land
   (*e*) Flash
6. What is draft with reference to cavity ?
7. Write short notes on the following:
   (*a*) Venting (*b*) Shrinkage
   (*c*) Moulding cycle
   (*d*) Factors affecting compression
   (*e*) Loading of compression moulds.
8. Describe various types of moulds for compression moulding.
9. Methods of heating a mould in compression moulding.
10. Describe the various compression moulding presses.
11. Write short notes on with reference to compression moulding
    (*a*) Cure time variables
    (*b*) Material charge
12. State advantages and disadvantages of compression moulding.
13. What is feed system in injection moulding ? Sketch and describe a typical feed system to feed four cavities.
14. Define the following with reference to injection moulding
    (*a*) sprue (*b*) runner

(*c*) gate (*d*) sprue puller
(*e*) locating ring

15. Sketch and describe any three types of gates used in injection moulding.
16. Sketch and name the various parts of an ejector plate used in injection moulding.
17. Describe any three methods of ejection used in injection moulding.
18. What are inserts? Sketch and describe :
    (*a*) Cavity insert (*b*) Core insert.
19. Discuss with reference to injection moulding
    (*a*) Mould filling. (*b*) Venting.
    (*c*) Mould cooling.
20. What is die casting?
21. Sketch and describe
    (*a*) Hot chamber die casting machine.
    (*b*) Cold chamber die casting machine.

15

Typical Problems

15.1. Optimum included Angle of *V*-Locator

The included angle between two surfaces of a *V*-locator governs the position of circular sections of varying diameters.

Consider a *V*-locator (Fig 15.1) with an included angle of 2θ. Let it locate a circle of radius R_1 with centre A and radius R_2 with centre B. The distance between centres is C.

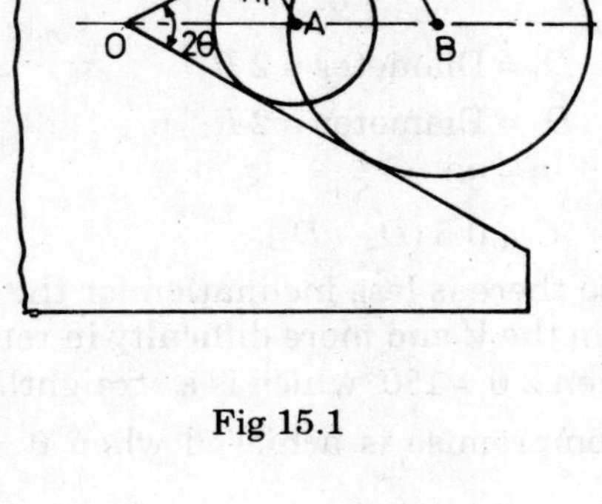

Fig 15.1

$$2\,\theta = \text{Included angle}$$
$$AK = R_1$$
$$BM = R_2$$
$$C = \text{Distance between } C \text{ centres}$$
$$= AB$$

From similar triangles OAK and OBM

$$\frac{R_1}{OA} = \frac{R_2}{OB} = \frac{R_2}{OA + AB} = \frac{R_2}{OA + C}$$

Now $$OA = \frac{AK}{\sin\theta}$$
$$= AK \text{ cosec. } \theta$$
$$= R_1 \,.\, \text{cosec}\,\theta$$
$$\frac{R_1}{OA} = \frac{R_2}{OA + C}$$
$$OA + C = \frac{R_2 \times OA}{R_1}$$
$$C = \frac{R_2 \times OA}{R_1} - OA$$
$$= OA\left[\frac{R_2}{R_1} - 1\right]$$
$$= OA\left[\frac{R_2 - R_1}{R_1}\right]$$
$$= R_1 \text{ cosec}\,\theta \times \frac{(R_2 - R_1)}{R_1}$$
$$= \text{cosec}\,\theta\,(R_2 - R_1)$$
$$= \frac{\text{cosec}\,\theta\,(D_2 - D_1)}{2}$$

where $D_1 = \text{Diameter} = 2\,R_1$

$D_2 = \text{Diameter} = 2\,R_2$

Now when $\theta = 90$

$$C = 0.5\,(D_2 - D_1)$$

In such case there is less inclination for the circular section to seat positively in the V and more difficulty in retaining it. Further when $\theta = 90°$ then $2\,\theta = 180°$ which is a straightline.

The best compromise is achieved when $\theta = 45°$ and included angle of $V = 90°$.

15.2. Surface Roughness Representation

The surface roughness obtained depends on the following factors.

(*i*) Type of machining

(*ii*) Condition of cutting tool

(*iii*) Type of workpiece material

(*iv*) Quality and quantity of coolant used

(*v*) Rigidity of machine tool.

The surface roughness is indicated by the symbol shown in Fig. 15.2.

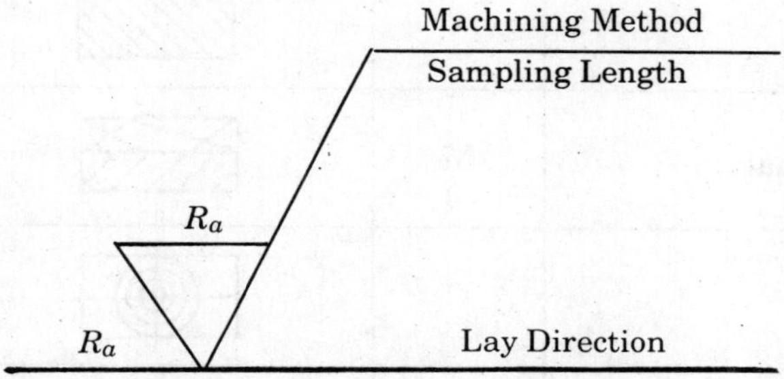

Fig. 15.2

where R_a = average surface roughness value

Fig 15.3 shows a typical value of R_a as 0.16 with a cut off length of 0.40 and direction of lay perpendicular and method of machining as lapping.

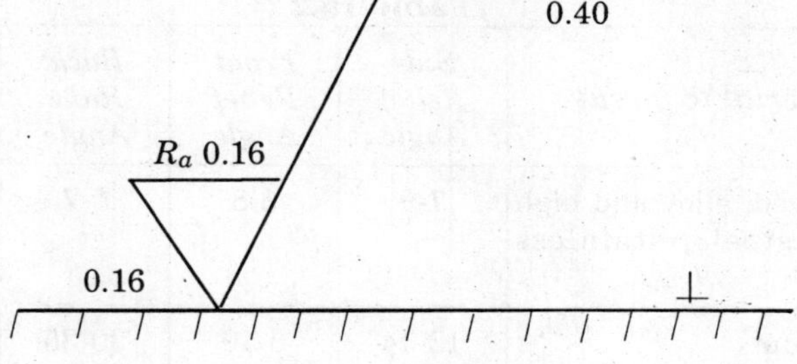

Fig. 15.3

The direction of lay is represented by the following symbols are indicated in Table 15.1.

Table 15.1

Type of Lay	*Symbol*	*Direction*
Parallel	=	
Perpendicular	⊥	
Angular	×	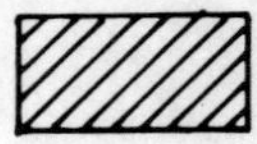
Multi-directional	M	
Circlar	C	
Radial	R	

Parallel lay means parallel to the boundary line of nominal surface.

Cutting tool angles. Table 15.2 indicates the values of various angles for single point cutting tool made of high speed steel to cut some of the commonly used materials. The angles are in degrees.

Table 15.2

Material to be cut	*Side Relief Angle*	*Front Relief Angle*	*Back Rake Angle*	*Side Rake Angle*
High speed, alloy and high carbon steels, stainless steels	7-9	6-8	5-7	8-10
Aluminium	12-14	8-10	30-35	16
Bakelite	10-12	8-10	0	0
Brass bronze	10-12	8-10	0	1-3

(Contd...)

Material to be cut	*Side Relief Angle*	*Front Relief Angle*	*Back Rake Angle*	*Side Rake Angle*
Cast iron	8-10	6-8	3-5	10-12
Copper	12-14	12-14	14-16	18-20
Copper alloy shard	8-10	6-8	0	0
Copper alloys-soft	10-12	8-10	0-2	0
Fibre	14-16	12-14	0-2	0
Nickel steel	14-16	10-12	6-8	12-14
Monel and nickel	14-16	12-14	8-10	12-14
Nickel silvers	10-12	10-12	8-10	0-(-2)
Rubber-hard	18-20	14-16	0-(-2)	0-(-2)

Table 15.3 indicates the values of angles for a single point. Cutting tool made of cement carbide.

Table 15.23

Material	*Normal End Relief*	*Normal Side Relief*	*Normal Back Rake*	*Normal Side Rake*
Aluminium and Magnesium alloy	6-10	6-10	0-10	10-20
Copper	6-8	6-8	0-4	15-20
Brass and bronze	6-8	6-8	0-(-5)	-8-(-5)
Cast iron	5-8	5-8	0-(-7)	-6-(-7)
Castings steel	5-10	5-10	0-(-7)	+6-(-7)
Carbon steels	5-8	5-8	0-(-7)	+6-(-7)
Alloy steels	5-8	5-8	0-(-7)	+6-(-7)
Free machining steels	5-10	5-10	0-(-7)	+6-(-7)
Stainless steels-Austenitic	5-10	5-10	0-(-7)	+6-(-7)
Stainless steel-Hardenable	5-8	5-8	0-(-7)	+6-(-7)
Titanium alloys	5-8	5-8	0-(-5)	+6-(-5)

Blank diameter

Table 15.4 indicates the value of blank diameter to make some types of cup shaped components from metallic sheet.

Table 15.4

Shape of Body	*Diameter of Blank*
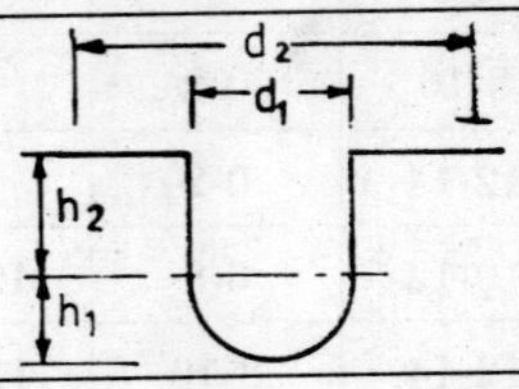	$\sqrt{d^2 + 4(h_1^2 + d_1 h_2)}$
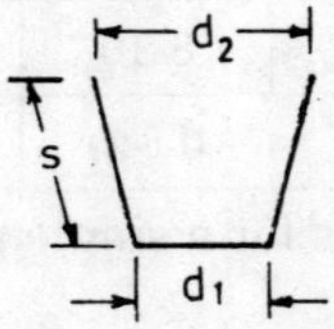	$\sqrt{d_1^2 + 2s\,(d_1 + d_2)}$
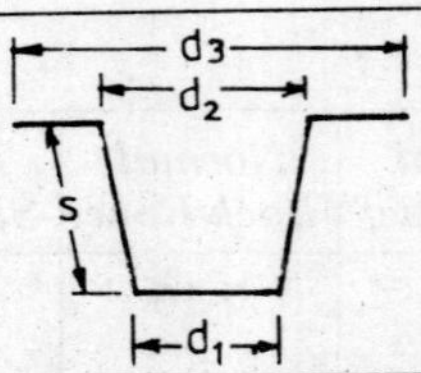	$\sqrt{d_1^2 + 2s\,(d_1 + d_2) + d_3^2 + d_2^2}$
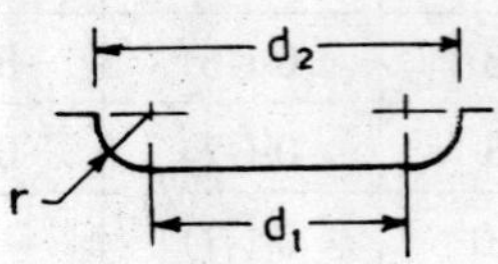	$\sqrt{d_1^2 + 6.28rd_1 + 8r^2}$ or $\sqrt{d_2^2 + 2.28rd_2 - 0.56r^2}$

d_1 = Diameter of the component

d_2 = Diameter

S = Tapered length

r = Radius.

15.3. Scrap Web Allowance

Table 15.5 indicates the scrap web allowance for curves adjacent to straight lines (Fig. 15.4) for machining metallic sheet components.

Table 15.5

One-pass single station dies			*One-pass single station dies*		
T = Stock thickness			*T* = Stock thickness		
D (inches)	*G or H*	*Smallest G or H (inches)*	*D (inches)*	*G or H*	*Smallest G or H (inches)*
TO 1	$\frac{3}{4}T$	$\frac{1}{32}$	TO 1	T	$\frac{3}{64}$
1-3	T	$\frac{3}{64}$	1-3	$1\frac{1}{4}T$	$\frac{1}{16}$
3-6	$1\frac{1}{4}T$	$\frac{3}{32}$	3-6	$1\frac{1}{2}T$	$\frac{3}{32}$
6-10	$1\frac{1}{4}T$	$\frac{1}{8}$	6-10	$1\frac{1}{2}T$	$\frac{1}{8}$
10-15	$1\frac{1}{2}T$	$\frac{1}{8}$	10-15	$1\frac{3}{4}T$	$\frac{5}{32}$

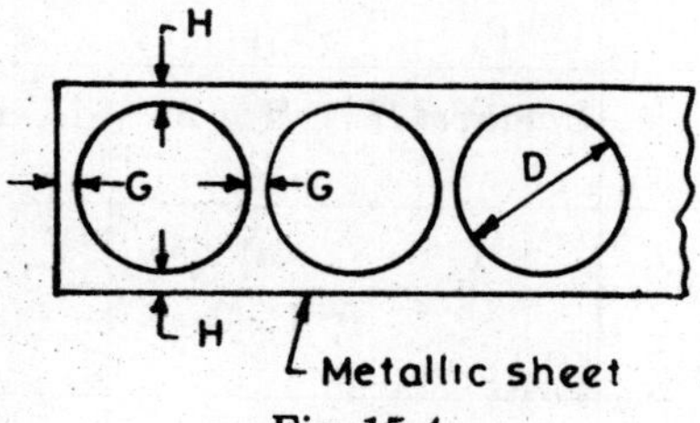

Fig. 15.4.

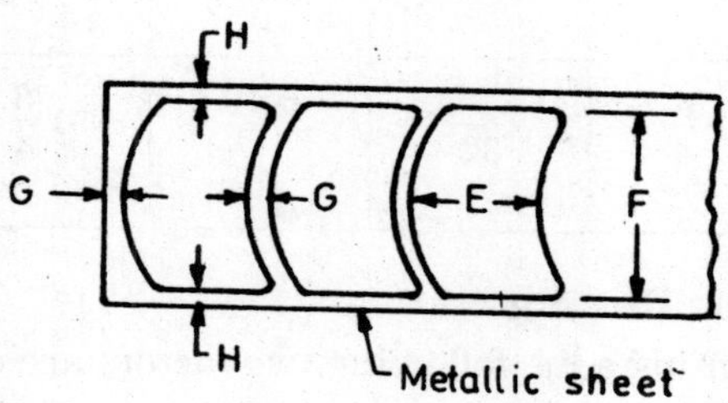

Fig 15.5

Table 15.36 indicates the scrap web allowance for webs with edges parallel as shown in Fig 15.5

T + metallic sheet thickness

Table 15.32.

One-pass Single Station dies			*One-pass Progressive dies*		
T = Stock thickness			*T = Stock thickness*		
E or F (inches)	*G*	*Smallest G (inches)*	*E or F (inches)*	*G*	*Smallest G (inches)*
0-2	T	$\frac{3}{64}$	0-2	$1\frac{1}{4}T$	$\frac{1}{16}$
2-6	$1\frac{1}{4}T$	$\frac{1}{16}$	2-6	$1\frac{1}{2}T$	$\frac{5}{64}$
6-10	$1\frac{1}{2}T$	$\frac{5}{64}$	6-10	$1\frac{3}{4}T$	$\frac{3}{32}$

E or F	*H*	*Smallest H*	*E or F*	*H*	*Smallest H*
0-2	$1\frac{1}{4}T$	$\frac{1}{16}$	0-2	$1\frac{1}{2}T$	$\frac{1}{16}$
2-6	$1\frac{1}{2}T$	$\frac{5}{64}$	2-6	$1\frac{1}{2}T$	$\frac{3}{32}$
6-10	$1\frac{3}{4}$	$\frac{3}{32}$	6-10	$1\frac{3}{4}$	$\frac{1}{8}$

15.4. Multi-hole Box Jig

While designing a jig, following two factors are important:

(*i*) Body of Jig should be lighter in weight,

(*ii*) Chip removal should be easier.

Fig. 15.6 shows a box jig for drilling holes in more than one plane in the component. The jig is provided with same number of drill bushes as the number of planes.

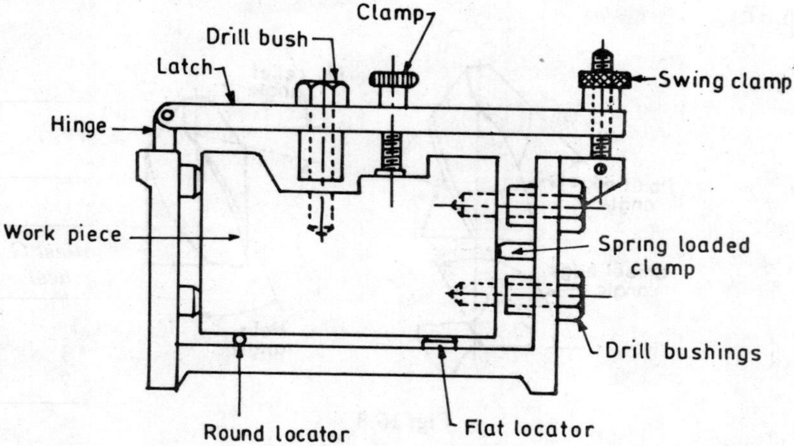

Fig. 15.6

Jig is fitted with a latch to provide opening for loading and unloading of the component.

15.5. Centralizer

It is used during clamping a workpiece in jigs and fixtures. Fig. 15.7 shows a linkage controlled centraliser.

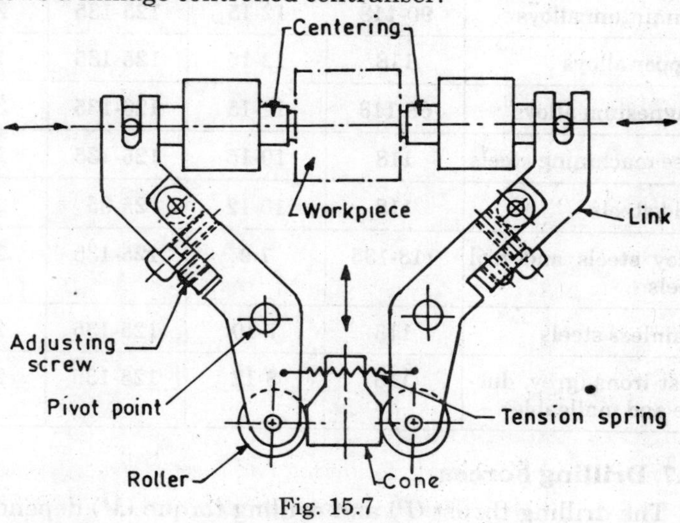

Fig. 15.7

The workpiece is held in position by two pivoted links.

15.6. HSS Drill Angles

Fig. 15.8 shows the angles of high speed steel drill. The commonly used angles to cut various materials are indicated in table 15.37.

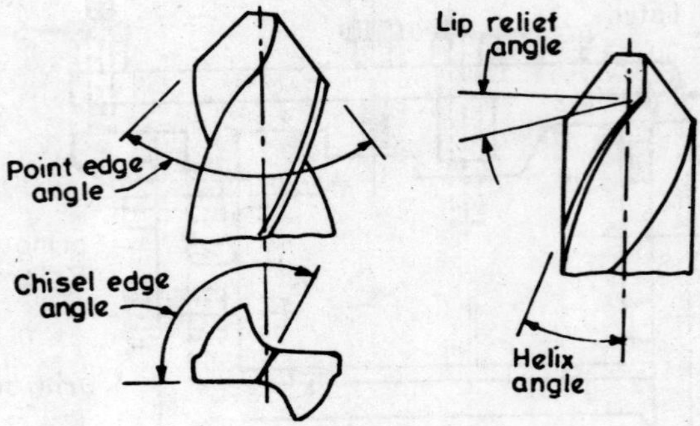

Fig. 15.8

Table 15.37

Work piece material	*Point angles (deg)*	*Lip relief angle (deg)*	*Chisel edge angle (deg)*	*Helix angle (deg)*
Aluminium alloys	90-118	12-15	125-135	25-40
Copper alloys	118	12-15	125-135	10-30
Magnesium alloys	68-118	12-15	120-135	30-45
Free machining steels	118	10-15	125-135	25-30
Mild steels	118	10-12	25-35	25-30
Alloy steels and tool steels	118-135	7-9	125-135	25-30
Stainless steels	118	7-10	125-135	25-30
Cast irons (grey, ductile and malleable)	118	8-12	125-135	25-30

15.7. Drilling Forces

The drilling thrust (*P*) and drilling torque (*M*) depend on the following factors (See Fig. 15.9).

(*i*) Workpiece material hardness
(*ii*) drill diameter
(*iii*) feed rate
(*iv*) point angle of drill

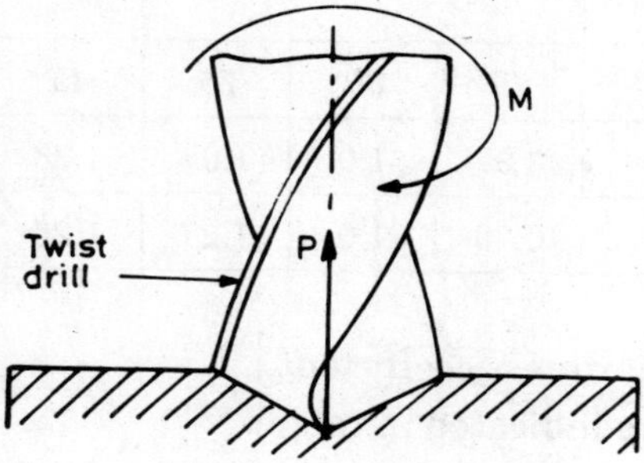

Fig. 15.9.

$$P = 9.806\, C_1\, K_1\, K_2\, d^{x1}\, f^{y1} \text{ in N.}$$

$$M = 9.806\, C_2\, K_1\, K_2\, d^{x2}\, f^{y2} \text{ in N–mm}$$

where d = Drill diameter in mm

f = Feed rate mm/rev.

C_1 and C_2 are material constants

x_1, x_2, y_1 and y_2 are exponents.

The values are indicated in table 15.38.

Table 15.38

Materials	C_1	C_2	x_1	x_2	y_1	y_2
Carbon steel : σ_u = 735 N/mm^2	85	34	1	1.9	0.7	0.8
C.I. *HB* = 190	52	20	1	1.9	0.8	0.8
Bronze	31	12	1	1.9	0.8	0.8
Alloy steel : σ_u = 112 N/mm^2	270	75	1.15	2.1	0.77	0.76
σ_u = 686 N/mm^2	163	55	1.0	2.0	0.62	0.76

K_1 = Drill point angle coefficient.

The values are as follows (see table 15.39.).

Table 15.39.

$\frac{1}{2}$ *point angle degree*	*P*			*M*		
	45	*60*	*75*	*45*	*60*	*75*
Steel	0.97	1.0	1.04	1.23	1.0	0.82
Cast Iron	0.73	1.0	1.27	1.25	1.0	0.88

K_2 = Brinell hardness coefficient.

The values are indicated in table:

Values of Factor K_2 for C.I.

HB	130	150	170	190	210	220	250	270
K_B	0.80	0.87	0.94	1.00	1.96	1.13	1.18	1.25

Values of Factor K_2 for Carbon Steel

σ_u (N/mm^2)	441	490	588	735	1128	1324	1471
K_B	0.67	0.79	0.89	1.0	1.2	1.28	1.36

15.8. Forces for Milling

The specific energy consumption during plain milling (Fig. 15.10) is determined as follows :

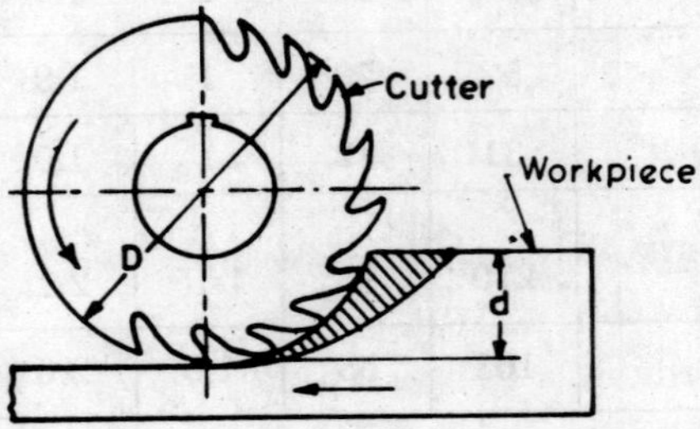

Fig. 15.10

U = Specific energy

$$= \frac{C_1 \times 10^{-3}}{\left(s_o \sqrt{\frac{d}{D}}\right)^{\lambda}} \text{ kW/mm}^3$$

$$= \frac{C_2 \times 10^{-6}}{60\left(s_o \sqrt{\frac{d}{D}}\right)^{\lambda}} \text{ kW/mm}^3$$

s_o = feed per tooth

$$= \frac{s}{zn}$$

where s = feed rate, mm/min.

z = number of teeth,

n = rev./min

d = depth of cut, mm

D = cutter diameter, mm

Average tangential cutting force,

$$P_t = \frac{C_p}{\pi}\left(\frac{B\, s_0^{1-\lambda} d^{1-\frac{\lambda}{2z}}}{D^{1-\frac{\lambda}{2}}}\right) N$$

where B = width of cut, mm

C_1, C_2 and λ = material constants. Their values are indicated in table 15.11.

Table 15.11

Material	C_1	C_2	λ
Alloy steel	0.03-0.04	2100	0.28
Mild steel	0.02-0.03	1400	0.28
Bronze	0.006-0.007	400	0.40

The cutting force approximately can be determined using following relations

P_R = Radial thrust = (0.5 to 0.6) Pt

P_Z = Horizontal force = (0.8 to 1.0) Pt

P_V = Vertical force = 0.2 Pt

15.9. Angles of H.S.S. End Mill Cutter

Fig 15.11 shows various angles of an end mill cutter.

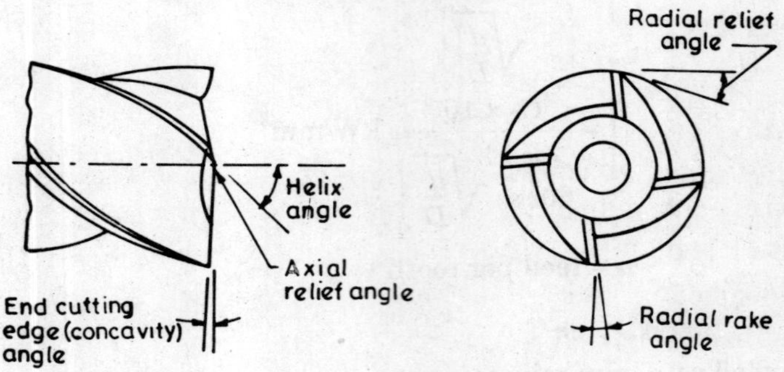

Fig. 15.11.

Table 15.38 indicates recommended angles of high speed steel (HSS) end mill cutter.

Table 15.12

Material	*Helix angle (deg)*	*Radial rake angle (deg)*	*End cutting edge (concavity) angle (deg)*	*Axial relief angle (deg)*	*Radial* relief angle (deg)*
Free machining steels, mild steels and medium carbon steels	28-30	10-20	3	5-7	M
Alloy steels	30	15	3	5-7	M
Tool steels	30	10-12	3	5-7	M
Stainless steels	30	15	3	5-7	M
Cast irons (grey, ductile and malleable)	30	12	3	5-7	M
Aluminium alloys	30-45	15-20	5	7-12	N
Copper alloys	30	10-20	5	7-12	N
Magnesium alloys	30-45	15-20	5	7-12	N

* Radial relief angles for various diameters of end mills are indicated below :

Diameter (mm)	*6*	*10*	*12*	*16*	*25*
M	12°	10°	10°	9°	8°
N	15°	14°	13°	12°	1°

15.10. Jig Bodies

Jig bodies should be of proper strength. It should be economical to manufacture the jig body. The jig bodies may be

(*i*) built up body (Fig. 15.12 *a*)

(*ii*) welded body (Fig. 15.12 *b*)

(*iii*) cast body (Fig. 15.12 *c*)

The cast bodies are quite commonly used.

(*a*) Built up body

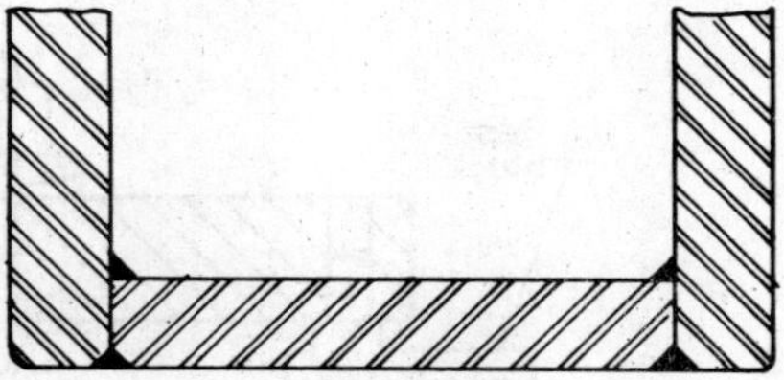

(*b*) Welded body

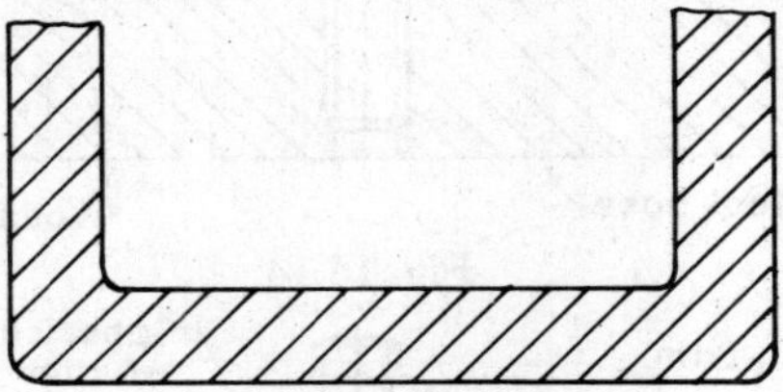

(*c*) Cast body

Fig. 15.12.

Example 15.1. *Sketch typical following types of clamping devices*

(*a*) *Strap clamp using hexagonal head screw.*

(*b*) *Strap clamp using a locating pin*

(*c*) *Cam clamp.*

Solution. Fig. 15.13 shows a strap clamp using hexagonal head screw whereas Fig. 15.14 shows a strap clamp using a locating pin and Fig. 15.15 shows a cam clamp.

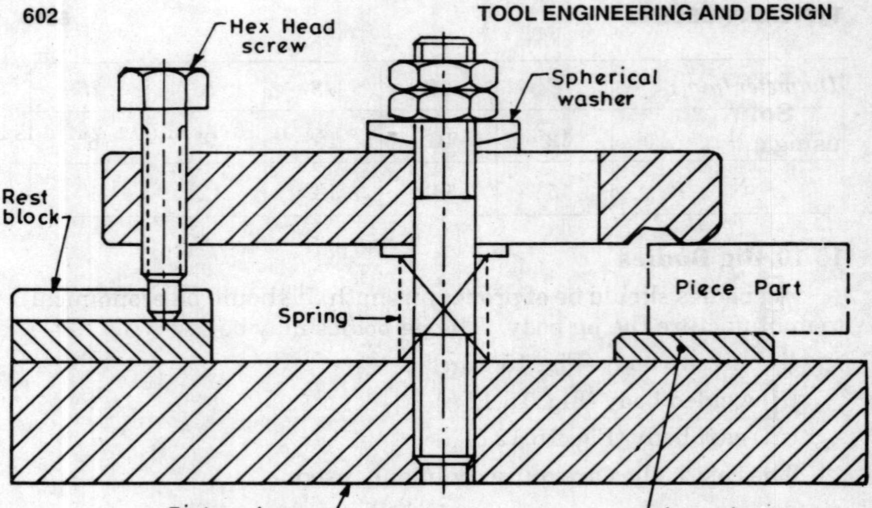

Fig. 15.13.

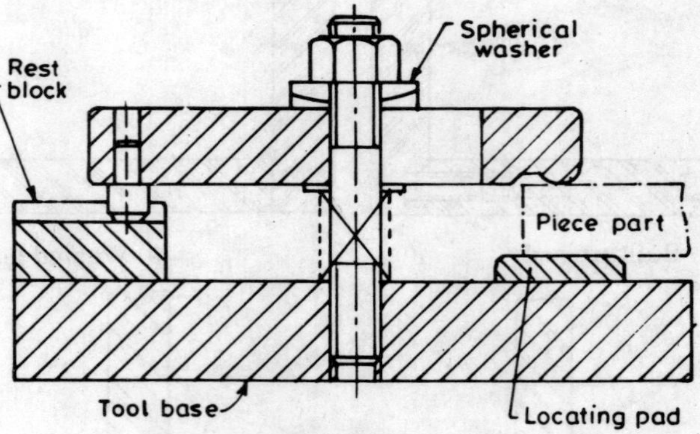

Fig. 15.14.

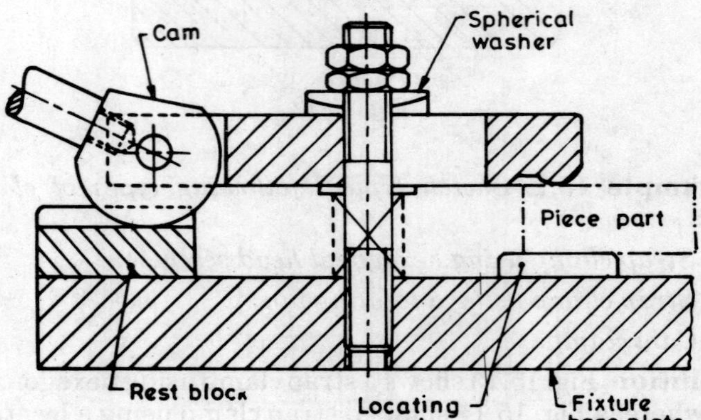

Fig. 15.15.

Example 15.2. *Sketch four types of latch clamping devices.*

Solution. Fig. 15.16. shows four types of clamping devices using a latch.

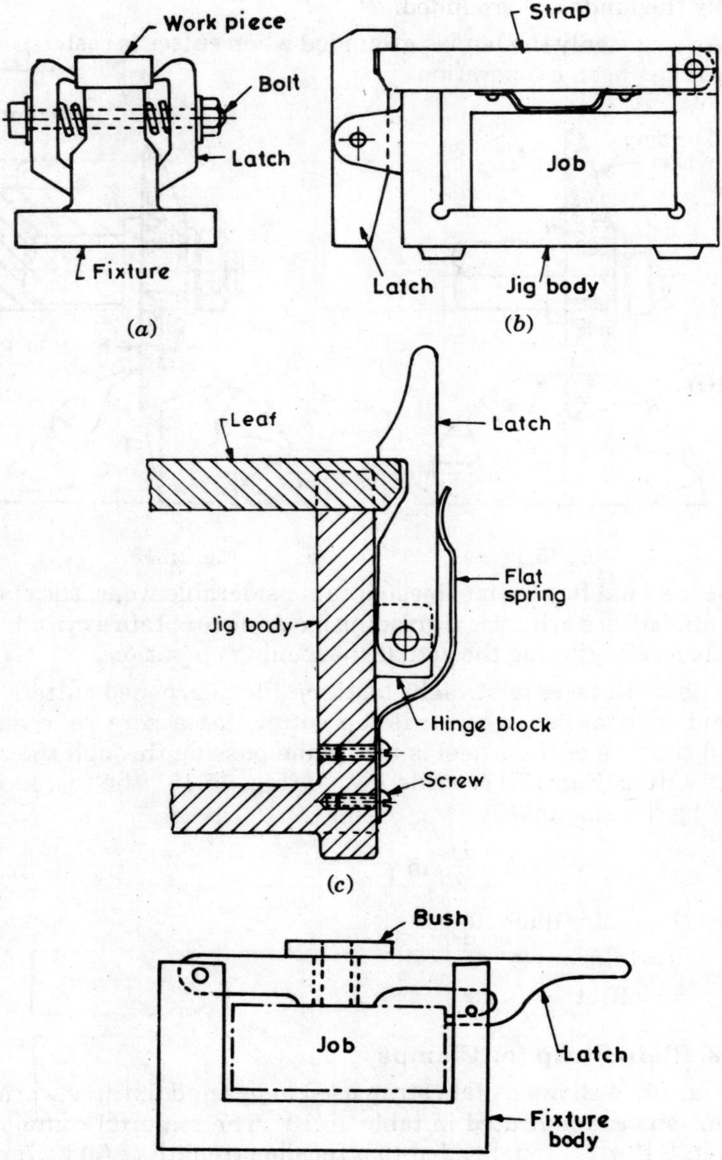

Fig. 15.16.

15.11. Sharpening of Milling Cutters

Sharpening of milling cutters is carried out in following order. Firstly tooth faces are grounded, then the external surfaces and finally the lands are grounded.

As a rule only the land is grounded when cutter is resharpened after it has been in operation.

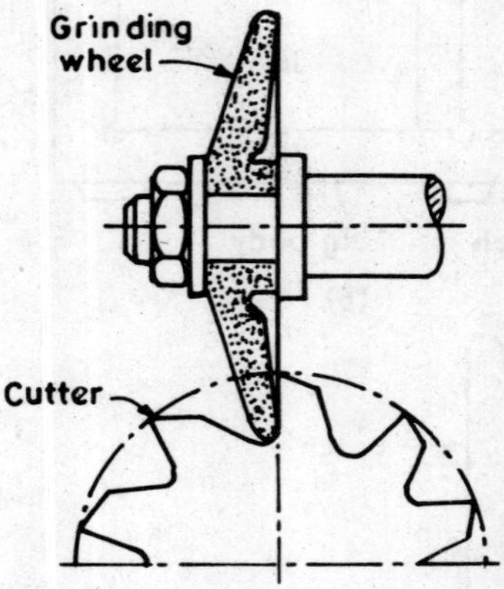

Fig. 15.17.

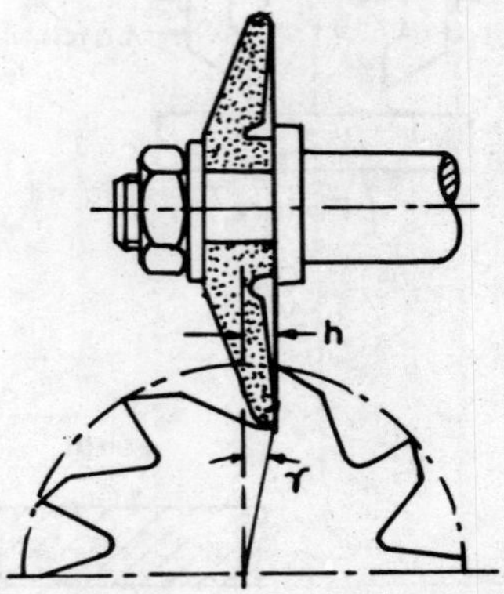

Fig. 15.18.

If the land has been subjected to considerable wear, the cutter is grounded on a cylindrical grinding machine to obtain a cylindrical land before beginning the actual sharpening operation.

The tooth faces of straight-tooth profile-sharpened cutters are ground with a dish wheel. If the cutter has a zero rake angle ($\gamma = 0$) the face of the wheel is in a plane passing through the axis of the cutter (Fig. 15.17) while if $\gamma > 0$ (Fig. 15.18), the tool face is offset by the amount

$$h = \frac{D}{2} \sin \gamma$$

where D = cutter diameter

γ = rake angle

h = offset

15.12. Plain Strap for Clamps

Fig. 15.14 shows a plain strap used in jigs and fixtures, various dimensions are indicated in table 15.13. The material commonly used in C45 steel toughended to a tensile strength of 60 kgf/mm^2. The strap should be free from crackes, burrs, and pits etc.

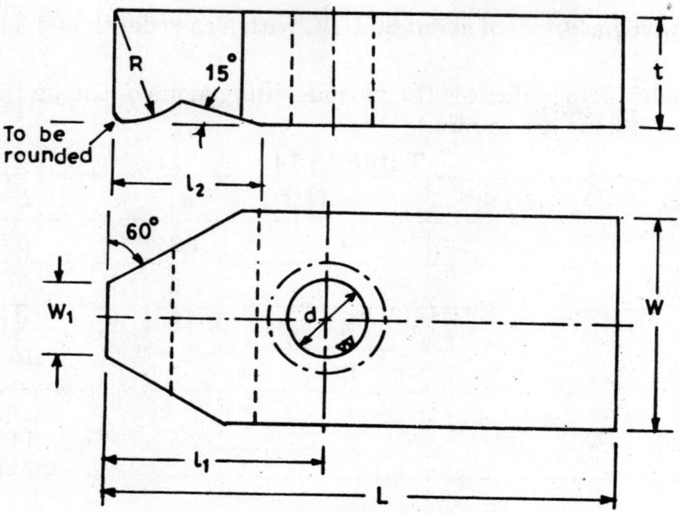

Fig. 15.19.

Table 15.13

d	*L*	*L₁*	*L₂*	*W*	*t*	*Screw size*	*W1*	*R*
6.6	50	20	14	20	12	M6	6	13
9	60	23	18	25	16	M8	8	14
11	70	30	20	30	16	M10	10	16
14	80	35	25	40	20	M12	14	20
18	100	45	28	50	23	M16	18	25
22	120	50	28	50	25	M20	18	25

15.13. Jig Button

Fig. 15.20 shows a jig button. Jig buttons are commonly made from case hardening steel such as 16 Mn Cr 5 or 20 Mn Cr 5, C15.

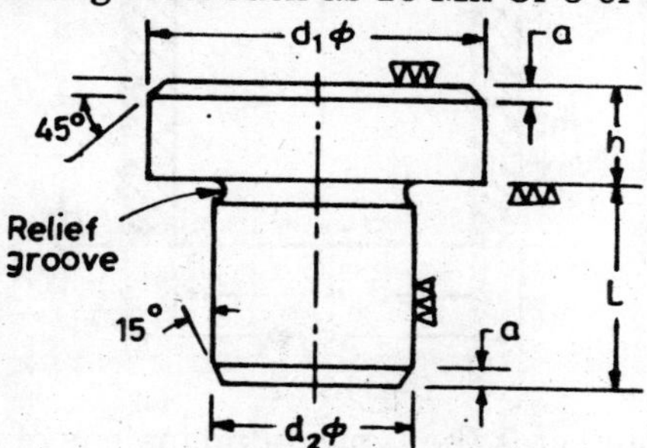

Fig. 15.20.

They have hardness of about 60 HRC with a case depth of 0.3 to 0.5 mm.

Table 15.14 indicates the various dimensions of the jig button (all dimensions are in mm.)

Table 15.14

d_1	$d_2(n6)$	$h(h_9)$	a	L
6	4	9	1.2	6
10	6	8	1.6	8
16	8	5	2	10
		13		
25	12	8	2.5	14
		20		
40	20	13	3.2	20
		32		

15.14. Jig Bush

Fig. 15.21 shows a liner bush used in jigs. The materials commonly used for making bush may be direct, hardening type steel such as

(*i*) En 31 (*ii*) T 90 (*iii*) 20 Mn V8

The hardness is usually 60 ± 2 HRC with a case hardened depth of 0.5 to 0.8 mm.

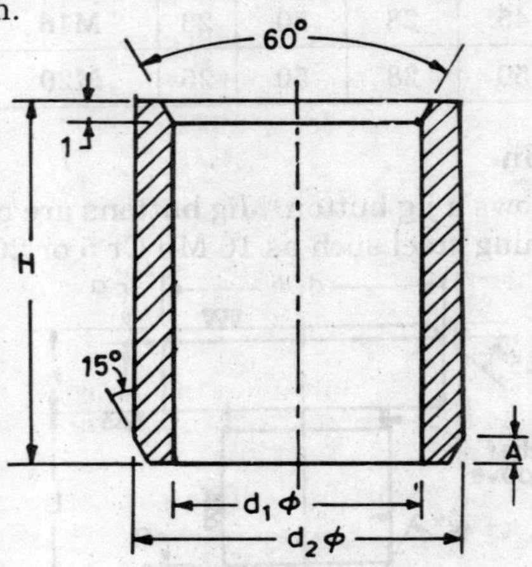

Fig. 15.21.

Table 15.15 indicates the typical dimensions of the liner bush. The dimensions are in mm.

Table 15.15

<table>
<tr><th rowspan="2">d_1
(H_7)</th><th colspan="2">H</th><th rowspan="2">$d_2(m6)$</th><th rowspan="2">A</th></tr>
<tr><th>Short</th><th>Long</th></tr>
<tr><td>8</td><td>8</td><td>12.5</td><td>12</td><td rowspan="2">1.5</td></tr>
<tr><td>10</td><td>10</td><td>16</td><td>18</td></tr>
<tr><td>15</td><td>12.5</td><td>20</td><td>20</td><td rowspan="2">2</td></tr>
<tr><td>22</td><td>16</td><td>25</td><td>26</td></tr>
<tr><td>28</td><td rowspan="2">20</td><td rowspan="2">32</td><td>36</td><td rowspan="2">2.5</td></tr>
<tr><td>33</td><td>40</td></tr>
<tr><td>46</td><td rowspan="2">25</td><td rowspan="2">40</td><td>56</td><td rowspan="2">3.0</td></tr>
<tr><td>53</td><td>70</td></tr>
</table>

15.15. Design Considerations for Die Cast Components

Some of the considerations while designing a die cast component are as follows :

(*i*) section thickness should not vary much

(*ii*) sharp corners should be avoided

(*iii*) Fillet radii should be as large as possible

(*iv*) Proper draft should be provided

(*v*) Material concentration should be avoided

(*vi*) Ribs should be of minimum thickness.

Since cost of casting increases with the increase in weight, the designer should use thinnest sections that can meet

(*i*) strength and

(*ii*) stiffness and other design requirements.

Thin sections cool quickly in the die. Hence die can be opened sooner than thicker sections and casting cycle time is reduced. Thinner sections are likely to be smoother and have minimum surface porosity. Ribs are mainly incorporated into a die cast component to reinforce it structurally replacing heavy sections that would otherwise be necessary. Whenever possible losses should be cored and ribs may be applied to stiffen the boss and walls around it. The boss should be moved away from the wall and connected to the wall with a short rib of the same thickness as shown in Fig. 15.22.

Table 15.16 indicates die-casting wall thickness.

Table 15.16.

Surface area cm^2	*Minimum Recommended Wall Thickness, mm*			
	Zinc Alloys	*Al Alloys*	*Mg Alloys*	*Cu Alloys*
0-25	0.38-0.75	0.75-1.30	0.75-1.30	1.50-2.00
25-100	0.75-1.30	1.30-1.80	1.30-1.80	2.00-2.50
100-500	1.30-1.80	1.80-2.20	1.80-2.20	2.50-3.00
500-2000	1.80-2.20	2.20-2.80	2.20-2.80	—
2000-4000	2.20-4.60	2.80-6.30	2.80-6.30	—

Sharp internal corners in a die cast component should be avoided because when the metal shrinks induces stresses are concentrated at sharp corners instead of being distributed through the surrounding mass thus making the parts weaker at such corners. Therefore radii and fillets should be as generous as possible and should be around 1.5 times wall thickness for both internal and external radii as shown in Fig. 15.23. The value of radii (R) may be taken as: $R = 1.5\,t$, where t = wall thickness

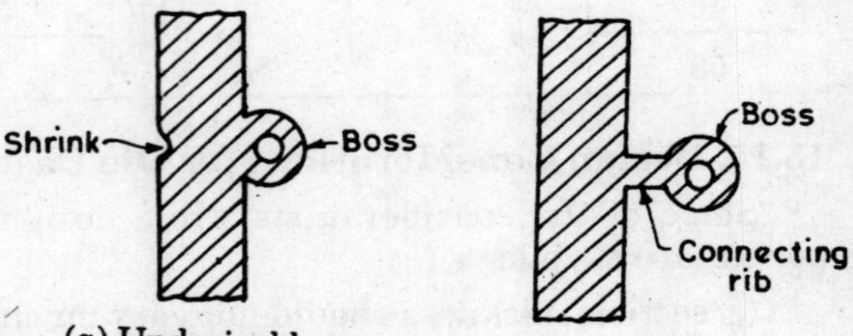

(*a*) Undesirable

Fig. 15.22.

The side walls of die cast components and other features perpendicular to the parting line must be tapered/drafted as much as possible to facilitate removal from the die. Draft angle depends on: (*i*) type of metal being cast and (*ii*) wall depth.

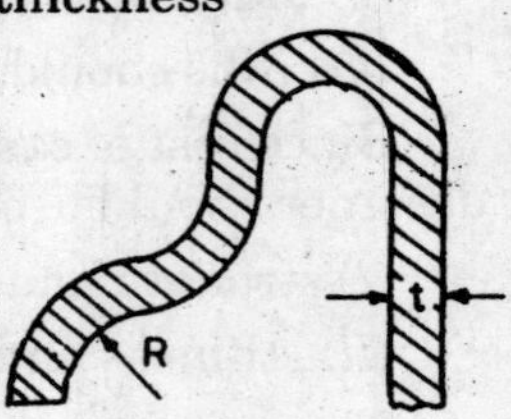

Fig. 15.23.

Draft angle varies inversely with wall depth. Table 15.17 indicates typical values of draft angle in degrees for aluminium alloys and zinc alloys.

15.16 Turning Fixture

A turning fixture is shown in Fig. 15.24. The base of the fixture is clamped to the face plate or back plate of the lathe. The work piece is located, supported and clamped on the fixture. As shown a spring operated strap clamp may be used to clamp the work piece. To compensate for the unbalanced loading over the lathe spindle, a balance weight is provided on the fixture base.

Table 15.17.

Wall Depth (mm)	Draft angle	
	Aluminium alloys	Zinc alloys
7.5-15	3	1.8
15-25	2.2	1.5
25-50	1.5	1.0
50-100	1.0	0.7
100-200	1.0	0.5

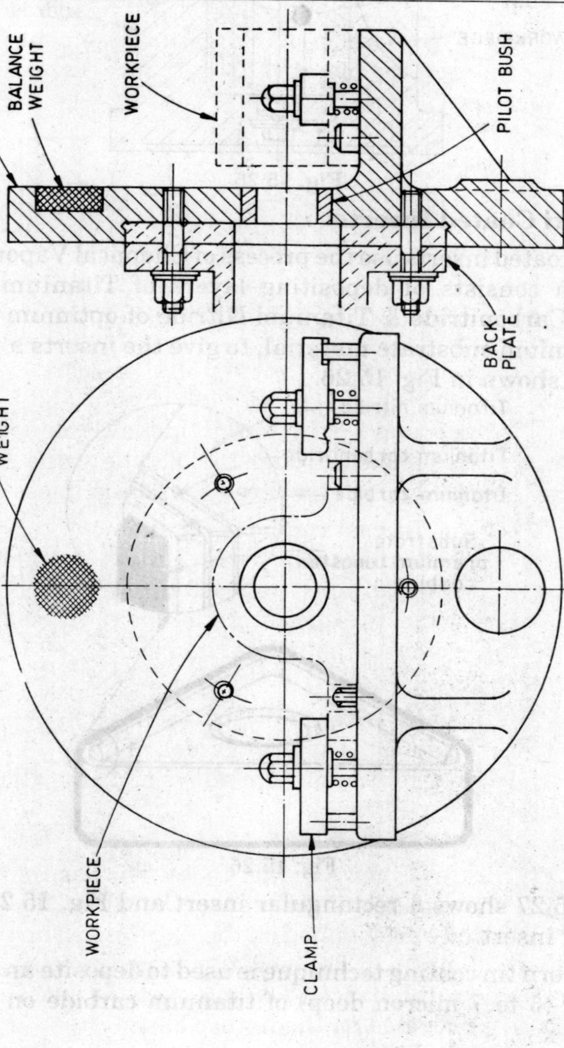

Fig. 15.24

15.17 Pot Jig.

Fig. 15.25 shows a pot jig. It is suitable for use with circular components having both external and internal diameters. The body of the jig is in the form of a pot.

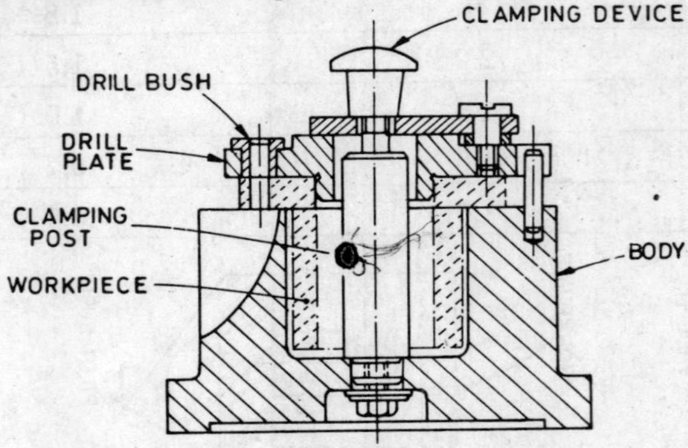

Fig. 15.25

15.18 Multi Coated Inserts

Multi coated inserts use the process of Chemical Vapour Deposition which consists of depositing layers of Titanium Carbide. Titanium Carbonitride & Titanium Nitride of optimum thickness over a premium substrate material, to give the inserts a prolonged tool life as shown in Fig. 15.26.

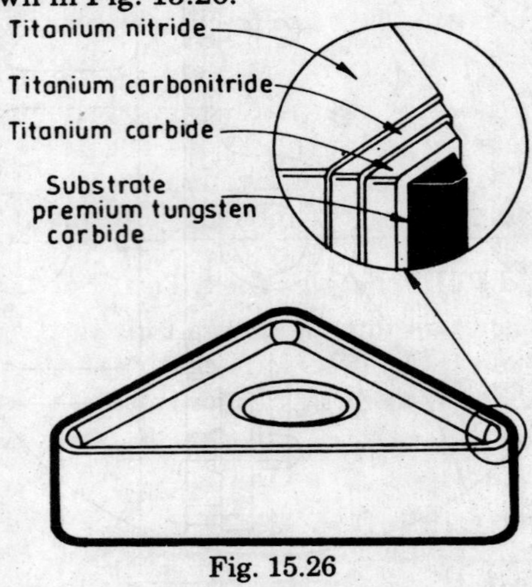

Fig. 15.26

Fig. 15.27 shows a rectangular insert and Fig. 15.28 shows a triangular insert.

A modern tin coating technique is used to deposite an extremely thin layer (5 to 7 micron deep) of titanium carbide on otherwise wholly processed inserts. Thus a good toughness is combined with very high wear resistance in the same insert. Working with the same cutting data the cutting edge of a coated carbide insert may last 3 to 4 times longer than that of a conventional carbide insert. For the same tool life coated carbide can be used at about 40% higher cutting speed. Coated carbides improve the total quality of cemented carbide cutting edges.

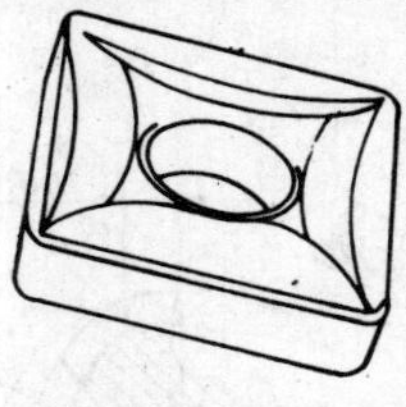

Fig. 15.27

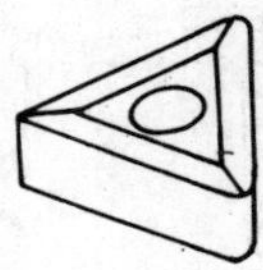

Fig. 15.28

15.19 Thread Cutting Dies

Dies are quite successfully used to cut external threads. Fig. 15.29 shows a thread cutting die. The quality and accuracy of threads cut by dies are moderate but is acceptable for most mass produced articles.

Threading dies are of two general types : (*i*) Adjustable dies and (*ii*) Die head with chasers

Adjustable dies consist of two pieces which are held in a collet or mounted directly in a die stock.

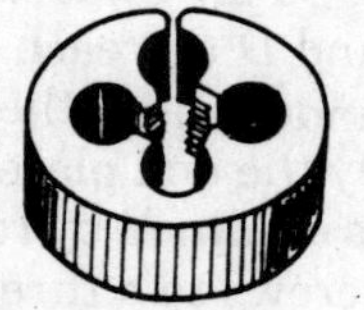

Fig. 15.29

Die boxes are used for high production of external threads on capstan and turret lathes. Die heads contain dies or chasers and each is suitable for a given range of sizes. The dies open automatically when the required length of thread is cut.

15.20. Rake and Relief Angles for a Tap

Fig. 15.30 shows various parts of a tap. Fig. 15.31 shows zero rake angle, positive rake angle and negative rake angle for the tap teeth. Fig. 15.32 shows relief angles for the teeth of tap.

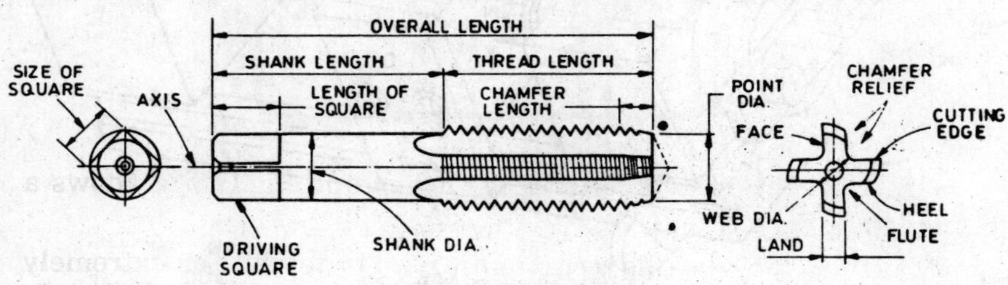

Fig. 15.30

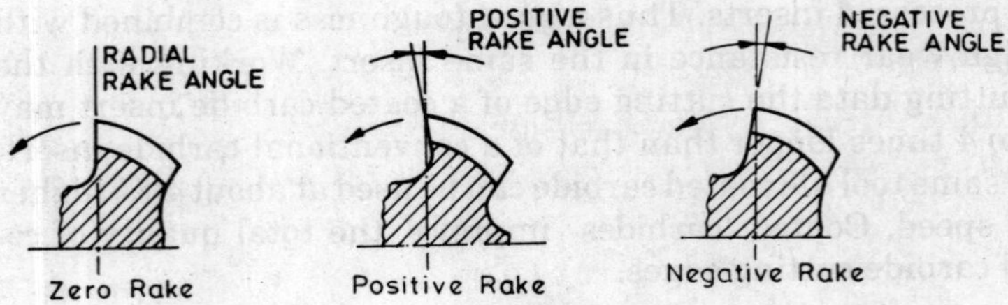

Fig. 15.31

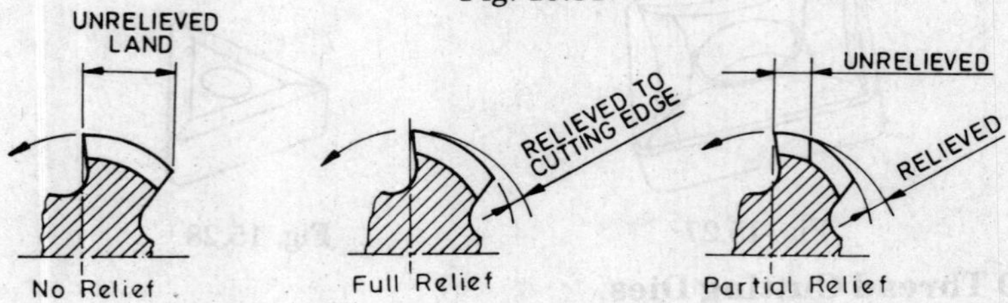

Fig. 15.32

15.21 Soldered Joint Testing Jig

Fig. 15.33 shows a soldered joint testing jig. The two blocks *B* and *D* are each secured to the base *A* by four cap screws from the underside of the base. Block *E* is to slide along the base and is guided by the end plates *C* in groove in the base. The movement of block *E* is obtained by rotating the hand lever which is attached by two set screws to a threaded shaft *K*.

The shaft and block *B* have a clearance fit but the shaft engages with internal threads in block *E*. The test piece is fitted on the two

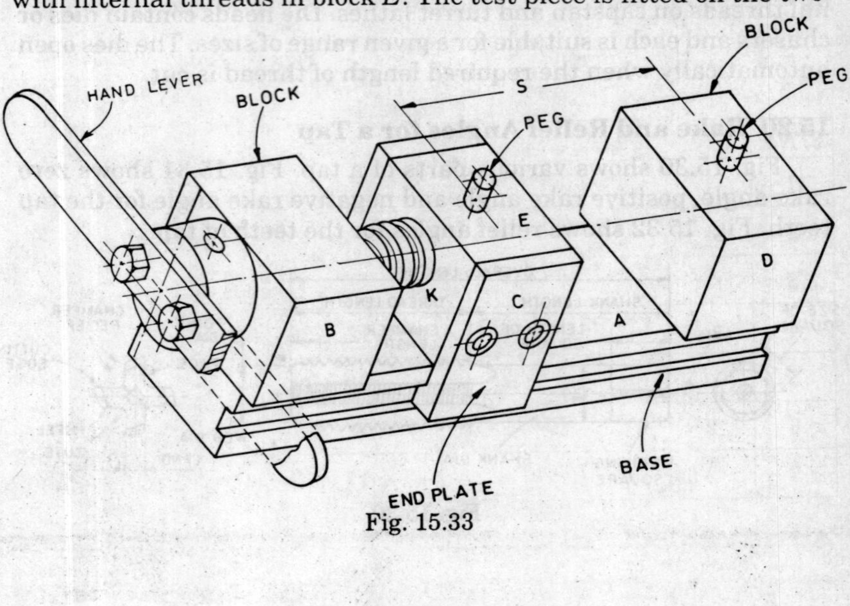

Fig. 15.33

pegs having a central distance S. The base A and blocks B, E, D are made of cast iron whereas screens, threaded shaft K, hand lever and pegs are made of mild steel.

Example 15.1. *Design and draw a template drilling jig for the mild steel component shown in Fig. 15.34 to drill four holes 5 mm diameter at 70 P.C.D.*

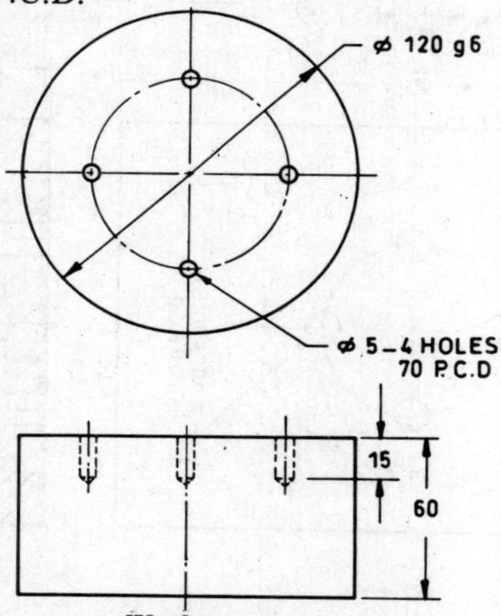

Workpiece

Fig. 15.34

Solution.

Fig. 15.35 shows the various typical parts of template drilling jig and Fig. 15.36 shows the assembly of the jig.

Table 15.18 indicates bill of materials.

Table 15.18.
Bill of Materials

S. No.	*Qty.*	*Part Description*	*Size*	*MAT.*	*Remarks*
1	1	WORK PIECE	ϕ 120 × 60	MS	—
2	1	NEST LOCATOR	240 × 240 × 60	C.I.	—
3	1	TEMPLATE	170 × 240 × 60	MS	—
4	2	CLAMPLING SCREW	ϕ 12 × 30	STD	—
5	4	DRILL BUSH	ϕ 20 × 32	HCS	HRC48
6	2	NUT	$M8 \times 1.5$	STD	—
7	2	T-BOLT	ϕ 12 × 50	STD	—

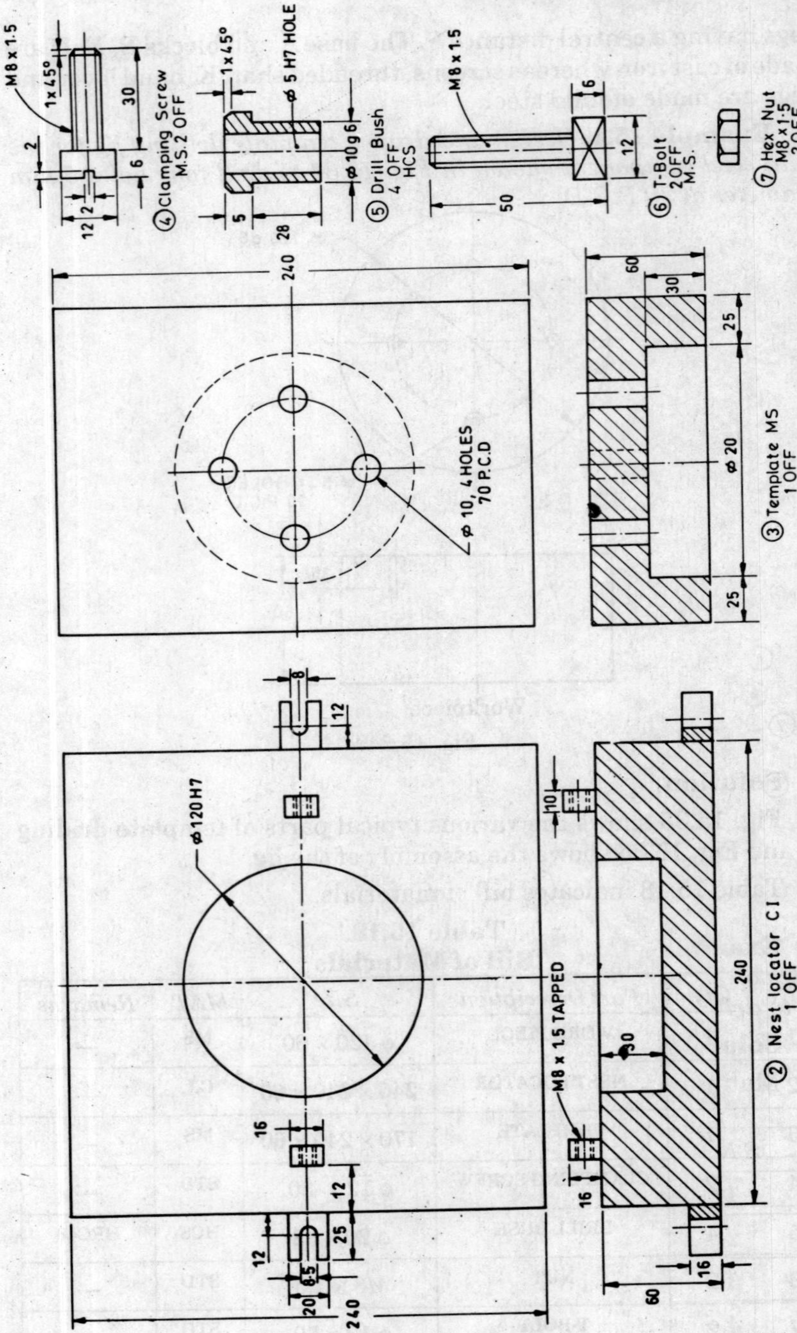

M8 x 1.5
1x45°
30
2
6
12
2
④ Clamping Screw
M.S. 2 OFF
1x45°
ø 5 H7 HOLE
ø 10 g 6
5
28
⑤ Drill Bush
4 OFF
HCS
M8 x 1.5
6
12
50
⑥ T-Bolt
2 OFF
M.S.
⑦ Hex Nut
M8 x 1.5
2 OFF
M.S.
240
ø 10, 4 HOLES
70 P.C.D
60
30
25
ø 20
25
③ Template MS
1 OFF
8
12
ø 120 H7
10
M8 x 1.5 TAPPED
30
240
16
12
16
25
12
6.5
20
240
16
60
② Nest locator CI
1 OFF

Fig. 15.35

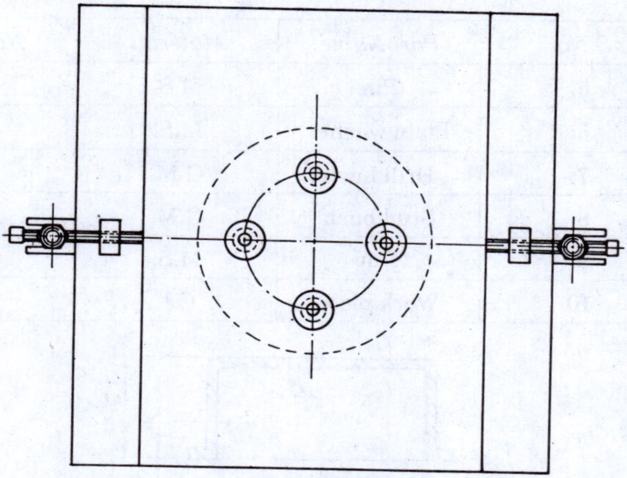

Top View

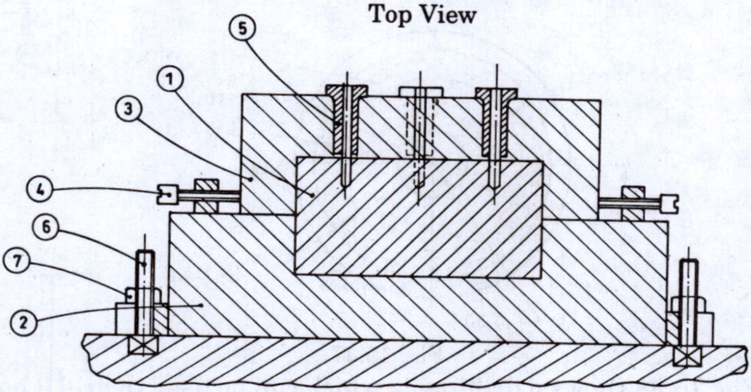

Front View

Fig. 15.36

Example 15.2. *Fig. 15.37 shows a C.I. component in which 3 holes of 12 mm diameter are to be drilled. Draw a typical drilling jig to drill holes.*

Solution.

Materials for the various parts of jig shown in table 15.19.

Table 15.19. Material list

S.No.	*Part Name*	*Material*	*No. OFF*
1.	Body	C.I.	1
2.	Plate	C.I.	1
3.	Stud	M.S.	1
4.	C-Washer	M.S.	1

(*Contd...*)

S.No.	*Part Name*	*Material*	*No. OFF*
5.	Pin	M.S.	1
6.	Plain washer	M.S.	1
7.	Drill bush	G.M.	3
8.	Stud bush	G.M.	1
9.	Nut	M.S.	2
10	Work piece	C.I.	1

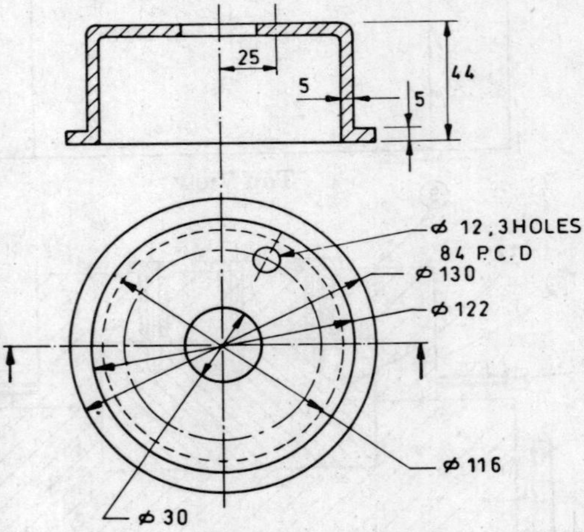

Fig. 15.37

Fig. 15.38 shows a drilling jig which can be used to drill 3 holes in the component of 12 ϕ placed at 84 P.C.D. and equi-spaced.

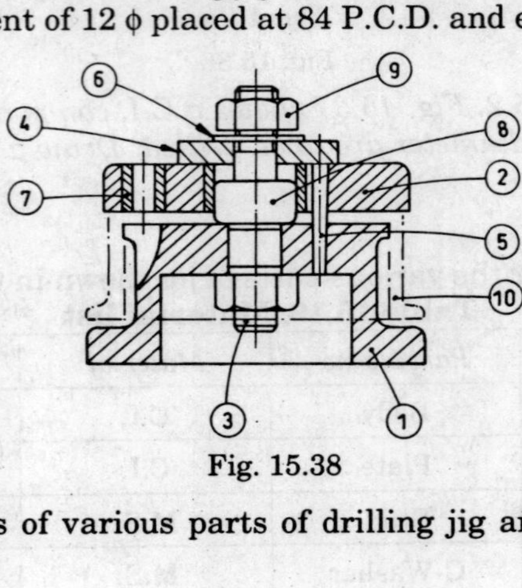

Fig. 15.38

The details of various parts of drilling jig are shown in Fig. 15.39.

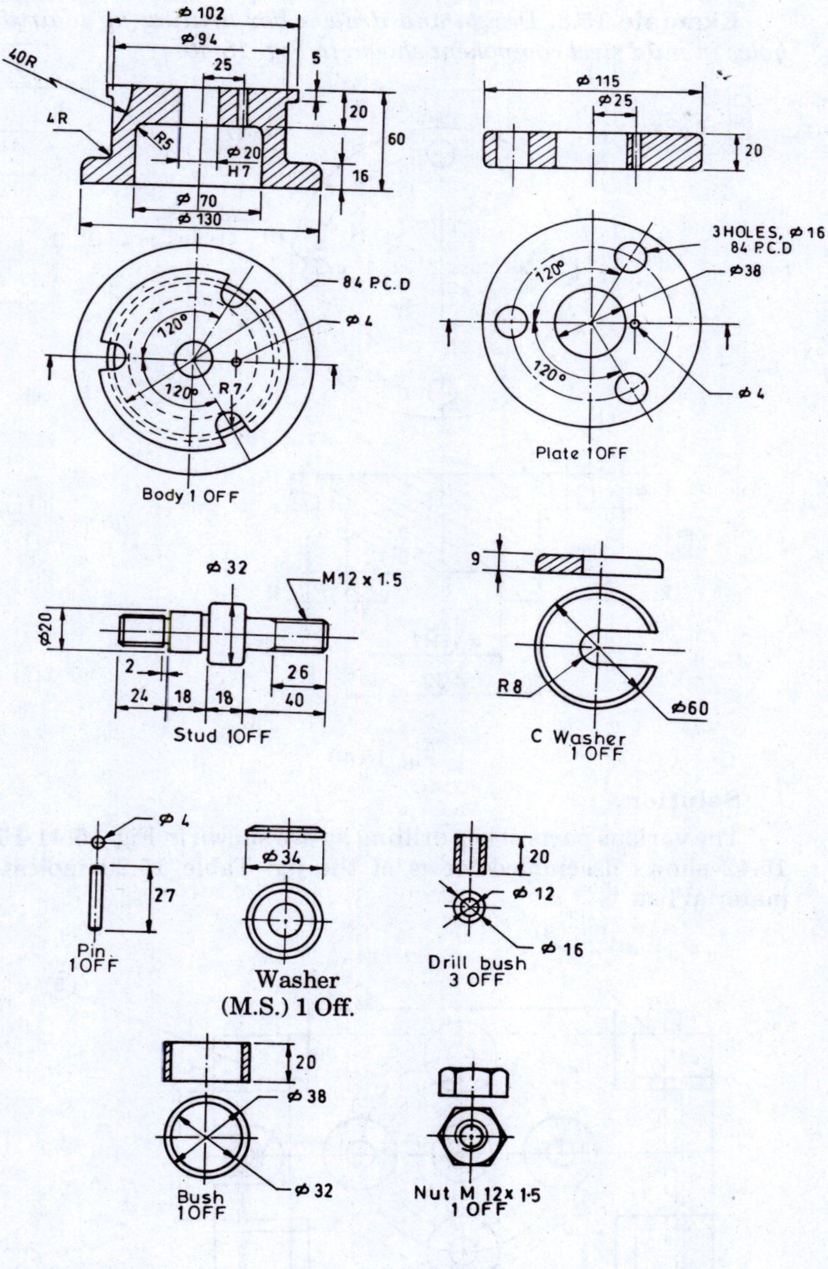

ϕ 102
ϕ 94
40R
25
5
20
60
16
4R
R5
ϕ 20
H7
ϕ 70
ϕ 130
84 P.C.D
ϕ 4
120°
120°
R7
Body 1 OFF
ϕ 115
ϕ 25
20
3HOLES, ϕ 16
84 P.C.D
ϕ 38
120°
120°
ϕ 4
Plate 1OFF
ϕ 32
M12 x 1.5
ϕ20
2
26
24
18
18
40
Stud 1OFF
9
R8
ϕ60
C Washer
1 OFF
ϕ 4
27
Pin
1OFF
ϕ 34
Washer
(M.S.) 1 Off.
20
ϕ 12
ϕ 16
Drill bush
3 OFF
20
ϕ 38
ϕ 32
Bush
1OFF
Nut M 12x 1·5
1 OFF

Fig. 15.39

Example 15.3. *Design and draw a box drilling jig to drill 4 holes in mild steel component shown in Fig. 15.40.*

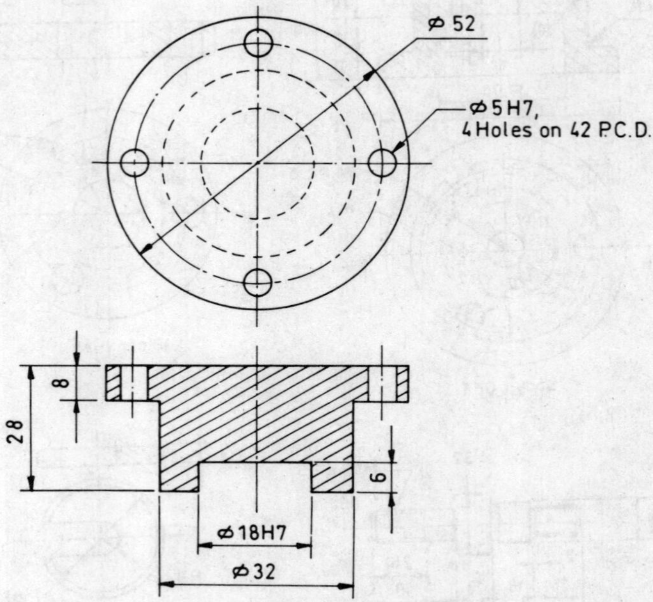

Fig. 15.40

Solution.

The various parts of box drilling jig are shown in Fig. 15.41. Fig. 15.42 shows assembled views of the jig. Table 15.20 indicates material list.

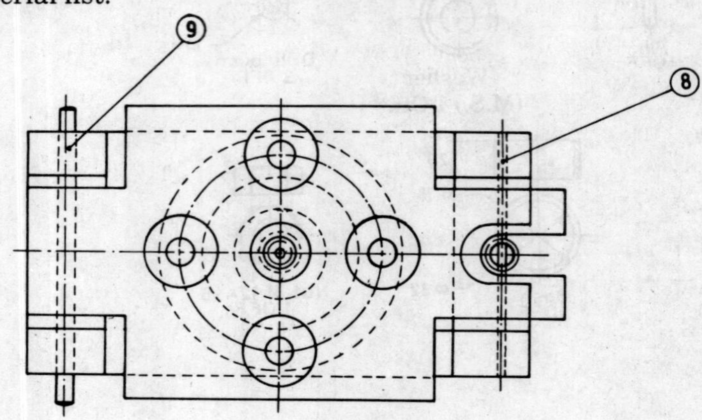

Fig. 15.41 (Contd...)

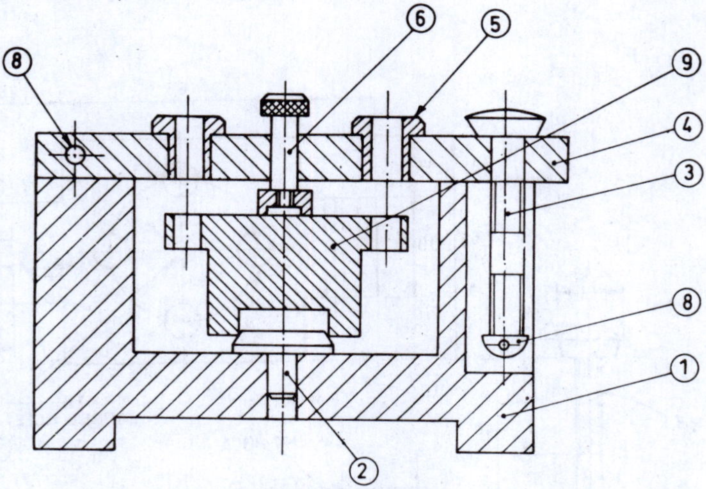

Fig. 15.41

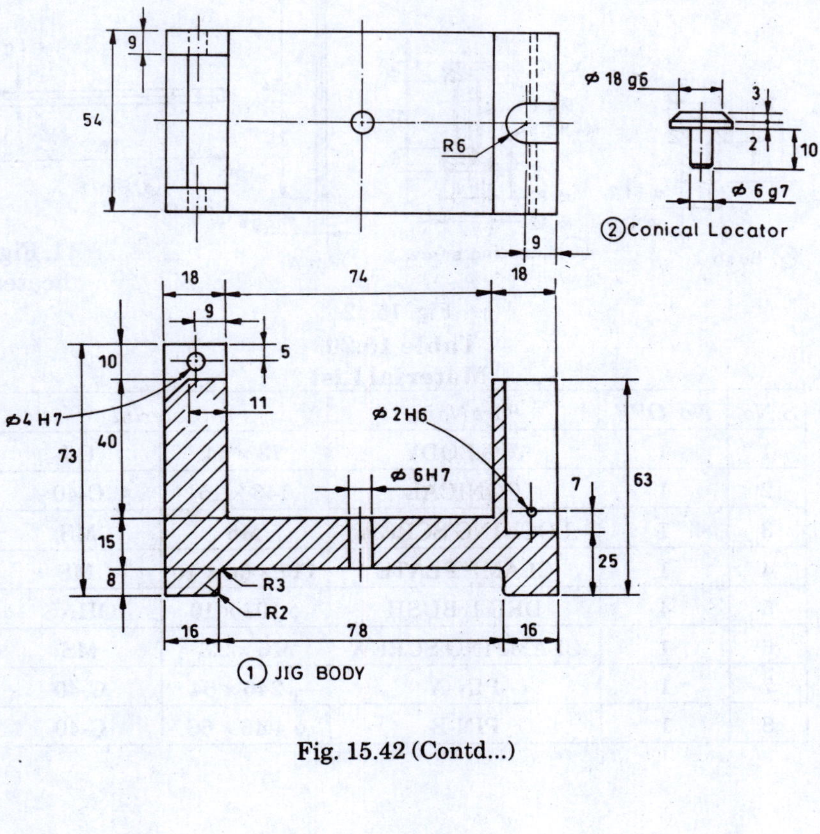

Fig. 15.42 (Contd...)

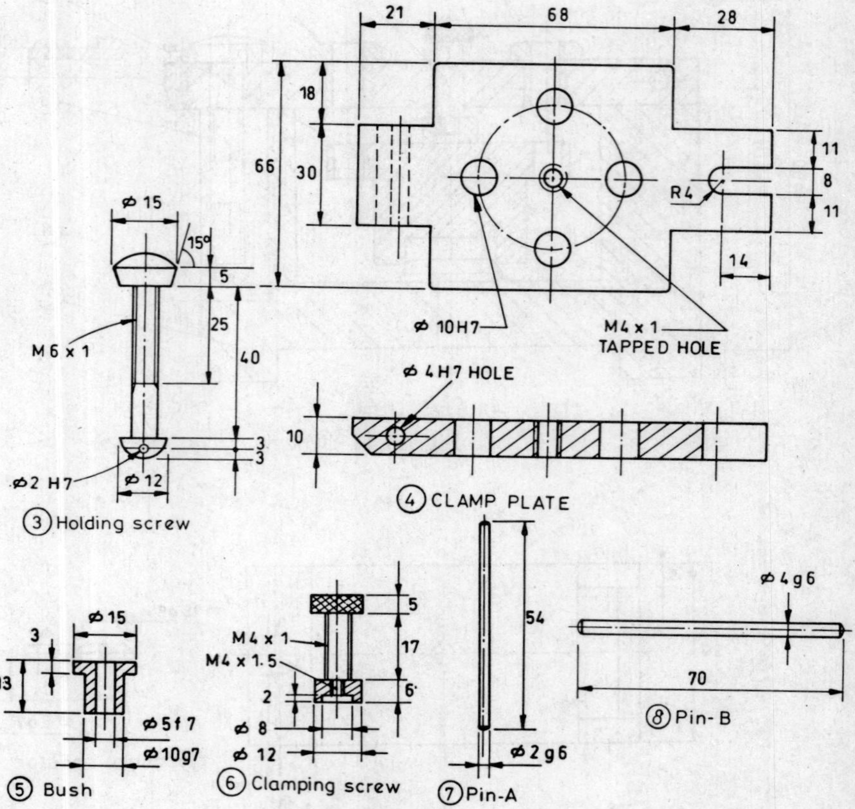

Fig. 15.42

Table 15.20.
Material List

S.No.	*No. OFF*	*Part Name*	*Material*	
1	1	JIG BODY	73 × 54	C.I
2	1	CONICAL	143 × 15	C-40
3	1	LOCKING SCREW	M6	MS
4	1	CLAMP PLATE	117 × 66 × 10	MS
5	4	DRILL BUSH	ϕ 107 × 10	OHNS
6	1	CLAMPING SCREW	*M*6 × 2.8	MS
7	1	PIN-A	ϕ 246 × 54	C-40
8	1	PIN-B	ϕ 4.46 × 66	C-40

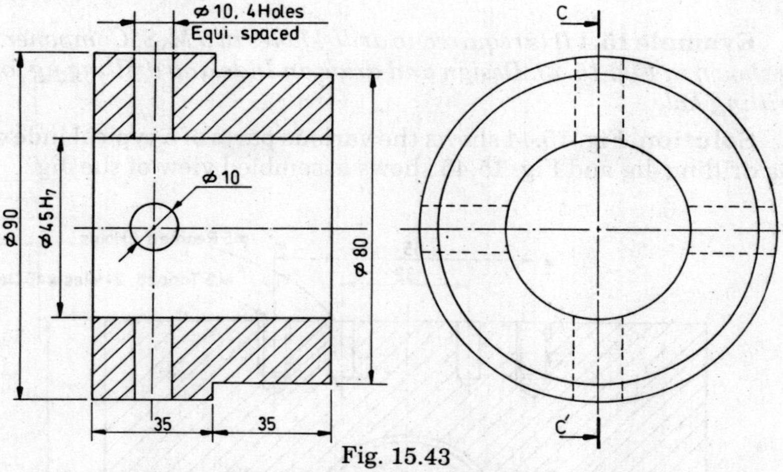

Fig. 15.43

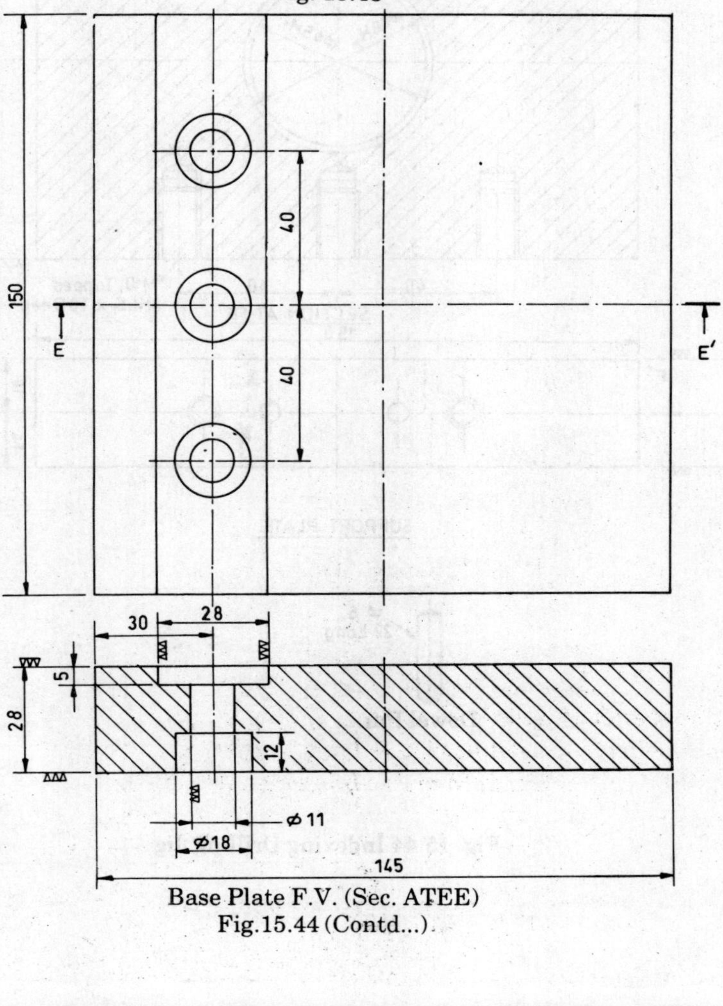

Base Plate F.V. (Sec. ATEE)

Fig.15.44 (Contd...)

Example 15.4 *It is required to drill 4 holes in a M.S. Component as shown in Fig. 15.43. Design and draw an Indexing drilling jig for drilling hole.*

Solution. Fig. 15.44 shows the various parts of a typical indexing drilling Jig and Fig. 15.45 shows assembled view of the Jig.

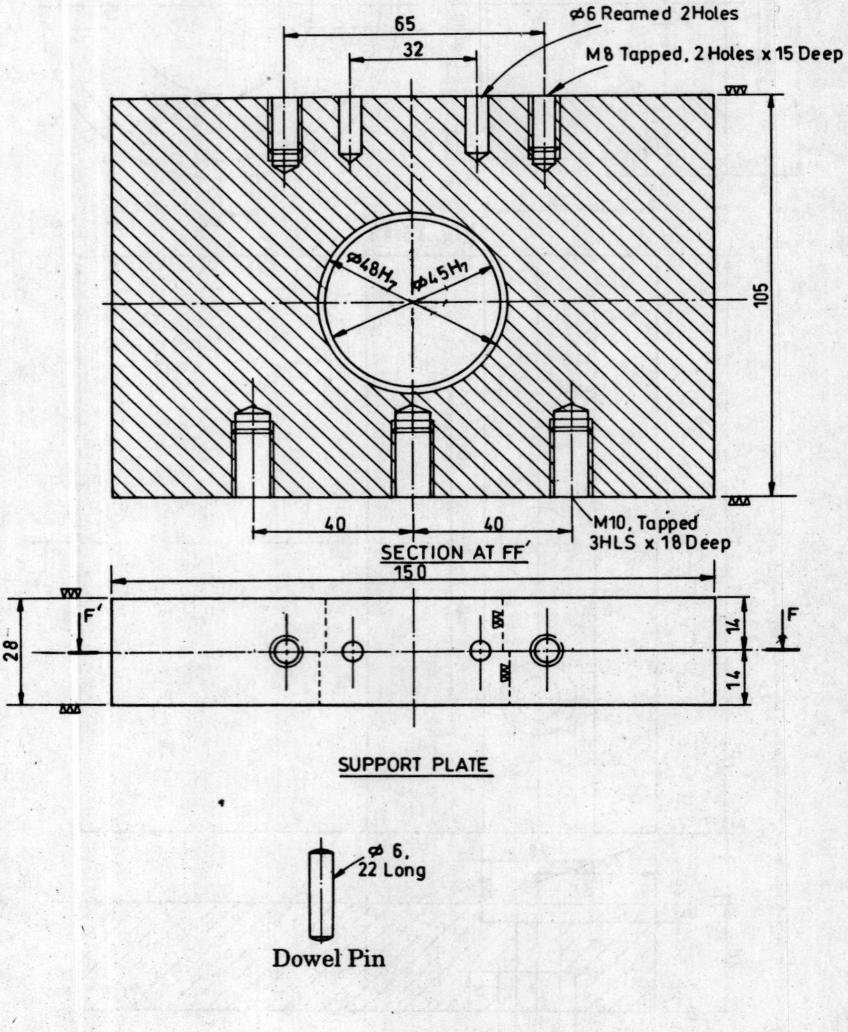

Fig. 15.44 Indexing Drilling Jig

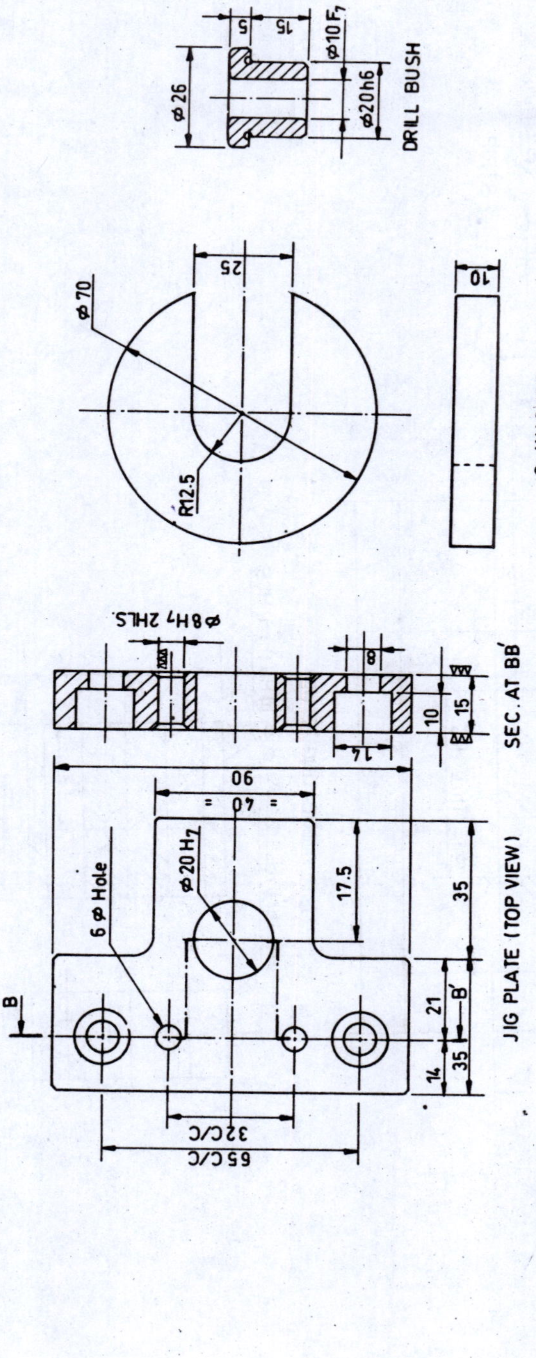
DRILL BUSH
ø26
ø20h6
ø10 F7
5
15
C-WASHER
ø70
R12.5
25
10
JIG PLATE (TOP VIEW)
6 ø Hole
ø20 H7
40
90
17.5
35
21
14
35
32C/C
65C/C
B
B'
SEC. AT BB'
ø8H7 2HLS.
8
14
10
15

Fig. 15.44

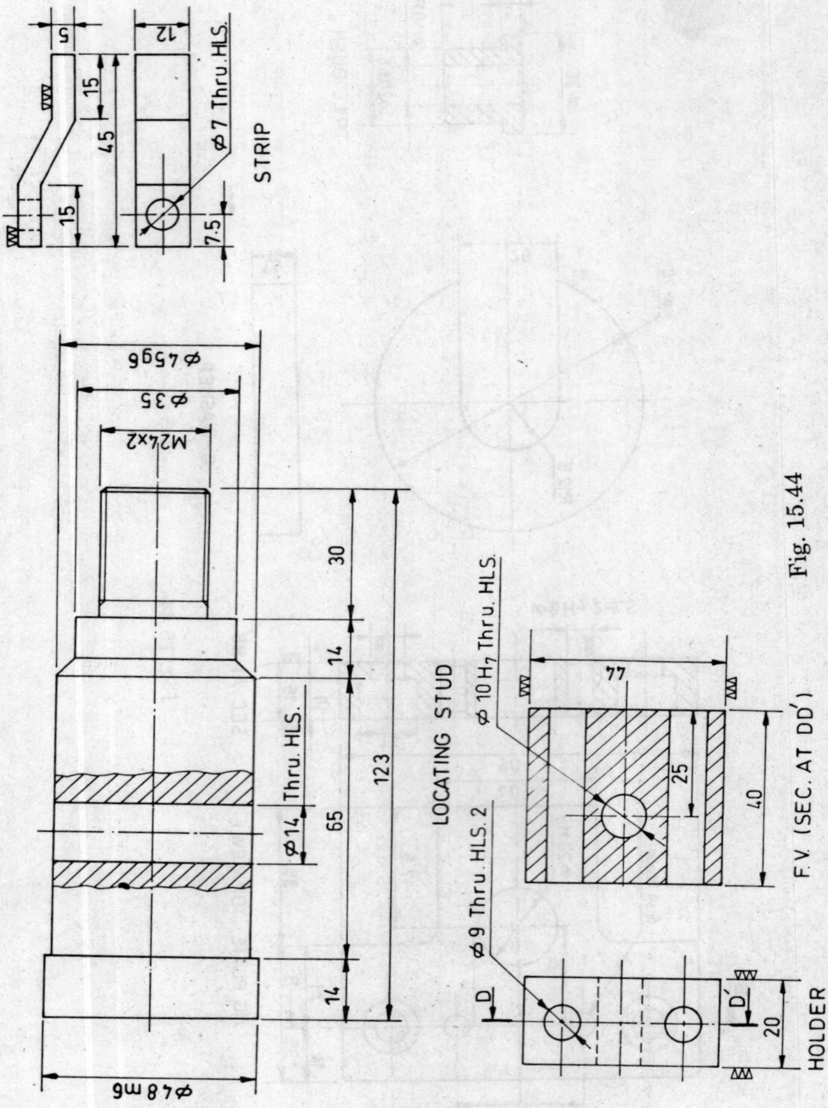
STRIP
⌀7 Thru. HLS.
5
12
15
45
15
7.5
⌀45g6
⌀35
M24x2
30
14
65
123
14
⌀14 Thru. HLS.
⌀48 m6
LOCATING STUD
⌀9 Thru. HLS. 2
⌀10 H7 Thru. HLS.
77
25
40
D
D′
20
F.V. (SEC. AT DD′)
HOLDER

Fig. 15.44

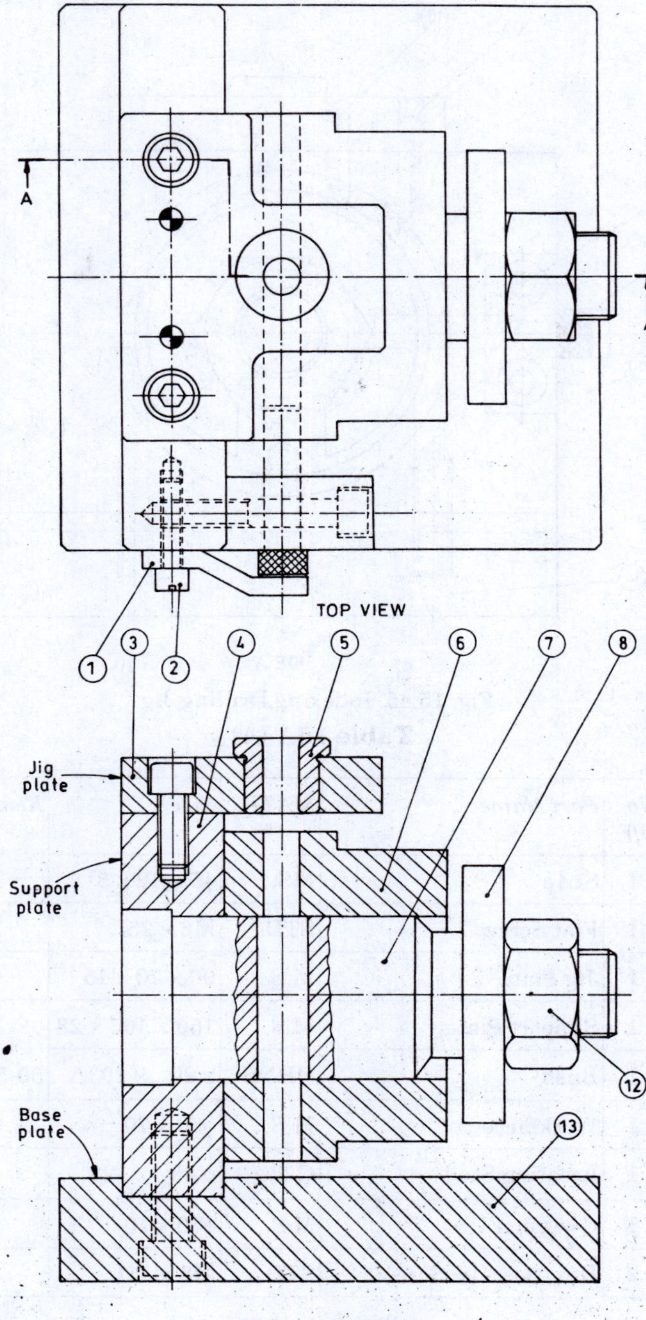
A
A′
TOP VIEW
1
2
3
4
5
6
7
8
Jig plate
Support plate
Base plate
12
13
FRONT VIEW (SEC. AT A-A′)

Fig. 15.45

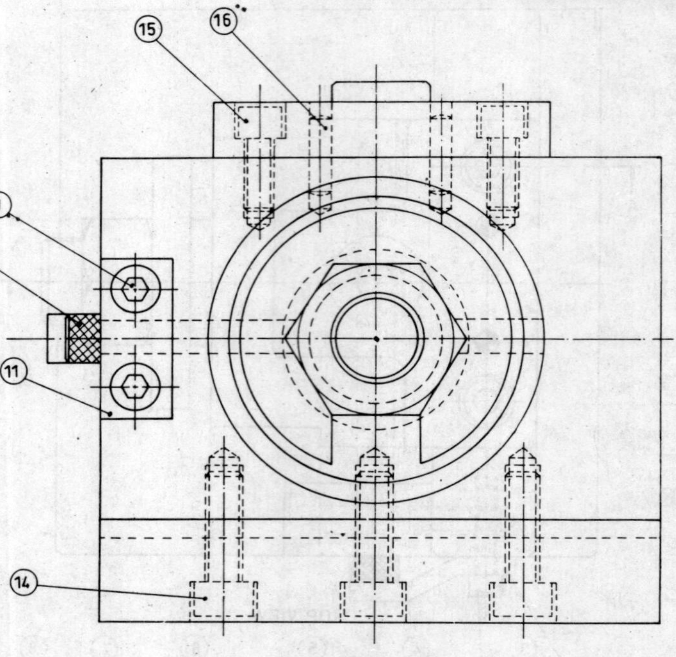

Fig. 15.45. Indexing Drilling Jig

Table 15.1 *(A)*

S. no.	*No. Off*	*Part Name*	*MATL.*	*Size*	*Remark*
1.	1	Strip	MS.	45 × 12 × 5	
2.	1	Flat Screw	STD.	M6 × 25L	
3.	1	Jig Plate	M.S.	90 × 70 × 15	
4.	1	Support Plate	M.S.	150 × 105 × 28	
5.	1	Bush	OHNS	$\phi\ 20_{h_6} \times 20$	50-55 HRC
6.	1	Workpiece	M.S.	$\phi 90 \times 70$	
7.	1	Locating Stud	C-35	$\phi\ 45_{g_6} \times 123$	
8.	1	C-washer	M.S.	$\phi 70 \times 10$	
9.	2	Hex. Soc. Hd. Screw	STD.	M8 × 45L	

(Contd...)

S. no.	*No. Off*	*Part Name*	*MATL.*	*Size*	*Remark*
10.	1	Pin	C-40	φ 10 × 40	50-55 HRC
11.	1	Holder	M.S.	44 × 40 × 20	
12.	1	Hex. Nut	STD.	M24 × 2	
13.	1	Base Plate	M.S.	150 × 145 × 28	
14.	3	Hex. Soc. Hd. Screw	STD.	M10 × 30L	
15.	2	Hex. Hd. Soc. Hd. Screw	STD.	M8 × 20L	
16.	2	Dowel	MS	η 6 h_6 × 22	45-48 HRC.

15.22 Elements of a twist drill

Fig. 15.46 shows a twist drill with parallel shank.

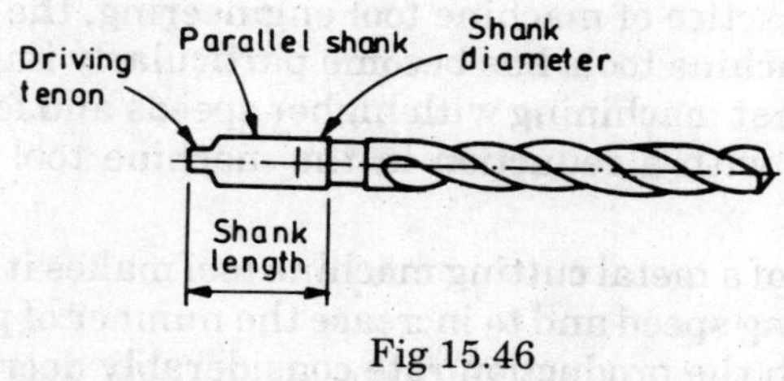

Fig 15.46

Fig. 15.47 shows a twist drill with taper shank.

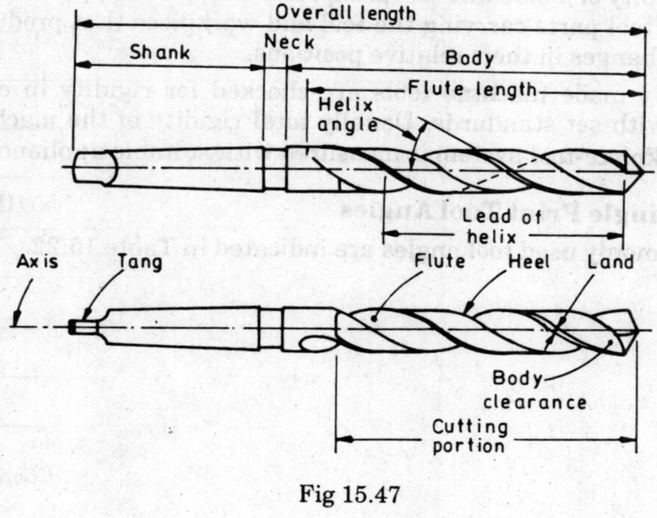

Fig 15.47

Fig. 15.48 shows various angless and other terms for a twist drill.

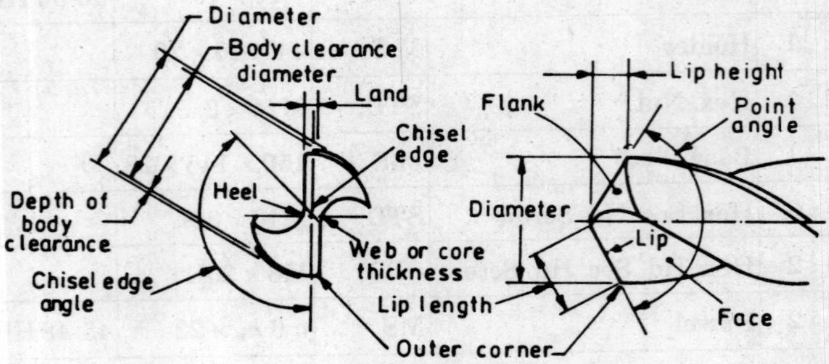

Fig. 15.48

15.23 Rigidity of machine tool

In modern practice of machine tool engineering, the increased rigidity of the machine tools has become particularly important in view of the fact that machining with higher speeds and forces finds wide application with a reduction in the machine tool weight to drive capacity.

Poor rigidity of a metal cutting machine tool makes it necessary to lower the cutting speed and to increase the number of passes due to vibrations with the production rate considerably decreased and the machining accuracy and surface roughness impaired as a result.

Risgidity of a machine tool is expressed as a load applied to the machine tool parts carrying the tool and workpiece that produces specific changes in their relative positions.

Newly made machine tools are checked for rigidity in compliance with set standards. Usually total rigidity of the machine tool-workpiece-tool system is measured with suitable appliances.

15.24. Single Print Tool Angles

Commonly used tool angles are indicated in Table 15.22.

Table 15.22

Work material	*Hardness, BHN*	*Tool material*	*Back rake angle*	*Side rake angle*	*End clearance angle*	*Side clearance angle*	*Side and end cutting edge angle*
Free machining steels	85 to 225	HSS	10	12	5	5	15
		Brazed carbides	0	6	5	5	15
		Throwaway carbides	–5	–5	5	5	15
Mild steels Medium carbon steels	225 to 325	HSS	8	10	5	5	15
		Brazed carbides	0	6	5	5	15
		Throwaway carbides	–5	–5	5	5	15
Alloy steels Tool steels	325 to 425	HSS	0	10	5	5	15
		Brazed carbides	0	6	5	5	15
		Throwaway carbides	–5	–5	5	5	15
	$45R_c$ to $58R_c$	HSS	0	10	5	5	15
		Brazed carbides	–5	–5	5	5	15
		Throwaway carbides	–5	–5	5	5	15
Cast iron	200 to 300	HSS	5	8	5	5	15
		Brazed carbides	0	6	5	5	15
		Throwaway carbides	–5	–5	5	5	15
Grey, ductile and malleable	300 to 400	HSS	5	5	5	5	15
		Brazed carbides	–5	–5	5	5	15
		Throwaway carbides	–5	–5	5	5	15

(Contd...)

Work material	*Hardness, BHN*	*Tool material*	*Back rake angle*	*Side rake angle*	*End clearance angle*	*Side clearance angle*	*Side and end cutting edge angle*
Aluminium	30 to 150	HSS	20	15	12	10	5
		Brazed carbides	3	15	5	5	15
		Throwaway carbides	0	5	5	5	15
Magnesium alloys	40 to 90	HSS	20	15	12	10	5
		Brazed carbides	3	15	5	5	15
		Throwaway carbides	0	5	5	5	15

15.25 Recommended angles for milling cutters

Table 15.23 indicates recommended angles for various types of milling cutters.

Table 15.23

	H.S.S. Cutters		*Carbide Cutters*	
	Rake Angle	*Clearance Angle*	*Rake Angle*	*Clearance Angle*
Type N-Cutters	10°	10°	–5°	8°
Type S-Cutters	25°	10°	15°	10°
Type H-Cutters	6°	8°	–10°	8°

Type-H cutters are used for hard materials like cast iron. For softer materials, higher rake and clearance angle are provided on the cutter.

Commonly used profile sharpened cutters are as follows :

(*i*) *Angle Cutters* : Single-angle and double-angle cutters are usually made light with light duty teeth and are used for light cuts. These are used for cutting dovetails, grooves, notches or other angular slots.

(*ii*) *Cylindrical Cutters* : They are cylindrical in shape and have teeth on the periphery only. The usual helix angle of the cutters is 25–30°. These cutters shear material rather than cut and are best suited for thin metals, copper bars etc.

(*iii*) *End Mills* : These are designed for milling slots, keyways and pockets where the ordinary arbor type milling cutter cannot be used.

(*iv*) *T-Slot Milling Cutters* : A T-slot milling cutter is like a side and face cutter joined to a taper shank with a neck.

(*v*) *Metal Slitting Saws* : These resemble small circular blades and have teeth on their circumference. They are used for cutting off and for slotting.

(*vi*) *Side and Face Cutters* : These are very widely used ones. They have cutting teeth on the periphery and on one side. The staggered-teeth side and face cutters have alternate teeth arranged in an alternating helix pattern. They are used for cutting slots or side and face-milling of die plates, punch plates, etc.

(*vii*) *Shell End Mills :* These tools bridge the gap between the shank type end mills and large face cutters and their normal function is that of face cutting.

(*viii*) *Woodruff Keyseat Cutters :* They are used to cut keyways in shafts, etc.

(*ix*) *Forn-Relieved Cutters :* Any particular from can be made on a form cutter and can be used for that particular purpose. There are some standard form cutters, namely :

(*i*) Concave cutters. (*ii*) Convex cutters.

(*iii*) Corner rounding cutters. (*iv*) Involute gear cutters.

Example 15.4. *Name the carbon steel used for making tools.*

Solution. Carban tool steels : Table 15.24 indicates the carbon steels for making diffrent tools.

Table 15.24.

Tools	*Carbon %*
Coldchisels, Press tools	0.7–0.8
Large taps, reamers, wood working tools	1.0
Drills, reamers small taps	1.15
Turning tools	1.3
Files	1.4

Example 15.5. *Sketch the variation of specific cutting resistance with feed for carbon steels.*

Solution. Fig. 15.49 shows the variation of specific cutting resistance and feed for carbon steels.

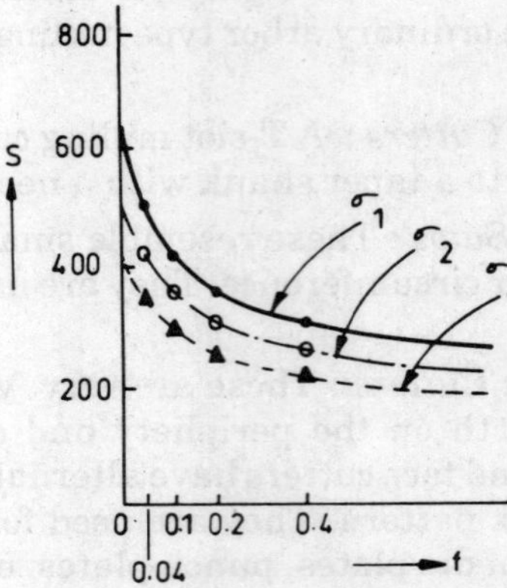

Fig. 15.49

The specific cutting resistance increases with increase in tensile strength of steels.

s = specific curring resistance kg/mm^2

f = feed (mm/rev.)

σ_1 = tensile strength = 80 kg/mm^2

σ_2 = 60 kg/mm^2

σ_3 = 40 kg/mm^2

Example 15.6. *Discuss the fundamental techniques for more efficient metal removal while using carbide inserts (tips).*

Solution. Following fundamental techniques should be followed for more efficient metal removal during machining of metals.

1. Select the largest side cutting or end cutting edge angle the workpiece can allow.

This will help to

(*i*) produce thinner ships

(*ii*) protect nose radius

(*iii*) reduce insert notching

(*iv*) dissipate heat faster

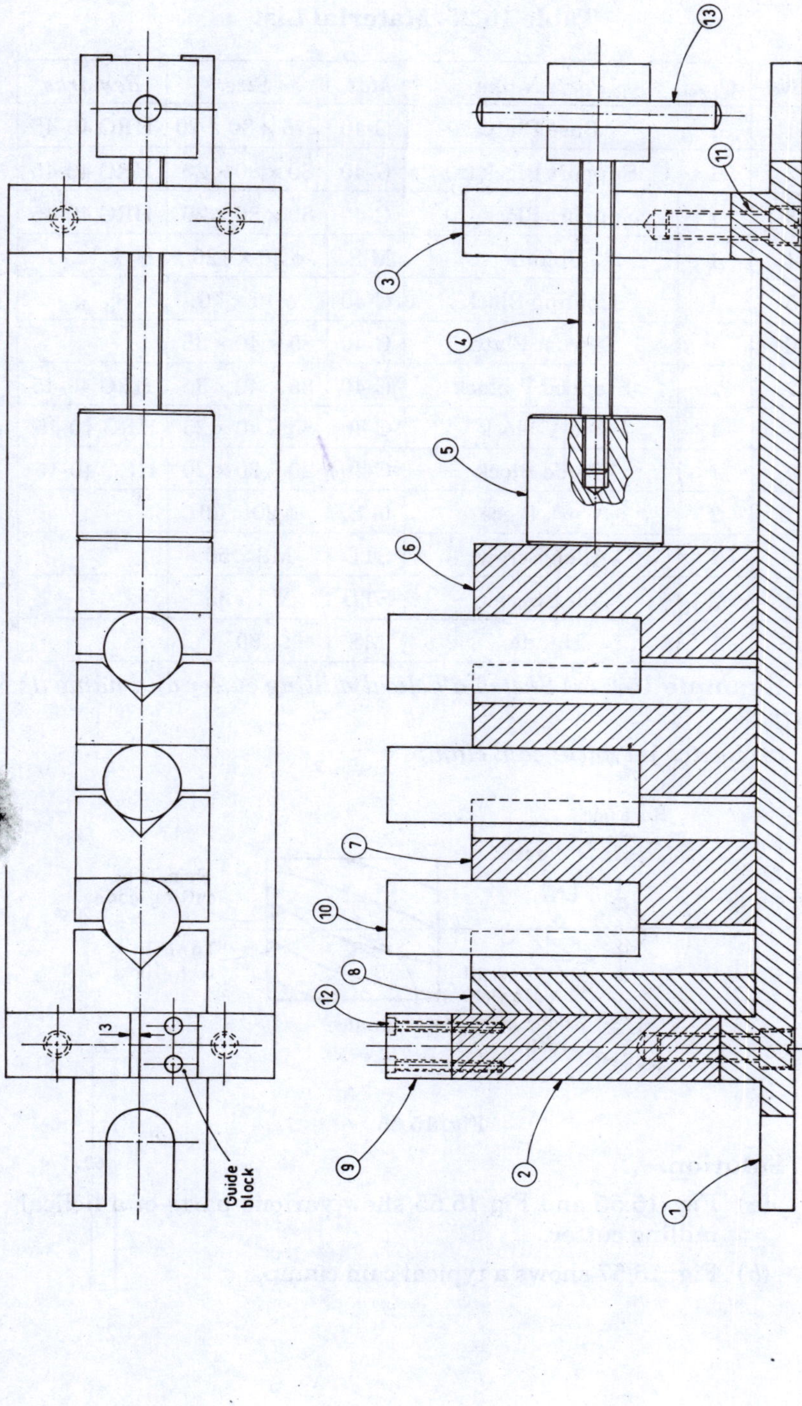

Fig. 15.54.

Table 15.25. Material List

S.No.	*Qty.*	*Parts Name*	*Mat.*	*Size*	*Remarks*
1	1	Base Plate	C-40	275 × 80 × 20	HRC 40-45
2	1	Support Block (a)	C-40	80 × 80 × 20	HRC 40-45
3	1	Support Block (b)	C-40	80 × 80 × 20	HRC 40-45
4	1	Spindle	M.S.	ϕ 30 × 120	
5	1	Holding Block	C-40	ϕ 40 × 40	
6	1	Thrust Plate	C-40	85 × 40 × 35	
7	2	Stepped V-block	C-40	85 × 40 × 35	HRC 40-45
8	1	Std V-block	C-40	85 × 40 × 25	HRC 40-45
9	1	Guide Block	C-40	20 × 20 × 20	HRC 40-45
10	3	Work Piece	M.S.	ϕ 20 × 60	
11	4	Allen Screw	STD	M8 × 50	
12	2	Allen Screw	STD	M3 × 35	
13	1	Handle	MS	80	

Example 15.9 (*a*) *Sketch a helical milling cutter and name its parts;*

(*b*) *Sketch a typical cam clamp.*

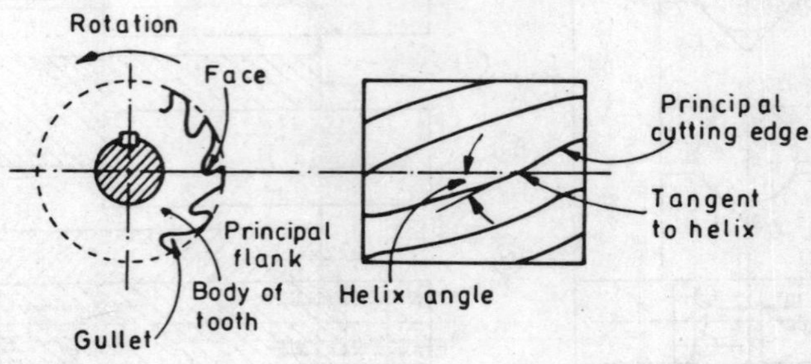

Fig. 15.55.

Solution.

(*a*) Fig. 15.55 and Fig 15.55 show various parts of a helical milling cutter.

(*b*) Fig. 15.57 shows a typical cam clamp.

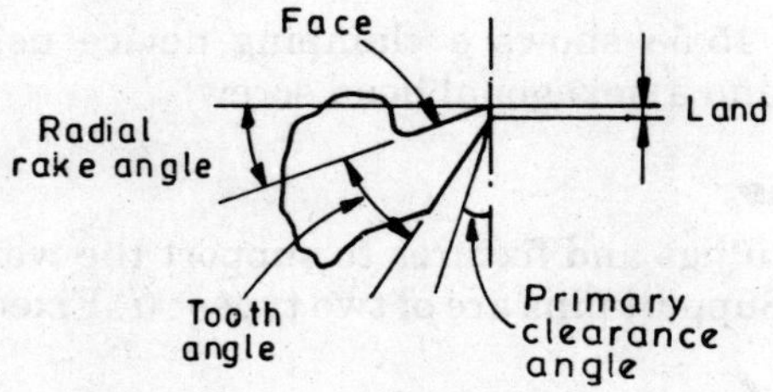

Fig. 15.56.

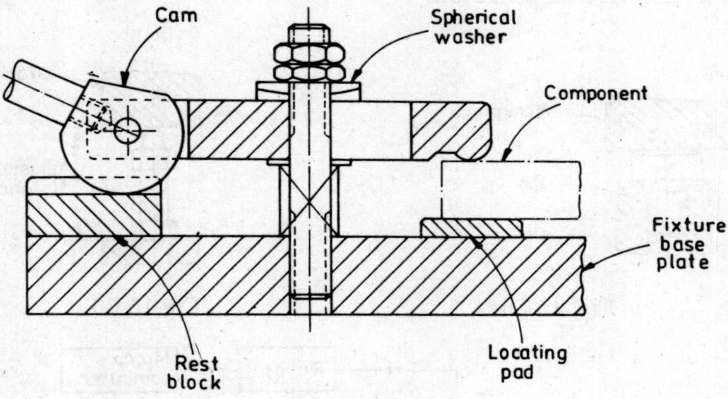

Fig. 15.57.

Example 15.10. *Sketch a clamping device using hexagonal head screw and spring bolt system with a strap.*

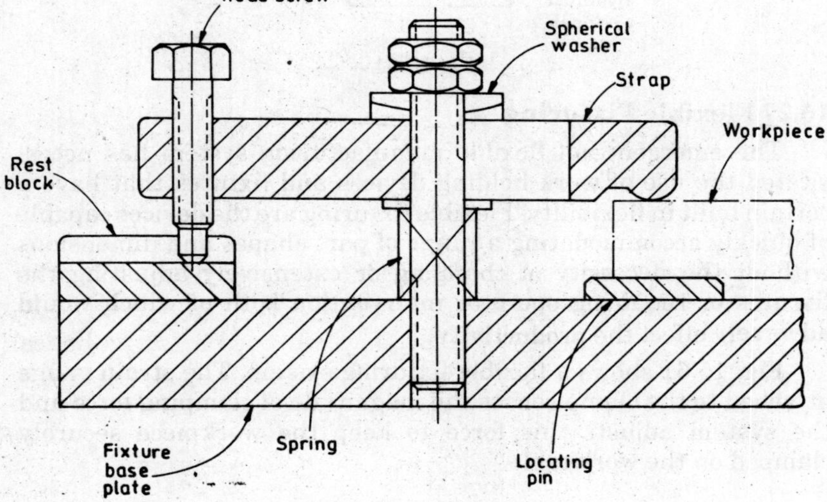

Fig. 15.58.

Solution. Fig. 15.58 shows a clamping device using strap, spring bolt system and a hexagonal head screw.

15.26 Support pins

They are used in jigs and fixtures to support the workpiece at convenient points. Support pins are of two types : (*i*) Fixed type and (*ii*) Adjustable type.

Fixed type support pin is shown in Fig. 15.59 and adjustable type is shown in Fig. 15.60.

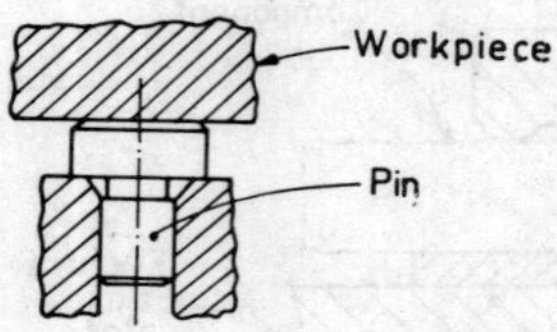

Fig. 15.59.

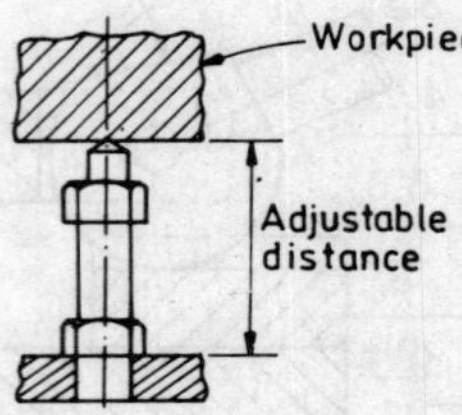

Fig 15.60.

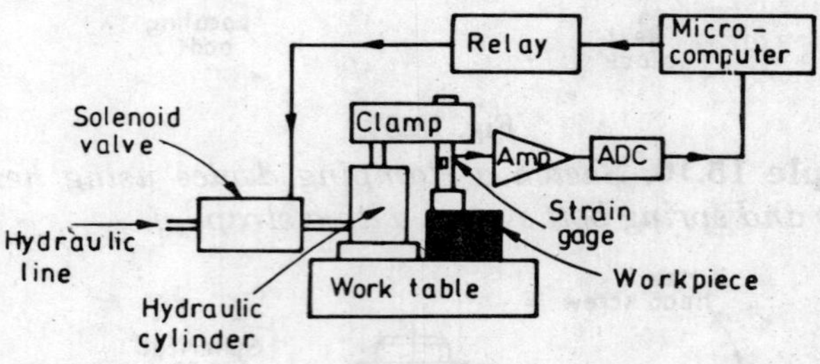

Fig 15.61

15.27 Flexible Fixturing

The emergence of flexible manufacturing system has necessitated the use of work holding devices and fixtures that have a certain built in flexibility. Flexible fixturing are the devices capable of quickly accommodating a range of part shapes and dimensions without the necessity of changing or extensively adjusting the fixtures or requiring operator intervention both of which would adversely effect the productivity.

Fig. 15.61 shows a flexible fixturing system. The strain gauge attached to the clamp senses the magnitude of clamping force and the system adjusts this force to keep the workpiece securely clamped on the work table.

15.28 Dimensions of Pilots

They are used for locating the workpiece in jig and fixture. Fig. 15.62 shows acorn type pilot and Fig. 15.63 shows flattened point type pilot. Table 15.26 indicates the dimensions of pilots.

Table 15.26

Nominal A mm	*B mm*	*C mm*	*D mm*	*E mm*
		Acorn Type		
3.15	3.15	0.8	6.3	2.5
4.75	4.75	1.18	6.3	3.15
6.3	6.3	1.6	11.2	4.75
8	8	2	11.2	5.6
9.5	9.5	2.5	12.5	6.3
11.2	11.2	3.15	12.5	7.1
12.5	12.5	4	12.5	8
16	16	4.25	16	9
18	18	4.75	16	9.5
		Flattened Point Type		
19	19	11.2	16	9.5
22.4	22.4	14	19	11.2
25	25	16	19	15.5
31.5	31.5	19	25	16
35.5	35.5	22.4	25	18
37.5	37.5	25	31.5	19

$F = 1.6$ mm or thickness of stock whichever is greater.

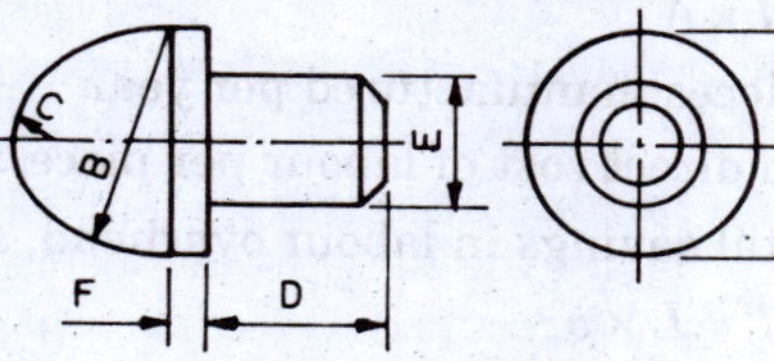

Acron Type

Fig. 15.62.

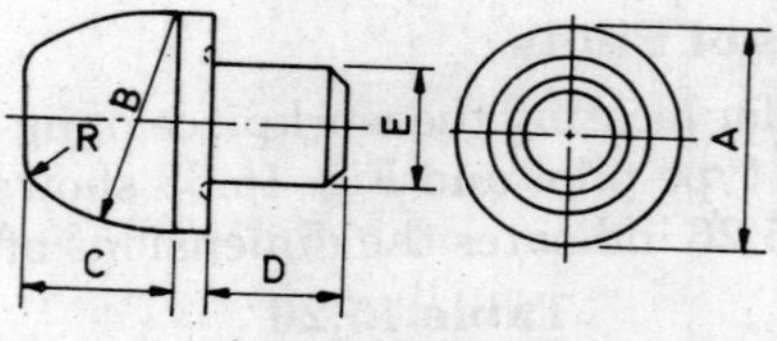

Fig. 15.63.

Example 15.11

(*a*) *Sketch and describe two types of template jigs.*

(*b*) *Discuss savings that can be achieved by using jigs and fixtures.*

Solution. (*a*) Fig. 15.64 and Fig. 15.65 show template jigs.

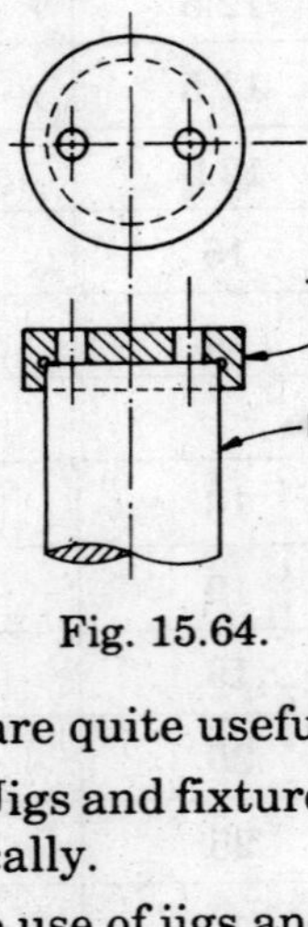

Fig. 15.64.

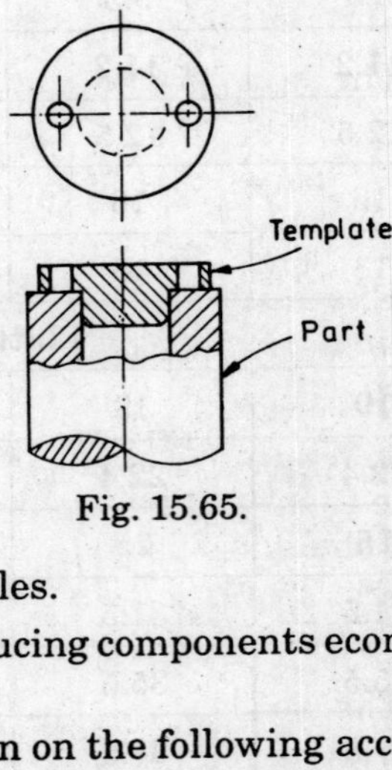

Fig. 15.65.

They are quite useful for drilling holes.

(*b*) Jigs and fixtures helps in producing components economically.

By the use of jigs and fixture we gain on the following account:

(*i*) Yearly total saving in direct cost of labour, say

Rs. $L = N \times A$

where N = No. of pieces manufactured per year

A = saving in direct cost of labour per piece.

(*ii*) Yearly total savings in labour overhead, say

Rs. $T = L \times p$

where p = percentage of overhead on labour saved.

(*iii*) Yearly profits to be made in excess of fixed charges say Rs. *P*.

The amount spent on account of using jigs and fixtures is

(*i*) yearly % allowance of interest on investment, say *X*.

(*ii*) yearly % allowance for such fixed charges as insurance, taxes, etc. say *Y*.

(*iii*) yearly % allowance for up-keep, say *Z*.

(*iv*) yearly % allowance for depreciation and obsolescence on the basis of uniform depreciation, say, 1/*H*.

where *H* = No. of years required for amortisation of investment out of earnings.

(*v*) estimated initial cost of jig and fixture, *i.e.* cost of installed and ready to run including drafting and tool room material and tool room overhead, say Rs. *I*.

(*vi*) yearly cost of set-ups, say Rs. *K*.

The savings will equal total fixed charges per year when

$$N = \frac{I\left(X + Y + Z + \dfrac{1}{H}\right) + K}{A\,(1 + p)}$$

Example 15.15. *Discuss materials used for making patterns that may be made of (i) wood, (ii) matals and (iii) plastics.*

Solution.

1. **Wood.** Wood is the most commonly used pattern material. It is the easiest of all the pattern materials to work. Properly direct wood should be used. It may be kiln dried or air dried. It must have straight grains and free from knots, cracks and sap.

The woods available are as follows :

(*i*) *White pine* : It is most widely used wood in pattern making because of its

(*a*) straight grain

(*b*) light weight

(*c*) softness

(*d*) easy to work

(*e*) unlikely to warp.

(*ii*) *Mahogany* : It is harder and more durable wood than white pine. It is less likely to warp than some of other woods.

(*iii*) Maple, birch and cherry are harder and heavier than white pine. They tend to warp in large sections and therefore are perferred for marking small patterns.

Wood in general has a cellular structural called fibres. The cells are tubular and hollow and contain mostly air and water.

Moisture in wood is calculated by taking a piece of wood and heating it in an oven at about 212° F until the dry weight reaches a constant value.

$$M = \frac{(W_1 - W_2) \times 100}{W_2}$$

M = % Moisture; W_1 = Weight of green wood

W_2 = Weight of dry wood.

2. **Metals.** Metals used for making patterns are as follows :

(*i*) *Cast Iron* : Cast iron with fine grains may be used. It is cheaper and more durable.

(*ii*) *Brass* : It has a smooth closed pored structure. It can be easily worked and built up by solder or larze. However it is expensive.

(*iii*) *Aluminium* : It is quite commonly used metal for making patterns because it

(*a*) can be easily worked (*b*) is light in weight

(*c*) is corrosion resistant

Although it is subjected to shrinkage and wear by abrasive action especially when used in same mould.

(*iv*) *White metal (tin base)* : These alloys have

(*a*) low shrinkage (*b*) can be easily cast

(*c*) low melting point (*d*) low weight

3. **Plastics.** Plastics are also used for marking patterns. They have the following advantages:

(*i*) They are durable

(*ii*) They do not change in size or shape appreciably

(*iii*) They do not absorb moisture

(*iv*) They can be quickly finished when the pattern is removed from the mould.

Example 15.13. *Sketch and describe the purpose of sprue, gate and gate basin.*

Solution. In sand casting process the sprue is usally made circular in cross section. It should be as small as possible. It should allow enough metal to flow.

Gate is to feed the casting at a rate consistent with the rate of solidification. All edges of the gate should be rounded to prevent pieces of sand from breaking off and being carried into the mould cavity.

The gate basin acts as a reservoir for molten metal. It prevents turbulent molten metal from entering the gate and traps loose sand and particles which are undesirable.

Fig. 15.66 shows the sprue, gate and gate basin.

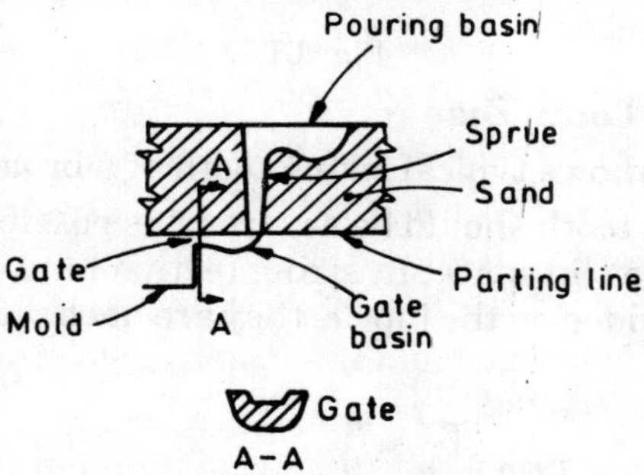

Fig. 15.66.

15.29 Tool Wear Land

Fig 15.67 shows wear land for a single point cutting tool.

The worn area, called wear land is usually taken as a measure of the amount of wear and can be readily determined by means of a tool maker's microscope. It extends from the top to a distance on the flank surface, which is abraded away as cutting continues.

Table 15.27 indicates the allowable wear land for various machining operations using high speed steel tool and carbide tools.

Table 15.27

Operation	*Allowable wear land (mm)*	
	High speed steels	*Carbide*
Turning	1.6	0.4
Force milling	1.5	0.4
End milling	0.3	0.3
Drilling	0.4	0.4
Reaming	0.15	0.15

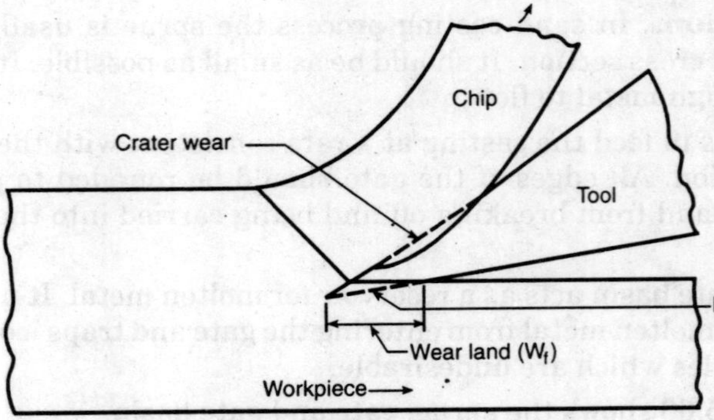

Fig. 15.67

15.30 Broach Tooth Size

Fig. 15.68 shows typical sizing tooth of a broach.

The broach tooth should be as strong as possible while allowing for a reasonable clip space. In sizing teeth a land of about 0.25 mm in width is provided on the top *i.e.* they are not beached off to a sharp edge.

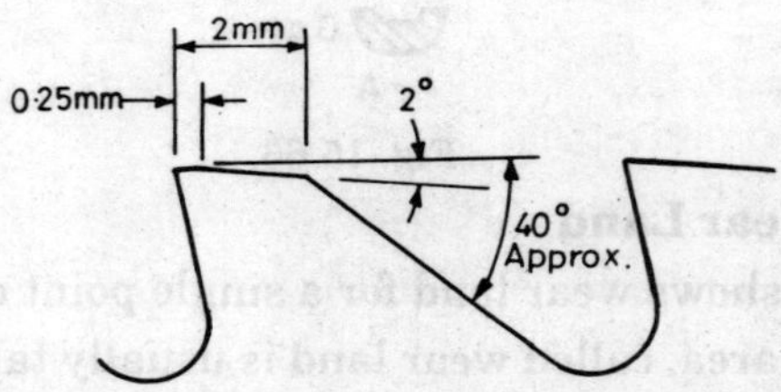

Fig. 15.68. Sizing tooth

The cutting teeth (Fig. 15.3) should be ground to a sharp cutting edge and them bached off approximately 0.075 mm on the diameter in a length of 2.5 mm.

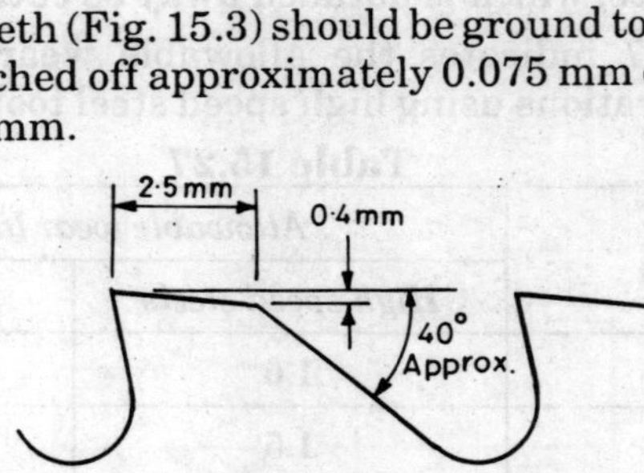

Fig. 15.69. Cutting tooth

15.31 Average Cut Per Tooth

Table indicates average cut per tooth of broach while cutting steel, cast iron and aluminium.

The average cut per tooth may be upto 0.5 mm while cutting bronze because of its free cutting qualities.

Table 15.28 shows rise per tooth and cutting speed for broaching operation.

Table 15.28

Work material	*Rise per tooth (mm)*	*Cutting speed (m / min.)*
	0.1	10
Mild steels	0.1	6-10
Medium carbon steels	0.08	4-8
Alloy steels	0.08	5-10
Tool steels	0.05	3-7
Stainless steels	0.075	4-7
Cast irons (grey, ductile and malleable)	0.1	7-10
Aluminium alloys	0.15	10-15
Copper alloys	0.125	8-10
Magnesium alloys	0.15	8-15

15.32 Forces acting at Cutting Edges in Milling

Fig. 15.70 shows forces acting at cutting edges for conventional milling.

Radial force (R) = ON or CT

Circumferential force (P) = OA or CE. It steadily increases with thickness of chip.

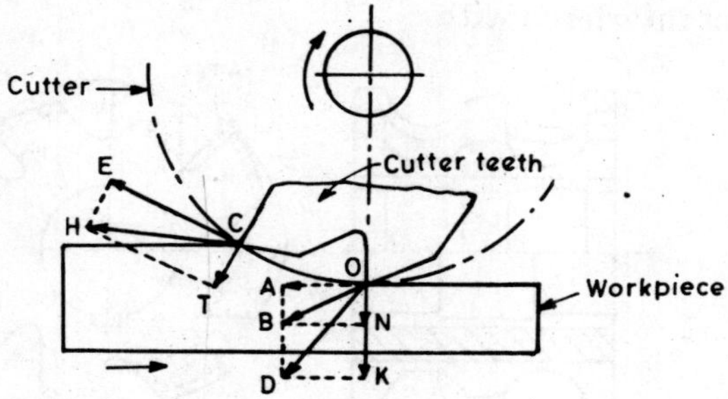

Fig. 15.70

Resultant (Total) force (F) = OB or CH. It may be directed downwards or upwards, depending upon the point of the action of the cutting edge. In down cut milling (Fig. 15.71) the forces acting are as follows :

Radial force $R = ON$ or CT

Circumferential force $P = OA$ or CE

Total force $(F) = OB$ or CH.

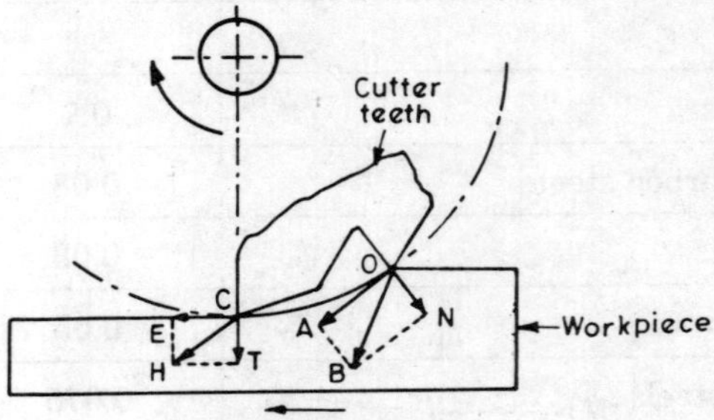

Fig. 15.71

Circumferential force is being same as in conventional milling but is directed every where downwards. The radial force is smaller because of the favourable start of the cut and is also directed down wards along with the resultant force.

15.33 Form-relieved Cutter

Figure 15.72 shows a typical form-milling cutter which is backed off or relieved in such a manner as to maintain the accuracy of its form after regrinding. This type of cutter is relieved on what is known as a relieving lathe and which has a cam-operated tool slide. It has a relief of 4 mm. By relieving the cutter in this manner the cutting form is maintained right through the tooth. When sharpening the cutter, the teeth are ground on the front only and the cutting form is not interfered with.

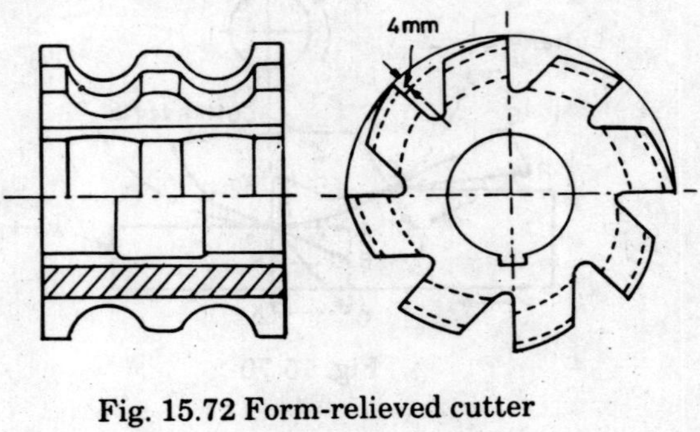

Fig. 15.72 Form-relieved cutter

15.34 Circular Form Tools

Circular form tool is used either on the front or back side, is fixed to the holder by a bolt and prevented from rotating when cutting by serrations formed on a boss on one side of the tool which fit in similar serrations on the tool holder. Fig. 15.73 shows a circular form tool.

Circular tools may or may not be provided to the top rake.

In both cases with or without top rake the tool control is always set above the work piece centre to give the required clearance angle.

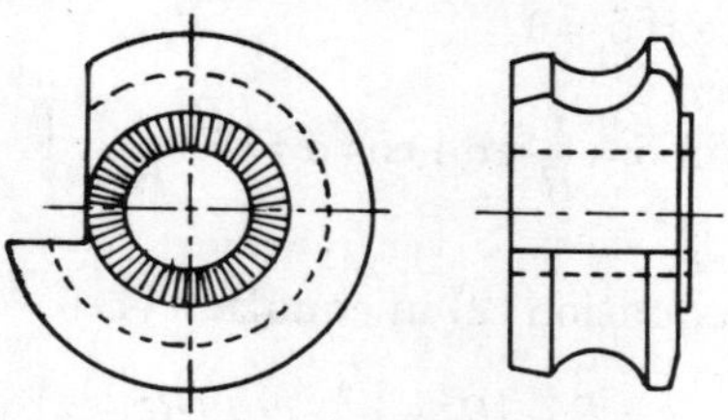

Fig. 15.73

(*i*) Circular form tool without top rake

Fig. 15.74 shows a circular form tool without top rake.

θ = clearance angle

x = Differential in centre height of workpiece and tool

R = Radius of tool

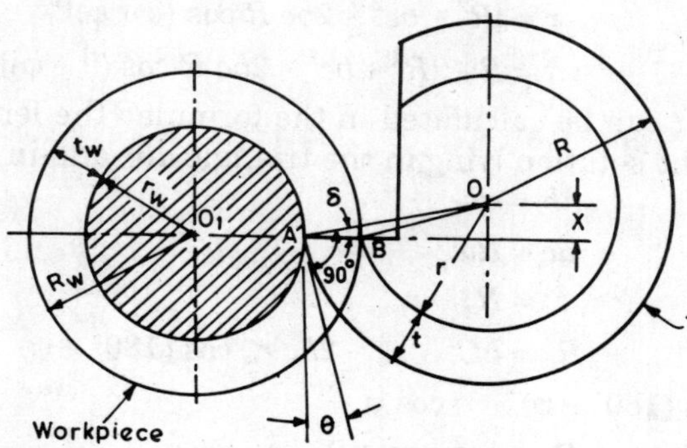

Fig. 15.74

In Δ *OAC*

$$x = R.\sin\theta$$

In Δ ABC, Let $AC = R$

$$BC = r$$

In Δ ABC

$$AC = R$$
$$BC = r$$
$$AB = a = t\omega$$

we have $r^2 = R^2 + a^2 - 2aR \cos \delta$ and $t \doteq R - r$

Therefore $t = R - (R^2 + a^2 - 2aR \cos \delta)^{\frac{1}{2}}$ ...(1)

If angle θ has not been previously calculated, then angle δ is not a known quantity, but x and R are usually standard figure for the machine, therefore if $\delta = \theta$

Then, $\sin \delta = \dfrac{x}{R}$ and $\cos \delta = \left(\dfrac{R^2 - x^2}{R}\right)^{1/2}$

...(2)

Substituting equation (2) in equation (1)

$$t = R - [R^2 + a^2 - 2a\,(R^2 - x^2)^{\frac{1}{2}}]^{\frac{1}{2}}$$

(*ii*) **Circular form tools with top rake :**

It is again necessary to calculate, t. It is shown in Fig. 15.75.

In Δ obc, $ob = R$, $oc = r$

$$t = ob - oc$$

Now, $oc^2 = ob^2 + bc^2 - 2bc\,.\,ob\,.\cos(\theta + \varphi)$

$$r^2 = R^2 + bc^2 - 2bc\,R \cos(\theta + \varphi)$$
$$r = [R^2 + bc^2 - 2bc\,R \cos(\theta + \varphi)]^{1/2}$$
$$t = R - [R^2 + bc^2 - 2bc\,R \cos(\theta + \varphi)]^{1/2}$$

Before t can be calculated in the formulae the length bc must be found, the solution lying in the triangle abc and in this triangle is $ab = rw$

$$ac = Rw$$

and $t_w = R_w - r_w$

Now, $R_w^2 = bC^2 + r_w^2 - 2bc\,r_w \cos(180° - \varphi)$

but $\cos(180° - \varphi) = -\cos\varphi$

Therefore $R_w^2 = bc^2 + r_w^2 + 2bc\,r_w \cos\varphi$

resolving quadratic equating to find bc,

$$bc = -r_w \cos\varphi + \left(\frac{4r_w^2 \cos^2\varphi + 4R_w^2 - 4r_w^2}{4}\right)^{\frac{1}{2}}$$

$$bc = -r_w \cos\varphi + [r_w \cos^2\varphi + t_w\,(R_w + r_w)]^{\frac{1}{2}}$$

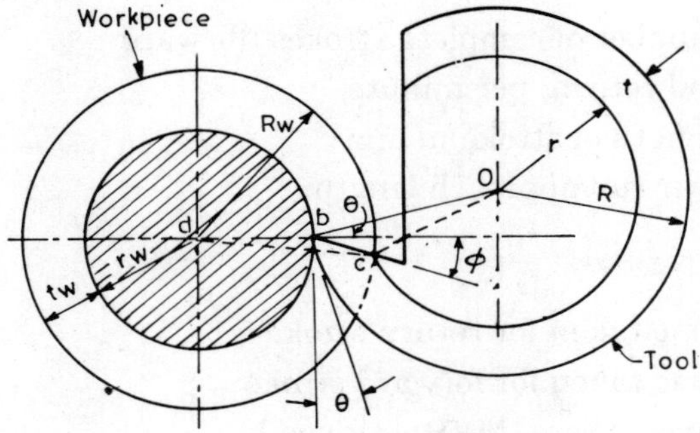

Fig. 15.75

15.35 Shaping and Planing

The shaper is also called shaping machine and it is used to produce a flat surface with the help of a single point cutting tool reciprocating over the stationary workpiece. as shown in Fig. 15.76.

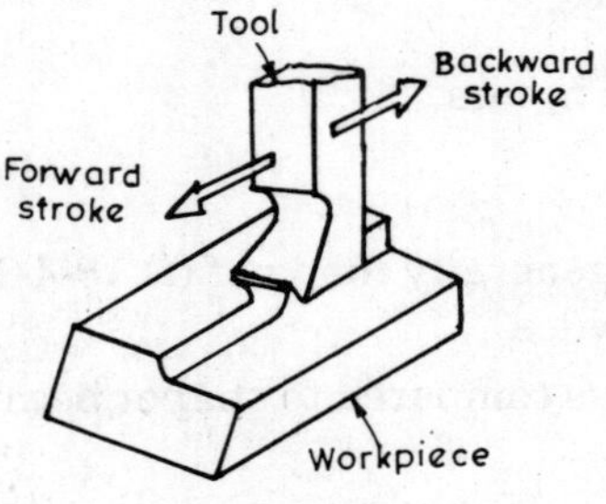

Fig. 15.76

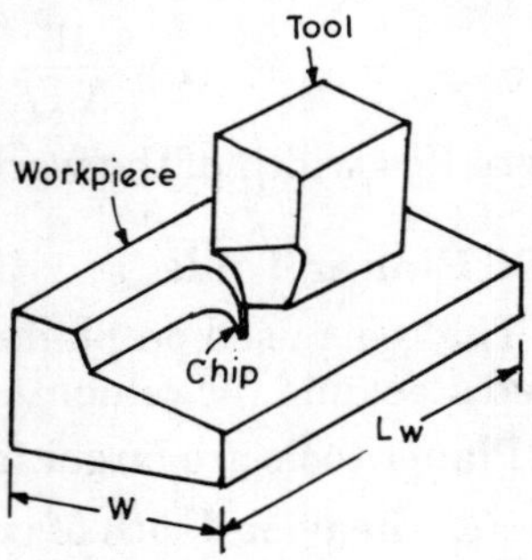

Fig. 15.77

The planer is also used to produce flat surface using a single point cutting tool. In this case the tool is stationary and the work piece reciprocates as shown in Fig. 15.77.

Planer can handle bigger jobs as compared to shaper and the depth of cut is more in case of planer.

Planer size is expressed by

(*i*) width of table in mm

(*ii*) Maximum distance of the table to the cross rail in metres

(*iii*) Maximum stroke of the table is mm.

In shaping or planing machining operation the cutting speed is given by the following formula :

$$V = \text{cutting speed} \quad = \frac{N\,(L + A)\,(1 + n)}{1000}\,\text{m/min}$$

where N = Number of complete strokes (forward and return) per minute

L = Length of stroke in mm

A = over run/approach length

$$n = \frac{t_1}{t_2}$$

where t_1 = Time taken for return stroke

t_2 = Time taken for forward stroke

Metal removal rate (MRR) is given by

$$\text{MRR} = f \,.\, d \,.\, N \,.\, L_\omega \text{ mm}^3\text{/min}$$

where f = Feed in mm

d = Depth of cut in mm.

L_ω = Length of work piece.

Cutting time (T) is calculated as follows

$$T = \frac{W}{N \,.\, f} \text{ minutes}$$

where W = width of the workpiece in mm.

15.36 Planer Tools

The tools used on planer are generally made of (*i*) 18-4-1 high speed steel and (*ii*) cemented carbides.

Planer tools are larger in size as compared to shaper because of

(*i*) heavier depth of cut

(*ii*) larger cutting strokes.

Planer tools may be classified as

(*i*) roughing tools (see Fig. 15.78)

(*ii*) finishing tools (see Fig. 15.79)

(*iii*) grooving tools (Fig. 15.80)

(*iv*) T-slot cutting tools (Fig. 15.81)

(*v*) Dove tail side cutting tools (Fig. 15.82)

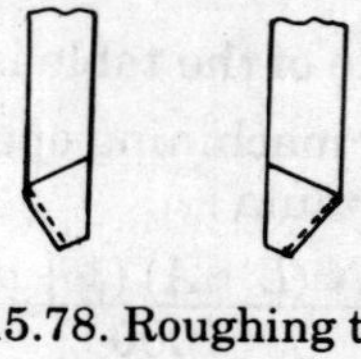

Fig. 15.78. Roughing tools

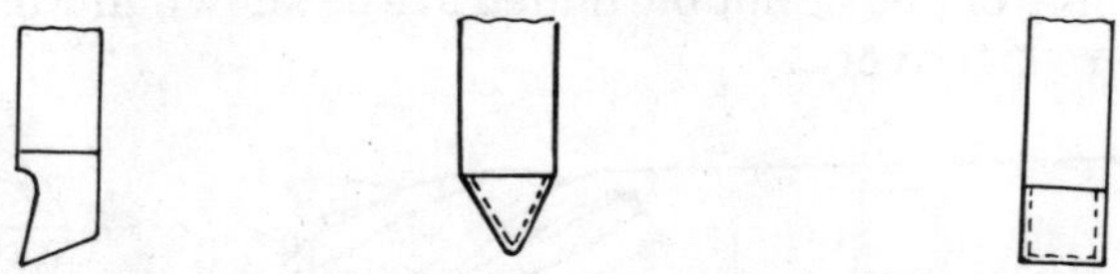

(*i*) Straight. (*ii*) Round nose. (*iii*) Square nose.

Fig. 15.79 Finishing tools.

Fig. 15.80 Grooving tool.

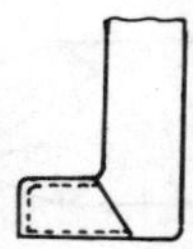

Fig. 15.81 T-slot cutting tool.

Fig. 15.82 Dovetail slide cutting tool.

15.37 Classification of End Mill Cutters

The work performed by end mills is usually of a light character. Two types of end mills are as follows:

(*i*) *Right hand spiral cutter* :- It is for right hand cutting. The blades are made with a right hand spiral usually not more then 20° and have a front cutting rake angle of 10°. It is quite commonly used. It has a tapped hole at the end of the shank so that the cutter can be held firmly into its socket (see Fig. 15.83).

(*ii*) *Left hand spiral cutter* :- It has spiral angle of 10°. Font rake angle should not exceed 7°. (see Fig. 15.84).

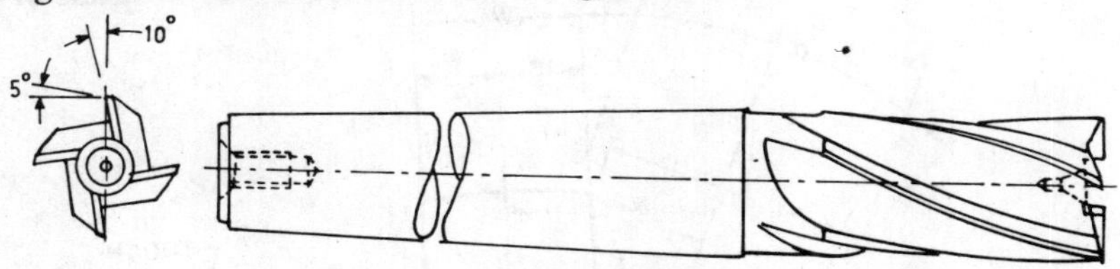

Fig. 15.83

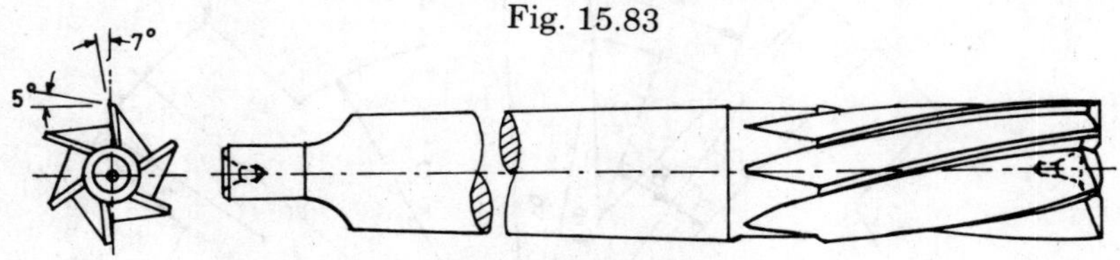

Fig. 15.84

The solid end mills may be of

(*i*) Two flued end mills when they have two cutting edges

(*ii*) Multiple flued end mills when they have three cutting edges, for cutting edges, etc.

(*iv*) Single ended or double ended are as shown in Fig. 15.85 and Fig. 15.86 respectively.

Fig. 15.85

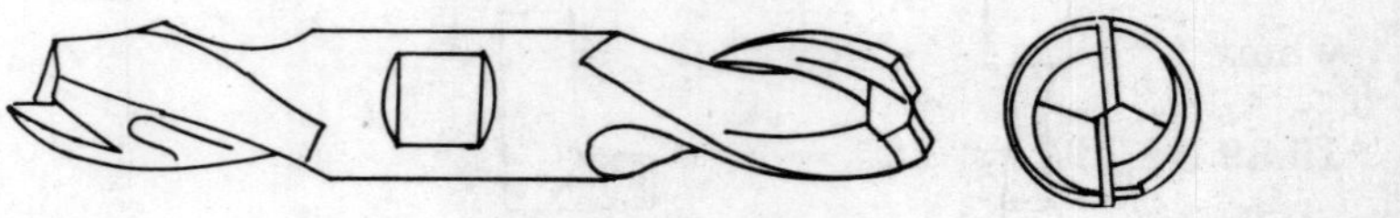

Fig. 15.86

(*iv*) They may be centre relieved (Fig. 15.85) or they may be of centre cutting end mills (Fig. 15.86) in which case the cutting edges on the end of end mill meets in the centre.

15.38 Spline Cutter

Fig. 15.87 shows the typical dimensions of a spline cutter.

$$\sin\beta = \frac{W}{D_1} \quad ; \quad \theta = \frac{\alpha}{2} - \beta$$

$X = D_1 \sin\theta$ = dimension across sharp corners of cutter.

where D_1 = Root diameter.

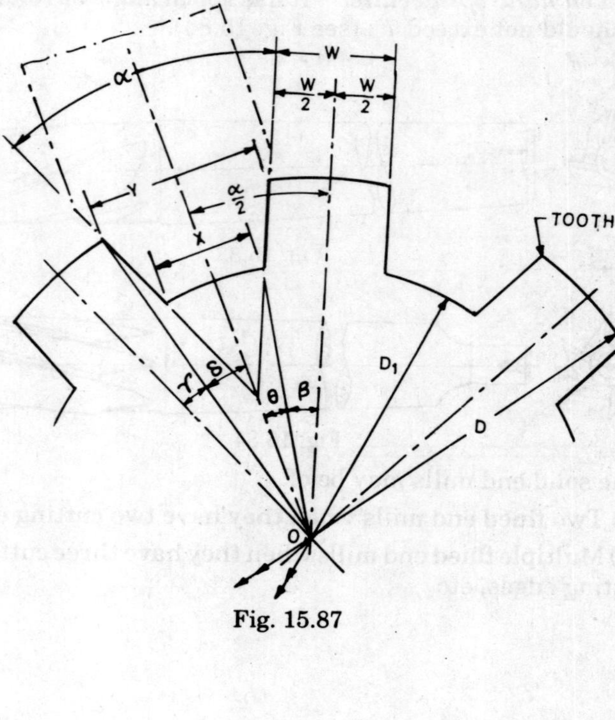

Fig. 15.87

The checking dimension Y (which may be measured with gear tooth calipers) is determined as follows :

$$\sin \gamma = \frac{W}{D} \text{ and } \delta = \frac{a}{2} - \gamma$$

$\therefore$ $Y = D \sin \delta$ = dimension of cutter at to of spline.

where D = outside diameter of cutter

15.39 Key Way Broaching

In key way broaching the simple broaching fixture are of various spigots Fig. 15.88 shows a typical spigot for key way broaching. The diameter A is made to fit the hole in the machine table, and the flat B is located against a shoulder or plate on the table to prevent movement of the spigot. Diameter C is made a push fit in the component, whilst the bottom of the groove D controls the depth of key way to be cut- the total depth of the groove plus the depth of key way required equalling the maximum depth of the broach at the largest end. By using a hardened shim similar to that shown at E, it is possible to cut a key way deeper than the total cutting depth of the broach. The broach is pulled through the work in the usual manner, and then the shim is placed in the bottom of groove D and the broach is pulled through again. The lip shown on the shim bears against the end of the spigot and prevents the shim being pulled through the slot by the friction of the broach.

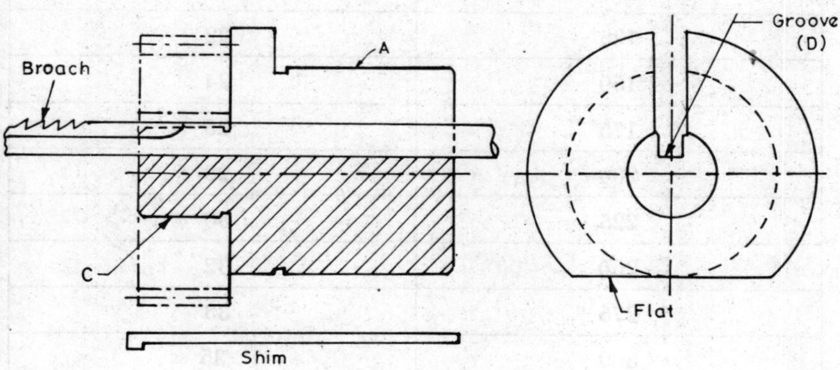

Fig. 15.88

Fig. 15.89. Shows a spigot for broaching key way in a taper hole.

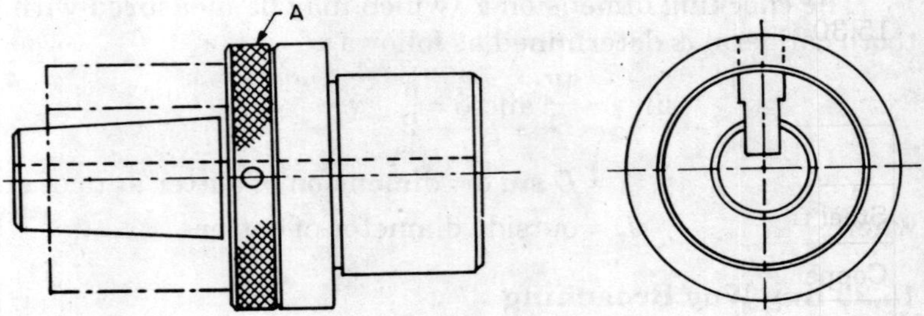

Fig. 15.89

15.40 Pitch of Broach Teeth

The pitch of teeth of broach mainly depends on *(i)* length of the workpiece to be broached and *(ii)* material of the workpiece.

Table 15.29

Hole length (mm)	*Pitch of teeth (mm)*
25	10
50	14
75	16
100	20
125	22
150	24
175	26
200	28
225	30
250	32
275	33
300	35

The pitch should be such that at least two to three teeths are cut at any given time.

p = Pitch (mm)

$= 2\sqrt{2}$, where L = length of hole in mm

Table 15.29 indicates pitch for various work lengths. Table 15.30 indicates front cutting angle for some of the work materials.

Table 15.30

Material	*From cutting angle*
Steel tubes	12–15°
Copper	15°
Aluminium	10–12°
Steel forgings	7–10°
Cast steel	7–10°
Cast and malleable iron	0.5°
Bronze	0°

15.41 Cut per Tooth

Average cut per tooth for broach is indicated in table 15.31 when components are made of cast iron, steel or aluminium.

Table 15.31

Type of broach	*Chip thickness (mm)*
Round holes	0.05 mm
Splines	0.06 mm
Key ways	0.085 mm

For bronze components cut per tooth may be upto 0.15 mm.

Example 15.14. *Sketch a typical punch-die set for blanking and frequency operation, also name the parts..*

Solution. Fig. 15.90 shows various parts which are indicated in Table 15.32.

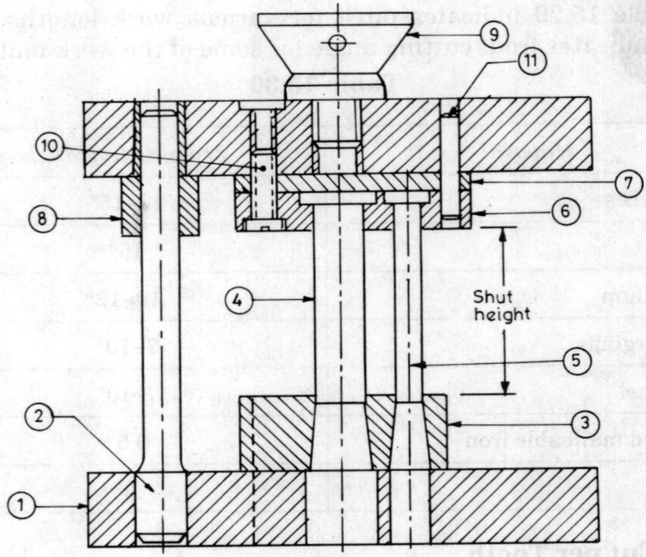

Fig. 15.90

Table 15.32

Sl. No	*Part Name*	*Material*	*Hardness (HRC)*
1.	Bottom Bolster	M.S.	
2.	Guide Piller	OHNS	50-52
3.	Die Plate	HCHCr	60-62
4.	Blanking Punch	HCHCr	60-62
5.	Piercing Punch	HCHCr	60-62
6.	Punch Holder	M.S.	—
7.	Thrust Plate	M.S.	—
8.	Guide Bush	OHNS	50-52
9.	Shank	M.S.	—
10.	Allen Bolt	C-35	45-50
11.	Dowell Pin	C-40	48-50

Example 15.15. *(a) Sketch and describe two types of core drills.*

(b) Sketch and describe a side and face milling cutter.

Solution. Fig. 15.91 shows two types of core drills.

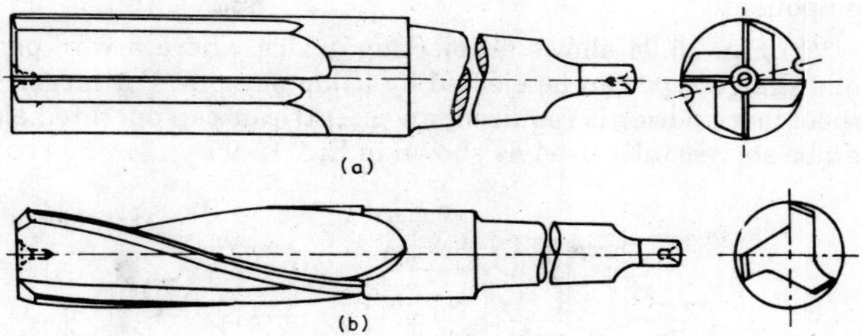

Fig. 15.91 Core drills.

(*b*) Fig. 15.92 shows a side and face milling cutter. It is a general type of milling cutter and can be used for milling faces with a edge beneath, or a slot, or in gangs for milling either side of one or more bosses at the same time.

Angle of cleance is nearly 5° to 7° whereas angle of rake is about 7°

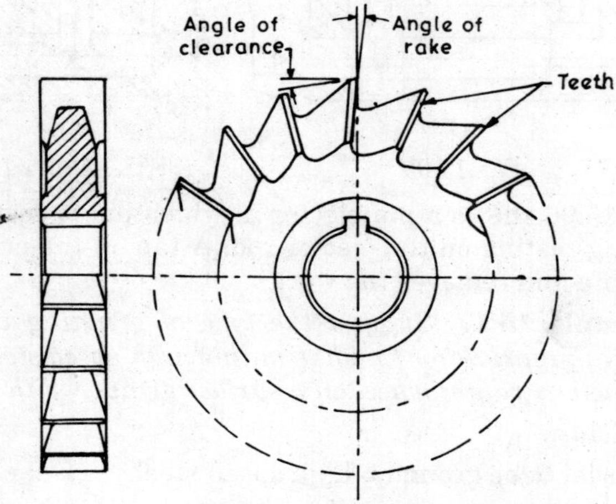

Fig. 15.92

Example 15.16. *(a) Sketch and explain a drill bush for guiding and clamping*

(*b*) *Sketch and explain three work ejecting devices.*

Solution. (*a*) Fig. 15.93 shows a bush for grinding the tool and clamping the work piece. The recessed end of the bush fits over a boss on the work piece and is clamped by the spring plunger acting on the handle. This is depressed to rause the bush and release the component.

(*b*) Fig. 15.94 shows an ejecting device where a workpiece of solid flange type can be ejected by using one pin. For larger work wheel more power is required; an eccentric or can operated ejector can be successfully used as shown in Fig. 15.95.

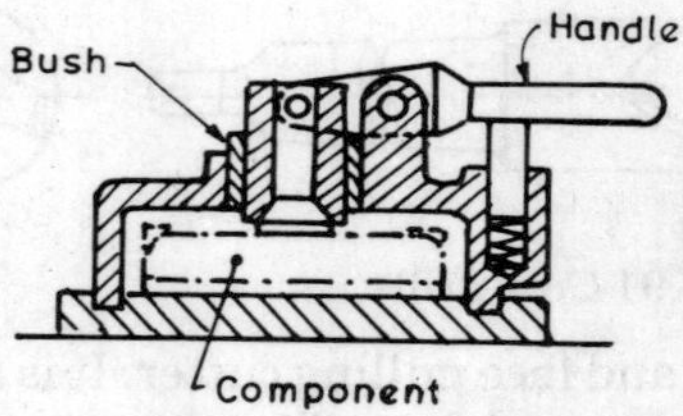

Fig. 15.93 Bush for guiding and clamping.

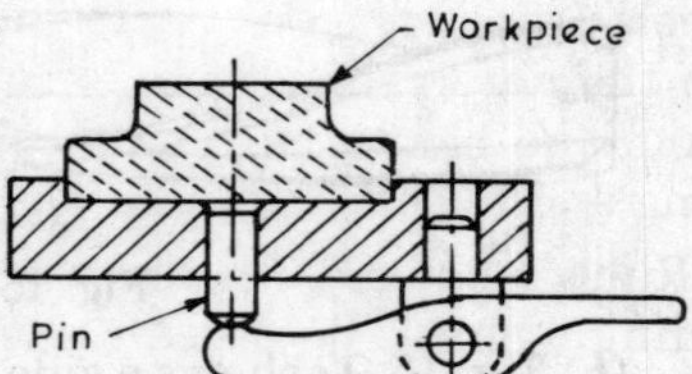

Fig. 15.94

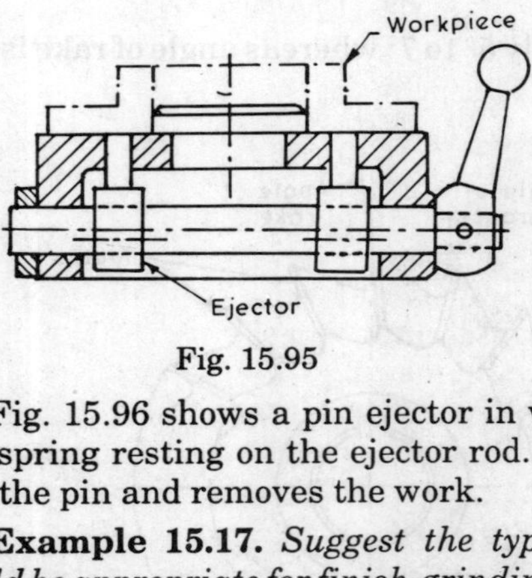

Fig. 15.95

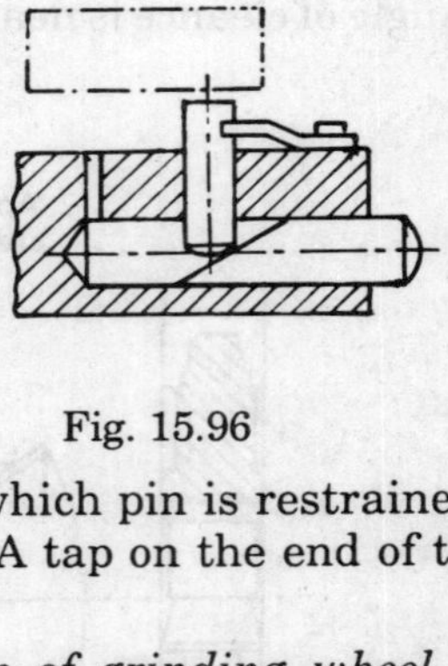
Fig. 15.96

Fig. 15.96 shows a pin ejector in which pin is restrained by a leaf spring resting on the ejector rod. A tap on the end of the rod lifts the pin and removes the work.

Example 15.17. *Suggest the type of grinding wheel which would be appropriate for finish-grinding high-speed steel with a 150 mm diameter straight wheel on a surface grinder with no coolant.*

Solution.

Material to be ground = high speed steel.

Grinding wheel suggested = A 60 k6

where A stands for aluminium oxide grit and 60 indicates grit size. K indicates grade of grinding wheel which is of a softer grade. This is suitable for high speed steel which is quite hard.

For surface finish, the grinding medium structure should be used. This 6 structures may be used.

For cylindrical grinding 8 structures should be used for roughing operation and a 5 structures for finishing operation.

Surface grinding requires a more open structure than cylindrical grinding.

Example 15.18. *Compare the applications of following types of grinding wheels*

(a) Resinoid bonded (ii) Rubber bonded (iii) Shellac bonded (iv) Oxychloride bonded and Celluloid bonded grinding wheels.

Solution. Resinoid bonding material is an organic bond. Wheels so bonded are made by mixing powdered synthetic resin with the abrasive, pressing the mixture into the wheel form in a mould, and baking it in an electrical oven. These wheels are very strong and may be operated at surface speeds of upto 3000 mpm.

Rubber-bonded wheels use natural or synthetic rubber as a bonding agent. The process consists of mixing the abrasive with rubber, rolling the mixture into sheets of the desired thickness, cutting the sheets into the desired diameters, and vulcanizing them. Because of their flexibility they can be used at high surface speeds (5000 mm) for high surface finish. The flexibility also makes it possible, the manufacturing of wheels under 1 mm thick. These wheels may be used as cutoff wheels.

Shellac bonds are also used for high-finishing and thin cutoff wheels. These wheels are baked at low temperatures and because of the low-temperature bond breakdown high finishes are possible.

Oxychloride-and celluloid-bonded wheels are not very common. Abrasive grains and magnesium oxychloride (oxidizing oil) are mixed and compressed in moulds into wheel shapes. Celluloid-bonded wheels are formed by rolling the mixture of the celluloid and the abrasive into sheets and then cutting them into the desired diameters.

Example 15.19. *State the factors which effect the selection of cutting fluids during metal cutting.*

Solution. Metal cutting fluids are widely used in machining operations.

Cutting fluids are used to

(*i*) increase tool life
(*ii*) reduce cutting forces
(*iii*) reduce power consumption
(*iv*) reduce cost per unit volume of material removed
(*v*) obtain desired cutting temperature
(*vi*) obtain good surface finish

Selection of cutting fluid depends on the following factors

(*i*) work piece material
(*ii*) Machining operation

(*iii*) tool material
(*iv*) cutting fluid properties
(*v*) heat-generated during cutting
(*vi*) machining variables such as
(*a*) cutting speed (*b*) feed and (*c*) depth of cut

Example 15.20. *Explain the importance of machinability*
(*a*) *of a material*
(*b*) *state machining process input and output variables.*

Solution. (*a*) Machinability is a measure of case with which a work material can be satisfactorily machined. The machinability aspect is of considerable importance, so that machining process can be planned in an efficient manner. Machinability helps in proper selection of: (*i*) cutting tool (*ii*) cutting fluid and (*iii*) proper material for making a component.

The machinability of engineering materials has a marked influence on the production cost. Machinability assessment is carried out with respect to

(*i*) cutting tool life
(*ii*) cutting forces
(*iii*) specific energy consumed
(*iv*) surface finish desired
(*v*) dimensional accuracy of the processes surface
(*vi*) size and form of chips
(*vii*) machining process

(*b*) A machining process is defined by
(*i*) input and (*ii*) output variable.

The input variables are

(*i*) work material and its properties
(*ii*) tool material and its geometry
(*iii*) machine tool rigidity and capacity
(*iv*) cutting conditions
(*v*) cutting fluid.

The machining process output variables are

(*i*) tool life
(*ii*) cutting forces
(*iii*) specific energy consumed
(*iv*) surface finish
(*v*) dimensional accuracy of the processed surface
(*vi*) types of clips

Example 15.21. (*a*) *Discuss applications of diamond grinding wheels,* (*b*) *State the purpose of cutting fluids during grinding and* (*c*) *State the factors which are considered while selecting a grinding wheel.*

Solution.

(*a*) Diamond wheels are used to grind or cut materials such as carbide, glass, stone, marble, and ceramics. The diamonds are opaque and are also used for industrial purposes. They are crushed with heavy manganese steel rollers and then sorted into various grain sizes. In varied degree of concentrations, they are mixed with a bond. Longer life and better finishes are achieved with lower concentration of diamond grit. The reduction in production costs for the lower concentration of diamond grit more than offset the cost of the wheels with higher degrees of diamond grit concentration.

(*b*) The grinding operation generates a great deal of localized heat at the contact point of the wheel and the work. Since grinding is a true cutting process, chips are created. The use of cutting fluids (Soluble oils) will, if properly applied, wash away the chips to prevent clogging the pores. The fluid also reduces the localized heating. Fine surface cracks may develop from localized heating of the material . Failure to remove the chips may result in scratched work surfaces or glazing.

(*c*) The grinding wheels is the cutting tools used in grinding operation, high rates of metal removal as accomplished with a tool bit is not possible. However many materials which can not be cut with the conventional cutting tools can be machined with the use of a grinding wheel. Five factors which are considered while selecting a grinding wheel are as follows :

(*i*) Type of abrasive such as
  (*a*) Aluminium oxide (A) (*b*) Silicon carbide (C)
  (*c*) Diamond (*D*)

(*ii*) Grit size such as
  (*a*) coarse (*b*) medium
  (*c*) full (*d*) very full

(*iii*) grade such as
  (*a*) soft (*b*) medium and (*c*) hard

(*iv*) Structure
  (*a*) close, (*b*) medium and (*c*) wide

(*v*) Bond such as
  (*a*) Vixtified (V) (*b*) Resenoid (B) (*c*) Rubber (R)
  (*d*) Shellac (E) (*e*) Silicate (S)

For example in a grinding wheel specified by, *A* 60 *K* 8 *V G*

(*i*) *A* indicates aluminium oxide abrasive

(*ii*) 60 indicates grit size

(*iii*) *K* indicates grade

(*iv*) 8 indicates structure

(*v*) *V* indicates vitrified bond

(*vi*) *G* indicates manufacturer's code

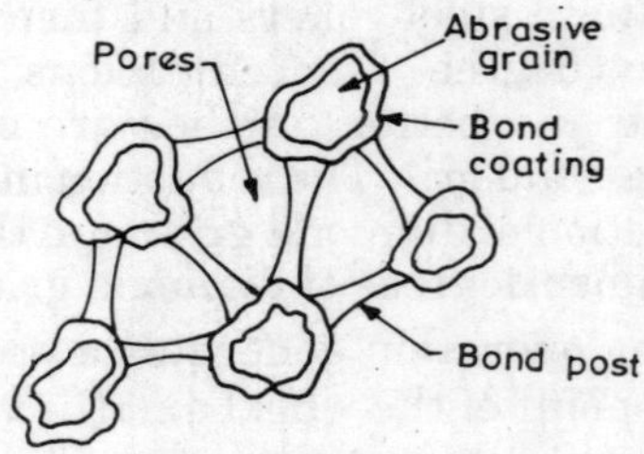

Fig. 15.97.

The hardness of a wheel refers to the strength of the bond, not to the hardness of the grit. The grit is held in position by the bond posts as shown in Fig. 15.97. If the bond posts break easily, the wheel is said to be soft even though the abrasive is diamond. The range of harness of the bond increases from *A*, soft, through *Z*, hard

(1) Rough-grinding jobs require grades from the middle to the end of the alphabet (the harder grades). Precision grinding dictates the softer bonds at the beginning of the alphabet. (2) In general the harder the material to be ground, the softer should be the grade to be used. (3) The smaller the area of contact between wheel and work, the harder is the grade permitted.

In general, coarse grains should be selected for grinding soft or ductile materials or when fast grinding is desired. The finer the grain size, the higher is the finish achieved. Fine grain wheels also should be used on brittle and hard materials.

Example 15.22. (*a*) *Why centre point of twist drill should be at the centre of rotation of drill*

(*b*) *State the applications of natural abrasives and synthetic abrasives.*

Solution.

(*a*) The centre point of twist drill should be at the centre of rotation of drill as shown in Fig. 15.98. This is essential to produce hole of exact size. In the case

$$\alpha_1 = \alpha_2 \text{ and } L_1 = L_2$$

If the centre point of drill is not at the centre of rotation a side thrust will be developed and the drilled hole will be larger than drill diameter it self.

(*b*) Natural abrasives include

(*i*) Emery (*ii*) Quartz

(*iii*) Sandstone (*iv*) Garret etc.

The synthetic abrasives are

(*i*) Aluminium Oxide (Al_2O_3)

(*ii*) Silicon Carbide Sic

(*iii*) Diamond.

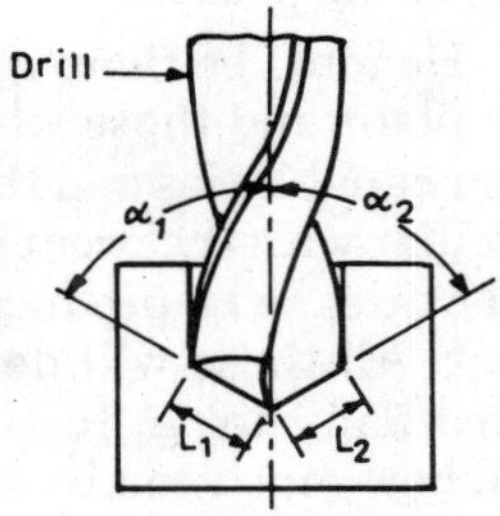

Fig. 15.98

The natural abrasives are not widely used for precision grinding because of the impurities in their structure. The synthetic abrasives, products of the electric furnace, are controlled so that the impurities are held to a minimum, and the physical properties of the grains may also be controlled during manufacturing. The abrasive material is charged into an electric furnace with other products (coke, salt, etc.) and heated to high temperature until it fuses. The fused material is crushed between rollers and graded.

The physical properties of aluminium oxide compared with silicon carbide are :

(*i*) Silicon carbide is harder than aluminium oxide.

(*ii*) Silicon carbide is more brittle and therefore not as tough as aluminium oxide.

(*iii*) Aluminium oxide can withstand greater stresses than silicon carbide.

(*iv*) Aluminium oxide wheels are used to grind high-tensile-strength and tough materials such as steel, malleable and wrought iron ; whereas, the silicon carbide wheels are used to grind low-tensile strength materials and nonmetallic materials such as gray iron, stainless steel, soft nonferrous materials, marble, stone, or rubber and many hard materials such as carbide.

Diamond abrasives are used to grind carbides and other very hard or highly abrasive materials such as marble, gems, stone, etc.

Example 15.23. *Discuss the requirements of a tool engineer.*

Solution. The production of a part or an assembly can be a very complicated endeavour. The tool engineer is the professional who has the job of assisting the product engineer in the design and refinement of the product, in designing or purchasing the machinery, tools, fixtures, dies and gauges, to be used in producing the parts and in their assembly into the final product. He is responsible for maintaining the quality consistent with minimum cost of the product.

He must be thoroughly familiar with the available machines in the plant and those which may be purchased. He must also know their capabilities and their limitations. He must then be thoroughly familiar with the product to be manufactured, the precision desired, quantities to be produced, job lot sizes, lead times, and cost limitations. All these will determine how the product will be manufactured and this, in turn, will determine the kind of tooling needed and how much can be spent on this tooling.

Tool Engineer must be familiar with all available standard parts ; what is available as standard but can be altered to meet job needs ; what can be cast, welded, or stamped ; and what needs to be machined. Unless parts are needed in very large quantities, in most instances it is cheaper to buy standard parts than it is to make them.

When it comes down to the actual design of the tools, jigs, fixtures and machines, the tool engineer must follow a plan of action or design procedures.

Example 15.24. *State the factors which effects the quality of finished components.*

The quality of work produced in a factory greatly depends on the accuracy and suitability of

(*i*) Machine tools (*ii*) Cutting tools

(*iii*) Jigs & fixtures (*iv*) Gauges used

(*v*) Inspection

The inspection equipment available to the tool inspector must be capable of much greater precision than that used for normal inspection in he workshop. Inspection should be concerned with every thing entering the factory from the raw material to the finished assembly.

Good design and standards lead to good quality. Inspection system should be such that it should ensure (*i*) adequate quality and (*ii*) reliability without incurrng the cost of an unnecessary elaborated inspection system.

Example 15.25. *Fig. 15.99 shows a single point cutting tool having*

Front relief angle = 6°

Side relief angle = 7°

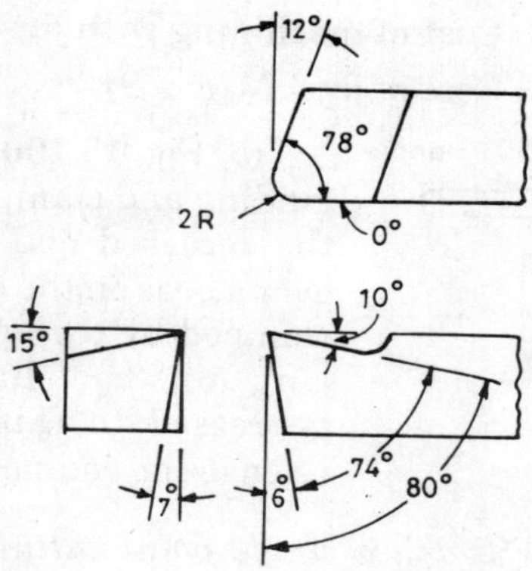

Fig. 15.99

Back rake angle = 10°

Side rake angle = 15°

Nose radius = 2 mm

End cutting-edge angle = 12°

Side cutting-edge angle = 0°

Indicate the following angles

(*a*) Lip angle, (*b*) Cutting angle and

(*c*) Nose angle

Solution.

$$\text{Lip angle} = 90 - (10 + 6) = 74°$$

$$\text{Cutting angle} = 90 - 10 = 80°$$

$$\text{Nose angle} = 90 - (12 + 0) = 78°$$

Example 15.26. *(a) Discuss economics of using jigs and fixtures in machining (b) sketch and describe a jig bush for guiding and clamping.*

Solution. (*a*) The main functions of jigs and fixtures are

(*i*) to reduce cost by the elimination of manual location of components.

(*ii*) to assure interchangeability of machined parts

(*iii*) to enable high grade work to be performed by unskilled labour.

When planing a machining operation consideration should be given to the cost of machining the work with jig and without jig.

Let N = Number of components.

E = Cost of machining without jig

S = Cost of machining with jig

C = Cost of jig = $N(E - S)$

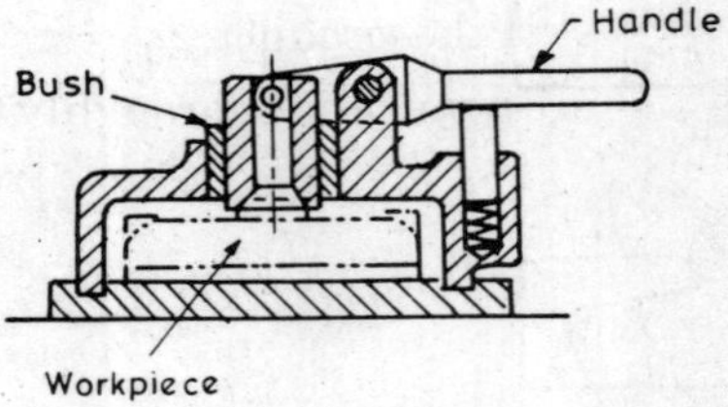

Fig. 15.100

(*b*) Fig. 15.100 shows a bush for guiding and clamping. In this bush the recessed end of the bush fits over a boss on the component and is clamped by the spring plunger acting on the handle. This is depressed to raise the bush and release the component.

Example 15.27. *Sketch a single point cutting tool with rake, positive back rake and negative back rake.*

Solution. Figure 15.101 shows a tool with zero back rake. Fig. 15.102 one positive back rake ; and Fig. 15.103 (*c*) one with a negative back rake. A zero rake will project a line from the top of the tool through the center of the work, as shown. Positive rake sets up a "scooping" action. Negative rake sets up a "bulldozer" action. Tools may also have negative side rake or combinations of positive and negative back and side rakes.

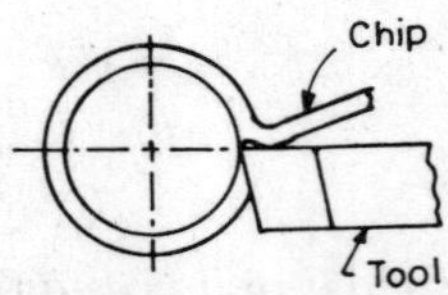

Fig. 15.101

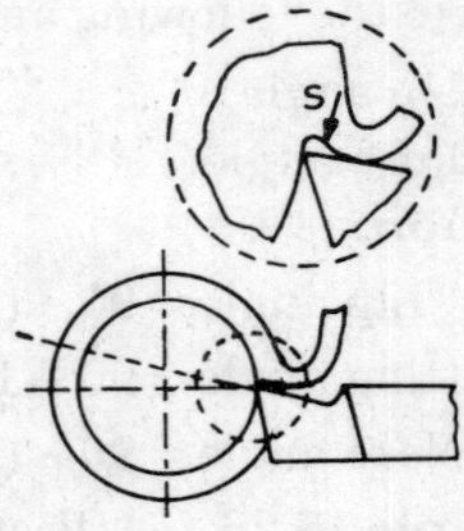

Fig. 15.102

Figure 15.102 (*b*) shows the shearing force of the material acting on the tip of the tool. In Fig. 15.103 (*c*) the shearing force is greater but acts back of the tip where the strength of the tool is greater. The shear force (S) is acting as shown.

Example 15.28. *(a) Sketch and describe three types of cemented carbide tools*

(*b*) *Sketch and describe three types of diamond turning tools.*

Solution. (*a*) Fig. 15.104 shows three types of cemented carbide tools. The shank is made of carbon. Steel with carbon 0.5%.

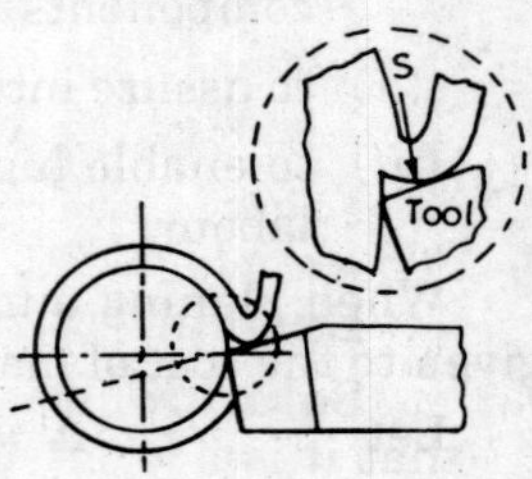

Fig. 15.103

Tools shown at (*b*) and (*c*) are used for heavy cutting where as tool shown at (*c*) is used for light turning and facing where a belt finish is required.

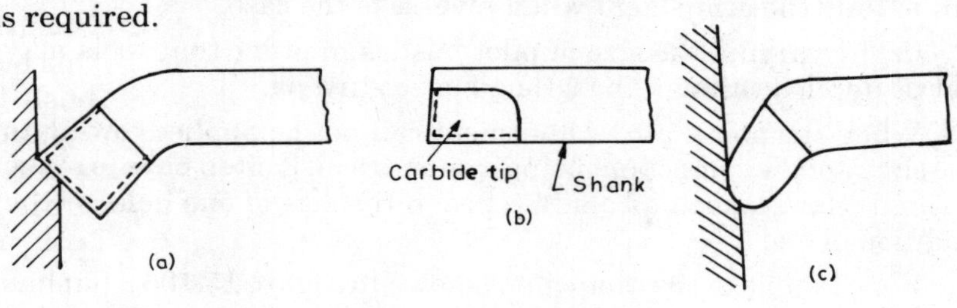

Fig. 15.104

(*b*) **Diamond turning tools**

Diamonds are shaped and polished to suitable angles and mounted in holders. The tools be suitably mounted and used for light cuts up to 0.125 mm deep at high speed. The cutting edges for boring and turning may be classified as shown in Figure 15.105 (*a*) with one cutting edge, (*b*) with a circular cutting edge, and (*c*) with several facets around the contour of the tool nose.

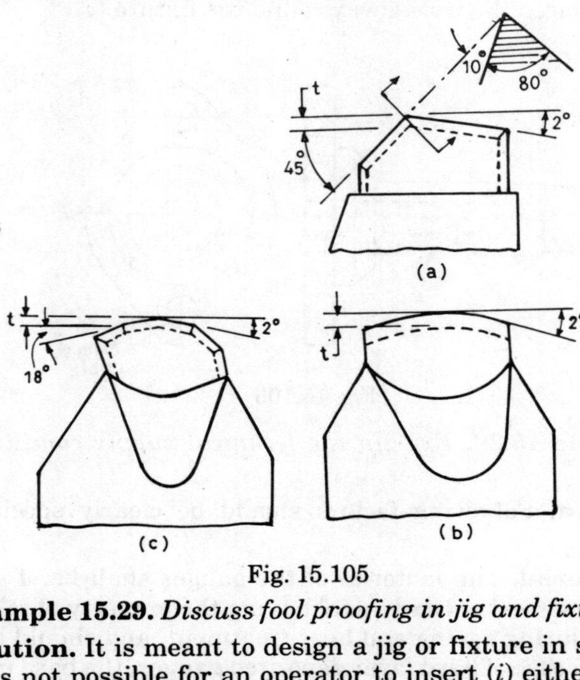

Fig. 15.105

Example 15.29. *Discuss fool proofing in jig and fixture.*

Solution. It is meant to design a jig or fixture in such a way that it is not possible for an operator to insert (*i*) either the work piece or (*ii*) the cutting tool in any position other than the correct position.

This can be achieved (*i*) by placing a pin or abutment in a position to clear the component when it is in correct relative position but fouling the component when reverse is the case.

(*ii*) by varying the size of pilot bushes in order that tools may not be applied through the wrong bushes in a jig.

When the above pin or abutment can not be applied, owing to the shape of the component being symmetrical, it often pays to make a small change, such as a difference in the size of one hole, or the addition of one hole.

For example in the component shown in Figure 15.106 a flat has to be millled at *A*, and the fixture is arranged so that a number stand on the flange in line and an end mill of the correct width is passed along them using a horizontal milling machine. The flat has to be in correct relationship with the hole at *B*. Because of the component being originally symmetrical, it is possible to place the parts in the fixture so that the flat is machined on the opposite positive to the hole *B* with the result that components are not rejected. By changing the size of one of the holes in the flange from 7 to 8 mm and altering the locating pins in the fixture to suit the components cannot be placed the wrong way round the fixture.

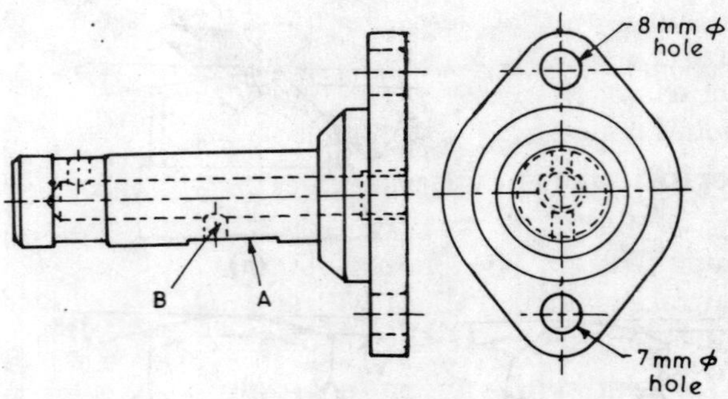

Fig. 15.106

Example 15.30. *Explain the technical supply conditions for gauges.*

Solution. Following factors should be clearly specified for gauges.

(*i*) **Material.** The material of the gauges shall be of suitable quality gauge steel or hard metal having the property of relatining dimension during ageing and heat treatment, and should be wear resistant. In case of hard layer deposited gauges, the base material should be of good quality.

Suitable examples of steel from IS : 1570-1961 are given below:

Sl. No.	*Designation*
1	T215Cr12
2	T105Cr1Mn60
3	T105Cr1
4	T90V23
5	T90Mn2W50Cr45
6	17Mn1Cr95

(*ii*) **Hardness.** The measuring surface of the gauges shall have a hardness of 60 HRC minimum. In case of hard layer deposited gauges, hardness should be checked using a micro hardness tester.

(*iii*) **Tolerances**

(*a*) For dimensions without tolerances on gauges with plain and cylindrical surfaces, the medium class of deviations according to IS : 2102-1969 'Allowable deviations for dimensions without specified tolerances' shall apply.

(*b*) The form tolerance of the gauging surface on working gauges shall be maximum one grade less than the manufacturing tolerance of the gauge dimensions. In case of accuracy grade 7 and above for the manufacturing tolerances of the gauge dimensions, the form tolerance should not be greater than IT5.

(*iv*) **Inscriptions.** The inscriptions shall be legible and free from burrs.

(*v*) **Surface Finish.** The average roughness value (Ra) for the measuring surface given in Table 15.33 depends upon the manufacturing tolerance for the measuring surface.

Table 15.33. Permissible average roughness value (Ra) for measuring surfaces in microns

Manufacturing Tolerance for the 'Gauge Dimension'		*Average Roughness value (Ra)*	
Above	Up to	Plain	Threaded
± 0.8	± 1.5	0.04	0.1
± 1.5	± 4	0.063	0.16
± 4	± 10	0.1	0.25
± 10	± 25	0.16	0.4

(*vi*) **Workmanship ;**

(*a*) The gauges and gauge members shall be well-finished, free from defects which may effect their serviceability and shall be consistent with the grade of the product.

(*b*) The gauges and gauge members shall be demagnetized.

(*c*) All sharp corners and edges of measuring surfaces shall be broken burrs.

(*vii*) **Marking.** The gauges shall be marked with the following:

(*a*) Nominal size ;

(*b*) Class of tolerance with type of deviation and amount of tolerance ;

(*c*) The word 'GO', 'NO GO' on GO and NO GO gauges respectively ;

(*d*) Manufacturers trade mark.

The 'NO GO' gauges shall be painted with red paint.

(*vii*) **Packing.** The gauges shall be suitably protected against climatic condition by application of a suitable anti-corrosive coating. The gauges may then be packed in suitable cases to prevent damage in transit or storage.

Example 15.31. *Sketch and describe open type blanking die with guide posts.*

Solution. Fig. 15.107 shows open type blanking die with guide posts. When punch is in top most position its end is flush with

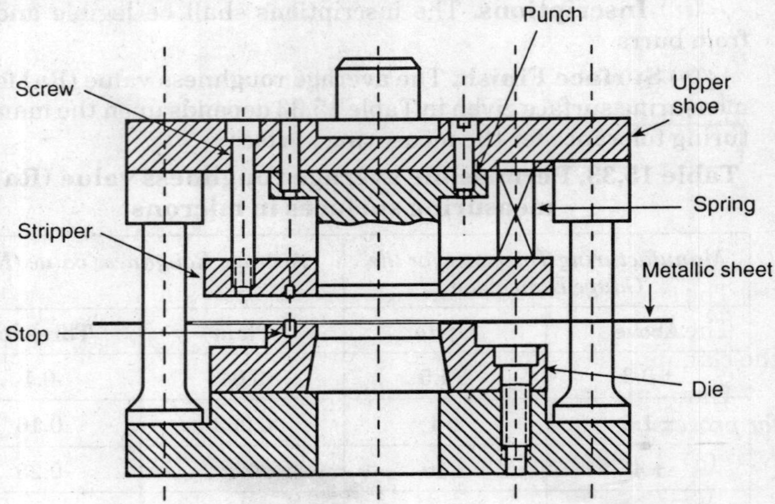

Fig. 15.107

stripper. As the punch moves down the stripper presses the metallic strip against die, during which punch blanks cut the component.

At this moment springs get compressed between the upper shoe and the stripper. The stop is provided to ensure equal spacing between balanced components.

Example 15.32. *Sketch and describe a clamp for drilling machine.*

Solution. Fig 15.108 shows a typical clamp for drilling machine.

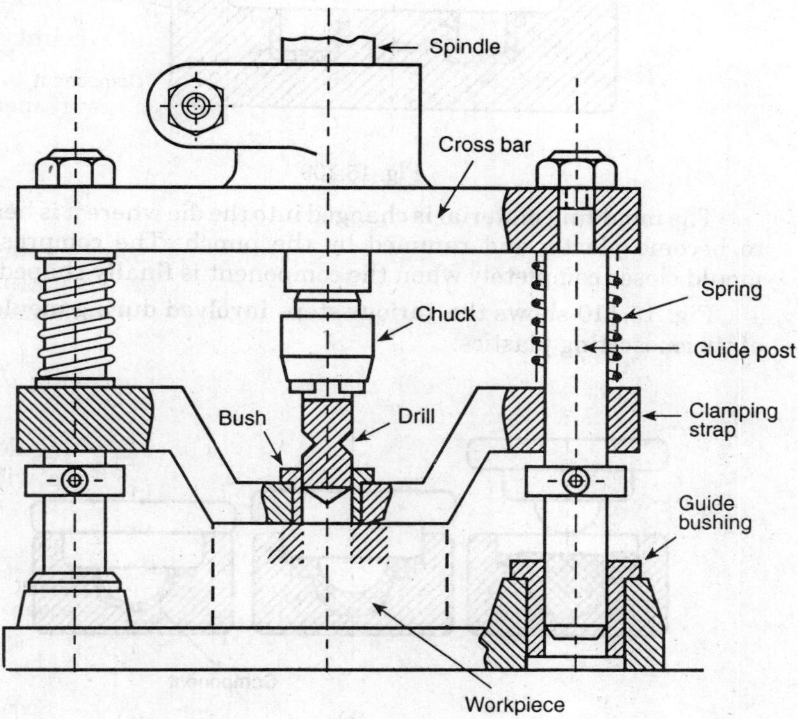

Fig. 15.108.

The cross bar is held in position by nut, bolt and spring system.

The drill is moved into the workpiece by the guide provided by the clamping strap and bush.

Example 15.33. *Sketch and describe following types of moulds for processing plastic materials.*

(*a*) *Compression mould* (*b*) *Transfer mould*

(c) *Injection mould*

Solution

(*a*) Fig. 15.109 shows compression mould.

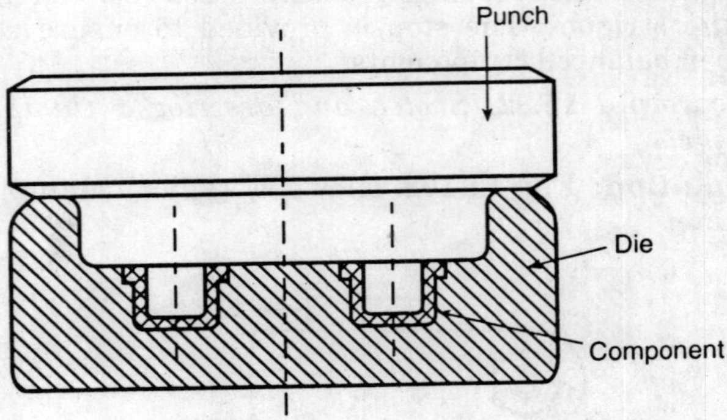

Fig. 15.109.

The moulding material is changed into the die where it is heated to become plastic and rammed by the punch. The compression mould closes completely when the component is finally shaped.

Fig. 15.110 shows the various steps involved during moulding of thermosetting plastics.

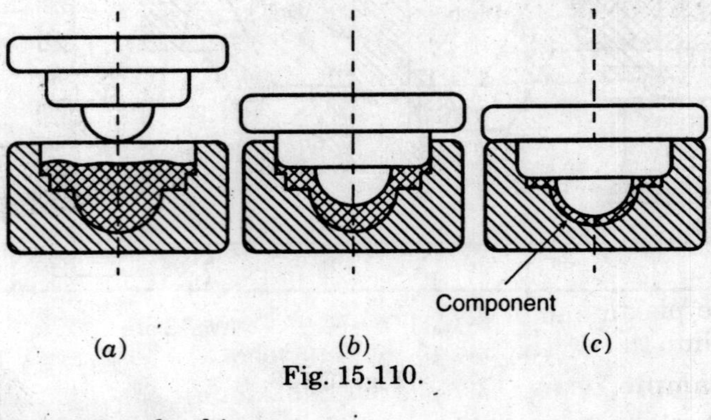

Fig. 15.110.

The steps involved in are :

(*a*) Prior to moulding (*b*) Moulding begins

(*c*) Moulding is complete

To press the thermosetting plastics it is necessary to develop the specific pressure of 30 to 100 megapascals depending on the grade of plastics and the design of the mould.

Plastics are divided into two principal classes: *thermoplastic materials* which soften under heat and reharden when the heat is removed (these include polystyrene, polyethylene, capron) and *thermosetting plastics* which harden or cure by the application of heat; further heating has no softening effect on it.

(*b*) Transfer mould is shown in Fig. 15.111. In this process the shaping cavity is made separately from the loading chamber and is completely clamped prior to filling it with material.

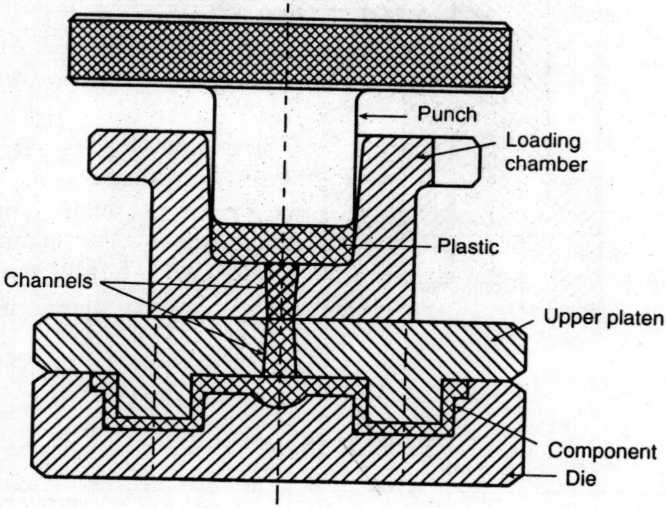

Fig. 15.111.

(*c*) Fig. 15.112 shows injection moulding process for thermoplastics.

The plastic material is heated in cylinder and is pushed by piston into the cavity to form the component.

Example 15.34. *Discuss draft angle for die cast components.*

Solution. Draft angle depends on types of alloys and varies inversely with wall depth.

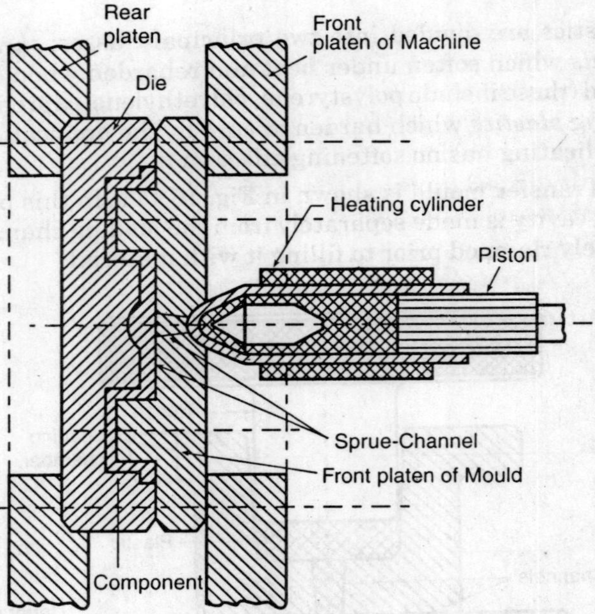

Fig. 15.112.

TABLE 15.34

Depth of Wall, mm	*Draft Angle Requirement for Side Walls, Deg*		
	Cu Alloys	*Al Alloys*	*Zinc Alloys*
0.25–0.50	16.0	15.0	10.0
0.50–1.00	14.0	12.0	7.0
1.00–2.00	10.0	8.0	5.0
2.00–4.00	7.0	6.0	3.5
4.008.00	5.0	4.0	2.5
8.00–2.00	3.5	3.0	1.8
2.00–25.00	2.5	2.2	1.5
25.00–50.00	2.0	1.5	1.0

The sidewalls of die cast component and other features which are perpendicular to the parting line must be tapered/drafted as much as possible to facilitate removal from the die. Draft angle should be large enough, as without it even the slightest depression in the drafted surface of the die will prevent ejection without causing drag marks in the surface of the casting. Various values are indicated in table 15.34.

Example 15.35. *State the values of feed for drilling and reaming for hole diameters upto 40 mm*

Solution :- The commonly adopted values of feed for H.S.S. drill and reamer are as indicated in Table 15.35.

Table 15.35

Hole dia. (mm)	Feed *(mm/rev.)*	
	Drilling	*Reaming*
1-2	0.04-0.05	0.08-0.1
2-4	0.05-0.1	0.1-0.2
4-6	0.05-0.15	0.15-0.3
6-8	0.1-0.20	0.2-0.4
9-15	0.15-0.2	0.3-0.5
15-20	0.2-0.3	0.5-0.70
20-30	0.25-0.3	0.61-0.80
30-40	0.28-0.40	0.71-0.90

Example 15.36. *Calculate the axial cutting force required during broaching using the following data. Axial cutting force (kgf) per millimetre of cutting edge length = 15 kgf/mm.*

General correction factor = 1.15

Length of surface being broached = 60 mm.

Pitch of roughing teeth = 12 mm.

Maximum tooth diameter of broach = 55 mm.

Length of Surface to be broached = 60 mm

Solution :- F = Axial cutting force

$$= Q \,.\, \Sigma L \,.\, K$$

where Q = Axial cutting force per millimeter of cutting edge length

= 15 kgf/mm

ΣL = Total length of cutting edges of all the teeth participating in the cutting work simultaneously

$= \pi D \dfrac{Z_C}{Z_S}$ for round broaching

where D = Maximum tooth diameter of broach = 55 mm

Z_C = Number of teeth participating in cutting simultaneously

$= \dfrac{l}{p} + 1$

where l = length of surface being broached = 60 mm.

p = pitch of roughing teeth = 12 mm

$$Z_C = \frac{60}{12} + 1 = 6$$

Z_S = Number of teeth per section = 2 (say)

$$\Sigma L = \pi \times 55 \times \frac{6}{2} = 518 \text{ mm.}$$

K = General correction factor = 1.15

F = Axial cutting force

$= Q \,.\, \Sigma L \,.\, K = 15 \times 518 \times 1.15$

= 8935 kgf

or = 8935 × 9.81

= 87652 Newtons.

Example 15.37. *State the formula to calculate locking force for die casting.*

Solution.

The locking force for a diecasting is calculated as follows.

$$R = \frac{Ap}{1000}$$

where R = locking force in metric tonnes

P = specific injection pressure in kg/cm^2

A = projected area of the casting plug sprue, sleeve, runners, gates and overflows (cm^2).

The specific injection pressure is dependent on the alloy cast, the nature of the casting. Castings are classified into three categories for this purpose as indicated in table 15.36 for zinc (Zn) and aluminium (Al) and magnesium parts.

Table 15.36

Specific Injection Pressure (kg/cm^2)		
	Zinc	*Al or Mg*
Decorative parts	100–200	200–400
Engineering parts	200–300	400–600
Pressure-tight parts	250–400	800–1000

Example 15.38. *State typical values of*

(*a*) *Velocity of metal flow in gate*

(*b*) *Cavity fill time.*

(*c*) *Gate area for die casting.*

Solution.

(*a*) Table 15.37 indicates typical values of gate velocity corresponding to thickness.

U = Velocity of molten metal in gate (m/s).

T = Thinnest wall dimensions any where on the casting (mm.)

Table 15.37

T(mm)	*U(m / s)*
0.75	45-53
1.27-1.52	43-52
1.90-2.28	40-49
2.54-2.79	37-46
2.85-3.8	34-43
4.65-5.0	30-40
6.5	28-32

(*b*) Table 15.38 indicates optimum cavity fill time (t) and metal temperature and die temperature.

Table 15.38

		Metal Temp.	*Die Temp.*
Zinc Alloy		*390°C*	*204°C*
Mg & Al Alloy		*650°C*	*330°C*
Thickness mm (in)	*Fill time (sec.)*	*Thickness mm (in)*	*Fill Time (sec)*
0.5	0.007	2.5	0.03
1.0	0.015	3.0	0.04
1.5	0.02	3.5	0.05
2.0	0.03	5.0	0.07

(*c*) A = Gate area $= \dfrac{Q}{U}$

where Q = Cavity fill rate $= \dfrac{V}{t}$

where V = Volume of Casting $= \dfrac{\text{Mass}}{\text{Density}}$

t = Cavity fill time

U = Gate velocity

Gate thickness should not be less than 0.4 mm and should not be more than half the wall thickness.

Example 15.39. *Explain (a) cutting time*

(*b*) *Metal removal rate (MRR)*

(*c*) *Depth of cut for boring operation.*

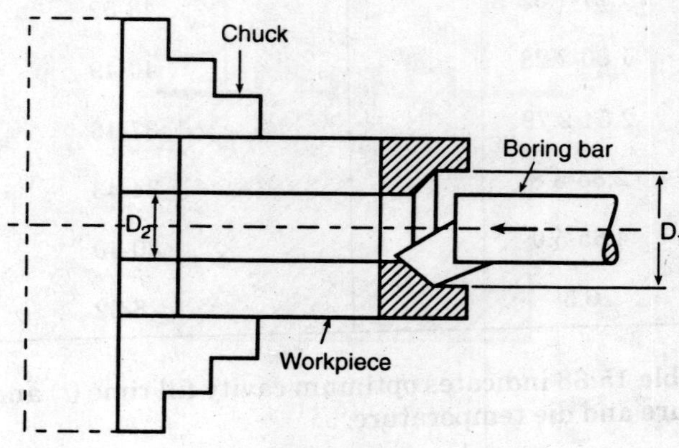

Fig. 15.113.

Solution :- Boring is the process of enlarging a hole that has already been drilled. The tool is fed parallel to the axis of the work piece as shown in Fig. 15.113.

(*a*) t = cutting time $= \dfrac{L + A}{f \times N}$

where $N = R.P.M.$

L = Length of cut, mm

A = Allowance, mm

f = Feed, mm/rev

(*b*) The metal removal rate, (MRR) is given as

or $$MRR = \frac{\pi}{4}(D_1^2 - D_2^2)\, f \quad N, \frac{\text{mm}^3}{\text{min}}$$

(*c*) d = Depth of cut $= \dfrac{D_1 - D_2}{2}$

where D_1 = Diameter of bore

D_2 = Original diameter of hole.

Example 15.40. *Explain the following*

(*a*) *Embossing and*

(*b*) *Redrawing*

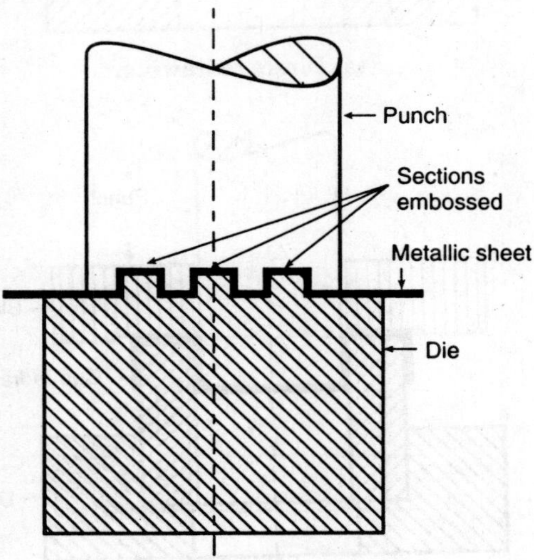

Fig. 15.114.

Solution.

(*a*) **Embossing.** It is the operation in which impressions are made on metallic sheets. It finds applications in making name plates, medals or aesthetic design in metallic sheets.

Fig. 15.114 shows embossing operation, here down ward moving punch applies the required force.

(*b*) **Redrawing.** It is carried out when it is difficult to draw a cup in one draw.

Redrawing is of two types as shown in Fig. 15.115.

(*a*) Direct redrawing (*b*) Reverse redrawing.

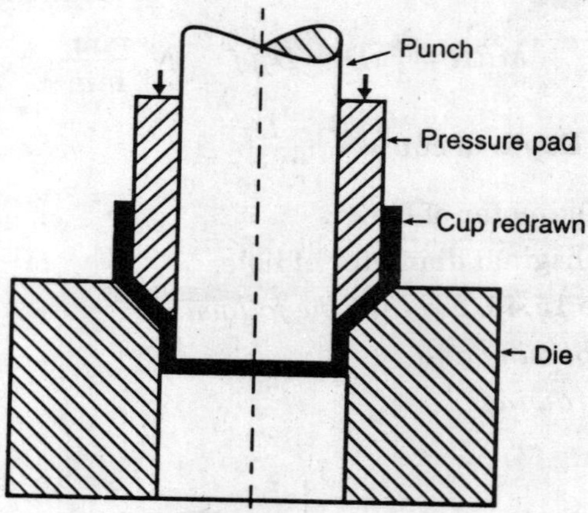

(a) Direct redrawing.

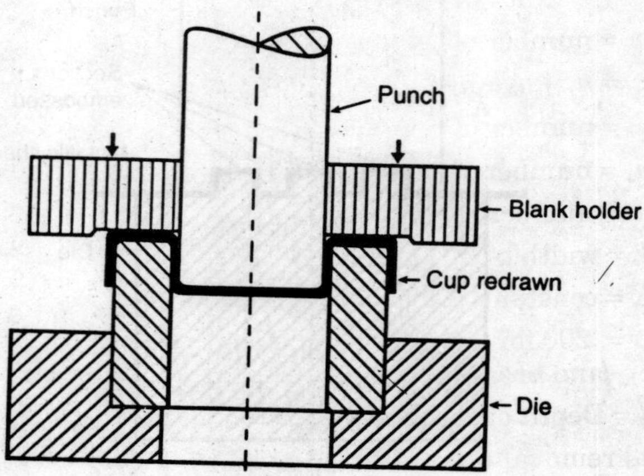

(b) Reverse redrawing

Fig. 15.115

Example 15.41. *Explain the following for a broach.*

(*a*) *Rise per tooth (RTP)*

(*b*) *Depth of cut*

(*c*) *Cutting time*

(*d*) *Broaching force*

(*e*) *Metal removal rate (MRR)*

(*f*) *Power required for broaching operation.*

Solution :- Fig. 15.116 shows rise per tooth (RPT) and depth of cut.

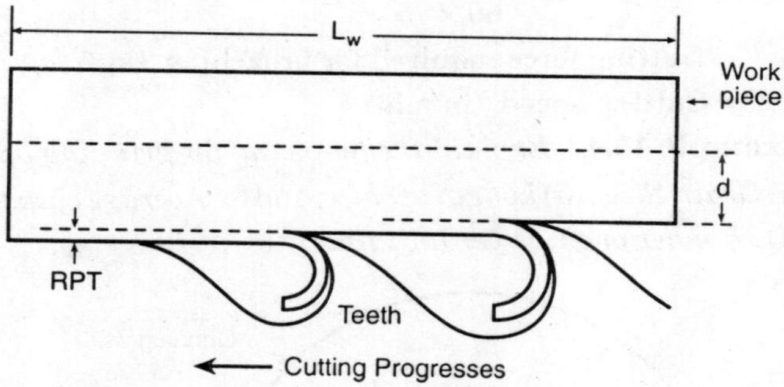

Fig. 15.116.

Broaching force :- It is the force required for broaching operation.

Minimum force required to operate a broach is given by,

$$F = KndW, \; Kgf \qquad ...(15.25)$$

where n = number of teeth cutting at a time

$= n_r + n_s + n_f$

where n_r = number of roughing teeth

n_s = number of semi–finishing teeth

n_f = number of finishing teeth

W = width of cut, mm

K = constant 400 for mild steels and cast iron

= 200 for non-ferrous materials such as aluminium, zinc, and brass.

d = Depth of cut.

Metal removal rate (MRR) is given by

$$MRR = 12t \times W \times V_n, \quad \text{in}^3/\text{min}$$

where W = width of broach tooth

n = number of roughing teeth in contact with part

$$= \frac{L_w}{P}$$

where L_w = Length of cut on workpiece

P = Pitch

Majority of the material is removed by roughing teeth.

The power required for broaching is given as

$$\text{Power} = \frac{FV}{60 \times 75} \quad HP$$

where F = Cutting force required for broaching. (kgf)

V = Cutting speed, (m/min).

Example 15.42. *Explain the following for grinding operation (a) Grain Size ; (b) Length of chip* ; and *(c) Average chip thickness (d) Number of chips per unit time.*

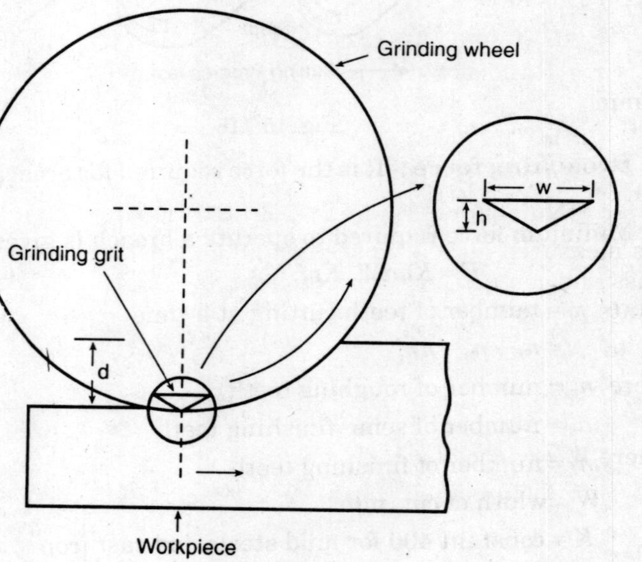

Fig. 15.117.

Solution.

(a) Grain size. Fig. 15.117. shows grit

Grain sizes used in grinding wheels range from 8 to 240 grit per inch. 8 to 16 grit per inch is very coarse: 16 to 30 grit is coarse: 36

to 60 grit is medium; 80 to 120 grit is fine: and 150 to 240 grit is extra fine. Usually coarse grits are used for soft materials and fine grits for hard materials.

(*b*) *Length of chip*

The length of the chip, L is given as

$$L = \sqrt{Dd}\text{, mm}$$

where D = Diameter of grinding wheel, mm

d = Depth of grind (cut), mm

(*c*) *Average chip thickness*

$$t = \sqrt{\frac{4v}{Vcr}\left(\frac{d}{D}\right)^{1/2}}$$

where t = Chip thickness, mm for surface grinding

v = Work speed, m/min

V = Peripheral speed of wheel (cutting speed), m/min

$$= \frac{\pi DN}{1000}$$

N = R.P.M. of grinding wheel

r = Ratio of width (w) to height (h) of grit both are expressed in mm

$$= \frac{w}{h}$$

c = Number of grinding wheel active grits per m^2

c is measured by rolling the grinding wheel on a piece of smoked glass and counting, under a microscope, the marks left where grit points pierce the smoke film.

(*d*) *Number of chips*

$$n = \frac{VWC}{1000}$$

where W = width of wheel, mm

n = Number of chips per unit time

Problems

1. Derive an expression for optimum included angle of v- locator used in jigs.
2. (*a*) State the various surface roughness symbols.

(*b*) Sketch and describe surface roughness representation symbol.

3. Sketch and describe a Box Jig used for drilling holes in different planes in a component

4. Write short note on :

(*i*) Centraliser used in Jigs

(*ii*) Scrap web allowance for metallic sheet components.

5. Sketch the geometry of HSS drill indicating various angles.

6. Write short notes on the following :

(*a*) HSS twist drill angles

(*b*) Twist drill forces

(*c*) Forces on milling cutter

(*d*) Angles for HSS end mill cutter

7. Sketch and describe various jig bodies.

8. Discuss sharpening of milling cutters.

9. Discuss the various considerations for die cast components.

10. Write short notes on the following :

(*a*) Turning fixture (*b*) Pot Jig

(*c*) Multicoated inserts (*d*) Soldered joint testing jig.

11. Write short notes on the following

(*i*) Tool wear land (*ii*) Broach tooth size

(*iii*) Average cut per broach tooth

(*iv*) Form relieved cutter.

12. Discuss the forces at cutting edge of milling cutter.

13. (*a*) Sketch a circular form tool.

(*b*) Discuss clearance angle for circular form tool.

14. Write short notes on the following

(*i*) Cutting speed in shaping and planing

(*ii*) planer tools.

15. Explain various types of end mill cutters.

16. Write short notes on the following

(*i*) Spline cutter (*ii*) Key way broaching

(*iii*) Pitch of a broach tooth.

17. Sketch and describe the following

(*a*) Diamond turning tools (*b*) Cemented Carbide tools.

11

Objective Type Problems

1. Tick mark the correct answer :

(*A*) The metal cutting wedge is fundamental to the geometry of

(*a*) Hand tools only

(*b*) Power driven tools only

(*c*) Sheet metal cutting tools only

(*d*) All cutting tools.

(*B*) Continuous chips are formed when cutting

(*a*) Brittle materials

(*b*) Ductile materials

(*c*) Amorphous plastic materials

(*d*) Free cutting non ferrous alloys only.

(*C*) The rake angle of a cutting tool

(*a*) Controls the chip formation

(*b*) Prevents rubbing

(*c*) Determines the profile of tool

(*d*) Determine whether the cutting action is oblique or orthogonal

(*D*) Back rake angle for H.S.S. single point cutting tool to machine free cutting brass is

(*a*) 15° (*b*) 0°

(*c*) 5° (*d*) 10°

2. In the list of processes given below tick (√) mark the chip removal processes

(*a*) Die casting (*b*) Extruding

(*c*) Forging (*d*) Rolling

(*e*) Broaching.

3. In the list of processes given below tick (√) mark the non-chip removal processes

(*a*) Grinding (*b*) Spinning on lathe

(*c*) Thread cutting (*d*) Drilling

(*e*) Milling.

4. State whether the following statements are true or false :

(*a*) For a given cutting speed cemented carbide tool removes more work material than H.S.S. tool.

(*b*) Optimum rake angle of a tool is not a function of the properties of work material.

(*c*) Cemented carbide is more tough than high speed steel.

(*d*) In oblique cutting the edge of tool is not perpendicular to the cutting direction.

(*e*) Chip reduction coefficient is always more than unity.

(*f*) Larger value of chip reduction coefficient indicates poor machinability.

(*g*) Grinding wheel is a single point cutting tool.

(*h*) Decreasing wedge angle of tool reduces mechanical strength of tool.

5. Fill in the blanks.

(*a*) The point angle of twist drill to machine steel is .....

(*b*) The cutting speed of H.S.S. twist drill to machine grey cast iron is ....

(*c*) The cutting speeds of H.S.S. milling cutter to machine aluminium is .....

6. Tick mark the correct answer

(*A*) A twist drill has its point thinned in order to

(*a*) Reduce the hole diameter

(*b*) Increase the rake angle

(*c*) Locate in the centre punch mark

(*d*) Reduce the axial (feed) pressure.

(*B*) A reamer used to correct the

(*a*) Size and roundness of a drilled hole

(*b*) Size and position of a drilled hole

(*c*) Finish and position of a drilled hole

(*d*) Finish and depth of a drilled hole

(*C*) An oversize hole is produced by a drill if

(*a*) Lips of drill are of unequal length

(*b*) Feed is too high

(*c*) Insufficient coolant is used

(*d*) Cutting speed is too high.

(*D*) Cemented carbide tipped tools can machine metal even when their cutting elements get heated up to the temperature

(*a*) 1650°C (*b*) 1400°C

(*c*) 1000°C (*d*) 1800°C.

(*E*) Cemented carbide tools are usually provided with

(*a*) Positive back rake angle (*b*) Neutral back rake angle

(*c*) Negative back rake angle.

7. State whether the following statements are true or false :

(*a*) The rates of feed and cutting speeds for twist drill are lower than for most other machining operations

(*b*) Like any other cutting tool the twist drill must be provided with correct tool angles

(*c*) A twist drill produces a hole of fine finish and accurate size

(*d*) No cutting fluids are used for carbide tipped milling cutters.

8. Tick mark the correct answer

The time taken to drill hole through a 20 mm thick plate at 300 R.P.M. and at a feed of 0.2 mm/revolution is

(*a*) 15 seconds (*b*) 12 seconds

(*c*) 20 seconds.

9. State the usually recommended value of rake angle for machining aluminium with cutting tools made up of

(*a*) High speed steel tool (*b*) Cemented carbide tool

(*c*) Diamond tool.

10. Two major factors which determine the r.p.m. of milling cutter are the material being cut and

(*a*) Number of teeth in cutter

(*b*) Diameter of cutter

(*c*) Time allowed to complete the job

(*d*) Depth of cutter.

11. Mark against each statement according to the key given below :

Mark A - If the condition produces discontinuous chips

Mark B - If the condition produces continuous chips

Mark C - If the condition produces built up chips

(*i*) Brittle materials and slow cutting speeds

(*ii*) Ductile materials and high depth of cut

(*iii*) Ductile materials with coarse feed

(*iv*) Ductile materials with fine feed

(*v*) Mild steel with sharp cutting edge of tool

(*vi*) Mild steel with high cutting speed

(*vii*) Mild steel with low rake angle.

12. Friction between chip and tool may be reduced by

(*a*) Increased sliding velocity (*b*) Increased shear angle

(*c*) Use of low tool finish

13. State whether the following statements are true or false :

(*a*) Aluminium oxide abrasives are used for grinding high tensile strength materials

(*b*) Silicon carbide abrasives are used for grinding low tensile strength materials

(*c*) Selection of grinding wheel does not depend on the work piece material

(*d*) Fine grain wheels are used to grind soft ductile materials

(*e*) Hard and brittle materials and finishing cuts require dense structure in grinding wheel

(*f*) Grade of grinding wheel is denoted by a number

(*g*) Structure of grinding wheel is denoted by alphabets.

14. State whether the following statements are true or false :

(*a*) Machinability index implies the degree of easiness in machining

(*b*) Free cutting steel cannot be easily machined

(*c*) Heat resisting steels possess low machinability

(*d*) Cast iron does not permit as high a cutting speed as structural carbon steel (*e*) A most machinable metal one which permits fastest removal of largest amount of material per grind of the tool.

(*f*) For the same amount of applied force orthogonal cutting removes more metal

(*g*) For the same amount of metal removal the shear stress induced in orthogonal cutting is more than in oblique cutting

(*h*) In orthogonal cutting the cutting edge of the tool remains inclined to the direction of the work feed.

15. The studs used as a coolant in general machine shop consists of :

(*a*) A solution of detergent and water

(*b*) A straight mineral oil

(*c*) An emulsion of oil and water

(*d*) A chemical solution

16. State whether the following statements are true or false :

(*a*) A cutting fluid should have low conductivity.

(*b*) Use of cutting fluids promotes a better surface finish.

17. State whether the following statements are true or false :

(*a*) The structure of a grinding wheel indicates the relative spacing of grains in the wheel.

(*b*) The grade of a grinding wheel indicates the relative strength of the bond which hold the abrasive grains in place.

(*c*) About 75% of grinding wheels have vitreous bonds.

(*d*) Corundum contains more aluminium oxide than emery.

18. Select the suitable peripheral speeds for following grinding operations given in column A form the Column B and indicate in the space provided.

A		*B*
Type of grinding operation		*Speed in metres / min.*
(*i*) Cylindrical grinding	☐	(*a*) 1200-1800
(*ii*) Internal grinding	☐	(*b*) 2700-48000
(*iii*) Snagging off hand grinding with vitrified wheel	☐	(*c*) 600-1800
(*iv*) Surface grinding	☐	(*d*) 1600-1950
(*v*) Rubber,shellac and resinoid bonded wheel.	☐	(*e*)1500-1800

19. Match the words of column A with the words of column B and fill in the space provided.

Column A		Column B
(*i*) Emery	☐	(*a*) To machine external cylindrical surfaces.
(*ii*) Silicon carbide	☐	(*b*) Artificial abrasive
(*iii*) Surface grinding	☐	(*c*) To machine flat surfaces
(*iv*) Centre type cylindrical grinding	☐	(*d*) Natural abrasive
(*v*) Symbol used for silicate bond	☐	(*e*) E
(*vi*) Symbol used for shellac bond	☐	(*f*) S.

20. State whether the following statements are true or false :

(*a*) Cast iron is often ground dry.

(*b*) The workpiece is supported between the centres during centreless grinding

(*c*) Surface grinder is used to grind flat surfaces.

21. Milling cutter is sharpened on :

(*a*) Tool and cutter grinder (*b*) Centreless grinder

(*c*) Cylindrical grinder (*d*) Surface grinder.

22. State whether the following statements are true or false :

(*a*) Ordinarily the surface finish improves the cutting speed.

(*b*) An increase in back rake angle of a cutting tool deteriorates surface finish.

(*c*) Some degree of roughness which may be extremely small is always present on any machined surface.

23. Arrange the following machining process in the increasing order of good surface finish

Milling, filling, hand grinding, drilling , surface grinding, lapping, sawing, super finishing, turning.

24. (*a*) V-locators are widely used because their construction permits automatic location of workpiece.

(*b*) Bushings are made of C.I.

25. State the degrees of freedom possessed by the parts given below, indicate translation by *T* and rotation by *R*.

(*a*) Single point tool operating in lathe tool post.

(*b*) Arm of radial drill.

(*c*) Plug gauge in component bore.

26. Identify the following tools as single point cutting tools or multi point cutting tools.

(*i*) Twist drill (*ii*) Grinding wheel

(*iii*) Roughing tool of shaper (*iv*) Parting tool in lathe

(*v*) Milling cutter (*vi*) Reamer.

27. Emery is a :

(*a*) Artificial abrasive (*b*) Natural abrasive

(*c*) Type of cloth.

28. Grinding is :

(*a*) Metal fusing operation.

(*b*) Metal powdering operation

(*c*) Metal finishing operation.

29. Grinding is done wherever :

(*a*) Other machining operations cannot be carried out

(*b*) A large amount of materials is to be removed

(*c*) High accuracy is required

30. Name the abrasives to be used (Aluminium oxide or Silicon carbide) to grind the following materials :

(*a*) Steels (*b*) Cast iron

(*c*) Aluminium (*d*) Wrought iron

(*e*) Copper (*f*) Non-metallic materials

(*g*) Bronze.

31. State four properties of work material which affect the cutting tool life.

32. State three requirements which should be fulfilled for all cutting tools.

33. State three conditions for the formation of continuous chips with built up edges.

34. The Young's modulus of carbide tools is about

(*a*) Three times than for steel

(*b*) Six times than for steel

(*c*) Nine times than for steel

(*d*) None of the above.

35. Twist drills are usually considered suitable for machining holes having a length less than

(*a*) Two times their diameter

(*b*) Five times their diameter

(*c*) Ten times their diameter.

36. A hard grade grinding wheel is suitable for grinding :

(*a*) Hard materials (*b*) Soft materials

(*c*) Both hard and soft materials (*d*) None of the above.

37. The relative motion of workpiece in planning is :

(*a*) Rotary (*b*) Translatory

(*c*) Rotary and translatory (*d*) None of the above.

38. The accuracy obtained by the grinding process can be of the order of :

(*a*) 0.25 mm (*b*) 0.025 mm

(*c*) 0.00025 mm.

39. The feed used for reamers is about :

(*a*) One time (*b*) Three times

(*c*) Six times

That employed for drilling.

40. The cutting speed in reaming should be less than drilling by about :

(*a*) 75 % (*b*) 50 %

(*c*) 25 % (*d*) None of the above.

41. *Statements :*

(*i*) With carbide tools better cutting conditions can be achieved with negative rake and high cutting speeds.

(*ii*) In metal cutting it is always desirable to obtain a shortest possible shear plane because for a fixed shear strength reduction in shear plane area reduces the shearing forces required to produce sufficient stress.

42. Name H.S.S. commonly used for making tools.

43. The diameter (D) of a plain milling cutter is approximately related to arbor diameter (*d*) as

(*a*) D = 2.5 to 3 *d* (*b*) D = 4.5 *d* to 6 *d*

(*c*) D = 1.5 to 2 *d*.

44. Knock outs are used to remove components which adhere to:

(*a*) Punch (*b*) Die.

45. *Statements*

(*i*) The larger the cutting angle and the smaller the thickness of uncut chip, the more tightly the chip will curl (the smaller its radius of curvature will be).

(*ii*) The use of cutting fluids reduces the radius to which the chip curls.

(*iii*) An increase in nose radius leads to greater chip contraction.

(*iv*) Greater the cutting angle (or smaller the positive rake angle) the greater is chip contraction.

46. State the factors which affect the chip contraction.

47. Name four fine finishing operations.

48. Name the cutting fluids used for machining, the following metals :

(*i*) Cast iron (*ii*) Mild steel and free cutting steel

(*iii*) Aluminium and aluminium alloys.

49. State whether the following statements are true or false

(*a*) A cutting tool with large back rake angle is weak and tool point may break off readily.

(*b*) A cutting tool with negative back rake angle has better heat conductivity.

(*c*) Negative back rake angles are specially provided on cemented carbide tipped tools because the cemented carbide possesses very high compressive strength and comparatively very low tensile and shear strengths.

(*d*) Nose radius provided on cutting tool imparts strength to the cutting point.

(*e*) Manually operated machine tools are economical for smaller batch size production.

(*f*) Transfer machines are economical for larger batch size production.

(*g*) During drilling the chips produced are removed automatically out of drill hole by helical flutes.

50. State the type of twist drill to be used for machining the following material :

(*a*) Laminated plastics (*b*) Brass

(*c*) Cast iron (*d*) Steel

(*e*) Copper (*f*) Aluminium alloy.

51. State whether following statements are true or false :

(*a*) Excessive positive rake angle weakens the cutting end of tool.

(*b*) Drawing speed should be less for harder and less ductile materials.

(*c*) After fine blanking no further machining is needed.

52. Name three types of die sets.

53. What is the difference between forming and generating.

54. State the difference between embossing and coining.

55. Name three force transmitting media in bulging dies.

56. Name three components manufactured by coining process.

57. Name three types of components produced by drawing.

58. Die block should never be thinner than :

(*a*) 7 to 10 mm (*b*) 3 to 5 mm

(*c*) 15 to 20 mm (*d*) None of the above.

59. Punch plate is made of :

(*a*) Mild steel (*b*) High speed steel

(*c*) Cast iron (*d*) None of the above.

60. Piercing punch is made of :

(*a*) Medium carbon steel (*b*) Tool steel T 160

(*c*) Cast iron (*d*) None of the above

61. Stripping force (F) is about

(*a*) 5--20% of P (*b*) 2--5% of P

(*c*) 25--30% of P, where P = cutting force

(*d*) None of the above.

62. Shear provided on punch or die is :

(*a*) $2t - 3t$ (*b*) $t - 1.5t$

(*c*) $0.5t - t$ (*d*) None of the above

where t = Metal thickness.

63. State whether the following statements are true or false :

(*a*) If a hole is to be pierced, shear should be ground on the punch face. If the operation is blanking the shear should be applied to the die.

(*b*) In forging the operation of securing dies in the hammer is known as set up.

(*c*) In forging draft angle is smaller on outside surface than in side surfaces.

64. Define pitch of a progressive die.

65. In forging the draft angle for outside faces is about :

(*a*) 10--15 (*b*) 5--7

(*c*) 2--3 (*d*) None of the above.

66. Name the materials for the following :

(*a*) Hot trim dies (*b*) Cold trim dies

(*c*) Cold trim punches (*d*) Hot trim punches.

67. Define die set.

68. For forgings the width to thickness ratio is

(*a*) 3.1 to 5 : 1 (*b*) 2.2 to 2.5 : 1

(*c*) 8.1 to 10.1 (*d*) None of the above.

69. In forgings the draft of inside faces is :

(*a*) 2--3° (*b*) 7--10°

(*c*) 12--15° (*d*) None of the above.

70. Machining allowance for steel forgings (up to 5 kg) is :

(*a*) 1.5 mm per side (*b*) 2.5 mm per side

(*c*) 3.5 mm per side (*d*) None of the above.

71. In forging rib height should not exceed.

(*a*) 4 times the rib width (*b*) 2 times the rib width

(*c*) 8 times the rib width (*d*) None of the above.

72. The number of degrees of freedom for any work piece in space are :

(*a*) 12 (*b*) 3

(*c*) 6 (*d*) None of the above.

73. To minimum number of locators to locate the workpi ce are:

(*a*) 2 (*b*) 3

(*c*) 1 (*d*) 6.

74. Statements :

(*a*) An irregular surface does not allow more than three contact points for location.

(*b*) Table of machine acts as reference plane for location from plane surface of a component.

75. Locating pins of longer length are called

(*a*) Plugs (*b*) Set screws

(*c*) Shaft (*d*) None of the above.

76. Buttons are used for

(*a*) Vertical location (*b*) Horizontal location

(*c*) Inclined location (*d*) None of the above.

77. Scremed type of locating buttons are where the buttons are liable to be subjected to :

(*a*) Less wear and tear (*b*) More wear and tear

(*c*) None of the above

78. Locating pins are generally used in fixtures for :

(*a*) Vertical location (*b*) Horizontal location

(*c*) Inclined location (*d*) None of the above

79. *Statements :*

(*a*) Slip renewable bushings are usually knurled to aid in their removal whereas fixed renewable bushings are not knurled.

(*b*) Renewable bushings are based with liners.

80. Name two types of renewable jig bushings.

81. What is meant by 3--2--1 principle of location.

82. What is the best method to locate a rough surface.

83. Drill bushes are made of :

(*a*) High speed steel

(*b*) High carbon steel, hardened and ground

(*c*) Low carbon steel

(*d*) Aluminium.

84. State five criteria for classification of presses.

85. State three advantages of hydraulic presses.

86. Drill bushes have a headness (HRC) of about.

(*a*) 60-64 (*b*) 45-48

(*c*) 40-45 (*d*) None of the above.

87. The base plate of milling fixture is made of :

(*a*) High speed steel (*b*) Medium carbon steel

(*c*) Cast iron (*d*) Aluminium.

88. State the main principle to be observed while designing a clamping device.

89. State four design features to be considered with respect to clamping.

90. Name three main types of end cutting tools used for quantity production.

91. Name four elements to be considered while designing a drilling jig.

92. Statements

(*i*) The size of chips cut is very small for grinding as compared with milling.

(*ii*) The punch force in drawing is limited to the maximum tensile load which can be carried by the wall of the cup and this sets a limit to the depth of flange which can be drawn.

93. What are throw away carbide tips.

94. State the commonly used values of the following for H.S.S. twist drill.

(*i*) Point angle (*ii*) Lip relief of angle

(*iii*) Helix angle (*iv*) Margin.

95. Define a form tool. State three type of form tools.

96. State two advantages of broaching.

97. State the purposes of nose radius on cutting tools.

98. Pilots are usually hardened upto

(*a*) HRC 57 to HRC 60 (*b*) HRC 40 to HRC 50

(*c*) HRC 70 to HRC 80 (*d*) None of the above.

99. Stripping force ranges between

(*a*) 30 to 40% (*b*) 50 to 60%

(*c*) 5 to 20% of cutting force.

100. *Statements :*

(*a*) In sufficient clearance increases pressure on the punch and die edges and has marked effect on die life.

(*b*) Punch holder thickness varies from 25 to 75 mm.

(*c*) In press work the maximum length of punch is generally kept up to 100 mm.

(*d*) In press work 9 to 10 mm screws are used on die components up to 150 mm square.

101. In drawing operation the blank holder force (F) is given by

(*a*) F = P (*b*) F = P/3

(*c*) F = 2 P (*d*) None of the above.

where P = Drawing force

102. *Statements*

(*a*) The carbide tools can be used as brazed tip tools or throw away tip tools. The throw away tip tools are commonly used because the tool setting time is reduced.

(*b*) Flank wear occurs at the cutting edge of tool.

(*c*) Flank wear occurs due to increase in temperature at the cutting edge of tool during machining.

103. State three characteristics of ceramic tools.

104. State four functions of a cutting fluid.

105. In piercing operation on a press the clearance is provided on

(*a*) punch (*b*) die

(*c*) punch and die (*d*) none of the above.

106. Bending operation on a press is performed

(*a*) Parallel to the direction of grains

(*b*) Perpendicular to the direction of grains

(*c*) At any angle to the grain direction

107. Statements (True or False)

(*a*) Elastic stresses remaining in the bend area after bending pressure is released cause a slight decrease in the bend angle.

(*b*) Spring back phenomenon in bending depends on the following factors.

(*i*) Type of material (*ii*) Material thickness

(*iii*) Hardness of material

108. Name two methods of overcoming the phenomenon of spring back in bending.

109. Name three shaping operations for metals.

110. Name four auxiliaries of a jig or fixture.

111. Name three methods of manufacturing jigs and fixtures.

112. Die shoe is made up of

(*a*) Cast iron (*b*) Mild steel

(*c*) Aluminium (*d*) None of the above.

113. Punch holder thickness varies between

(*a*) 5 to 25 mm (*b*) 25 to 75 mm

(*c*) 75 to 125 mm (*d*) 150 to 200 mm.

114. *Fill in the blanks*

(*A*) Punch dimensions must be checked for

(*i*) .... (*ii*) ....

115. Permissible deflection in die springs is

(*a*) 50 to 25% of free length (*b*) 10 to 15% of free length

(*c*) 5 to 8% of free length.

116. Nitriding process of surface treatment for steel tools is used for tools taking:

(*a*) Light cuts (*b*) Medium cuts

(*c*) Heavy cuts.

117. At very low cutting speeds the tool wear is due to

(*a*) Plowing action (*b*) Transfer.

ANSWERS

1.	(A) (*a*)	(B) (*b*)	(C) (*a*)	(D) (*b*).
2.	(*e*).	**3.** (*b*).		
4.	(*a*) True	(*b*) False	(*c*) False	(*d*) True
	(*e*) True	(*f*) True	(*g*) False	(*h*) True.
5.	(*a*) 118°	(*b*) 25--40 metre/min		
	(*c*) 180--240 metre/min.			
6.	(*A*) (*d*)	(*B*) (*a*)	(*C*) (*a*)	(*D*) (*c*)
	(*E*) (*c*).			
7.	(*a*) True	(*b*) True	(*c*) False	(*d*) True
	(*e*) True.			
8.	(*e*).			
9.	(*a*) 35°	(*b*) 15°	(*c*) 0°.	
10.	(*c*)			
11.	(*i*) (*a*)	(*ii*) (*c*)	(*iii*) (*c*)	(*iv*) (*b*)
	(*v*) (*b*)	(*vi*) (*b*)	(*vii*) (*c*).	
12.	(*a*).			
13.	(*a*) True	(*b*) True	(*c*) False	(*d*) False
	(*e*) True	(*f*) False	(*g*) False.	
14.	(*a*) True	(*b*) False	(*c*) True	(*d*) True
	(*e*) True	(*f*) False	(*g*) True	(*h*) False.
15.	(*c*).			
16.	(*a*) False	(*b*) True.		
17.	(*a*) True	(*b*) False	(*c*) True	(*d*) True.

18. (*i*) 1600--1950 (*ii*) 600--1800

(*iii*) 1500--1800 (*iv*) 1200--1800

(*v*) 2700--4800.

19. (*i*) (*d*) (*ii*) (*b*) (*iii*) (*c*) (*iv*) (*a*)

(*v*) (*f*) (*vi*) (*e*).

20. (*a*) True (*b*) False (*c*) True.

21. (*a*).

22. (*a*) True (*b*) False (*c*) True.

23. (*i*) Sawing (*ii*) Hand grinding

(*iii*) Falling (*iv*) Turning

(*v*) Milling (*vi*) Drilling

(*vii*) Surface grinding (*viii*) Lapping

(*ix*) Super finishing.

24. (*a*) True (*b*) False.

25. (*a*) 2 T (*b*) 1 T, 1 R (*c*) 1 T, 1 R.

26. Multipoint cutting tools are twist drill, milling cutter grinding wheel and reamer.

27. (*b*). **28.** (*c*). **29.** (*c*).

30.

Material	*Abrasive used*
(*a*) Steel	Aluminium oxide
(*b*) Cast iron	Silicon carbide
(*c*) Aluminium	Silicon carbide
(*d*) Wrought iron	Aluminium oxide
(*e*) Copper	Silicon carbide
(*f*) Non-metallic material	Silicon carbide
(*g*) Bronze	Silicon carbide

31. The properties of the work material which affect the cutting tool life are as follows :

(*i*) Shear strength of the metal

(*ii*) Coefficient of friction between the chip and the cutting tool.

(*iii*) Hardness and strain hardenability of the work material.

(*iv*) Micro structure particularly the presence of hard constituents.

32. Requirements to be fulfilled for all cutting tools follows :

(*i*) High hardness (*ii*) More life

(*iii*) Low cost

33. (*a*) Low rake angle (*b*) Low cutting speed
(*c*) High feed.

34. (*a*). **35.** (*b*). **36.** (*b*). **37.** (*b*).

38. (*c*). **39.** (*b*). **40.** (*a*).

41. (*i*) True (*ii*) True.

42. 18--4--1 H.S.S. is commonly used for making cutting tools. It contains

18% Tungsten

40% Chromium

1% Vanadium

43. (*a*). **44.** (*b*).

45. (*i*) True (*ii*) True (*iii*) True (*iv*) True

46. The main factors affecting chip contraction are as follows :

(*a*) Geometric elements of cutting tool point (chiefly cutting angle and nose radius)

(*b*) Cutting variables such as cutting speed and feed

(*c*) Cutting fluid

(*d*) Workpiece material

(*e*) Mechanical properties of workpiece material

47. (*i*) Lapping (*ii*) Honing (*iii*) Precision turning
(*iv*) Precision boring

48. (*i*) Dry machined
(*ii*) Mineral oil, lard oil, inactive E.P. oil
(*iii*) Mineral oil, inactive E.P. oil

49. (*a*) True (*b*) True (*c*) True (*d*) True.
(*e*) True (*f*) True (*g*) True

50. (*a*) (*H*) (*b*) (*N*) (*c*) (*N*) (*d*) (*N*)
(*e*) (*S*) (*f*) (*S*).

51. (*a*) True (*b*) True (*c*) True.

52. (*i*) Back-pin type die set
(*ii*) Centre-pin type die set
(*iii*) Diagonal-pin type die set

53. In forming the shape of the surface obtained is a replica of the shape of tool (punch and die) whereas in generating the shape of the surface depends on direction of the motion of the tool with relation to the work and is practically independent of the tool shape.

54. Coining differs from embossing in that in coining the metal flows whereas in embossing the metal does not change in thickness to any great extent following.

55. (*i*) Rubber (*ii*) Urethane (*iii*) Oil.

56. (*i*) Metal buttons (*ii*) Medals

(*iii*) Coins.

57. (*i*) Cups (*ii*) Shells (*iii*) Boxes

58. (*a*) **59.** (*c*) **60.** (*b*)

61. (*a*) **62.** (*b*)

63. (*a*) True (*b*) True (*c*).

64. The linear travel of the strip stock at each press stroke is called the progression, advance or pitch and is equal to the inter station distance.

65. (*b*).

66. (*a*) Unhardened medium carbon alloy steel for heavy trimming jobs.

Mild steel for light duty service

(*b*) Tough alloy tool steel hardened to HRC 52--54

(*c*) Tough alloy tool steel hardened to HRC 45--47

(*d*) Medium carbon alloys hardened to HRC 38--40.

67. Die sets are used to hold and aid in the alignment of the cutting members.

68. (*a*) **69.** (*b*) **70.** (*a*)

71. (*c*) **72.** (*a*) **73.** (*b*)

74. (*a*) True (*b*) True

75. (*a*) **76.** (*a*) **77.** (*b*)

78. (*b*) **79.** (*a*) True (*b*) True

80. (*i*) Fixed renewable bush

(*ii*) Slip renewable bush.

81. According to 3--2--1 principle of location to locate a workpiece fully, it has to be placed and held against three points in a base plane, two points in a vertical plane and one point in a plane square with the first two. It is required that the planes should be square with each other and point should be placed as far apart as possible.

82. To locate a rough surface of work piece it is desireable to use relieved locators which offer means of getting close to the average plane of rough surface and holds the workpiece in stable position as shown in Fig. 11.1.

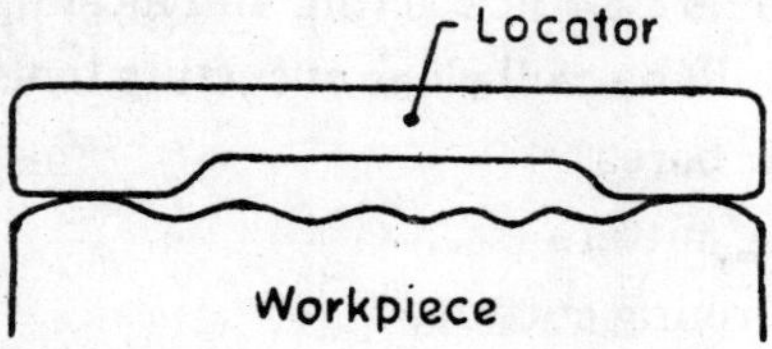

83. (*b*).

84. (*i*) Purpose for which they are made such as blanking, drawing, coining etc.

(*ii*) Type of drive to the tool slide such as :

(*a*) Crank drive

(*b*) Cam drive

(*c*) Toggle drive

(*d*) Rack and pinion drive

(*iii*) Source of power

(*iv*) Type of construction

(*a*) Straight sided press

(*b*) Open back inclinable press

They may be single action or double action presses.

(*v*) Tonnage of press.

85. (*i*) Static pressure can be applied to the work at any stage of operation.

(*ii*) Operation of press is smooth

(*iii*) The stroke is easily adjustable.

86. (*a*) **87.** (*b*), (*c*).

88. The main principle to be observed while designing clamping device is that the fixture, work piece and location features should not be distorted or strained. The clamping force should not be excessive but sufficient to hold the workpiece rigidly and should be applied at points where the workpiece has the support of solid metal of the fixture body.

89. (*i*) Clamps should be applied to the components where it is rigid and well supported.

(*ii*) Clamping forces should not be large enough to distort the locators, workpiece and fixture.

(*iii*) Clamps should be quick acting and as simple as possible.

(*iv*) Clamps should be well clear of cutting tools.

90. (*i*) Counter bores

(*ii*) Spot facing cutters

(*iii*) Counter sinking cutters.

91. When a drilling jig is being designed the following four elements must be considered :

(*i*) For locating the component

(*ii*) For clamping the component

(*iii*) For guiding the cutting tools

(*iv*) For holding the whole together as an assembly

92. (*i*) True (*ii*) True.

93. Throw away carbide tips are clamped firmly to the tool holder. These tips are available in thickness ranging from 3 to 12 mm and in size from 10 to 25 mm square. They prove to be economical because four to six edges of tips can be used before they are thrown away.

94. Point angle = 118°

Lip relief angle = 12°

Helix angle = 29°

Margin = 0.4 to 1.6 mm.

95. From tools are used an caps tan, turret and automatic lathes for machining profiles of different shapes by feeding the tool radially into the workpiece. They are made from HSS or tungsten carbide tips.

Three types of form tools are as follows :

(*i*) Flat form tool

(*ii*) Circular form tool

(*iii*) Dovetail form tool.

96. (*i*) Accurate holes and key ways can be easily cut

(*ii*) Production rate is high.

97. The nose radius on cutting tool is provided to increase the surface finish of the cutting tip of the tool. Small radii will produce smooth finish and are used on this cross sections of work. Large radii strengthen the tool and are used on cast iron and castings where the cuts are interrupted.

98. (*a*) **99.** (*c*)

100. (*a*) True (*b*) True (*c*) True (*d*) True

101. (*b*).

102. (*a*) True (*b*) True (*c*) True.

103. (*i*) Ceramic tools can operate at high cutting speeds.

(*ii*) They have high compressive strength

(*iii*) They are brittle in nature.

104. (*i*) To carry away heat

(*ii*) To provide lubrication at the cutting edge of tool

(*iii*) To flush away swarf (chips)

(*iv*) To protect newly machined surface from rusting.

105. (*b*). **106.** (*b*).

107. (*a*) True (*b*) True.

108. (*i*) Overbending

(*ii*) Corner setting :- This means coining (squeezing) the metal slightly at the corner in order to relieve elastic stresses.

109. (*i*) Bending (*ii*) Forming (*iii*) Drawing.

110. (*i*) Screws (*ii*) Handles (*iii*) Washers

(*iv*) Bushings.

111. (*i*) Machining (*ii*) Casting (*iii*) Welding.

112. (*a*). **113.** (*b*).

114. (*i*) Strength (*ii*) Deflection.

115. (*a*) **116.** (*a*) **117.** (*a*).

[illegible]

[illegible] Small [illegible] [illegible] [illegible] [illegible] will [illegible] [illegible] [illegible] [illegible] cross sections [illegible] [illegible] [illegible] [illegible] and [illegible] cast iron and [illegible] [illegible] are [illegible]

[illegible]

[illegible] True [illegible] True [illegible] True [illegible] True

[illegible] True 1[illegible] (ii) True [illegible] True.

10[illegible] [illegible] can [illegible] at high cutting speeds.

[illegible] They have high [illegible] strength.

(iii) The carbide is [illegible]

10[illegible] [illegible]

(i) The [illegible] cutting edge of [illegible]

(ii) To [illegible]

(iii) To [illegible] surface from rubbing

10[illegible]

107. (i) True (ii) [illegible]

108. (i) [illegible]

(i) [illegible] This [illegible] on [illegible] slightly at the [illegible] in order to relieve elastic stresses.

109. (i) Bending (ii) Forming (iii) Drawing

110. [illegible] (ii) Headless (iii) [illegible]

(iv) Bushing

111. (i) Machining (ii) Casting (iii) Welding

112. (a) 113. (b)

114. (i) Strength (ii) Deflection

115. (c) 116. (a) 117. (a)